When published in 1982, this translation of Professor Jacques Gernet's masterly survey of the history and culture of China was immediately welcomed by critics and readers. This revised and updated edition makes it more useful for students and for the general reader concerned with the broad sweep of China's past.

Written with an elegant and flowing narrative, the essential virtue of Jacques Gernet's book is to see the history of Chinese civilization as a whole. Yet within the synthesis of the trends — social, political, religious, scientific, artistic — that make up China's past and present, the author never loses sight of the telling detail that brings history to life. *A History of Chinese Civilization* is illustrated by a wide range of photographs, many maps, line drawings and tables. A detailed and updated chronological table and full bibliography complement the text and the expanded index now includes Chinese characters.

A History of Chinese Civilization

A History of
Chinese Civilization
Second Edition

Jacques Gernet

Collège de France

translated by J. R. Foster
and Charles Hartman

 **CAMBRIDGE**
UNIVERSITY PRESS

PUBLISHED BY THE PRESS SYNDICATE OF THE UNIVERSITY OF CAMBRIDGE
The Pitt Building, Trumpington Street, Cambridge CB2 1RP, United Kingdom

CAMBRIDGE UNIVERSITY PRESS
The Edinburgh Building, Cambridge CB2 2RU, United Kingdom
40 West 20th Street, New York, NY 10011-4211, USA
10 Stamford Road, Oakleigh, Melbourne 3166, Australia

Originally published in French as *Le Monde Chinois*
by Librairie Armand Colin, Paris 1972
and © Librairie Armand Colin 1972
First published in English by Cambridge University Press 1982
as *A History of Chinese Civilization*
English translation © Cambridge University Press 1982
Reprinted 1982, 1983
First paperback edition 1985
Second edition 1996
Reprinted 1996, 1997

Printed in the United States of America

Typeset in Times

Library of Congress Cataloguing-in-Publication Data is available

ISBN 0-521-49712-4 hardback
ISBN 0-521-49781-7 paperback

Contents

Plates

Maps

Tables

Figures

Preface to the New Edition

First published in French in 1972, *Le monde chinois* was twice corrected, rearranged, and enlarged for new French editions that appeared in 1980 and 1990. An English translation first published by the Cambridge University Press in 1982 made the work known to the English-speaking world. That translation was based upon the French text of 1980. But since the English translation is now out of print, the North American Branch of Cambridge University Press has taken the initiative for this new edition. This second English edition is, to some extent, a new book. Although based on the French text of 1990, important improvements have been made, including overall additions, corrections, and changes. There are also several entirely new portions and an index with the Chinese characters so necessary for sinologists.

Professor Charles Hartman of the State University of New York at Albany has made numerous translations from the French and undertaken a complete overhaul and updating of the bibliography that now gives priority of place to works in English. I hope that in its new form this book will better serve the needs of both nonspecialist and specialist readers alike.

The spirit that inspired the first publication of this book remains. As the first note in the introduction states, it aims 'to bring out the links between the different aspects of China's evolution: society, political system, economy, relations of the Chinese with the other civilizations of Eurasia, technology, intellectual life, and so on.' But it aims also to stress the significant changes that China has undergone in its long history.

I would like in particular to express my gratitude to Professor Charles Hartman for his valuable assistance and to the devoted staff of the North American Branch of Cambridge University Press.

Jacques Gernet

Acknowledgements

The publisher would like to thank the following for permission to reproduce illustrations in their possession:

Ashmolean Museum, Oxford, Pl. **42, 45**; Bibliothèque Nationale, Pl. **60**, Fig. **1/2, 1/4, 1/5, 1/6, 1/7, 1/8, 1/9**, and Fig. **14**; British Museum, Fig. **1/1**; Camera Press, Pl. **1, 3, 10, 18, 21, 22, 23, 24, 27, 28, 33, 47, 49, 57, 61, 62, 74, 75, 76, 79, 80, 81, 82, 83, 85, 86, 87, 88, 90, 91, 92**; J. Allan Cash, Pl. **32, 55**; Charbonnier-Réalités, Pl. **84**; Collection Viollet, Pl. **67, 71, 78**, Fig. **10**; Dominique Darbois, Pl. **34**; Harlingue-Viollet, Pl. **70, 73**; Keystone Collection, Pl. **72, 89**; Mansell Collection, Pl. **17, 38, 39, 40, 41, 46, 50, 51, 52, 53, 77**; Musée Cernuschi, Paris, Fig. **15**; Musée Guimet, Paris, Pl. **13, 56, 58, 59, 63, 64, 65, 66**, Fig. **1/3**; Popperphoto, Pl. **19, 20, 31**; Robert Harding Associates, **2, 4, 5, 6, 7, 8, 9, 11, 12, 14, 15, 25, 26, 29, 30, 32, 36, 37, 54, 55, 68**; The School of Oriental & African Studies, University of London, Pl. **16**; The Syndics of the Fitwilliam Museum, Cambridge, for the jacket illustrations; The University of Pennsylvania Museum, Pl. **35**.

Grateful thanks are also due to the author and Armand Colin for offering every assistance in publishing the English translation of this book; to Professor D. C. Twitchett for advice and encouragement; to Dr Michael Salt for help with the maps and to Reginald Piggott for drawing and lettering them; to Stephen Jones for preparing the index; to Mervyn Adams Seldon and Sam Addington for work on the bibliography; to Edward Binet and Robert Seal for picture research; to Angela Turnbull and Robert Seal for editing and proofreading.

Translator's Preface

I should particularly like to thank the author for his ready co-operation and help in preparing this translation. My thanks are also due to Professor D. C. Twitchett, who put me on the right lines in the matter of converting the Pinyin romanization of Chinese into Wade–Giles, to my secretary, Fräulein E. Jewan, who retyped some rather tricky parts of the manuscript, and to the publisher's editor, Mrs A. Turnbull, who made a number of useful suggestions. For the deficiencies that doubtless remain I am solely responsible.

As I have already implied, in spite of the Chinese government's recently expressed preference for Pinyin, Chinese names have on the whole been transliterated according to the Wade–Giles system. However, where a traditional, Anglicized form of a Chinese name exists, I have used that. I doubt whether I have succeeded in being entirely consistent in following this dual system and I therefore beg the reader's indulgence for any discrepancies in this thorny field of nomenclature.

J. R. Foster
Luxembourg,
October 1981

'During the days when I did not see you,' he said, 'I have read a great deal, in particular a Chinese novel with which I am still occupied and which seems to me very remarkable.'

'A Chinese novel,' I said, 'that must be rather curious.'

'Not as curious as one might be tempted to think,' replied Goethe.

'These people think and feel much as we do, and one soon realizes that one is like them. . . .'

'But,' I said, 'perhaps this Chinese novel is a rather exceptional one?'

'Not at all,' said Goethe, 'the Chinese have thousands of the kind, and they even had a certain number of them already when our forebears were still living in the woods.'

Goethe's Conversations with Eckermann,
Wednesday, 31 January 1827

Introduction

The object of this book—or rather its ambition—is to serve as an introduction to the history of the Chinese world, to depict the various stages in the development of this world, its successive experiences, the contributions—from every part of the globe—which have enriched it down the centuries, the influence which it has exerted, and its contribution to world history.[1]

The present state of China is the product and culminating point of a long history, and just as one could not claim to know the countries of Europe if one were totally ignorant of all the factors that have contributed to their formation since the Renaissance, the Middle Ages, and antiquity, so one cannot form any real conception of what China is today if one strips it of its tremendous historical dimension.

The importance of China is not confined to the number of its inhabitants and to the power, still largely untapped, of this nation of over one billion people. It is of a more general nature and proceeds quite as much from the past as from the present: Chinese civilization was the guiding spirit of a very large section of humanity, giving it its writing, its technology, its conceptions of man and of the world, its religions and its political institutions. The land of China itself, Korea, Japan, and Vietnam all form part of the same cultural community. But China's influence radiated far beyond that. It made itself felt among the Turkish, Mongol, and Tungus peoples of Mongolia and the Altai, in central Asia, in Tibet, and in all South-East Asia. It also impinged on more distant countries. The

---

1. Account had to be taken of the paucity of standard textbooks and of the elementary level of such knowledge of China as exists, not to mention misconceptions and prejudices. Hence the need to proceed step by step, putting the facts in their historical context and trying to bring out the links between the different aspects of China's evolution: society, political systems, economy, relations of the Chinese world with the other cultures of East Asia and the other civilizations of Eurasia, technology, intellectual life, and so on.

West, which has borrowed from China right down to our day without realizing it, is far from recognizing its sizable debt to her, but for which we ourselves would not be what we are.

To achieve such a synthesis is an arduous task and the present book can be only an attempt to do so; for although the sum total of the studies devoted by Chinese, Japanese, and Western scholars to the history of the Chinese world and of Chinese civilization cannot be compared with the immense labours accomplished in acquiring our present knowledge of classical antiquity and of the countries of Europe, the works that do exist are nevertheless already too numerous for any one person to know and draw upon. Gaps, imperfections, and errors are inevitable when it comes to embracing so rich and varied a range of events extending over three and a half millennia.

Besides this handicap, there are difficulties of a different sort. Anyone trying to familiarize himself with the countries of the Far East is bound to lack a whole fund of elementary knowledge which comes as much from the unconscious apprenticeship of daily life as from education in the technical sense of the term. Although a third of humanity lives in this part of the world, and although in the shrunken globe of today these people are now our neighbours, our culture remains resolutely 'Western'. It requires a considerable effort of the imagination to adopt a point of view from which Europe appears simply as an appendage of the Eurasian continent and its history as a particular aspect of the history of Eurasia.

Lands and peoples

The history of the Chinese world involves a vast and far from homogeneous geographical area extending from Siberia to the Equator and from the shores of the Pacific to the heart of the Eurasian continent. These immense spaces display a wide range of differing geographical conditions, and some familiarity with them is essential to an understanding of Chinese history. However, we shall confine ourselves here to recalling the essential points: the massive character of the continent as a whole, emphasized to the south-west by the tremendous complex of very high mountains and high plateaux formed by the folds of the Himalayas, stretching in an arc from the Hindu Kush to the Indo-Chinese peninsula; the great zone of steppe (or, to be more precise, of prairie), interrupted by deserts, which covers the area between the Siberian forests and the cultivated regions of North China; the existence of fertile plains formed by the alluvial deposits of the great rivers (the Sungari and Liao basins in Manchuria; the great central plain of North China, which covers more

Plate 1.   Section of pagoda roof, Summer Palace, Peking

than 300,000 square kilometres [115,000 square miles]; the middle and lower Yangtze; the plain of the Canton region; the Red River basin in Vietnam and other river basins of the Indo-Chinese peninsula, and so on); the enormous length of coastline from the mouth of the Amur to the Malay peninsula, and the existence of an uninterrupted chain of large and small islands from the Japanese archipelago to the more extensive range of big Indonesian islands (the Philippines, Borneo, Celebes, Java, and Sumatra). Climatic conditions add to this diversity: the eastern and southern regions are subject to the alternating influences of the monsoon, while the interior of Asia has a dry, continental climate. The effects of differing latitude are no less important. China is as much a country of Siberian cold and harsh winters as one of damp, heavy tropical heat.

The peoples who inhabit these regions are extremely diverse and they all have their own modes of life, their own individual cultures and languages. The linguistic differences are probably those that spring to mind first.

The languages spoken in the Far East and the People's Republic of China belong to five different linguistic groups, the geographical distribution of which is relatively clear, except in South China and the Indo-Chinese peninsula, where the linguistic situation is an extremely tangled one.

1. From Siberia to those regions of North China where a population of Chinese language and culture is in the majority, we find peoples who have overflowed from central Asia and beyond, and whose languages belong to the Turkish, Mongolian, and Tungus groups (languages formerly known as 'Ural-Altaic').

2. Korean and Japanese, radically different linguistically from Chinese and the languages related to it, constitute a separate group, although they both seem to have some affinities with the Turkish, Mongolian, and Tungus languages.

3. The peoples speaking Sino-Tibetan languages occupy all the high mountains and high plateaux of the Himalayas, the countries of the Indo-Chinese peninsula and China proper, the China of the twenty-one provinces extending from the valley of the Amur and Mongolia to the frontiers of Burma, Laos, and Vietnam. Because of the number of individuals who speak them, the Chinese dialects naturally form the dominating linguistic group in this vast, diverse complex.

4. The Mon-Khmer languages, spoken by a few small minorities in south-west China, are much more in evidence in the Indo-Chinese peninsula.

Table 1. The languages of the Far East[1]

'Altaic' Languages			Languages of North-East Asia	
Turkish group	*Mongolian group*	*Tungus group*	*Korean*	*Japanese*
Uighur	Mongolian	Manchu		
Kazak	Daghur	Sibo		
Uzbek	(Mongor)	Hoche (Nanay)		
Tartar	(Tung)	Oronchon		
Salar		(Evenki)		
Kirghiz				
Yuku				

Sino-Tibetan Languages			
Tibeto-Burmese group	*Thai group*	*Miao-Yao*	*Chinese group*
Tibetan dialects	Siamese	Languages of	Dialects of the north
Burmese	Laotian	the minorities	Wu dialects
Languages of the	Languages of the	of south-west	Cantonese dialects
Tibeto-Burmese	Thai minorities	China and the	S. Fukien dialects
minorities of south-west	of south-west	Indo-Chinese	N. Fukien dialects
China and the Indo-	China and the	peninsula	Hakka dialects
Chinese peninsula	Indo-Chinese		Hunan dialects
	peninsula		

Austro-Asiatic Languages (Mon-Khmer)	'Malayo-Polynesian' Languages
Khmer (Cambodian)	Malay
Cham (minorities of the east coast of Viet-	Javanese
nam and Cambodia)	Other 'Malayo-Polynesian' languages
Mon (lower Burma)	of Indonesia
Languages of the Mon-Khmer minorities	Languages of the ethnic minorities
of Yunnan, the Indo-Chinese peninsula	of Taiwan
and the Nicobar islands	

1. Apart from Japanese, all the linguistic groups figuring in this table are represented in the People's Republic of China and in Taiwan.

For the sake of completeness it is worth also mentioning the Indo-European languages, which in 1957 were represented in the P.R.C. by 15,000 Tadjiks (who speak an Iranian language) and by 9,700 Russians.

5. Finally, further south, Malaya and the big islands of South-East Asia are the domain of the languages known as 'Malayo-Polynesian', a domain which in fact extends eastwards to Melanesia, northward to the island of Taiwan (Formosa) and westward to Madagascar.

The distribution of the various groups of languages in the Far East preserves the memory of a long history of which it represents the culminating point. It is hardly possible to know what the situation was like in the far distant past, but we are familiar with the broad lines of its evolution. Since the beginning of the first millennium B.C. the languages their archaic, ancient, or modern forms, have spread from the valley of the Yellow River to the basin of the Yangtze, then towards South China and North-East Asia; the Thai, Tibeto-Burmese, and Mon-Khmer languages have moved and spread from the valley of the Yangtze and the Sino-Tibetan borders towards South China and the Indo-Chinese peninsula; and the Malayo-Polynesian languages have spread out from the coasts of southern China towards South-East Asia and beyond. Finally, a number of Indo-European languages (for example, Khotanese and eastern Iranian dialects) which were represented in the oases of central Asia during most of history have completely disappeared from them in our day.

The Han Chinese

In the vast geographical and human complex of the Far East the peoples of Chinese language and culture, the Han Chinese, today form the most important group. Their field of expansion extends over nearly fifteen million square kilometres (six million square miles), from Siberia (54° N) to Timor (10° S) and from Mindanao (126° E) to the heart of the Eurasian continent (73° E, the meridian of Bombay, on the west coast of India). The distance from Singapore, a city which is three-quarters Chinese, to the valley of the Amur is the same as that from Dublin to the western frontier of the People's Republic of China.

These people amount in all to more than a billion human beings. They are the majority in the twenty-one provinces that form China proper – but they continue to expand beyond the borders of these provinces – and occupy a continuous geographical area of about 4,600,000 square kilometres (1,775,000 square miles), an area as large as Europe up to the frontier of the U.S.S.R. These twenty-one provinces, to which constant reference will be made in this book, cover on average areas ranging between that of the United Kingdom and that of Greece. In 1975 the density of their populations was roughly comparable with that of European countries. At that time the only province that was more thickly populated than the Netherlands was Kiangsu (Shanghai now has 10.5 million inhabitants, Nanking 1.6 million, and several towns in Kiangsu more than half a million).

However, there is also an overseas China consisting of the large Chinese communities which have established themselves in most of the countries of South-East Asia (Indo-Chinese peninsula, Indonesia, and the Philippines). These communities are very numerous in Malaysia,

Table 2. Han populations in East Asia outside of the People's
Republic of China (1986 estimates)

Taiwan	19,400,000
Hong Kong	5,600,000
Macao	300,000
Singapore	1,800,000
Thailand	11,000,000
Malaysia	6,400,000
Indonesia	5,100,000
Vietnam	1,500,000
Total	51,200,000

where they form more than a third of the population, in Sarawak (on the north-east coast of Borneo), and in Thailand; and they are also far from negligible in Vietnam, Cambodia, Java, and the Philippines. Singapore, Penang, and Malacca in Malaysia, and Cholon in Vietnam are Chinese cities.[1]

Far from forming a homogeneous whole, the various peoples of Chinese language and culture differ in traditions, customs, ethnic composition, and the dialects they speak. The absence in China of national boundaries, which in Europe enable us to distinguish so clearly between Frenchmen, Spaniards, Italians and Romanians, conceals a diversity that is the product of history and that was once no doubt more marked than it is today, when education and relatively easy communications are tending to blot out the original character of the different regions. But the history of the Han settlement of China and the ethnographical charting of the different peoples of Chinese language and culture would be an immense task which has never yet been tackled in a systematic fashion and for which documentation would often be lacking.

Although they are called dialects – a term which for us suggests the form assumed by a national language in a limited region – the principal Chinese dialects are spoken by millions of individuals. They differ from each other just as markedly as European languages belonging to the same linguistic group and in reality they each form complexes within which we meet important variations.

It should be noted, however, that there is one relatively homogeneous block, that of the northern dialects, spoken in 1953 by 387 million people and consisting of three distinct groups. The relative uniformity of these dialects is explained by the mingling of peoples which occurred in the

1. It should be noted for the record that there are also Chinese communities in India, Madagascar, South Africa, Europe, and both North and South America.

Table 3. Comparative areas of the provinces with a
Han majority and the countries of Europe
(in square kilometres)

Chinese provinces		European countries
Szechwan	569,000	
	550,800	France
	504,900	Spain
Heilungkiang	463,600	
	449,200	Sweden
Yunnan	436,200	
Kansu	366,000	
	311,700	Poland
	301,100	Italy
	244,800	United Kingdom
	243,400	Romania
Kwangtung	231,400	
Kwangsi	220,400	
Hunan	210,500	
Hopei	202,700	
Shensi	196,750	
Hupei	187,500	
Kirin	187,000	
Kweichow	174,000	
Honan	167,000	
Kiangsi	164,800	
Shansi	157,100	
Shantung	153,300	
Liaoning	151,000	
Anhwei	139,900	
	132,500	Greece
	127,800	Czechoslovakia
Fukien	123,100	
	110,950	Bulgaria
Kiangsu	102,200	
Chekiang	101,800	
	93,000	Hungary
	69,000	Ireland
	41,300	Switzerland
Taiwan	35,960	
	30,560	Belgium

course of history in all the regions between Mongolia and the basin of the
Yangtze and also by the mainly recent settlement of the north-eastern provinces (Manchuria) and the south-western ones (Yunnan and Kweichow).
On the other hand, the diversity of the southern and south-eastern dialects, and also the archaic character of several of them, bears witness to
the relative stability of the peoples established in these regions. These
features are also explained by the successive waves of colonization which
carried the Han population there from the end of ancient times onward.
Like the peoples of Europe, those of China are the product of the con-

Table 4. Population of provinces and town areas with a Han majority,
and of territories with a Han minority
(1957 censuses and 1986 estimates)

	1957	1986	areas (in km2)
PROVINCES			
Szechwan	72,160,000	101,880,000	
Honan	48,670,000	77,130,000	
Shantung	54,030,000	76,950,000	
Kwangtung	37,960,000	62,530,000	
Kiangsu	45,230,000	62,130,000	
Hunan	36,220,000	56,220,000	
Hopei	44,720,000	55,480,000	
Anhwei	33,560,000	51,560,000	
Hupei	30,790,000	49,310,000	
Chekiang	25,280,000	40,300,000	
Kwangxi*	19,390,000	38,730,000	
Liaoning	24,090,000	36,860,000	
Kiangsi	18,610,000	34,600,000	
Yunnan	19,100,000	34,060,000	
Heilungkiang	14,860,000	33,110,000	
Shensi	18,130,000	30,020,000	
Kweichow	16,890,000	29,680,000	
Fukian	14,650,000	27,130,000	
Shansi	15,960,000	26,270,000	
Kilin	12,550,000	22,980,000	
Kansu	12,800,000	20,410,000	
Chinghai	–	4,070,000	
TOWN AREAS			
Peking	–	9,600,000	16,800
Shanghai	–	12,170,000	6,200
Tientsin	–	8,080,000	11,300
TERRITORIES with Han minority			
(Autonomous Regions)			
Inner Mongolia	9,200,000	20,070,000	1,177,500
Uighurs of Sinkiang	5,640,000	13,610,000	1,646,900
Tibet	1,274,000	1,990,000	1,221,600
Hui of Ning-hsia	2,050,000	4,150,000	66,400

* The official name of this province is 'Kwangsi Chuang Autonomous Region.'

stant intermingling of races caused by wars, invasions, colonization,
transfers of population, and contacts between neighbours. Turkish,
Mongol, Tungus, Korean, Tibeto-Burman, Thai, Miao, Yao, and Mon-
Khmer strains have all contributed to the formation of the Han peoples;
sometimes even more distant peoples from the borders of India, Iran,
and South-East Asia have added their share. The ethnic composition of
North China has been constantly renewed in the course of history by the
contributions of Altaic-speaking peoples from the steppes and northern
Manchuria; and that of the western provinces by intermarriage with the
mountaineers of the Himalaya and the Tibetan plateau, and with the

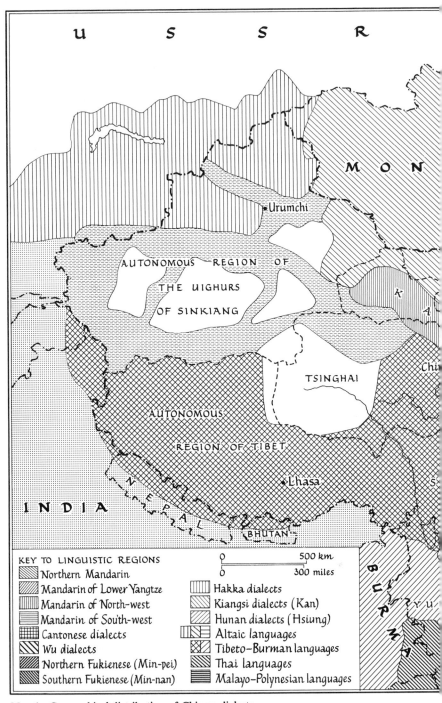

U S S R

M O N

•Urumchi

AUTONOMOUS REGION OF

THE UIGHURS

OF SINKIANG

K

A

Chi

TSINGHAI

AUTONOMOUS

REGION OF TIBET

•Lhasa

S

I N D I A

N E P A L

BHUTAN

B U R M A

Yü

KEY TO LINGUISTIC REGIONS

0 .... 500 km
0 .... 300 miles

Northern Mandarin
Mandarin of Lower Yangtze
Mandarin of North-west
Mandarin of South-west
Cantonese dialects
Wu dialects
Northern Fukienese (Min-pei)
Southern Fukienese (Min-nan)
Hakka dialects
Kiangsi dialects (Kan)
Hunan dialects (Hsiung)
Altaic languages
Tibeto–Burman languages
Thai languages
Malayo–Polynesian languages

Map 1 Geographical distribution of Chinese dialects

Table 5.   Chinese dialects
(1953 statistics, in millions)

Northern dialects (4 groups)	387
Wu dialects (4 groups)	46
Cantonese (Kwangtung) dialects (5 groups)	27
Hunan and Kiangsi dialects	26
Hakka dialects	20
Southern Min (Fukien) dialects	15
Northern Min (Fukien) dialects	7
Total	528

These figures do not take into account the Han Chinese of Taiwan (seventeen million today, the majority of whom speak a Southern Min [Fukien] dialect) or the Chinese colonies in South-East Asia (some fifteen million people, who speak Cantonese, Hakka, or Min dialects, according to their origin).

semi-nomadic inhabitants of Tsinghai. Ethnic intermixture has been just as important in South China, where colonization has gone on for more than two millennia down to our own day. In the whole of the south-west (the provinces of Kweichow, Yunnan, Hunan, Szechwan, Kwangsi, and Kwangtung) there are still very numerous non-Han elements.

Non-Han minorities

While the Han Chinese form the vast majority of the population of the People's Republic of China, Chinese citizens belonging to other nationalities nevertheless amounted in 1957 to between forty-two and forty-five million people. More than fifty of these nationalities are officially recognized and enjoy a certain degree of political autonomy.

Thus it becomes clear not only that the Han peoples are far from forming the homogeneous block that one might imagine *a priori*, but that in certain provinces the ethnic diversity is extreme. Racial groups speaking Malayo-Polynesian tongues also exist in the north and east of the island of Taiwan. These non-Han peoples form the last remnants of a history marked by the constant progress of the peoples of Chinese language and culture, and by the triumph of a mode of life and culture which has been changed, enriched, and diversified by its conquests and by its contacts with more distant civilizations. Racial intermixture, borrowing from other peoples, assimilation—for example, some Han Chinese adopted the mode of life of nomadic shepherds, others that of the aborigines of South China, while on the other hand certain racial groups in the southern provinces are now scarcely distinguishable from the Chinese

Table 6. Principal non-Han peoples of the People's Republic of China
(1957 censuses)

Name	Ethno-linguistic group	Habitation	Number
Chuang	Thai	Yunnan, Kwangtung	7,800,000
Uighurs	Turkish	Sinkiang, Western Kansu	3,900,000
I	Tibeto-Burman	Yunnan, Hunan	3,260,000
Tibetans	Tibetan	Tibet, Szechwan	2,770,000
Miao	Miao-Yao	South-western provinces	2,680,000
Manchus	Tungus	North-east, Mongolia, Peking area	2,430,000
Mongols	Mongol	Mongolia, North-east, Kansu, Tsinghai	1,640,000
Puyi	Thai	Yunnan	1,320,000
Koreans	Korean	North-east	1,250,000

— lead us to emphasize the capital importance, from a historical point of view, of modes of life and of cultures.

Modes of life and cultures

The linguistic situation in East Asia and the People's Republic of China, in which all the linguistic groups of this part of the world are represented, itself reveals the complexity of the population, but other factors make it possible to put into sharper focus the nature of human life in the Far East. In one form or another gathering, hunting and fishing, livestock rearing and agriculture are the basic activities of humanity, since men have first of all to feed themselves. Complemented by predatory (raiding, pillage, piracy) and commercial activities, these means of life are closely connected with the culture for which they have served as a basis. Thus modes of life provide the foundation for any general interpretation of history.

The basic facts are geographical. It is geography that forms this or that mode of life and defines its limits. Above a certain altitude and outside certain climatic conditions wheat gives place to barley and millet. The vast grasslands of Mongolia are more propitious to cattle rearing than to agriculture; wet rice cultivation is best carried out in the irrigated plains of the tropical and subtropical regions. But we must not let ourselves be carried away by a sort of geographical determinism: by means of terraced fields wet rice cultivation can climb the hills and, thanks to irrigation, take over arid zones; northern China and southern

Mongolia lend themselves as well to agriculture as to the raising of cattle, sheep, and horses. The latitude thus granted to modes of life accounts for their advance and retreat as well as their coexistence, phenomena which have had great historical importance and partly explain the contacts and borrowings between different cultures. But this deep-rooted tendency of human societies to extend the modes of life to which they are attached beyond their natural limits, this relative freedom which geographical conditions permit human activity are not in contradiction with a general distribution of modes of life and consequently of types of culture and civilization. In the huge geographical area of East Asia four big groups of cultures, linked to specific modes of life, can be discerned:

1. That of sedentary peoples with a highly developed agriculture which forms their predominant activity. It is to this kind of culture that the peoples of Chinese civilization and all those that have undergone their influence belong.

2. That of the nomadic cattle-raisers of the grasslands and desert regions which extend from the Siberian taiga to the agricultural lands of northern China, and from Manchuria to the lower basin of the Volga.

3. That of the mountain peoples of the huge Himalayan–Tibetan complex and its borderlands, who practise both livestock raising and agriculture.

4. That of the mixed cultures of the tropical zone which combine hunting and cattle rearing with more or less primitive forms of agriculture. These cultures, once highly developed, are now in process of disappearing.

For the sake of completeness we should add to these four big groups that of the sedentary trading peoples of the central Asian oases.

The sedentary peoples with a highly developed agriculture forming their predominant activity

As in other parts of the world, it is the most highly developed forms of agriculture that have allowed the biggest growths of populations, the building up of substantial reserves, and the formation of organized states. That is how the great civilizations began. However, in this group, which has spread over all the plains, valleys, and fertile high plateaux of East Asia, winning over to its mode of life peoples living in analogous geographical conditions, two different kinds of agriculture can be distinguished:

1. A 'dry' agriculture, which goes back to Neolithic times and grows by way of cereals barley, wheat, and various different species of millet. Irrigation has occasionally been practised in the 'dry' zone corresponding with northern China and has made it possible to increase both yields and the regularity of harvests. In spite of the predominance of agriculture in these regions the rearing of livestock (cattle, sheep, horses) was relatively important early on (second and first millennia) and long retained a far from negligible place. But unlike the nomads and mountain peoples the sedentary agriculturalists did not care for drinking milk and progressively reduced the proportion of meat in their diet.

2. The wet cultivation of rice, which developed only very slowly in the course of the first ten centuries of our era and was not in full swing until the end of this period. This is an agricultural technique which probably originated simultaneously in several different places (mainly northern India and the lower basin of the Yangtze) but was to prove a great success, spreading to all the warm, damp regions where irrigation was possible (plains and valleys of tropical and sub-tropical China, districts of the Indo-Chinese peninsula, Indonesia, Korea, and Japan). The development of rice growing represents a new stage in the history of the peoples of East Asia: it gave a sort of second wind to the civilizations of this part of the world from the seventh to tenth centuries onwards.

The history of the highly developed forms of agriculture in the Far East is in any case rich and complex. It is marked by a whole series of advances and transformations. Not only have the techniques of rice growing been perfected, but the selection of species, the introduction of sorghum in the thirteenth century and of American plants from the sixteenth century onwards (sweet potato, ground-nut, maize, tobacco, potato) have been causing radical changes for a thousand years.

The nomadic livestock-raisers of the steppe zone

These speakers of 'proto-Altaic' and 'Altaic' languages played a vital part in the history of the Chinese world and exerted a profound influence on its civilization. Their main characteristics are:

1. The mobility of the dwellings (yurts), of the herds (oxen, sheep, horses, camels, yaks), and other property (the women's jewels form one of the nomads' movable forms of wealth). The moves between summer pastures in the plains and winter pastures in sheltered valleys seldom ex-

ceed a hundred miles. But in case of need pastoral tribes can undertake long journeys and in general do so when threatened by more powerful tribes.

2. A mode of life which is a permanent training for war (drilling of horses, hunting, practising on horseback with bows and guns).

3. An economy in which animal products suffice for essential needs (milk, koumiss, cheese, butter, wool and hair, hides and furs, dried dung for fuel). Raiding (expeditions against sedentary peoples in neighbouring tribes, pillage of caravans), the gifts of sedentary peoples, and trade made it possible to add certain complements to this economy: metals, cereals, silks, luxury objects, tea from the tenth century onwards. The object of raids is to obtain a complementary ration of cereals in winter, but also very often to force sedentary peoples to open markets. Yet nomadic livestock-raisers are not ignorant of the cultivation of barley, corn and millet, and in certain periods they practised metallurgy. Furthermore, the presence of sedentary peoples – agriculturalists and artisans – among nomads is a constant factor in history.

4. The important intermediary role played by the peoples of the steppe between free hunters of the Siberian forests, sedentary producers of cloths and metals, mountain peoples of the Himalayan complex, sedentary traders of the chain of oases which runs from north-western China (province of Kansu) to Transoxiania, and the peoples of the Middle East and eastern Europe. The expansion of the steppe peoples extended to all these regions.

5. A tribal society founded on the subordination of the weak tribes to the powerful tribes and on the opposition between an aristocracy that owns the herds and groups of slaves or serfs.

6. The unstable character of the federations of tribes and the political units, in which it should be noted that the power of the elected chief is limited by assemblies of warriors on horseback and under arms. The contacts and commercial relations with sedentary peoples are at the root of economic and social borrowings and changes which at first tend to strengthen the political organization of the steppe societies and to enrich them, but in the long run cause tensions and internal ruptures as a result of the 'sedentarisation' of part of the tribes or of their aristocracy.

*The mountain peoples of the Himalayan complex
and its borderlands*

The area of occupation of the mountaineers extends to about four million square kilometres and its population could be estimated in 1957 at three or four million people. A cereal agriculture, with poor but hardy cereals (mainly barley, but also millet, rye, buckwheat, sometimes wheat in sheltered valleys) is combined with the raising of cattle, yaks, horses, sheep, and goats. Cattle raising on the grand scale, like that of the herdsmen of the steppe zone, is not unknown on the high plateaux of Tibet and Tsinghai, but mountain rearing, with the animals moved to stables in winter, predominates in the hilly regions. The diversity of the natural conditions (high plateaux, mountains, and valleys) explains the specialization of the livestock-raisers and agriculturalists or the combination of livestock rearing and agriculture by the same peoples. The black tents of the livestock-raisers contrast with the stone, flat-roofed houses of the cultivators, which are sometimes built in the shape of towers with several storeys. Warlike in their habits, the mountain peoples of the Himalayan complex (Tibetans, Ch'iang or Tangut, Tyarung, I, Nasi or Moso) used to raid caravans and make incursions into the lands of settled agriculturalists. In the course of history they have overflowed towards the east, into the present provinces of Kansu, Szechwan and Shensi, as well as towards the north, into the oasis zone.

The mixed cultures of South China and South-East Asia

These cultures, which are today in retreat, once extended over a wide area up to the valley of the Yangtze and in South-East Asia. They combined gathering, hunting, livestock raising, forms of agriculture less developed than those of the Han Chinese, and coastal and river fishing. Their gradual withdrawal towards the mountainous regions before the rice-cultivators of the plains and their general retreat towards the south make the reconstruction of past ages difficult. In adapting themselves to more difficult natural conditions some groups have had to modify their mode of life and to change over to a form of shifting agriculture very anciently attested in the Far East and still practised today by a whole group of ethnic minorities of South China and the Indo-Chinese peninsula: Yao and Miao of Kwangsi, Kwangtung, Kweichow and Yunnan, Meo or Mhong of northern Vietnam, Li of the mountainous regions of the island of Hainan. This rudimentary agriculture proceeds by burning brushwood or forest and involves moving villages as the land becomes exhausted after four or five years. It grows tubers (taro, yam) sown with the digging stick, 'dry' cereals, mountain rice and, for the last few centuries, maize. Some of these ancient peoples, especially those who lived by the sea and made fishing their principal activity, have disappeared or merged with sedentary peoples with a more highly developed agriculture, who have adopted their maritime techniques. Some groups changed over to irrigated rice growing—such is the case with the substantial Thai minority of south-west China, the Chuang, who in 1957 numbered 7.8 million, with the Shans of Burma, the Thais of Vietnam (Tho, black and white Thais, Nong) – and founded organized states in the deltas of the big rivers of the Indo-Chinese peninsula. The history of these peoples, who were acquainted with writing, is relatively well known and makes it possible to follow their migrations from the Sino-Tibetan borders and South China towards the more southerly regions (the Burmans coming down the valley of the Irrawaddy, the Thais down the Chao Phraya valley, the Khmers down the Mekong valley and the Vietnamese down the Red River valley).

Although historical evolution brought the extension of irrigated rice growing from the valley of the Yangtze right to Java, and thus profoundly modified the original situation, South China remains closely connected historically by its peoples, its languages, and its ancient cultures to South-East Asia. The same ethnic minorities – Tibeto-Burman, Thai, Miao, Yao and Mon-Khmer – are found both in southern China and in the mountainous regions of the Indo-Chinese peninsula.

Certain characteristics of these peoples of different cultures, characteristics known through the written sources and archaeology, have persisted until our day: shifting agriculture, dwellings on piles, buffalo rearing, the preparation of fermented fish as seasoning, use of betel, use of the mouth-organ (the Laotian *khene* and the Chinese *sheng*) and of the bronze drum, myths of the creation of the various races and of the deluge, cult of serpents and dragons, of the dog and the tiger, shamanism, and so on. Some of these cultural characteristics are even very widespread among the most highly developed people of South China and the Indo-Chinese peninsula.

The sedentary cultures and the traders
of the Central Asian oases

There is a continuous chain of oases linking western Kansu to the basins of the Syr-Darya and the Amu-Darya (known to the Greeks as the Oxus) on each side of the Takla Makan desert and on the far side of the Pamirs: Chiu-ch'üan, An-hsi – Hami, Turfan, Kucha, Aksu to the north, Tunhuang, Charkhlik, Niya, Khotan, Yarkand to the south – Kashgar, Kokand, Tashkent, Samarkand, Bukhara. Peopled by sedentary agriculturalists and traders, these oases were the meeting-places of all the peoples of Asia: Indo-European speakers (Kucheans, Khotanese, Sogdians), 'Altaic' speakers (Hsiung-nu, Turks, Uighurs, Mongols) and Sino-Tibetan speakers (Chinese, Tibetans, Tanguts). The diversity of the paper manuscripts of the fifth to tenth centuries found in 1900 near the town of Tun-huang, in the extreme west of Kansu, reveals the cosmo-politan character of the population of these oases, control of which was continually disputed all through history by the Chinese, the nomads of the steppe, the mountain peoples of the Himalayan complex, and the empires established beyond the Pamirs. Alongside the mass of Chinese manuscripts we find a number of texts in Tibetan and also documents in Uighur Turkish, Sogdian (eastern Iranian), Tangut, Khotanese and Kuchean, Sanskrit and Prakrit.

Once very busy, these oases were one of the principal paths for the introduction into the Far East of the influence of Iranian, Indian, Near Eastern, and Mediterranean peoples.

The main routes of the Eurasian continent

Finally, an important place must be given to the influence of distant civilizations. The Far East in general and the Chinese world in particular were in contact throughout their history with the western and southern parts of the Eurasian continent. These contacts pose three series of close-ly connected problems: that of the great commercial currents — maritime and caravan traffic; that of the great military expansions and of diplomatic relations; and that of the spread of the great religions and of pilgrimages. It was not the same routes that were most frequented in every age, and consequently it was not the same parts of the world that were in contact with the different regions of the Far East. The oasis routes played a major role from the end of Chinese antiquity (third century B.C.) to the ninth century A.D. The steppe routes, further to the north, linked Mongolia and North China closely to Europe and the countries of the Middle East in the thirteenth and fourteenth centuries. The various periods of maritime expansion — Indo-Iranian from the second to the eighth century, Islamic from the eighth to the fourteenth, Chinese from the eleventh to the fifteenth, European from the beginning of the sixteenth century onwards — also had very important consequences for the history of the civilizations of Eurasia.

The commercial centres situated at the ends of the main routes across the Eurasian continent and on the borders of the Chinese world were fre-quented by merchants, embassies, and missionaries from the lands of central Asia, from India, and from the Middle East. In the same way, the ports on the Chinese coast were the meeting places of sailors and mer-chants from the most varied regions: Koreans and people from Liaotung on the coasts of Shantung and Kiangsu, Japanese in Chekiang, people from South-East Asia and the Indian Ocean (Indians, Iranians, Arabs), Westerners (from the sixteenth century onwards) in Kwangtung and

Fukien. The length of the journeys involved and the annual rhythm of the monsoons explain why foreign colonies, hubs radiating influences from distant lands, grew up in these parts and in the urban centres on the great commercial axes of the Chinese world (the roads that link the valley of the Wei, in Shensi, to the region of the lower Yangtze, roads from Canton to the middle Yangtze via the basin of the Kan River in Kiangsi, the valley of the Yangtze and the big canals which connected the Hangchow region to those of K'ai-feng and Peking, and so on). The big Chinese cities—especially the capitals—have always been in every age cosmopolitan cities. But conversely Chinese armies, embassies, pilgrims, merchants, and craftsmen visited almost every region of Asia.

A schematic typology of the modes of life and cultures of the Far East, with a reminder of the outside influences that have been involved, makes it possible to understand the complexity and richness of human life in this part of the world. Like the 'provinces' of Europe, every region of China proper and the neighbouring countries has its own history, which is that of its population, and of the political entities of which it has formed part down the centuries, and of the influences which it has received from the aboriginal inhabitants and from neighbouring or distant peoples. Languages, customs and traditions, and human types everywhere preserve the memory of a past that goes back to more or less ancient epochs.

The Chinese world, more than any other, has been in contact and maintained permanent relations with peoples whose modes of life and culture were very different from its own. Similarly, the civilizations from which it has received contributions (ancient Mesopotamia, pre-Islamic Iran, India, Islam, the Christian West) were profoundly alien to it by their very nature. Because of the very different elements which have shared in its foundation and in the course of time enriched and transformed it, Chinese civilization has been, like the other great civilizations of history, a perpetual creation.

Outline of the historical evolution of the Chinese world

The fundamental difference between the history of China and that of the Western countries, from antiquity until our day, is a difference of analytical precision. It is not that the materials are lacking; they are so rich and plentiful that their exploitation has scarcely begun. But while the history of France or Italy in the sixteenth century, for example, is known year by year and the study of the historical changes which took place in that century has been carried as far as it can be taken, that of

China is so poorly known in the West that people very often still refer to long periods of three or four centuries. Thus the Ming period (1368–1644) is sometimes alluded to as a homogeneous whole in which it is only possible to pick out a few important events. But the *history* of this period, year by year and region by region, still remains to be discovered, for China of the Ming period, from the tropics to Siberia, covered an area ten times that of France. Until the development of medieval studies it was believed that our Middle Ages had been a period of darkness and stagnation; but the labours of historians have revealed a rich and complex evolution and have given life, colour, and movement to what seemed dead. The history of China is like our own unexplored Middle Ages, and the repeated accusations of stagnation, periodical return to a previous condition, and permanence of the same social structures and the same political ideology are so many value judgements on a history that is still unknown. No doubt the considerable amount of work devoted to it since the beginning of this century in China, Japan, and the Western countries has rendered possible great progress in our knowledge. Nevertheless, even if there could be no question of going into details as small as those available for the history of the West, we are still far from attaining a level of analysis sufficient to enable us to think of comparing the evolution of the Chinese world with that of Europe.

However, it is possible to distinguish in the course of this evolution forms of socio-political organizations that were very different. For example, the religious, warrior monarchy of archaic times (roughly 1600–900 B.C.) has nothing in common with the centralized empire, administered by paid civil servants subject to dismissal, which was established at the end of the third century before our era. The society of the tenth to seventh centuries B.C., with its numerous principalities, whose chiefs were assisted by high dignitaries drawn from noble families, and its hierarchy of family cults, is something quite original. But the changes that took place in the centralized state from the time of its creation onwards were more important than is generally supposed, for they are masked by the uniformity of the vocabulary. The establishment, in the empires of the Yangtze valley between the second and sixth centuries, of an endogamous aristocracy with manors and dependants, which imposed its authority on the central power, is a phenomenon without parallel in any other epoch or any other region of China. The political system of the early Sung period (960–1279), with its party struggles in civil service circles, and the authoritarian empire created at the end of the fourteenth century by the first Ming emperor are worlds apart. Thus it is quite false to see the elimination of the Sino-Manchu dynasty in 1912 as the end of a two-thousand-year-old political system. Although there were always emperors and dynastic lines between the first one of all, Shih Huang Ti of the Ch'in (221–210 B.C.) and the last, the Manchu P'u-i, who came to the throne when still a child under the reign name of Hsüan-t'ung (1908–12), there were also profound differences between one epoch and another, differences connected with the organization of the state and the social groups who often held the real power (aristocracies, army leaders, highly educated families living on the rent from estates, eunuchs, and so on). It is a grave error of method to try to characterize the Chinese imperial system as a whole and throughout its existence, for political systems are living organisms which continually adapt themselves to social and economic changes except for the brief periods when they are in contradiction with them.

The distinction which we are accustomed to make between monarchy and democracy is too absolute. Just as history does not present any models of pure democracy, so the monarchical institutions of the Chinese world were very far from excluding any moderating mechanism and any form of popular expression. The exploitation of the weakest, arbitrary behaviour and violence are not inventions of the Chinese world and, when all is said and done, no more justice and humanity are to be found among the other peoples of history. It is possible to paint the social and political history of China in the darkest colours; but the same enterprise would be just as easy in the case of Europe.

A general framework will help to crystallize our ideas about the successive changes in the political forms of the Chinese world from the remotest antiquity down to our day.

I. Antiquity

c. *1800(?)–900*. This is the epoch of a palace civilization of which the Middle East[1] provides analogous examples during the same period. The king, leading member of the noble class whose exclusive activities are making sacrifices and waging war, is head of the armies and chief priest. All activities are dependent on the royal palace, which vaguely assumes functions which are simultaneously political, religious, military, and economic.

c. *900–500*. A system of aristocratic cities, sometimes allies, sometimes

---

1. The Anglo-Saxon term 'Middle East' has been adopted in this book to designate the vast geographical area which extends from the plains of northern India to the Mediterranean, as opposed to the term 'Near East', the connotation of which is limited to the countries bordering the eastern Mediterranean.

rivals, replaces this form of archaic royalty. The leaders of the principalities are united among themselves, within a hierarchy based on kinship and privileges in the field of worship, by family, religious, political, military, and economic ties. But the system declines at the end of this period simultaneously with the establishment of big kingdoms which come into conflict with each other.

c. *500–220*. This crisis in the aristocratic society was resolved by the development of monarchical institutions and ended in the creation of a type of centralized state which leaned directly, thanks to the suppression of the chiefs and the elimination of the upper ranks of the nobility, on the peasantry, a source of economic and military power.

II. The first unified state, its decline, and the Middle Ages

220 B.C. – 190 A.D. This kind of state was extended by the general conquest of all the former kingdoms. But it evolved fairly rapidly. The centralization of power favoured the palace at the expense of the civil service and this provoked two successive crises, the second of which ended in complete political anarchy.

190–310. The leaders of independent armies which contended for power ended by sharing all the Chinese lands: North China, the lower Yangtze and Szechwan. A military dictatorship was set up in North China but came up against the growing power of the rich landed families with autarchic estates and dependants, the development of which went back to the first and second centuries.

310–590. The non-Chinese peoples who had been settling in North China since the beginning of the Christian era founded kingdoms with institutions which were a mixture of the governmental and military traditions of the Chinese world and those of the nomads of the steppe or those of the mountain-dwellers of the Sino-Tibetan borders. However, in the valley of the Yangtze the big landed families with manors and dependants gradually began to form an endogamous aristocracy which dominated the fairly weak central power. Becoming more and more sinicized and leaning on a military aristrocracy of mixed blood, the kingdoms and empires of the North finally gave birth to a unified empire which seemed in its early stages like a prolongation of these kingdoms and empires.

590–755. The Sino-barbarian autocracy which was dominant at the start of the new empire came into conflict with a new class of civil servant created to reinforce the administrative framework of the state. The system of allotment of land to the peasantry and of supervision of landed properties which had persisted in North China since the formation of the centralized state was in decline and was to be replaced, at the end of the eighth century, by a system of taxes on harvests; rights over men and their work were replaced by rights over cultivated lands. In a similar fashion, conscription for a specified period was soon to give way to permanent mercenary forces.

755–960. The warlike aristocracy which had reunited the Chinese lands was eliminated simultaneously with the new class of civil servants which had grown up in the course of the preceding period. Military adventurers enrolled armies of mercenaries and divided the Chinese lands between them.

III. The Mandarinal state and its restoration after the Mongol occupation

960–1280. Reunification was the work of one of these army leaders. But the need for an administrative apparatus and the upsurge of the state's economy caused the rapid development of the civil service and the perfecting of the political and administrative machinery. The rapid reproduction of writing through printing five centuries before Europe favored the spread of education and the growth of a lettered class that came to dominate Chinese political life until the present century. Put aside under the Mongols, this class consequently often entered into conflict with the central power.

1280–1370. Big non-Chinese empires which borrowed their institutions from China had come into being on the northern borders during the course of the previous period. They were eliminated from the beginning of the thirteenth century onwards by the growing power of the Mongols, whose authoritarian and feudal regime presents special characteristics and rested on largely non-Chinese personnel. This regime was extended by the conquest of the whole of China at the end of the thirteenth century, but it was swept away by popular uprisings which began in the middle of the following century.

1370–1520. The empire which grew out of the popular revolts of the end of the Mongol period displayed from the start very strong autocratic tendencies. The central power distrusted its own agents and supervised them by means of a secret police.

1520–1650. Tension grew sharper as the result of a new economic and intellectual upsurge. The contradiction between the rigidity of the political institutions and the profound social and economic changes of the sixteenth century caused from about 1600 onwards a serious social and political crisis which was soon followed by insurrections of mercenaries and peasants.

IV. The Manchu empire

1650–1800. Sinicized peoples who had taken possession of the northeastern territories (Manchuria) in the course of the first half of the seventeenth century took advantage of the anarchy prevailing in China to overcome the old Chinese governing classes and take their place. The military and feudal regime established immediately after the invasion was progressively relaxed as the new rulers adopted in all essentials the institutions of the preceding dynasty, seeking at the same time to win over the old scholarly classes. Through the collaboration of these classes the new dynasty was enabled to avoid the dangerous tensions which had arisen in the first half of the seventeenth century. An unprecedented prosperity contributed to social peace.

1800–1900. But a financial crisis, the development of corruption, and an economic recession caused the situation to worsen from about 1800 onwards. This deterioration, which continued during the first half of the nineteenth century, ended in a fearsome social explosion between 1850 and 1870. In the last thirty years of the nineteenth century the economic and military pressure of the Western nations, soon to be joined by Japan, caused the decomposition of the state and society, the collapse of the economy, and the loss of national independence.

V. Contemporary China

1900–1950. New political currents appeared, the most important of them represented by the commercial middle class which had grown up as a result of the foreign settlements in the big ports and in South-East Asia. But real power lay in the hands of leaders of new armies supported by the foreign powers. This long crisis was partially resolved by the creation of a military dictatorship which was to be finally swept away through the development of peasant militias, whose leaders founded in 1949 the People's Republic of China.

1950–1993. The new regime, modeled on that of the Soviet Union, restored the economy and committed itself to a radical transformation of society. This pace quickened with the Great Leap Forward (1958–1959) inspired by the utopian ideas of Mao Tse-tung. Natural catastrophes during 1960–61 and the break with the USSR forced a return to realism and practicality until the terrible Cultural Revolution of 1966–70, whose disastrous consequences began slowly to attenuate only after the death of Mao Tse-tung in 1976. The tragedy at T'ien-an Men Square in 1989 cruelly disappointed hopes, born from a moderate liberalization of the economy, for a democratization of the political system. Finally, although the form of the central government remains unchanged, the development at the end of the 1980s of the maritime provinces, a consequence of the massive injection of capital from the wealthy countries of East Asia, and the rapid increase in speed of the economic take-off at the beginning of the 1990s seem to portend profound changes and turmoil.

This much-simplified outline of the political history of the Chinese world does not take account of other important aspects of its evolution; for example, the expansion of peoples of Chinese language and culture, the enlargement of the political units, periods of military expansion and colonization.the little Chinese cities of remote antiquity were only enclaves in the midst of vast extents of uncultivated land and did not extend beyond the limits of the lower basin of the Yellow River. The exploitation of the plains of North China dates only from the fourth to first centuries B.C. The colonization of the southern provinces was a long-lasting affair which began at the end of the third century B.C. The warlike China of the sixth to eighth centuries A.D. turned towards central Asia and succeeded in extending its authority to the regions beyond the Pamirs, while China of the twelfth and thirteenth centuries was a maritime, trading land threatened by the advance of the empires of the steppe. The Sino-Manchu empire which in the eighteenth century dominated the major part of China attached more importance to continental problems than to the very active commerce which occupied its maritime provinces in the south and south-east.

Nor does this outline take account of the successive advances in technology which were always followed by fresh increases in population. In ancient times the population of the Chinese lands was doubtless only a few million; the great advances in technology (agricultural, metallurgical, and mechanical) of the fourth to second centuries B.C. were probably responsible for the clear increase in population revealed by the first census known to us, which gives a figure of 57 million in A.D. 2. The second great period of technical innovation lies between the eighth and eleventh centuries A.D. (progress of rice growing in flood conditions, selection of species, printing, paper money, new machines, appearance of the big high-seas junk) and brought a new demographic upsurge; between the eleventh and fifteenth centuries the population expanded to more than a hundred million. Finally, the introduction of American plants and the progress made in certain branches of technology (weaving, ceramics, printing) from the beginning of the sixteenth century onwards made possible the biggest increases in history between that century and about 1830. More recent developments date from our own day and run parallel to those in other parts of the world.

If the history of ideas, of religions, and of literature occupies a place in this book, it is not as an appendix to a political, economic, and social history which would be self-sufficient on its own, but because these two kinds of history really form one and the distinction often made between them is an artificial one. It was important to show or remind the reader that the Chinese world has an intellectual *history,* that is, that in all the domains of knowledge and thought there has been that accumulation of successive experiences, that process of assimilation of the new to the old, of deepening and development which is characteristic of all history. It is necessary to emphasize the specific orientation, the originality of Chinese intellectual traditions, and at the same time the influence of the contributions from abroad which link China to the rest of the world and account for the very general parallelism of developments. It is difficult not to be struck by the analogies which ally the great impulse of Buddhist fervour in China to that of medieval Christianity and the distant affinities which unite the great Chinese thinkers of the seventeenth and eighteenth centuries to the 'philosophers' of the century of the Enlightenment in Europe. Thus what the West has been able to contribute to China in recent times is not so radically new as the man in the street tends to imagine: mathematics, moral and political philosophy, sociology, historical and textual criticism all developed there in the course of a long history and China found herself, in many domains, on a level with the West when the latter discovered her.

The general characteristics of Chinese civilization

Chinese civilization seems to be tied to a brand of highly developed agriculture which confined itself almost exclusively to the plains and valleys. Mountains are scarcely utilized in Chinese or sinicized lands and remain the realm of different types of population. Moreover, the rearing of grazing animals is limited to essential needs in the way of draught- and pack-animals. While in India, in the Middle East, in the Mediterranean basin, and in Europe the grazing animal—the ox, the horse, the camel, the sheep, and the goat—plays a major role in the economy and in people's conceptions, and while in all these regions agriculture and livestock raising are closely associated with each other, the Far East is the only part of the world where there is such a sharp division between livestock-raisers and tillers of the soil. This antithesis, which alone would suffice to indicate the originality of the Far East and which has had extremely important consequences, is doubtless the expression of one of those choices which are proper to civilization, but it was also formed by geography; the great stock-farming regions lie to the north-west and north of the big fertile plains of the Yellow River basin.

Modern writers have insisted on the predominance of an agricultural economy in Chinese lands. But it looks as if a recent exceptional state of affairs led them to emphasize too exclusively the rural character of the Chinese world and to draw general conclusions from it. It was in fact a severe economic recession that caused China to become in the first half of the twentieth century an unorganized conglomeration of village communities which lived with some difficulty on the resources of agriculture alone. In the eyes of the other peoples of the Far East and in those of the rest of the world, China was distinguished until a quite recent period by other characteristics than the agricultural foundation of her economy.

One of her most outstanding merits is to have developed, in the course of a long process of evolution, complex forms of political organization which were the most highly perfected in the history of human societies. It is in fact astonishing and remarkable that it should have been possible to extend a unified administrative system so early to a world as vast as Europe and containing human beings of comparable diversity. One has only to think of Mirabeau's description of pre-1789 France: 'An unorganized aggregate of disunited peoples'! The Chinese world was also among those which took the most trouble to organize their living space in a systematic way, with roads, staging posts, granaries, walled cities, walls for defence, regulated water courses, reservoirs, canals, and so on. The development of the political sphere in the Chinese world and its pre-eminence over all the other (military, religious, economic) is one of its most characteristic marks.

But Chinese civilization is also first and foremost a technical civilization. Unlike the nomadic stock-raisers who use skins and felt, it soon invented weaving techniques requiring considerable skill: silk weaving by the end of the second millennium B.C., cotton by the end of the thirteenth century A.D. But it also displayed at the same time remarkable aptitude in the arts involving the use of fire, on the one hand in the techniques of pottery – the history of Chinese ceramics is one of the richest in the world and the art of making porcelain had reached perfection in China by the twelfth century – and on the other hand in metallurgy: Shang bronzes from the end of the second millenium B.C. are the finest ever produced; the production of cast iron had become a big Chinese industry by the fourth century B.C.; and Chinese smelters succeeded in regularly producing steel some centuries later. Although Chinese civilization has recently been described as a 'vegetable civilization', for all the peoples of Asia, China was the land of the most skilled metallurgists.

Chinese craftsmen and engineers were called to Persia and even to Russia. Up to the nineteenth century China was a big exporter of luxury products, the traffic in which was world-wide: silks from the third century B.C. to the nineteenth century, ceramics, cotton goods, tea. Nor should we forget bronze mirrors, lacquer ware, hardware, furniture, books, and paintings. It was because there was a great deal of commercial activity in the Far East that the maritime nations of Europe were drawn to that part of the world from the beginning of the sixteenth century onwards. A China with an exclusively rural economy would have held no attraction for them.

The view that people usually hold of the Chinese world is thus false; yet it reflects a general truth that is felt in a somewhat confused way, namely that because of the pre-eminence of the political function—the organization of living space and society—economic activity could not attain in China, any more than religious or military activities, the same degree of autonomy or specificity as in other civilizations. No doubt there existed in the Chinese world independent forms of religious life, military circles with their own traditions, a very active mercantile sector which escaped the hold of the state, but no clergy, no military caste, no merchant class ever succeeded in gaining political power. This is certainly one of the constants and one of the great original aspects of the Chinese world, one that distinguishes it from all others.

We find in China neither that subordination of the human order to the divine order nor that vision of the world as a creation born of ritual and maintained by ritual which are part of the mental universe of India. Nor can the stock-raiser of the steppe see or understand the world as it is seen by a Chinese, the product of a civilization of farmers and craftsmen. The nomadic herdsman knows what the appropriation of property means because he practises it every day. Property acquired as booty, slavery in the strict sense of the term, the power of command, the division of pastures, wealth and men captured on raids determine the social and political order of nomadic stock-raisers. They call up before the mind's eye a world founded on force and right, attitudes of mind and modes of behaviour which seem more familiar to us, because of our Indo-European—Latin, Celtic, and German—past than that of the Chinese. Among these peoples, who only adopted writing in the transitory periods when they formed states, the spoken word possesses value and power which are the prerogative of the written word in the Chinese world.

Political power, generally conceived as the power of constraint and command, was seen in China as the principle that gave life and order, even if this conception did not exclude recourse to force and brutal interventions. But constraint is always accompanied in China by the idea of moral correction. It would be a mistake to see in the insistence laid on the regulation of morals only a pretext, a sort of alibi for a tyrannical regime; it is in fact the expression of a privileged mode of political action which has lasted down to our day. Thus we should only be deceiving ourselves if we thought that we had torn away the mask from a power that was simply autocratic.

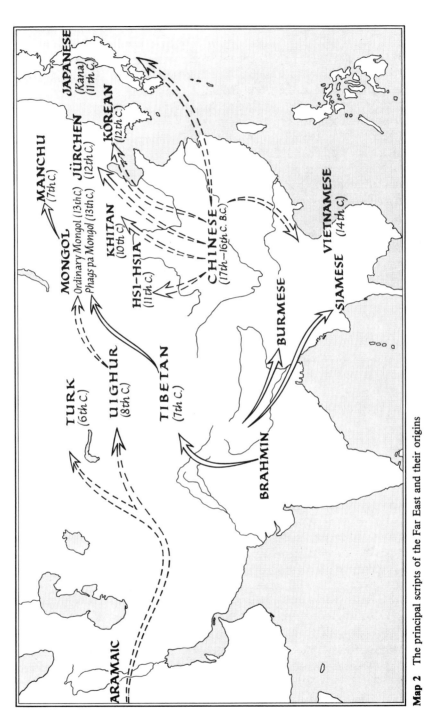

Map 2 The principal scripts of the Far East and their origins

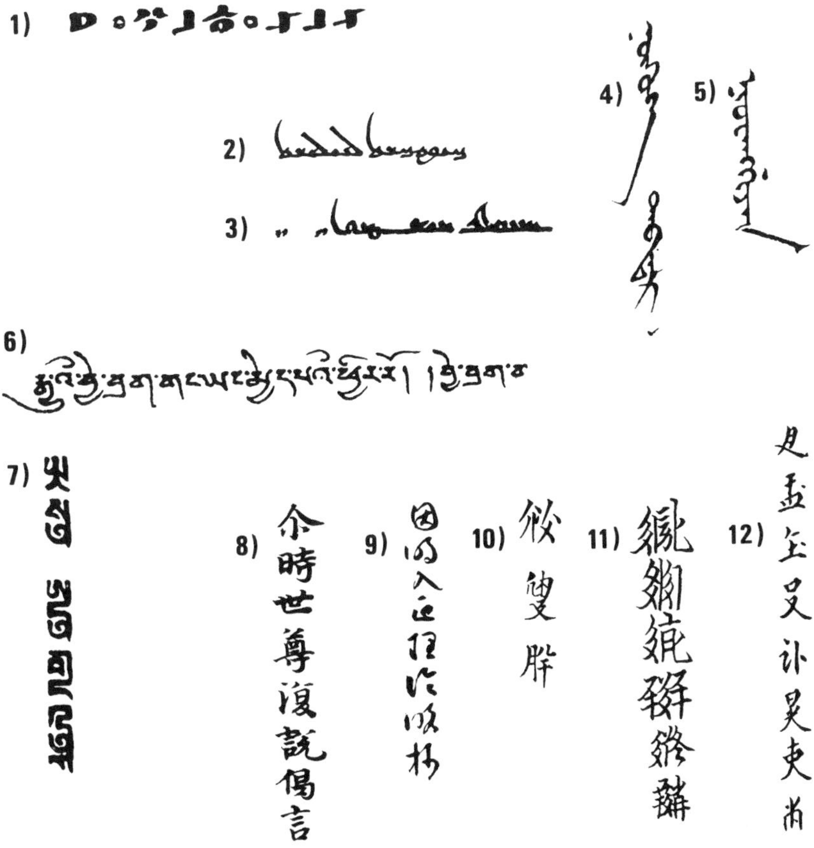

Figure 1 Types of script found in China and the border areas. 1. Turkish from the Orkhon River region; *scripts derived from the Aramaic alphabet*: 2. Sogdian; 3. Uighur; 4. Standard Mongol; 5. Manchu; *scripts derived from the Indian*: 6. Tibetan; 7. Mongol 'phags-pa; *scripts derived from Chinese*: 8. Chinese, regular style; 9. Chinese, cursive style; 10. Khitan; 11. Hsi-Hsia; 12. Jürchen

This remark leads us on to the dangerous ground of the general characteristics of Chinese thought. We must know exactly what we are talking about: which period, which sector of human activity, which social milieu. Yet it is quite clear to all those who have been in contact with this world that it is quite different from the one in which we ourselves have been moulded and that it remains so today. Its fundamental traditions — political, religious, aesthetic, juridical — are different from those of the Indian world, of Islam, of the Christian world of the West (in any case, the civilizations whose domains stop short of the fearsome barrier of the Himalayas have had numerous and frequent contacts with each other). China does not know the transcendent truths, the idea of good in itself, the notion of property in the strict sense of the term. She does not like the exclusion of opposition, the idea of the absolute, the positive distinction between mind and matter; she prefers the notions of complementarity, or circulation, influx, of action at a distance, of a model, and the idea of order as an organic totality. She does not have recourse to exhaustive inventories after the fashion of the Mesopotamian world or to neatly boxed classifications in the Indian style; for Chinese thought, the order of beings and of the world is best translated by systems of variable, dynamic symbols. Her logic does not proceed from an analysis of language. It is based on the handling of signs with opposing and complementary values. Perhaps Chinese writing is not unconnected with these deep-rooted tendencies which have ended by giving a privileged position to the written sign at the expense of the spoken word.

Writing

There are close links between writing and civilization. Without this means of recording and transmitting facts and ideas, which gives man a hold over space and time, the great civilizations would not have been able to develop. But the sort of writing used has had profound effects on the general orientation of these civilizations. Chinese writing enables us better than any other to appreciate this very important fact. It provides the only example of writing totally original in its principle—every sign corresponds as a rule to a semantic unit—and consequently extremely complex, which has nevertheless served as means of expression to such a large part of humanity. Its complexity no doubt redounded to the advantage of the social classes which were able to have access to it, but much less than one would be tempted to think: persons capable of reading have never formed in any society anything but a small minority, and the proportion of educated people seems to have been generally higher in the Chinese world than in the West, even though the process of becoming familiar with the Latin alphabet did not require a particularly protracted effort. The paradox is explained by the importance attached in China to a knowledge of writing and to book knowledge.

On the other hand, in several domains the original nature of Chinese writing had fundamental consequences, to the extent that this writing was unaffected by the phonetic changes that occurred in the course of time, by dialectal variations, and even by differences in linguistic structure. After the unification of the script imposed by Ch'in in the Chinese lands at the end of the third century B.C. this writing became one of the most effective instruments of political unification. The development in

China of a written language designed for the eye and accessible to all the Chinese lands was due to reasons that were at the same time linguistic (the diversity of the dialects), political, and administrative. In principle there was no obligatory oral standard until our own day and the same text can be read aloud in different dialects. Whenever people cannot communicate orally the written text permits mutual comprehension. Thus by virtue of its very nature Chinese writing became a sort of universal means of expression in every part of Asia subject to Chinese civilization or influence.

Peoples whose languages were profoundly different from Chinese (Korean, Japanese, Vietnamese) adopted Chinese writing, which they used to read, and still do read, in their own way and in accordance with their own linguistic habits. Written Chinese remained the cultural and administrative language of Vietnam until the French conquest and that of Korea down to the Japanese annexation, just as it had been that of Japan during the centuries when the influence of China was preponderant in that country. Thus there exists a whole literature in Chinese whose creators — poets, historians, novelists, philologians, and philosophers — were not Chinese at all, but Korean, Japanese, and Vietnamese. It is consequently legitimate to say that in East Asia there was a real community of civilization characterized by use of the Chinese script.

Another consequence of the original nature of this script concerns the sort of learning and culture which grew up in the Chinese world and in the lands affected by Chinese civilization. Its indifference to phonetic changes made possible a continuity of written tradition which is not to be found in any other civilization; though the style may vary according to the period and the kind of text, it is scarcely more difficult, and sometimes less so, to read a text written in the second century B.C. than to read a work written in the classical language in the contemporary period. This is the explanation of the traditional character of Chinese learning and its astonishing accumulation down the centuries. The realm of expression has seen the growth of an inexhaustible repertory of formulas, an endless store of binomials *(tz'u)*, the result of the continuous contributions of generations of poets, political writers, historians, moralists and scholars. The extraordinary continuity of the written tradition means that the reading of the texts requires above all enormous erudition, the acquisition of which takes far longer than that of the writing itself. This continuity explains not only the role of writing as an instrument of government and administration but also the great prestige of the 'lettered person', the man of culture and taste, qualified to exercise political functions. The art of oratory, so highly prized in the Graeco-Roman world, occupies only a subsidiary position in the lands belonging to Chinese civilization. Through its intimate links with the political, social, aesthetic, and intellectual aspects of the Chinese world, the script itself forms an introduction to the understanding of its civilization.

But finally a strange paradox must be mentioned: this complicated and apparently inconvenient script was in fact, in much simplified cursive forms, the first shorthand in history. Commonly used to note down on the spot conversations, political discussions, legal proceedings, the torrent of words uttered by people possessed by spirits, Chinese writing made possible very early on and very widely something that alphabetic scripts achieved less easily, the immediate notation of the spoken word. An Arab work written at Baghdad in 988 records the astonishment of the famous Mohammed al-Razi (850–925) when he saw a Chinese, no doubt passing through the Abbasid capital, translate and note down as they were dictated the works of Galen, one of the fathers of Greek medicine (second century A.D.).

Far from forming some kind of exception, Chinese writing inspired the creation in East Asia of scripts of the same type (Khitan in the tenth century, Tangut Hsi-Hsia in the eleventh century, Jürchen in the twelfth century, Vietnamese *chunom* in the fourteenth) and its cursive forms served as the foundation of the Japanese syllabaries and the Korean alphabet.

Part 1

From the Archaic Monarchy to the Centralized State

Chapter 1

The Archaic Monarchy

The Neolithic antecedents

Numerous archaeological discoveries made in the second half of this century in all regions of China as well as on its borders have particularly enriched our knowledge of the most ancient history and often confirmed written evidence.[1] These discoveries have drastically modified the traditional image of the origins of Chinese civilization, which seems to have been the product of diverse cultures native to East Asia.

We still know little about that period, around 8,000 B.C., when a still primitive agricultural economy replaced that of populations that lived exclusively by hunting, gathering, and fishing. But archaeological evidence is not lacking for the following millennia: remains of dwellings dating from 6,500 to 5,000 are numerous in the valleys of the Wei River (modern Shensi) and the middle Yellow River and reveal an already well-developed agriculture (cultivation of millet *Setaria italica* and *Panicum miliaceum*, domestication of pigs and dogs, perhaps of chickens) along with varied implements of stone and bone. Ceramic works are still rather coarse, although there are perceptible regional differences in form and decor. But it is in Southern China that the oldest ceramic fragments have been discovered, decorated for the most part with corded motifs. These multiple remains furnish proof of the existence, unsuspected till recently, of a great southern Neolithic tradition largely anterior to 5,000.

1. This section owes much to information supplied by Mr. Alain Thote.

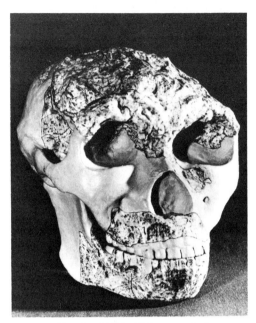

Plate 2.   Middle Pleistocene skull,
the so-called Lan-t'ien man

For the period after this date, the recent discoveries have brought to light several great, distinct cultures spread over vast geographical groupings:

1. Yangshao culture, known from several hundred sites (carbon 14 dates from 5,150 to 2,960), stretched from Kansu to the central plain and comprised the southern regions of Shansi and Hopei. This is the zone of loess, a fine dust deposited probably in the Pleistocene and still present today in thick layers in northwest China. This far from homogeneous culture was characterized in a general way by the importance of agricultural economy, combined nevertheless with hunting, fishing, and gathering; stone tools including hoes, spades, knives, and wheels; and the breeding of pigs, dogs, and perhaps bovines. Ceramic works present a large regional diversity of production techniques and of painted or corded decoration. The most attractive pottery is ornamented with geometric designs and sometimes with highly stylized drawings of fish in black or red.

2. Ta-wen k'ou culture (4,746–3,655) covered the Shantung peninsula and a part of the large alluvial basin of the Yellow River. Its economy was based, as was that of Yangshao, on the cultivation of millet. The form

of their vessels is more elaborate and the decoration is made up of open-work, appliqué, or impressions from basket making. The range of shades and the homogeneity of the paste shows that there has been a selection of different clays.

3. Four other cultures nearly contemporary with those at Yangshao and Ta-wen k'ou and of a comparable technical level can be distinguished in the middle and lower valleys of the Yangtze. But a very different geographical context distinguishes these cultures: rice in the two species *Oryza sativa japonica* and *Oryza sativa indica* constituted the main cereal from about 5,000 B.C. The domestication of the buffalo is attested to have taken place during the same time as that of the dog and the pig. Wooden and bone implements preponderate over those in stone, and the construction of houses involved recourse to a skilled wooden joinery using mortise and tenon. It is also in the lower Yangtze that the earliest shuttles for weaving have been discovered. Toward the end of the fourth millennium the firing temperature for ceramics reached 950 to 1,000 degrees.

4. Further south, in the maritime provinces of Fukien and Kwangtung as well as Taiwan, populations that seem to have come to agriculture somewhat later appear to have practiced a primitive form of gardening. These cultures are not yet well known.

A Hsia dynasty

As the different cultures of the middle Neolithic developed and spread, contacts and exchanges between them multiplied, and more extended and homogeneous groupings came into being. There is proof of significant progress during the fourth and third millennia (elaborate working in jade, handicrafts in bamboo, silk weaving, and hemp in the lower Yangtze; improvements in stone, shell, bone, and wooden implements, greater use of the potter's wheel, and the appearance of extremely refined and elegant ceramic wares in North China). Certain characteristics already preview the bronze age: the form of certain vessels, a divinatory practice in which animal bones were heated with fire, buildings erected on the ground itself and no longer partially subterranean, major embankments of rammed earth, sacrifices connected to foundations and tombs. . . . Copper or an alloy containing a high proportion of copper began to be worked. Although there is still no archaeological evidence that can be precisely linked to the Hsia dynasty (traditional dates: 2,207–1,766), for which history preserves only a list of sovereigns, there is here an assemblage of characteristics that is already that of the bronze age and that renders very probable the existence of this dynasty. It is in this context of evolving Neolithic cultures and in the midst of rather dense populations that the city-palace very likely appeared. Later in the second millennium, these city-palaces developed into centers of power based on the possession of bronze weaponry. These general conditions are analogous to those that gave birth to the first civilizations in Mesopotamia, the Indus valley, and Egypt, all of which appeared likewise in great river basins. It is therefore justifiable to trace the first city-palaces and the first manifestations of Chinese civilization to the end of the third millennium.

The archaic monarchy

The most recent archaeological discoveries have brought to light bronzes much older than those of the 'An-yang' period (fourteenth to eleventh centuries B.C.), and the appearance of bronze in the lower valley of the Yellow River has lost the character of suddenness which had struck archaeologists before the Second World War. Nevertheless the Bronze Age in China does not seem to have been preceded by the long period during which pure metals were used that we find in the western parts of the continent. It also appears later than in the Middle East. On the other hand, in the second half of the second millennium B.C. its technology achieved a degree of perfection which was to remain unknown elsewhere. Certain peculiarities of the Far East help to explain this remarkable technological success. The mastery of the potters of Lungshan, the high temperatures which they seem to have been capable of obtaining, and the restricted role of hammering and forging in the technical traditions of the Far East all incline one to favour the idea of an independent discovery of bronze metallurgy. And while we should not rule out entirely any possibility of influences from afar, it is clear that in the case of bronze, as in that of other elements of civilization, these influences were very quickly integrated into the culture of archaic China. There had grown up in the lower valley of the Yangtze by the end of the Neolithic Age a nucleus of civilization which possessed its own original characteristics and was to make its influence felt all over the Far East.

There are good reasons for connecting the Bronze Age civilization with the Lungshan culture, for they possess certain characteristics in common:

1. the process of ramming earth in successive layers;
2. the fortification of urban sites by thick walls of rammed earth;
3. divination by means of animal bones subjected to the action of fire;
4. very typical shapes which appear in closely related versions both in

the fine black pottery of Shantung (Lungshan) and in the bronze vessels of the Shang period.

Finally, historical tradition, according to which the earliest dynasties moved their capitals from east to west, is in harmony with the respective positions of the centre of the Lungshan culture in Shantung and of the capitals, which lie further to the west, of the Shang period.

The first dynasty of the Bronze Age: the Shang or Yin

Although it is extremely probable that forms of political organization prefiguring the monarchy of the Shang period preceded it and that the traditions relating to the existence of a Neolithic dynasty—that of the Hsia—are not entirely without foundation, it remains true that the rapid development of bronze technology coincided with a remarkable upsurge in archaic civilization. The remains of the last capital of the Shang/Yin (in the north-east of Honan, close to present-day An-yang), which was occupied from the fourteenth century B.C. to the end of the eleventh century, reveal an already highly developed civilization, in possession of a whole range of skilled techniques and knowledge, the antecedents of which are not very well known. On the whole, writing, the chariot, architectural techniques, the practice of divination, the art of working in bronze, various kinds of sacrificial vessel and decorative motifs all appear in the lower basin of the Yellow River in forms that are already very elaborate. The discoveries made since 1950 have enabled us to go much further back in time and to understand better than before the process of development which made it possible to attain, in each domain, the degree of refinement and complexity characteristic of the last Shang period. We are probably justified in dating the beginning of this dynasty — and doubtless the early days of the Bronze Age — to the middle or end of the seventeenth century B.C., but in describing Shang civilization we are forced to refer principally to the excavations at An-yang.

The site of Ta Shang or Ta-yi Shang, the last capital of the Shang (or Yin, according to a name in use during the last period), was occupied during the reigns of the last eleven kings of this dynasty, which, according to tradition, comprised about thirty monarchs and experienced six changes of capital in the area between western Shantung, southern Hopei, western Honan, and northern Anhwei. The remains are spread over a wide area. The excavations have uncovered a small citadel, with walls of rammed earth running east-west and north-south as in the Chinese cities of later ages in North China; pits containing bones and tortoise-shells that had been used for divination by fire and often bear inscriptions; the remains of foundations and of rectangular buildings with stone bases and bronze cushions intended to support pillars; funerary pits containing human victims and dogs (the sacrificed men, arranged outside the buildings and turned outwards, were equipped with battle-axes, *ge*, and had bronze vases by them); and five graves containing harnessed chariots with their drivers. In some graves the remains of decapitated men were found, in others heads without bodies. Finally, some large tombs, obviously royal tombs, have also been brought to light. Most of these discoveries, which suggest the existence of rites connected with building and the sacrifice of prisoners of war, were made between 1927 and 1936.

Since 1950 numerous other sites of the Shang age have been discovered in North China. The most important one was found in 1953 in the suburbs of Chengchow in Honan. Archaeologists have uncovered there the base of a wall of rammed earth sixty feet thick, the remains of dwellings, workshops and furnaces, with moulds for producing bronzes, and a great deal of pottery. No big tomb of the sort found at An-yang has been brought to light, but as in the last capital of the Shang/Yin monarchs the prevailing orientations are north-south and east-west. The bronze objects are simple in workmanship, but the technical mastery displayed already surpasses that of the oldest remains of bronze art in the Middle East.

The only objects cast in bronze in these remote times were weapons, vessels connected with worship, and fittings of chariots and harnesses. Those of the end of the Shang age bear a complex and refined decoration, the style and motifs of which, relatively constant and limited in number, recur in an identical form on objects made of ivory, jade, or wood. The decoration consists of highly stylized drawings and shapes of animals arranged symmetrically on each side of a median axis. This animal art, which is entirely absent in the Neolithic Age, appears quite suddenly and seems to be typical of the Bronze Age in North-East Asia. It is found as far north as southern Siberia and in particular in the Karasuk culture (upper valleys of the Ob and Yenisei), which seems to have been in contact with Bronze Age China at the end of the Shang era and at the beginning of the Chou period. Analysis of the Shang bronzes reveals varying proportions of copper and tin according to the kind of alloy needed for different objects. The objects contain 5 to 30 percent of tin and 2 to 3 percent of lead. The finest pieces are obviously religious vessels, which exist in a large variety of shapes, each corresponding to a particular ritual use. In the Shang age these vessels still bear only very short inscriptions or marks which are doubtless the equivalent of family coats of arms. This kind of mark also appears on weapons, the most characteristic of which is the *ge*, an axe or dagger with a handle found

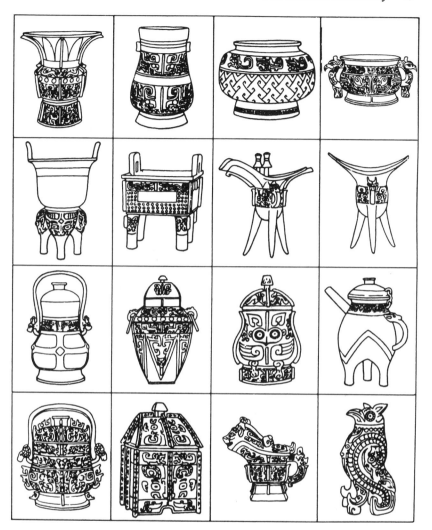

Figure 2   Different types of vessels connected with worship

only in the Far East and serving to hook on to the enemy and deliver the first blows.

The chariot, light and strong, with big, many-spoked wheels, is already of the type used in the following age, but seems to have been less widespread. Very close to the kinds of chariots known in the western parts of Asia in the Bronze Age (it should be remembered that the chariot and the domestication of the horse for draught work appear in Anatolia and Syria towards the seventeenth century B.C.), it is a vehicle with a square frame and curved shaft, drawn by two horses harnessed by a yoke round the withers, the only method of harnessing used in the world before the invention of the breast-strap and horse-collar. It was a weapon of war and an object to parade, restricted to the king and the upper ranks of the nobility. The ancient poets of the *Shih-ching* were to describe in the ninth to sixth centuries the beauties of parade chariots and their harnessed horses.

The chariot and some of the weapons used for war (in particular a composite retroflex bow which seems to have been very powerful) were also employed in the hunt, a sort of royal rite often alluded to in inscriptions. Big game (various kinds of deer, wild oxen, bears, tigers, and wild boars) was plentiful.

Archaeological data and inscriptions make it possible to form at least a general idea of what the society of the Shang age was like. Comparison with later evidence reveals at the same time a general concordance and numerous analogies — the society of the Chou age certainly seems to have been derived from that of the Shang age — and also distinctive characteristics.

The walled city, the chariot, and the bronze weapons and vessels are typical of an aristocratic class which can be defined by its participation in sacrifices and in war. It is about this class that the excavations and inscriptions have given us most information, for one can only glimpse the existence of a peasantry whose culture and tools (stone knives and wooden spades with curved handles) do not seem to have been very different from those of the Neolithic Age. The royal palace is the centre of all the activities of an aristocratic society dominated by the person of the king, who is on a much higher plane. Moreover, there is a close connection, or to be more accurate a positive lack of any distinction, between religious, military, political, administrative, and economic functions. The royal house is at the head of a clan-like organization in which the heads of families are at the same time heads of the family worship. There exist already territorial powers which seem to have been analogous to the fief as it is known in later ages. These powers, which correspond to the titles of *hou* and *po*, are normally exercised by members of the royal clan, but sometimes also by families with a different name. The Shang domain extended to the whole of the central plain and at certain points beyond it toward the valley of the Yangtze. Peoples alien to the Shang and regarded as barbarians coexisted in this area with the Bronze Age people, with whom they were most often on hostile terms. These peoples were particularly numerous in the north of Kiangsu and in the valley of the Huai.

It is by its religious practices and their predominant role that the Shang civilization is most clearly distinguished from that of the following age. The factors which should be emphasized are these: the importance of a kind of divination by fire which was to play only a secondary role in the following ages; the privileged position occupied by the cult of dead kings and the sumptuous nature of the sacrifices; and the practice of making human sacrifices, which tended to disappear under the Chou monarchs.

Divination and sacrifices

The custom of applying heat to the bones of sacrificed animals for purposes of divination is peculiar to the Far East, which was unfamiliar with the practice of examining entrails, so common in the western parts of the Eurasian continent. The custom, already attested in the Neolithic Age, was perfected and developed much further in the Bronze Age, becoming one of the most important aspects of royal activity and giving rise to a positive service of divination which was the prerogative of colleges of specialists. The bones used for divination were now prepared with more care and contained superimposed circular and oval cavities which made it possible to obtain through the action of the fire T-shaped cracks (the character *pu* designates this very ancient kind of divination). Towards the end of the An-yang period the use of the ventral shells of tortoises became general. More than 100,000 bones and tortoise-shells bearing inscriptions have been found since the beginning of the twentieth century. They all come, except for a very small number, from the site of the last capital of the Shang/Yin. Of this total, more than 50,000 inscriptions have been published and studied. The first engraved pieces appeared in chemists' shops, where they were sold as dragons' bones. They attracted the attention of the epigraphist Wang I-jung (1845–1919) and were identified by his friend Lin E (1857–1909) as documents of the Shang dynasty. Since that time numerous Chinese scholars have devoted themselves to the study of these divinatory inscriptions (*pu-tz'u,* or *chia-ku wen*: 'inscriptions on shells and on bone'). At the same time scientific knowledge of the Shang sites progressed with the excavations carried out by the Academia Sinica from 1927 to 1936 and with the discoveries made since 1950. Thus the religious, political, and social aspects of the Shang monarchy in its last period could be investigated in detail and although many uncertainties remain the knowledge acquired is considerable.

Engraved after the fire test and serving as a sort of commentary on the signs obtained, the inscriptions were intended to form archives which made possible the development of the service of divination. These archives constitute the oldest form of historiography in China and they imparted to it from the start its essential characteristics: its close link with

Plate 3.   Oracle tortoise-shell, c. 1000 B.C., reputed to be China's earliest miniature carving

political activity and the aspect which made it a sort of science of precedents. Divination had a bearing on all the activities connected with the royal function: worship of ancestors and divinities, military expeditions, appointments to official posts, summonses to court, construction of towns, agricultural campaigns, meteorology (rain, drought, and winds), illnesses, journeys, dreams, births, and the propitious or unpropitious nature of the decade or night to come.

Study of these inscriptions furnishes the most ancient forms of the Chinese written characters and reveals the extraordinary continuity of the graphic tradition, even if we take into account the important changes which occurred between the Shang and Chou ages. Quite a large number of characters belonging to the script in use today have come down by a process of uninterrupted evolution from the fourteenth to eleventh centuries B.C. Already very complex and containing nearly 5000 characters, of which 1500 have been reliably interpreted, this archaic writing is familiar with most of the principles of formation which were to make subsequent developments possible: alongside simple signs (*wen*) (conventional signs or very much stylized drawings of objects or parts of objects) we already find signs employed by association (*tzu*). But it can also happen, as in the oldest scripts of the Middle East, that certain signs are employed for their phonetic value independently of their original meaning.

The colleges or groups of soothsayers and scribes who were entrusted with the royal divination (different schools of innovators and traditionalists grew up in the course of the An-yang period) were preoccupied by questions of number and questions relating to the calendar. We already find in the inscriptions on bones and shells the two forms of numeration which were to be used throughout the history of the Chinese world: a continuous decimal numeration represented by means of ten simple signs from 1 to 10 and a sign for 100, to which a sign for 10,000 was to be added; and two series of more complex signs, one of ten symbols and the other of twelve, the combination of which was to serve to form a cycle of sixty double signs. These signs were used simply for the notation of the days; the cycle of sixty was only applied to the years as well from the second century B.C. onwards. The decade of ten days and combinations of the decade are the basis of the division of time in the Shang period and it is noticeable that the names of the kings always include one of the signs denoting the decade. It seems that it corresponded to the day on which sacrifices had to be made to them.

There were a large number of sacrifices occurring either at a fixed date or more irregularly. The most important ones were related to the worship of dead kings, a cult in which the queens were sometimes associated. Inscriptions have enabled us to draw up a complete list of the Shang kings which goes back even beyond the foundation of the dynasty. The succession ran from elder brother to younger brother and when all the brothers were dead from maternal uncle to nephew. Thus although the list of Shang kings enumerates thirty sovereigns the number of generations is only eighteen. This list coincides, apart from a few details, with the one preserved by subsequent tradition and to be found in the *Historical Records* (*Shih-chi*) of Ssu-ma Ch'ien, which were completed at the beginning of the first century B.C.

Oxen, sheeep, pigs, and dogs were sacrificed in large numbers. Offerings of thirty or forty oxen for one single ancestor are not infrequent. Certain characters in the script serve to denote sacrifices of a hundred oxen or a hundred pigs and sacrifices of various animals in tens. The abundance of victims, which does not recur in later ages, suggests that stock farming occupied a relatively important place in the economy of this archaic society. On the occasion of big banquets worship ensured a redistribution of wealth. It could also involve massive slaughters, especially at the funerals of kings.

The most striking picture of China in the Shang period is afforded by the big royal tombs discovered at An-yang between 1927 and 1936.

Plates 4-9.   Shang ritual implements

Cruciform in plan, they comprise a big rectangular grave on a north-south axis, with a smaller, deeper, central grave. Two, and sometimes four, access ramps fifteen to twenty yards long lead down to the level of the main excavation. The royal coffin, made of wood, lay above the central grave, in which a dog had been sacrificed. On the access ramps and on the platform surrounding this grave were found the remains of men-at-arms—doubtless the companions and servants of the king—his chariot with its horses and their drivers, pottery, bronze vases, and other objects of value. The custom of sacrificing a royal person's closest servants at his funeral, a custom which also demands that the king should be surrounded by his most precious goods and by the insignia of his rank (mainly his chariot and horses), recurs in numerous other Bronze Age civilizations.

The divinatory inscriptions deal also with other cults. An important sacrifice bearing the name of *ti* or *shang-ti* (the term was adopted later to denote the mythical sovereigns of the earliest ages and was to be used by the first emperor to create the new term *Huang Ti* at the end of the third century B.C.) seems to have given birth to the idea of a superior deity, guarantor of the political order (protector of towns and armies) and of the natural order (rain, wind, droughts). But there are also less important deities: the mother of the east, the mother of the west, the lords of the four cardinal points of the compass, the source of the river Huan, which passes near An-yang, the Yellow River, certain sacred mountains, and so on. Shamans of some sort (*shih*: this term, which also means 'corpse', indicates the representative of the dead man in the funerary ritual of the Chou period) and sorcerers (*wu*) seem to have played a part in certain cults.

Human sacrifices appear to have been one of the characteristics of the civilization of the Shang age; some seem to be connected with the consecration rites of buildings, others to be linked to the funerary cult or to form part of the sacrifices made in honour of dead kings. The only practice which was to survive, and that in a sporadic way, was the one that required the prince's closest companions and his concubines to follow him in death, and these human victims were to be replaced more and more often in the course of the first millennium by mannekins or figurines.

Chapter 2

The Age of the Principalities

The decline of the archaic monarchy

According to a tradition which there is no reason to doubt, a state by the name of Chou, in Shensi, put an end to the Shang/Yin dynasty. It looks as if the event can be dated to round about 1050 or 1025 B.C. Situated outside the Shang domain, this city, which was in permanent contact with the barbarian peoples of these western regions, seems to have been able to take advantage of geographical conditions favourable to horse breeding: in subsequent periods the upper valley of the Ching and the north-east of Kansu were regions given over to stud-farms. The Chou, doubtless more warlike than the Shang, seem to have made wider use of the chariot and to have invented a new kind of harness with four horses abreast.

The first few centuries of the Chou

The story of the replacement of the Shang by the Chou as recorded by tradition merits a brief retelling because of the prestige which was to be enjoyed by the founders of the Chou dynasty in the Lu school of letters, that is, in the so-called 'Confucian' tradition.

Led by the man known to later history as King Wen, so the story goes, the people of Chou marched on Honan just when the last Shang sovereign was occupied by a war against the barbarians of Huai. In the course of the victorious Chou advance King Wen died in a fight and was succeeded by King Wu. The Shang were finally beaten at the battle of Mu-ye, to the north of the Yellow River, and the last Shang king, Chou-hsin was beheaded. Kings Wen and Wu were honoured as liberators by the former subjects of the Shang and the barbarian peoples who had suffered the tyranny of Chou-hsin. After his victory King Wu entrusted the administration of the cities of the central plain to Wu-keng, the beheaded tyrant's son, and returned to Shensi, where he soon died. Disturbances occurred under his successor, King Ch'eng, of which Wu-keng, in alliance with the barbarians of Huai, took advantage to rebel against the authority of the Chou. The young King Ch'eng's uncle, the duke of Chou (Chou-kung), organized the defence and the counter-attack. Shang was destroyed and the barbarians of Huai offered their submission. From then on Chou had two capitals, Chou-tsung, near the present Sian in Shensi, and Ch'eng-chou, near the present Loyang in Honan. To secure their domination over the former Shang territories the Chou put members of their own line or of related families in charge of the old cities and of the new ones created in this period.

Traditional history then speaks—and this much can be accepted as reliable—of revolts by alien but assimilated peoples in the reigns of King Ch'eng's two successors, of efforts by the Chou to penetrate towards the north-west (Kansu and probably present-day eastern Sinkiang) in the reign of King Mu (middle or end of the tenth century?), and of this prince's battles against peoples called the Ch'üan-jung ('barbarian dogs') in the north-east and against the inhabitants of northern Kiangsu.

According to the sites and inscriptions discovered since 1950, it certainly seems that the beginning of the first millennium B.C.was a period of expansion. The Chou's colonizing efforts then reached the region of present-day Peking, the north-eastern extremity of Shangtung and the plains of the lower Yangtze.

On the other hand, the end of the ninth century and the eighth century were almost certainly a period of weakness and decline which can be related to attacks by foreign peoples: incursions under Hsüan-wang (827–782) by the Yen-yün, a steppe people who perhaps already rode horses, invasions of Shensi by the Ch'üan-jung in the reign of You-wang (781–771). It is just when the royal house of Chou is entering its period of decline, under King Li (878–828), that we begin to have at our disposal a precisely dated history. The first date in Chinese historiography is 841 B.C.

Traditional chronology

Traditional historiography divides the Chou age into two parts: one in which the kings of this dynasty had their main capital in the valley of the Wei (this period is known as the period of the Western Chou, from the end of the eleventh century to the year 771); and a second one which extends from the transfer of the capital to Ch'eng-chou (near present-day Loyang in Honan) to the destruction of Chou by the kingdom of Ch'in in 256 B.C. (this period is known as that of the Eastern Chou). But there are other traditional divisions; one is based on the existence of the annals of the kingdom of Lu in Shantung, which cover the years 722–481. Hence the name given to this period, Ch'un-ch'iu (Springs and Autumns), which is borrowed from the title of these annals. Finally, the age which precedes the imperial unification of 221 B.C. is known as the period of the Warring States (Chan-kuo) because of its incessant wars. The beginning of this period is sometimes fixed at the factual division of power in 453 B.C. with Chin (a kingdom which covered Shansi and part of Hopei and Honan), sometimes at the official recognition by the king of Chou in 403 B.C. of this division and of the kingdoms which had arisen out of it (Han, Wei, and Chao).

Seeing that rituals, religious traditions, and family hierarchies had been preserved in essentials down to the second half of the fifth century and had then been abolished, the ancient Chinese historians contrasted the Ch'un-ch'iu period with that of the Warring States. In fact the complex process of evolution which leads from the archaic monarchy — the main characteristics of which persist at the beginning of the Chou period — to the centralized state and the imperial unification does not present any real break in continuity.

From the principalities to the kingdoms

What we know of Chou society comes principally from a chronicle added as a sort of commentary to the *Annals of Lu*. This chronicle is called the *Traditions of Tso* (*Tso-shih-chuan* or *Tso-chuan*) and was no doubt put together in the fifth and fourth centuries B.C. But these traditions appear faithful enough to enable us to reconstruct, with the help of the other written sources and of the archaeological evidence, the kind of society which seems to have existed in the Chinese principalities of the ninth to seventh centuries.

The nobiliary society of the ninth to seventh centuries B.C.

The term 'feudal' has been so often misused that it has lost all meaning. It is better to do without it and to confine ourselves to characterizing by its specific institutions the political and social system which in the long history of the Chinese world was to come closest to the system to which the historians of the West first gave this epithet. In any case, the Chinese version is quite original because of the close links which cause the political organization to depend on the system of family cults and which unite the military function with the religious function. Arising out of the archaic monarchy, it is still closely bound to it.

It was based on a hierarchy of domains and family cults, with the royal domain and the worship of the ancestors of the Chou at its apex. The king bore the title of *T'ien-tzu* ('Son of Heaven') and was regarded as holding his post from the 'Lord on High' (*shang-ti*), to whom he alone had the right to make sacrifices. The capital, Chou-tsung in the valley of the Wei, was the great religious centre of the whole community of Chou cities. It was there that the temple of the deceased kings was situated.

Power was held in each city by families who owed their authority to the number of their chariots, their religious privileges (the right to perform certain sacrifices and particular hymns and dances), the age of their traditions and their links with the royal house, and the possession of emblems and treasures (bronze vases, pieces of jade, carillons of resonant stones and bells, and so on). In order to preserve the memory of rights acquired, the custom had been adopted since the reign of King Mu (middle or end of the tenth century) of inscribing accounts of the ceremonies of investiture or donation on the bronze vessels used for the ancestral cult. Thus we know that the grant of a fief, of a township, or of a responsibility was accompanied by various gifts: garments, cloth, bronze weapons, chariots, sacrificial vessels, cowries, servants, animals, and so on.

Territories were enlarged by a sort of 'swarming' process. The fief system, which made it possible to grant to an aristocratic family a power both religious and military over a precisely defined domain (the term *feng* which denoted the fief alluded to the earth banks, *feng*, which marked its limits), was in the last analysis only a replica of royalty within a vast hierarchy of families and domains. It was the order of family cults, divided into principal branches (*ta-tsung*) (that of the royal house and those of the princely houses) and secondary branches (*hsiao-tsung*) which ensured the cohesion of the whole. In each clan the head of the principal cult was the descendant in direct line of a founding father who continued to be venerated from generation to generation, like all his direct successors, while the heads of secondary branches were authorized to worship, in their family, only four generations of ancestors (father, grandfather, great grandfather, and great-great grandfather). In all noble families the rule, at any rate from the end of the Shang period onwards, was that the first-born son of the principal wife succeeded to the responsibilities and religious privileges. This is the explanation of the importance attached to the institutions of son-and-heir and principal wife.

The organization of the principalities (*kuo*: the term denotes a city surrounded by walls) reproduced that of the royal house: around the head of the principality, who bore the title of *kung*, 'lord'—a title which was later to be incorporated in an aristocratic hierarchy with five degrees of nobility—were grouped barons (*tai-fu*) and great officers (*ch'ing*). The oldest meaning of the word *ch'ing* reveals the simultaneously domestic and religious character of the office; it denoted the president of the big sacrificial banquets. The illustrious families whose heads, *ch'ing* and *tai-fu*, filled, alongside the lord, offices which became practically hereditary received as benefits, at the same time as their responsibilities, townships (*i* or *ts'ai-i*) in the territories outside the walled city (*pi*). Barons and great officers had under their authority the ordinary gentlemen (*shih*), descendants of the cadet branches, whose main function was to serve in the chariot units. The peasants provided the infantry (*t'u*) and tilled certain lands, the harvests of which were reserved for the nobility.

Outside their responsibilities to the heads of the principalities and their presidency of their own family cult, high-ranking officers and barons, like the heads of principalities, who were important dignitaries of the royal court, had the duty of participating in battles and furnishing contingents of chariots and soldiers at the request of their superior. The organization of the armies was thus modelled on the political and family organization.

One can see faintly how this society founded on hierarchies of family cults and the maintenance of ancestral privileges arose out of a more ancient state in which the royal authority seems to have been all-powerful. Whereas under the Shang the cult of the deceased kings and the prestige of their line seem to have animated and dominated from a much higher level the social and political organization as a whole, the much more complex and unstable system subsequently established implies that the royal authority no longer acted as anything more than an arbiter. In principle, the responsibilities and privileges conferred by the king were revocable, but the development of the principalities and the strengthening of the families of great dignitaries tended to make them hereditary and to crystallize an order which was no doubt originally more supple and entirely dependent on the royal power. Then again the process of evolution was hastened in the first half of the eighth century by the attacks made by the peoples of Shensi and the reduction in size of the royal domain. Alongside Cheng, which was the main ally of the kings of Chou when the capital was moved but soon lost its preeminent position, other powerful principalities had grown up in the central plain: Sung, Wei, Lu, Ts'ao, Ch'en, Ts'ai, and others. There were to be a dozen of them in the eighth century, amidst a very large number of small cities. Moreover, the

Plate 10.   Western Chou jade chisel
carved in the form of a slave,
discovered in 1967

Plates 11 – 12.   Western Chou ritual implements

Plate 13.   Western Chou ritual vase

system of princely lines had grown more complicated since the foundation of the Chou, for alongside families bearing tne same name as the Chou (*t'ung-hsing*) and attached to their line there were other lines with different names (*i-hsing*), whose ancestors had been the former companions-in-arms of the first kings. Even the Shang line had not been interrupted; it lived on in the principality of Sung, in the west of Honan, where the ancient traditions of the An-yang monarchy were preserved.

In this constellation of weak or powerful principalities it was no longer the religious and military sovereignty of the kings that was the dominant factor, even if it remained customary to refer to them for arbitration and to lean on their moral authority; ritual practices and the knowledge of precedents formed the foundation of a new order. They governed the relations between these allied yet rival cities, united and also divided by war, vendetta, matrimonial alliances, treaties, and the exchange of goods and services. With the development of the principalities and the weakening of the royal power a new society and new manners made their appearance: a nobility jealous of its privileges and attentive to questions of protocol, the ideal of the noble warrior, an ethic of honour and prestige.

A society of this sort would obviously seem to be transitory and unstable in as far as the system of hierarchies of worship and of rites which ensured its cohesion was linked to the preeminence of the royal line. The decline of the monarchy, a geographical dispersal which accentuated regional differences, and the tendency of the principalities to grow larger and to form big political units were gradually to impair the equilibrium between the cities and to force the world of aristocratic principalities into a path which led to its ruin.

The decline of nobiliary institutions

In the course of the Ch'un-ch'iu period a general antithesis became perceptible between the ancient cities of the central plain whose princely lines went back to the foundation of the Chou dynasty—the 'principalities of the centre', *chung-kuo*, a term later applied to China—and the peripheral cities which begin to form more extensive and powerful political units. The parcelling-out of the territories is always more marked in the old regions than in the new ones. These big kingdoms in process of establishment were Chin, in the valley of the Fen, in Shansi, a mountainous land favourable to horse breeding, where the political organization was an extension of the military organization; Ch'i in northwest Shantung, a maritime land enriched by the trade in salt, fish, silks, and metals; and Ch'u in the region of the middle Yangtze and the valleys of Hupei, whose princes bore the title of king (*wang*) like the sovereigns

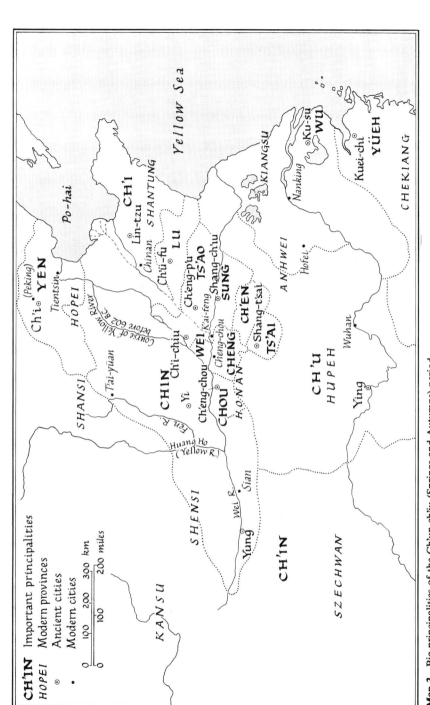

Map 3 Big principalities of the Ch'un-ch'iu (Springs and Autumns) period

of Chou and reigned over vast territories inhabited by aboriginal tribes. This kingdom, with its semi-barbarous culture and a language that belonged to a different linguistic group from that of the Chinese, had expanded by 704 B.C. into the south of Honan.

External circumstances were to strengthen the power and authority of these kingdoms. The incursions of peoples settled in North China, which already posed a considerable threat in the eighth century, grew worse in the second half of the seventh century and led the princes of Ch'i and Chin to play the part of leaders of confederations and protectors of the Chinese lands. It is possible that these attacks by non-Chinese tribes were brought about by the pressure exerted on these tribes by the first communities of nomadic herdsmen of the steppes, who had probably already mastered the art of horse-riding. In any case they favoured the rise of the hegemonies (*pa*). The hegemony of Ch'i was asserted on the occasion of the oath of alliance (*meng*) presided over by Prince Huan (685–643) in 651, that of Chin at the time of the coalition formed by Prince Wen (636–628) in 632.

But the nature and meaning of the hegemonies changed at the beginning of the sixth century after the defeat inflicted on the armies of Chin in 597 by King Chuang of Ch'u. From this time onwards the most powerful kingdoms enforced their will on the weaker ones and the oath, sworn under duress, became a means of legalizing a situation achieved by force.

With the development of big regional units the struggle between kingdoms tended to assume a new character. It was no longer a series of family quarrels which allied, yet rival, principalities, united by the same traditions and the same type of culture, strove to settle by force of arms; confrontation in war became the outward sign of a deeper conflict. The kingdoms of Ch'i in Shantung, of Chin in Shansi, of Ch'in in Shensi each had original characteristics and a personality largely due to particular geographical conditions (mountains or plains, amount of stock farming, proximity of the sea and importance of fishing, ease of communications and commercial activities, relations with close or distant alien peoples, and so on). But these three kingdoms of the north were too near to the cities of the central plain to differ greatly from them. It was not the same with the kingdom of Ch'u, whose original civilization seems to have been the product of a synthesis between autochthonous traditions of the 'barbarian' peoples of the middle Yangtze and the 'Chinese' traditions of the principalities of the centre, the *chung-kuo*. In addition, the spread of the Bronze Age civilization in the south-east was to give birth to two other kingdoms whose culture was no less distant from that of China of the Yellow River. These were the kingdoms of Wu and Yüeh. Wu was situated in the region of plains and lakes which lies to the south of the lower reaches of the Yangtze and Yüeh on the northern coast of Chekiang. The rise of these kingdoms of sailors and boatmen at the end of the sixth century B.C. caused the decline of Ch'u, their neighbour to the west. Under King Fu-ch'a (496–473) Wu spread towards the middle Yangtze and southern Shantung. But his rival, King Kou-chien of Yüeh (496–465), was finally to gain the upper hand and put an end to the kingdom of Wu, taking over its conquests. Ch'u and Yüeh continued to threaten the peace and independence of the little states of the central plain in the following period, that of the Warring States.

The preponderance of military factors in a society whose foundations were of a religious and ritual nature was destined to change its character, and in fact it was not only the traditional relationships between the principalities that were affected but also, because each social system formed a homogeneous whole, relationships between great families within the city-states themselves. Signs of a crisis in the nobiliary society grow more and more frequent from the years round about 600 onwards. In the course of the sixth century we see the appearance of new institutions intended to strengthen the prince's power and his independence. The first forms of agrarian taxation are recorded in Lu in 594 and 590 and in Cheng in 543 and 538; the old *service d'ost* (*fu*), which consisted in providing the prince with a contingent of armed men, tends to be replaced by a contribution in weapons and cereals; and the first laws inscribed on bronze appear in the second half of the sixth century. Laws and taxes were rightly regarded by the scholars in ritual of the Lu school as the first attacks on the traditional customs which formed the basis of the old order; they were a sign of the struggles between the great families which had access to the exercise of power. These struggles grew more bitter from the beginning of the fifth century onwards. In Lu, in western Shantung, three powerful families of barons, the Meng-sun, Shu-sun, and Chi-sun, seized control of the principality and left only a nominal role to the legitimate line of rulers whose ancestors had been enfeoffed by the founder of the Chou dynasty. In Chin, the six families of high officers (the six *ch'ing*) who commanded the kingdom's three armies fought with each other for power; their struggles ended in 453 in the destruction of Chin and the division of its territory to form three independent political units governed by the Han, Wei, and Chao families. In Ch'i all the prerogatives of the princely line were usurped once and for all in 386 by the T'ien family.

These internal conflicts and usurpations were the prelude to the wars of the period of the Warring States. They already herald the changes to come: the concentration of power in the hands of one individual and the establishment of the centralized state.

Chapter 3

The Formation of the Centralized State

The age of the Warring States, from the end of the fifth century to the imperial unification of 221 B.C., is one of those exceptional periods when successive and concomitant changes, provoking and reinforcing each other, speed up the course of history and cause a complete transformation of society, manners, economics, and thought. The movement was slow at first; scarcely perceptible in the sixth century, it accelerates as we approach the end of the third, to such an extent that differences grow deeper from one generation to the next.

The point of departure was certainly the crisis of aristocratic society, of its institutions and beliefs, revealed in the sixth and fifth centuries by the struggles between families belonging to the upper ranks of the nobility and by the first measures to concentrate power in the hands of the heads of principalities or kingdoms. If one had to sum up the basic tendency of the last three centuries before the imperial unification, one could say that political power was trying to free itself from the matrix in which it was imprisoned — that is, from the family and religious context of which it formed an integral part in the ninth to seventh centuries — and that as it gradually broke loose it was conceived more and more clearly as a specific factor. To say that the prince sought to free himself from the weighty tutelage of the families of high dignitaries does not take account of the whole reality: in fact it was power itself that changed its nature during the course of this struggle between tradition and the new demands of the age.

The acceleration in the changes

This tendency of political power to define itself as such and to strengthen its authority cannot be isolated from a sort of military expansionism. The struggles of the central power against the families of great dignitaries are echoed by the wars fought by the kingdoms to extend their territories, increase their resources and achieve hegemony. This close relationship between the internal problems and external wars was the real motive force of the great changes of this period. Thus the age of the Warring States thoroughly deserves its name; it was military dynamism that forced the Chinese nations of the end of antiquity on to the road to the centralized state.

There can be no question here of going into the details of the wars and alliances that filled this whole period. The main contestants were seven in number: the 'three Chin', that is, Han, Wei, and Chao, which had arisen out of the partition of Chin; the rich and ancient kingdom of Ch'i, governed by the T'ien family; two kingdoms which had only recently revealed their power: Yen in Hopei, the capital of which was situated in the Peking region, quite close to the steppes and their nomadic herds- men, and Ch'in in Shensi, land of the first Chou princes, rich in horses and rough and warlike in manners; and finally Ch'u, in the valleys of the middle Yangtze and Han, a kingdom that was only half Chinese. These were the 'seven powers' (the *Ch'i-hsiung*) between which alliances of brief duration were to be made and unmade, giving the advantage now to Wei, now to Ch'in — for these were the two principal adversaries in this period of bitter warfare. In the course of the fighting the little states of the cen- tral plain, repositories of the most ancient traditions, were to be ab- sorbed by the powerful kingdoms which surrounded them.

Ancestral customs now look more than ever at odds with the needs of the age: if the prince — legitimate or usurper — wished to preserve his power, he had to be able to command resources, armies, and suitable ex- ecutive agents. He therefore had to appeal to new men, to whose advan- tage he would divest the big noble families of their hereditary respon- sibilities.

The changes in political power

In the principalities of the Ch'un-ch'iu period there had grown up a class of minor officials whose tasks were mainly connected with sacrifices and war, but also with the administration of the princely house and the management of his estates. For besides the highest posts, filled from one generation to the next by the great families of barons and high officers (the posts of *ssu-t'u*, head of the administration, *ssu-ma*, minister of war, *ssu-k'ung*, the official in charge of public works, *ssu-k'ou*, chief law officer) and differing in detail from one principality to another, there were numerous less illustrious but indispensable jobs, those, for example, of grand scribe, scribe of internal affairs, and director of ancestral affairs. These jobs required numerous subordinates (intoners of prayers, soothsayers, augurs, master of the ritual ballets, and so on). Then there were also the personal servants of the prince: squires, coachmen, superintendents of the chariots, food-tasters, and so on. The holders of these offices came from a class whose social status and economic circumstances were far inferior to those of the families of barons and high officers. The offspring of the families of younger sons and of sons of second-class wives (*shu-tzu*), they belonged to the mass of small gentry (*shih*). But the role of this minor nobility, men at arms, guardians of the written traditions, specialists in various branches of knowledge, was to be decisive. These were the people from whom the prince was to recruit his first executive officials. It thus becomes understandable why, at the end of the process of evolution which ended in the centralized state, the term *shih*, which in the Ch'un-ch'iu period had denoted the 'knight', the fighting gentleman, finally acquired the sense of 'lettered person', qualified to exercise political functions of an essentially civil character.

At the same time as a new type of central power was tending to come into being, territorial powers were changing radically. While the ancient custom of the royal gift of townships (*ts'ai-i*) or fiefs (*feng*) which often accompanied the grant of responsibilities at the court and outside — favours which the inscription on religious vessels sought to emphasize as being hereditary in character — was the sole source of territorial authority in the principalities of the central plain, a new term had appeared in the peripheral kingdoms of Ch'in, Chin, and Ch'u. Conquered townships, doubtless placed under the direct authority of the head of the kingdom, had there received the name of *hsien*. The first uses of this term in this particular sense date from the years 688–687. The innovation had no immediate consequences, for the *hsien* soon became, in accordance with the traditional system which still prevailed in the Ch'un-ch'iu period, the hereditary property of the families of barons or high officers. But what distinguished the *hsien* in principle from the villages of the older type, namely the fact that it was conquered territory, was later to provide the key to a radical transformation of territorial powers: when the head of the kingdom broke free from the tutelage of the great families by relying on the minor nobility, the newly conquered territories were preserved from the traditional appropriation by the upper ranks of the nobility and kept directly dependent on the central power. The *hsien* then became the model for a new type of territorial power – the administrative district controlled by representatives of the central power – and this model could be extended to the whole of the kingdom as soon as the prince was powerful enough to overthrow the old families of the high officers and barons. This is what was done for the first time in Ch'in, under Hsiao-kung (361–338), at the time of the reforms of Shang Yang. The administrative system which was later to be adopted by the Ch'in and Han empires was then installed. A hierarchy of territories corresponds to the hierarchy of officials; the *hsien*, 'counties', are grouped in larger units called 'commanderies' (*chün*), and the *hsien* and *chün* each have their seat of government and their administrative head (*hsien-ling* in the *hsien, t'ai-shou* in the *chün*).

Such was the direction of the process of evolution. It ended in a political system characterized by the existence of a body of selected civil servants, paid and subject to dismissal, under the control of the central power, of which they were a sort of extension, and by the division of the whole territory into administrative districts. But it was only in the reign of Prince Wen (445–395) in Wei and in that of King Hui-wen (337–225) in Ch'in that the new office of Chancellor (*hsiang*) appeared and with it the habit of distinguishing systematically between civil and military functions; and it was only in the course of the fourth century that the first districts administered by civil servants were set up. To complete the radical changes involved in the advent of the centralized state, the process of political evolution which was taking shape in the midst of the struggles between great families and the efforts of the central power to break away from the hold of tradition had to be joined by the concomitant action of other factors which also contributed to the formation of the new state.

Changes in the nature of war

In remote antiquity and in the Ch'un-ch'iu age war was an aristocratic activity. The possession of chariots, horses, and weapons of bronze was restricted to the small number of men who took part in the battles, tournaments in the open countryside which tested the valour of the conflicting noble houses. The infantry, composed of peasants, played only a secondary part. But by injecting more bitterness into the struggles the decline of the traditional rites and hierarchies began to modify the nature of the battles in the fourth and fifth centuries. It was no longer a matter of winning fame by giving proof of bravery and, if need be, of generosity, but of winning and conquering territory. Thus from this time onwards war mobilized more and more energies and resources. At the end of the Ch'un-ch'iu period the number of chariots increased, campaigns, previously confined to a few confrontations, grew longer, and the fourth and third centuries were to see the development of siege warfare. The command of armies tended to become no longer the affair of nobles, for whom the profession of arms was a tradition parallel to the practice of the religious cult, but that of specialists in tactics and strategy. The quest for efficiency as an end in itself was at the root of the changes in warfare; this process of evolution is reflected both in the composition of the armies and in the new importance attributed to reserves. From the fifth to the third centuries the development of the infantry was gradually to reduce the role of the chariots and was eventually to destroy the aristocratic mode of life bound up with the driving of teams. Certain innovations contributed to this change in the form of combat, namely the appearance of the sword, probably borrowed from the steppes in the middle of the sixth century, the crossbow, and cavalry. More powerful and accurate than the retroflex bow, with its double curve, used in antiquity and by the nomads, the crossbow, put under tension with the foot, was to be one of the most commonly used weapons in the Chinese world and was to be constantly improved up to the Sung period (tenth to thirteenth centuries). Its entry into general use has been attributed to the second half of the fifth century B.C. by the historian of technology, Yang K'uan, but it may have been a little later. As for cavalry, swifter and more mobile than chariots, it appears in the fourth century B.C. in the northern kingdoms, where it was adopted in imitation of the nomads at the same time as the dress of the horsemen of the steppes (tunics and trousers).

The development of infantry units from the sixth century B.C. onwards — in Chin at the time of the battles in mountainous country against the tribes of Shansi, and probably also in Wu and Yüeh, where the terrain was scarcely any more suitable for chariots because of the lakes and numerous watercourses — down to the huge armies of foot-soldiers of the third century was to have very important consequences, and one may say that the advent of the centralized state was closely linked to this change in the technique of warfare. By giving more importance and in the end a decisive role in battle to the old footsloggers (*t'u*), who in the Ch'un-ch'iu period had acted as a sort of domestic staff for the noble combatants, the leaders of kingdoms greedy for conquest and hegemony were led to grant them at the same time a status and dignity which until then had been denied them. The centralized state saw the simultaneous promotion of the peasantry to the rank of independent farmers and combatants. The right to own land and the right to honours acquired on the field of battle go hand in hand.

But the duration and violence of the clashes from the sixth to fifth centuries onwards and the 'realistic' attitude of leaders of kingdoms and their advisers in the fourth and third centuries were also at the root of a new interest in economic questions or, to be more precise, of a growing awareness of the economy as a specific reality. Victory belonged to the man who had at his disposal the largest number of men and the most extensive resources and reserves of grain.

The changes which affected political power and warfare had an economic and social background, the great importance of which must be emphasized.

Upsurge of the economy and technical innovations

The fourth and third centuries before our era were a period of rapid economic development and technical inventions in the Chinese world. It was at this time that the valley of the Wei, the central plain, and the basin of Ch'eng-tu in Szechwan became continuously cultivated areas, thanks to intensive clearing operations encouraged by the heads of kingdoms. At the same time a skilled husbandry was developed (use of manure, distinction between different types of soil, attention to the date of ploughing and sowing, drainage). The drying-out of marshy regions and drainage of salty terrains form one of the most important aspects of this deliberate policy of agricultural development. The great irrigation operations of this period aimed as much at bringing new land into cultivation as at making water available in times of drought. The most famous of these operations were those of the Ye region, near Han-tan (in the southeast of present-day Hopei), of the Ch'eng-tu region in Szechwan and of the valley of the Wei in Shensi. The names of the hydraulic engineers who organized these great works are recorded by history: Hsi-men Pao and Shih Ch'i in Wei; Li Ping and his son Cheng Kuo in Ch'in.

It was in the fourth and third centuries B.C. that the first great increase in the population of the Chinese world began to occur. Although we hardly possess the means to evaluate the population in the Ch'un-ch'iu age, all the evidence indicates that it was very sparse and that even in the area where the Chinese cities were most numerous — along the course of the Yellow River and in the central plain — agricultural technique did not permit a high density. On the other hand, third-century texts (particularly the *Han Fei-tzu*) speak of a great increase in population which continued during the time of the First Han rulers. This explains the figures

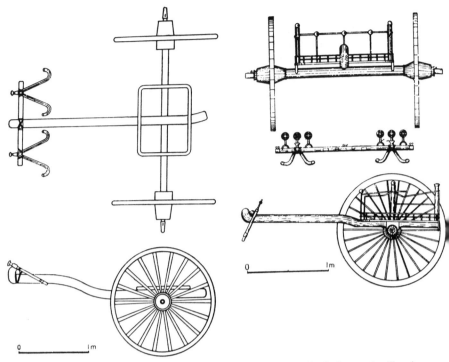

Fig. 3 **Left:** diagram of a chariot from the site of An-yang (end of second millennium B.C.). **Right:** diagram of a chariot from the site of Hui-hsien (Honan Province) (fifth century B.C.)

provided by the first census known to history: 57,671,400 taxable individuals in A.D. 2, or in other words rather more than the estimates given for the whole of the Roman Empire at about the same time.

The clearing and exploitation of new lands contributed considerably to the strengthening of the central power and helped it to free itself from the tutelage of the great families. They furnished it with new, regular resources thanks to the taxes extracted from the families of farmers and at the same time they ensured its direct control of the population, since the peasants settled on the new lands were no longer dependent, as they were in the old villages, on the local grandees. The clearings made it possible to extend the administrative districts. But the promotion of agriculture was favoured at the same time by the development of technology. Modern historians, among others the Chinese Yang K'uan and the Japanese Masubuchi, have stressed the decisive role, in the fourth and third centuries, of the spread of iron tools, which replaced at this time wooden and stone ones, made deeper ploughing possible and facilitated clearing operations and other substantial works. These tools were not made of wrought iron but of cast iron. It seems in fact that the Chinese world, thanks to its experience in the arts involving the use of fire, arrived directly at casting iron, without passing, as the European countries did, through the long intermediary stage of forging it. The first allusion to an object made of cast iron possibly dates from 513 B.C. and it implies that at this time the technique of casting iron had already been mastered and was commonly used.

The archaeological evidence is later and only starts to appear round about 400, at a time when casting iron had become a positive industry. Remains of objects made of cast iron (axes, spades, knives, swords, and so on) dating from the age of the Warring States have been found in large numbers in sites excavated since 1950. Moulds used for making objects of cast iron have also been unearthed, particularly on the sites of the ancient capital of Yen, near Peking. Cast iron, more breakable and taking a less sharp edge than bronze, had the great advantage that it could be produced in quantity, especially in regions such as Shansi and Shensi which were rich in minerals. Moreover it seems that, thanks to the combination of casting and forging, iron weapons began to compete with bronze weapons (which, however, remained in more general use) as early as the age of the Warring States.

People have been surprised at China's 'lead' in the realm of iron and steel technology; the Chinese were capable of producing steel in the first to second centuries A.D., whereas the first successful attempts at casting iron were not made in Europe until the end of the Middle Ages, and steel came later still. The difference in the time-scale, which reveals not so much a lead or backwardness as the originality of the technological traditions of different civilizations, is sufficiently explained by the experience acquired in the Chinese world in the casting of bronze (it was lack of copper and tin that first caused the switch to iron) and by the perfecting of bellows at the time of the Warring States. However, it seems that it was not until later, under the Han rulers, that the double-action piston bellows made its appearance. This device makes it possible, by a system of valves, to obtain a continuous current of air and consequently higher temperatures. This type of bellows, noted by Europeans as early as the sixteenth or seventeenth century, was to remain in use in China until our day.

One of the effects of casting iron was to accustom the Chinese world very early to the idea of mass-producing the same model of tool, an idea which has only become familiar to us since the development of modern

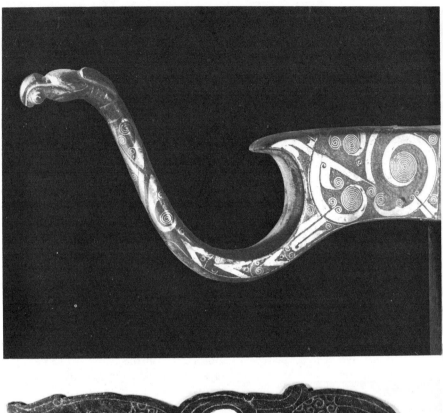

Plates 14–15.   Warring States period silver and bronze implements

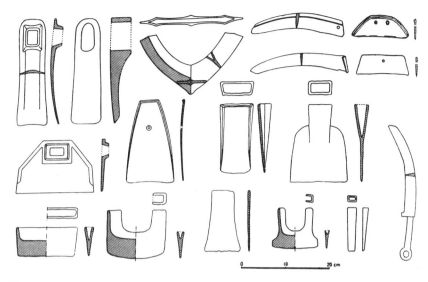

Fig. 4 Cast-iron implements from the fourth–third centuries B.C.: hoes, ploughshare, sickles, axe, and knife

industry. While in antiquity each bronze vessel was usually a unique piece, the moulds used for casting iron were used for mass production and were often designed to produce several examples of the same object in one single operation.

Other aspects of technical progress concerned means of transport. The cart with a pole and two horses harnessed with a neck-yoke gave way at the time of the Warring States to the cart with two shafts. And it seems that at the same time the neck-yoke — which was to remain for a very long time the only method of harnessing known in the rest of the world — was replaced by the breast harness. This new device, and also the horse-collar, which was to appear between the fifth and ninth centuries A.D., were important pieces of progress in the field of animal traction. By freeing the horses from the pressure of the yoke, which tended to choke them, they made driving easier and rendered it possible to pull heavier loads. One single horse would suffice where formerly two or sometimes even four were required. It is noteworthy that the casting of iron and more rational methods of harnessing, attested in the Chinese world at the time of the Warring States, both appear in Europe at the end of the Middle Ages. Although it cannot be proved clearly in either case, it is extremely probable that both procedures were passed on from China to the West.

It was also in the fourth and third centuries B.C. that the custom spread in China of fixing spokes at a slight outward angle to the circumference of the wheel; this increases resistance to lateral shocks.

If the age of the Warring States is one of the richest known to history in technical innovations, this is no doubt due to the needs created by wars that became more and more bitter. To ensure their independence and to increase the military power of their kingdoms, princes were not concerned merely to increase agricultural production. They were on the watch for new resources. The lands which had remained on the fringe of the cultivated fields, areas of marsh, woodland or forest, open till then to the peasants, who came to collect wood, to fish or to hunt there, were gradually appropriated and exploited by the heads of kingdoms for their animal, vegetable, and mineral products. Taxes were instituted on merchandise and market stalls. But commercial and craft activities, now in full swing, were to give rise to a new class of merchants. Whereas in the Ch'un-ch'iu age commerce remained confined to luxury products such as pearls and jade and was the province of merchants who had special relations with the princely courts, the following age saw the development of a considerable trade in ordinary consumer goods (cloth, cereals, salt), and in metals, wood, leather, and hides. The richest merchants combined with this kind of commerce big industrial enterprises (iron mines and foundries in particular), employed increasing numbers of workmen and commercial agents, and controlled whole fleets of river boats and large numbers of carts. These new activities lay outside the traditional framework of the palace economy with its bodies of craftsmen controlled by palace nobles: potters, cartwrights, bow-makers, curriers, basket-makers, builders, and so on. But the big merchant entrepreneurs were the social group whose activities made the biggest contribution to the enrichment of the state. As allies and sometimes advisers of the heads of kingdoms, they seem to have exerted considerable influence on the development of political thought at the end of antiquity.

The capitals of the kingdoms were no longer simply the seat of political power. They tended to become big commercial and manufacturing centres, and the most recent excavations have disclosed that their walls were enlarged at the end of the age of the Warring States. Among these prosperous cities may be mentioned Lin-tzu in Ch'i, in north-west Shantung, one of the biggest and richest agglomerations of this period, Han-tan in Chao, in north-eastern Hopei, Wen in Wei, Ying in Ch'u, Lo-yi in Chou, and Jung-yang in Han. In fact the object of the wars of the third century was often the conquest of these big commercial centres.

The upsurge of commerce and private industry which explains the growth of the cities also stimulated the use of metal coins, the earliest specimens of which go back to the fifth century. Excavations have revealed that these coins, of four different types, circulated in fairly well defined geographical areas which no doubt corresponded with big economic units. The *pu*, shaped like an iron spade, was used in Han, Wei, and Chao, the three kingdoms which had arisen out of the partition of Chin; the *tao*, shaped like a knife, was current in the north-eastern regions, Ch'i, Yen, and Chao; the 'ant's nose' *(i-pi)*, shaped like a cowrie—that archaic 'coin' which combined the functions of ornament, jewel and talisman—in the land of Ch'u, in Hupei and in Honan; and the circular coins with a hole in the middle in the north-western regions, in Chou, Ch'in, and Chao. In Ch'i it was the state itself which began to cast money, but the coins shaped like spades and knives, which often bear the name of the city in which they were issued, may have been due to the initiative of rich merchants.

The effects of the economic upsurge were not limited to the Chinese lands. Commercial relations with neighbouring peoples were intensified in the course of the last two centuries before the empire. Yen, the capital of which was situated in the region of present-day Peking, traded with the tribes of Manchuria and northern Korea, and Chao and Ch'in with the nomads of the steppes. It seems in fact that it was in the fourth and third centuries B.C. that the silks of Ch'in reached northern India (hence the Indian name 'Cina' to indicate the land of silks). In the south, Ch'u seems to have developed its commercial relations with the aboriginal peoples of the tropical zone in the same period. In the reign of King Ching-hsiang (298–263 B.C.) a military expedition was sent to Szechwan (lands of Pa and Shu), Kweichow (Ch'in-tsung) and the region of the present K'un-ming in Yunnan (land of Tien). According to tradition some of the soldiers of Ch'u settled there and married local women. This commercial expansion by the big peripheral kingdoms, a factor which helped Chinese colonization in the border lands (southern Manchuria, Mongolia, and the present southern and north-western provinces), prepared the way for the big military expansions of the Ch'in and Han empires.

Social upheavals

Although the two centuries which preceded the unification of the Chinese lands in 221 B.C. were a period of economic upsurge and innovation, they were also a time of social upheavals.

The old aristocratic society could resist neither the blows inflicted on it by the new heads of state seeking to monopolize power nor the deeper and more powerful influence of economic changes. The great families who traced their descent from remote antiquity were ruined, removed

Figure 5 Drawing of motifs decorating a bronze *hu* vase discovered in 1965 at Ch'eng-tu in Szechwan province. Height 39.9 cm. Late 6th–5th century B.C.

Upper register: two interpretations, either a scene depicting the picking of mulberry leaves or the selection of tree branches for the making of bows.

Middle register: scenes of archery and of hunting; scenes of a dance with long spears (?); a banquet in a pavilion; an orchestra composed of bells and chimes, mouth organs, pan-pipes, etc.

Lower register: a naval battle; siege of a city or of a camp (?).

Wen-wu 1976.3, pl. 2; Wen Fong, ed., *The Great Bronze Age of China* (New York, 1980), no. 91.

(There exist several other vases with this style of decoration from the same period. This example is one of the most abundantly decorated. These are the earliest known examples of storied decoration from China.)

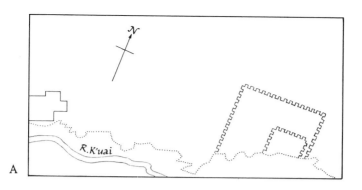

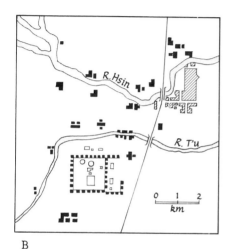

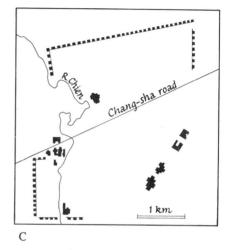

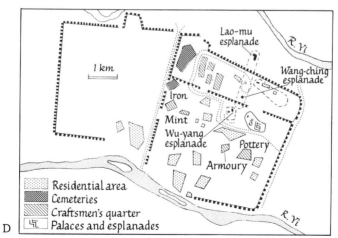

Map 4 Cities of the age of the Warring States
A: Wu-kuo, near present-day Ch'ü-wo (kingdom of the Chin)
B: Wang-ch'eng, near Lo-yang (Honan)
C: Han-tan (Hopei)
D: Hsia-tu (kingdom of Yen, in Hopei)

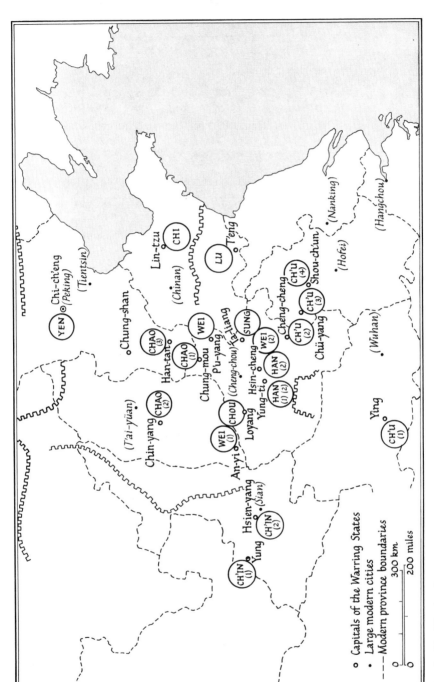

Map 5 The Warring States

from their positions of power and finally destroyed. The cults which they had preserved so jealously down the ages disappeared at the same time as their estates and cities, which were swallowed up in the territory of the kingdoms.

However, the decline of the upper ranks of the nobility and the simultaneous strengthening of the central power attracted to the courts of the heads of kingdoms a large number of minor gentry in search of jobs. These men, who cultivated various arts and made a display of their talents in the hope of being called to serve the prince, besieged his closest advisers. Thus round the princely courts and in the retinue of ministers there formed groups of clients (*pin-k'o,* 'guests', *she-jen,* 'people of the house') who were sources of prestige and power. The great historian Ssuma Ch'ien, in his *Historical Records (Shih-chi)* (beginning of the first century B.C.), was to give the biographies of four of these advisers who were famous for having attracted, by their generosity and sense of honour, several thousand clients. These four were the lords Meng-ch'ang in Ch'i, P'ing-yüan in Chao, Hsin-ling in Wei and Ch'un-shen in Ch'u. It was in such circles that political and moral philosophy, the science of stratagems, the art of oratory, and so on all developed. The times were propitious to the appearance of sects and schools whose interests were indissolubly bound up with the social and political realities of the epoch.

The upper and lower nobility were not the only classes affected by the change. The dim world of the countryside, on which the oldest texts shed only a fleeting light (collective labour under the control of superintendents, group marriages at the time of big religious festivals, classification by kinship, religious life linked to the rhythm of the changing seasons) underwent a profound transformation that was to facilitate the change in its status (participation in battles and right to own land).

The economic upsurge which caused the appearance of a small class of merchant entrepreneurs and big landed proprietors was not of equal benefit to all; on the contrary, it accentuated inequalities. Poor peasants fell into debt and in the end were driven from their land. The result was a growth in the number of tenant farmers, agricultural labourers, and people enslaved for debt—the only form of slavery, apart from penal slavery, known to the Chinese world. The landless peasants were employed in the industries which were now growing up (mines, iron foundries, salt-works, craft workshops) or settled on new lands which the heads of kingdoms were striving to bring into cultivation. All these changes split up the big undivided peasant family and caused the ruin of the old village communities. Conditions were now favourable to the great reforms that made it possible to lay the foundation of the centralized state.

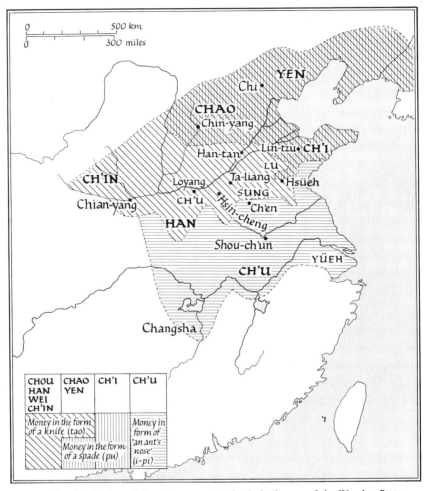

CHOU HAN WEI CH'IN	CHAO YEN	CH'I	CH'U
Money in the form of a knife (tao)			Money in form of 'an ant's nose' (i-pi)
	Money in the form of a spade (pu)		

Map 6   The distribution of the different sorts of coin in the age of the Warring States

The state revolution

I brought order to the mass of beings and put to the test deeds and realities: each thing has the name that fits it.
Stele erected by the first Ch'in emperor.

The reform movement which was to give birth to the centralized state is only one of the currents flowing through the age of the Warring States and cannot therefore be isolated from the whole mass of differing tendencies apparent in this period, one of the richest in the intellectual history of China. But the reformers who were later called 'Legalists' (*Fachia*) had the merit of devising the basic institutions of the new state and consequently those of the empire itself, since the reforms, applied at first in the most systematic manner in Ch'in, were extended to all the Chinese lands in the course of the conquests made by the north-western kingdom in the years 230–221.

The foundation of the centralized state

While the realistic and practical current of thought to which the legalists belonged became more and more conscious of its aims, its means, and its philosophical implications, and reached its climax in one of the greatest thinkers of the third century, Han Fei (280?–234), at the same time it responded in principle to the two practical considerations which dominated the whole political life of the two centuries preceding the empire, namely the idea of 'enriching the state' (*fu-kuo*) (giving the prince the material means of power) and that of 'strengthening the armies' (*ch'iang-ping*) (giving the prince by force of arms a universal hegemony or sovereignty). More than any other kingdom, Ch'in seems to have presented conditions favourable to the application of radical reforms which were to make it a powerful state and one of a kind profoundly different from those hitherto known to the Chinese world. Isolated in the basin of the Wei and fairly well protected against attacks from outside, Ch'in was a poor and relatively backward country, where it was easy to extend the administrative districts by clearing new land and the nobility does not seem to have been very powerful. Advisers who favoured a realistic, absolutist policy followed one another there, from the aristocrat Shang Yang (390?–338) to the rich merchant Lü Pu-wei, minister to the last prince of Ch'in, the founder of the empire.

Related to the princely family of the little city of Wei in Honan (a different Wei from that of the big kingdom that arose out of the partition of Chin), Kung-sun Yang, lord of Shang, better known under the name of Shang Yang, was the architect of the first great reforms in the kingdom of Ch'in. At first adviser to King Hui of Wei at Ta-Liang (the present-day K'ai-feng), he must have arrived in Ch'in in 361. The first reforms inspired by Shang Yang were probably promulgated in 359. They consisted in instituting paramilitary groups of five and ten families with a collective responsibility, in taking as the basis of the fiscal system not the undivided family but the restricted family, in creating ranks of nobility for great deeds in war (these ranks foreshadow the twenty-one degrees of nobility of the Ch'in and Han empires), in encouraging land clearance and agricultural production, in reducing to the status of ordinary private individuals those members of noble families who had won no glory in war, and in granting lands, slaves (the idle were reduced to slavery), and clothes to the holders of the new noble ranks. A fresh series of reforms seems to have been put into effect in 350, after the transfer of the capital to Hsien-yang (to the northwest of the present Sian, on the left bank of the Wei). They proclaimed the abolition of the large undivided family, the creation of administrative districts (*hsien*), a new division of lands, and the unification of weights and measures.

After Ch'in's victory over Wei in 340 Kung-sun Yang was to receive the land of Shang as a reward for his services. But the reformer, who had aroused the hatred of the old nobility, was quartered on the death of the prince whose adviser he had been. Others were to carry on his work.

Distinctive characteristics of the new state

The appearance of the centralized state and the parallel destruction of the old society can best be described as a revolution. Because it provided the basis of the imperial power and continued to inspire the most fundamental political conceptions of the Chinese world, the creation of the centralized state in Ch'in in the middle of the fourth century B.C. occupies in the history of East Asia a place comparable with that of the creation of the Greek city (*polis*) in the Western world. There are in fact, as well as profound differences, some remarkable analogies. In China, as in Greece, the crisis of aristocratic society ended in a 'democratization' of aristocratic institutions. Promoted to the rank of combatants and freed from the tutelage of the great noble families, the peasants were given access to a hierarchy of ranks which was a transposition into the new context of the centralized state of the old aristocratic hierarchies. In the same way, it is significant that the term which formerly denoted the equivalent of our medieval *service d'ost* (the *fu*, a contribution in men and chariots from the holders of fiefs and villages, converted into a contribution in goods at the end of the Ch'un-ch'iu age) was applied in the end to the capitation fees and dues imposed on each individual by the power of the state.

If the evolution was different, and in the last analysis very original in the Chinese world, that is because the institutions of the Ch'un-ch'iu age could show nothing comparable with the practice so characteristic of the Indo-European world and archaic Greece, the assembly of warriors with equal rights, of which the city assembly seems to have been a sort of transposition.

One of the most important results of the reforms was to make the peasants, formerly the dependants of the noble families, the foundation of the economic and military power of the new state. This combination of the function of production with the military function does not occur in such a systematic way in any other civilization. It was to remain, with some interruptions, the basis of the political and social system of the Chinese world until the ninth century A.D. But these fighting farmers were neither the subjects of a despot with discretionary powers, used to suit his own whims, and the power of life and death over every individual, nor citizens with equal rights deciding in common affairs of their city. It would be a mistake to see in the new political system defined in the fourth century only a banal form of despotism. In fact the prince did not exercise, properly speaking, an arbitrary power of command; rather he embodied the power of setting things in order and of prompting action.

The notion of law which emerges and takes shape in the age of the Warring States has nothing in common with what we generally understand by this term. It does not arise out of custom or out of common practice in settling disputes. Nor is it the result of a convention translating a common will. Objective, public, superior to all men and excluding any divergent interpretation, it is the means of ordering individuals hierarchically in accordance with a general scale of dignities and indignities, merits and demerits. At the same time it is the all-powerful instrument which makes it possible to guide everyone's activity in the direction most favourable to the power of the state and the public peace. Intended to create order, it cannot be in contradiction with the nature of things and beings. Han Fei, who died in 234, speaks of 'testing' the laws and attaches great importance to the prince's being perfectly informed of the state of his kingdom by means of a rational critique of all the evidence. Source of a universal harmony, the law has affinities with the resonant tubes (*lü*) which are at the basis of all musical scales and the name of which summons up the ideas of pattern and rule (under the empire the term *lü* was to be applied to the penal codes).

The reforms were the expression of a mode of thinking which may be described as rational. They aimed at substituting uniform rules for the multiplicity of rights, privileges, and customs which characterized the old society—one is almost tempted to say the *ancien régime*—with its aristocratic lines of descent, its bonds of dependence, and its hierarchies. State institutions—civil and military officers, a system of rewards and punishments meted out in accordance with rules that excluded any injustice or favouritism, honorific ranks granted for services rendered, collective responsibility and the obligatory denunciation of crimes within the family groups, a uniform system of weights and measures — replaced the customs, rites, and ethical system of days gone by. The great characteristic of the new state is that its functioning was based on objective criteria.

The effects of the state revolution were profound and extended to every sphere. In the process the Chinese world no doubt lost much of its past, and much of its past gradually became incomprehensible to it. But if the upheaval was early and radical in Ch'in the changes were less rapid and came later in the other Chinese lands, and this delay permitted the survival of certain traditions in spite of the extension of the centralized state to the whole of the contemporary Chinese world and in spite of the first emperor's efforts to destroy all that recalled the old society. In the eastern regions, the old cultural centres of Ch'i and Lu in Shantung seem to have succeeded in preserving, in the whirlwind, part of their traditions. This is the explanation of the resurgence of these traditions in a context very different from that of the centuries preceding the empire, in the Han age.

Chapter 4

The Heritage of Antiquity

The written documents which have come down from antiquity have had an importance in Chinese culture equal to that of the biblical and classical traditions in the West. These writings – or rather what has survived with alterations and forged interpolations – have been the subject of voluminous exegeses from the second century B.C. to our own day and have served as the basis of education and as the foundation of philosophical, political, and moral reflection. The history of Chinese thought is largely that of the various points of view and conceptions adopted down the ages with regard to this venerable heritage in which the Chinese world has ceaselessly sought the traces of lost wisdom. Often represented as the expression of an immutable orthodoxy, the textual and philosophical interpretation of the ancient texts has in reality been the subject of excited and contradictory debates with very important consequences and echoes reverberating down to our own day. All in all, the best analogy seems to be with our own Christian tradition.

Traditions of the tenth to sixth centuries B.C.

The classics

The oldest documents transmitted by written and oral tradition come from the circles of scribes and annalists of the royal court of the Chou and the princely courts. They date from the ninth to sixth centuries. This means that they are pieces of a political, religious, or ritual character, in harmony with the sort of society that we can glimpse at the beginning of the first millennium and in the age of the principalities: a nobility whose main occupations are war and sacrifice, anxious to assert the antiquity of its rights and privileges. The majority of these documents seem to come from the royal court. They are partly archives, similar in language and content to the inscriptions on bronze dating from the same epoch (deeds of investiture or donation, decisions arising out of legal proceedings), but there are also fragments of the scenarios of ritual dances. These texts were assembled in a collection called the *Shu* (*Writings*) or *Shang-shu*, of which about half is today regarded as authentic. Some chapters of this collection reproduce parts of a libretto relating to a war-dance cele- brating the victory of King Wu of the Chou over the last sovereign of the Shang. Analogous pieces, coming from ritual ballets acted at the Shang court, the tradition of which had been preserved in the principality of Sung, also seem to have been incorporated in the *Shang-shu* at the same time as speeches, harangues, and the text of oaths.

Hymns that accompanied sacrifices and ritual ceremonies such as ban- quets or the rite of shooting with the bow formed the major part of another collection bearing the name of *Shih* ('poems' or 'odes'). These poems consisting of regular stanzas were sung at the court of the kings of Chou to the accompaniment of dancing and of music in which the domi- nant sounds were those of chimes of bells and resonant stones. Their themes seem to have become more varied in the eighth to sixth centuries and to have been enriched by a new genre, the 'songs of principalities' (*kuo-feng*), which appear to have been inspired by the alternating choruses of peasant youths and girls at the spring festivals. These love- songs, more supple and more free in form than the old religious hymns, are composed of themes and popular refrains which combine with the sentiments expressed by the opposing choirs the various moments in the life of nature and of the village groups.

Coming from the same circles as the archives, the scenarios of ritual ballets and the sacrificial hymns, the Annals are also one of the original forms of the most ancient written traditions. Consisting of the record of events which seem to have been announced in their temple day by day, month by month, season by season and year by year, to the ancestors of the royal or princely lines, they may be described as ritual documents. They seem to have succeeded the divinatory archives of the An-yang age and to have had as their object the construction of a science of diplomatic, religious, astronomical, and natural precedents. This no doubt explains the precision of the terms and dates, as well as the ex- treme dryness and stereotyped character of the notes. In the mode of thought which governs the writing of the Annals temporal conjunctions are indissoluble from events; space and time are treated as being endowed with special virtues.

The most ancient Annals seem to go back to the ninth century. Basing himself on documents which have disappeared since his time, Ssu-ma Ch'ien gives as the first precise date in history the year 841 B.C. One single set of state annals has been preserved in very large part, the *Annals of the Kingdom of Lu* in Shantung, known, after the reference to seasons which appear in the headings to paragraphs, as the *Springs and Autumns (Ch'un-ch'iu)*. The parts which still exist refer to the years 722–481. The Annals of Chin and Ch'u, which are mentioned in certain works, had disappeared by the end of antiquity; those of Ch'in were incorporated in the *Historical Records* of Ssu-ma Ch'ien at the beginning of the first century B.C. Finally, the discovery of the tomb of a prince of Wei in 279 A.D. made it possible to recover the Annals of this kingdom in Shansi. The text of these documents on thin sheets of bamboo (hence their name, *Chu-shu chi-nien, The Bamboo Annals*) has been much altered in transmission and was only reconstructed in part in 1917 by the scholar Wang Kuo-wei.

Even though it is reasonable to assume that these most ancient forms of history in the Chinese world are a sort of extension of the divinatory archives on bones and tortoise-shells, divination itself developed autonomously in the time of the first kings of Chou. In parallel with divination by fire, which was to persist for a very long time because of its venerable character, a new procedure which was both more convenient and more complex came into use. It consisted in the manipulation of light sticks made of yarrow stems. Even or odd numbers of these make it possible to construct figures composed of six continuous or broken lines, continuous lines corresponding to odd figures and broken ones to even figures. These hexagrams, up to the number 64, translate all the possible structures of the universe and are endowed with a dynamic force thanks to the possible mutations of the lines, male (*yang*) or female (*yin*), in their ascent or decline. Carrying on the tradition of the soothsayers of the Shang epoch, the specialists in divination by yarrow (*shih*) were to define the first elements in a conception of the world as a totality of opposing and complementary forces and virtues, and contribute to the first developments in mathematics. Their reflections were the basis of the sciences and of philosophy in the Chinese world.

Each city seems to have possessed its own traditions in divination, but only the manual in use at the Chou court was destined to be preserved. It received the name of *I*, usually translated as *The Book of Changes*. The most ancient rules of interpretation, couched in a concise, obscure language rich in technical terms the meaning of which has been lost, were endowed during the course of the first millennium with a whole series of glosses and commentaries which bear witness to the continual enrichment of the divinatory tradition.

Such are the four collections (*Shu, Shih, Ch'un-ch'iu, I*) in which were preserved the most ancient traditions of the world of scribes, annalists, and soothsayers of antiquity. The scholars of Lu who seem to have been responsible for their transmission added to them the rituals (*Li*) giving the detailed rules which had to be observed in every circumstance of life, and also a treatise on music (*Yüeh*) which was lost in the Han period. Assembled in different versions by oral or written tradition, reworked and enlarged with apocryphal texts, these six works were to be promoted under the Han rulers to the rank of Classics (*Ching*).

Relatively late character of the classical traditions

The most ancient writings, couched in extremely concise language that is difficult to interpret, form only a very small part of the legacy of the ancients. Other more substantial texts were added to them between the fifth and third centuries by way of complement and commentary. These texts belong to an age in which the old society was already in decline or on the point of collapse. Thus while linking up with older traditions these works present novel characteristics; one can see in them the influence of the theories and moral concepts of the age. Thus the influence of the classifying theories of the specialists in *yin, yang* and the Five Elements (*yin-yang wu-hsing chia*) is perceptible in the *Kung-yang-chuan*, a commentary on the *Annals of Lu* which seems to have been written in the fourth or third century at the same time as the *Ku-liang-chuan*, another commentary on these Annals. While recording some very ancient traditions, the *Chou-li* (*Rites of the Chou*) or *Chou-kuan* (*Officials of the Chou*), compiled about the same time as the other Rituals (*I-li, Li-chi*) and *Ta-tai Li-chi*) (fourth and third centuries) give much space to an administrative utopia. The *Tso-chuan*, a composite work consisting of incomplete texts reworked at the end of antiquity, consists for the most part of a semi-fictional chronicle of the struggle between the kingdoms of Chin and Ch'i.

Thus what China was to preserve of its most ancient legacy comes in essentials from fifth- to third-century traditions collected and often altered in the Han age and down to the third and fourth centuries of our era. This means that at the very beginning of the classical tradition we meet a problem that simply cannot be ignored, that of their interpretation and of later additions.

The awakening of moral and political reflection

Confucius, patron of the school of 'literati'

Those who were considered in the Han age as belonging to the school of 'literati' (*ju-chia*) quoted as their authority a sage by the name of K'ung Ch'iu, which the Jesuit missionaries of the seventeenth century were to latinize as Confucius (K'ung *fu-tzu*, 'Master K'ung'). The literary remains of this sage are limited to a few more or less authentic traditions and a small collection of his *dicta*, the *Analects*, *Lun-yü*, the text of which was established by his disciples after his death. What may be described at a pinch as the 'Confucian tradition' consists of a number of texts varying considerably in nature and content which include the Classics, the most ancient commentaries on them, the *Analects of Confucius*, and works of the third century B.C. reflecting original orientations typical of this period of profound social and political upheavals. If the term 'Confucianism', coined by Westerners, has any meaning at all, it is clear that it goes far beyond the actual personality or teachings of the great sage.

Doubtless one can date from Confucius and his age the beginning of a process of moral reflection which seems to have been provoked by the crisis of aristocratic society and the decline of ritual. As is shown by the place given in his teaching to the writings of antiquity, Confucius links up with the traditional circles of scribes and annalists. Shocked by the constantly increasing attacks on the ancient customs and rules, these circles must have been tempted by the idea of returning to ritual correctness both in behaviour and in the use of terminology (this is confirmed by the subsequent development of an archaizing ritualism, apt to be utopian, and of the theory of the 'rectification of names', *cheng-ming*). It seems natural that an effort should have been made in these circles to define the 'good man' (*chün-tzu*), independently of the prevailing situation. Such at any rate is the general orientation which is just perceptible. Head of a little school that aimed at forming good men, Confucius (his traditional dates are 551–479 B.C.) attaches great importance to exercises in ritual behaviour, which forms the basis of a process of individual self-improvement rendering possible the mastery of one's movements, actions and feelings. His ethical system, which is the fruit of continual reflection about men, is devoid of any abstract imperative. It is practical and pragmatic, the master taking account of each particular circumstance as well as of the individual character of each of his disciples. Thus the qualities which make an accomplished man, the first of them being *jen* (which may be described as an affectionate and indulgent disposition of mind), cannot be defined once for all; they are the subject of approaches which differ with each case and each individual. Wisdom can only be acquired, after an effort lasting every minute of one's life, by control of the smallest details of conduct, by observation of the rules of life in society (*i*), by respect for others and for oneself and by the sense of reciprocity (*shu*). The master is not aiming at an abstract science of man but at an art of life embracing psychology, ethics, and politics. Virtue is the fruit of a personal effort (and no longer an intrinsic quality of the nobly born). In contrast to the spirit of competition which animated the great nobles of his age, Confucius preaches the probity, trust, and good understanding which seemed to him to have governed human relations in days of old. He identifies personal culture with the public good.

Thus a body of teaching which aimed primarily at being faithful to tradition in fact threw up ideas that were new. They were to be developed and to assume new significance in a different historical context with Meng-tzu (Mencius) (second half of the fourth century) and Hsün-tzu (*c.* 298–235). The high reputation which the sage enjoyed under the Han rulers, and to an even greater extent from the Sung period (tenth to thirteenth centuries) onwards, was largely due to the theoretical and doctrinal additions made to his thinking after his own lifetime.

Mo-tzu, founder of a sect of preaching brothers

Mo-tzu, who flourished about sixty years after Confucius (*c.* 480–390), seems to have been the leader of a sect of minor gentry (*shih*) which, unlike the humble school of Confucius, was to enjoy tremendous success in the fourth and third centuries. Stirred by the conflicts of his age and hostile to the class spirit whose disastrous effects were becoming more and more clearly perceptible, Mo-tzu wanted to create a new egalitarian society based on a sense of mutual aid and devotion to the common good (*chien-li*). He condemns the lust for profit, luxury, the accumulation of wealth, the development of military power, and war, which in his view is only a form of brigandage. He suggests as remedies for the evils of his age an ideal of universal frugality, the uniform regulation of expenditure, strict respect for the laws, and fear of the gods and spirits. Taking the view that family selfishness was the principal cause of quarrels and conflicts, he preaches a generalized altruism (*chien-ai*). His disciples, animated by sectarian fervour, lived in penury and intervened to avoid wars and to defend by force of arms cities unjustly attacked (curiously enough, it is these convinced pacifists who give us the most precise information about the military art in the age of the Warring States). The work compiled under Mo-tzu's name consists for the most part of moralizing discourses, the themes of which were probably the subjects of sermons: 'On Frugality', 'Against Aggression', 'The Will of Heaven', 'On the Existence of Spirits', 'Against the Scholars'. A believer in an authoritarian power based on the lesser gentry, Mo-tzu would like this power to impose a sort of moral conformism on everyone.

This strange sect, which seems to have made numerous converts in the two centuries preceding the imperial unification, was to leave little impression on the history of Chinese thought. Its most noteworthy contribution was to the art of oratory. Mo-tzu and his disciples cultivated rhetoric for preaching purposes, thus contributing to progress in the articulation of ideas and to greater suppleness in sentence construction. They aimed to illustrate the themes of their sermons with the help of examples and to amplify them by the use of analogy.

Intellectual currents of the fourth and third centuries B.C.

The social and economic changes which began to make themselves felt in the fifth century and the tendency of the central power to rely on the class of minor gentry explain the proliferation of groups of clients, sects, and schools. Gentlemen in search of jobs sought to distinguish themselves in arts likely to win them the patronages of the powerful, in an age when heads of states were on the lookout for any formula, stratagem, or technique that would allow them to strengthen their power and defeat their rivals. These arts concerned first and foremost the running of the state. Some, such as the science of diplomatic combinations, the art of persuasion, and the knowledge of secret tricks of government, were of a civil character (*wen*); others, such as tactics, strategy, and swordsmanship, were of a military nature (*wu*). There were also the techniques that made it possible to enrich the kingdom (agronomy, hydrology) or to procure for the prince a surfeit of vital power which would enable him to achieve sanctity. Eminent masters of these arts and techniques appeared and collected varying numbers of disciples. Going round from kingdom to kingdom offering instruction, they were sometimes lodged permanently at the courts of princes or in the houses of their advisers. But this multiplication of schools and this proliferation of knowledge only becomes really noticeable in the fourth and third centuries, and we should no doubt regard Confucius and Mo-tzu himself, if not his disciples, as belonging to an age when this future development was still only adumbrated.

The essentially practical aim of these schools of teaching and their close links with the political, social, and economic preoccupations of their time explain the eclectic character of most of them and the facility with which reciprocal influences made themselves felt. We are not dealing here with systems, with disinterested philosophical constructs, but with currents of thought between which it is sometimes difficult to establish clear lines of demarcation. However, this practical bias does not impair the value and the intrinsically philosophical interest of the questions which Chinese thinkers of this age put to themselves; the abstract, logical way of philosophizing is not the only one.

The theorists of the state

Of all the currents of thought abroad in the fourth and third centuries, the most important was almost certainly the one represented by the thinkers later christened 'Legalists' (*Fa-chia*). It is at any rate the one which, being in harmony with contemporary changes in the state and society, made the most effective contribution to them. Yet the history of Legalism is not well known. The book attributed to Shang Yang, author of the reforms in Ch'in in the middle of the fourth century, the *Shang-tzu* or *Shang-chün shu*, is reckoned to be a forgery compiled several centuries after his time. A composite work written at the time of the Warring States and ascribed to Kuan Chung, a minister of Prince Huan of Ch'i in the seventh century B.C., encouraged the bibliographers of the Han period to turn this semi-legendary personage into the first of the Legalists. And as for Shen Pu-hai and Shen Tao, who were counted under the Han rulers among the Legalists, their ideas are not very well known and we are not even certain who they were. Only the *Han Fei-tzu*, the work of the eminent thinker Han Fei (Fei of Han) (280?–234), seems to be for the most part authentic. In this book Legalist thinking appears in its most elaborate form, as the result of a process of synthesis and reflection applied to a whole series of experiences relating to the government and administration of the state. These touch diplomacy, war, and economics as much as administration and respond to the concern, very general in the fifth to third centuries, to reinforce the economic and military power of the various kingdoms.

But the merit of the Legalists was to have understood that the basis of the very power of the state resided in its political and social institutions; their originality lay in their desire to subject this state and its subjects to the sovereignty of the law.

According to Han Fei, it is important that the prince should be the sole dispenser of gifts and honours, punishments and penalties. If he delegates the smallest part of his authority he runs the risk of creating rivals who will soon usurp his power. In the same way, it is essential that the functions of the state's agents should be very strictly defined and divided, so that no conflict about competences can arise and officials profit from the vagueness of their spheres of action to arrogate undue power to themselves. But the functioning of the state must be assured first and foremost by the establishment of objective, binding, and general rules. In its philosophy, Legalism is distinguished by a constant effort to attain objectivity. Not only must the law be public, known to everyone and exclude any divergent interpretation, but its very interpretation must be made impervious to the uncertain and variable judgement of men. To measure the honour won in war, and to calculate the degree of bravery shown, by the number of heads cut off the enemy may seem a somewhat crude procedure, but it has the advantage of removing from the sphere of discussion what, in the absence of any objective standard, would be only a matter of opinion. The whole spirit of Chinese law was to remain marked by the original direction given to it by Legalism. The role of the judge, a high administrative official, is not to weigh the evidence for and against, to estimate according to his own conscience the gravity of the crime and to decide on the punishment in a purely arbitrary fashion, but simply to define the crime correctly. His task is limited solely to this, for this definition involves automatically the corresponding sanction, which is provided for in the code of law. In the civil service the strict execution of orders is ensured by recourse to the written word (accounts of management, inventories, daily situation reports), to calculations, and to objective modes of proof (seals, emblems in two parts, which need only to be put together to reveal the authenticity of the emblem by the matching of the markings). The value of institutions and that of the state's agents are to be judged solely by the effectiveness of the results they produce.

The problem of the choice of men, which is a fundamental question for moralists who favour government by virtue, is of no importance for the Legalists. The prince has no use for exceptional men and no need either to rely on luck; it suffices to employ anyone who offers his services, since the mechanisms already installed must necessarily ensure the good running of the state and society. Moral qualities are worse than useless because they can lead the state to ruin by giving virtuous men a power which endangers the sovereignty of the prince and the law. According to the *Shang-tzu*, which in spite of its late date remains true to the Legalist tradition of the fourth and third centuries B.C., politics is not a matter of morality. It is only the body of positive means and stratagems which ensure and maintain the power of the state.

Legislative measures are not concerned simply with reforming radically the political organization; they aim at remoulding society as a whole. The establishment of a scale of crimes and a scale of honorific ranks, which together form an indissoluble whole, should result in the creation of a continuous social hierarchy, always liable to modification, which directs all the activities of the state's subjects and enlists them in its service, favouring those whose activities are considered useful (soldiers and producers of cereals) and penalizing the rest (vagabonds, parasites, manufacturers of luxury articles, speechifiers, and philosophers). In fact historical circumstances – the evolution of armies in which the peasantry had finally come to furnish the main combatants, and the necessity for sufficient reserves to fight long campaigns – caused the allocation of absolute priority to agricultural production. Agriculture is therefore regarded as the source (*pen*: the 'root' or 'trunk') of all economic and military power, as opposed to the secondary and subordinate activities (the 'branches', *mo*), industry and commerce, the disorderly development of which can involve the weakening and ruin of the state. It is important to put a brake on all activities that divert the population from its essential tasks, to combat speculators, to control the price of vital raw materials and to keep a grip on the currency. Thus we can already see in the fourth to third centuries B.C. the beginnings of a political economy which in the Chinese world underwent a large and precocious development.

Although the prince is the sole source of the rewards and punishments which determine the social hierarchy, this does not imply that he can use his power as the fancy takes him. His power is confined to the erection of institutions and objective criteria known to all. His impartiality is complete, like that of the natural order, and in this point the influence of the Taoists is clearly perceptible in Han Fei.

Other influences also affected the development of Legalism. Even before the consolidation of a theory of the state founded on the sovereignty of the prince and of the law, those who had in mind the success of diplomatic combinations sought to take advantage of favourable opportunities and situations (*shih*) by means of expedients that were kept secret (*shu*). This concept of political action based on the idea of concrete, specific times and places seems to have been the first to be adopted when heads of kingdoms wished to take advantage of the upheavals in aristocratic society to free themselves from the tutelage of the great noble families and make an attempt to achieve hegemony. The Legalists were to find a place, alongside the body of laws intended to ensure the functioning of the state and the general organization of society, for this idea of secret devices and stratagems; indeed the prince owed part of his personal power to them.

Finally, the development of Legalism was influenced by the mentality of the great merchant entrepreneurs, some of whom served as advisers to heads of kingdoms in the fifth to third centuries; for example, Fan Li in Yüeh about 500 B.C., one of the first men to preach the 'enrichment of the state and the strengthening of the armies', *fu-kuo ch'iang-ping*, Pai Kuei in Wei in the fourth century and Lü Pu-wei, adviser to the prince of Ch'in at the end of the third century. Recourse to calculations and to objective means of proof and the very idea of secret stratagems are common to the Legalists and commercial circles.

What most struck their contemporaries and men of the Han period about the ideas of the Legalists was the equality before the law which they wished to impose on everyone. 'They do not distinguish', writes Ssu-ma T'an in the second century B.C., 'between kin and strangers, they make no difference between nobles and the common people; they let them all be judged by the law, so that relationships based on affection and respect are abolished.'

Nevertheless, in spite of subsequent changes in the Chinese world, the contribution made by the Legalists in the realms of law and of political, social, and administrative organization was a fundamental one. Legalism has continued to inspire Chinese political thinking down to our own day.

From religious practice to philosophy: the Taoists

The fourth and third centuries, a period of anxiety and of social disturbance and upheaval, were to be particularly favourable to the development of religious currents. The sect led by Mo-tzu had already made itself conspicuous in the fifth century by its religiosity and its ambition to ensure universal salvation. For those who were later called 'Taoists' (*tao-chia*), the salvation of each and every one does not lie in collective action but in retirement and in the practice of procedures which permit one to withdraw from the world and to master it. These people have left us collections of fables, symbolic tales, and discussions. The most important of them, the *Chuang-tzu*, is for the most part the work of a writer of genius, probably one of the greatest in the long history of Chinese literature, namely Chuang Chou, who lived *c.* 370–300. Another, later collection, the *Lieh-tzu*, seems to have been compiled in imitation of the *Chuang-tzu*. In addition to these two works there is a smaller one, the *Lao-tzu Tao-te ching*, containing sybilline sayings probably intended to serve as themes for meditation. The obscurity of these sayings has tempted numerous translators.

Many passages hint at recourse to magico-religious practices which were probably much more ancient. As Marcel Granet has emphasized, the point of departure of the Taoist thinkers is not philosophical but religious. The aim was to preserve and increase one's vital force by recourse to various disciplines: dietary, respiratory (breathing in a closed circuit), sexual, gymnastic, and no doubt already alchemical. These disciplines as a whole were known as *yang-sheng* ('nourishing the vital principle'). *Yang-sheng* was a means of refining the body so as to render it invulnerable (water, fire, and wild beasts are powerless against the saint), of acquiring the ability to disport oneself freely in the universe on ecstatic voyages, of delaying indefinitely the process of growing old. All these techniques, better known from the Han period onwards, seem to have been the privilege of schools of magicians (*wu*) whose existence is attested in the remotest antiquity.

It is on this basis of magical tradition and under the influence of the other currents of thought, but in complete opposition to them, that the Taoist philosophy seems to have developed. The Taoist thinkers contrast the ideal of an independent, natural, free and happy life with the constraints of morality, ritual, and political organization, and with the sacrifices preached by the gloomy disciples of Mo-tzu. All the world's miseries come from the distortion, hindrances, and superfluous adjuncts imposed on nature by culture; these things cause a weakening of the vital principle. To live a full and whole life we must avoid all waste of energy, rediscover the perfect simplicity (*p'u*) of a being in its natural state, conform to the rhythm of universal life, alternate between long periods of hibernation and periods of untrammelled merry-making, imitate the games and dances of the animals who know instinctively how life should be lived. One must be, like the great All, silence, repose, and complete indifference. Those who agitate themselves, busy themselves in search of fortune and glory, try to save the world, or devote themselves to the service of the state are only fools who waste their vital force and deny themselves all hope of achieving true holiness.

In the same way one must reject all discursive thought, for language, a social institution, is one of the first obstacles to the free communication of the being with the great All. All distinctions are arbitrary. Life and death are only two alternating phases of the same reality. The *Chuang-tzu* borrows the sophists' dialectic to demonstrate the total vanity of linguistic antitheses. All teaching which employs the spoken word is illusory, and the writings of the ancients are only, so to speak, their droppings. The saint instructs and transforms his disciples in a direct way, by his imperceptible influence, without uttering a word. The fact is that, outside the immediate, universal knowledge conferred by perfect repose and indifference, there are only fleeting, chance, impermanent, relative truths. The sole true reality is the power of indefinite transformation, the immanent principle of cosmic spontaneity embodied in the Tao.

Taoism was to have an extremely important and often predominant influence on Chinese thought and on the development of religious movements in the Chinese world. It made a considerable contribution to the formation of scientific concepts and to certain discoveries. Its influence has even been perceptible both in the concept of political authority, one of the bases of which was the possession of magico-religious powers, and in theories of government.

Mencius

In contrast to the innovators, preoccupied with the actual functioning of the state and installation of the institutions necessary for its development, we find those who thought that the foundation of power lay in the virtue of the prince, an old idea to which the progress of moral concepts tended to give a completely new lease of life in those who quoted Confucius as their authority. According to these thinkers, virtue is no longer inherent in artistocratic families; it has become a normal quality which can be acquired by anyone. In the view of Meng-tzu (Mencius; second half of the fourth century B.C.), the prince capable of displaying a virtue equal to that of the legendary heroes of remote antiquity (Yao, Shun, and Yü, founder of the Hsia) and of the first kings of Chou, epochs when perfect social harmony reigned, will necessarily impose himself on all the Chinese lands as universal sovereign. It is no longer a question of patrimonial power with a religious basis, but more simply of generosity and concern for each individual's well-being. What is important is not lands, of which there are always enough, or wealth or warlike power — these things mean nothing without the adhesion and support of the minor gentry and the common people — but men. Yet greed, selfishness, and the lust for power led princes to multiply the constraints and sufferings of the humble and thus alienate the sympathy of the people. He among the great ones of this world who dared, in this age of violence and unbridled appetites, to offer a bold challenge and to return to the humanitarian mode of government of the ancient kings would provoke a sort of revolution; all the oppressed peoples would run to him as to their saviour.

This theme, developed at length in the work which recounts the Master's conversations (it also contains advice of an economic and fiscal nature: Mencius suggests going back to the old practice of the 'common field' idealized in the *ching* system — the division of the allotments into squares of nine equal plots — and reducing commercial taxes) is combined with an optimistic view of human nature. Men possess in embryo at their birth the moral qualities needed to make them into good men, namely *jen,* humanity, *i,* sense of duty, *li,* politeness, and *chih,* knowledge.

These seeds can either be developed by education or stifled by the pernicious influence of the environment.

A thinker of no great originality, Mencius was not to enjoy much success until the ninth to eleventh centuries, when he became popular because of the analogies between his conception of human nature (*hsing*) and certain Buddhist theories (the nature of Buddha is innate in every being) and because of the general harmony of his political ideas with the philosophical and moral tendencies which were to develop in the Sung period. *Mencius* was to become one of the basic texts of the 'neo-Confucian' orthodoxy adopted by the authoritarian, paternalist Ming (1368–1644) and Ch'ing (1644–1911) empires.

Hsün-tzu

Much more profound and original than Mencius, Hsün-tzu (*c.* 293–235 B.C.), together with his contemporary Han Fei, was one of the most powerful minds of the third century. His thought owes much to the Legalists as well as to the Taoists. Probably the first man in history to recognize the social origins of morality, Hsün-tzu refuses to see anything in raw human nature but a complex of anarchical and irrational tendencies: goodness and reason are born of the discipline automatically imposed by life in society. It is society which, by its constant repression of the natural appetites, violence, and selfishness of individuals, canalizes these lively forces, tames them and turns them to the advantage of each and all. Society is the great educator of individuals. Duties (*i*) and rules of conduct (*li*, 'rites') teach each individual self-control and give him a sense of what is fitting and just. Festivals and ceremonies, music and dance are a training in mutual understanding. Institutions make the man.

But far from being the arbitrary work of a legislator, *i* and *li*, conceived no longer as moral qualities but as objective realities, are the natural product of history. Thus they incorporate a principle of rationality, and society is itself the source of all reason (*li*). Social order and reason merge into each other.

Without a distribution (*fen*) of ranks and conditions that is in conformity with equity (*i*) and recognized by all, quarrels and disputes would ruin the social cohesion which makes possible the collective power of human groupings. It is therefore essential that this distribution should be clear and that names should correspond with realities. We find in Hsün-tzu one of the best expositions of the theory of the 'rectification of names' (*cheng-ming*). The theory of *cheng-ming*, developed by the scribes and annalists, who saw in a use of terms that was in conformity with ritual tradition the means of expressing a moral judgement, became the instrument of a new order based on merits and demerits. By 'designating' – that is, by creating titles and ranks – the prince 'secretes' the order which ensures the regular functioning of society as a whole. Since he does this, he does not intervene in quarrels; he contents himself with installing a mechanism which avoids them because it is based on the universal consensus. We find here the same approach as in Han Fei: the prince does not issue commands or intervene directly; being completely impartial, he is the source and guarantor of universal order. We do not meet in Hsün-tzu any more than in other Chinese thinkers the idea which seems to some extent to be a constituent element of Western thought, namely that the principle of order is the power of constraint and individual command. In the Ch'un-ch'iu age the source of order lies in the complex of ritual rules and of hierarchies of family cults. In Mencius it is the effect of the virtue of the holy man; for Hsün-tzu it is the product of objective mechanisms arising out of life in society; and for Han Fei the result of general rules established by heads of state. The idea that order can only result from a sort of spontaneous, organic adjustment recurs in cosmological conceptions: no individual power is in command of nature, whose equilibrium is ensured by interplay of opposing, complementary forces or virtues, the growth and decline of which are expressed in the succession of the seasons. One can understand the difficulties of the dialogue when the Chinese and European civilizations came into contact with each other in the seventeenth century. In the notion of *T'ien* (Heaven, natural order) Christian missionaries saw – according to their own tendencies – either a simple mechanistic conception or the trace of a monotheistic cult.

Sophists and specialists in the 'five elements'

The rhetoric which was one of the original features of the school of Motzu was based on analogies, lengthy comparisons, and repetition. Heavy and involved, it was scarcely suitable for the debates of the princely courts and diplomatic negotiations in which the object was not to preach but to gain your point in a few words. On these occasions speech was lively, allusive, forceful, or ironical. The opposing parties would use any means available to gain their end: moral and ritual precepts, anecdotes, fables, historical precedents, paradoxes and trains of reasoning that led to absurd conclusions. To embarrass and surprise one's opponent it was quite legitimate to make use of fallacious arguments. Thus political circumstances in the age of the Warring States favoured the development of a kind of sophistry which is quite original in character and distinguished by its essentially pragmatic aim from that of the Greek world, which was bound up with the practice of making speeches in law courts and political assemblies. The time available for speaking was strictly limited. Hindered by having to use a language that could not distinguish between singular and plural, abstract and concrete, the Chinese Sophists (*Pien-che*) scarcely had the leisure to push their analysis of language very far or to develop a logic of speech. Hui Shih (*c.* 380–300) and his better-known successor Kung-sun Lung (*c.* 320–250) are the only ones who have left a few fragments — or even a name — behind them. We are indebted to them for a series of paradoxes based on analysis of the ideas of size, time, space, movement, unity, and multiplicity. These paradoxes had some success at the time but represented an attempt to reflect on abstract ideas which was never carried any further.

Chinese logic was not to develop along these lines. It followed the path taken by the specialists in divination, who were the founding fathers of mathematics in the Chinese world. The manipulation of numbers and the combination of signs suited to translate the correct values of space-time were to serve as the basis of philosophical theories and of the sciences. Less irrational than many others, this mode of apprehending the world was to demonstrate its heuristic worth down the years in many fields (chemistry, magnetism, medicine, and so on). It seems in fact to have been the period of the Warring States that saw the systematization of the classificatory theories inherited from soothsaying circles. These theories correlate and reassemble in spatio-temporal groups fundamental properties or forces that are both in opposition and complementary to each other (*yin* and *yang*, male and female powers, Five Elements). The growth and decline of these forces, as well as their succession, make it possible to interpret both the natural order and history. They explain the birth, zenith, and decline of political power. These theories, which corresponded with the needs of an age of social and political upheavals but were also to be very popular in the Ch'in and Han empires seem to have been cultivated particularly in the 'academy' of Chi-hsia at Lin-tzu (the modern Itu in Shantung), the capital of Ch'i, where representatives of various different schools rubbed shoulders. Tradition ascribes to one Tsou Yen (*c.* 305–240) the credit for systematizing these cosmological conceptions.

Literature

The men who have been called the Chinese philosophers (*chu-tzu*) of the age of the Warring States refer to a rich oral literature from which they borrow anecdotes, fables, stories, allegories, and riddles that are found in various different versions. Part of this literature must have been put down in writing at the same time as the other traditions of this period in the second and first centuries B.C., in the form of chronicles or fictional biographies and collections of speeches and remarks ascribed to famous men. The content of these collections is often somewhat heterogeneous. The *Mu-t'ien-tzu chuan*, found in Honan in 279 in a tomb of the age of the Warring States, recounts the legendary travels of King Mu (traditional dates: 1001–947) in the western regions. The *Yen-tzu Ch'un Ch'iu* is a collection of anecdotes arranged according to type. The *Wu-tzu* is a work on strategy put under the name of a famous general of the kingdom of Wei. The *Kuan-tzu*, attributed to Kuan Chung, a minister of Ch'i in the seventh century B.C., is a treatise of politics and economics consisting of disparate sections. The *Kuo-yü* and *Chan-kuo-ts'e* are histories intermingled with speeches relating sometimes to the Ch'un-ch'iu age, sometimes to that of the Warring States.

It is reasonable to suspect that this extremely varied literature betrays the influence of an international folklore explained by the historical circumstances of the epoch (the presence of Indo-European peoples in central Asia, the expansion of Seleucid Persia to Transoxiania in the fifth century, the relations of fifth- to third-century China with the Indian world). The mythical geography of India seems indirectly to have inspired the cosmology of Tsou Yen, who gives a central place to Mount Kunlun, the Chinese equivalent of Mount Sumeru, and Zeno of Elea's paradox of the arrow recurs in the Chinese Sophists.

But just as mythical geography was soon to be abandoned in favour of positive concepts, so the most ancient myths of the Chinese world began to be remoulded as secular history. The construction of this history continued in the Han period. It recasts and inserts into a continuous chronology going back to the beginnning of the third millenium before Christ fragments of myths and legends and religious themes, the significance of which it transforms into historical data. Civilizing heroes who had been adopted as patrons by the various sects and schools of the fifth to third centuries (Huang-ti the Yellow Emperor, Fu-hsi and his sister Nü-kua, Shen-nung the Divine Ploughman, Yao, Shun, Yü the founder of the Hsia, and so on) and to whom humanity owes its basic institutions and the adaptation of its environment, find themselves assigned places in a dated history in perfect continuity with succeeding ages.

In a quite different field, the end of the period of the Warring States was marked by the appearance of a new kind of poetry originating in Chu and rich in elements borrowed from autochtonous cultures. Springing no doubt from a much more ancient tradition, it was given lustre for the first time at the beginning of the third century by a noble of the kingdom of Ch'u called Ch'ü Yüan. This poetry is religious in inspiration and lyrical in character; its free rhythms, sometimes halting, sometimes majestic, are punctuated by exclamations. Some pieces describe the shaman's journey in search of the divinity invoked and recall the trips of the 'perfect man' (*chen-jen*) who, according to Chuang-tzu, rides the wind and the clouds, straddles the sun and the moon, and voyages outside the universe. The poems (*fu*) of Ch'ü Yüan were to be imitated by his nephew Sung Yü and by Chin Ch'a before being transmuted in the Han age into poetic descriptions precious in style and mannered in vocabulary.

Part 2

Rise, Evolution, and Decline of the First Centralized State

Prologue

During the course of the Han period (from the beginning of the second century before our era to the end of the second century of our era: official dates, 206 B.C.–A.D. 9 for the First Han dynasty and A.D. 25–220 for the Later Han dynasty) an important process of evolution took place affecting society, the division of political power, the distribution of the population, the relations of the Chinese world with the steppe, and the economy. Moreover one can distinguish different stages in the continuous process of change undergone by the centralized state, as it had been defined by the first Ch'in emperor, between the civil war of the years 210–202 B.C. which put an end to his empire and the period of anarchy and struggles between leaders of armies in which the Second Han dynasty came to an end in A.D. 190–220.

The first sixty years of the second century B.C. were a period during which the central power was strengthened. This phase was succeeded by the great military expansion of the reign of the emperor Wu Ti (141–87), which was accompanied by a tremendous effort to develop the northern and north-western territories. The power of the empire was based on the mass of small farmers liable to conscription. But the autocratic tendencies which had developed under Wu Ti caused after his death a divorce between the corps of civil servants and the court, which became the centre of intrigues organized by the families of empresses. These intrigues ended in the usurpation of power by Wang Mang during the years A.D. 9–23. However, the political crisis of the last fifty years of the First Han dynasty had been accompanied by social and economic changes and by the slow assimilation of a certain proportion of former nomads. These diverse factors had favoured the growth of a class of rich landed proprietors, a general withdrawal of the colonies established on the northern and north-western borders, and the rapid reduction of the class of small farmers. In fact the empire restored after Wang Mang's interregnum rested on the new class of eminent citizens or gentry, which furnished its administrative and political cadres. After relative prosperity difficulties arose once again, first in the shape of a conflict between court circles, represented by the eunuchs, and the leading families, then in the form of a peasant crisis which found expression in big, popular, Taoist-inspired insurrections. These weakened the central power and favoured the rise of the army leaders entrusted with the task of suppressing them. From 190 onwards the power of the Han emperors was purely nominal and the general anarchy caused the decline of the urban economy.

Chapter 5

The Conquering Empire

From the Ch'in to the Han

The unification of the Chinese lands
and the first expansionist tendencies

The first great military exploit of Ch'in after its reorganization by Shang Yang was its victory over the nomads of the north in 314 B.C. This victory was followed in 311 by the occupation of the plain of Ch'eng-tu (land of Shu) in Szechwan and by the advance of the Ch'in armies into the mountainous regions, peopled by non-Chinese tribes, of eastern Szechwan (land of Pa). The occupation of the upper valley of the Han (Han-chung was taken in 312) made it possible for Ch'in to expand in Hupei at the expense of Ch'u in the years 278–277. The capital of Ch'u, Ying (the present-day Chiang-ling), fell at this time into the hands of General Pai Ch'i. There followed a series of offensives against Ch'in's eastern neighbours, Han, Wei, and Chao. The armies of Ch'in advanced as far as Han-tan, the capital of Chao in the extreme southeast of Hopei, but were forced to raise the siege of this city in 257. In 249 Ch'in annexed the small realm of the eastern Chou in Honan and thus put an end to the venerable line of the kings of Chou.

The man who was to unify the Chinese lands by force of arms and to found the first empire in China's history, Prince Cheng of Ch'in (259–210), came to power in 247. In ten years of campaigning he destroyed Han (223), Chao (228), Wei (225), Ch'u (223), Yen (222), and Ch'i (221). Having completed by 221 the conquest of all the Chinese lands, he took the title of 'august sovereign' (*huang-ti*), which was to remain the normal

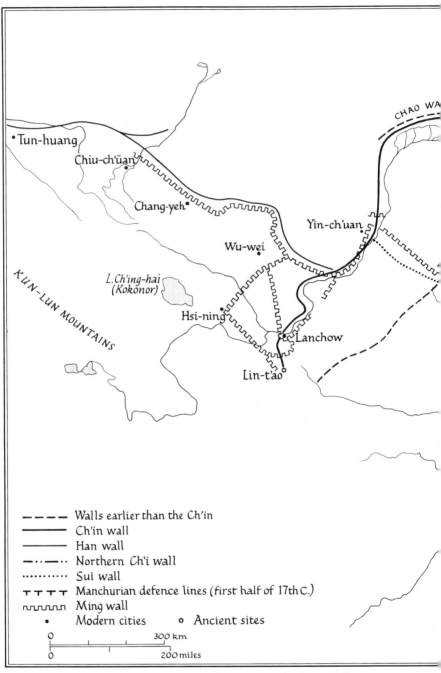

Map 7 The Great Wall of the Ch'in and the lines of successive Great Walls

The following labels appear on the map:

CHAO WA[LL]

•Tun-huang

Chiu-ch'üan

Chang-yeh•

Yin-ch'uan•

Wu-wei•

L.Ch'ing-hai
(Kokonor)

Hsi-ning•

Lanchow

Lin-t'ao°

KUN-LUN MOUNTAINS

Legend:

- – – – – Walls earlier than the Ch'in
- ———— Ch'in wall
- ———— Han wall
- – ·· — ·· Northern Ch'i wall
- ············ Sui wall
- ⊤ ⊤ ⊤ ⊤ Manchurian defence lines (first half of 17th C.)
- ⌐⌐⌐⌐⌐⌐ Ming wall
- • Modern cities ° Ancient sites

0 ———————— 300 km
0 ———————— 200 miles

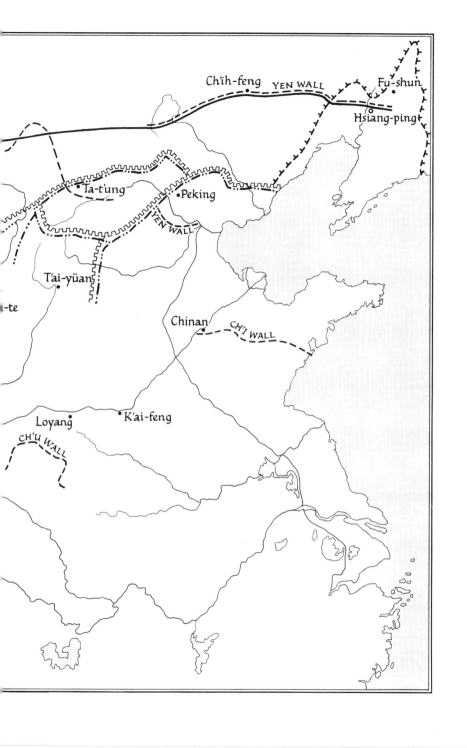

帝　皇　始　秦

Plate 16.   Idealized portrait, *c.* 1640 A.D., of
Ch'in-shih-huang-ti, the first Chinese emperor

appellation of the emperors. However, he himself was to be known to
history as the 'First Emperor' (*shih huang-ti*).

With the help of his Legalist adviser Li Ssu, who had succeeded the
merchant Lü Pu-wei (banished in 237) in this capacity, the First Emperor
extended the administrative system in use in Ch'in to the whole of the existing Chinese world. A whole series of unifying measures accompanied
the division of the territories into thirty-six 'commanderies' (*chün*), soon
increased to forty-eight. These measures included the creation of one
single type of circular copper coin with a square hole in the middle, a pattern which remained in use until our own day; the unification of the
measures of length and capacity; the creation of new standard characters
intended to replace the various types of writing hitherto in use in the
Chinese lands; and the standardization of the gauge of cart-wheels. The
ancient walls which the different kingdoms had built on their frontiers to
defend themselves against their neighbours were pulled down and the
possession of arms was made illegal (twelve giant statues were cast in the
capital out of the metal from the weapons which were confiscated). A
tremendous effort was made to develop the country as a whole: a network of imperial roads and irrigation canals was constructed and a Great
Wall was erected on the northern frontier. This wall was intended to protect the empire against the invasions of the Hsiung-nu, nomadic cattle-

A

B

Figure 6 Chinese writing of the Ch'in and Han periods. **A.** Standardized style of the Ch'in empire (copies dating from the 8th and 10th centuries); **B.** Official style of the Later Han (1st–2nd centuries)

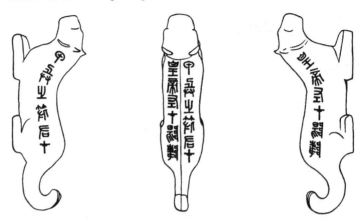

Fig. 7   Two-part emblem of the Ch'in dynasty (221–206 B.C.) The inscription on the two sides of the tiger reads: 'Two-part emblem for the armies. The right-hand part is in the Imperial Palace, the left-hand part at Yang-ling.' This type of emblem appeared during the Warring States period and was used until the T'ang (7th–9th centuries). The fact that the two halves tallied guaranteed that military orders were genuine.

raisers of the steppes. It followed the line of the ancient fortifications built round about 300 B.C. by the kingdoms of Ch'in, Chao, and Yen, reinforcing them and prolonging them continuously from southern Kansu to the northern part of the peninsula of Liao-tung (i.e. from the 104th to the 123rd degree of longitude). In 213 an expeditionary force of 100,000 men was dispatched by General Meng T'ien against the Hsiung-nu settled in the Ordos region. Other operations were carried out in the barbarous lands of South China and Vietnam, where new commanderies were created. The centres of these commanderies were P'an-yü (the modern Canton), Kweilin, in the north-east of the province of Kwangsi, and Hsiang (Hanoi). The Ch'in offensives against the aboriginal peoples of Fukien (the Yüeh of the land of Min: Min Yüeh) resulted in the creation of yet another commandery in the region of present-day Foochow. Peopled by exiles, these distant territories, where the Chinese garrisons had to contend continually with the guerilla activities of the native population, broke away from the empire at the time of the disturbances which followed the death of the First Emperor. Nevertheless they had already been permeated by Chinese products and explored by merchants and adventurers in the period of the Warring States and they preserved the traces of this Chinese implantation. Descendants of the soldiers and exiles of the time of the First Emperor were still there a century later.

Collapse of the Ch'in empire and advent of the Han

The First Emperor's tyranny seems eventually to have been rendered intolerable by a combination of factors: the number of military operations

Plate 17.   Burning the books, by order of Emperor Ch'ih-shih Huang Ti,
B.C. 213, from a Western reconstruction

conducted, from Kansu to Korea and from Fukien to Vietnam; the extent of the big public works undertaken (construction of towns, roads, post houses, canals, Great Walls), not to mention the installation of a huge palace in the capital (Hsien-yang, on the left bank of the Wei, in Shensi) and the excavation of an immense hypogeum inside Mount Li (thirty miles east of Hsien-yang); and finally the extreme rigour of the penal system. The popular discontent was accompanied by the hatred of the old nobility, which had been deprived of its rights and deported (120,000 'rich and powerful families' were moved to the region of the capital). Nor were scholarly circles any happier; in his desire to eliminate speech-makers who took it upon themselves to criticize the new state, the First Emperor banned all books except treatises on medicine, agriculture, and divination. In 213 came the notorious 'burning of the books', which was followed by the execution at Hsien-yang of over four hundred opponents of the regime. The first insurrections occurred immediately after the First Emperor's death, when his youngest son succeeded him under the name of Second Emperor (Erh-shih Huang-ti). In 209 came the popular rebellions led by Ch'en Sheng and Wu Kuang, which the ancient nobility of Ch'u, headed by the Hsiang family, soon joined.

Liu Pang, a minor Ch'in official of lowly birth, found his authority as head of the insurgent bands growing. He was at first under the orders of Hsiang Yü (232–202), who had made him prince of Han, but he soon quarrelled with his associate. In 207 he led his troops across the Ch'in-

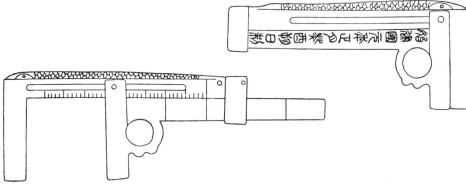

Figure 8   Callipers (shoemakers' size-sticks) made in 9 A.D. They are graduated in *ts'un* (tenth part of a *ch'ih*) and in *fen* (tenths of a *ts'un*). The face shown on the right bears the inscription: 'Made on *kuei-yu* day, on the new moon of the fifth month, first year of *Shih-chien-kuo*'

ling and in the following year, 206, the theoretical date of the foundation of the new Han empire, crushed the Ch'in army in the valley of the Wei. In 202 Liu Pang eliminated his rival, proclaimed himself emperor and fixed his capital at Ch'ang-an (the present-day Sian), to the south-east of Hsien-yang. Like Hsiang Yü before him, Liu Pang distributed titles of nobility and fiefs to his old companions-in-arms.

Permanence of Legalist institutions

The Legalist state, as initiated in the kingdom of Ch'in from the middle of the fourth century onwards and extended on the same principles by the First Emperor to the whole of the Chinese lands, was based on a faceless administrative and military organization which ensured the control and utilization of the peasantry. It was this direct relationship between the peasantry and the state that formed the essential characteristic of this new conception of power and society. In spite of appearances, the First Han emperors were the heirs of the Ch'in rulers and continued their work. Traditional history enjoyed presenting the Ch'in empire in the blackest light. The tyrant, Cheng (the First Emperor), so the story ran, had declared war on the literati, while under the Han dynasty their influence was to be preponderant. But the foundations of the Han power were no different in origin from those of the Ch'in kingdom and empire. The same conceptions predominate in the philosophical and religious domain, namely a system of correspondences of a scholastic character furnishing a general explanation of the universe and of the changes undergone by society, and Taoist beliefs springing from the soothsayers and thaumaturges of Shantung and the coast of Hopei. Outside the empire, general conditions remained the same from one period to the next and the great expansion of Emperor Wu's reign (141–87) towards Mongolia, Korea, central Asia, South China, and Vietnam merely continued, after an interval of about a century, the offensives and expeditions of the First Emperor.

It was only in the long run and as a result of a complex process of evolution that the Han empire departed further and further from its origins. All kinds of factors were involved in this evolution: economic expansion, changes in the relationship between the Chinese world and the world of the steppe, strengthening of the palace at the expense of the civil service, weakening of the state's hold on the peasantry, rise of the families of the rich and gentry, and so on.

Although the Han founder considerably softened the extreme harshness of the penal laws of the first empire, the political and administrative organization that Liu Pang put in place differed little from that of the Ch'in. We find the same division of the territory into commanderies (*chün*) and prefectures (*hsien*), and the same tripartite division of functions both in the capital and in the provinces: civil affairs, military affairs, and inspection and supervision of the administration. In short the same 'Legalist' empire was perpetuated not only in the territories directly dependent on the central power but also in the 'fiefs' (*feng-kuo*) granted first to the founder's companions-in-arms and later to relatives of the imperial family. Its power was based on the direct control of peoples and individuals by the state. This implies recourse to accurate censuses, and in fact those which have been preserved from the Han period are reckoned to be among the most precise in history. Every subject was liable to a personal tax payable in coin (this tax was levied even on children of tender years), to annual stints of forced labour and to military service. In addition, the Legalist system of rewards and punishments (grants of rank, promotions, amnesties, judicial condemnations) made it possible to classify the whole population in the continuous hierarchy of the twenty-four degrees of dignity (*chüeh*). Promotions were conferred for military exploits or for deliveries of cereals to the state; and they could also be purchased. Punishments involved demotion, while the possession of grades ensured a reduction of the penalties in the case of an offence. Amnesties, which sometimes cancelled debts and were accompanied by promotions, were used to correct the excesses of too harsh legislation. In the case of an amnesty the administration would present alcohol and sacrificial oxen to the peasant communities (the 'villages', *li*) for their annual banquets in honour of the god of the soil (*she*). By the social cohesion and moral pressure which they exerted

Plate 18. The Great Wall: from a watch-tower

Plate 19. The Great Wall: archway through a wall

Plate 20. The Great Wall: panorama

Plate 21. The Great Wall: near the Mongolian border; these four views of the Great Wall depict sections constructed in the fifteenth century

at the local level, these communities reinforced the state's hold on the population. They were headed by leading elder citizens and enforced a morality based on the subordination of the younger to the elder and on the respect for hierarchies.

The Legalist empire was based on the breakdown of human groupings into very small units, and in fact the existence of large communities, of important local cults, and of numerous private retinues formed the biggest obstacle to its activities. Thus the hold of the central power was firmest where the settlement was most recent; in the long-settled regions the imperial administration had to come to terms with the great families. Such was the case in Shansi, where inter-clan rivalries were at the root of constant vendettas which the representatives of the central power were powerless to end. This sheds light on one of the main reasons for transfers of population: it was in the state's interest to move influential families, to shift them from their surroundings, in order to rob them of all power. Similarly, it was also in the state's interest to extend the areas of land clearance and colonization, for it is easier to keep in hand a population consisting of displaced persons—convicts, freedmen, soldiers, and bankrupt peasants.

Transfers of population also happened to serve economic and military ends as well as political ones. Relieving the most densely inhabited areas of their excess population, they made it possible to develop the arid lands of the northern provinces and the frontier with Mongolia. This in turn facilitated the provisioning of the armies entrusted with the task of repulsing invasions from the steppe. As early as 198 B.C. over 100,000 persons belonging to the rich and influential families of the ancient lands of Ch'i, in northern Shantung, and Ch'u, on the middle Yangtze and in the lower valley of the Han, were deported to the region of the capital. This was the first of a long series of analogous measures which went on until the end of the first century B.C. They were substantial enough to affect the distribution of the population in North China and more particularly the north-west, where military colonies (*t'un-t'ien*) peopled by soldiers and their families multiplied during the reign of Wu Ti (141–87).

Like the Ch'in, the first Han rulers pursued a policy of undertaking big public works, the majority of which were strategic or economic in character. In 192 and 190 B.C. peasants and their womenfolk from the valley of the Wei were conscripted for the construction of the walls of the new capital, Ch'ang-an. In each of these two years there were nearly 150,000 people at work. But subsequently more and more use was made of soldiers and convicts. In 132 B.C. 100,000 soldiers were drafted to repair a breach in the dykes of the Yellow River. It was soldiers and convicts who in 102 B.C. extended the Great Walls from the north-east of

Lan-chou to Yü-men-Kuan, at the western end of Kansu. The same labour force built fortifications in Mongolia in the region of Chü-yen (Etsingol), to the north and north-east of the commanderies of Chiu-ch'üan and Chang-yeh. In 76 B.C. another line of fortifications was built in southern Manchuria by 'young good-for-nothings and civil servants guilty of misdemeanours' who had just been deported to that area. Besides ramparts and forts, canals and roads were also built. These reinforced the hold of the central power on the regions but also corresponded to economic needs. In 129 B.C. ninety miles of canal were dug between Honan and Shensi to connect the basin of the Wei with the Yellow River; 95 B.C. saw the opening of a canal some sixty miles long linking the course of the Wei to that of the Ching further north. But innumerable irrigation works were carried out in the whole of North China during the reigns of Wu Ti and his immediate successors. Among the great roads constructed under the first Han emperors were the one linking the capital to Ch'eng-tu via the valley of the Pao-Hsieh, through the Chung-nan-shan massif, and the one started in 130 B.C. from Szechwan towards the rich plains of Kwangtung. The technical difficulties, which often made it necessary to build roads with an overhang (*chan-tao*) over precipices, were aggravated in the south-west by mutinies among the workers recruited on the spot from the aboriginal tribes.

The reduction of the 'fiefs' and the reining-in
of the imperial nobility

However, although the Han empire inherited all its institutions from the Ch'in empire and possessed all the characteristics of a 'Legalist' state, its initial weakness necessitated certain compromises.

The Han power had been born in a climate of anarchy and general insurrection. The regionalist tendencies inherited from the age of the Warring States had remained very much alive during the short period of unification imposed by the Ch'in kingdom and empire between the years 230 and 210. Thus the imperial administration of the Han rulers could at first be applied directly only to part of the ancient Chinese lands. Of the fifty-four 'commanderies' into which the empire was divided at the beginning of the second century B.C., thirty-nine, or nearly two-thirds of the whole territory, formed part of the fiefs (*feng-kuo*) allocated in 201 to the founder's old companions-in-arms. The majority of these 'kingdoms', the administration of which was identical with that of the imperial territories and was supervised by imperial commissioners, were situated in the eastern regions of the Yangtze. It would certainly be a mistake to see in the creation of these 'kingdoms' a sort of resurgence of the fiefs of antiquity; the ancient 'feudalism' had disappeared for good. Nevertheless the relative freedom which the heads of these kingdoms enjoyed constituted a threat to the central power, which strove to eliminate them during the course of the second century.

In the reign of the empress Lü (187–180), the old companions-in-arms placed in control of the fiefs by the empire's founder, who were showing too much independence of the central power, were eliminated to the benefit of the empress's relations. In the time of her successor, Wen Ti (179–157), the advisers Chia I (200–168) and Ch'ao Ts'o (?–154) suggested reducing the excessive power of the princes. Finally, under Ching Ti (157–141), a crisis arose which ended in the rebellion of the 'Seven Kingdoms' led by the princes of Wu and Ch'u, whose fiefs lay in the present-day province of Kiangsu. The imperial armies defeated this rebellion in 154, thus asserting the authority of the central power over the regions most distant from the capital thirteen years before the beginning of the great reign of Wu Ti (141–87). In 124, Liu An, prince of Huainan, a fief in Anhwei, tried in his turn, but in vain, to shake off the control of the emperors. He was executed two years later. As early as 127 B.C. a law was adopted which was to lead to the final breakup of the fiefs and the downfall of the imperial nobility. It ended the rule by which the title and possessions were passed on to the sole legitimate heir and it enjoined that they should be shared out equally between all the sons. By the end of Wu Ti's reign the princes had lost all territorial power; the only advantage which they still enjoyed was the right to levy taxes in grain on a certain number of peasant families. It thus becomes apparent that Wu Ti's reign was not only a period of unprecedented military expansion but also one of internal consolidation.

Thus the general tendency throughout the second century was towards increased centralization. The influence at court acquired by the literati as advisers and the toning down of the legislation inherited from the Ch'in rulers did not affect this basic orientation. The harshest laws of the Ch'in period were in fact abolished between the years 191 and 167. In 191 possession of the books banned by the First Emperor was once again authorized, and in 167 mutilation as a punishment disappeared from the legal code. On the other hand, while the equality of all before the law – one of the great principles of Legalism – was at first maintained in the early days of the Han dynasty, the tendency to introduce distinctions based on social position (*kuei-chien* or *tsun-pei*) and degree of kinship (*ch'in-shu*) began to appear through the influence of powerful advisers who appealed to the scholarly tradition. As early as 176 a memorandum by Chia I drew attention to the drawbacks of a too uniform application of the law: imperial majesty falls on those close to the sovereign through

their position or ties of blood and it is therefore fitting to spare important personages the dishonour inseparable from ordinary punishments.
It is considerations of this sort that explain the custom finally adopted of
authorizing, as a special favour, dignitaries liable to capital punishment
to commit suicide. However, a long process of evolution was required to
produce the system of penalties graduated according to degree of proximity (a proximity reflected in the nature and duration of the mourning
required in each case) and according to the status of the guilty person and
the victim. The same is true of the procedures peculiar to the categories
of guilty persons belonging to the aristocracy and the mandarinate (the
pa i, 'eight deliberations'). The whole system attained its most elaborate
form in the T'ang code of the seventh century, the first collection of
penal laws which has come down to us complete. The legislators of the
periods between the Han and Sui dynasties were the authors of this admirable systematization of the law.

The great expansion of the Han in Asia

One may say that the whole policy of the First Han emperors was
dominated and directed by the problems of the steppe. Invasions of
horsemen using the bow who came from the steppe were doubtless
nothing new, for they had already threatened the kingdoms of Ch'in,
Chao, and Yen from Kansu to Manchuria at the end of the fourth century, and caused the construction of the first defence walls. But the
danger increased at the end of the third century B.C. It was in fact just at
the time of the rebellions which marked the end of the Ch'in dynasty and
during the civil war between the various claimants to supreme power that
a great confederation of nomad tribes led by the Hsiung-nu was formed
in the steppe zone.

There have been long and fruitless debates on the question whether the
Hsiung-nu and the Huns were of the same origin; the similarity between
the names may be deceptive. In any case the question has no interest for
history in view of the lapse of time between the two periods concerned.
Like the other empires of the steppe, that of the Hsiung-nu, which extended from Baikal to Balkhash, and southward to the neighbourhood
of the fortieth parallel, united tribes of diverse origins whose languages
belonged to the 'Altaic' group of Mongol, Turk, and Tungus languages
known to us at a much later date. The name of the most powerful
tribes — those which had placed themselves at the head of the confederation — was extended to these peoples as a whole; the same thing happened
in later times with the Juan-juan, the Turks, and the Mongols. Founded

Table 7.   The Han expansion round about 100 B.C.

136	Beginning of the exploration of the roads from Szechwan to Burma via Yunnan, and from Szechwan to Kwangtung via Kweichow.
135	First attacks on the Yüeh kingdom in Fukien.
133	Expedition against the Hsiung-nu in Mongolia by an army corps of 300,000 men with chariots and cavalry.
130	Fresh efforts to advance along the roads from Szechwan to Burma and from Szechwan to Kwangtung.
128	Offensive against the Hsiung-nu. First campaigns in Manchuria and the north of Korea.
124	First big offensive against the Hsiung-nu.
123	Fresh offensive in Mongolia.
121	Second big offensive against the Hsiung-nu.
120	Expedition against the K'un-ming tribes in western Yunnan.
119	Third big offensive in Mongolia and great victory over the Hsiung-nu.
117	Creation of the commanderies of Tun-huang and Chang-yeh in western and central Kansu.
115	Creation of the commanderies of Chiu-ch'üan and Wu-wei in the same regions.
112– 111	Expedition against the kingdom of the Yüeh in the south (Kwangtung and northern Vietnam), and division of their lands into nine commanderies.
110	Expedition against the Yüeh kingdom in Fukien and suppression of this kingdom.
109	Expeditions to northern and central Korea. Suppression of the kingdom of Tien in western Yunnan.
108	Creation of four commanderies in northern and central Korea. First expeditions to central Asia.
105	Han embassy in Seleucia on the Tigris.
104– 101	Campaigns in central Asia and the Pamirs.
102	Prolongation of the Great Walls to Yü-men-Kuan, in western Kansu.
101	Suppression of the kingdom of Ta-yüan, Ferghana, in the upper basin of the Syr-Daria.
97	Fresh campaign against the Hsiung-nu.
90	Campaigns in Mongolia and the Turfan region of central Asia.
86 & 82	Expeditions against the K'un-ming tribes of western Yunnan.
78	Expedition to Manchuria.
77	Fresh expedition to central Asia.
72–71	Campaign against the Hsiung-nu.
71	Intervention in Dzungaria, between Altai and Tianshan.
67	Expedition to Turfan.
56	Creation of the protectorate-general of the western regions (Hsi-yü-tu-hu).

by a certain Motu (209–174), the Hsiung-nu empire lasted from 204 to 43 B.C., at which date the steppe tribes split into the southern Hsiung-nu of inner Mongolia, who joined China, and the northern Hsiung-nu, who lived in the territories corresponding to present-day outer Mongolia. Even in the time of Motu the power of the Hsiung-nu extended as far as the basin of the Tarim. In the reign of his son Lao-shang (174–160), the Hsiung-nu exerted pressure on the Yüeh-chih, a big federation of tribes who spoke an Iranian dialect and lived in the region of the oases and in Kansu. Gradually pushed back towards the west, these Indo-European speakers finally settled on the north-western borders of the Indian world. These circumstances enable us to understand why Chinese expansion under the Han rulers was not confined simply to Mongolia but extended to the whole of central Asia.

Mongolia and central Asia

The rebellions and the civil war had halted the offensive policy inaugurated by the first Ch'in emperor. The Great Walls were left undefended between the end of the third century and the beginning of the second. The nomads living in Mongolia and the Ordos area were quite free to make incursions into northern China. They took two main routes. One gave access, through present-day Ta-t'ung in the extreme north of Shansi, to the valley of the Fen; the other led to the Ch'ang-an region through the Ordos and the valleys of Shensi. A defeat incurred by the Chinese armies in 201–200 caused a general retreat south of the Great Walls which lasted until about 135. The Han rulers were forced to adopt a policy of appeasement known as *he-ch'in,* 'peace and friendship'. In 198 a Chinese princess was given in marriage to the head of the Hsiung-nu, the *shun-yü,* to whom every year the emperor sent substantial gifts of silks, alcohol, rice, and copper money. But as early as the time of Wen Ti (179–157) two of the emperor's principal advisers, Chia I (200–168) and Ch'ao Ts'o (?–154) criticized this policy of appeasement. The continual incursions of the Hsiung-nu, the number of Chinese who went over to them and the increased demands which they made provoked a change of attitude. The gifts handed over to the nomads increased both their power and their wealth. Once the central power had been consolidated it seemed possible to control the intruders' access routes on the far side of the Great Walls and to adopt once again the policy of expansion favoured by the First Emperor. The advocates of a strong policy defeated those who preached compromise at the discussions which took place at court in 133 B.C. The famous mission of Chang Ch'ien some years later must also have helped to convince people of the need for a general offensive, by showing that the Han could find allies in central Asia. Chang Ch'ien had set out from the west in 139, in search of the Yüeh-chih, old enemies of the Hsiung-nu. Kept prisoner for ten years by the nomads, he eventually escaped and reached the upper valley of the Syr-Darya and the land of Ta-yüan, Ferghana. From there Chang Ch'ien went on to Bactriana, to the south of the Amu-Darya, where he found the Yüeh Chih, who had adopted a settled life and were known at that time to the Greeks by the name of Indo-Scythians. Returning to Ch'ang-an in 126, Chang Ch'ien set off again in 115 for the land of the Wu-sun, horse-breeders who lived south-east of Lake Balkhash. He visited Ferghana again, then Sogdiana and the oases of central Asia. He returned convinced of the lively interest of all these countries in Chinese products, especially the most prized of them, silks. All these lands, he said, could be won over to the side of the Han by gifts. What Chang Ch'ien's journeys revealed to the China of that period was the existence of commerce in silks and other Chinese products in central Asia and the regions beyond the Pamirs.

It seems therefore that the factors which led to the Han expansion in the reign of the great emperor Wu Ti (141–87) included not only the consolidation of the central power and the organization of powerful armies but also a degree of wealth and an economic expansion which enabled China to assert its prestige among all its neighbours. We should not forget that diplomatic activity played just as big a part as military conquest in the Chinese advance into Manchuria, Mongolia, central Asia, and the tropical regions.

The first big victorious offensive against the Hsiung-nu took place between 127 and 119. Expeditionary forces of more than 100,000 men, both horse and foot, set out for Mongolia in 124, 123, and 119. From 115 onwards the Han empire had scarcely any further worry about its northern frontiers. In 108, after the creation of the four commanderies in northern and central Korea, it extended from the Sea of Japan to the region of K'un-ming in Yunnan, and from Tun-huang to the region of Tourane in Vietnam.

However it should not be imagined that the Han rulers were able to install a regular administration everywhere. In many places it was a matter merely of Chinese infiltration, which was protected by garrisons controlling the roads and passing-places, in the midst of populations whose loyalty was often dubious. It was in Korea and on the northern frontier that the Han emperors tried to gain a more solid hold by founding military colonies (*t'un-t'ien*), which had the double task of developing the conquered territories by clearing and irrigating the land and ensuring the defence of the area to their rear.

In Kansu the commanderies of Tun-huang and Chang-yeh were created in 117 and those of Wu-wei and Chiu-ch'üan in 115. From this time onwards a big effort was made to colonize the north-western regions, and the number of people settled there in the reign of the emperor Wu Ti may be estimated at two million. A few figures will suffice to bring home to us the scale of these transfers of population. In 127, 100,000 peasants were settled in Shuo-fang, north-west of the Ordos bend, right in Mongolia; in 102, 180,000 soldier-farmers went off to people the Chiu-ch'üan and Chang-yeh commanderies; and in 120, after big floods in western Shantung, 700,000 victims of the disaster were transferred to Shensi. These transfers of population were numerous enough to affect the distribution of the population in North China and doubtless had a beneficial effect on the agrarian economy in the most thickly populated areas of the Yellow River basin.

Manchuria and Korea

The Han expansion in Mongolia and central Asia was accompanied by efforts to advance towards the north-east (Manchuria) and Korea. These efforts aimed at putting an end to the domination exerted by the Hsiung-nu over the Tung-hu and Wu-huan, horse-breeding peoples of south-eastern Mongolia and the basin of the Liao (southern Manchuria), and at securing for the empire control of the trade routes in these regions. In any case Chinese colonization in Manchuria had been going on for a long time and went back at least to the age of the Warring States (fifth to third centuries B.C.). Remains have been found in Manchuria that must be attributed to colonists of the kingdom of Yen, the capital of which lay in the neighbourhood of present-day Peking. Moreover maritime relations between the coast of Shantung and the peninsula of Liaotung, which are only about 75 miles apart (the distance from Sicily to Tunisia), and doubtless also between Shantung and Korea, were established before the Han age. It thus becomes clear why the Han rulers made a systematic attempt at the end of the second century B.C. to incorporate the plains of southern Manchuria and the peninsula of Korea in the empire. After a victory over the Tung-hu in 128, Han commanderies were set up in Manchuria. Between 109 and 106 most of Korea was conquered, and commanderies were created in Le-lang in the north-west, Chenfan in the south-west, Lint'un in the north-east and Hsüan-t'u in the north, astride the river Yalu. The west coast of Korea remained Chinese until the beginning of the fourth century A.D. This period of Chinese infiltration explains the abundance of archaeological remains of the Han

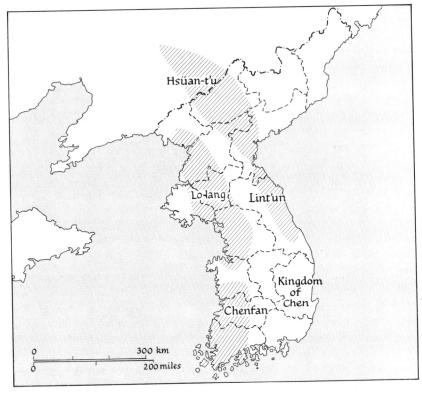

Map 8 The Han commanderies in Korea

age in the Korean peninsula. Until the recent discovery of other sites, it was the Chinese tombs at Lo-lang in Korea that had furnished the finest specimens of wall paintings from this period.

The organization of the armies of the north

It would be simplistic to see in the Great Walls a sharp divide between the world of the nomadic cattle-raisers and that of the Chinese farmers and townspeople. The northern frontiers of the Chinese world formed a zone where the opposing modes of life of the farmer and the herdsman mingled and combined. Down the centuries sometimes the pasturages would advance and the cultivated land shrink, sometimes the arid lands would be conquered and developed by the sedentary peoples. Just as certain tribes of herdsmen changed over to agriculture, so some Han adopted the nomads' mode of life. The problems of defence against incursions from the steppe must be seen in a context which is as much cultural, political and economic as military, thanks to phenomena of assimilation, diplomatic combinations, and commercial exchanges. The Great Wall formed only one element in a much vaster complex: allied tribes who collaborated in the defence against incursions; outposts, forts, and advanced garrisons; military colonies; lands developed by deported populations; horse breeding, and so on.

The organization of the Han armies and defence system on the northern frontier is fairly well known to us thanks to the discovery of a substantial number of manuscript texts on wood and bamboo and to the excavations carried out on the Chinese *limes* in the Han period since the beginning of the century. These texts come from the region of Etsingol (Chü-yen) in western Mongolia and from the neighbourhood of Tun-huang, in the west of Kansu. About 10,000 in number, they consist of reports, communiqués, inventories, soldiers' letters, fragments of legal texts, and so on. They take the form, current at the time, of strips of wood or bamboo, usually bearing one single column of characters. The dates mentioned in them run from about 100 B.C. to A.D. 100.

Two kinds of troops were to be found near the frontiers: farmer-soldiers, known as soldiers of the irrigation canals (*he-ch'ü-tsu*) or soldiers of the granaries (*k'u-tsu*), and soldiers on garrison duty in advanced posts. Look-out duty, patrols, and training occupied a considerable part of the time of troops serving in the first lines of defence. Each post was in permanent contact with neighbouring posts and with the rear, thanks to a system of signals: red and blue flags, smoke by day and fires by night, rendered more easily visible by long pivoting poles rather like Egyptian shadoofs. This system of signals, which made possible, thanks to a fairly complex code, the swift transmission of relatively precise information about troop movements and attacks, is mentioned in the texts as early as 166 B.C. All messages sent and received were recorded in writing. The head of each post was obliged by a very formalistic administrative routine to write a large number of letters and to keep extensive records which deal not only with military activities but also with victualling and the weapons kept in magazines—bows, arrows, crossbows, and catapults. On their patrols the soldiers were often obliged to level wide strips of earth or sand to detect traces of the nomads. They were responsible for the maintenance of buildings, for the manufacture of bricks made in a mould and dried in the sun, for collecting fuel and making arrows, and also acted as customs officers and police. Everything that passed the frontier posts—men, herds and merchandise—was subject to strict supervision. When a fugitive was being hunted, an accurate description of him was passed to the troops. The use of the passport, the antecedents of which go back to the age of the Warring States, is well attested in the Han period, as is the use of police dogs. The frontier posts also had to supply the needs of diplomatic caravans. Contemporary documents thus reveal the diversity of the tasks incumbent on the garrisons of the Chinese *limes*. Military activities proper formed only one of the aspects of the relations between the Chinese world and that of the nomadic herdsmen.

The Han armies were based on the system in use in the Ch'in kingdom and empire, namely conscription. Able-bodied men were enrolled at the age of thirty and were obliged to serve for one year in their local commandery. That at any rate was the system in the areas near the capital; conscripts recruited in the frontier regions stayed there permanently. But we also find paid mercenaries on the frontiers. As for the expeditionary forces of Wu Ti's time, they were composed of strong contingents of barbarian auxiliaries, of Chinese mercenaries and of convicts allowed to serve their time in the army. After Wu Ti there was a tendency to reduce the number of conscripted troops; the armies of the Second Han dynasty consisted mainly of veterans, mercenaries and very large bodies of barbarian auxiliaries.

The Han advance into tropical lands

The Chinese expansion south of the Yangtze is one of the great phenomena of the history of East Asia, both because of its long duration — nearly three millennia — and because of the changes which accompanied it, to wit, movements of whole populations, intermixture of races, the disappearance or transformation of ancient cultures, reciprocal borrowings, and so on. What remains today of the ancient ethnic units forms no more than a sort of residue which cannot give us any precise idea either of these ancient cultures — in spite of the remarkable permanence of some features — or of the distribution of the different ethnic units in ancient times. Some peoples seem to have disappeared completely. Big princedoms and substantial kingdoms with distinctive civilizations were gradually destroyed or greatly reduced by the Chinese expeditions and by progressive assimilation. Archaeology alone has finally been able to shed a clear light on some of these original cultures. Thus the real nature of the kingdom of Tien, which is briefly mentioned by sources of the Han period and whose political centre lay in the plain of present-day K'un-ming in Yunnan, was abruptly revealed in 1956 and the following years by some astonishing archaeological discoveries. This kingdom, whose economy was based on large-scale cattle-breeding and agriculture, was in contact at the end of the age of the Warring States and in the second century B.C. with the warlike Yeh-lang tribes to the east (who controlled the roads between Szechwan and Kwangtung), the K'un-ming tribes in western Yunnan and the Chinese of the plain of Ch'engtu. It occupied the crossing places between the upper Yangtze and Burma. Its commercial wealth explains how it came to develop an original bronze art showing a mixture of many different influences, the clearest of which, and possibly the most unexpected, are those of the Ordos region and the steppe. The excavations at Shih-chai-shan, south-east of the Lake of K'un-ming, produced from 1955 to 1960 remarkable bronze vessels adorned with cowries — the palladia of the princely families — the lids of which are decorated with scenes in relief which constitute valuable evidence about the economy, religious cults, and daily life of the inhabitants. The kingdom of Tien was crushed by the Han armies in 109 B.C. Its prince was allowed to retain his title until the reign of Chao Ti (87–74), but the title was suppressed after a rebellion. Chinese colonization was to eliminate all trace of this distinctive civilization.

In 86 and 82 B.C. expeditions against the K'un-ming tribes of western Yunnan extended Chinese penetration up to the approaches to Burma. Tribute was sent to Loyang by the Shan kingdom of northern Burma round about A.D. 100 (embassies of the years 94, 97, and 120).

Another site, Dong-son in Thanh-hoa, about ninety miles south of Hanoi, discovered in 1924, has revealed yet another Bronze Age civilization which seems to have been more or less contemporary with that of Tien. It was a civilization of fishermen-cum-hunters-cum-agriculturalists who lived in houses built on piles. It was characterized by the use of bronze drums with decorations showing religious scenes in which dancers adorned with feathers appear. Among the musical instruments employed was the *khene,* a mouth-organ found over a wide area of the tropical zone. It was the ancestor of the Chinese *sheng.* Influences both from the steppe and from China are perceptible in the Dong-son civilization. Articles imported include a vase and a sword of the age of the Warring States and also coins dating from the time of Wang Mang (9–25).

What is true of Tien and Dong-son is probably also true of other ancient kingdoms of which we have no archaeological traces. Fukien — facing the sea and cut off by its mountains — and southern Chekiang formed one of these independent kingdoms in the third and second centuries B.C. The Yüeh of Min (the old name of Fukien and the Foochow River) were one of the numerous fishing peoples who had occupied since antiquity the whole coastline from the estuary of the Chekiang to the region of the Hue in Vietnam. The first Ch'in emperor's expeditions had been only temporary affairs without lasting consequences, but the Han rulers advanced in force into this area at the end of the second century and destroyed the kingdom of the Yüeh of Min in 110 B.C.

All the maritime lands with big fertile plains (basin of the Hsi-chiang in the region of Canton, delta of the Red River), i.e., Kwangtung and

Vietnam down to the neighbourhood of present-day Da-nang (Tourane), had been penetrated by Chinese traders as early as the age of the Warring States (fifth to third centuries). After his expeditions towards the south in 221–214, the First Emperor had installed garrisons in the areas of present-day Kweilin (north-eastern Kwangsi), Canton, and Hanoi. However, after the collapse of the Ch'in empire an independent kingdom had been set up there; its ruling family bore the name of Chao and may have been half Chinese. This state was known as the 'Kingdom of the Yüeh of the south' (Nan-yüeh-Kuo), a term which corresponds, according to Chinese syntax, to the name 'Vietnam' (Namviet). The principal activities of this kingdom, whose inhabitants must have been ancestors of the Thais and Mon-Khmers, seem to have been trading and fishing. Its most important ports were Canton, Hep'u (in the pearl-fishing area, to the west of the peninsula of Lei-chou in Kwangtung) and a port on the Gulf of Tonkin. It traded in ivory, pearls, tortoise-shells, rhinoceros horns, textiles made from vegetable fibres, and slaves from the islands. After several military interventions, the earliest of which took place in 181, Han expeditionary forces advanced into the Canton area and the delta of the Red River in 113, and two years later the territory of the kingdom of the Nan-Yüeh was transformed into Chinese commanderies.

Nevertheless there was a permanent atmosphere of insecurity in the tropical, unhealthy regions controlled by the Han rulers in South China and Vietnam. The vegetation and the often mountainous contours of the country lent themselves admirably to guerrilla warfare and there were continual raids and skirmishes. At the time of the troubles which marked the reign of Wang Mang (9–23) and the first years of the Han restoration, Chinese emigration to Yunnan, Kwangtung and north and central Vietnam increased considerably. But from A.D. 40 onwards revolts in the delta of the Red River became widespread and led to the insurrection of the inhabitants of the whole of the north and centre of present-day Vietnam, as well as those of the Hep'u region in the west of Kwangtung. Two sisters, Tru'ng Thac and Tru'ng Nhi, the elder of whom soon assumed the title of queen, were the leaders of this great rebellion. They were to be venerated in our own time as the heroes of Vietnamese national independence. However, Ma Yüan (14 B.C. to A.D. 49), appointed 'general and tamer of the waves', succeeded in crushing this revolt in A.D. 43.

The first breakthrough to South-East Asia
and the Indian Ocean

The establishment of the Han in Kwangtung and Vietnam extended Chinese influence to South-East Asia. Bronze axes found in Cambodia are modelled on Chinese axes, and fragments of Han pottery dating from the first century A.D. have been found in eastern Borneo, western Java, and southern Sumatra. At the same time this expansion of the Han commanderies towards the south enabled the countries of South-East Asia and the Indian Ocean to enter for the first time into direct relations with the Chinese world. A passage in the *History of the Han* (chapter 28B) provides the first list of maritime routes towards the South Seas and the Indian Ocean in the first century B.C. However, these relations did not really start to develop in earnest until the first centuries of the Christian era, as a result of the maritime expansion of the Indo-Iranians, which was followed from the third century onwards by greatly increased maritime activity in South China. Archaeology (for example, tombs in the Canton region, at Kuei-hsien in Kwangsi and at Ch'ang-sha in Hunan) reveals the import of overseas products under the Han rulers: glass, amber, agate, and cornelian. Traffic in slaves from South-East Asia is attested by certain funerary statuettes. Jasmine (*mo-li*), a plant introduced from abroad, began to be planted in the Canton region in the third century. Indian embassies came to the Han court between A.D. 89 and 105. The first mention of official relations between China and the island of Java dates from 132.

The development of Indo-Iranian maritime trade, which was probably due to a number of factors — progress in navigational techniques, the increase in exchanges between India, the Middle East, and the Mediterranean, the spread of Buddhism (a merchant's religion which removed the fear of pollution), the discovery of new gold-producing countries at a time when the roads across northern Eurasia were cut — was almost certainly one of the great events in the history of Asia in the first few centuries of our era. It was the root cause of the conversion to Hinduism of the coastal plains of the lands of South-East Asia. It also accounts for the episodic contacts which Han China had with the eastern regions of the Roman Empire. One of the great ports of call for this Indo-Iranian trade seems to have been a port in the old Cambodian kingdom of Funan (Phram) in the delta of the Mekong. On the site of this ancient town, among remains dating from the second to sixth centuries, have been found a Roman coin struck in A.D. 152 bearing the head of Antoninus Pius (138–161) and another bearing the head of Marcus Aurelius (161–180). The *History of the Liang* (502–557), chapter 54, recalls that in the time of the Han emperors the merchants of Ta Ch'in (the term 'Great Ch'in' denoted the eastern regions of the Roman Empire) frequently visited Funan. In 120 a gift of dancers and jugglers, who had arrived in East Asia by sea from the land of the Ta Ch'in, was sent by a kingdom in Burma to the court of Loyang. In 166 an 'embassy' of Roman merchants, possibly Syrians from Palmyra, who had landed on the coast of central Vietnam, is mentioned by Chinese sources. Two other similar embassies are referred to, one in 226 at Nanking and one in 284 at Loyang.

These long-distance relations between the eastern Mediterranean and South China have more than mere curiosity value. They reveal the existence of commercial exchanges which had some economic importance and were stimulated by the attraction of Chinese silks.

Chapter 6

Causes and Consequences of the Expansion

Just as the power of the great nomad empire of the Hsiung-nu in the steppe zone was very probably created and strengthened by the import of iron and silks from China, so the Han expansion in Asia was certainly due fundamentally to the economic upsurge of the Chinese world. Not only were Han China's strength and prestige abroad based on this economic prosperity, but it was also the trade with Mongolia, Korea, central Asia, South China, and northern India that, by attracting the attention of China's rulers, stimulated the military and diplomatic expansion. However, the Chinese world's superabundance of wealth and the policy adopted by the Han of distributing gifts to their neighbours gradually modified the original situation and led to the incorporation of the 'barbarians' in the empire. The result was that from the end of the first century B.C. onwards it was no longer necessary to maintain the same effort to expand, and the flow of Chinese colonization towards the north and north-west started ebbing back.

These changes in the Han empire's relations with its immediate neighbours, together with the economic upsurge, also caused the progressive disintegration of the class which had formed China's strength in the time of Emperor Wu (141–87), namely the soldier-peasants and small farmers. It was the families of the leading citizens, whose wealth and power had never ceased to grow, who were the architects of the Han restoration in A.D. 25, after the brief reign of the usurper Wang Mang.

Economics and politics

Commerce and expansion

As early as the fourth to third centuries B.C., trade seems to have developed in the kingdoms of Chao and Ch'in with Mongolia and central Asia, in the kingdoms of Yen and Ch'i with Manchuria and Korea, and in that of Ch'u with Szechwan and Yunnan. Numerous knife-shaped coins (*ming-tao*) dating from the age of the Warring States were found during excavations in Manchuria and Korea. They prove the existence of trade between the kingdom of Yen, which lay in the region of present-day Peking, and the north-eastern territories. On the other hand, all the evidence seems to indicate that the silks of the kingdom of Ch'in were exported towards the west, and it was probably as a result of these exports that the land of silk came to be known in India. The name 'Cina' seems to go back to the fourth–third centuries B.C.

This trade between Chinese lands and various areas of the Asiatic continent increased under the Han rulers, and numerous pieces of evidence suggest a connection between the Han expansion from the end of the second century B.C. onwards and the discovery or knowledge of the main trade routes which linked the Chinese world of those days with South China, South-East Asia, central Asia, and the borders of India and Iran. It was Chang Ch'ien's report indicating the interest shown in Chinese silks by the peoples of central Asia and the areas north and south of the Amu-Darya that determined the great policy of expansion towards the basin of the Tarim and the Pamirs. It was the same Chang Ch'ien's surprising discovery, when he was staying in Bactriana, of bamboo and cloth which had come from Szechwan via Burma and northern India that led Emperor Wu to launch expeditions into Yunnan in order to control the roads of these regions. It was T'ang Meng's deductions about the existence of a trade route betwen Szechwan and the Canton region (P'an-yü) – on his mission to Kwangtung in 135 B.C. he had come across a sauce made with fruit imported from Szechwan – that were at the root of the Han expeditions into Kweichow.

China's political expansion in the second century B.C., as well as its economic prosperity at this time, was naturally bound to increase the importance of trade and to draw still tighter the bonds that linked commerce, war, and diplomacy. The installation of Chinese garrisons from Korea to the heart of Asia, the establishment of diplomatic relations, and the control of the important trade routes created a particularly favourable situation for merchants. The caravans that crossed the steppes in the Han period were like towns on the move. In A.D. 84 an embassy from the northern Hsiung-nu travelling towards Ch'ang-an and including the *shanyü* himself and princes of his family was accompanied by a herd of 100,000 head of cattle. During the course of a raid in the winter of A.D. 135, the Wu-huan seized more than a thousand carts driven by Chinese merchants from Hopei. Big markets were set up in the frontier towns and the soldiers of the resident garrisons took part in the trade. The city situated on the site of present-day Chang-chia-k'ou (Kalgan), to the north-west of Peking, where the Wu-huan and the Hsien-pei came to trade at the end of the Second Han dynasty, is an example of these big commercial centres on the frontiers. At the end of the second century it profited from the influx of refugees caused by the revolts of the Yellow Turbans in 184.

In these 'international' exchanges, it is difficult to distinguish between what could at a pinch be regarded as private trading and the form of official commerce constituted by tribute, an exchange of goods intended to strengthen the political and sometimes family links which the Han maintained with their neighbours. Merchants slipped into the official caravans and profited like them from the protection of the Chinese garrisons; some of them who came from distant kingdoms even went so far as to proclaim themselves the authorized representatives of their countries. The opening-up of central Asia by the Han armies at the time of the emperor Wu was followed by a rush of Chinese merchants into the oasis region. In any case, the Han emperors seem to have based their whole foreign policy on the exchange of gifts and more particularly on the exchange of valuable goods. By eliminating the intermediaries on the borders of the empire, who were enriching themselves and increasing their prestige through the trade in Chinese products (especially silks), the Han rulers aimed not so much at extending their direct domination as at developing their diplomatic relations. For this reason they confined themselves at first and most often to controlling the trade routes and installing garrisons at the points where the caravans of merchants passed. Such was the case not only in the oases of central Asia, always threatened by incursions of people from the steppe, but also in the mountainous regions of south-west China, which were inhabited by aboriginal tribes whose loyalty could never be relied upon.

Policy of gifts and the trade in silk

In order to extend their influence among their neighbours, to win them over and to provoke dissensions among their enemies, the Han practised a policy of ostentatious generosity which surprises us by its extremely high cost and systematic character. Probably no other country in the world has ever made such an effort to supply its neighbours with presents, thus elevating the gift into a political tool. During the four centuries of the Han period, the peoples of the steppe and the oases – and to a smaller extent those of the mountainous regions of south-west China – received an incalculable amount of silk, China's principal commercial wealth, and other Chinese products. These gifts were very substantial as early as the beginning of the second century B.C., but they increased rapidly in the second half of the first century and reached their maximum under the Second Han emperors. A few figures will illustrate the increase:

Table 8.   Han gifts of silk in the first century B.C.

	floss-silk in pounds (*chin*)	rolls of silk
51 B.C.	6,000	8,000
49 B.C.	8,000	8,000
33 B.C.	16,000	18,000
25 B.C.	20,000	20,000
1 B.C.	30,000	30,000

In A.D. 91 the total value of gifts of silk to the southern Hsiung-nu amounted to 100,900,000 pieces of currency (*ch'ien*), and in the same year the value of the gifts received by the kingdoms of the oases was 74,800,000 pieces. But by the time of Chang Ch'ien's second trip to Dzungaria and the Pamirs, that is, the end of the second century B.C., Chinese products and silks were so plentiful in central Asia that in those regions they had lost a considerable part of their attraction and value.

It has been estimated that the annual revenue of the empire from the first century B.C. to about A.D. 150 amounted to roughly ten milliard coins, excluding the emperor's private income of eight milliard. Of these ten milliards, three or four were absorbed every year by the annual gifts to foreign peoples. One can imagine the consequences of this substantial levy on China's wealth – it must have simultaneously stimulated production and weakened the general economy of the empire – and its enlivening effect on trade between East Asia, northern India, Iran, and the Mediterranean basin.

Although it is clear that the trade in Chinese products pre-dates the unification of the country by the first Ch'in emperor, these gifts to the Hsiung-nu and the kingdoms of central Asia almost certainly gave the phenomenon an unprecedented volume. This great trade in silk across the Eurasian continent grew even greater under the Second Han rulers, in the first and second centuries A.D. The lands involved were China, central Asia, northern India, the Parthian Empire, and the Roman Empire. The famous 'silk route' which linked the valley of the Yellow River to the Mediterranean passed through the cities of Kansu, the oases of what is now the autonomous territory of Sinkiang, the Pamirs, Transoxiania, Iran, Iraq, and Syria. The oasis of Khotan, rich in jade, on the road which skirts the southern edge of the desert of Takla-Makan, seems to have been one of the great transit centres for silks. Fragments of silk material dating from the Later Han have been discovered at Niya, an oasis to the east of Khotan, and these silks have considerable similarities to those discovered in the tombs at Palmyra, which are reckoned to date from 83–273. However, India seems often to have served as a half-way house in the silk trade between China and the Mediterranean. Chinese silk, doubtless made in Szechwan or travelling via that area, was already known in the plains of the Ganges and the Indus in the fourth and third centuries B.C. as a product of China, that is, of the kingdom of Ch'in. But to judge by certain pieces of archaeological evidence the Han expansion in central Asia in the time of Wu Ti seems to have strengthened relations with north-western India. Some at any rate of the silks which arrived in the Roman Empire must have been imported directly from the Indus valley. Since the Parthians, and more particularly the Nabataeans, who levied a 25 per cent tax on goods, controlled the trade between Transoxiania, Iran, and the Mediterranean, in the first and second centuries Rome encouraged sea trade by the south, a route which made it possible to skirt the Parthian empire. Moreover, it is known that Kan Ying, sent by the Han rulers in A.D. 97 to Ta Ch'in, a term which denoted the eastern Roman empire, had been discouraged by the Parthians from continuing his journey.

Although a large proportion of Chinese silks took the road to the Near East and the Mediterranean basin, it should not be forgotten that in fact the trade extended to the whole of Asia, as is proved by archaeological discoveries. Silk materials have been found, far from the 'silk route', at Etsingol in Inner Mongolia, at Noin-Ula, which is eighty miles north of Ulan Bator, at Ilmova-Pad in Buryat Siberia, and even at Kersh in the Crimea.

The sinicization of the barbarians and their integration in the empire

These gifts to the barbarians were part of a conscious, long-term policy. The idea was first to seduce them, to detach them from the powerful

Hsiung-nu confederation which dominated the whole steppe zone and the oases of central Asia, and then, in the long run, to corrupt them by accustoming them to luxury.

Sumptuous receptions accompanied by exceptionally fine gifts were organized for the leaders of the Hsiung-nu, the *shan-yü,* and for the central Asian princes who came to the Han court. The first visits of the *shan-yü* who had declared their loyalty to Ch'ang-an were great political events. But subsequently the Chinese came to fear these rather too frequent displays of allegiance because of the very high expenditure which they involved. In 3 B.C. the Han declined to receive the *shan-yü* of the southern Hsiung-nu. In A.D. 45 they refrained from extending the tribute system — which cost the empire more than it cost its neighbours — to eighteen central Asian kingdoms which were preparing to send gifts and hostages to Loyang.

The grant of official titles, the gift of seals from the emperor, and the recognition of specific rank in a hierarchy governed by protocol and covering all the countries allied to the empire were other by no means negligible advantages for foreign princes. But it was an exceptional distinction to be linked by ties of blood to the Liu family. The practice of reinforcing political alliances by marriages was to be followed by numerous Chinese or sinicized empires down to the Manchu period. Chinese princesses introduced into foreign countries the manners, customs, culture, and luxury of China. Their presence in these countries justified the coming and going of embassies. But one of the most frequent practices in the Han age was that of sending hostages (*chih*) to the imperial court. As a token of their loyalty, princes of central Asian kingdoms and leaders of tribal confederations would offer their own sons, who were lavishly entertained in the capital at the emperor's expense, received a Chinese education and were often appointed to posts in the imperial guards or in the domestic administration of the palace. Having been converted to the mode of life and culture of the Chinese, when they returned to their own countries they acted as agents of Han influence. Besides forming a guarantee against the breaking of alliances, the hostage system thus also provided a means of interfering more easily in the dynastic affairs of the countries allied to China.

Combined with the military offensives, the diplomatic activity of the Han, the gifts of silks and other Chinese products — the tombs of the Hsiung-nu leaders have yielded a large amount of lacquer ware, jade, pottery, bronze mirrors, coins, and pieces of silk — the grants of titles, the matrimonial alliances, and the hostage system all bore fruit in the long run. Regular relations were established between the Han and the 'dependent kingdoms' (*shu-kuo*) formed by the peoples who supported

China, from Manchuria to central Asia. The confederation of tribes of different origins which the Hsiung-nu had created at the end of the third century B.C. began to fall apart in the middle of the first century. In 60 B.C. the Hsiung-nu split into five hostile groups, and the adhesion to the Han in 51 B.C. of one of the principal chiefs, the *shan-yü* Hu Han-yeh, accelerated the process of disintegration. In 43 B.C. the division of the peoples of the steppe into southern Hsiung-nu, attached to the Chinese, and northern Hsiung-nu, hostile to the empire, finally crowned the efforts of nearly a century. The neighbouring tribes, those of the regions corresponding more or less to what is now Inner Mongolia, formed a buffer between the world of sedentary farmers and that of the most bellicose tribes, who led a nomadic existence further north, up to the vicinity of Lake Baikal. By 36 B.C. the Han had for all practical purposes settled the threat from the people of the steppe for a century.

The development of the inhabitants of the northern borderlands of the Chinese world was uneven. It was swift in the north-west among the Ch'iang, who paid tribute to the Han from 98 B.C. onwards and were half converted to a sedentary life, adding the resources of agriculture and commerce to those of cattle raising and raiding. On the other hand, it was scarcely perceptible in what is now Outer Mongolia before the first and second centuries A.D. The Wu-huan, a tribe of north-eastern Mongolia in contact with sedentary people, were quite soon permeated by Chinese influences and incorporated *en masse* in the Han armies, in which they formed cavalry units. However, their neighbours to the north, the Hsien-pei, remained faithful to their nomadic mode of life and proved more aggressive. They made an incursion in A.D. 140, obliging the Han to cede a substantial slice of territory, and were active again in 156–76.

After obtaining the adhesion of big groups of tribes who had placed themselves under their protection, the Han rulers strove to increase their control over their 'dependent kingdoms' (*shu-kuo*), who in principle were simply allies, free to follow their own customs, and were not taxed. The process of converting the *shu-kuo* first into military territories (*pu*), then into ordinary administrative districts (*chün hsien*), continued in all the frontier territories of the empire between the time of the emperor Wu Ti and the second century A.D. As early as the end of the second century B.C. ordinary districts formed out of peoples allied or subjected to the Han had been created in southern Mongolia, Kansu, Korea, Yunnan, Kwangtung, and northern Vietnam. But the tendency to incorporate the former nomadic herdsmen more and more completely into the empire continued to grow during the two Han dynasties. It was favoured by internal changes in the tribes themselves: their enrichment, the increase in

Plate 22. Han terracotta rider, from recently discovered tomb (photo 1980)

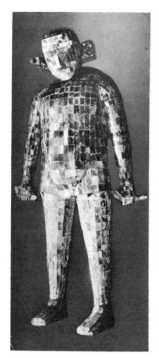

Plate 23.   Han jade suit, threaded with gold wire, from the
tomb of Liu-sheng and his wife Tou-wan (photo 1968)

Plate 24.   Han terracotta warriors, among the 3000 figures excavated from
a recently opened tomb in Shansi province (photo 1980)

their numbers, their propensity to adopt a sedentary or semi-sedentary mode of life. About 50 B.C. the total number of Hsiung-nu attached to China seems to have amounted to between 50,000 and 60,000 individuals. By A.D. 90 it had reached the figure of 237,000. Chinese officials strove to convert the former nomads to the agricultural activities which were a source of supplementary revenue for the empire, while the incorporation of former nomads in the armies went on apace. The wives and children of the men conscripted were kept as hostages behind the lines and executed in case of treason.

Exploited by the Chinese administration and by ordinary private citizens, who exacted services, forced labour, and taxes—for example, the Hsiung-nu of Shansi were employed as farm labourers by the rich families of the T'ai-yüan region, and the Ch'iang of Kansu were subjected to heavy requisitioning for transport—the tribes of the interior sought to shake off the heavy yoke laid on them as early as the first century B.C., and the whole Second Han dynasty was troubled by their revolts. The injustices suffered by these tribes seem all the more flagrant when we remember that the nomads of Outer Mongolia, whose incursions formed a threat to the Han, continued to receive rich presents from China.

Economy and society

The increase in production, the progress in technology, and the development of mercantile activities formed the background to the military, diplomatic, and commercial expansion of Han China. These different aspects of historical evolution cannot really be separated. By the same token they involve the whole social history of the second and first centuries B.C.

Progress of technology and upsurge of the economy

From the second half of the second century B.C. onwards the Chinese world displayed a remarkable vitality confirmed by both the literary and the archaeological evidence. It profited from the progress made in the two centuries preceding the empire, a period rich in innovations, and from the advantages accruing from political unification.

The progress in iron metallurgy continued under the Han. One has to wait until the sixth century A.D. to find a description of an open hearth process, the ancestor of the modern Siemens-Martin process, but the

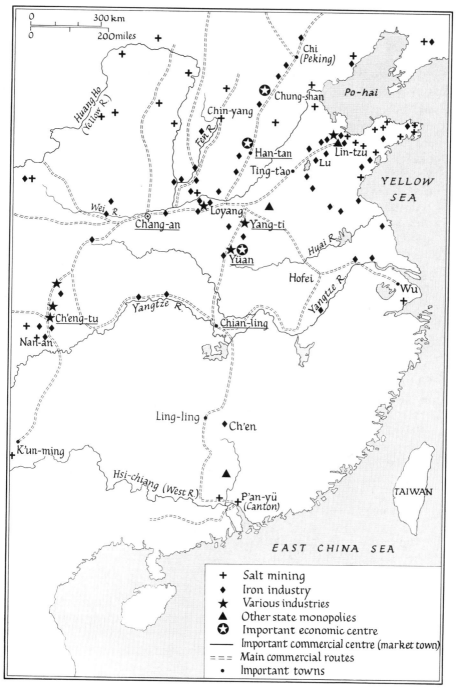

Map 9 Economic centres of China under the First Han emperors

Chinese could produce steel as early as the second century A.D. by heating and working together irons with different carbon contents. As early as this time steel weapons replaced bronze weapons, the only ones known, so it seems, in the age of the Warring States, when cast iron was used mainly for the production of agricultural tools. Swords, halberds, and crossbow mechanisms of the Han age found in the course of excavations are made of iron. The evidence of Pliny the Elder (A.D. 23–79), who praises the quality of the iron produced by the Seres, corroborates the allusions in Chinese texts to clandestine exports of iron and to the diffusion of the iron and steel technology of the Han age in the oases of central Asia. Moreover the working of iron was the most active and important craft of this period. When the state monopoly in iron and salt was instituted in 117 B.C., forty-eight foundries were established by the government, each of which employed a labour force of some hundreds to a thousand workers. Known in private foundries as *t'ung-tzu*—a term applied to adolescents and suggesting a servile condition—these workers were conscripts or convicts frequently compelled by their living conditions to rebel.

Outside the two big sectors of salt and iron, where in any case the state monopoly was strictly enforced for less than a century, private and public enterprises existed side by side. The same is true of silk weaving. Both in the capital (Ch'ang-an) and in the provinces there were big state workshops, which were very expensive to run and the output of which must have been largely used for the gifts to foreign peoples. At Lin-tzu, the former capital of the kingdom of Ch'i, in north-west Shantung, these workshops employed several thousand workers. But there were also private enterprises created by families of rich merchants. It was the same with lacquer ware, which was produced mainly in Szechwan and Honan. Some pieces found on archaeological sites bear the name of the master craftsman who directed production; others bear no mark and could come from private workshops. Archaeological discoveries and allusions in certain texts suggest that private enterprise played an important part in the economy of Han China.

Another important craft was copper work. The principal products were coins, which it was very early forbidden to cast privately, and bronze mirrors. In the first century A.D. these mirrors became export articles, and it is noticeable that from this time onwards the designs and inscriptions on them change. Numerous specimens have been found from Siberia to Vietnam, and even in the south of Russia.

Clear progress was made in agricultural production and techniques. Iron tools were of better quality than they had been in the fourth and third centuries B.C., and the use of a plough drawn by oxen became general. A great effort was made at the time of the emperor Wu to increase the area of irrigated land and to develop new lands in North China. Agricultural experts were entrusted with the task of spreading new methods of cultivation, and some officials tried to convert to cereal growing the nomadic tribes who settled inside the Great Wall from the end of the first century B.C. onwards. A kind of rotation of crops – strips of land with alternating crops (*tai-t'ien*) – was practised from 85 B.C. onwards. However, the principal crops remained those of antiquity – barley, wheat, millet. Soya and rice were also grown, but were still relatively unimportant. From the end of the second century onwards lucerne (the plant *mu-su*), imported from the western regions, made it possible to extend horse breeding to North China.

The reign of Wang Mang (9–23) saw the appearance of the water-mill. Usually this consisted of a battery of pestles (*tui*) activated by a horizontal axle with a cam, which was turned by a wheel probably placed vertically in a current of water. However a text of A.D. 31 mentions the application of hydraulic power to piston bellows in forges.

A rational method of harnessing horses, the breast-strap, had made its appearance in the age of the Warring States (fifth to third centuries B.C.), at a time when the cart with two shafts was beginning to replace the chariot with a single pole. The Han age took full advantage of this great technical innovation in the realm of transport. But another invention must also be mentioned, that of a vehicle which might be regarded – wrongly – as of secondary interest. We have written evidence of the wheelbarrow in Szechwan in the third century A.D., but figurative representations of it go back to the first and second centuries. It is an extremely useful tool wherever ways of communication are reduced to narrow paths. Thanks to a centre of gravity near the axle of the wheel, the wheelbarrow makes it possible to transport without great effort loads of up to 300 pounds.

Unlike the China of today, Han China – and T'ang China, too – had at its disposal an abundance of draught and pack animals – horses, oxen, and donkeys. The breed of horses, which were ridden or harnessed but were used solely for the transport of persons and for warfare, was improved from the end of the second century B.C. onwards by crossbreeding with stallions imported from Ferghana and the territory of the Wu-sun, in the valley of the Ili. As for the donkey, an animal of western origin introduced into North China by the Hsiung-nu, it was much appreciated in all classes of society because of its robust nature and moderate price.

Plates 25–26. Western Han craftsmen were noted for their exquisite animal ware

Rich merchants and gentry

The technical progress of the second and first centuries B.C., the increase in production, and the development of important commercial activities were bound to affect contemporary society. As the heir to Legalist traditions, the Han empire tried to put a brake on the ambitions of rich families and to establish a substantial state sector (foundries, salt works, silk factories) for the needs of its diplomacy and military expansion. But it was unable to maintain this effort for more than a century; the relaxation of controls grew more marked from the middle of the first century B.C. and became general in the time of the Later Han emperors (25–220). This period saw the final triumph of the rich provincial families.

However, if the truth be told, even at the time when state control of the empire's economy had been most effective, the central government had to reckon with the local leading citizens. One of the social peculiarities of the Han period as a whole was in fact the existence of very rich families who combined agricultural enterprises (cereal or rice production, cattle raising, fish farming) with industrial undertakings (cloth mills, foundries, lacquer factories) and commercial businesses, and who had at their disposal a very large labour force. In the areas where agriculture was the principal resource the rich families confined themselves to exerting pressure on poor peasants by making loans at exorbitant rates of interest and inducing their debtors to let or sell their land. Such was no doubt the case with the thousand eminent citizens, petty rural despots, who were arrested and convicted in 129 B.C. at the command of Wang Wen-shu, an official of Legalist tendencies. But wherever economic conditions allowed it, other resources were added to agricultural revenues.

One may regard as quite typical from this point of view the case of the region of Ch'eng-tu in Szechwan known to geographers as the Red Basin. It was one of the richest and most active regions of Han China. The exploitation of salt mines, iron smelting, the production of lacquer ware (lacquer ware made in Szechwan has been found in Han tombs in western Korea, nearly two thousand miles from Ch'eng-tu) and brocade, the trade in cloth, oxen, and iron all explain how big fortunes came to be made there as early as the second century B.C. The Cho family, one of the richest in Ch'eng-tu, owned huge expanses of cultivated land, fish-ponds, and game parks. It possessed ironworks and steelworks in which it employed 800 slave workers and grew rich through the iron trade with the aboriginal inhabitants of the south-west, barbarians with a head-dress in the shape of a mallet. This trade between Chinese and aboriginal tribes seems very often to have taken the form of an exchange of gifts, a concept no doubt better adapted to the mentality of the aborigines than commercial practices which keep an exact account of the value of the merchandise. The case is quoted of a substantial gift of silks and other Chinese products which was subsequently repaid by a consignment of horses and oxen.

But what is true of Szechwan is also true of many other regions of Han China and bears witness to the existence of a class of rich citizens who furnished the empire with its administrative cadre. Far from being solely agricultural, the economic base of this class was very often industrial and commercial. This is probably what explains the relatively large number of 'slaves' in Han China, convicts and bankrupt debtors who were employed for the most part in the big workshops which needed skilled craftsmen.

The concentration of land ownership which accompanied the economic expansion in the course of the first century B.C. must have proved a serious problem for the government towards the beginning of the Christian era. It was this problem that the usurper Wang Mang was unable to solve in the years 9 to 23 and that was one of the principal causes of his failure.

Freedom or a controlled economy?

The hostility towards merchants which had such profound effects on the fate of the Chinese world, and which has given Chinese civilization its own particular character, is explained by a number of different and complex factors. Even before the empire, the literati, and the Mohist, Taoist, and Legalist traditions were at one in condemning luxury and pointless exploitation, but the reasons for this condemnation differed from school to school. An indication of dissipation, arrogance, and lack of virtue according to the tradition of the literati, the taste for luxury appears already in Mencius as one of the indirect causes of peasant poverty. For Taoist thinkers, luxury was a source of artificiality and a cause of disorder, and it was condemned by the disciples of Mo-tzu in the name of an idea of austerity, universal frugality, and general levelling down. But the deepest reasons for this hostility seem to have been those adduced by the rulers and the state: mercantile activities were, they felt, a factor leading to a maladjusted society, since merchants' wealth enabled them to secure domination over the poor, to buy up peasant lands and to employ as slaves in their mining, iron and steel, or manufacturing enterprises the cultivators whom they had reduced to destitution. Mercantile activities, by inciting people to useless expenditure, distracted them from the activities fundamental and indispensable to the survival of the state, namely the production of the cereals and cloth necessary to maintain the armies and to back a diplomacy which counted on gifts of silks as one of its most effective tools. Defence activities in general and public works also suffered. Thus the damage caused by the merchants and craftsmen was simultaneously social, political, and economic. The vigour and vitality of Han China were largely based on the technological progress made since the age of the Warring States and on the expansion in the production of cereals, iron, salt, and cloth. To abandon these sources of wealth to the merchants, or to leave them in exclusive control of them, seemed like accepting the decline and disintegration of the empire. Peace and unity were only possible if the political power could control and share out the principal resources.

As early as 199 B.C., right in the middle of a civil war, measures were taken to reduce the merchants' style of life. They were forbidden to wear silk garments, to ride horses and to carry arms. This rigorous policy, which bears witness to the merchants' wealth (for only what is already practised is forbidden), was not relaxed until the empress Lü, already all-powerful, grasped the reins of power. The imperial ladies often showed favour to the big merchants and connived with them, because the organization of the administrative services of the women's quarters, and possibly also certain much older traditions, made this complicity inevitable. The anti-mercantile reaction did not set in strongly until the end of the second century B.C., at the time of Wu Ti and under the pressure of a deficit caused by a policy of military and diplomatic expansion which was extremely costly. Hence the imposition in 119 B.C. of a uniform tax on boats and carts and the creation in the same year of a state monopoly in salt and iron. In 117 this monopoly was extended to the whole empire. Since the age of the Warring States iron and salt had been the two most active and profitable industries, and this measure—imitated later by other Chinese empires—seems to have reduced for a time the power of the big merchants who headed industrial and manufacturing enterprises. However, it should be noted that under Wu Ti the imperial power was relatively independent of any contributions which the big merchants might make to its resources. It did not need to turn to the rich business men, as was to be the case under the T'ang, Sung, and Ming emperors, and to give them the task of keeping the armies of the north supplied with grain, forage, and other products, for these supplies were ensured in essentials by the military colonies (*t'un t'ien*). The salt and iron monopolies were complemented in 98 B.C. by the less important alcohol monopoly. It is clear in any case that the state's measures to control the economy and its hostility to the merchants were closely bound up with the state of the empire's finances. The anti-

Plate 27.   Han acrobats

Plate 28.   Han zither, with 25 strings, bridges and winding pegs, from a recently excavated tomb

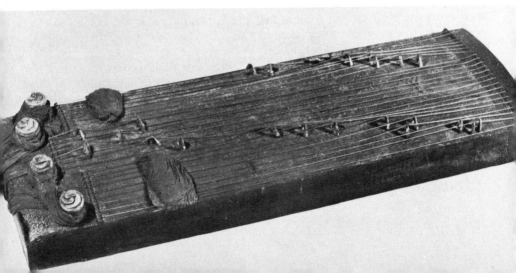

Plates 29–30. Western Han objets d'art

mercantile traditions simply adduced arguments to support the policy suggested by the difficulties of the moment. This is proved by the criticisms provoked by the monopoly system after Wu Ti's death, on the occasion of the discussions which took place at the court in 81 B.C. concerning its maintenance or abolition. The voluminous account of these discussions, published some ten or twenty years later, between 73 and 49, has fortunately been preserved under the title of *Yen-t'ieh-lun* (*Discussions about Salt and Iron*).

Chapter 7

The Rise of the Gentry and the Crisis in Political Institutions

From palace intrigues to usurpation

The fall of the First Han rulers at the beginning of our era was the result of internal developments which had begun more than a century earlier. In the reigns of Wen Ti and Ching Ti, from 179 to 141 B.C., the collaboration of the civil servants and the emperor's ministers and advisers in the management of affairs had made it possible to consolidate the imperial power, but in the long reign of Wu Ti (141–87) autocratic tendencies made their appearance and triumphed during the regency of General Huo Kuang, the recipient of Wu Ti's last wishes. What Huo Kuang established from 80 onwards was his own dictatorship, with members of his own family in all the governing posts. The reaction which followed his death in 68 (there was a great trial in 66 which ended in the execution of all his relatives) did not call into question the concentration of power in the hands of the emperor alone. Deprived of the support and counterweight formed by the administrators and advisers as a whole, the imperial power soon became the pawn of palace plots and of struggles between the empresses' families. Autocratic, omnipotent power necessarily falls under the thumb of favourites, women, and eunuchs. One of these empresses' families, which were so powerful at the end of the First Han dynasty, succeeded in pushing on to the throne one of its own members, the usurper Wang Mang, who founded the ephemeral dynasty of Hsin, 'the new dynasty' (A.D. 9–23).

Another parallel cause of the fall of the First Han dynasty seems to have been the increasingly rapid development in the countryside. The concentration of land in the hands of the richest men (local gentry, merchants, great families) was the source of a social tension in rural areas and of economic difficulties which the advent of Wang Mang was far from resolving. The first edicts aimed at limiting the extent of private estates date from the last few years of the first century B.C. They were to be followed down to the end of the third century A.D. by a long series of other similar edicts which seem to have been generally ineffective, thus bearing witness to the difficulties which the state met in maintaining its control and protection of the small farmer.

Wang Mang tried to remedy the difficult situation which he had inherited by means of radical measures. He 'nationalized' all the estates and all the slaves (who probably represented, however, only a hundredth of the population and enjoyed a very different status from that of Roman slaves), carried out successive monetary reforms and issued new coins of ancient type. The advent of the new dynasty also involved changes in all titles and all institutions. This mania for reform, all the stronger because power had been usurped, was of course inspired by contemporary cosmogonic theories, but also by archaizing notions. Wang Mang based his reforms on a work since regarded as suspect and of late composition, but abounding in details that are doubtless very old. This work was the *Chou-li* (*Rites of the Chou*) or *Chou-kuan* (*The Officials of the Chou*), which draws a very systematic picture of the Chou administration and divides all the official posts between officials of Heaven, of Earth, and of the four seasons.

The radical measures taken by Wang Mang were ineffective and upset the rich landowners without easing the agrarian crisis. The redistribution of estates which ought to have followed their confiscation by the state could not be put into effect, and the manipulation of the currency caused general economic disorder. Bands of rebellious peasants, led by a woman skilled in witchcraft, 'Mother Lü', appeared in Shantung in A.D. 17. Others who appeared the following year had as their leader a certain Fan Ch'ung. As a result of floods in the lower basin of the Yellow River the insurrections spread to the whole of the central plain. The rebels, who painted their faces so as to look like demons, were known as the 'Red Eyebrows' (*ch'ih-mei*). Their spiritual leader was a certain 'King Ching of Ch'eng-yang' in Shantung, who claimed to be related to the Lin branch of the Han and expressed himself through mediums. The aim of the movement, which possessed its own distinctive political and administrative organization, was in fact the restoration of the Han. The new dynasty was threatened not only by this agitation and these peasant revolts but also by the resistance and rebellions of the old Han nobility and the big landed families. It was the combination of these two forces which finally won the day in 23. After the defeat and death of the usurper, one of the representatives of the old Lin line from the region of Nanyang, in the south of Honan, assumed power and restored the Han dynasty. This Lin Hsiu, who reigned under the name of Kuang Wu Ti (25–57), reduced the remnants of the rebellious peasants to submission and destroyed the independent kingdoms which had been set up in eastern Kansu under Wei Hsiao and in Szechwan under Kung-sun Shu.

The new bases of the restored empire

The First Emperor (Shih Huang Ti of the Ch'in line) had at his disposal a faceless administrative and military organization which he had extended to the conquered lands, and the First Han rulers, faithful to this policy of direct control of the peasantry by the state, had managed in less than a century to eliminate all those who might form an obstacle to the activity of the central government. The Later Han emperors, on the other hand, leaned on the new social class which had carried them to power, namely the big landed families of the central plain and particularly of Honan. The transfer of the capital from Ch'ang-an to Loyang is explained not only by the economic development of the regions to the east of the passes between Shensi and Honan but also by the existence of this new clientele. In order to fight the power of the holders of fiefs, of eminent citizens, and of the rich families, the First Han had striven for the support of the small farmers. But at the end of the first century B.C. and under the Second Han the evolution of society, internal migrations and revolts were to reinforce the power of the big landowners — relations and collateral kinsmen of the imperial family, high officials, and provincial gentry.

Movements of population accelerated in the first quarter of the first century A.D. They were due to a general retreat from the lines of defence established in the north and north-west in Wu Ti's time by means of military colonies and transfers of population. This retreat was in turn due to the settlement of tribes of nomadic herdsmen and mountain-dwellers from the Sino-Tibetan borders inside the Great Wall and the frequent revolts of these people, who had been converted to a sedentary life and were exploited by the Chinese administration. The main areas to profit by the exodus were the southern part of the central plain, the Red Basin of Szechwan and to a smaller extent the valley of the Yangtze (the population of the commandery of Ch'ang-sha in Hunan, 235,825 at the census of A.D. 2, was 1,054,372 by 140). The influx of uprooted peasants and former military colonists in quest of land enlarged the labour force of the big estates. This was the origin of a series of people dependent on the rich families — 'guests' (*k'e*), that is, resident farmers; the personal guards later known by the name of *pu ch'ü;* and servants or slaves (*nu-pi*). Simultaneously the state's hold on the small farmers, to whom the First Han rulers had owed a large part of their power, was weakened. The future Kuang Wu Ti, founder of the Second Han dynasty, was a typical representative of these big provincial landed families, who only succeeded in seizing power, after several fruitless rebellions against Wang Mang, thanks to the peasant revolts. The huge domain that he owned near Nanyang was protected by walls with gates in them, and he had his own market. A private militia looked after defence. This social class, which retained a dominant position at the start of the new dynasty and came into conflict with the palace eunuchs in the second century, showed a good deal of initiative in agricultural affairs, irrigating vast expanses of land, developing cattle raising and fish farming, and thus ensuring complete economic independence in times of trouble. Some of its members seem to have accumulated immense fortunes. When the great minister Liang Chi, a relation of the emperor by marriage, was executed in 159, the sale of his properties is said to have brought into the treasury three thousand million pieces of coinage, enough to make it possible to suppress half the grain taxes for a year. These big landowning families already point forward to the aristocracies of the time of the Chin and the southern dynasties, whose power was favoured by the decline of the urban economy.

At the same time as the social and political context, the empire's relations with the border peoples had changed radically since the reign of the emperor Wu and the dictatorship of General Huo Kang. The empire had hardly any further worries about Mongolia; the power of the Hsiung-nu had continued to decline since the time of their division, and this decline was to be accentuated by Pan Ch'ao's offensive in Mongolia and central Asia at the end of the first century A.D. Between the peoples who had preserved the nomadic mode of life and the sedentary tillers of the soil, tribes which were more or less thoroughly sinicized and settled served as a protection for the empire. Almost the only dangerous incursions by the northern Hsiung-nu mentioned are those of 89–90; and the more powerful attacks from the steppe in the second century, those by the Hsien-pei in Hopei and Shansi in 140 and 156–78, do not seem to have had serious consequences. On the other hand the Han had grave difficulties with the former nomadic tribes settled in China itself and with the proto-Tibetan mountain peoples of the western and north-western borders, who had settled in Kansu and Shensi. Their revolts never ceased under the Second Han dynasty and multiplied in the second century. As early as 107, as a result of the Ch'iang rebellions, some advisers were even considering a general retreat from the north-western defence lines between the commercial centres of Wu-wei (Liang-chou) in central Kansu and western Shensi. These foreign peoples, who had been integrated in the empire and incorporated *en masse* in the Chinese armies, were the ancestors of those who, from the beginning of the fourth century onwards, formed independent kingdoms in North China.

Progress of commercial relations in the first and second centuries A.D.

The measures taken under the First Han emperors to curb the power of the merchants seem in the end to have had little effect. But the general relaxation of controls inside the country and at the frontiers under the Second Han, and the decentralization of the monopoly system at the time when Kuang Wu Ti was restored, increased the importance of private business and smuggling. Never do foreign merchants seem to have been so numerous as in the first and second centuries, and the presence of these foreigners probably explains why outside influences were so active under the Second Han rulers. It should be recalled that it was at this time – which also marked the high point of the silk trade in Eurasia – that Buddhism began to make its way into China. As for smuggling activities, they were bound up with the veto on the export of what might be described as goods of strategic value – mainly iron and weapons. A few pieces of archaeological evidence confirm what we are told by the texts: weapons bearing inscriptions in Chinese and iron tools have been found in a barbarian tomb in the north of Liaoning dating from the time of the emperor Wu. A crossbow mechanism exhibited since 1915 in the museum at Taxila (near Peshawar) in Afghanistan and originating from the ruins of the second Parthian palace of Sirkap, which was reconstructed after A.D. 30, has recently been identified as Chinese. Moreover the protective measures taken by the Han did not succeed in preventing the diffusion of the Chinese iron founders' technical secrets in Asia. Ch'en T'ang, a general of the end of the First Han dynasty, asserts that the Wu'sun of the valley of the Ili had recently learned how to make tapering weapons. The same thing seems to have been true of the people of Ta-yüan, in Ferghana. Perhaps it was only a question of iron forgings imported from China. But more decisive proof is furnished by the iron foundries discovered at the oasis of Niya, to the east of Khotan. The iron and steel industry was to persist in the Tarim basin; its products were imported into the Chinese borderlands at the time of the Western Chin (265–314).

The development of the new empire from its foundation
to the insurrection of 184 A. D.

The first three reigns of the restored dynasty, from 25 to 88, were a period of stability at home and expansion abroad. The empresses' families and the eunuchs who had been at the root of Wang Mang's usurpation of power were kept at a distance from the business of government. In the basin of the Red River and in central Vietnam the situation became potentially dangerous when the aboriginal inhabitants revolted, but it was restored by General Ma Yüan (14 B.C.–A.D. 49) in 43–44. The Hsiung-nu, too badly divided to take advantage of the empire's weakness during the civil war in Wang Mang's time, were no longer a serious threat to North China. In central Asia, the expeditions organized — usually on his own initiative — by General Pan Ch'ao (32–102) made it possible to regain control of the oases between 73 and 94. A garrison was installed in 73 at Hami (Yiwa) and the road through the Pamirs, closed since A.D. 16, was opened up once again by the Han armies. More than fifty central Asian kingdoms sent tribute to Loyang in 94. But subsequently the Han only succeeded in re-establishing their domination in central Asia during the years 125–50.

In the capital the political climate began to deteriorate from the reign of Ho Ti (88–105) onwards. The families allied by marriage to the imperial line, those known as the *wai-ch'i* ('outer relationships') took advantage of the succession to the throne of a series of children and weaklings to recapture the ascendancy which they had lost. Under Ho Ti (88–105) it was the Tou family, under An Ti (100–125) the Teng family, and under Shun Ti the Liang family. At the same time the eunuchs succeeded in asserting themselves: in 135 they were authorized to adopt sons, and their power grew with their wealth. Owning large agricultural domains (the case is quoted of a eunuch who owned 31 houses and some 1500 acres of tilled land), they turned to big business and controlled their own slave workers. The authority held at the court by these palace servants from the lower classes and the unhealthy consequences of their influence on the emperor's policies, and on the recruitment of state officials, provoked a reaction on the part of the big landed families and the literati in the civil service belonging to them. A party was formed which the eunuchs succeeded in overcoming in 167; all its members were relieved of their posts and sent into exile. But this defeat did not discourage the great landed families, whose power was still intact in the provinces. The struggle ended at the time of the big peasant revolts which began in 184. Weakened for a little while, the eunuchs regained power thanks to the agrarian troubles, but were finally eliminated in 189 by Yüan Shao, member of an important Honan family, who, after gaining control of Loyang, massacred over two thousand eunuchs, while Ho Chin, commander of the imperial guards, was the victim of his own indecision.

The Messianic revolutionaries

The last few years of the second century were in fact marked by an agrarian crisis of exceptional gravity. From about 170 onwards bands of wandering peasants had begun to threaten the peace of the provinces. Soon, as a result of floods along the lower Yellow River, a vast Messianic movement, Taoist in inspiration, developed on the borders of Shantung and Honan. It ended in 184 in the fearsome rebellion of the Yellow Turbans (*Huang-chin*). The leaders of the rebels were one Chang Chiao, chief patriarch of the Taoist sect of the Great Peace (*T'ai P'ing* – the term evokes the idea of a golden age brought into being by complete equality and the common ownership of goods), and his two brothers, Chang Pao and Chang Liang. A talented propagandist and healer – epidemics consequent on the floods were raging in the lower valley of the Yellow River – Chang Chiao was the pope of a religion centred on the lord Huang Lao, a synthesis of the mythical sovereign Huang Ti ('the Yellow Emperor') and a deified Lao-tzu. Organized on military lines, by 184 the sect had 360,000 supporters under arms. Supreme power was assumed by the trinity of Chang Chiao and his brothers, 'Lords general of Heaven, Earth, and Men'; under their orders they had a whole hierarchy of leaders whose functions were simultaneously military, administrative, and religious. The communities devoted a large part of their time to religious activities – feasts and ceremonies which lasted several days and bore the name of 'assemblies' (*hui*) or 'fasts of purification' (*chai*). In the course of these religious proceedings the participants made a public confession of their sins and gave themselves up to collective trances which were encouraged by interminably repeated prostrations, the accompanying music, and the collective excitement thus generated. There were sometimes orgiastic scenes in which men and women 'mingled their breath' (*Lo ch'i*). Distributions of healing amulets and medical charms took place at the spring and autumn equinoxes. According to the doctrine of *T'ai-p'ing-tao,* diseases were the consequence of sins. Combining the cosmological theories of *yin-yang* and the Five Elements with Taoist traditions and the cult of Huang-lao, this salvationist religion revered as its sacred texts Lao-tzu's *Tao-te-ching* and a revealed text of more recent origin, the *Canon of the Great Peace* (*T'ai-p'ing ching*).

A sect whose organization and doctrines were similar to those of the Yellow Turbans developed at the same period in West China; however, it was destined to remain confined to Szechwan and the upper valley of the Han. Founded by the master magician Chang Tao-ling (or Chang Ling), who was reckoned to have subjected to himself the genii of air, earth, and water, it required of its devotees a contribution of five bushels of rice (hence its name, *Wu-tou mi tao,* 'doctrine of the five bushels of rice'). Like the Yellow Turbans, the devotees of *Wu-tou mi tao* resorted to the practice of 'possession' and believed in the virtues of amulets, the efficacy of the confession of sins, and the religious origin of diseases. Sick persons were kept apart and lived in cabins. But measures of mutual help seem to have been developed to a greater degree: there were free store houses for travellers, and roads were maintained as a labour with expiatory value. Moreover, private property seems to have been abolished.

The rebellion of the Yellow Turbans was launched wherever the movement had taken root at the second moon of 184, a year marked by the cyclical signs known as *chia-tzu,* the first of a new sexagesimal cycle. The rebels, recognizable by the yellow turban (*huang-chin*) which they wore on their heads, seized the towns of Shantung and Honan, in spite of the resistance organized at Loyang by General Ho Chin. After the death of the three Changs, who were killed at the start of the rebellion, the movement spread in 185 to the region of T'ai-hang-shan, which divides Shansi from Shantung, in 186 to Shensi, Hopei and Liaotung, and in 188 to Shansi. About 190 the devotees of the sect of the Five Bushels of Rice succeeded in establishing an independent state in southern Shensi, under the leadership of Chang Lu, grandson of Chang Tao-ling.

The empire a prey to the soldiery

One may say that at this period the emperor's authority was purely nominal. The real power belonged to the army leaders entrusted with the task of suppressing the Yellow Turbans. Some of these generals had taken part in the *coup d'état* of 189. Those concerned were Tung Cho, an adventurer from eastern Kansu; Yüan Shu, a cousin of Yüan Shao; Ts'ao Ts'ao (155–220), the adopted grandson of a eunuch and a native of Anhwei; and Sun Ts'e (175–200), elder brother of the Sun Ch'üan who was to found the kingdom of Wu at Wu-ch'ang in 222. Immediately after the execution of the eunuchs in 189, Tung Cho led his troops to Loyang and put on the throne the last Han emperor, Hsien Ti. In the following year his army, which included, like that of Ts'ao Ts'ao, large contingents of barbarians, sacked and burnt Loyang. The imperial library and the Han archives disappeared in the fire, and the loss seems to have been much more serious than that involved in the famous 'burning of the books' under the first Ch'in emperor. However, in 192, two years after moving the capital to Ch'ang-an, Tung Cho, notorious for his excesses and cruelty, was assassinated. Ts'ao Ts'ao now began to assert his own power. He gradually eliminated his rivals in North China—Yüan Shu, for example, who had founded an independent kingdom in 197— and laid the foundations of a new empire, which remained confined, however, to the central plain and the northern provinces.

The destruction caused by the peasant revolts, and still more the ravages due to the wars between rival army leaders from 190 onwards, led to a decline in the urban economy, a decline that was particularly noticeable in the valley of the Wei and northern Honan. Together with the collapse of the state and the triumph of the army leaders, this economic decline, occurring after the great manufacturing and urban upsurge of the Han period, was one of the signs which heralded the start of a new period. By the end of the Han age we are already in the Chinese 'Middle Ages'.

Chapter 8

The Civilization of the Han Age

The scholastic philosophy of the Five Elements

The Han age witnessed the triumph of a kind of thinking which seems to have been supreme in the interpretation of presages and in the occult sciences. It was a kind of scholastic philosophy based on a system of spatio-temporal correspondences which provided a complete explanation of the universe. It was what is known as the theory of *yin, yang,* and the Five Elements (*Yin-yang Wu-hsing shuo*). Modes of being or fundamental powers, the Five Elements and the female (*yin*) and male (*yang*) virtues follow each other through phases of growth, zenith, and decline. The soothsaying schools of antiquity, interpreters of the sixty-four hexagrams and the three trigrams, were at the root of these concepts, which were systematized in the age of the Warring States, mainly in Shantung. Their most famous theorist was Tsou Yen of Ch'i (305–240), who seems to have extended his system of interpretation to all spheres of knowledge — astronomy, divination by the stars, geography, history, and politics. According to Tsou Yen's fundamental thesis, the rise and fall of political power was related to that of the Five Elements, the old always being destroyed by the new, in the order earth–wood–metal–fire–water.

These theories were dominant at the time when the Chinese lands were unified by the kingdom of Ch'in. They are the ideas which we find in one of the chapters of the Rituals, the *Yüeh-ling,* the text of which is adopted by the *Lü-shih ch'un-ch'iu* (*Springs and Autumns of Master Lü*), a work which was reckoned to represent the sum total of human knowledge, a synthesis of all the schools. It was compiled by the clients of Lü Pu-wei, a rich merchant of Honan who was adviser to the prince of Ch'in and afterwards a minister of the First Emperor until 237. Lü Pu-wei had assembled a sort of private court which included nearly three thousand men of talent from Ch'i, Tsou Yen's country, and Taoist magicians from Chao and Ch'u. But there was more to it than that. The whole new ritual of the Ch'in empire was based on the theories relating to the Five Elements and on the system of correspondences between elements, cardinal points, planets, colours, notes of the scale, moral qualities, tastes, feelings, internal organs, and so on. Since the advent of the new dynasty marked the triumph of the fundamental virtue or quality of water over that of fire, by which the Chou emperors had reigned, all the empire's institutions had to be in harmony with this new virtue. It dictated the colour black for flags, justified the severity of the laws, and was the reason for the constant recourse to the figure 6, which determined even the length of contracts and the shape of ceremonial hats.

Diversity of the traditions

Emphasis has often been laid on the 'Confucianism' which is supposed to have followed the obscurantist period of the Legalist Ch'in empire. It is true that under the Han rulers classical studies were systematically encouraged by the state. They became the source of an official ideology, the orthodoxy of which it was important to establish. As early as 136 B.C. a corps of 'Scholars ('literati') of vast knowledge specializing in the five classics' (*wu-ching po-shih*) was created. There were 50 of these literati in the reign of the emperor Wu (141–87), 100 in that of Chao Ti (87–74) and 200 in that of Hsüan Ti (37–7). They became even more numerous under the Second Han rulers and exerted considerable influence at court and on the political system. It is also true that, in public morality, under the Han the accent was put on the virtue of submission to one's elders and on respect for the classification of people according to their age. Filial piety became one of the criteria for the choice of civil servants and acts contrary to it were liable to the most severe penalties. Village meetings in honour of the god of the local soil were encouraged because they were regarded as a means of reinforcing social cohesion and of making manifest to everyone the hierarchies based on age and on titles granted by the state (a notion which seems moreover to be in complete conformity with the Legalist tradition).

However, we must beware of making categorical distinctions which would be in contradiction with the spirit of the age. Towards the end of the period of the Warring States and during the first century of the Han dynasty, it is very difficult to distinguish between specialists in *yin* and *yang,* magicians, Taoists, and literati versed in the ancient writings of the Chou era—sages who are denoted by the various terms *fang-shih, shu-shih, tao-jen, ju.* The First Emperor, who had banished speechifiers, sophists and theorists, had none the less retained a college of seventy representatives of the various schools of the age of the Warring States. This college already foreshadowed the imperial academy of the Han dynasty, and it could justifiably be argued that the emperors and governing circles of this period were just as keenly interested in Taoist concepts and techniques as they were concerned to establish a 'Confucian' orthodoxy.

The Taoist current, so strong in the reign of the First Emperor, flowed on under the Han rulers. It was a belief in the secrets of longevity which made it possible to achieve the survival of the body through various techniques (alchemy; dietetic, sexual, breathing, and gymnastic techniques; and so on), belief in the existence of immortals who manifested themselves under different forms down the ages, belief in the isles of the blessed in the eastern seas. The Taoist magicians (*fang-shih*) of Shantung and the coast of Hopei retained at the Han court the prestige which they had enjoyed under the First Ch'in Emperor. Taoism was favoured by the emperor Hui Ti (195–157), by the empress Tou, wife of Wen Ti (180–157), and by scholars like Lu Chia (time of Kao Tsu, 206–157), author of the *Hsin-yü,* a work explaining the metaphysical reasons for the fall of the Ch'in dynasty and the triumph of the Han. Other devotees of Taoism were Ssu-ma T'an, father of Ssu-ma Ch'ien, and later still Yang Hsiung (53 B.C.–A.D. 18), who wrote a Taoist work called the *Supreme Mystery* (*T'ai Hsüan*). Taoist philosophy was in fashion at the court of Prince Liu An of Huainan at the end of the second century B.C.

We know too that the religious forms of Taoism played an important role in the life of the lower classes. The last and most powerful Taoist risings, those of the Yellow Turbans and the Five Bushels of Rice at the end of the second century A.D., were marked not only by faith in a millenarian utopia but also by the existence of an organized church, of religious worship, and of moral teaching. The influence of these popular currents of thought reached as far as the Han court via the empresses and imperial concubines, who themselves sprang from the people. The cult of Huang-lao was introduced at the court a few years before the start of the Yellow Turban revolt, and Taoism appeared there in the form of a political theory which aimed at that state of perfect social harmony denoted by the term 'Great Peace' (*t'ai p'ing*).

Thus it is impossible to attribute a sort of supremacy to 'Confucianism' or to refrain from emphasizing the eclectic character of intellectual life at the Han court.

The rise of esoteric interpretations

The most remarkable thing is that the whole thought of this period is permeated by the scholastic doctrine of the Five Elements. This in itself meant that there was no break between the Ch'in period and the one that followed it. If it is permissible to speak of a renewal of classical studies and of 'Confucianism', this renewal took place under the aegis of the theories of *yin* and *yang*. Consequently it was profoundly original.

The scholastic doctrine of the Five Elements was in fact to serve as the foundation for a new interpretation of the classics which had been preserved by the oral tradition and reappeared as early as the second century B.C. The founder of this new school of exegesis was Tung Chung-shu (*c.* 175–105 B.C.), whose principal work, the *Ch'un ch'in fan-lu,* is at the same time an explanation of the *Annals of Lu* (the *Ch'un-ch'iu*), and of the commentary on them by Kung-yang, and an exposition of his own theories. But Tung Chung-shu borrowed his main inspiration from the scholastic philosophy of *yin, yang,* and the Five Elements, the keys to the vault of the universe and the principles of moral, social, and political order.

The Classics, venerable products of remote antiquity, the works of eminent sages, were reckoned by the men of this period to contain secret knowledge, and their interpretation had therefore to be confined to schools of specialists, who transmitted their secret meaning from one generation to the next. The cosmological theories, almost cabalist in nature, which had been popular since the time of Chou Yen satisfied both the need for synthesis and general explanation which seems to be characteristic of the age and the preoccupations of the interpreters of the Classics. One can understand why their texts, often so concise as to be positively obscure, were very soon regarded as collections of prophecies and why esoteric commentaries (*ch'an wei*) multiplied under the first Han emperors. The *ch'an wei* abound in speculations about numbers, auspicious and inauspicious omens, the relations between sectors of the sky and regions of the earth (*fen-yeh*), the events of history and the rise and fall of dynasties. They devote great attention to the symbolical diagrams of heaven and earth (the *t'u*), the most famous of which — *the Writing of Lo,* brought to the emperor Yü by a divine tortoise, and the *Table of the River,* given to the legendary sovereign Fu-hsi by a horse-dragon that emerged from the Yellow River — form the subjects of two important esoteric commentaries (*Lo-shu-wei* and *Ho-t'u-wei*).

The taste for esoteric commentaries and prophecies and also the use of omens for political ends seem to have been at their height at the end of the first Han dynasty, round about the beginning of the Christian era.

The tendency was not without effect on scientific knowledge. The care devoted to the observation of natural phenomena was certainly very old, but the systematic notation of spots on the sun began in 28 B.C. The resulting lists are not without interest for the astronomers of today. It was also in the Han period—in A.D. 132—that the first seismograph in the history of the world was invented by Chang Heng. The apparatus devised by Chang Heng was theoretically intended to make it possible to pin-point earthquakes, which were regarded as signs of disorder in nature. It is supposed to have detected a shock which had occurred in Kansu. Rapid progress was also made in the Han period in the field of astronomical instruments. An equatorial circle was invented by Keng Shouch'ang (*c.* 75–49) and presented to the emperor in 52 B.C., while in A.D. 124 Chang Heng produced a celestial globe, with equatorial circle, ecliptic, and median and horizontal planes. A daily revolving mechanism controlled by a water-clock was added to it in 132.

Links between the scholastic philosophy and the realities of the time

Because it exercised a real dominion over all minds, the scholastic philosophy of the Five Elements—or at any rate its categories and basic antitheses—is also to be found in the interpreters of omens, the commentators on the Classics, thinkers in the Taoist tradition (the *Huai-nan-tzu*, a collection of Taoist, mystical writings compiled at the end of the second century B.C. is as much permeated by it as are the works of Tung Chung-shu), and even in those very writers who criticize the abuse of esotericism and the excessive reverence for superstition.

It is permissible to wonder why this philosophy was so successful. It may be that the development of a doctrine that claimed to give a complete explanation of the universe was favoured by political circumstances. With the creation of the empire, the substitution of administrative districts for the old principalities and the disappearance of the ancestral cults of heads of cities, authority seemed to be deprived of any religious foundation and may well have felt the need to seek the support of a cosmology of a magical nature based on elements borrowed from archaic thought. These elements were then incorporated in systems which could also vary considerably. For example, as well as the theory which explained the succession of the five elementary virtues or powers as the destruction of the obsolete virtue by a new one, there was also the theory that regarded each virtue as born from the preceding one. While it was in conformity with a very ancient tradition that the prince's activity should be regarded as an ordering of the cosmos, under the empire the context was quite new: it was the positive laws and regulations of the Legalists that acquired the magico-religious value of the ancient rites. The First Emperor explicitly defined himself as the demiurge who had shaped the world by imposing on it his own norms, his own measures of length and capacity, and a new script. He had likewise shaped society by the creation of a continuous hierarchy of ranks and by the institution of a graduated scale of rewards and punishments.

Under the influence of the dominant theories of *yin* and *yang,* the system which the Legalists had devised as the privileged instrument of the political and social order was enriched with a magico-religious significance: bounties and amnesties were auspicious things (*chi*), penalties and punishments were inauspicious things (*hsiung*). The emperor's duty was to use a suitable mixture of strict and kindly measures so that neither the auspicious nor the inauspicious should endanger the cosmic harmony by their presence in excess. The emperor, in an empire conceived as universal, and his officials, in their commanderies and prefectures, were the inspirers of, and the persons responsible for, a total order manifested in the abundance of the harvests, good understanding between men, and the absence of natural calamities, wars, and brigandage.

Rivalries between different schools;
opposing tendencies

The diversity of the scriptural traditions and of the schools of interpreters under the First Han dynasty was to be reduced fairly quickly to a conflict between two dominant tendencies. While most exegetes based themselves on the texts transmitted orally and written down in the script of their own time (*chin-wen*), copies of the Classics written before the empire in ancient scripts (*ku-wen*) were found. These archaeological discoveries were to unleash a quarrel, the scope of which went far beyond the mere question of the authenticity of the texts. Its repercussions made themselves felt right down to the nineteenth century. According to some people, the first big discovery was made as early as the time of the emperor Chin Ti (156–140 B.C.); according to others, it dates only from 93 A.D. However that may be, copies of new versions of the *Classic of History* (*Shang-shu*), of the *Treatise on Rites* (*Li-chi*), of the *Analects of Confucius* (*Lun-yü*) and of the *Classic of Filial Piety* (*Hsiao-ching*) were discovered in a wall of Confucius's house. A descendant of the Master's family, one K'ung An-kuo, who lived in the time of the emperor Wu Ti

(141–87), was the first to take an interest in these texts, the deciphering of which, so it is said, presented some difficulties. But the specialists in texts written in ancient characters fairly soon gathered round them all those who criticized cabbalistic interpretations and refused to regard the Classics as collections of prophecies. It looks as if the champions of the texts in the new script can be connected with the cosmological, divinatory tradition of the land of Ch'i, a tradition of which Tsou Yen had been one of the most famous representatives, while their opponents belonged rather to the moralizing, ritualist — but also very much rationalist — tradition of the land of Lu, the native country of Confucius. However, the new tendencies were slow in asserting themselves. At the time of the discussions at court in 57 B.C. between representatives of the opposing schools, it was Tung Chung-shu's interpretations which were triumphant, and at the end of the First Han dynasty the champions of the traditions recorded in *ku-wen* were still fairly isolated figures. One of them was Liu Hsin (32? B.C.–A.D. 23), the imperial librarian and great editor of texts antedating the imperial unification. At this time the argument was no longer simply about dissimilar versions of the same texts, but about works containing different doctrinal contents. Thus Kung-yang's commentary on the *Annals of Lu* is typical of the *chin-wen* school because of the interest shown in it by Tung Chung-shu and its esoteric background, while Tso Ch'iu-ming's big chronicle, the *Tso-chuan*, regarded as a commentary on the *Annals of Lu*, and the *Rites of the Chou* (*Chou-li*) are works characteristic of the *ku-wen* school. The favours granted to the champions of the *ku-wen* school by the usurper Wang Mang were to do them no good at the time of the Han restoration, but the movement soon gained breadth and the most famous commentators of the Second Han dynasty based their studies on texts in the old characters. Such is the case with Chia K'uei (30–101), author of commentaries on the *Tso-chuan*, the *Chou-li* and the *Discourses on the Kingdoms* (*Kuo-yü*); with Ma Jung (79–166), who wrote among other things a comparative study of the three commentaries on the *Annals of Lu* (*Ch'un-ch'iu san-tsuan i-t'ung shuo*); and with the famous Cheng Hsüan (127–200), to whom we owe commentaries on the *Book of Odes* (*Shih-ching*), the *Memorandum on the Proprieties* (*I-li*), the *Chou-li*, the *Li-chi*, the *Lun-yü* and the *Shang-shu*. The only important representative of the *chin-wen* tradition under the Second Han emperors was Ho Hsiu (129–82), whose work was concerned with Kung-yang's commentary. But his theories were refuted by Cheng Hsüan. The texts first compiled in ancient characters dominated the scene after the Han age, mainly at the Liu-Sung court in 457–65 and the Liang court in 502–20, in the Yangtze region of China, and then later in the Sui empire (589–618). The triumph of *ku-wen* was to cause the almost total disappearance of the vast esoteric literature of the Han period, and it was only in the eighteenth and nineteenth centuries that certain scholars and philosophers took it into their heads to rehabilitate the forgotten tradition represented by the works of Tung Chung-shu, Kung-yang's commentary on the *Annals of Lu,* and the writings of Ho Hsiu.

The decipherment of texts in ancient scripts was probably at the bottom of a new interest in epigraphy. The first Chinese dictionary—for one can hardly regard as a dictionary the *Erhya,* a work earlier than the empire but of unknown date and taking the form of an encyclopaedia and a series of glosses—appeared about A.D. 100. This was the *Shuo-wen chieh-tzu,* by Hsü Shen. In it the simple and compound signs of the still relatively archaic script devised by Li Ssu before the imperial unification are analysed. The work contains 9353 characters classified under 540 keys.

Another tendency which should no doubt be connected with those which find expression in the devotees of the traditions recorded in ancient scripts is the rationalist reaction which becomes apparent at the end of the First Han dynasty. It is represented by men like Yang Hsiung (53 B.C.–A.D. 18), author of *fu* and a specialist in the *Book of Changes,* Huan T'an (beginning of the first century A.D.), a musician and naturalist, and above all Wang Ch'ung (27–97), author of the *Lun-heng,* a large work devoted to criticism of the superstitions of his time. While these writers could not insulate themselves from the modes of thought of their age (the system of correspondences, the opposition between *yin* and *yang,* Heaven and Earth, and so on), it cannot be denied that they possess a keen sense of logical reasoning and a pronounced taste for logical explanations. Wang Ch'ung shows a lively interest in questions of physics, biology, and genetics. He does appeal sometimes to the authority of the ancients, but he likes to use arguments drawn from experience and tries to explain phenomena by natural causes alone. A materialist, like Huan T'an, he denies that anything can exist after death: just as fire needs fuel, so the mind, senses, and perceptions cannot exist independently of the body. Criticizing the notion of individual destiny (*ming*) in which people believed so firmly in his time, he sees the diversity of human destinies as the result of three independent factors: innate physical and intellectual aptitudes, the chance combination of circumstances and accidents, but also—and here Wang Ch'ung shows how much he remains a prisoner of his age—the astral influences which acted on the individual at his birth.

*The zenith of classical studies and the intellectual
renaissance of the end of the Han period*

Classical studies shone with their greatest lustre under the Second
Han emperors, with eminent commentators such as Ma Jung (79–166),
author of a comparative study of the three commentaries on the *Annals
of Lu* (*Kung-yang-chuan, Ku-liang-chuan* and *Tso-shih-chuan*), and
the great Cheng Hsüan (127–200). The text of the Six Classics (*I,
Shih, Shu, Ch'un-ch'iu, Li, Yüeh*) established by Ts'ai Yung (133–92)
was engraved on stelae in the capital in 175. Soon circumstances were
not to be so favourable: classical studies and 'Confucianism' were
to enter a long period of decline and lethargy which lasted practically
until the rise of a new moral and metaphysical philosophy in the eleventh
century.

The political and social crisis of the end of the Han dynasty already
favoured the appearance of new tendencies marked by a return to the
traditions of the age of the Warring States – the philosophical Taoism of
the *Chuang-tzu* and the *Lao-tzu,* nominalism, the dialectic of the school
of Mo-tzu, and Legalism. As in the fourth to third centuries B.C., men's
minds seemed to be divided between the two antithetical attitudes of
withdrawal into oneself and aspiration towards an imposed order, between the two options of anarchy and dictatorship. Thus the *Ch'ien-fu-
lun* of Wang Fu (*c.* 90–165), the very title of which (*Remarks of a Her-
mit*) suggests precisely this refusal to become committed in a corrupt
world, is a criticism of the political morality of the period and of the excessive room taken by commercial and manufacturing activities. The
reviving influence of Legalist theories can already be felt in this book.
But the *Treatise on Politics* (*Cheng-lun*) by Ts'ui Shih (*c.* 135–70) is even
more the work of a convinced partisan of the strengthening of the state
by the application of Draconian laws indifferent to *de jure* or *de facto*
privileges.

The new tendencies which make their appearance at the end of the Han
period were to blossom in the third and fourth centuries, when the great
religious movement which was to dominate all Chinese thought in the
Middle Ages began to take shape. China of the fourth to eighth centuries
was to be a Buddhist China.

*The advent of history as a synthesis
and as moral and political reflection*

The slow progress of historiographical traditions since the beginning of
the annals of kingdoms and the epoch of the first inscriptions on bronze

(ninth to eighth centuries) finally produced about 100 B.C. a synthesis which was the work of one of China's greatest historians. The *Historical Records* (*Shih-chi*) of Ssu-ma Ch'ien (135?–93?), who carried on the work of his father Ssu-ma T'an, took advantage of all earlier progress in the field and at the same time provided the model for a long series of official histories which were produced right down to the time of the Sino-Manchu empire. Ssu-ma Ch'ien inherited the very precise chronological framework of the annals of kingdoms (recording of events by day, month, and year of reign) which has given the work of Chinese historiographers such precision from the first events dated, in 841 B.C., down to our own epoch. He also inherited the ancient custom of religiously reproducing to the letter the solemn enactments of the royal power. Finally, he makes great use of the art of narrative, anecdote and discourse which had developed in the diplomatic interviews and disputes between different schools of the time of the Warring States. A whole oral literature, the memory of which had not yet been lost, was thus collected and recorded in the Han epoch: Tso Ch'iu-Ming's great chronicle, which soon came to serve as an illustration of, and commentary on, the *Annals of Lu,* the *Stratagems* (or rather *Writings on Bamboo*) *of the Warring States* (*Chan-kuo-ts'e*), the *Discourses on the Kingdoms* (*Kuo-yü*). Aided by one of the finest styles in the literary history of China and by a great capacity to synthesize, Ssu-ma Ch'ien paints for the first time, thanks to the oral traditions, texts, archives, and contemporary witnesses, a picture of the whole Chinese world from its origins down to his own time. A work of political and moral reflection, the *Historical Records* were to inspire the authors of the great dynastic histories which followed, the first of them being the *History of the Han* (*Han-shu*) completed about A.D. 82 by Pan Ku and his sister Pan Chao. We meet again in these works the three main divisions adopted by Ssu-ma Ch'ien: annals of the sovereign, treatises (on rites, music, astronomy, administration, geography, the armies, the canals, the economy, law, and so on), and biographies, which include the very valuable remarks about foreign countries.

Chinese prose seems to have reached full maturity in great writers like Ssu-ma Ch'ien, Chia I (201–168) or Tung Chung-shu (*c.* 175–105), all historians or authors of political essays and memoranda to the throne. Equally adapted to exposition, narrative, and discourse, it is justly famed for its vigorous yet elegant conciseness, its suppleness and its evocative power. It seems to have profited from all the various experiments in very different genres made in the age of the Warring States. It was this Han prose that Liu Tsung-yüan and Han Yü wanted to reinstate in a position of honour about A.D. 800, and which the writers of the Ming and Ch'ing epochs strove to imitate.

A court literature

The princely courts of the second century B.C. — mainly those of Liang, Wu, and Huainan — were, like the imperial court, centres of an intellectual, literary, scientific, and artistic activity which in some ways recalls that of the principalities of the age of the Warring States. Princes and emperors maintained in their entourage a retinue of jugglers, acrobats, musicians, soothsayers, writers, and scholars. It was the followers of Prince Liu An of Huainan, executed in 122 B.C. for rebellion, who compiled the work of Taoist tendencies known as the *Huainan-tzu*. But their work is exceptional in its depth and seriousness. The general tendency was to produce amusements and refinements for court life, and these needs account for the success of a kind of literature which was much cultivated between the second century B.C. and the third century A.D., namely the *fu*. Derived from the lyrical poems of the land of Ch'u (the *Ch'u-tz'u*), the *fu* takes the form of a description in a rhythmic and sometimes quite grand style of the hunts, parks, palaces, and entertainments of the imperial and princely courts. This genre, which is not classified as poetry by the Chinese tradition, is also marked by its exaggerations, hyperboles, and lyricism as well as by its preciosity and by the learned, far-fetched character of its vocabulary. It was prized so highly in the Han epoch that there was hardly a famous writer who did not try his hand at it. The best known authors of *fu* are Chia I (200–168; his works were inspired, when he was in exile in Hunan, by the memory of the great Ch'ü Yüan), Ssu-ma Hsiang-ju (179?–117), a man from Szechwan whose *fu* were much imitated, Yang Hsiung (53 B.C.–A.D. 18), another native of Szechwan, and the historian Pan Ku (32–92), author of the famous *Fu of the Two Capitals* (*Liang-tu-fu*), which was imitated later on by the learned astronomer Chang Heng (78–139) in his *Erh-ching-fu*.

These refinements did not exclude a pronounced taste for popular music and song and for anything that came from exotic countries after the great expansion of Wu Ti's time. Founded by men of the people, the Han empire long retained the traces of its plebeian origin. With a view to the composition of new hymns for the temple of the imperial ancestors, an Office of Music (*Yüeh-fu*) was set up under Wu Ti, with the task of collecting popular and exotic music and songs. The themes of peasant songs and the dances, tunes and musical instruments of central Asia thus found ready access to the cultivated society of the age. Suppressed in 7 B.C. at the instigation of orthodox scholars hostile to novelties, the Office of Music was to have a profound influence on the development of Chinese poetry. A new poetic form, the antique poem (*ku-shih*), with verses of five characters (seven from the end of the Second Han dynasty onwards), made its appearance in the first and second centuries of our era. Borrowing its first subjects from popular songs, this new genre was to have a tremendous future and to end, after a long process of evolution, in the regular poem (*lü-shih*), the rules of which were fixed in the T'ang period (seventh century). The admirable *Nineteen Ancient Poems* (*Ku-shih shih-chiu-shou*) were the first step in the long and illustrious career of classical poetry in China.

The very strong influence of popular traditions, of magical and religious Taoism, and of foreign civilizations on the art of the Han epoch explains its vigour and vitality. These qualities are to be found in the mural paintings discovered in Korea, Manchuria, Hopei, and Shantung, in the scenes and personages carved in stone in tombs, temples, and porticoes (for example, the sculptures of Shantung, Szechwan, and Honan), and in the realistic, lifelike funerary figurines (various personages and pictures of buildings).

Part 3

The Middle Ages

Prologue

The period which begins at the end of the Han dynasty is related in some respects to our own European Middle Ages. It is marked right from the start by the decline of the state, the collapse of the urban economy, and the dismemberment of the empire. While North China, the richest and most densely populated part of the Chinese world in those days, was parcelled out at the beginning of the fourth century among several kingdoms whose governing classes were of barbarian origin, a powerful aristocracy, jealous of its privileges, became established in the valley of the Yangtze and imposed its will on the central power. In the intellectual field, the dominant philosophy of the Han period became completely forgotten and classical literature was scarcely cultivated any longer. Individualistic tendencies and a purely aesthetic conception of literature and the arts asserted themselves. These Chinese Middle Ages were also a period of great religious fervour, and it is legitimate to say that the China of this epoch was Buddhist in the same way as medieval Europe was Christian.

However, the analogy probably stops there, for very soon in the north — by the middle of the fifth century — there was a renewal of the centralized state; and the age of the southern dynasties, in the valley of the Yangtze, was one of the most brilliant in the history of China in the realms of literature, art, and thought. On the other hand, the resurgence of the merchant economy from the end of the fifth century onwards was to cause the rapid decline of the southern aristocracy, which disappeared in the course of the wars of the middle of the sixth century. In the north, this resurgence favoured the consolidation of the power of the state. While there was a complete change of atmosphere and a perceptible break between the Han age and that of the northern and southern dynasties (317–589), the Chinese Middle Ages, on the contrary, lasted on into the 'aristocratic empire' of the Sui and the T'ang. In its institutions, its governing classes, its literature, its arts, and its religious fervour, this new empire was certainly the heir and continuer of the northern and southern dynasties.

Table 9. Chronological table of the period 220–589

North China	Szechwan	Yangtze and South China
Three Kingdoms (San-Kuo) (220–265)		
Wei (Ts'ao-Wei) at Loyang 220–265 absorb Shu-Han in 263 →	Shu-Han at Ch'engtu 221–263	Wu at Nanking 222–280
Western Chin at Loyang (265–316) succeed Ts'ao Wei in 265 absorb Wu in 280 fall back to Nanking in 317		
Dynasties of the North and South (Nan-Pei-Ch'ao) (317–589)		
Sixteen Kingdoms of the Five Barbarians 304–439	Ch'eng Han at Ch'engtu 304–347 absorb Szechwan in 347	Six Dynasties (Liu-Ch'ao) after Wu (222–280), at Nanking, Eastern Chin (Tung Chin) 317–420
← absorb Szechwan in 347		
Northern Wei (Pei Wei or Toba-Wei) 386–535 unify North China in 439; capital at Loyang from 493 onwards		Sung (Liu-Sung) 420–479 Ch'i (Nan Ch'i) 479–502

North-East China	*North-West China*	
Eastern Wei (Tung Wei) (534–550) at Yeh (South Hopei)	Western Wei (Hsi Wei) (535–557) at Chang'an The Hsi Wei absorb Szechwan in 553	Liang 502–557
Northern Ch'i (Pei Ch'i) 550–577 at Yeh	Northern Chou 557–581 at Ch'ang-an	
← absorb the Pei Ch'i in 577		Ch'en 557–589
Sui 581–618 succeed the Pei Chou at Ch'ang-an in 581		
absorb Ch'en (South China) in 589 →		

Chapter 9

Barbarians and Aristocrats

Generalities

The history of the period from the end of the Han dynasty to the unified Sui and T'ang empires, that is, from the beginning of the third century to the end of the sixth, is so complex that it will be helpful to stand back for a moment from the multiplicity of events and to underline certain basic factors that remained valid throughout the period. Some of these concern North China, others concern the valley of the Yangtze.

1. The conversion of the nomads into sedentary peoples was a process that began at the end of the first Han dynasty and went on in the kingdoms and empires that shared out, or succeeded in unifying, North China between the third and sixth centuries. This slow, complex transformation of nomadic cattle-breeders into sedentary peoples in Inner Mongolia, Manchuria, and north and north-west China has been one of the great constants in the history of East Asia down to our own day.

2. The centralizing, statist tendencies which seem to be bound up with the problem of defence against incursions from the steppes, but also with the needs of colonization, distribution of land and the irrigation of dry zones, lasted in North China, and especially in the north-west, from the Ch'in and Han periods down to those of the Sui and T'ang. These tendencies are just as characteristic of the kingdom of the Ts'ao Wei as of that of the Northern Wei, and it looks as if the 'Legalist' tradition, according to which the state should play an active part in the distribution of the population and in social and economic organization, was typical of North China.

3. Another tendency peculiar to the states of North China was their military expansionism, which was caused by the threat from the steppes.

The kingdom of the Ts'ao Wei, the 'Sixteen Kingdoms of the Five Bar-barians' (fourth century) established in the valley of the Wei and in Kansu, and the empires of the Northern Wei and Northern Chou in the fifth and sixth centuries all had designs on central Asia, Mongolia, Man-churia, and Korea, just like the Ch'in and Han rulers before them and the Sui and T'ang rulers after them. Their diplomatic and military activities aimed at reinforcing their defence system against incursions and at con-trolling the main commercial routes.

The southern lands also had characteristic features which remained relatively constant until the sixth century.

1. The aboriginal peoples — Thais, Tibeto-Burmans, Miao-Yao and possibly still Mon-Khmers in the interior and Malayo-Polynesians on the coasts — occupied most of the territory, for the peoples of Chinese language and culture had begun to populate only the plains of the Yangtze basin, the southern coast of the bay of Hangchow, and the plain of Canton. Decimated, pushed back into the mountains, conscripted and incorporated in the Chinese armies because of the lack of labour and soldiers, permeated by Chinese trade, these ethnic groups with their dif-fering and original cultures were slowly sinicized and assimilated as the territory controlled by the Han Chinese expanded. These contacts be-tween the Chinese and aborigines resulted in many mutual borrowings, the extent of which is still not very well known; it seems to have been con-siderable.

2. Since the Han occupation of the Yangtze basin and South China occurred in successive waves, rivalry between new immigrants and old colonists created difficulties which could only be eliminated progres-sively. In every case the oldest established colonists strove to impose an inferior status on the newcomers.

3. The thin population of Yangtze China and South China, their rela-tive poverty (commercial activities only began to develop at the end of the southern dynasties and there was little progress in the cultivation of rice until the T'ang dynasty, and in the seventh and eighth centuries), the large distances involved and the colonial character of these areas were at least partly responsible for a socio-political morphology which seems to have been remarkably stable. The weakness of the central authority and the power of the great families were characteristic of the empires estab-lished in Nanking between the end of the Han and the fall of the Ch'en. The period from the fourth century to the middle of the sixth saw the birth and development of an aristocracy of great families which only married among themselves, held the most important posts and made the central government recognize their special privileges.

The case of Szechwan, or to be more precise, of the valley of the Min-chiang, the Red basin, was a special one. Its marked tendencies to autonomy are accounted for by its relative isolation from the other Chinese lands, by its wealth, which was due to the fertility of its soil and its climate, and also to its mining resources and its position at an international crossroads – the plain of Ch'engtu lies at the intersection of the roads leading to Yunnan, Burma and north-eastern India, Kweichow and Kwangtung, the valley of the middle Yangtze, the upper valley of the Han and the basin of the Wei, Tsinghai and the oases of central Asia. The plain of Ch'engtu is in fact connected to the ancient lands of Ch'u and Ch'in by only two main routes, which are difficult of access and easily controlled. Towards the north there are narrow mountain roads connecting Szechwan with the valley of the Wei; and towards the east the course of the Yangtze, squeezed between gorges with dangerous rapids, forms the only means of access to the middle and lower Yangtze. This special situation explains why, apart from numerous periods of complete autonomy, Szechwan was dependent sometimes on the states established in the valley of the Wei and sometimes on the kingdoms or empires of the middle or lower Yangtze. As a result we find two distinct sets of influences there, those of north-west China and those of the Yangtze region.

Szechwan had been independent between 25 and 36 A.D., at the time of the rebellions of the Red Eyebrows, and it was independent again between about 180 and 215, when Chang Tao-ling and his grandson Chang Lu organized a sort of religious state there. After the epoch of the Three Kingdoms, in the course of which the kingdom of Shu-Han existed from 221 to 263, Szechwan enjoyed a fresh period of independence between 304 and 347, under the rule of a family of Ti mountain-dwellers of proto-Tibetan origin. It was Han of the Ch'eng family (Ch'eng-Han) who formed one of the 'Sixteen Kingdoms of the Five Barbarians'.

From the military dictatorship to anarchy (A.D. 190–317)

The Three Kingdoms:
the Ts'ao-Wei in North China

Although the Han dynasty was not abolished until 220, it was Ts'ao Ts'ao who held the real power in the valley of the Wei and the central plain by the beginning of the third century, and the start of the kingdom of Wei (220–65) could be placed in the year 219. By that time Ts'ao Ts'ao had unified the whole of North China under his own aegis. His ambitions had extended to the conquest of the Yangtze valley, but the famous battle of the Red Cliff (*Ch'ih-pi*), on the course of the great river in Hupei, had put a stop to this policy of expansion. The serious defeat inflicted on Ts'ao Ts'ao by the allied troops of Sun Ch'üan (185–252) and Liu Pei (161–223) was the prelude to the division of the Chinese lands into three kingdoms (San-Kuo), that of the Wei of the Ts'ao family, that of the Han of Szechwan (Shu-Han) (221–63), founded by Liu Pei, and that of Wu (222–80), founded by Sun Ch'üan.

The policy pursued by Ts'ao Ts'ao was in harmony with the tendency which had been most in evidence in intellectual circles towards the end of the Han period. It was typically 'Legalist', that is, centralizing and authoritarian, and the state founded by Ts'ao Ts'ao had all the appearances of a military dictatorship. One of the most notable features of this new policy was the creation of numerous agricultural colonies (*t'un-t'ien*). At a time when insurrections and civil wars had led to a clear decrease in agricultural production the institution corresponded to economic and fiscal needs. Unlike the *t'un-t'ien* of the first Han period, those established by Ts'ao Ts'ao were therefore not always peopled by soldier-farmers but often by dispossessed peasants. They were not all situated on the northern frontiers but extended to the interior of the empire. There were some very large ones, comprising several tens of thousands of men, in eastern Honan, and they were to be found even in the valley of the Huai. Subject to a paramilitary organization, the inhabitants of the *t'un t'ien* received agricultural tools and draught animals from the state.

The creation and extension of the agricultural colonies helped to set the economy going again and to strengthen the defences. They were accompanied by a great effort of reconstruction – drainage and irrigation works, the building of reservoirs, and so on. But they also had a more important aim, namely the taking in hand of an unstable, peripatetic population which escaped the control of the state and tended to settle on the estates of the rich landowners. Himself the adopted grandson of a eunuch, without any connection with the aristocracy of the end of the Han period, Ts'ao Ts'ao sought to strengthen his own position at the expense of the great families of gentry who had occupied the forefront of the political stage since the assassination of the eunuchs in 189.

Ts'ao Ts'ao's armies originally consisted of a heterogeneous collection of mercenaries, former bandits and vagabonds, and of both Chinese and barbarians – Hsiung-nu, Hsien-pei, Wu-huan, Ch'iang. All his power depended on these armies. In order to ensure a regular form of recruitment for his growing empire, Ts'ao Ts'ao instituted families of profes-

sional soldiers, the *shih-chia,* who could only marry among themselves
and in the long run would have perhaps constituted a sort of military
caste. As in days gone by in Ch'in, military vocations were encouraged by
grants of titles and material advantages. But Ts'ao Ts'ao also reorganized
his armies on the basis of still greater recourse to the former nomadic
herdsmen settled in North China. It was they who provided his best
troops and especially the most skilled mounted bowmen. This massive recruitment and also the favours granted to steppe tribes — Ts'ao Ts'ao
authorized a large group of Hsiung-nu to settle permanently in south-
eastern Shansi — resulted in the acceleration of a process of assimilation,
the consequences of which were to appear at the beginning of the fourth
century, when the sinicized former nomads formed independent
kingdoms in North China.

Another aspect of Ts'ao Ts'ao's policies was a strengthening of the
penal legislation, as a reaction to the relaxation which had occurred
under the Second Han emperor. It was under the Ts'ao Wei emperors — whose accession to the throne was proclaimed in 220, on the
death of Ts'ao Ts'ao, by his son Ts'ao P'ei — that the first synthesis of all
the juridical work accomplished in the four centuries of Han rulers was
compiled. The New Code (*Hsin-lü*) of the Wei marked an important date
in the history of Chinese law. It was to inspire the editors of the Chin
Code, published in 268, during the T'ai-sheh period. Much more detailed
than that of the Han — it comprises 2926 articles — the Chin Code was to
be the subject of commentaries by two remarkable interpreters of the
law, Tu Yü (222–84), famous for his skill as an engineer and for his commentary on the *Tso-chuan*, and Chang Fei (date unknown).

The concern for efficiency and political centralization which marked
the work of Ts'ao Ts'ao and his successors reappeared in the adoption of
a new system of promotion for civil servants. Intended in principle to
favour the best and guarantee impartial selection, it consisted in the
classification of all officials in nine grades, the *chiu-p'in*.

However this system very soon began to favour the great families who
had been able to win distinction in the armies, and it was in fact from
these families that the danger for the Ts'ao was to come. To judge by the
Ssu-ma family, their rise was very rapid. Ssu-ma Yen, whose great uncle
had led several expeditions into Szechwan against the Shu-Han and had
destroyed the independent kingdom founded by the Kung-sun in Liaotung, and whose father had organized the Wei armies and commanded
the troops which put an end to the Shu-Han empire in 263, was to seize
power two years later at Loyang and found the new Chin dynasty
(265–316).

Shu-Han and Wu
(Szechwan and the valley of the Yangtze)

The birth of the two ephemeral empires of Szechwan and the Yangtze valley is explained not only by the troubles and economic recession of the end of the Han dynasty but also by geographical and social factors. It was the secession of colonial China south of the Yangtze which was to give the struggle carried on by the Sun, mere army commanders and rivals of Ts'ao Ts'ao, the significance of a war of independence. Thus it is no doubt the influence in the Wu kingdom of the great families of the Chiang-han (the expression denotes the regions to the south of the lower Yangtze) that explains the transfer of the capital, which was at first Wu-ch'ang, at the confluence of the Yangtze and the Han, to Nanking in 229. As early as the time of the Yellow Turban rebellions these rich colonial families had shaken off the tutelage of the central government. They were organized for their own defence and if need be could call on the 'Yüeh of the mountains' (*Shan-yüeh*), native inhabitants pushed back to the high ground by colonization and fugitives who had sought refuge there. All that had been needed for the appearance of an independent state in the valley of the Yangtze was an aggravation of the troubles in North China and the willingness of the soldiers and colonists to join forces.

A similar phenomenon occurred in Szechwan, a rich and relatively iso-lated land where the aboriginal inhabitants were equally numerous. It was favoured by the prestige of Liu Pei, a descendant of the Han im-perial family, and by the political and military genius of his adviser, Chu-ko Liang (181–234). But while the kingdom of Wu was ruled by a sort of confederation of the most powerful families of the Yangtze valley, cen-tralizing tendencies won the day in Szechwan: like Wei, Shu-Han was a military state governed by 'Legalist' advisers. However its power declined after the death of Chu-ko Liang and it was annexed by Wei in 263.

The civil war and the revolt
of the sinicized mercenaries

The rise to power of the Ssu-ma clan marked the victory of the great families—the Ssu-ma, the Ts'ui, the Hsia-Lou, and others—over the authority of the state and was to make efforts at political centralization difficult. Even before seizing power the Ssu-ma had applied themselves to suppressing the colonies (*t'un t'ien*) which the Ts'ao had created and on which their power was based. Thus the arrangements made by the new empire to strengthen itself—the publication of a new penal code, measures to prevent the great families monopolizing the political and administrative posts, limitation of the extent of big estates and of the number of dependants—turned out to be ineffective. Right from the start of the dynasty, twenty-seven kinsmen of the emperor—apart from members of the families not related to the imperial house—were endowed with large incomes (the highest in rank received the taxes paid by several thousand peasant families), had the right to appoint their own officials in the territories given to them as fiefs, and were authorized to keep up private militias whose strength varied between 1500 and 5000 men. After the death in 290 of the founder, who had succeeded ten years earlier, in 279–80, in reuniting the valley of the Yangtze (kingdom of Wu) with the empire, the rise of a great family by the name of Chia caused dissensions among the nobles and their provincial clients. The troubles lasted from 291 to 305, and for seven years a positive civil war, known as 'the Rebellion of the Eight Princes', brought the princes of the imperial family into conflict with each other. The situation deteriorated rapidly from the first few years of the fourth century onwards as a result of droughts and invasions of locusts, which caused famine in the regions already ravaged by the civil war. In addition the tribes of mountaineers and cattle-breeders installed in the north and north-west, and incorporated *en masse* in the armies, took advantage of the general chaos to rebel and form independent political units. As early as 304 a family of proto-Tibetan Ti founded the kingdom of the Ch'eng Han in Szechwan, while the Hsiung-nu of southern Shansi proclaimed themselves independent and adopted the dynastic name first of Han, then of Chao. In 311 the Hsiung-nu chieftain Liu Ts'ung seized Loyang, and in 316 Ch'ang-an fell in turn to the assault of another Hsiung-nu leader called Liu Yao. It was the end of the ephemeral empire of the Western Chin.

The famine and the political, economic, and administrative chaos that prevailed in North China at the beginning of the fourth century, and the tribal rebellions that occurred there, caused an exodus of the Chinese population. It went on after the establishment of the Eastern Chin dynasty at Nanking (Chiang-h'ang) in 317, but seems to have reached its climax around 309. The flood of refugees flowed in two parallel currents: one from Hopei and Shantung towards the valley of the Huai, the lower Yangtze, Chekiang and Fukien, and the other from Shensi and Shansi towards the middle Yangtze, Yunnan and the Red River valley in Vietnam. A small number of refugees from Hopei made for southern Manchuria. Altogether more than a million people, so it seems, emigrated like this in the first quarter of the fourth century. The activities of non-

Chinese peoples seem to have had only secondary effects on this phenomenon, which, like the other great crises of history, accelerated the Chinese diaspora. It is moreover inaccurate to compare, as is sometimes done, the barbarian insurrections in North China at the beginning of the fourth century with the great invasions experienced by Europe a century and a half later. It was not foreign invasions that caused the fall of the Chin rulers and the withdrawal of the Chinese dynasties towards the lower Yangtze, but primarily disorder and destitution. The 'barbarians' simply took advantage of the anarchy; they were already settled in China when they seized power. Far from having remained crude mountaineers and nomadic herdsmen, they were already much influenced by the customs, institutions, and mode of life of the Chinese. The thrust of the Huns towards southern Russia, Europe, and the eastern Mediterranean in 444–54, like that of the Chionites earlier towards Iran in 356, was the work of true nomads, probably from the Altai region. These invasions cannot be linked to events in China at the end of the Western Chin dynasty. Thus whether the Hsiung-nu and the Huns were to some extent related, as some people have thought, or whether they were not related at all is of no interest to history, for the only things that matter are modes of life, socio-political forms, and cultures.

The reign of the aristocracies in the Yangtze basin

The political climate changed as a result of the Chin withdrawal to the valley of the Yangtze. There was no longer any question of centralization, except, in a sporadic way, during the Sung (420–79) and Ch'i (479–502) dynasties, which tried without much success to break the power of the great families. On the contrary, what we find is the development of an endogamous, hierarchical aristocracy which held the real power at court and in the provinces until the middle of the sixth century. Consisting of descendants of the great families who had emigrated from the north at the beginning of the fourth century and of the richest colonial families of the Yangtze valley and the coasts of the bay of Hangchow, this aristocracy was to be recognized and confirmed by the imperial power and exempted from taxes and requisitions. And as it was essential to prove the antiquity and fame of one's family in order to qualify for posts and privileges, people strove to compile genealogical registers (*chia-p'u*). The formation of this aristocracy was sufficiently advanced at the end of the Sung dynasty for legislation to put the seal on the rules in use by forbidding marriages between nobles (*ming-chiu,* 'illustrious families') and commoners (*han-men,* 'poor families'). The formation of this endogamous aristocracy with its own letters patent, its rise and then its swift decline from the middle of the sixth century onwards constitutes the most original social phenomenon of the southern dynasties.

The Eastern Chin

The new state founded at Nanking in 317 by a prince of the Ssu-ma family found itself faced right at the start with the difficult question of the immigrants. The newcomers were so numerous that it was decided to register them separately (they were recorded in white registers, *pai-chi,* and the original residents in yellow registers, *huang-chi*), and in some regions 'commanderies of immigrants' (*chi'iao-chün*) were created. The government was unable to prevent the rapid development which soon made the lower-class immigrants dependent on the rich families. They became 'guests' (*k'o*) and servants of the big landowners. The state was too weak to dream of imposing limits on the size of estates, as in North China, or of controlling the number of dependants. In any case affairs were controlled by the big families; the Wang, the Yü, and the Huan succeeded each other in positions of power after desperate struggles.

Yet, in spite of their weakness, the Eastern Chin succeeded not only in resisting attacks from the north and in halting Fu Chien's offensives (on the river Fei in 383), but even in annexing Szechwan in 347. They thus opened up a route towards central Asia for the Nanking dynasties.

The crisis which was to put an end to the Chin illustrates both the power of the big provincial families and that of the army chiefs. In the second half of the fourth century the valley of the Kan in Kiangsi and part of Hupei were already virtually out of the central government's control. However, the Nanking government's efforts to enroll the private guards (*pu-ch'ü*) and the dependants of the great families seems to have created latent discontent in the regions between Lake T'ai-hu and the northern coasts of Chekiang. This situation must have favoured the outcome of a rising that started about 400 in the Ning-po region. Its leader was one Sun En, a mixture of pirate and magician affiliated like his father, a native of Shantung, to the Taoist sect of the Five Bushels of Rice (*Wu-tou-mi-tao*). Sun En recruited his followers from the sailors, fishermen, and pirates of the coast of Chekiang, but he was also almost certainly in contact with the big landowners of the modern regions of Hangchow, Shao-hsing, and Ning-po. Embarked in 'boats with decks' (*lou-ch'uan*) and forming 'armies of demons', the rebels ravaged the coastline from bases in the Chousan Islands and soon threatened Nanking. They were crushed in 402 and the defeat resulted in a number of mass suicides in their ranks. However, the struggle against Sun En's insurrection had facilitated the rise of the army leaders entrusted with the task of suppressing it. A certain Huan Hsüan had taken advantage of the situation to usurp power at Nanking, where he was killed in 404 by a rival called Liu Yü, whose victorious campaigns against the kingdoms of the north had won him great popularity. This Liu Yü founded a new dynasty, that of the Sung, known as the Southern Sung (Nan Sung) or Sung of the Liu family (Liu Sung).

The Sung

It seems that at the time when Liu Yü came to power in Nanking the difficulties caused by the immigrations of the early fourth century had been smoothed over and the northerners had merged into the rest of the population. In fact as soon as they ascended the throne the Sung suppressed the distinction between yellow and white registers in order to standardize the fiscal system. The first few years of the dynasty were disturbed by attacks from the kingdoms established in Shensi and Hopei, but subsequently the Yangtze empire enjoyed relative tranquillity during the *yüan-chia* era (424–53) and was able to develop its relations with central Asia and the Japanese principalities. This period of peace did not last: the efforts of the Liu, a family of humble origin carried to power by a military *coup d'état*, to take in hand again the administration of the regions provoked resistance from the big noble families. At the same time the attacks launched by the Wei empire of the north, whose armies reached the Yangtze, helped to weaken the dynasty. A general by the name of Hsiao Tao-ch'eng, who had suppressed a rebellion by one of the imperial princes, took advantage of the central power's decline to put one of his creatures on the throne and finally to seize power himself in 479.

The Ch'i

Two important facts need to be mentioned in connection with the short dynasty—the Ch'i (479–502)—founded by Hsiao Tao-ch'eng: the strengthening of the central government at the expense of the aristocracy and the great expansion of commerce in the valley of the Yangtze and South China. Falsification of the census registers which served as the basis for taxation was severely punished, while the new government strove to favour the promotion of commoners to positions of authority.

It was in fact excessive repression of the aristocracy which led to the downfall of the dynasty. Massacres of nobles caused disturbances in the last few years of the fifth century and a cousin of the emperor, who held a fief in the strategic area of the Hsiang-yang, in the north of Hupei, marched on Nanking and eventually forced the cession of power to himself. This was Hsiao Yen, the future Emperor Wu of the Liang dynasty (502–57).

The Liang

The awakening of Yangtze China to mercantile activities from the end of the fifth century onwards was to have important social consequences. The commercial upsurge was to contribute to the ruin of an aristocracy which drew part of its power from the partition of the regions and the economic autarchy of the big estates. This commercial awakening, which was no doubt connected with the development of trade in the South Seas and the Indian Ocean, marked the beginning of a process of evolution which ended in the great economic upsurge of the Yangtze basin and the maritime provinces of the south in the tenth to thirteenth centuries. At the end of the fifth century there was certainly increased commercial activity on the Yangtze, and the presence is recorded of numerous foreign merchants from South-East Asia and the Indo-Iranian world. The towns on the great river, and also Canton in the extreme south, grew in size, and the state began to draw considerable revenues from commercial taxes.

This expansion of the economy continued and was consolidated in the long reign of the emperor Wu of the Liang dynasty (502–49), who surrounded himself with able advisers in the persons of Shen Yüeh (441–513), known especially for his works on phonetics, and Hsü Mien (466–535), the author of political works. The first half of the sixth century was an epoch of prosperity and peace, the golden age of the aristocratic civilization of the southern dynasties. Buddhism, which had adapted itself to the social forms of Yangtze China and was favoured by the court and the great noble families, experienced an unprecedented upsurge. However a very serious crisis, which was to lead to the disappearance of the southern aristocracy, was soon to arise.

The institution of families dedicated to the profession of arms (*shih-chia* or *ping-lu*), a practice inaugurated by the Ts'ao, was kept up under the Eastern Chin, and the state had more or less retained control of the armies in the fourth century. This situation did not continue in the fifth century, for from the time of the Sung (420–79) onwards the government began to use half-official, half-private armies consisting of mercenaries recruited in the provinces by the local officials and the big aristocratic families. The formation of these armies of rascals and bandits, which call to mind the 'great companies' of the European Middle Ages and were led by military adventurers, a species of *condottiere,* was to endanger the central government and cause the fall of the Liang in the middle of the sixth century. One Hou Ching, a general in the service of the Western Wei (north-west China), moved over to the service of the Liang, rebelled in 548 and led his troops on Nanking. During the course of the disturbances which ensued until his death in 552, the Western Wei launched a series of victorious offensives against the Liang empire from the valley of the Wei in Shensi. In 553 they occupied Szechwan, thus cutting the communications between Nanking and central Asia, seized the strategic point of Hsiang-yang, which commands access to the valley of the Han, and advanced into western Hupei as far as Chiang-ling on the middle Yangtze, where they installed a prince of the reigning family of the Hsiao, whom they had taken prisoner at Hsiang-lang. This new kingdom of Later Liang in Hupei was to be controlled by whatever power was established in the valley of the Wei—the Western Wei (535–57), the Northern Chou (557–81) and the Sui (581–618), who put an end to it in 587. After the Western Wei had gained control of Szechwan and Hupei the civil war went on in the lower valley of the Yangtze. Ch'en Pa-hsien, an army leader whose fief was in the Wu-ch'ang area—more prosperous at that time than the Nanking area—seized power in 557 and founded the last of the southern dynasties, that of the Ch'en (557–89).

The Ch'en

The product of military rebellions and the civil war of the end of the Liang period, the Ch'en empire was different in kind from the previous Nanking dynasties, for the aristocracy had been forced out of power and only a few of its numbers survived the massacres. Just one small section of the old Liang nobility was able to find refuge in Ch'ang-an, with the Western Wei. The empire, bereft of its western provinces and generally weakened, could now count only on its armies. It was threatened to the west by the attacks of the Later Liang, and to the north by those of the Chou and the Northern Ch'i. The victory which it gained in retaking Shou-yang (the modern Shou-hsien, 125 miles north of Nanking) led to nothing. It was to collapse in the swift campaign directed against Nanking in 589 by the first Sui emperor.

Kingdoms and empires of the
sinicized 'barbarians' in North China

The Sixteen Kingdoms of the Five Barbarians (fourth century)

The revolts at the end of the Western Chin dynasty by non-Chinese peoples living in North China soon ended in the division of North China—from southern Manchuria to the eastern oases of central Asia and from Szechwan to Shantung—into several small kingdoms whose ruling classes were most often natives of the northern and north-western borders. Thus the early fourth century saw the opening of a period the political history of which is extremely confused. This period did not end until 439, when North China was reunited by the descendants of a Hsien-pei tribe. The various annexations, the successive emergence of new powers, and the frequent changes of capital—for example, between 407 and 431 the Hsia moved their political centre from northern Shensi to Hsi'an, then to T'ien-shui in eastern Kansu, and finally to the upper valley of the Ching, north-east of T'ien-shui—make any clear, connected narrative impossible. The multiplicity of racial groups, their degree of intermarriage with the Han Chinese, their varying stages of evolu-tion—they were more or less sinicized and sedentary—add to the com-plexity of the political history. However, it is worth noting that these racial groups, which Chinese historians call the Five Barbarians (Hsiung-nu, Chieh, Hsien-pei, Ch'iang, and Ti) belong to two different peoples. The Ch'iang and the Ti were related to the Tibetans and Tangut of later ages, came from the north-western border, and spoke Sino-Tibetan languages. The other three tribes were descendants of the nomadic cattle-raisers of the steppes and their languages belonged to the group which in-cludes Turkish, Mongolian, and Tungus. It looks as if their forms of social and political organization were fairly different: the Ch'iang and the Ti were strangers to the aristocratic, tribal system of the nomads and seem to have had only a military organization.

These peoples—or, to be precise, their élites—thus combined their own political and social traditions with large borrowings from Chinese concepts and institutions. Their ruling classes were so thoroughly sini-cized that they regarded themselves as the heirs to the old political units of North China. The Hsiung-nu of Shansi adopted the name of the great Han dynasty, and ancient names from the period of the Warring States also reappeared in the fourth century: the Sixteen Kingdoms of the Five Barbarians bore the name of Ch'in in Shensi, of Chao in Shansi, and of T'en in Hopei and Shantung. The only exceptions were the kingdoms

Table 10. The Sixteen Kingdoms of the Five Barbarians (*Wuhu shih-liu-kuo*)

Name of the kingdoms	Origin of the ruling class and region	Kingdoms which succeeded it	Dates
Earlier Chao (Han)	Hsiung-nu (Shansi)	Later Chao	304–329
Ch'eng Han	Ti (Szechwan)	Eastern Chin	304–347
Later Chao	Chieh (Hopei)	Earlier Yen	319–351
Earlier Liang	Han (Kansu)	Earlier Ch'in	314–376
Earlier Yen	Hsien-pei (Hopei)	Earlier Ch'in	349–370
Earlier Ch'in	Ti (Shensi)	Western Ch'in	351–394
Later Yen	Hsien-pei (Hopei)	Northern Yen	384–409
Later Ch'in	Ch'iang (Shensi)	Eastern Chin	384–417
Western Ch'in	Hsien-pei (Kansu)	Hsia	385–431
Later Liang	Ti (Kansu)	Later Ch'in	386–403
Southern Liang	Hsien-pei (Kansu)	Western Ch'in	397–414
Northern Liang	Hsiung-nu (Kansu)	Northern Wei	401–439
Southern Yen	Hsien-pei (Shantung)	Eastern Chin	400–410
Western Liang	Han (Kansu)	Northern Liang	400–421
Hsia	Hsiung-nu (Shensi)	Northern Wei	407–431
Northern Yen	Han (Liaoning)	Northern Wei	409–439

established in Kansu, which took the name of Liang (the modern Wu-wei) in the centre of this province. In the reigning families, intermarriage with the Han Chinese who formed the majority of the population was so frequent that it is impossible to distinguish between Chinese and non-Chinese. Thus no conclusions can be drawn from the fact that, of the sixteen kingdoms which succeeded each other in North China between the early years of the fourth century and 439, three are supposed to have been founded by families of Han origin: the Earlier Liang of 314–76, the Western Liang of 400–21 and the Northern Yen of 409–39.

The only outstanding event in the extremely confused political history of North China in the fourth century was the foundation of a big kingdom by a family of proto-Tibetan origin, that of the Earlier Ch'in (351–94). The greatest sovereign of this kingdom centred on Ch'ang-an, in the valley of the Wei, was Fu Chien (357–85), who succeeded in unifying North China during the years 370–76 into a powerful military state and even threatened the Western Chin empire in the valley of the Yangtze. According to tradition, in 382 Fu Chien mounted a formidable expedition against the South—the figures given by the historical texts, 600,000 infantry and 270,000 cavalry, are exaggerated—but suffered a decisive defeat on a river in central Anhwei. This was the famous battle of the Fei (383).

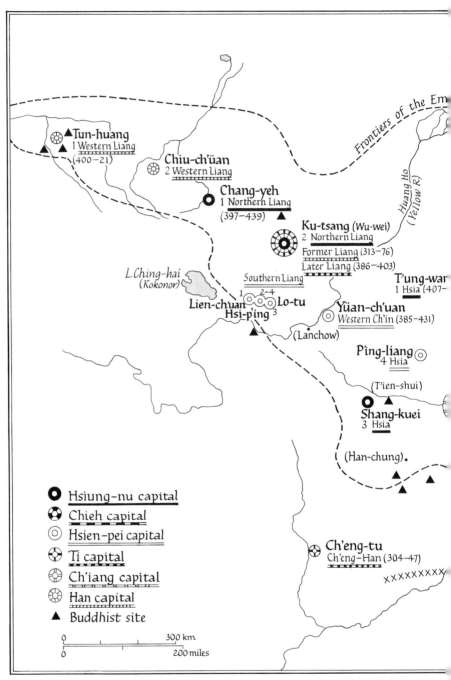

Map 10 The partitioning of North China in the fourth century: the Sixteen Kingdoms of the

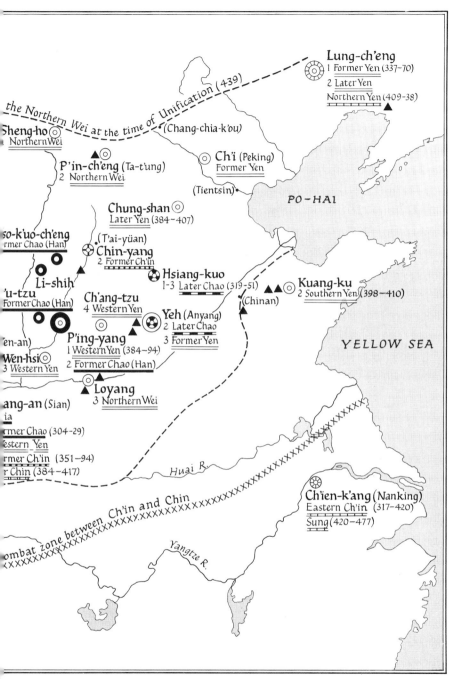

Lung-ch'eng
1 Former Yen (337–70)
2 Later Yen
Northern Yen (409–38)

the Northern Wei at the time of Unification (439)

Sheng-ho
1 Northern Wei

(Chang-chia-k'ou)

P'in-ch'eng (Ta-t'ung)
2 Northern Wei

Ch'i (Peking)
Former Yen

(Tientsin)

PO–HAI

so-k'uo-ch'eng
rmer Chao (Han)

(T'ai-yüan)
Chin-yang
2 Former Ch'in

Chung-shan
Later Yen (384–407)

Li-shih
'u-tzu
Former Chao (Han)

Hsiang-kuo
1–3 Later Chao (319–51)

Kuang-ku
2 Southern Yen (398–410)

(Chinan)

Ch'ang-tzu
4 Western Yen

Yeh (Anyang)
2 Later Chao
3 Former Yen

YELLOW SEA

en-an)

Wen-hsi
3 Western Yen

P'ing-yang
1 Western Yen (384–94)
2 Former Chao (Han)

Loyang
3 Northern Wei

ang-an (Sian)
ia
rmer Chao (304–29)
estern Yen
rmer Ch'in (351–94)
r Chin (384–417)

Huai R.

Ch'ien-k'ang (Nanking)
Eastern Ch'in (317–420)
Sung (420–477)

ombat zone between Ch'in and Chin

Yangtze R.

arbarians

The rise of the Tabgatch (Toba) and the formation
of the empire of the Northern Wei

The rise of the little Toba kingdom and the conquest of North China in the first half of the fifth century are a typical illustration of the evolution of the peoples of nomadic origin resident in these regions. The political units in which the process of conversion to a sedentary existence was most advanced, and whose ruling classes were most thoroughly sinicized, soon found themselves threatened by peoples who had retained the war-like manners of the nomadic herdsmen and had so far borrowed from China only the institutions indispensable for the formation of a state. These peoples, whose territory lay in the borderlands between the agricultural zone and the steppe, controlled the commercial routes and easily found recruits for their armies.

The Eastern Chin (265–318) had sought the alliance of the Hsien-pei, tribes of nomadic herdsmen from southern Manchuria who had settled in south-eastern Mongolia in the third century. They had ceded some land in northern Shansi to the Toba, one of the three groups of Hsien-pei tribes (Toba, Yü-wen, and Mu-jung), and in 315 granted the Toba chief the title of Prince of Tai. The Toba (the term is the Chinese transcription of the tribe's own name for itself, Tabgatch) thus occupied a strategic position on one of the principal invasion routes into North China. By the end of the fourth century they had succeeded in gaining control of all the lands between the Ordos and the basin of the Siramuren, to the north-east of Peking. Adopting the ancient name of Wei — they are known to history as the Northern Wei — and fixing their capital in 386 at Ta-t'ung, in the extreme north of Shansi, they expanded into Hopei at the expense of the Later Yen Kingdom and were encroaching on Honan by the beginning of the fifth century. Assisted by the Eastern Chin attacks on the northern kingdoms, the Wei promptly launched a series of victorious offensives which enabled them to unify North China. The Hsia who occupied northern Shensi were annexed in 431, the Northern Yen of Liaoning (southern Manchuria) in 439, and the Northern Liang of Kansu in the same year. In 440 the Wei gained control of the region of Wu-wei (Liang-chou) in Kansu, which gave them access to central Asia.

The Northern Wei followed a 'Legalist' policy marked by state intervention in the control and distribution of the population, but this policy was aggravated by the roughness and severity of warriors of the steppes: nomads had a certain tendency to regard sedentary people as so much cattle. State employees were practically kept prisoner in their workshops and were not allowed to contract marriages outside their caste. Even free workers were closely watched. The peasantry was controlled by a military kind of organization reminiscent of the Ch'in age: five families

Table 11. Deportations carried out by the Northern Wei
(first half of the fifth century)

Year	People	Number	Destination
398	Hsien-pei of Hopei and northern Shantung	100,000	Ta-t'ung
399	Great Chinese families	2,000 families	Ta-t'ung
399	Chinese peasants from Honan	100,000	Shansi
418	Hsien-pei of Hopei	?	Ta-t'ung
427	Population of the kingdom of Hsia (Shensi)	10,000	Shansi
432	Population of Liaoning	30,000 families	Hopei
435	Population of Shensi and Kansu	?	Ta-t'ung
445	Chinese peasants from Honan and Shantung	?	North of Yellow River
449	Craftsmen from Ch'ang-an	2,000 families	Ta-t'ung

formed a 'neighbourhood' (*lin*), five *lin* formed a 'village' (*li*) and five *li* formed a 'commune' (*tang*). At each level leaders responsible to the government were appointed. In order to increase the reclamation of arid areas, the Northern Wei employed an authoritarian system of dividing up land according to the number of men of an age to cultivate it. The Sui and T'ang were to resurrect this system in the seventh century. The Wei also posted to Buddhist monasteries convicts and state slaves, who were known as 'community families' (*seng-ch'i-hu*) and given the job of bringing waste land back into cultivation. But above all they made use of deportation in order to populate the region round the capital, Ta-t'ung, and lands in Shansi.

During the reign of Tao Wu Ti alone (386–409), the total number of persons deported from the regions east of the T'ai-hang-shan to the neighbourhood of Ta-t'ung amounted to 460,000.

These deportations, which usually took place immediately after the conquest of new territory, contributed to a slow transformation of the economy, of institutions, and of manners which was to make its effects fully felt in the sixth century. In fact several factors combined to assist the progress of Chinese influences after the capital had been installed at Ta-t'ung at the end of the fourth century. As the empire encompassed more numerous sedentary populations, so the need to employ Chinese institutions and to appeal to Chinese advisers made itself felt more sharply. In this connection an important role was played at the court of Ta-t'ung by the great adviser Ts'ui Hao (381–450), who introduced Chinese administrative methods and the Chinese penal code into the Northern Wei

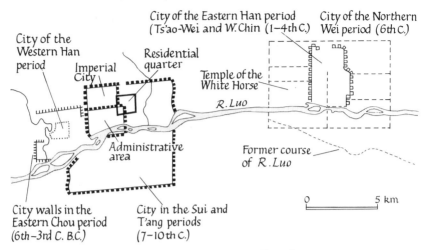

City of the Eastern Han period
(Ts'ao-Wei and W.Chin (1–4th C.)

City of the Northern
Wei period (6th C.)

City of the
Western Han
period

Imperial
City

Residential
quarter

Temple of the
White Horse

R. Luo

Administrative
area

Former course
of *R. Luo*

City walls in the
Eastern Chou period
(6th–3rd C. B.C.)

City in the Sui and
T'ang periods
(7–10th C.)

0   5 km

Map 11   Successive sites of Loyang, Han dynasty to T'ang dynasty

kingdom. The incursions of the nomads of Outer Mongolia (the Juan-juan or Jou-jan, a people probably related to the Avars who invaded Europe in the sixth to eighth centuries), the need for a counter-offensive (the Northern Wei launched a great expedition against the Juan-juan in 429), and the strategic and commercial importance of controlling the oases of central Asia all put the Northern Wei in the same position as previous Chinese empires. The gradual conversion to a sedentary existence, the decline in the importance of the horse as a result of the role played by infantry in the wars against the Yangtze empires, and the growing importance of revenues with an agricultural origin (cereals and cloth) gradually changed the empire's economy. Finally, the attraction of the products of Chinese craftsmen, the taste for luxury, the prestige of Chinese culture, and the preponderant influence of Buddhism transformed the mentality of the Toba aristocracy.

By the end of the fifth century the process of evolution had gone so far that it became clear that it was essential to shift the capital. In 494 the court abandoned Ta-t'ung, on the border of the steppes, and moved to Loyang, right in the centre of the big agricultural zone. Six hundred miles due south of Ta-t'ung the Northern Wei had rebuilt in the previous year, near the site of the old capitals of the Han and the Ts'ao Wei, abandoned since 311, the new walled city of Loyang, which was to be enlarged in 501.

The progress of Chinese influences, which the transfer of the capital to Loyang would have stimulated in any case in the ruling classes of nomadic origin, was to be accelerated by the policy of systematic sinicization adopted by the emperor Hsiao Wen Ti (471–99) on his arrival in Honan and continued by his successors. Hsien-pei clothes, the Hsien-pei language, and even family names of Hsien-pei origin were forbidden. The imperial house set an example by taking the Chinese name of Yüan. Marriages between the Hsien-pei aristocracy and great Chinese families were encouraged, and all over the realm there was a rapid and thorough conversion of the governing classes to Chinese manners and customs. The warlike traditions of the steppe were soon no more than a distant memory, while the taste for luxury was given free rein in the sumptuous buildings erected by the empress Hu in the reign of Hsiao Ming Ti (515–28) and by the great families of the Hsien-pei aristocracy. Buddhist monasteries and storied towers rose everywhere, and were furnished with bells and statues. The religious fervour which took hold of high society in this period was characterized by lavish spending on outward display. The city of Loyang, which was the great centre of Buddhism in East Asia, un-folded its marvels and its wealth inside its huge ramparts, which ran for six miles from east to west and for four and a half miles from north to south. A description of this metropolis with its '1367 large and small monasteries' has been preserved in the shape of the *Treatise on the Bud-dhist Monasteries of Loyang* (*Loyang ch'ieh-lan chi*) by Yang Hsien Chih, published some years after 543.

One phenomenon which was to favour the assimilation of the old Hsien-pei aristocracy to the Chinese mode of life was the economic up-surge which made itself apparent from the end of the fifth century on-wards both in North China and in the Yangtze basin. In spite of their political division, the two halves of the Chinese world lived at the same pace and there was considerable trade between them. In North China the renewal of commerce with central Asia explains the flow of foreign mer-chants to Loyang (a whole district of the city, the Mui-li, was reserved for them), while at Yeh, the capital of the Northern Ch'i (550–77), in southern Hopei, numerous Sogdian traders from the basin of the Amu-Darya were to be seen.

Tensions in North China:
its breakup and division (534–577)

The process of evolution which went on throughout the fifth century, and increased in pace at the beginning of the sixth, was at the root of the tensions which became more and more evident in Hsien-pei society. The change-over to Chinese culture and the Chinese mode of life mainly af-fected court circles and the upper ranks of the nomad aristocracy in general; the armies which guarded the northern frontiers and the tribes which continued to live as nomads on the outskirts of the agricultural zone remained faithful to the old traditions of the steppe in spite of Chinese influences. Feelings of hostility and resentment towards the court and the upper ranks of the civil service seem to have built up in this military and pastoral world as changes in the economy and in society pushed it into the background. At the time of the conquests, in the first half of the fifth century, the combatants, who came mainly from pastoral tribes, were treated with honour and generosity, but after the transfer of the capital to Loyang the government began to show less and less interest in military questions.

In 523 the armies—consisting of Hsien-pei, Juan-juan and Tölös Turks—which protected the empire against incursions from the steppe up to the neighbourhood of the forty-first parallel finally rebelled. This was the rebellion of the 'Six Garrisons' (*liu-chen*); it was to be followed by a civil war which lasted ten years (524–34). When the empress regent Hu, whose extravagant expenditure on Buddhism had led to banditry and revolts, caused the emperor Hsiao Ming Ti to be assassinated in 528 and put a child on the throne, the armies and tribes of Shansi moved south and seized Loyang. The empress Hu and her child emperor were drowned in the Yellow River and two thousand courtiers were murdered. These events were followed by a very confused period, in which two army leaders asserted their power. They shared the Wei empire between them in 534–35. This geographical division reflected the political and social antagonisms which had produced the civil war. The empire of the Eastern Wei, which was founded in 534 at Yeh (southern Hopei) under the aegis of General Kao Huan (496–547), was traditionalist, hostile to Chinese influences, and dominated by soldiers of nomadic origin; on the contrary, the empire of the Western Wei, the first head of which was installed by General Yü Wen T'ai (505–56) at Ch'ang-an in 535, was governed by the survivors of the sinicized aristocracy of Loyang and depended largely on the Chinese for its civil service and for the recruitment of its armies.

One can imagine that these empires, in which the generals held the real power, did not last very long. On the death of Yü Wen T'ai, in 556, his eldest son inaugurated the new Chou dynasty (Northern Chou, 556–81); similarly, in the next year, a cousin of Kao Huan seized supreme power at Yeh and founded the new Ch'i dynasty (Northern Ch'i, 557–77), which lasted until it was annihilated by the Chou. Finally, a relative of the imperial house on the distaff side, Yang Chien by name, usurped the imperial power at Ch'ang-an, creating the new Sui dynasty and ending in 589 the long division between North China and Yangtze China which had begun for all practical purposes in 222.

The Sui empire and the T'ang empire in its early days were in every way heirs to the empires centered on Ch'ang-an from 535 to Yang Chien's usurpation. Most of their institutions originated with the Western Wei and the Northern Chou. One of the most important of these concerned the organization of the armies: they were militias (*fu-ping*), the creation of which is generally attributed to Yü Wen T'ai in 550. In spite of changes of dynasty, the governing personnel, political conceptions, and society in general did not change much between Yü Wen T'ai's time and the middle of the seventh century. Thus if it is legitimate to see in the reunification of China in 589 the end of a great historical period, it remains true none the less that there is a clear thread linking Sui and early T'ang China to the northern dynasties, and more especially to the Western Wei and Northern Chou empires.

Contacts, influences, and foreign relations

A general survey of the history of the Chinese world would not be complete without some reference to the constant enrichment ensured by the contacts of the Han Chinese with peoples alien to them in culture and mode of life. The contributions of the steppe, of the Sino-Tibetan borders, and of South China were crucial in the formation of Chinese civilization. The influence of neighbouring cultures made itself felt in every domain—methods of harnessing horses, use of the saddle and the stirrup (fifth century), ways of building bridges and mountain roads, the science of medicinal plants and poisons, seafaring, and so on. The Chinese mouth-organ, the *sheng,* is a borrowing from the peoples of the tropical zone and in principle is nothing other than the Laotian *khene.* Later, in the thirteenth century, it was the aboriginal inhabitants of the southern provinces who taught the Han Chinese the cultivation and weaving of cotton, which were to spread in the Mongol epoch and become one of the great Chinese industries. Even the religious traditions of the Han Chinese bear the mark of borrowings from neighbouring peoples: the myth of the dog P'an-hu, born from the primordial egg and creator of all human races—a myth which has lived on down to our own day among numerous ethnic groups of South China and the Indo-Chinese peninsula—passed into Chinese folklore between the age of the Warring States and that of the Han dynasties. The poems of Ch'u (*Ch'u-t'zu*) (fourth to third century B.C.) have preserved the memory of shamanist traditions which do not seem to be of Chinese origin. These few examples will suffice to indicate Chinese civilization's debt to its neighbours. The contributions of more distant civilizations were no less important. In the long history of these contacts and borrowings the 'Chinese Middle Ages' were certainly one of the richest and most fruitful periods.

South China, South-East Asia, and the Indian Ocean

Although it is impossible to retrace the history of the process in all its details, the advance of peoples of Chinese language and culture into the tropical regions south of the Yangtze valley seems to have made clear progress during the period of the southern dynasties (i.e., the Six Dynasties: Wu, Eastern Chin, Sung, Ch'i, Liang, Ch'en). The Wu and Shu dynasties in the third century, and the Eastern Chin in the fourth, sought to exploit the wealth of the still little-known regions which extended to the south of their realms: Yunnan, Kweichow, Hunan, Kwangsi, Kwangtung, and the north and centre of modern Vietnam. Lacking labour and soldiers, they organized expeditions against the aboriginal inhabitants and conscripted them. In the fifth century the Sung were to fight some hard battles against the tribes whose territories they had annexed.

South and south-west China began to be better known from the fourth century onwards. The year 304 saw the appearance of a treatise—one of the first Chinese works on botany—devoted to the trees, plants, fruit, and bamboos of Kwangsi and Chiao-chih (the basin of the Red River in Vietnam). This was the *Nan-fang Ts'ao-mu Chuang*. After the conquest of Szechwan in 347 by the Eastern Chin, a certain Ch'ang Ch'ü compiled a geographical and historical work which covers the regions of Kweichow, Yunnan, Szechwan and southern Shensi; it is entitled the *Treatise on the Kingdom of the Hua-yang* (*Hua-yang Kuo-chih*). In it is to be found information about the flora, fauna, products, and customs of these countries, most of which were still inhabited by aboriginal tribes.

However the efforts at colonization and the armed expeditions passed beyond the limits of South China and Vietnam, and reached overseas lands. The Wu rulers already possessed a navy in the third century and attacked Taiwan (unless the sources mean to indicate the Ryukyu Islands) (I-chou), Hainan (Chu-ya) and the island of Quelpaert to the south of Korea (Chi-chou-tao). The Wu dynasty had political and commercial ambitions in the South Seas, and strategic interests in the north-eastern seas. About 228 it sent an embassy by sea to the kingdom of Funan (Phnam), in the Mekong delta, which was frequently visited by foreigners from the countries on the Indian Ocean and from the Middle East. The leaders of this Chinese mission to ancient Cambodia, Chu Ying and K'ang T'ai, who met there an envoy from the Indian empire of the Kusanas, left travel notes: the former wrote a *Treatise of the Curiosities of Funan* (*Funan I-wu chih*), the latter an *Account of Foreign Kingdoms in the Time of the Kingdom of Wu* (*Wu-shih wai-kuo chuan*) and also a work on the *Customs of Cambodia* (*Funan T'u-su*).

Yangtze China's relations with South-East Asia and the Indian Ocean were to develop from the fourth to the sixth centuries. The Sung, Ch'i, and Liang dynasties were in contact with Lin-i – a Hinduized kingdom on the south-east coast of Vietnam known later as Champa – and with Funan, the island of Java, India, and Ceylon. Embassies from Indian kingdoms and from Ceylon were frequently to be seen in Nanking between the end of the fourth century and the middle of the sixth. As in the other periods of great maritime expansion (eleventh to thirteenth and sixteenth to nineteenth centuries), this expansion of the Chinese world's relations with South-East Asia and the Indian Ocean took place in a much wider context. The Nanking dynasty's interest in overseas countries was contemporaneous with the expansion of Indo-Iranian seafaring activities and with the development of commercial routes between the Middle East, the Indian Ocean, and South-East Asia. This is the explanation of the progressive conversion to Hinduism of the coastal plains of the Indo-Chinese peninsula and Indonesia, as well as of the presence in the cities of South China and of the Yangtze valley of more and more foreigners from South-East Asia and the Indian Ocean – people from Vietnam, from Champa (Lin-i), Cambodia, Ceylon, northern and southern India, and eastern Iran. These foreigners, travelling via the southern seas, were to contribute to the spread of Buddhism in the Chinese world.

Manchuria, Korea, and Japan

The struggle between Wei and Wu in the third century had given a new importance to the regions which lay to the north-east of the Chinese world. The Han expansion had favoured the foundation of Chinese colonies in southern Manchuria and in Korea. At the end of the second century the Kung-sun, the family which governed Liaotung, had taken advantage of the Yellow Turban disturbances and of the civil war ravaging North China to establish in the south of Manchuria a sort of kingdom independent of the Han emperors. Its chief wealth seems to have come from breeding and selling horses. Between 231 and 238 the Ts'ao Wei put an end to this kingdom and subsequently gained a foothold in Korea, where they re-established the two commanderies of Le-lang and Tai-feng in the western part of the peninsula. The Chinese presence in Korea was to be maintained until about 313.

Succeeding the Han dynasty as great power in the north-east, the Ts'ao Wei had also entered into relations with the Japanese principalities. In the Han period numerous chiefdoms of Wo-jen — the 'dwarf', to use the Chinese expression — had acquired the habit of sending tribute to the Han emperors. These chiefdoms were very probably situated in the north of Kyushu, where excavations have yielded numerous relics of the Han period — bronze mirrors, iron objects, and coins from the time of Wang Mang. A seal of investiture given by a Han emperor to a 'king of the dwarf slaves' (Wo-nu-wang) was even discovered in this area in 1784. Long considered a forgery, this seal has been recognized as authentic since the recent discovery (in 1956) of a similar seal originating from the ancient kingdom of Tien in eastern Yunnan. In the third century relations between the Ts'ao Wei, then in conflict with the kingdom of Wu, and the Japanese principalities seem to have grown closer. Four Japanese embassies to Wei and two Wei embassies to Japan are mentioned between 238 and 247, and archaeology bears witness to this continuity of exchanges by the number of silks, gold objects, and Chinese mirrors of the Wei period found in Japan. It is worth noting that the *San-kuo-chih* (*History of the Three Kingdoms*) compiled by the Szechwan writer Ch'en Shou (233–97) is the first document to describe the route from the south-east coast of Korea to the Japanese archipelago via the Tsushima and Iki islands.

The relations between North China and Japan were to grow looser from the beginning of the fourth century onwards as a result of the partition of the Western Chin empire (260–316) and the formation of the three Korean kingdoms of Koguryo (Kao-chü-li) in the north of the peninsula, Paekche (Pai-chi) in the south-west and Silla (Hsin-lo) in the south-east.

The kingdom of Wu (222–80) lacked horses and also sought an alliance with the Kung-sun against its powerful northern neighbour; this explains the dispatch of several embassies by sea to Manchuria. One of them is said to have numbered nearly eight thousand men embarked in a hundred ships. It may have been an expeditionary force intended to bring help to the Kung-sun, threatened by the attacks of the Ts'ao Wei. A monk from the Eastern Chin empire centred on Nanking is supposed to have been the first to introduce Buddhism to the court of Paekche in 384. Finally, in the fifth and sixth centuries, the Japanese principalities, worried by the designs of Koguryo, which was allied to the Northern Wei, on the two Korean kingdoms in the south of the peninsula, sought an alliance with the Nanking dynasties. These political factors drew Japan closer to Yangtze China at this period.

Mongolia and Central Asia

The influence of the steppe cultures on North China was considerable and probably much more important than would at first appear. Since the end of antiquity there had been numerous borrowings from the people of the steppe—the technique of training horses for the cavalry, breeding techniques, trousers, the saddle, and the invention of the breast-harness between the fourth century B.C. and the Han age, the stirrup in the fifth century A.D., and the horse-collar between the fifth and ninth centuries. Even if the nomads settled in North China became more and more rapidly sinicized from the Han age onwards, the inverse phenomenon was almost certainly just as important: the warrior tradition and certain institutions were borrowed from the world of the steppe. However, this synthesis of Chinese and nomad culture was discreetly veiled. In fact, after the Northern Wei had made Loyang their capital at the end of the fifth century, everything which could remind the ruling classes of their nomad origin was completely discredited. The history of the Wei (*Wei-shu*), compiled from 551 to 554, strives to present the Tabgatch dynasty as typically Chinese, and reading it one would never imagine that this dynasty consisted of the descendants of barely sinicized herdsmen of the steppe. The strongly marked tendency from about 500 onwards to censor anything in institutions and customs that might appear to deviate from Chinese norms led writers to blend into the continuous, homogeneous fabric of the dynastic histories the very distinctive period of the 'barbarian' kingdoms and empires of the fourth and fifth centuries. The aristocracy of mixed blood which held the levers of power at the beginning of the T'ang dynasty (seventh century) doubtless retained this prejudice of parvenus ashamed of numbering among their distant ancestors illiterate nomads who dwelt in tents and lived on cattle breeding and raiding. Thus the histories of the north compiled in the seventh century cannot tell us what the Sixteen Kingdoms of the Five Barbarians and the Tabgatch empire of the Wei before its capital was transferred to Honan were really like; only cross-checking, involuntary evidence, and induction can throw any light on this whole period.

The settlement of peoples from Manchuria, Mongolia, and the Sino-Tibetan borders in North China resulted in the modification of the ethnic composition of this part of the Chinese world and at the same time in the transformation of mentalities and traditions. Marriages between Han Chinese and people of the steppe or mountaineers were common in the lower classes and multiplied in the upper classes from the beginning of the sixth century onwards as a consequence of the policy of systematic sinicization adopted by the Northern Wei. They ended in the creation of an aristocracy of mixed blood. Numerous great families of the Sui and T'ang periods—the very ones who were the most loyal supporters of the imperial power round about 600 and well into the eighth century—bear names of Turkish or Hsien-pei origin—Yü-wen, Mu-jung, Ling-hu, Tu-ku, Yü-ch'ih, and so on. But in many cases 'barbarian' origins were concealed by the adoption of a Chinese family name. The T'ang themselves, who bore the thoroughly Chinese name of Li, were half Turkish.

The 'Chinese Middle Ages' come between two great periods of expansion in central Asia, the Han period, from the end of the second century B.C. to the middle of the second century A.D., and the T'ang period, in the seventh and eighth centuries. However, the relations of the Chinese lands with the oases in the Tarim basin and at the foot of the Kunlun were not interrupted between these two great periods of conquest, during which Chinese armies ventured as far as the Pamirs and sometimes even into Transoxiania. The Ts'ao Wei strove to regain a foothold in these oases. The prestige of the Western Chin at the end of the third century explains the number of embassies sent to Loyang between 268 and 289 not only by the kingdoms of central Asia but also by the countries of South-East Asia. There was tribute from Shanshan (the modern Charkhlik), Khotan, Kucha, Karashahr and Ferghana in the years 271, 273, 285, and 287, and embassies from Lin-i (Champa) and Funan (Cambodia) in the years 268, 284, 285, 287, and 289. In 285 a Chinese ambassador was sent to Ferghana to confer on the sovereign of this land the title of prince (*wang*). In the fourth century the kingdom of the Earlier Liang (316–76), which had its capital at Wu-wei, in the centre of Kansu, extended as far as the region of Turfan. After the year 376 and General Lü Kuang's expedition of 384, the great sovereign of the Earlier Ch'in, Fu Chien, was able to enforce his authority as far as the basin of the Tarim. The offensives of the Later Liang (386–403) were to take them to Karashahr and Kucha. When the kingdom of the Northern Liang (401–39) was annexed by the Northern Wei, the reigning family sought refuge at Turfan, where they founded the new kingdom of Kao-ch'ang. Finally, after their conquest of Kansu in 439–40, the Northern Wei were to impose their will on central Asia and receive tribute at Ta-t'ung from some twenty oasis kingdoms.

Moreover, contrary to what one might think in view of the distance and the natural obstacles involved, the Nanking dynasties of the fourth to sixth centuries were in contact with central Asia as well as with the countries to the north-east of the Ts'ao Wei and Northern Wei empires (Manchuria, Korea, and Japan). The T'u-yü-hun, a cattle-raising people of Tsinghai (Kokonor), served in fact as intermediaries between the

Yangtze empires and the oasis principalities. These relations even became closer under the Liang of Nanking during the first half of the sixth century as a result of the expansion of the T'u-yü-hun towards the oases of Shanshan and Ch'ieh-mo (the present-day Cherchen). They came to an end only when Szechwan was occupied by the Western Wei in 553.

The expansion of the T'ang in central Asia, and up to the borders of Iran, was not a sudden and unforeseeable affair; on the contrary, it was preceded at the time of the first Turkish incursions into North China by a period of great diplomatic activity between the empires established at Ch'ang-an from 535 onwards and the regions to the west of Yü-men-kuan and Tun-huang. This is proved by the number of embassies from central Asian kingdoms and Sassanid Persia which appeared in Ch'ang-an:

553   embassies from the Ephtalites and Persia
558   embassies from the Ephtalites and Persia
560   embassy from the kingdom of Kucha
564   embassy from Sogdiana (region of Samarkand)
567   embassy from Bukhara (valley of the Amu-Darya)
574   embassy from the kingdom of Khotan (tribute of horses)
578   embassy from Persia

Just as the cities of South China and the Yangtze valley welcomed a larger and larger number of foreigners from South-East Asia and the Indian Ocean during the age of the Six Dynasties (222–589), so the urban centres of North China saw the formation of colonies of traders from the oases of central Asia and the regions between the Syr-Darya and the present frontiers of India and Iran. There were people from Turfan, Kucha, Khotan, Kashgar, Samarkand, Bukhara, Bactria, and Peshawar; eastern Iranians, Kashmiris, and Indians from the valleys of the Indus and the Ganges. Merchants, official envoys, hostages, and missionaries who entered China by the southern ports and the roads through Kansu were to exert a decisive influence during this crucial age in the history of the Chinese world. After a period of acclimatization during the first few centuries of our era, Buddhism was to provoke in China, from the end of the fourth century to the end of the eighth, a huge wave of religious fervour, radically changing earlier traditions and leaving lasting marks on the Chinese world and the neighbouring countries. But Buddhist influences were not the only ones that made themselves felt; Indian, Iranian, and Hellenistic influences were at work at the same time in China and in the whole of East Asia.

Chapter 10

The Medieval Civilization

The period of four centuries from the decline of the Han dynasty to the
formation of the aristocratic Sui and T'ang empires was one of the
richest and most complex in the intellectual history of the Chinese world.
It was astonishingly fertile and abounded in innovations. It witnessed the
development of a metaphysics completely free of the scholasticism of the
Han age and enriched from the beginning of the fourth century by the
Buddhist contribution of the Great Vehicle, the doctrine of the universal
void. It also witnessed the affirmation of a sort of artistic and literary
dilettantism, a pursuit of aesthetic pleasure for its own sake which was in
complete contradiction with the classical tradition; the first, remarkable
attempts at literary and artistic criticism; the promotion of painting from
the rank of craft to that of a skilled art, rich in intellectual content; the
first appearance in world history of landscape as a subject for painting
and as an artistic creation; and an unprecedented efflorescence of poetry.
Finally, it saw the development of a tremendous wave of religious fervour with so many different aspects and such vast and numerous effects
that they can scarcely all be mentioned in a general history of the Chinese
world.

The complexity of the period's social and political history, the different ways in which North China and the Yangtze basin evolved, the
relative segregation of the different regions and the South's borrowings
from the North all add to the wealth and diversity of this intellectual life.
The ethical and philosophical evolution which took place between about
190 and the end of the third century makes this moment in history, when
the first of the Yangtze 'dynasties' appeared, into a watershed. By the
fourth century there were profound differences between warlike,
populist, almost illiterate North China, permeated by the influences of

the steppe and the Sino-Tibetan borders, and Yangtze China, aristocratic and refined, with its coteries, its hermitages, and its court life. This contrast was subsequently to grow less marked in the course of the fifth and sixth centuries. The Buddhist faith was to unite all sections of the old Chinese world in the same outburst of religious fervour from the moment when the Northern Wei, becoming more and more sinicized, transferred their capital to Loyang (494), the very spot which had been the centre of Chinese political power from the beginning of the first century to the beginning of the fourth.

The political and social circumstances of this period of more than three centuries do much to explain its moral atmosphere. The factional struggles between great families, the tendency of powerful clans to transform themselves into closed aristocracies, the weakness of the Nanking empires, and the emptiness of political activity certainly had something to do with the attitude of withdrawal and with the pursuit of art for its own sake which characterized cultivated circles between the third and sixth centuries. One can understand, too, in the Yangtze empires the predominance of coteries, the success of eremitical and monastic modes of life and finally the role of the court, last refuge in the troubled times of decline. As for the North, it is not difficult to account for the welcome accorded to the great foreign religion in a crude, violent, half-barbarian world, the patronage bestowed on Buddhism by the satraps who divided up among themselves the Ts'ao and Ssu-ma empire, and the rapid progress of Buddhist piety.

Metaphysics, aesthetics, and poetry

From Legalist nominalism to ontological speculations

At the time of the Han decline there was a break in scholastic traditions and a profound moral and political crisis which seems to have changed all outlooks. Classical studies shone with their last and finest lustre in the work of Ma Jung (79–166) and Cheng Hsüan (127–200), and the engraving in 175 on stelae at the Loyang academy (*t'ai-hsüeh*) of the text of the Six Classics established by Ts'ai Yung (133–92) acquires in retrospect a symbolic value, for these venerable texts, with the exception of the *Book of Changes* (the *I-ching*), were not to receive such care and attention for a long time. It is doubtless possible to cite the names of a few famous commentators on the Classics between the end of the Han dynasty and the great renaissance of the Sung age in the eleventh and twelfth centuries, but these scholars were only isolated individuals who carried on Han traditions and did not radically change either methods of textual interpretation or the philosophy implicit in them.

The disturbances of the end of the second century, and later the insurrections of the barbarian tribes at the beginning of the fourth century, played their part in this eclipse of scholarly traditions. The Han archives and the imperial library were destroyed when Loyang was sacked by Tung Cho's mercenary troops in 190, and the collections put together by the Ts'ao Wei suffered a similar fate in 311. It should be noted, by the way, that the imperial library of the Ts'ao Twei and the Western Chin, catalogued in accordance with the new system of classification in four categories (*ssu-pu:* classics, histories, philosophy, and literary works) which was subsequently to be adopted generally, had received some ancient documents on sheets of bamboo discovered in 279 in the tomb of a prince of the kingdom of Wei and dating from 299 B.C. Among these documents were the famous *Bamboo Annals* of the kingdom of Wei (*Chu-shu chi-nien*), of which only fragments have come down to us thanks to quotations in various works. However, it was mainly the moral crisis, perceptible by the end of the Han period, which, by provoking a renewal and deepening of political and philosophical reflection, directed intellectual life into new channels.

From the latter half of the second century onwards there had been a renascence of the currents of thought of the age of the Warring States (fourth and third centuries B.C.): Legalism, nominalism (the theory of the 'correctness of names', *cheng-ming,* that is, of the determination of statuses and social conditions), the metaphysically inclined Taoism of the *Lao-tzu.* But the point of view is quite different from that of the fourth and third centuries B.C.; the subjects for reflection which came to predominate in the first half of the third century A.D. concern the functional organization of society, its natural and necessary hierarchical shaping, the place of individuals in society as a whole, and their classification according to aptitudes and character. The idea that social order can only be assured when each is assigned the lot (*fen*) that suits him—a lot fixed by his individual destiny (*ming*)—was very generally shared by the thinkers of this period. We find it in Liu Shao (first half of the third century), the compiler of the *New Code* (*Hsin-lü*) of the Ts'ao Wei and author of a *Treatise on the Study of Character,* the *Jen-wu-chih,* in which Legalist concepts are closely associated with nominalist theories, and also in Kuo Hsiang (died in 312), the famous commentator on the *Chuang-tzu.* Wang Su (195–256), to whom we owe commentaries on the Classics which reject esoteric interpretations, is also preoccupied by the problem of social hierarchies.

One can see in these tendencies the influence of contemporary political conditions – Ts'ao Ts'ao and his successors had created a military dictatorship which was Legalist in inspiration – the influence, that is, of the theories which flourished so much in the Han period about the components of individual destinies, and also the influence of a particular administrative practice – the classification of candidates for public functions according to their behaviour and personality. This operation was the task of special magistrates (the *chung-cheng*) who summarizea their judgement in a short, incisive phrase. As early as the beginning of the third century the classification of personalities became one of the Chinese intelligentsia's favourite subjects of discussion in the free, disinterested talks known as 'pure conversations' (*ch'ing-t'an* or *ch'ing-i*). These conversations, in which the interlocutors vied with each other in producing witty remarks, amusing repartee, and polished epigrams, were gradually to extend their range from the study of character to literary, artistic, moral, and philosophical problems. The *ch'ing-t'an* became characteristic of the aristocratic coteries of the southern dynasties after the exodus of the early fourth century. Ancient examples of these 'pure conversations' have been preserved in a work of the first half of the fifth century, the *New Collection of Worldly Sayings* (*Shih-shuo hsin-yü*), by Liu I-ch'ing. On the other hand, a whole series of apologetics of the age of the southern dynasties was to borrow its form from the contemporary fashion for argumentative discussions. These treatises were one of the favourite weapons of the Buddhist literati and their adversaries in the fourth to sixth centuries, from the *Mou-tzu or Doubts Resolved* (*Mou-tzu li-huo-lun*), a work compiled in Vietnam and of unknown date but certainly one of the first of its kind, down to the *Hung-ming-chi,* a big collection of disputations which appeared about 510.

Running parallel to the Legalist and nominalist current so characteristic of the third century, a fresh interest had arisen since the end of the second century in the esoteric work ascribed to Lao-tzu (the *Tao-te-ching*) and in the *Chuang-tzu*. This interest resulted in the third century in a new philosophical tendency which associated with these two works the ancient Chou manual of divination (the *Chou I* or *I-ching, Book of Changes*). This was what is known as the School of Mysteries (*hsüan-hsüeh*), whose most famous representatives were Ho Yen (died in 249), author of a *Treatise on the Nameless* (*Wu-ming-lun*) and of a *Treatise on Inaction* (*Wu-wei-lun*); Wang Pi (226–49), a philosopher of genius who died at the age of twenty-three after writing commentaries on the *Lao-tzu* and the *I-ching*; Hsiang Hsiu (223?–300), author of a big commentary on the *Chuang-tzu* which was to be added by Kuo Hsiang (died in 312) to his own commentary; and P'ei Wei (267–300), to whom we owe a *Treatise on the Pre-eminence of Being* (*Ch'ung-yu-lun*). What interested the members of the School of Mysteries were metaphysical problems. Among those that they tackled were the relations between 'being' and 'non-being', which were conceived not as mutually exclusive opposites but as indissociable, since 'being', which is determined, nameable, changing and diverse, has as its necessary reverse side, its ontological support, fundamental 'non-being', which is the source of all visible phenomena. Other questions discussed include the primacy of 'being' or of 'non-being'; the presence or absence of passions in the Wise Man; the relations between thought and language; the nature of music, and so on.

These ontological speculations, which in someone like Kuo Hsiang were closely associated with Legalist and nominalist interpretations, were to enjoy lasting success after the exodus to the south of the years round 310; and they were given fresh life by Mahayana ('Great Vehicle') Buddhism during the course of the fourth century. The Mahayana doctrine of the fundamental unreality of all phenomena was bound to attract the devotees of 'pure conversations' and of debates on being and non-being, substance (*t'i*), and function (*yung*). For nearly a century its apparent analogies with the ideas of the School of Mysteries were to mask the basic differences of this foreign philosophy from Chinese traditions.

Individualism, freedom, aesthetics, and poetry

The gnostic and ontological speculations of the School of Mysteries, often combined in the third century with conservative social theories, drew their inspiration from the two great works of the Taoist thinkers of the age of the Warring States, but they do not reflect in any way the basic tendencies of the Taoist movement. On the contrary, this movement expressed itself, in the world of the literati, in nonconformist attitudes — contempt for rites, free and easy behaviour, indifference to political life, a taste for spontaneity, love of nature. Independence and freedom of mind, a horror of conventions, a passion for art for art's sake are characteristic of the whole troubled age from the third to the sixth century. It would be legitimate to say that a sort of 'aestheticism' was dominant throughout the Chinese Middle Ages. The first figures to show signs of these tendencies, which were so clearly opposed to the classical tradition, were the ones who were to be christened the 'Seven Sages of the Forest of Bamboo' (*chu-lin ch'i-hsien*), a little group of Bohemian literati, the best known of whom is the poet and musician Hsi K'ang (223–62). The same attitudes of mind, the same taste for nature and freedom persisted in aristocratic circles after the exodus to the valley of the Yangtze. We find them in the group headed by the famous poet and calligrapher Wang Hsi-chih (*c.* 307–65), with whose name is connected one of the most famous episodes in the history of Chinese literature and calligraphy, the gathering at the Orchid Pavilion (*lan-t'ing-hui*) at Kuei-chi (in the neighbourhood of the present-day Shao-hsing in Chekiang), where, after many a libation, forty-one poets competed at improvising poems.

From the *Nineteen Ancient Poems* (*Ku-shih shih-chiu-shou*), the first examples of lyric poems, dating almost certainly from the Later Han, until the seventh to ninth centuries, the golden age of classical poetry, the development of Chinese poetry was continuous and was marked by a series of great names. While the works of the famous poets of the Chien-an age (196-220) — the *Chien-an ch'i-tzu* — and those of their contemporaries Ts'ao Ts'ao and his sons (Ts'ao P'ei, 187-226 — Emperor Wen of the Wei — and Ts'ao Chih, 192-232) are still the poems of men engaged in military and political activities, faithful to the simple, vigorous, popular themes of the Han *Yüeh-fu,* the poetry of the fourth and fifth centuries bears witness to the political apathy and the quest for beauty for its own sake which are a sort of special mark of the period of the southern dynasties. Taoistic tendencies, already perceptible in Hsi K'ang (223-62) and Juan Chi (210-63), are to be found again in the great bucolic poet T'ao Ch'ien (T'ao Yüan-Ming) (365-427), while the landscape poet Hsieh Ling-yün (385-433) was one of the first to be influenced by Buddhism.

The interest devoted to nature as it appears in Taoist concepts — as the abode of the immortals, a holy place where one can lead a pure, free life sheltered from the compromises of the century — was at the root of the parallel enrichment of both poetic and pictorial traditions. It was the fourth or fifth century which saw the appearance — alongside figures belonging to the scholarly or Taoist tradition, genii and demons, and scenes of life inside palaces — of mountain landscapes. Thus landscape painting, dominated by the themes and conceptions of Taoism and still retaining the memory of its dealings with magic, but already responding to purely aesthetic concerns, makes its appearance in China more than a millenium before the period in which it was to develop, in a very different context, in Europe. Progress in the pictorial domain doubtless grew more rapid from the moment when painting ceased to be the work of craftsmen, as it had been in the Han period, and became, in conjunction with calligraphy, one of the favourite arts of cultivated circles. Colours grew more varied and new representational conventions appeared, permitting more complex compositions (multiplication of the points of view, representation of the distant and the near by staggering the different planes, and so on). One of the first and greatest painters was born twenty years before T'ao Ch'ien and forty years before Hsieh Ling-yün. His name was Ku K'ai-chih (345–406).

The primacy accorded to the aesthetic value of works of art, quite independently of any moral judgement, and the concern to analyse them critically and to classify them, were one of the great novelties of the Chinese Middle Ages. Notable progress in the refinement of taste and standards was made between the Ts'ao-Wei period and the Liang period. The first work of literary criticism is the *Tien-lun,* by the poet Ts'ao P'ei (beginning of the third century), in which the respective merits of works in prose and in verse of the Han period are compared. Ts'ao P'ei's judgements are already made from an exclusively literary point of view and the same attitude is adopted by the great Taoist master Ko Hung, who declares in his *Pao-p'u-tzu* (*c.* 317) that morality and beauty are independent of each other. Much later, in the first half of the sixth century, Chung Jung, a writer of the Liang period, tried in his *Shih-p'in* to distribute one hundred and twenty-three poems ranging from the Han to the Liang ages into three classes, complementing this classification with numerous critical notes. But it was above all the *Wen-hsin tiao-lung* (*The Literary Spirit and the Engraving of Dragons*) of Liu Hsieh, at the beginning of the sixth century, and the publication of the famous anthology called the *Wen-hsüan* (*c.* 530) which marked one of the great moments in the history of literary criticism in China. The *Wen-hsüan,* compiled by a prince of the imperial Liang family, has remained until our own day one of the main sources for the history of Chinese literature during the period from the First Han to the beginning of the sixth century.

These attempts at literary criticism were paralleled by similar efforts to analyse and criticize pictorial art. Thus we owe to Hsieh Ho, who lived at the end of the Southern Ch'i dynasty (479–502), a *Classified Catalogue of the Ancient Painters* (*Ku-hua-p'in*), which deals with the works of twenty-seven painters of the third to fifth centuries. Yao Tsui of the Ch'en period (557–89) produced a sequel to this catalogue, the *Hsü-hua-p'in,* in which twenty painters of the Liang period are examined.

While the fourth and fifth centuries and the first half of the sixth may be regarded as an age of maturity and of important innovations in the literary history of the southern dynasties, a kind of decadence set in under the Ch'en (557–89). It is doubtless to be explained by the political and social conditions prevalent in this period. There was a tendency to concentrate on research into form. A style based on semantic antitheses and phonetic harmony, the regular combination of phrases of four and six characters, triumphed in prose works of the sixth century. Known by the name of *p'ien-wen* (coupled phrases) or *ssu-liu-wen* (phrases of four or six characters), this style had distant antecedents in the prose of the end of the period of the Warring States and of the Han period, but in the sixth century it acquired an artificial, systematic character which it had never possessed before. Finally, mention must be made of the success, in a neighbouring field, of a mannered, erotic brand of poetry at the court of the last Ch'en emperor. Its principal practitioners were poets like Hsü Ling (507–83) and Chiang Tsung (519–94). It looks as if by then the living springs drawn upon by such poets as T'ao Ch'ien, Hsieh Ling-yün, and Yen Yen-chih had dried up. However, these formal experiments of a decadent period were not to be valueless; the poets of the T'ang period were able to make use of them in their synthesis of all previous traditions.

Taoist circles

The gnostic and ontological speculations which the devotees of the School of Mysteries pursued by combining the study of the *Lao-tzu* and the *Chuang-tzu* with that of the Classic of Divination, the *I-ching,* were not in fact very Taoist at all. These members of high society, lovers of 'pure conversations', had no contact with the real religious, learned, technical current of Taoism which had flowed on separately since antiquity and the Han age. A more or less secret current, authentic Taoism was centred on circles sometimes affiliated to the big Szechwan sect of the Five Bushels of Rice (*Wu-tou-mi-tao*), circles which were the repositories of revelations made by mediums and of traditions relating to the avatars of the saints. These circles were based on the transmission from master to disciple of the loftiest secrets of the sect. These milieux gave rise to a hagiographic literature, the oldest example of which is the *Lieh-hsien-chuan,* compiled by Liu Hsiang at the end of the first century B.C. This kind of literature was imitated by Buddhist monks and was to be greatly expanded over the years. It was also these milieux which produced collections of stories of the supernatural that enjoyed great success after the appearance of the *Sou-shen-chi* (*Treatise on the Pursuit of Spirits*) by Kan Pao (317–420). In course of time these collections amalgamated tales of popular or Buddhist origin with stories of Taoist origin.

However, the main aim of Taoist circles was the quest for procedures capable of prolonging life (*ch'ang sheng*), of nourishing the vital principle (*yang sheng*), and of sublimating the body. The search for drugs that would confer immortality gave rise to a long series of experiments which went on through the greater part of history. According to Joseph Needham, these experiments were responsible for some of the Chinese world's most important discoveries (among others, that of the procedures for hardening steel). One of the most ancient documents on the history of this Chinese alchemy, which dealt in its operations with mercury, lead, sulphur, gold, and silver, is the *Chou-i ts'an-t'ung ch'i,* which was written in the second century A.D. The tradition was given lustre at the beginning of the fourth century by one of the greatest names in the history of learned Taoism, Ko Hung (283–343?), author of a work on Taoist techniques, the *Pao-p'u-tzu* (c. 317), and of a collection of biographies of the immortals, the *Shen-hsien-chuan*. Ko Hung seems to have mastered in particular the pharmacopoeia, alchemy, medicine, and astronomy. He may have initiated himself into the secrets of the aboriginal peoples during the course of long stays in the tropical regions, especially Canton. Ko Hung's principal heir in South China was T'ao Hung-ching (456–536). He too was a man with an encyclopaedic turn of mind, who assimilated all the knowledge of his time—mathematics, the theory of *yin* and *yang,* geography, alchemy, medicine, the pharmacopoeia, and not only the 'scholarly' but also the Buddhist literary tradition. He was responsible for a commentary on an ancient treatise on the pharmacopoeia, the *Pen-ts'ao-ching chi-chu.* Ko Hung's influence was felt in North China by K'ou Ch'ien-chih (363–448), a well-known member of a rich Ch'ang-an family who claimed to be connected with the line of Celestial Masters (*t'ien-shih*) whose first patriarch had been Chang Tao-ling, founder of the sect of the Five Bushels of Rice. In 424 K'ou Ch'ien-chih entered into relations with the court of the Northern Wei and succeeded in gaining the ear of the emperor T'ai Wu Ti (424–51), in whom he claimed to recognize the reincarnation of a Taoist divinity. He cooperated with the great scholarly civil servant Ts'ui Hao, T'ai Wu Ti's adviser, in measures against the Buddhist clergy. But the influence of the rival religion was already making itself felt; K'ou Ch'ien-chih was responsible for the first Taoist monastic institutions, which were inspired by the rules of the Buddhist discipline. This period saw the birth and rise of a Taoist priesthood which was to be largely a copy of the Buddhist priesthood, with its own sacred texts, its temples, and its liturgy.

The great enthusiasm for Buddhism

In geographical range and in the number and diversity of the peoples which it affected, from the borders of Iran to Japan and from central Asia to Java, the expansion of Buddhism in Asia was a far more extensive phenomenon than the almost contemporary spread of Christianity in the western parts of the Eurasian continent. The abundance of written traditions, the diversity of schools, and the wealth of cultural elements that Buddhism bore along with it add to the complexity of the phenomenon.

When Buddhism began to penetrate the Chinese world in the first and second centuries A.D., it already possessed a long history, during the course of which it had become steeped in Iranian and Hellenistic influences, not to mention all it owed to the autochthonous substrata of northern and southern India. It continued to develop in the Buddhist countries outside China during the period when religious fervour was at its height in China (fifth to eighth centuries). But its subsequent transformations also concern the history of China, in so far as it became, in the forms which it took in Tibet from the eighth century onwards, the great religion of the mountaineers of the Himalayan complex and of the nomadic cattle-breeders of the steppes. It is thus essential to take account of this process of evolution and of the diverse origins of Buddhist influences in East Asia. Although the Buddhism which entered China was in essentials the Buddhism of the central Asian oases and of the regions to the south-east of the Amu-Darya, schools which at certain periods exerted a wide influence and were localized in Kashmir, Ceylon, Sumatra, or the valley of the Ganges also influenced doctrinal development in China itself.

There is also yet another factor to be considered: the great religion which had arisen in north-eastern India had to adapt itself in China to a civilization profoundly different from the one in which it had been born. Buddhism was able to become acclimatized in the Chinese world to the extent that certain of its components corresponded with preoccupations and traditions native to the different strata in Chinese society of the end of the Han period and subsequent ages. A Buddhist church — a relatively autonomous body — with its religious communities, its centres of worship, its estates, and its dependants grew up as a function of the divergent interests of the aristocracy, the peasant communities, and the state. Thanks to its social, political, and economic role, to its real hold over men's minds from about A.D. 400 to the beginning of the eleventh century, and to its secret but profound influence on intellectual life down to our own day, Buddhism has been one of the basic elements in the formation of the Chinese world. Its intrusion both enriched and overturned religious, philosophical, literary, and artistic traditions.

The penetration of Buddhism into China

Buddhism conquered the greater part of the Asiatic continent, by travelling along the commercial routes, carried with the great flow of trade. One path was the chain of oases connecting the oases of the Amu-Darya valley with Kansu; the other consisted in the maritime routes followed by the trade between the Indian Ocean and South-East Asia. The upsurge of trade through the interior of the continent and the development of maritime relations were almost contemporaneous and occurred from the beginning of the Christian era onwards.

However, there were other prerequisites. Buddhism, which was born at the end of the sixth century B.C. on the middle Ganges, had to enrich itself with new elements, to stop being simply a means of holiness restricted to men who had broken with the world, and to become a religion of universal salvation open to everyone. Other preconditions were the development of a hagiography, which, by putting a miraculous halo round the historical Buddha, appealed to the taste of lay believers (for example, the cycle of previous lives of Sakyamuni, the *jataka,* which illustrated the altruistic virtues of the great sage); the definition of other Buddha-figures like him (first and foremost the figure of Maitreya, the saviour to come); and the creation of forms of worship (for example, the cult of relics, of the great sage himself, and of the immortalized Buddhist saints, the *arhats*). This process of evolution took place within the sects that had arisen out of the Master's teaching. However, round about the start of the Christian era, in north-western India, it was to result in a big innovatory current which, breaking away and taking the name of Great Vehicle (Mahayana; in Chinese, *ta-ch'eng*), infinitely multiplied the number of religious figures (past, present, and future Buddhas belonging to innumerable worlds and Bodhisattvas, 'beings of awakening', who through compassion for human beings delay their own entry into Nirvana in order to convert them and to save them from the eternal pains of transmigration). Buddhism thus became a layman's religion which was adopted by the merchants of the great trading area extending from the valley of the Indus to the valley of the Amu-Darya.

The Iranian and Hellenistic influences which had mingled for so long in this region with Indian influences seem to have lent powerful aid to this process of evolution. It was almost certainly at this crossroads of different civilizations that the Buddha was first represented in human shape and that a sculpture of Hellenistic inspiration developed (the school of Gandhara, in the Peshawar region in the north of Pakistan, whose influence spread eastward, giving rise to the school of Mathura, between Delhi and Agra). It was in these regions that the shape of the reliquary (pagoda) was modified, gaining in height, and that the custom of carving Buddhist sculptures in rock grew up. Some of the most famous examples of these are to be seen in the caves of Bamiyan, to the north-west of Kabul.

The expansion under Asoka (272–236) of the Indian empire of the Maurya up to the Hindu Kush had already strengthened the roots which Buddhism had put down in these regions (Asoka's inscriptions in favour of Buddhism are written in a variant of Sanskrit, Prakrit, in Aramaic and in Greek). But it was the formation of the Kushan empire (the Kushans were Indo-Scythians, Yüeh-chih from Kansu and Tokhares; their empire flourished from 50 to 250 A.D.) that seems to have played a decisive part in the expansion of Buddhism in central Asia and into the Chinese world. This empire, the capital of which was the great crossroads of Peshawar (Purushapura), controlled north-western India, Kashmir, present-day Pakistan, Afghanistan, the eastern borders of Iran, and the oases of the Amu-Darya valley and of the western end of the Tarim valley. Chinese expansion in central Asia and the development of trade between the Tarim valley and the Yellow River valley were also to favour the penetration of Buddhist influence into China.

Historical circumstances thus explain both the preponderance in the Chinese world of the very different traditions emanating from the regions between the valley of the Indus and the eastern parts of Iran, from Transoxiania, from Kashmir, and from the oases of central Asia (mainly Khotan and Kucha) and at the same time the fact that Buddhist influences first made themselves felt in the commercial cities of North China and in urban society. The first translators of Buddhist texts into Chinese were not Indians but Parthians, Sogdians and Indo-Scythians, or people born in China or the Chinese borderlands of Sogdian or Indo-Scythian parents.

The first allusion to a Buddhist community in the Han empire dates from A.D. 65. From its very eastern site in northern Kiangsu it can be inferred that Buddhism had already taken root in the commercial and cosmopolitan cities of Kansu (Tun-huang, Chiu-ch'üan, Chang-yeh, Wu-wei) and in the capitals (Ch'ang-an and Loyang), where foreigners were numerous.

The arrival of Buddhism in China by the sea route seems to have been later. Sea trade between the Indian Ocean and South-East Asia, which was to be the cause of the Hinduization and 'Buddhization' first of the river basins of the Indo-Chinese peninsula, then of the coastal plains of Sumatra (Palembang region) and Java, explains the presence in the north of modern Vietnam (Hanoi area), at Canton and in the Yangtze valley of merchants and priests from the regions between the Indus and eastern Iran and later from various provinces of India and the island of Ceylon. However, this phenomenon does not seem to have become perceptible until after the establishment of the kingdom of Wu (222–80) on the lower Yangtze and the development of commercial activities in the geographical and human unit formed by the Red River valley in Vietnam and the plains of the Canton area. The presence of numerous foreigners at Chiao-chou (Hanoi region) is indicated at the beginning of the third

century, and one of the first translators of Indian texts into Chinese,
K'ang Seng-hui, who arrived at Nanking in 247, was born in Vietnam of
a family of Sogdian merchants who had settled in that country.

Acclimatization

The penetration of Buddhism into China and its adaptation to the
Chinese world was a complex phenomenon, the different aspects of
which seem to have been relatively independent of each other. This
foreign religion did not present itself by any means as a monolithic creed
composed of indissoluble elements, but simultaneously and pell-mell as
the worship of statues, as a hitherto unknown kind of monastic life, as a
series of moral precepts, as various different doctrines, as techniques of
concentration or ecstasy. Worship and piety on the one hand and doctrines and philosophy on the other at first developed without any connection with each other. It was certain aspects of Buddhism which particularly attracted attention because of the analogies with them which
certain traditions peculiar to various circles of Chinese society presented.
In the first few centuries of the Christian era this foreign religion was
regarded as a variety of Taoism, and in time the idea even developed that
Buddhism was the product of ancient Taoist influences — hence the
theme of the conversion of the barbarians by Lao-tzu. But important as
the role of Taoism was, it was in a much more general way all the
religious, moral, and philosophical traditions of the Chinese world that
contributed, thanks to certain analogies, to this vast phenomenon of
assimilation which also affected the whole social and political history of
the second to eighth centuries.

The earliest reliable evidence of the presence of Buddhism in China is
the mention in A.D. 65 of a community established in P'eng-ch'eng, a
commercial centre in northern Kiangsu, and founded by a member of the
imperial family. On the occasion of ceremonies which took place at the
Han court in 166 Buddha appeared in association with the Taoist divinity Huang-lao. Another text reveals the erection in 193, again at P'eng-
ch'eng, by a sort of minor local lord, of a temple in the Buddhist style
and at the same time mentions the practice of holding religious banquets
(*chai*) and the Buddhist ceremony of baptizing statues. These pieces of
evidence reveal devotional activities the early stages of which are by no
means clear; but the part which they played was almost certainly
decisive. This religion from the west attracted attention through novel
characteristics which cannot have failed to arouse the curiosity and attention of urban circles — standing, squatting, or recumbent statues adorned
with sumptuous garments and ornaments, ceremonies accompanied by

strange psalmodies, chants and music, shrines in the form of towers, the height of which was at variance with the horizontal style of Chinese architecture, masts on the top of buildings, and so on. Devotional activities pose a basic and wide-ranging problem, that of the assimilation of Buddhism by the Chinese world's forms of religious life. Neither the philosophical and doctrinal borrowings nor even the half-fearful veneration of the semi-barbarian monarchs of North China for wonder-working monks suffice to explain the general impulse of intense fervour felt by the Chinese world from the end of the fifth century onwards. In short they do not explain how Buddhism became in China a great *religion*. There took place at the level of local cults and communities a subterranean activity about which very little is known. The results alone were to emerge into the light when Buddhism had become a Chinese religion with its priesthood, its faithful, and its places of worship.

On the other hand, we are much better informed about the series of partial absorptions of the intellectual or technical elements which were borrowed from Buddhism, thanks to certain analogies, in the course of the first four centuries of our era. It is possible to draw up a list of these borrowings and of their Chinese equivalents:

1. The Buddhist doctrine of *karma* (retributive destiny in the form of transmigration) and the Chinese concept of the individual lot (*fen*) and destiny (*ming*).
2. The Mahayana doctrine of the fundamental emptiness of phenomena and the ontological speculations of the School of Mysteries about being and non-being.
3. Buddhist altruism, purity, and morality (the five main 'prohibitions' condemn the murder of living beings, theft, adultery, lying, and drunkenness) on the one hand and traditional Chinese morality on the other.
4. The monastic life and the Chinese ideals of the wise man who retires from public life and of the saint cut off from the world.
5. The practices of Buddhist yoga (*dhyana*) (counting one's breathing, contemplation of the body as an object of putrefaction, visualization of coloured images) and Taoist techniques of inducing trances and ecstasies.
6. Buddhist and Chinese thaumaturgy (divination, medicine, and magic).

The first Chinese adaptation of an Indian text (the *Sutra in 42 articles, Ssu-shih-erh-chang ching*) dates from about A.D. 100, and translating activities in Loyang and Ch'ang-an towards the end of the Han period were far from negligible (especially after the arrival in the capital in 148 of the Parthian monk An Shih-kao). A good deal of translation was also done in the Ts'ao-Wei empire (220–65). Nevertheless, it looks as if the influence of Buddhism was at first limited to a very restricted range of people, namely those in direct contact with the colonies of foreign merchants, which doubtless included a fair number of persons born in China and already more or less assimilated (several of the translators of the first few centuries A.D. belong to this category of bilingual immigrants conversant with two cultures). The only notable event in Buddhism's very first days in China was the discovery in the second century by Taoist circles that the imported religion possessed new techniques of meditation and concentration. This accounts for the fact that a considerable proportion of the first translations dealt with the practices of *dhyana* prescribed by the 'Lesser Vehicle' (Hinayana). But it was only about A.D. 300 – after the period (268–89) during which the Western Chin empire had maintained close relations with central Asia and after the arrival at Ch'ang-an in 284 of the monk-translator Chu Fa-hu (Dhar-maraksha), born about 230 at Tun-huang of Indo-Scythian parents – that certain doctrinal elements in the Greater Vehicle (Mahayana Buddhism) began to penetrate the aristocratic coteries of the capital. It was the very moment when the School of Mysteries was enjoying something of a triumph with Hsiang Hsiu and Kuo Hsiang. From this time onwards, and after the exodus of the Chinese upper classes to the Yangtze valley, we find the circles devoted to 'pure conversations' showing great interest in the Buddhist doctrine of the void and in the doctrines of retribution for one's deeds and of the permanence of the being through its successive transmigrations. Thanks to this purely philosophical interest in Buddhism on the part of aristocratic circles, a sort of osmosis occurred between the lay world and the first communities of monks. Scholarly monks with a good grasp of Chinese culture – the culture of that time, in which exegesis of the *Lao-tzu* and *Chuang-tzu* occupied an important place – were fairly common. The Chinese monk Chih Tun (314–66) (Chih Tao-lin), whose influence was great in southern Kiangsu and nothern Chekiang as well as in the capital, may be regarded as a typical example of these scholarly monks.

This philosophical Buddhism, a mixture of the traditions of the School of Mysteries and of gnostic and ontological speculations borrowed from the texts of the Greater Vehicle (the *Prajnaparamita* and the *Vimalakirti*), enjoyed a success that lasted until the end of the Eastern Chin (420). However, it was unknown in North China, where learned traditions from the western regions did not begin to take root until the end of the fourth century. After the troubles which led to the dismemberment of the Chin empire in the northern provinces and the formation of barbarian kingdoms, it was the court of the Later Chao sovereigns Shih Le (319–33) and Shih Hu (333–49) in south-western Hopei that emerged as the most important Buddhist centre. A monk by the name of Fo-t'u-teng, who was almost certainly of Kuchean origin and was much appreciated by the two barbarian tyrants for his powers as a soothsayer and magician, was at the root of this first upsurge of Buddhism in North China after the exodus of the early fourth century. Worship and devotion, magic and interest in the techniques of yoga characterized the sort of religion patronized by the brief and brutal dynasties of nomadic or Tibetan origin which had established themselves in these regions. However the patronage of the state was to permit the rise of monastic centres and the progress of Buddhist studies. After the middle of the fourth century Ch'ang-an became the main centre of these studies. The Chinese monk Tao-an (314–84), a disciple of Fo-t'u-teng summoned to Ch'ang-an in 349 by Shih Hu's successor, was one of the most important figures in the history of Chinese Buddhism. He was interested in the Lesser Vehicle's techniques of concentration (the *dhyana*), the doctrine of the universal void contained in the *Prajnaparamita* (the *Perfection of Wisdom*) and the history of earlier translations (he was responsible for the first catalogue of Buddhist works in Chinese, which is accompanied by bibliographical notes of great scientific value, the *Tsung-li chung-ching mu-lu,* containing 600 titles). He founded a cult of the Bodhisattva Maitreya and he was the first to draw up a set of monastic rules and to study the scholastic classifications of the Lesser Vehicle. He was also the first to have been concerned to define the proper meaning of Buddhism in relation to the intellectual traditions of China. His influence was to be as considerable in the north, where his Ch'ang-an school was to be carried on at the beginning of the fifth century by the great translator Kumarajiva, and in Yangtze China (Tao-an lived in the middle of the Han valley, at Hsiang-yang, from 365 to 379; he maintained relations with the Buddhist centres of the Eastern Chin empire and several of his disciples went to settle in the Yangtze valley).

The great upsurge of Buddhism in China

The beginning of the fifth century, to which lustre was lent by the two great names of Hui-yüan (334–417) in Yangtze China and Kumarajiva (350–413) in North China, may be regarded as one of the decisive turning-points in the history of Buddhism in China. It was then that Buddhism came of age in every domain of the extremely complex reality that every religion forms. Acquaintance with the great Indian and Kashmiri schools grew wider and more precise, the quality and worth of translations made remarkable progress, and the contributions of the Greater Vehicle were no longer confined to a collection of philosophical notions. The spirit of devotion and of communion between the lay and religious worlds which made Buddhism a great religion of salvation began to permeate the Chinese world. The early years of the fifth century also saw the beginnings of an organized priesthood endowed with precise rules, thanks to the translations of the great treatises on monastic discipline (*Vinaya*), and an increase in the number of voyages by Chinese monks going to 'seek the Law' (*ch'iu-fa*) in the 'Indianized' lands, that is, to learn from foreign masters and to bring back still unknown texts.

All this progress was largely the result of the slow process of maturing which had gone on ever since the Chinese world had come into contact with the great religion of the foreigners of central Asia and the borders of India and Iran. But the work of the two eminent monks mentioned above, the Kuchean Kumarajiva and the Chinese Hui-yüan, also had something to do with it.

Born in northern Shansi of a scholarly family, in his youth Hui-yüan had received a classical education in Honan. Converted by Tao-an, he soon became one of his most brilliant disciples. About 380 Hui-yüan went to live on Lu-shan, a famous mountain to the south of Chiu-chiang, where he founded in the Tung-lin monastery the most important centre of Buddhism in the Yangtze valley. He was in touch with cultivated circles among the aristocracy of the end of the Eastern Chin period and kept up a learned correspondence about points of doctrine with Kumarajiva. Interested by the techniques of concentration which in the monastic tradition are a means of attaining Wisdom (spontaneous reflection of absolute, non-discursive reality), he initiated his lay disciples in the use of icons and in practices of visualizing the Buddhas as a method of concentration within the capacity of laymen. In 402 Hui-yüan assembled his whole community, both monks and lay people, in front of an image of the Buddha Amitabha, and together they vowed to be reborn in the western paradise (Sukhavati, the Pure Land, *ching-t'u*) which is the habitation of this great figure of Mahayana Buddhism. This was the first demonstration of a belief shared by all the faithful, the first context in which Buddhism appears as a religion of universal salvation. One of the characteristics of Hui-yüan's teaching seems to have been the wish to make Chinese educated circles understand what constituted the essence of Buddhism and distinguished it radically from the religious and intellectual traditions of the Chinese world.

Born at Kucha of a family of nobles of the oasis, Kumarajiva had been to study in Kashmir, where the Hinayana traditions of Sarvastivadin scholasticism and the practices of Buddhist yoga (the *dhyana*) were dominant. He had been converted to the Greater Vehicle in Kashgar. Returning to Kucha, he had been taken prisoner there by Lü Kuang, a general of the powerful Earlier Chin empire, who kept him at Wu-wei (Liang-chou) for seventeen years. When Yao Hsing, the 'Tibetan' sovereign of the Later Chin and a convert to Buddhism, conquered Kansu in 401, he seized this eminent monk and in the following year took him to his capital, Ch'ang-an. From this time onwards Kumarajiva organized and directed a team of translators whose activities extended to almost every domain of the vast collection of Buddhist scriptures. The great Mahayana sutras were translated or retranslated more accurately, and Chinese versions of treatises on discipline, manuals of *dhyana* and big scholastic and metaphysical works were produced. One of Kumarajiva's greatest titles to fame is to have made known in China the Madhyamika school of philosophy which had arisen out of the Greater Vehicle in the third or fourth century and was based on a sort of dialectic. According to this school, what is true from the point of view of the absolute is false from the point of view of the truths of appearance, and vice versa. It is constant recourse to this dialectic between the absolute and the phenomenal that makes it possible to arrive at the total liberation of the mind which is the very object of Buddhism.

Thus the age of Hui-yüan and Kumarajiva marks the point of departure of learned Buddhism conscious of its own originality and at the same time of a Buddhist piety that was to develop widely in all layers of Chinese society from the fifth to the eighth century. The beginning of the fifth century saw the emergence of the great religious figures of East Asian Buddhism, to which some of the most famous sutras of the Greater Vehicle correspond: the Bodhisattvas Maitreya (Mi-le), Avalokitesvara (Kuan-shih-yin or Kuan-yin), Manjusri (Wen-shu-shih-li), Samantabhadra (P'u-hsien); and the Buddhas Amitabha (A-mi-t'o fo) and Bhaishajyaguru (Yao-shih ju-lai). From this time onwards the religious currents began to form which were to give birth in the sixth to eighth centuries to truly Chinese Buddhist sects.

The year 440 may be regarded as an important date in the political and religious history of North China, for from then onwards the great Tabgatch empire of the Wei had direct access to the routes across central Asia. After a brief period (424–48) during which the court of the Northern Wei favoured the young Taoist Church sponsored by the celestial master K'ou Ch'ien-chih, Buddhism tended to become a sort of state religion. About 470 the monk T'an-yao was appointed head of the Buddhist priesthood and at the same period a special class of laymen depending directly on the church was instituted (the 'families of the Samgha', *seng-ch'i-hu*). Work on the famous Buddhist caves and sculptures of Yün-kang, to the west of Ta-t'ung, the capital, began in 489. After the transfer of the capital from Ta-t'ung to Loyang in 494, the new city became the most important Buddhist centre in Asia. It was at this time, so it seems, that Buddhist fervour reached its zenith both in the north and in the Yangtze valley. This period of intense faith, which was the period of empress Wu of the Northern Wei and of the 'Bodhisattva emperor' Wu of the Liang (first half of the sixth century), lasted until the reign of the empress Wu Tse-t'ien (690–705).

Religion, society, and religious policy

The curiosity displayed by the aristocratic coteries from about 300 onwards, the favours granted to the monks by sovereigns of barbarian origin such as Shih Hu (334–49) in North China, the first translations of Indian texts, and the first conversions did not imply the existence of a general movement of great fervour. On the contrary, when China began to be dotted with storeyed towers (stupa, *t'a*) and sanctuaries, when numerous Buddhist caves were carved out of rock, when the number of the faithful multiplied rapidly and the first mystical suicides took place (from the end of the fourth century onwards), the phenomenon had changed not simply in scale but in character. To understand this, we must consider the facts of social morphology—quarters of towns and villages, groups dependent on the great families, Chinese religious associations for making sacrifices to the God of the Soil (*she*), wider communal groupings (*i*). Conversion was not first and foremost a matter of individual conscience, but adhesion to a group of believers or to the community of monks. Far from replacing ancient forms of religious life, Buddhism infiltrated traditional groupings and created new ones modelled on them. That is how it became so thoroughly sinicized. The crucial event was this redistribution of the social mass round new places of worship (monasteries, sanctuaries, hermitages, places of pilgrimage), a change which had, besides the religious aspect, political, economic, intellectual, and artistic ones as well.

Buddhism adapted itself in the south to a society characterized by the power of an aristocracy with estates and groups of clients. The monasteries, with their domains and their families of dependants, modelled themselves on the secular world. In the north, on the contrary, the strength of the central power led Buddhism to seek the support of sovereigns who were the source of all favours. These social and political peculiarities explain why in the Yangtze valley and in South China the great Buddhist centres were dispersed (apart from Nanking, there were centres at Chiang-ling, Hsiang-yang, Lu-shan near Lake P'o-yang, in the Suchow region, the Shao-hsing area in Chekiang, the Canton region in the extreme south, Mount Emei in Szechwan, and so on), while in North China they corresponded with the capitals. It was not by chance that in the south a great monk like Hui-yüan (334–417) proudly asserted the Church's independence of the political power (his *Treatise explaining the reasons why monks are not obliged to pay homage to sovereigns, Sha-men pu-ching wang-che lun,* dates from 404), while Fa-kuo (who died in 419), director-general of the Buddhist priesthood with the Northern Wei, sought to identify the emperor with the actual person of the Buddha. The tendency to integrate the Buddhist church in the state made itself clearly evident on several occasions in North China during the fifth and sixth centuries. The reunified China of the Sui and T'ang inherited this double tradition – aristocratic and centralizing – in the field of religious policy, and it was the tendency towards a Draconian reduction of the clergy and its strict control – a tendency which manifested itself under the Northern Wei in 446 and under the Northern Chou in 574 – that finally triumphed in the ninth century.

Favoured by the political powers, the Buddhist church sought at the same time to assert its independence of the state (Hui-yüan, at the beginning of the fifth century, was the first to lay down the principle of the clergy's autonomy): the monks were not subject to the common jurisdiction either in the field of penal law or in the field of public obligations (forced labour, taxes, and capitation dues). Moreover, the Church's property was considered to be inalienable and was protected against any appropriation by prohibitions of a religious nature. These privileges implied in return respect for the monastic rules (tonsure, celibacy, observance of religious vetoes) and knowledge of the sacred rites and texts. While sponsoring the new religion and taking the initiative in pious acts (ordinations of priests, foundations of monasteries, various gifts and so on), the political authorities strove for their part to exercise some control over the Buddhist church, but the upsurge of this faith was so general and so powerful from the fifth century onwards that the phenomenon was to be at the root of numerous economic and political difficulties before which states in most cases found themselves powerless. The excessively large number of fictitious ordinations, which deprived the state of part of its income, of its labour force and of its soldiers, the growth in the number of peasants who sought the protection of the monasteries, the cornering of land through gifts or simulated sales, the very considerable expenses incurred in building, the upkeep of the priests and the organization of festivals, the shortage of metals caused by the casting of statues and bells, the economic power of the monasteries, which owned vast areas of cultivated fields and mountain land, water-mills and oil presses, the hidden power of the monks in touch with the imperial gynaeceum and the aristocracy, who were involved in all kinds of intrigues, the damage done to traditional morality by Buddhism (excessive expenditure, breaking of family ties, dispensation from duties to the state), the subversive character of certain sects – all these misdeeds due to the new religion's hold on people were periodically denounced by those civil servants who were most conscious of the interests of the state. This explains the efforts made from time to time to reduce the number of priests and monks and to restrict the amount of property owned by the Church. These efforts were known by the Buddhists themselves as the 'four persecutions' (under the Northern Wei in 446, under the Northern Chou in 574, under the T'ang in 842–45 and under the Later Chou in 955). The first two of these attempts to control Buddhism took place in North China, where they were encouraged by Taoist circles, who were jealous of the privileges enjoyed by the Buddhist church. The third took place, in the T'ang age, in a very different context, that of a 'nationalist' movement and of a reaction against the foreign influences which had permeated the Chinese world so widely during the course of the Middle Ages and in the first part of the T'ang period.

The pilgrimages

The written Buddhist traditions which had arrived in China had no coherence at all and came from various different sects or schools of the Greater and Lesser Vehicles. Moreover, the first translations, in which the authors had often made use of equivalents borrowed from Taoist traditions, were incomplete and difficult to read. Commentaries originally delivered orally were sometimes incorporated in them. These deficiencies and defects were to be felt more acutely when, at the end of the fourth century, people began to appreciate the extraordinary diversity of Buddhism. This was the essential reason for the pilgrimages; it was necessary to establish the true doctrine and to bring back from the 'Buddhist kingdoms' a larger number of texts. Thus the term 'pilgrimage', which evokes the idea of journeys made to holy places out of pure devotion, is scarcely adequate to describe the Chinese holy men's long travels across Asia. The attraction of the holy places and of the great sites in the history of Buddhism in north-eastern and north-western India was in fact to play only a secondary role in the vast pilgrimage movement, which was at its height from the end of the fourth century to the beginning of the ninth.

The first Chinese pilgrim known to us was one Chu Shih-hsing, who went to study in Khotan in 260 and remained there until his death. About the same time the famous translator Chu Fa-hu (Dharmaraksha) went on a journey to the oases of central Asia and returned to Ch'ang-an in 265. However most of those who journeyed westward at the end of the third century and during the course of the fourth remain unknown. It seems probable that the great monk Tao-an, who died in 385, drew on information furnished by the pilgrims of this period when he wrote his *Treatise on the Western Lands (Hsi-yü-chih)*. However, it was only from about A.D. 400 onwards that journeys by Chinese priests to central Asia and India grew frequent. The first pilgrim to gain fame by leaving an account of his extensive travels in the oasis region, India, and South-East Asia was Fa-hsien. Leaving Ch'ang-an in 399, when he was over sixty years of age, he was to visit Kucha, Khotan, Kashgar, Kashmir, the Kabul area, the Indus valley, and the cities on the Ganges. Taking ship at Tamralipti, a port on the Bay of Bengal, he landed in Ceylon and then at Sri Vijaya (near present-day Palembang, on the east coast of Sumatra). On the voyage home to Canton in 412 he was carried off course to the coast of Shantung. Bringing back with him numerous manuscripts, some of which he was to translate in Nanking with the Indian monk Buddhabhadra, Fa-hsien wrote an account of the fifteen years which he had spent in more than thirty kingdoms. This account is the *Fo-kuo-chi, Report on the Buddhist Kingdoms,* also known as the *Narrative of Fa-hsien (Fa-hsien chuan)*. It is the only description of travels in this age to have been preserved in its entirety. Most of the other journals written in the fifth and sixth centuries have either been lost or exist only in fragmentary form. Fragments of the *Li-kuo-chuan (Report on the Kingdoms Visited)* by Fa-yung, a Southern Sung monk who set out in 420 with twenty-five companions via Szechwan for the oases of central Asia and returned to China via the Indian Ocean, South-East Asia, and Canton, have come down to us. But nothing remains of the *Wai-kuo-chuan (Report on Foreign Kingdoms)* of Chih-meng, who left Ch'ang-an in 404 with fifteen other monks and returned to Wu-wei, in Kansu, in 424. But for the information which has been preserved by chance in the famous description of the monasteries of Loyang dated 547, the *Loyang ch'ieh-lan chi* by Yang Hsien-chih, we should have no precise information about the mission of Sung Yün, the ambassador sent by the Wei empress Hu, a religious fanatic, to a kingdom in north-western India. Leaving Loyang in 518 in the company of some Chinese monks, Sung Yün travelled via the territory of the Tu-yü-hun, Lobnor and the oasis of Khotan to the regions west of Kashmir — Udyana and Gandhara — and to the upper Indus Valley, where he stayed for two years. He was back in the Northern Wei capital in 522. His own account of his journey, the *Sung Yün chia-chi,* has disappeared.

The notes made on their travels by the Chinese pilgrims who went to

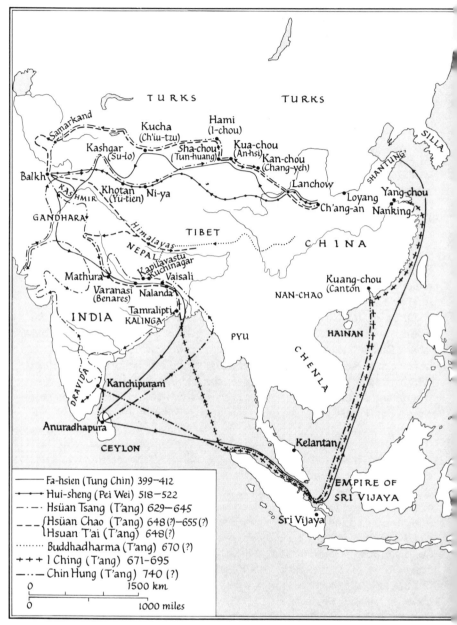

Map 12 Principal pilgrimages of Chinese Buddhist monks to India

central Asia, Kashmir, the north of present-day Afghanistan, the Ganges and Indus plains, southern India, Ceylon, Sumatra and the other countries of South-East Asia are, thanks to their precision and accuracy, our most valuable source for the history of these areas between the beginning of the fifth century and the end of the eighth. But for Fa-hsien's memoranda, the information collected in the *Shui-ching-chu* — historico-geographical commentaries compiled under the Northern Wei by Li Tao-yüan (?–527) at the beginning of the sixth century — that crucial work on Indian civilization in the seventh century, the *Shih-chia fang-chih,* completed in 650 by the monk Tao-hsüan (596–667), and the detailed notes of the pilgrims of the seventh and eighth centuries, we should know practically nothing of the history of 'Indianized' Asia at the beginning of our own Middle Ages.

Buddhist translations and literature in Chinese

The translation of Indian Buddhist texts (in Sanskrit, Prakrit, or Pali) into Chinese extended over nearly ten centuries. The first translations date from the second half of the second century, the last from the eleventh century. They cover all the Buddhist schools of India and of the countries converted to Buddhism and constitute a very considerable body of texts: about forty million Chinese characters and 1692 different works, some of which were translated several times at different periods. This literature is the richest and most extensive source of sutras (sermons attributed to the Buddha), treatises on discipline, commentaries, and scholastic texts that exists in all the various Asian languages which served as vehicles for the Buddhist scriptures.

After a first period of groping which produced the *Ancient Translations (ku-i),* when the versions were too free through making too many concessions to the Chinese public or clumsy and almost incomprehensible through being too literal, accuracy and style made great progress with the translating team assembled round the Kuchean monk Kumarajiva at the beginning of the fifth century, and later on with the team formed by Paramartha (Chen-ti, 500–69), an Indian monk who had stayed for a while in Cambodia and had been summoned from Canton to Nanking by the Liang emperor Wu in 548. This was the period of the *Old Translations (chiu-i).* A third stage was to be reached with the seventh-century translators, who developed a uniform terminology and a technical exactitude which, however, rob the *New Translations (hsin-i)* made in the T'ang period (seventh to ninth centuries) of the literary interest provided by the works of the previous period.

It seems that from the start the translating teams were assembled according to the principles in force in the fifth to eighth centuries: they were composed of a relatively large number of members, both priests and laymen, Chinese and foreigners (the tasks of each member tending no doubt to be more and more strictly defined), who translated the originals aloud, noted the translations down in writing, checked the accuracy of the sense, polished the style, and lastly made sure that the translation in its final form was accurate.

Prefaces, epilogues, colophons, and bibliographical lists give us valuable information about the conditions in which the texts were translated, about the men who introduced them into China, about the traditions surrounding the works themselves, their authors, and the Buddhist schools and sects of India and of the countries converted to Buddhism. It is thanks to these data, which bear witness to the deep-rooted liking of the Chinese for historical precision and exactitude, that we have been able to reconstruct the history of Buddhism in Asia. Between 515 and 946 no less than fourteen bibliographical catalogues of Buddhist translations in Chinese were compiled. They are accompanied by critical notes and various pieces of information. The most famous and the most precise are that of the monk Seng-yu (the *Ch'u-san-tsang chi-chi,* 515), which brings up to date the catalogue – now lost – of Tao-an (374), and that of the monk Chih-sheng (the *K'ai-yüan shih-chiao mu-lu*), one of the masterpieces of Chinese bibliography.

As well as the actual translations of Indian texts there is an abundant Buddhist literature in Chinese, which grew up from the fourth century onwards. It consists of works on the history of Buddhism in India and China, commentaries on canonical texts, collections of biographies of Chinese monks, histories of Chinese sects, apocryphal sutras, and so on. This huge production of religious texts, consisting both of translations and of works written in China itself, could not fail to influence Chinese secular literature.

Buddhism's contributions to the Chinese world

In the regions between India and Iran, Hellenistic influences had remained perceptible enough to exert a strong influence on Buddhist art, which, originally symbolic, became figurative. Thus an art consisting of a mixture of Indian, Greek, and Iranian influences spread from the Indus and Ganges valleys to the oases of central Asia, and from there to North China, Korea, and Japan. The distant memory of Greek sculpture preserved in the folds of the drapery, the poses and the faces of certain Chinese and Japanese Buddhist statues is one of the finest proofs of the unity of our world.

As well as sculpture, an architectural technique peculiar to the Indo-Iranian borders and to India also reached northern China, namely the technique of hollowing caves out of rock. These rock sanctuaries of India, Afghanistan, and central Asia—the Bamiyan site to the north-west of Kabul is one of the most famous examples—were noted by Fa-hsien on his pilgrimage at the beginning of the fifth century, by Sung Yün on the occasion of his mission to northern India at the beginning of the sixth century, by Hsüan-tsang at the beginning of the T'ang period, and by others. The first caves in the Thousand Buddha complex (*Ch'ien-fo-tung*) near Tun-huang must have been started in 366. Between the fifth and eighth centuries rock sanctuaries, the sometimes colossal statues of which have often been carved from the rock itself, multiplied in North China from Szechwan to Shantung and from Kansu to Hopei. The most beautiful and imposing of these sanctuaries, often built at the instigation of the emperors but with the collaboration of the faithful, testify, like the cathedrals of Europe, to the huge movement of religious fervour which took hold of the Chinese world in those ages. Good examples are the caves of Yün-kang, to the west of Ta-t'ung, where work went on from 489 to 523 and started again at the end of the Sui period (the biggest statues there are 130 to 160 feet tall); the caves of Lung-men, to the south of Loyang—the new capital of the Northern Wei, after Ta-t'ung, from the last few years of the fifth century onwards—where work went on almost continuously throughout the sixth and seventh centuries (the great Vairocana of Lung-men and his two acolytes were completed between 672 and 675); and the caves of Mai-chi-shan, near T'ien-shui in Kansu. But besides these three famous sites a long series of Buddhist grottoes was hollowed out of the rock in North China under the Wei, Ch'i, Chou, Sui and T'ang dynasties, during the course of the great period of Buddhist sculpture and architecture in China. The different influences emanating from Taxila, Mathura, the oases of Khotan, Kucha, Turfan, and so on doubtless explain the variations of style that can be noted from one site to another. Most of these sites preserve traces of later work dating from the Five Dynasties, the Sung and the Yüan—evidence of declining fervour and of an art that had lost some of its impetus and vigour.

The sides of caves and the walls of monasteries provided the surfaces for religious paintings (scenes from the Buddha's earlier life, Buddhist divinities, pictures of hell, and so on), the only important examples of which to survive damp and vandalism are to be found in the caves of the Thousand Buddhas (Ch'ien-fo-tung) near Tun-huang. A few paintings from the fifth and sixth centuries also exist in Astana, near Turfan. This popular art, influenced by central Asia and north-western India, helps us

Plate 31.   Ta-t'ung caves: Buddha in niche between grotto entrance and upper clerestory window

Plate 32.   Laughing Buddha, Ling-yin Ssu temple, near Hangchow

Plate 33.   Ta-t'ung caves: the Great Buddha, surrounded by Bodhisattvas

Plate 34.   Chien-fo-tung, near Tun-huang: detail from a Buddhist cave

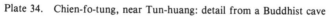

to imagine what the great Buddhist pictorial tradition was like—the tradition rendered illustrious by famous artists such as Wu Tao-hsüan (Wu Tao-tzu) (born *c.* 680), who was responsible for religious frescoes in the monasteries of Ch'ang-an.

Just as the Buddhist painting, so widespread in the fifth to eighth centuries, has left very slight traces, so there remain only a few examples of the most ancient Buddhist architecture, although the pattern of certain temples of the seventh and eighth centuries has been piously preserved in Japan. One of the most distinctive kinds of Buddhist buildings in China is, as is well known, the stupa (*t'a*) or pagoda, the only tall structure to be found in Chinese architecture. It takes the form of a storeyed tower or, more rarely, of an upturned bowl. The pattern evolved considerably in the course of centuries. Built at first of wood (second and third centuries), often of brick or masonry, sometimes of iron under the Sung, the stupa or pagoda was generally tetragonal in shape until the T'ang; later it became octagonal or decagonal. It had a varying number of storeys, the height of which diminished regularly from the base to the summit or else remained the same (tenth century). The most famous of these structures, such as the one nearly four hundred feet high erected in the Yung-ning-ssu at Loyang at the beginning of the sixth century, have all disappeared. Almost the only examples worth mentioning of really old ones that have survived until our own day are the stone stupa of the Sung-yüeh-ssu at Sung-shan (*c.* 520) and the two masonry stupa of Hsi-an erected in the T'ang capital in the seventh century.

No doubt we should not attach too much importance to the general effects of religious festivals and shows on the development of artistic activities. The point that has been made in connection with medieval Christianity is equally true of Buddhism: numerous artists, painters, metal-workers, sculptors, and architects lived on the commission given to them by monasteries, lay communities, or rich individual believers. Buddhist processions and shows, illuminations in the caves, periodical exhibitions of the treasures preserved in the big sanctuaries all served simultaneously to spread the faith, its legends and its essential dogmas, to strengthen social cohesion and religious feeling through activities involving the collaboration and participation of each individual, and to form a completely new aesthetic world. We can attribute to Buddhism a deep and general transformation of sensibility: the new religion introduced into the Chinese world a taste for ornamentation, for the tireless repetition of the same motifs (a religious practice which was to give birth to wood engraving), a taste for the sumptuous (statues coated with gold, precious cloths, and so on), but also for the gigantic, the colossal. All these tendencies were in opposition to the classical tradition, which aimed at stripping away inessentials, at vigorous conciseness, at exactness of line and movement.

The step from art to literature is an easy one to take and what is true of one is true of the other. The tendencies are identical and the enrichment just as considerable. The great Buddhist sutras of the Mahayana, which were much more widely diffused in fifth- to ninth-century China than the Classics, accustomed people to a longer-winded literature, to the repetition of the same themes, to the mixture of verse and prose; and Buddhist poetry, with its freer pace, influenced the development of Chinese poetry. Buddhism not only enriched the content of literature, bringing innumerable themes borrowed from the previous lives of the Buddha, from accounts of descents to hell, from the pilgrimages, from the stories of the great figures of Buddhism; it also gave birth to new literary genres—public sermons, conversations between master and lay or priestly disciples, representations of edifying scenes in which psalmody alternated with song. It thus contributed to the development of a literature in the vernacular and to the subsequent rise of the story, the novel, and the drama.

With the general triumph of Buddhism, the picture of the world itself was transformed into a vista of immeasurable, infinitely multiplied times and spaces, of a human destiny involved in a continuous cycle of rebirths intermingling the beings of the visible and invisible worlds (gods, men, beings of the underworld, animals and demons) and ineluctably subject to the mysterious phenomenon of the fructification of actions.

However, among the elements of Indian culture—sometimes coloured by Iranian and Hellenistic influences—which Buddhism carried along with it, the secular sciences of India certainly occupied a far from negligible place. Indian mathematics, astrology, astronomy, and medicine penetrated into the Chinese world between the fourth and eighth centuries thanks to translations of 'brahminical' works, the Chinese and Indian versions of which have unfortunately disappeared. An Indian medical work which dealt with 404 diseases figured among the translations made by the Parthian An Shih-kao, who arrived in Loyang in A.D. 147. The monk I-hsing (683–727), who in 721–25 organized a scientific expedition intended to note the length of the shadow on a sun-dial at the winter and summer solstices at nine points ranging from the centre of Vietnam to the frontiers of Mongolia (i.e., from the seventeenth to the fortieth parallel of latitude), was versed in Indian mathematics and astronomy. The influence of Indian science was to make itself particularly felt from about 600 to the middle of the eighth century.

The example of the Indians, past masters in grammar and phonetics, succeeded in stimulating an analysis of the sounds of the Chinese language, in spite of the insurmountable obstacles which seemed to be presented by the system of writing. The problems posed by the transcription of Indian terms and the need to reproduce as faithfully as possible the magic formulas of esoteric Buddhism (*mantra* and *dharani*) were also to contribute to the development of the study of phonetics in China. The notation of the pronunciation of the Chinese characters by means of other characters which gave the initial and the final letters (the *fan-ch'ieh* system) is attributed to Sun Yen of Wu (died *c.* 260) and no doubt developed without any Indian influence, but this is not the case with later researches. Those devoted to the rhyming system during the years 424–53 resulted with Shen Yüeh (441–513) in the first definition of the tones of old Chinese: the equal, ascending, descending, and 'returning' tones (words with a final occlusive). These researches made it possible to determine more strictly the rules for the composition of poems and were at the root of a whole series of dictionaries of rhymes:

> *Ch'ieh-yün* by Lu Fa-yen (601)
> *T'ang-yün* by Sun Mien (751)
> *Kuang-yün* by Ch'en P'eng-nien, printed in 1008
> *Chi-yün* by Ting Tu (53,525 characters); middle of the eleventh century
> *Wu-yin chi-yün* by Han Tao-chao of the Chin (1115–1234)

It was partly these valuable documents that were to provide the basis for the development, from the middle of the sixteenth century onwards, of learned research into historical phonology.

Finally, it should be noted – in a quite different field – that monastic circles served as the intermediary for the implantation in the Chinese world of certain financial institutions of Indian origin – loans on security, financial associations for the fructification of capital put into a common stock, auction sales, and, at a later date, lotteries.

To sum up, the contribution of Buddhism to China during the great period of contacts between the Chinese and Indian worlds (from the first few centuries of the Christian era to the ninth) would seem to be of the first importance, and during the whole period in which the monasteries, with their fine libraries of classical and religious works, were the main centres of instruction and knowledge one can speak of a positively Buddhist culture. This situation, which was to last longer in Japan, persisted in China until the great proscription of Buddhism and the dispersal of the religious communities in the years 842–45.

Part 4

From the Middle Ages
to Modern Times

Chapter 11

The Aristocratic Empire

The period which opened at the end of the sixth century and which was still completely immersed in its early days in what might be called the 'Chinese Middle Ages', to which it was linked by its men — aristocrats and dependants (*k'o, pu-ch'ü, nu-pi*) — its economy, its literature and art, its religious faith — for the T'ang period is reckoned to be the golden age of Buddhism — was in fact destined to be the period of transition from the medieval world to 'modern times' in East Asia. The signs heralding the changes to come were apparent immediately after An Lu-shan's great military rebellion, which lasted from 755 to 763. For this reason no account has been taken in this book of the traditional division into 'dynasties', which is based on the mystical notion of royal line, and the T'ang age has been broken up into two parts, with the second closely tied to the one that immediately follows it. For in fact it was not only the general atmosphere that changed after the rebellion but also the political climate, the economy, the institutions, and so on. The period known as the Five Dynasties, from 907 to 960, was only the logical continuation and result of the process of evolution which had begun at the end of the eighth century. The 'aristocratic empire', the foundations of which were established between 590 and 625, was succeeded by a period of 'transition to modern times'.

Because the accession of the Sui in 581 put an end to the empires of non-Chinese origin in North China and was followed, eight years later, by the reunification of all the Chinese lands, it is usually regarded as one of the great dates of history. But by putting the emphasis on political events of this sort traditional historiography achieves two contradictory results: it masks certain fundamental elements of continuity and at the same time it neglects the most profound and significant changes. Neither the usurpation of power by General Yang Chien (541–604) in the Northern Chou empire nor the accession to the throne of the Li family, founders of the T'ang dynasty in 618, was accompanied by radical changes in political personnel, type of society, or basic traditions. In any case the concepts of ethnic and cultural purity are myths; the empires of the Sui (581–617) and T'ang (618–907), which are normally regarded as genuinely Chinese as opposed to the barbarian kingdoms and empires of the fourth to sixth centuries, were based at the start on the political, social, ethnic, and cultural foundations of the already strongly sinicized empires of the Western Wei (535–57) and Northern Chou (557–81). On the other hand, it was the middle of the T'ang age and the end of the eighth century that saw the start of the great changes which were to give birth in the eleventh century to a world even more different from that of the sixth and seventh centuries than Renaissance Europe was from medieval Europe.

It is true that the reunion of Yangtze China with North China widened the vista, giving Sui and T'ang China an opening on the sea, the tropical zone, and the countries of South-East Asia. It is also true that the T'ang took over the valuable heritage of the literary and artistic traditions of the Nanking dynasties. But this reunion of North and South did not take place abruptly; the way had been prepared during the whole of the sixth century by progress in economic relations and human contacts, by the exchange of merchandise, men, and ideas. The Loyang of the first thirty years of the sixth century and the Nanking of the Liang emperor Wu belonged to the same golden age of medieval civilization, to the same aristocratic world animated by intense religious fervour, vitalized by the reawakening of the merchant economy, and permeated by the great commercial currents which flowed along the trails of central Asia and the sea routes of the Indian Ocean. Moreover, it is false to ascribe all the credit for the political reunification to the Sui dynasty alone; Szechwan was attached to the Western Wei empire as early as 553, and Hupei, where the Wei installed one of their creatures in the same year, also virtually formed part of it. The unification of North China, divided and ravaged by wars since about 534, must be put down to the Northern Chou, in 577. When the Sui destroyed the enfeebled Ch'en empire in 589, all they did was to carry to its inevitable conclusion a process which had begun thirty-six years earlier and one of the main factors in which was undoubtedly the worth of the military institutions created by the Western Wei.

The political history of the period 581-683

The Sui dynasty (581-617) was founded at Ch'ang-an after a *coup d'état* by General Yang Chien, leader of the aristocracy of the Wei valley and eastern Kansu and a relation by marriage of the reigning family of the Northern Chou. Yang Chien reigned from 581 to 604 under the name of Emperor Wen and in 589 put an end to the Ch'en empire, the last remnant of the Six Dynasties which had succeeded each other at Nanking since the beginning of the third century. Tradition contrasts him with his son, whom it paints in the blackest colours: usurping the imperial power, the emperor Yang (605-17) is supposed to have been led to destruction by his *folie de grandeur,* his taste for luxury, his vices, and his cruelty to the people. He is reproached for the big public works which he undertook and for his costly campaigns in Korea. But this is one of the favourite themes of official historiography: the last sovereign of a dynasty can only be a target for abuse. In fact the policy of the two Sui emperors displays a remarkable continuity, and the efforts which they made were to be continued at the beginning of the following dynasty. The construction of big canals and of huge granaries in the neighbourhood of Loyang and Ch'ang-an (Ta-hsing-ch'eng) began in the reign of the first Sui emperor, Wen, one of whose first undertakings was to build the two immense capitals of the Wei and Lo valleys. Great Walls 350 kilometres (220 miles) in length were built in the north-west in 585. The policy of maritime expansion which characterizes the reign of the emperor Yang (construction of a navy, development of Yang-tu, use of modern Yangchow as a second capital, expeditions to Formosa or the Ryukyu Islands, to Ch'ih-t'u-kuo in the region of Palembang in Sumatra, to Lin-i, later known by its Indian name of Champa, on the east coast of southern Vietnam) had already been initiated under Wen Ti. The first land and sea expedition against the Korean kingdom of Koguryo, a virtual ally of the Turks, took place in 598, thirteen years before Yang Ti's first Korean expedition. However, in the reign of the second Sui emperor this policy of power and prestige began to provoke growing difficulties: peasant revolts multiplied in Hopei and Shantung after floods on the lower Yellow River in 611. The situation grew worse as a result of the requisitions necessary for the three ill-starred Korean campaigns (612, 613, and 614). Relations with the Turks deteriorated in 613, the year in which the rebellion of Yang Hsüan-kan — the first organized by the aristocracy — broke out.

Li Yüan (565-635), the general responsible for defence against the nomads at T'ai-yüan, in the centre of Shansi, rebelled in 617 at the instigation of his son Li Shih-min (598–649), the future emperor T'ai-tsung, made an alliance with the Turkish tribes and marched on Ch'ang-an, where he founded the new T'ang dynasty. He became emperor under the name Kao-tsu (618–26).

The first few years of the T'ang dynasty were a time of internal consolidation. After all troubles had been quelled—a task which was completed in 628—there was an administrative reorganization. The empire was divided into ten big regions—to become fifteen in the eighth century—which were soon put under the control of inspectors of administration, finance, and justice. Much work was done in the fields of penal legislation, the agrarian system, taxation, the army, and education (academies and higher educational institutions were set up in the two capitals, Ch'ang-an and Loyang, and schools were established in the prefectures and sub-prefectures). This period of consolidation was followed from 626 to 683 by one of the greatest military expansions in the history of China. The Chinese armies inflicted a decisive defeat on the eastern Turks, whose capital lay in the valley of the Orkhon, to the south of Lake Baikal; crushed the Tölös Turks; secured the alliance of the Uighur Turks in eastern Mongolia and that of the T'u-yü-hun and the Tangut in the north-west; put an end to the kingdom of Kao-ch'ang in Turfan, which formed an obstacle to relations between Ch'ang-an, the Tarim basin, and Transoxiania; defeated the western Turks in the valley of the Ili; and opened and controlled the roads to the oases.

T'ang prestige in Asia reached its zenith: several countries of South-East Asia, such as the kingdom of Huan-wang (Champa) and Chen-la (Cambodia) recognized Chinese suzerainty. In Korea Koguryo was crushed and Silla reduced to submission. The T'ang created Chinese prefectures in Transoxiania and even intervened in northern India in the region of Patna (dynasty of Harshavardhana, 605–47, in Magadha).

This extraordinary expansion was based on political and economic institutions which merit description.

Political and economic foundations of the T'ang empire

Between the last few years of the sixth century and about 625 a great task was accomplished which was to provide the economic and institutional bases without which the Chinese expansion of the seventh and eighth centuries would have been impossible.

Plate 35. Bas-relief on the tomb of Emperor T'ai-tsung, T'ang dynasty, 626–49 A.D.

Big public works

Between 587 and 608 a network of navigable routes was constructed, consisting of canals and canalized rivers, in order to connect the valleys of the Yellow River and the Wei and that of the lower Yangtze as far as Hangchow. This network was extended in 608 by a canal guaranteeing communications between the Loyang area and the Peking area and was the first big canal system in the history of China. More than forty metres (130 feet) wide, with an imperial road running alongside, these canals were provided with relay-posts (there were about forty between Yangchow, north of the Yangtze, and Loyang). On the route between

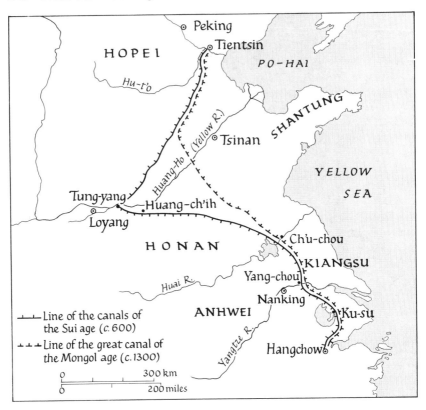

Map 13 The Grand Canal

Loyang and Ch'ang-an huge granaries were built. The biggest of them, at the confluence of the Lo and the Yellow River, had a capacity of 20 million *shih* (12 million hectolitres — 33 million bushels) of grain. Its remains have recently been discovered. Constructed for political and strategic purposes, and intended to facilitate communications between North China and Yangtze China immediately after the unification, this system of navigable routes carried only a small volume of rice to Loyang in the reign of T'ai-tsung (626–49) (12,000 tonnes) and much of the traffic consisted at that time of silks. However, as a result of the development of rice growing to the south of the lower Yangtze the tonnage was five to ten times greater a century later. Thus the big canals played a crucial role in the economic upsurge of the eighth and ninth centuries, and they allowed the T'ang government to maintain its position in the difficult conditions in which it found itself after An Lu-shan's rebellion (755–63). However, in spite of the work carried out on the section of four

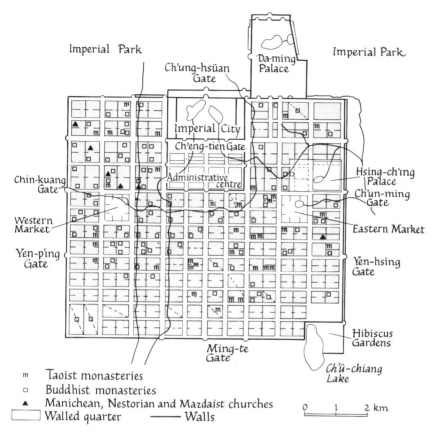

Imperial Park

Ch'ung-hsüan Gate

Da-ming Palace

Imperial Park

Imperial City

Ch'eng-tien Gate

Administrative centre

Chin-kuang Gate

Western Market

Yen-p'ing Gate

Hsing-ch'ing Palace

Ch'un-ming Gate

Eastern Market

Yen-hsing Gate

Hibiscus Gardens

Ming-te Gate

Chü-chiang Lake

m   Taoist monasteries
□   Buddhist monasteries
▲   Manichean, Nestorian and Mazdaist churches
☐   Walled quarter   ——— Walls

0   1   2 km

Map 14   Ch'ang-an during the Sui and T'ang dynasties

hundred kilometres (250 miles) connecting the two capitals, Loyang and Ch'ang-an, communications were never very easy because of the speed of the currents on the Yellow River and the mountainous nature of the borders of Honan and Shensi. Trans-shipment was unavoidable. In the case of famine in the Wei valley, the court and central government were obliged to move at great expense to Loyang, where supplies were easier to obtain.

The two capitals, Ch'ang-an and Loyang, were rebuilt on a grandiose scale round about the year 600. The outer ramparts of Sui and T'ang Ch'ang-an measured 9.7 kilometres (6 miles) from east to west and 8.2 kilometres (5 miles) from north to south. Rectangular in shape, the city had fourteen avenues running from north to south and eleven avenues running east to west. They varied in width from seventy to one hundred and fifty metres and were bordered by ditches planted with trees. These avenues marked off one hundred and ten walled quarters and two huge market places into which the canals ran. In the north of the city two big circuits òf walls protected the imperial palaces and the administrative district. However, it should be noted that the change of scale in the dimensions of the capitals dated from the construction of Loyang by the Northern Wei in 501. While the walls of Loyang under the Second Han dynasty measured only nine *li* (about 4.5 kilometres) by six (3 kilometres) those of the Wei capital already approached those of Sui Ch'ang-an in length. Perhaps this new conception of the city as a huge fortified camp reflects the influence of the peoples of the steppe. As for the new Loyang, the dimensions of which were somewhat smaller than those of Ch'ang-an, it too was built on a chessboard plan about the same time as Yang-tu, the great metropolis of the south-east, where foreign merchants seem to have been very numerous from the seventh to the ninth centuries. It was this latter city that the second Sui emperor, who seems to have had a sort of presentiment of the maritime and commercial expansion of lower Yangtze China from the tenth century onwards, wished to make his second capital after Loyang.

While the cities and waterways created round about the year 600 were to form the economic framework of seventh- to ninth-century China, the work accomplished in the field of legal, administrative, and military institutions was no less important or decisive. Heirs to the long tradition which went back to the Ts'ao Wei and the Northern Wei, the legislators of the Sui and early T'ang ages knew how to systematize earlier gains and to provide the new empire with one of the essential elements of its power.

The administrative system

In the seventh century the Chinese administration reached maturity. A learned and complex organism testifying to its long previous development, it deserves to be described here at least summarily.

The origins of the Chinese administrative system were ancient, since they dated from the time when palace duties, carried out by nobles of high rank, were replaced by public duties in the fourth and third centuries B.C. Thus the vocabulary sometimes recalled the personal and domestic character of the official posts of antiquity. However, from the foundation of the empire onwards, the administration tended to form a relatively autonomous corps whose wishes provided a counterweight to the factions which grew up at the court—eunuchs, empresses' families, generals—and also to the arbitrary power of the emperors. The machine was improved in the seventh century and made further progress in the eleventh century. It continued to evolve in the periods after the Sung (eleventh to thirteenth centuries), under the Ming and Ch'ing dynasties, in the direction of an authoritarian centralization which restricted its

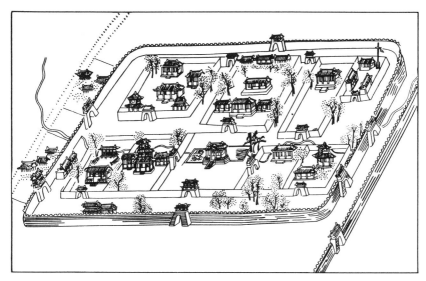

Fig. 9   Plan of a palace in Ch'ang-an

power and freedom both in the central government and in the provinces. The offices of the central administration under the T'ang occupied a walled area of four and a half square kilometres in Ch'ang-an. This area was called the 'imperial city' (*huang-ch'eng*) and lay to the south of the palace. The administration comprised four main organisms:

1. A Department of State Affairs (*shang-shu-sheng*), which grouped together six ministries (public administration, finance, rites, army, justice, and public works).

2. An imperial Chancellory (*men-hsia-sheng*), which acted as a centre for the transmission and checking of imperial decrees.

3. An imperial Grand Secretariat (*chung-shu-sheng*) responsible for producing official texts. These last two organs exercised a control over general policy.

4. A Council of State consisting of the emperor, great dignitaries, and important civil servants, who were usually presidents of the six ministries forming the Department of State Affairs.

There were also a number of services with more limited functions, the most important of which was the Court of Censors (*yü-shih-t'ai*), a sort of inspectorate-general of the administration. Its duty was to note abuses of every sort (corruption, extortion, fraud, and so on) and to hear complaints from the general public. The High Court of Justice (*ta-li-ssu*) gave the final decision in the most complex legal cases and was alone authorized to pronounce the death penalty. Other services looked after the administration of the waterways and canals, the arsenals, the imperial library, the state university (*kuo-tzu-chien*), the palace guards, the internal services of the palace and the crown prince's house, and so on.

Under the orders of this central administration was the whole administration of the provinces, or rather of the big regions (*tao* under the T'ang, *lu* under the Sung) into which the territory of the empire was divided. At the lowest level were the sub-prefectures (*hsien*), districts containing at the most a few tens of thousands of inhabitants. A number of sub-prefectures (four or five on average) formed a prefecture, the seat of which was in the principal urban centre in its territory. The prefectures were of varying importance. Most were known as *chou,* but some were designated higher prefectures (*fu*). Varying in size according to the density of their population (the most extensive were also the least heavily populated), the prefectures corresponded more or less to an average-sized French *département.* Officials of the imperial civil service appointed to the provinces were very few in number. A subprefecture usually had only one or two. The imperial officials were accordingly assisted by locally recruited staff. Strangers to the region, where they remained for only a few years, they had to secure the support of the local gentry and show flexibility in the execution of the central government's directives. On the other hand, their status as imperial officials assured them of considerable prestige.

Above the prefectures, and sometimes covering vast areas, there were certain specialized services, usually of a military or financial character, whose task was to coordinate and check the activities of the prefectures. These services were entrusted to officials of high rank.

Juridical institutions

Substantial collections of juridical and administrative documents from the T'ang age have been preserved; it has been possible partly to reconstruct some of them. Such is the case with the administrative ordinances and regulations collected by the great Japanese specialist in the history of Chinese law, Niida Noburu. The T'ang Code, first compiled in 624, revised in 627 and 637, and endowed with a commentary—the *T'ang-lü shu-i*—in 653, is the first Chinese legal code which has come down to us complete. Its direct ancestor was the code of the Northern Chou, published in 564, which was itself the heir to the less complete and less elaborate codes of the Ts'ao Wei and the Western Chin (268). The T'ang Code is an admirable composition of faultless logic in spite of its size and complexity. An analysis of the fundamental principles of this law, of its notions and categories, has never really been undertaken; it would certainly reveal a profoundly original psychology and set of ideas. In essentials it is law based on a continuous scale of penalties and one in which the gravity of the crime depends not only on its intrinsic nature but also on the position of the guilty person in regard to his victim. In the case of more or less close relations, this position is defined by the kind of more or less prolonged mourning required by the degrees of kinship, and in other cases by hierarchical relationships (the emperor, officials of various grades, ordinary private citizens, persons of servile status and so on). Apart from his role as examiner, and sometimes investigator, the magistrate did not have to weigh responsibilities or to 'lay down the law', but on the contrary to fix the precise nature of the offence on the basis of the models furnished by the code, proceeding by assimilation (*lun*) and conforming to a scale which provided for increasing or reducing the penalty according to the case and in a very strict way. These characteristics of Chinese law are ancient and take account of the absolute equivalence both in language and concept between the terms and ideas of offence and penalty (the language possesses only one word for the two, *tsui*). The range of penalties comprises a series of punishments which change in nature as they grow more severe — strokes of the cane, strokes of the bamboo, forced labour, exile accompanied by forced labour, strangulation, and decapitation. The code is distinct from other types of legislation and solely penal in character. The T'ang Code comprises more than five hundred articles divided into twelve sections:

1. General definitions and rules
2. Laws relating to passing into or through prohibited places (imperial palaces, town gates, walls, frontier posts)
3. Offences committed by officials in the exercise of their functions
4. Laws concerning peasant families (lands, taxes, marriages)
5. Laws relating to state stud-farms and storehouses
6. Laws relating to the raising of troops
7. Offences against the person and against property
8. Offences committed in the course of brawls
9. Forgery and counterfeiting
10. Various laws of a special character
11. Laws concerning the apprehension of guilty persons
12. Laws relating to the administration of justice

Agrarian regulations

The agrarian system of the T'ang age in the seventh century and the first half of the eighth was based on a very remarkable institution, namely a method of distributing land which for more than a century was to ensure the regularity of the revenue from taxes and to maintain a certain social stability. The practice of the equal distribution of plots of land as annuities (i.e. to be held only for the lifetime of the recipient) had made its appearance under the Northern Wei dynasty, where it had been officially adopted in 486. But while at that time it was a matter of encouraging the reclamation of land in dry areas by multiplying allotments, the agrarian ordinances (*t'ien-ling*) promulgated by the T'ang in 624 aimed at providing each peasant family with enough land to support it and to enable it to pay its taxes. The 'method of equal distribution of land' (*chün-t'ien-fa*) adopted at this time was in fact indissolubly linked to the fiscal laws enacted in 619. These laws defined three kinds of dues which, in accordance with a practice constantly followed since the end of antiquity, applied not to property, but to persons. There was the *tsu,* a tax paid in cereals; the *yung,* various kinds of *corvée;* and the *tiao,* a tax paid in cloth (silk, *chüan,* in the silk-producing areas; hempen material, *pu,* elsewhere and especially in the north-west). The tax in cereals and the tax in cloth were related to two basically different kinds of landed property which were carefully distinguished by the new agrarian regulations. On the one hand there were the big expanses growing corn, millet, or barley and on the other the small areas consisting of a house and garden and the plantations of mulberry trees or the hemp fields necessary for the cottage industries producing silk or cloth. While the big expanses of land had to be split up into 'life' plots (*k'ou-fen-t'ien*) according to the number of adult males in each family, the other properties, which were also limited in size, were regarded as permanent possessions (*yung-yeh*). Smaller shares of 'land held for life' (*k'ou-fen-t'ien*) were provided for old men, the seriously ill, the infirm, widows, traders and craftsmen, and monks and nuns. The plots were smaller in the 'cramped districts', where the population was dense, than in the 'districts with plenty of room'. Finally, there were numerous derogations for a whole series of lands not subject to distribution and excluded from the system established by the ordinances (public lands, official lands, lands granted as a gift by the emperor, monastery lands, military colonies, agricultural colonies).

This fiscal and agrarian system implied a very exact census of the population, a precise acquaintance with the cadastral survey of each district and the classification of individuals in legally defined age-groups — 'the yellow' (babies), 'the small' (children), 'the medium' (adolescents), adults, and old men. It was long thought that the 'method of equal distribution of land' existed only in theory, because of the complexity of the administrative control involved. However, the discovery of seventh- and eighth-century manuscripts at the oases of Tun-huang in Kansu and Turfan (Kao-ch'ang) in central Asia has proved that it did actually function. Some of the documents from Turfan refer to the granting and restitution of land in accordance with the system of 'life' shares, and the census registers of Tun-huang, which record the state of local families, with the age of each of their members and a precise note of the lands and their boundaries, date from a time when the system was already in decline but had not yet disappeared.

It is possible that the system could really be applied only in the 'dry zone', which extends from the northern provinces to the valley of the Huai; further south the rice fields formed units more difficult to split up and the investment needed to develop and irrigate them made the feeling of personal possession more acute. But the differences between wheat-growing China and rice-growing China were accentuated with the expansion of rice cultivation between the eighth and eleventh centuries. They were still noticeable in the Ming period (fourteenth to seventeenth centuries), when there was a dual taxation system corresponding approximately to this general contrast between the wheat and sorghum zone and the rice zone.

Armies

The core of the Sui and T'ang armies in the seventh century was aristocratic: it was the great families of Kuan-nei (Shensi and eastern Kansu) and, to a lesser extent, of the other regions of North China, who provided and officered the best troops. It was their men who served in the crack corps — the imperial guards and the palace troops. Contrary to traditional belief, the governing class of the sixth century and the class which arose out of it under the Sui and the first T'ang emperors was not a class of scholarly civil servants but an aristocracy with military traditions. These aristocrats' taste for military affairs, their love of horses, and the interest they took in breeding them are explained by their nomad descent and by the prolonged influence of the steppe cultures in North China. But for the military prowess, the sense of honour and the love of action innate in this aristocracy, the stirring deeds of the Sui and T'ang armies would not have been possible.

It is true that the efficiency of the military organization contributed to these successes, but this organization was originally conceived in terms of these families with military traditions. The system consisted of a series of militias (*fu-ping*), each of 800 to 1200 men, concentrated round the capital in Shensi, in the T'ai-yüan region in Shansi, on the route taken by Turkish incursions and on the northern frontiers. Under the Northern Chou this system of recruitment applied only to families devoted to the profession of arms, and it was not until the T'ang age that it was extended to the peasantry. It is significant that the regulations for the militias issued at the beginning of the T'ang dynasty laid down that cavalrymen should provide their own horses and part of their equipment. This would have been inconceivable if ordinary peasants had been concerned. Everything leads us to suppose that in that age, as in every other period of history, there was a division of tasks in the army: the peasants, unused to horses and poor riders, were not, with exceptions, warriors to rival the men of the steppes. On the other hand, they provided the bulk of the infantry and were suitable for holding fortified posts and occupying ground. They were often employed on the indispensable tasks of producing forage and cereals, or on transport and mail. The crack troops, the corps which could move into action rapidly, did not consist of peasants, but in the main of friendly and more or less sinicized nomads, or, as was the case in the sixth and seventh centuries, of Han Chinese cross-bred with barbarians, of Chinese half-converted to the habits and mentality of the people of the steppe.

A decisive role in the political offensive of the T'ang empire was played by an animal: the horse, the mount of riders armed with bows. Horse breeding was developed systematically in the seventh and eighth centuries. At the beginning of the dynasty the T'ang, if we are to believe the texts, had only a small number of horses at their disposal—a total of 5000, 3000 of which are supposed to have been taken from the Sui in the Ch'ih-an-tse marshes, to the west of Ch'ang-an, and 2000 from the Turks in Kansu. But very soon public stud-farms were set up and they must have quickly been successful, for by the middle of the seventh century the T'ang had 700,000 horses spread over the pasturages of Shensi and Kansu, which covered large areas. In addition there were the horses owned by private individuals. We do not know how many such horses there were, but private breeding seems to have been highly developed in North China, especially in eastern Kansu, Shensi, and Shansi. As we have seen, the regulations governing the militias (*fu-ping*) laid down that the soldiers—or at any rate some of them, those who belonged to the great aristocratic families—should provide their own horses. In the first half of the eighth century members of the imperial family, high officials, and generals owned herds of horses, oxen, sheep, and camels. The period during which the Chinese armies had the greatest number of horses corresponds with the period of the great offensives of the middle of the seventh century. Horses were numerous and cheap until about 665. Subsequently Turkish and Tibetan incursions disorganized the stud farms and breeding seems to have declined. In 713 there were only 240,000 animals on the imperial farms. The figure went up to 400,000 in 725, thanks to a resurgence of breeding and to purchases from the

Plates 36–37.   T'ang masterpieces

breeders of the steppes. A horse market was set up in 727 on the upper reaches of the Yellow River at Yin-ch'uan, whither the Turks came to sell their beasts in exchange for silks and metals. However, just before An Lu-shan's rebellion, in 754, the number of horses on the books of the stud-farm service had dropped to only 325,700. Up to this time the little Mongolian horse which was then common all over the steppes and in North China (it is now on the way to becoming extinct and exists only in Dzungaria) had been crossed with a large number of different breeds, thanks to the tribute offered by the central Asian kingdoms and by areas beyond the Pamirs. These horses from outside China included thoroughbred Arab steeds brought to the T'ang court in 703, wild ponies presented by the Tibetans in 654, horses from Kokand, Samarkand, Bukhara, Kish, Chack, Maimargh and Khuttal, horses from Gandhara, Khotan and Kucha, and Kirghiz horses from the Baikal area.

In the seventh and eighth centuries the northern aristocracy had a passion for horses. Members of high society rode about on horseback, and polo, doubtless imported from Iran, was tremendously popular in Ch'ang-an. This passion for horses no doubt explains the place they occupy in the painting—some painters, such as Han Kan (*c.* 720–780), specialized in equestrian painting—and sculpture of the T'ang age, as witness the magnificent bas-reliefs on the tomb of the emperor T'ai-tsung (626–49) and the funerary figurines. But the T'ang horse has characteristics which reveal the influence of imports and of crossing with Middle Eastern and Transoxianian breeds. These breeds were taller and more slender than the little Mongolian pony, which was to return in force after the T'ang, as is proved by the paintings of the Yüan (thirteenth and fourteenth centuries) and Ming (fourteenth to sixteenth centuries) periods.

The Tibetan incursions of 763, during which most of the horses on the public stud-farms were driven off, marked a decisive decline in breeding in north-western China. The T'ang could only turn to palliatives. These included the purchase of horses from private citizens (30,000 mares were acquired in the region of the capital for the palace stables) and from the nomads (horses to the value of 10,000 rolls of silk were bought in 815–16 in the Ordos area), and a not very successful attempt in 817–20 to set up state stud-farms—after expropriation of the peasants—in the agricultural areas of Shensi, Honan, and northern Hupei. The Uighurs, who had helped the T'ang in their battles against the Tibetans in 758–59, obtained in exchange an almost complete monopoly in the horse trade. Eager for profit, they sold bad horses at high prices to the Chinese government; at the end of the eighth century the price of an Uighur horse was forty pieces of silk.

The best areas for horse-breeding seem to have lain in eastern Kansu, in the Ching valley in Shensi, and in the western parts of Shansi. Once China was no longer in a position to protect these areas against the incursions of the mountaineers and nomads, it had lost one of the main means for its policy of intervention in central Asia and was condemned to retire towards Honan and the south-eastern regions. This was doubtless one of the causes of the weakness of the Sung up to the conquest of the north by the Jürchen between 960 and 1126.

The distribution of the Chinese armies is revealing – and the remarks that follow are valid not only for the T'ang age. They were concentrated round the capitals and along the northern and north-western frontiers. Their essential tasks were in fact to protect the empire against incursions and invasions from the borderlands and to defend the central government against rebellions arising in the provinces. The imperial guards posted to the south of the capital and the armies quartered to the north of the palace gave immediate protection against attempts at *coups d'état*. These guards also provided an escort for the emperor when he travelled and detachments for big ceremonies – shows simultaneously of force and pomp usually entrusted to crack troops. As for the frontier armies, they fulfilled, according to their nature, two different functions. They were either expeditionary corps, consisting chiefly of cavalry, or garrisons responsible for holding the lines of defence and centres of communication. The troops quartered in the provinces represented only a very small fraction of the total Chinese forces. The imperial government seems to have had few worries in this direction. As long as peasant revolts did not change into real rebellions, which sometimes received assistance from the upper classes, they did not form a serious or urgent danger. They consisted only of bands of uprooted peasants who lived on pillage and took refuge in difficult mountainous territory or hid in the marshy areas. Badly equipped, they were usually powerless against the walled towns where the representatives of the imperial power resided. All things considered, banditry was only a chronic and bearable evil. Besides, one could always negotiate with bandit leaders and win them over by granting them titles and official posts. In any case it is clear that the government did not rely primarily on force to keep the peace in the provinces. Usually the institutions sufficed. The grouping of the inhabitants in small units responsible for the acts of each individual, the obligation to denounce offences, the responsibility of the officials and of the heads of districts, villages, and families had formed since the early days of the empire such a general system of constraints, and one so well embedded in the Chinese way of life, that it was no longer even felt as such. Hence its remarkable efficacity.

The great expansion of the seventh century

From the end of the sixth century onwards the Chinese world grew stronger, richer, and better organized, and sought to extend its influence abroad and to push back the peoples who made incursions into its territory — the T'u-yü-hun of Tsinghai, the Tangut of the borders of Szechwan, Turks and other nomads from Mongolia and Dzungaria, the Kitan from eastern Mongolia and the valley of the Liao-ho in Manchuria, the people of the kingdom of Koguryo in Korea. It was stimulated both by the threats from outside, which forced it to build up its strength, and by the upsurge of its own power.

The events

The situation in the steppe zone had changed since the middle of the sixth century with the formation of a new confederation of nomad tribes led by the Turks (*T'u-chüeh*). These founders of a new empire of the steppes had put an end in 552 to the hegemony of the Juan-juan (or Jou-jan) in the regions extending from the valley of the Orkhon, south of Baikal, to that of the Ili. The Turkish threat, more dangerous than the one posed by their predecessors, was the basic cause of the second big period of building in the history of the Great Walls. The first period had been the third and second centuries B.C.; the third and last period was to come later, in the fifteenth century.

While the Northern Wei had confined themselves to strengthening in 423 the ancient walls of the Ch'in and Han periods, and to fortifying in 446 the area of Ta-t'ung, their capital, in the extreme north of Shansi, the Northern Ch'i, in 555–56, built new defence lines, which were partly doubled in 557 and 565 and followed a much more southerly route than the fortifications of the Ch'in age. The Ming were to adopt the same route in the fifteenth century.

When North China was unified by the Chou in 577, the relations between Turks and Chinese changed. Up to that date, while the two northern empires were fighting each other, it was to their advantage to seek the alliance of the Turks; but unification changed the terms of the problem. Unification formed the necessary precondition for the second great Chinese expansion in Asia (the first had taken place in the Han period).

The division of the Turks in 582 into two confederations — eastern Turks of the Orkhon valley and western Turks of the Altai — does not seem to have weakened their power: in the same year they passed inside the Great Walls *en masse* and in 585 the Sui were led to prolong westward the fortifications built by the Northern Ch'i. The new section extended for 350 kilometres (220 miles) from the Ordos to present-day Yin-ch'uan (Ning-hsia region), along the upper reaches of the Yellow River. The incursions stopped for a time following a treaty concluded in 584 and were followed in 594 by the gift of a Chinese princess in marriage to one of the Turkish khans. But the Turks took the offensive again about 600 and in 601 came as far as the approaches to Ch'ang-an. They were pushed back towards Kokonor in 608, but the threat which they posed was not removed until 630, the year of the great offensive which gave the T'ang control of the Ordos and of south-western Mongolia.

The year 630 marks in fact the start of the great T'ang expansion in Asia, during the reigns of T'ai-tsung and Kao-tsung (from 626 to 683). The defeat of the Turks opened the way to central Asia for the Chinese army and government in the years 630–45. Hami, Turfan (the kingdom of Kao-ch'ang, founded by Chinese colonists) in 640, Karashahr and Kucha in 658, then the oases of Transoxiania all passed successively under Chinese control. Chinese administrative districts were created on the far side of the Pamirs – the prefectures of Kang (Samarkand), An (Bukhara), Shih (Tashkent), Mi (Maimargh), Ho (Kushanika), Ts'ao (Kaputana), and Shih (Kish). In 648 General Wang Hsüan-ts'e organized an expedition to the Patna area of northern India, doubtless with Nepalese and Tibetan troops, in order to settle to China's advantage the succession to the throne of the little kingdom of Magadha. In the northeast, Manchuria and almost the whole Korean peninsula passed under T'ang control about 660. In 662 China intervened in the internal affairs of the Sassanid dynasty at Ctesiphon on the Tigris, just at the very time when the Persian empire was threatened by the advance of the Omeyyad Arabs. The extension of T'ang control to these vast territories led to the creation of six 'governments-general' (*tu-tu-fu* or *tu-hu-fu*) or military protectorates: those of An-nan at Hanoi, of Pei-t'ing (Beshbalik, region of present-day Urumchi, in the south of Dzungaria), of An-hsi in western Kansu, of An-tung in Liaoning (southern Manchuria), of An-pei in the north-west of the Ordos area, and of Shan-yü in the north-eastern part of the same area, in Mongolia.

The T'ang expansion from Korea to Iran and from the Ili valley to central Vietnam was undoubtedly the most important phenomenon in the political history of Asia in the seventh century. It implies a remarkable military and administrative organization, with quick-moving striking forces of cavalry, efficient horse breeding, the establishment of military colonies for the provisioning of the armies in central Asia, a system of relay stations and intense diplomatic activity. However, this extraordinary expansion, which made T'ang China the greatest power in Asia

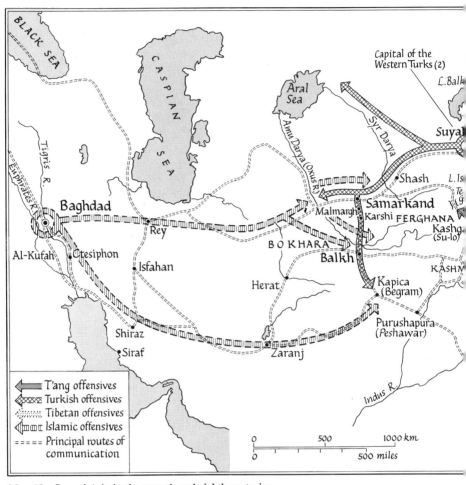

Map 15   Central Asia in the seventh and eighth centuries

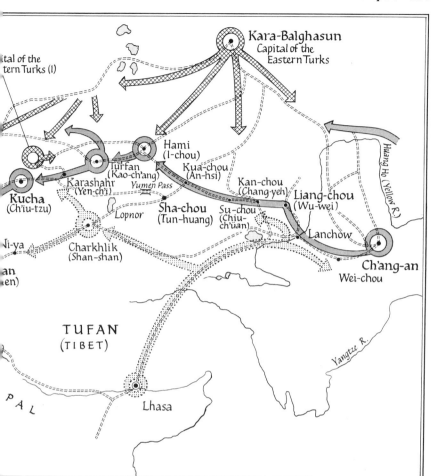

ital of the
tern Turks (I)

Kara-Balghasun
Capital of the
Eastern Turks

Hami
(I-chou)

Turfan
(Kao-ch'ang)

Kua-chou
(An-hsi)

Kan-chou
(Chang-yeh)

Liang-chou
(Wu-wei)

Karashahr
(Yen-ch'i)

Yumen Pass

Kucha
(Ch'iu-tzu)

Lopnor

Sha-chou
(Tun-huang)

Su-chou
(Chiu-
ch'üan)

Lanchow

Ch'ang-an

Wei-chou

Ji-ya

Charkhlik
(Shan-shan)

an
en)

Huang Ho (Yellow R.)

TUFAN
(TIBET)

Yangtze R.

PAL

Lhasa

at this time, was fragile. As in the Han period, the length and difficulty of communications between the capital and the areas controlled by China in central Asia explain the extremely precarious character of the Chinese occupation in these regions, where military colonies had to be maintained at great expense. Kashgar, the westernmost oasis of the Tarim valley, was nearly 5000 kilometres (3100 miles) from Ch'ang-an, and the tracks linking An-hsi to Hami and Turfan crossed desert areas where water was rare. The territories beyond the Pamirs, which were even more distant, could only be reached by mountain passes which it was a real exploit to cross.

Even though the submission of the T'u-yü-hun and of the Tanguts of Tsinghai and Kansu was obtained in the early days of the dynasty, and even though the Turkish problem was essentially settled first by the great offensive of 630 and later by the adhesion and progressive sedentarization of part of the steppe tribes, the incursions of nomads and mountaineers did not for all that come to a halt. They called into question the loyalty to the T'ang of the central Asian oases and threatened the safety of the garrisons and caravans. The T'ang were forced to mount an expedition into the valley of the Ili against the eastern Turks, and it was only in 748 that the Chinese armies destroyed their capital, Suyab, on the course of the river Tchou. Fresh difficulties made their appearance with the expansion of the Tibetans, who invaded the oasis zone between 670 and 678, occupying for a time Khotan, Yarkand, Kashgar, and Kucha. Then came the Arab expansion, which forced Chinese influence out of Iran and soon threatened the Chinese conquests in Transoxiania and in the Kashgar region.

The period 684–755: political history

The empresses Wu and Wei

The end of the seventh century and the first few years of the eighth were dominated by the astonishing figure of a former concubine of the emperors T'ai-tsung (626–49) and Kao-tsung (649–83), a woman called Wu Chao (624–705). Very influential from 654 onwards and empress in name the following year, she actually reigned after Kao-tsung's death in 683. Thrusting aside the legitimate heir, in 690 she took the name of Emperor Tse-t'ien and founded the Chou dynasty, of which she was to be the sole monarch—the first and only female emperor in the history of China. This interlude of fifteen years (or twenty-two if we take into account the whole period during which Wu Tse-t'ien actually wielded power) can only be explained by the political atmosphere of the time and by the tremendous influence of Buddhism. All the empress Wu's efforts, from the moment when she was in a position to affect the government, were aimed at removing from power the representatives of the north-western aristocracy, who had held all the levers of power since the beginning of the dynasty and in particular controlled the management of the state through the medium of the imperial Chancellory (*men-hsia-sheng*). Immediately after Kao-tsung's death in 684 Tse-t'ien ordered the execution of several hundreds of these aristocrats and of numerous members of the imperial family of Li. By transferring the normal seat of the court from Ch'ang-an to Loyang, she was able more easily to escape the control of the great families. But she also wished to further the formation of a new class of administrators recruited by competition. It is remarkable that the examinations and tests which under the Han had played only a secondary role in the recruitment and promotion of civil servants should not have been properly organized in a systematic way until the year 669. This institution, which was to have so considerable an influence in the Chinese world, was at first a political weapon in the hands of the empress Wu Tse-t'ien. When she became emperor in 690, she changed the whole official nomenclature and administrative organization, taking as her inspiration – as the usurper Wang Mang had done nearly seven centuries earlier – that suspect classic, the *Chou-li*. She also changed place-names and invented nineteen new written characters, the use of which became obligatory.

The extraordinary rise of Wu Chao, and especially her enthronement, could not have taken place but for the help and hidden support of the Buddhist church, which had been a great political and economic power since the beginning of the sixth century. Buddhist predictions made up to suit her marked out T'ai-tsung's former concubine as future emperor and as a reincarnation of the Bodhisattva Maitreya (Mi-le), the Buddhist saviour, a messiah whose expected coming had already given rise in the past to several millenary sects. Wu Chao herself had formerly embarked on the religious life as a nun in a convent, after T'ai-tsung's death, in 650. Bigoted and superstitious, she heaped favours on the Church (ordinations of priests, foundation of monasteries, building, casting of bells and statues, and so on). It was in her reign that the huge Vairocana, with his two acolytes, of the Lung-men Pass, to the south of Loyang, was carved out of the rock.

The period during which Wu Tse-t'ien was in power and the five years which followed the restoration of the T'ang in 705 – a time when the empress Wei was all-powerful – were an epoch of waste and general relaxation. Imperial princes and princesses, high officials, favourites and great monasteries all enriched themselves and enlarged their estates. The small peasantry with its 'life' plots was crushed under the weight of taxes and dues. The number of tenant farmers multiplied.

The golden age of the T'ang

The first half of the eighth century (or, to be more precise, the years 710–55) was the most brilliant period in the history of the T'ang dynasty. China's influence in Asia was at its zenith. The capital, Ch'ang-an, was the centre of a cosmopolitan civilization coloured by the influences of central Asia, of India, and of Iran. Classical poetry and Buddhist studies shone with their greatest lustre.

In 710 Li Lung-chi (685–762), son of the emperor Jui-tsung who had been pushed aside in 690 by Tse-t'ien, eliminated the Wei clan and put his father on the throne, before reigning himself from 712 under the name of Hsüan-tsung (712–56). This great reign began with the work of putting in order the finances, the administration and the conditions of political life. In 721 and 724 efforts were made to reconstruct the census registers, in order to remedy the dramatic reduction in the number of taxable families. The decline of the militia (*fu-ping*) system, which had made possible the T'ang expansion in central Asia in the seventh century, provoked a reorganization of the armies, and the reforms increased the autonomy and powers of initiative of the military leaders. Better management of the imperial stud-farms, which had been neglected in Tse-t'ien's reign, once again gave the government a plentiful supply of horses. The T'ang intervened in the Amu-Darya basin at the request of Tokhara and other kingdoms threatened by the Arab incursions. In 723 the kingdom of the Mohe, hunting tribes inhabiting the regions near the Amur, was transformed into a Chinese prefecture. From 745 onwards a vast counter-offensive was mounted to halt the Arab advance in Transoxiania and the valley of the Ili.

However, slow changes were taking place which were to end in one of the great crises of history. The agrarian system continued to deteriorate. The power of the army leaders grew with the creation on the northern frontiers of military regions (*fan-chen* or *fang-chen*) under the command of imperial commissioners (*chieh-tu-shih*). The formation of large armies of professional soldiers was a threat to the central government, yet state favours to the military leaders only increased during the reign of Hsüan-tsung. Money spent on the armies rose from 2 million bundles of 1000 copper coins in 713 to 10 million in 741, and in 755 it reached the figure of 14 to 15 million. In spite of all this, the T'ang had to yield to pressure from the Tibeto-Burmese kingdom of Nan-chao in Yunnan and hand over to it about 750 control of the south-western roads and territories, while the Chinese offensive in present-day Turkestan ended in failure: in 751 the T'ang armies commanded by the Korean general Kao Hsien-chih were crushed by the Arabs in the battle of the river Talas, to the south of Lake Balkhash. A kingdom of half-sedentarized Turks known as Uighurs grew up from 745 onwards in the Hami area, north-west of Tun-huang.

On the political plane, the restoration of the T'ang in 705 had been followed by the return to power of the ancient north-western aristocracy, which from then onwards had joined battle with the new class of officials recruited by competition. The conflict reached its height in 736, when the scholarly civil servant Chang Chiu-ling (673–740), a creole born in the tropics, was opposed by Li Lin-fu (?–752), the representative of the Wei valley aristocracy. Things grew more complicated when, at the end of his reign, Hsüan-tsung lost interest in the management of the state and under the influence of the concubine Yang Yü-huan, the famous '*kuei-fei* Yang' (*kuei-fei* = first class prostitute), who had entered the palace in 745, granted important posts to her family. On Li Lin-fu's death in 752, the imperial favourite's cousin, Yang Kuo-chung, competed with the general An Lu-shan for the post of prime minister. The award of this post to Yang Kuo-chung unleashed the great military rebellion of An Lu-shan at the end of 755.

The military rebellion of 755–763

In the reign of Hsüan-tsung (712–56) the military expansion and the suc-cess of the Chinese armies from Korea to Iran seem to have led to a sort of surrender to enthusiasm. The central government appears to have forgotten that in circumstances like these a kind of natural tendency leads to the formation of professional armies inspired by their own in-terests and ruled by a state of mind which becomes further and further removed from that of the civilians. To increase the autonomy of the ar-mies, to regroup commands and put oneself in the hands of the profes-sionals may be the way to secure the means of a victorious offensive policy, but it is also the way to weaken the state. Now the tendency in the first half of the eighth century to increase the powers of the army leaders was strengthened by considerations of internal policy: to counterbalance the power of the relatives of the concubine Yang Yü-huan, and more especially that of Yang Kuo-chung, who had carved himself out a sort of fief in Szechwan, the great minister Li Lin-fu, who directed the empire from 737 to 752, sought to favour the generals of the northern armies. Li Lin-fu put his money mainly on the generals of foreign descent, in the hope that they would be more manageable than the Chinese military men. This is how it came about that in the region of modern Peking, supplied directly by a great canal since the time of the Sui dynasty's Korean wars, General An Lu-shan, who was in sole command of three military areas, found himself heaped with favours by the court. An Lu-shan's father was a Sogdian and his mother was a Turk. His surname was one common among the Sogdians of Bukhara, to the north of the Amu-Darya, and his personal name a transcription of the Iranian name 'Roxana' ('light') — the name of the Bactrian princess whom Alexander the Great married. In the winter of 755–56 An Lu-shan marched at the head of his armies on Loyang and Ch'ang-an, which fell without striking a blow. An account of the dramatic events which followed — the emperor's flight to Ch'eng-tu, Shih Ssu-ming's succession to the leadership of the insurgent armies after An Lu-shan's death in 757, the difficult reconquest of the region of the two capitals by the new emperor Su-tsung with the help of the Tibetans and the Uighurs — has almost certainly no place in this book, where there is room only for a rapid survey of the history of China. On the other hand, it is important to underline the very serious consequences of this tragedy.

Chapter 12

The Transition to
the Mandarin Empire

The consequences of the rebellion

The rebellion of An Lu-shan and Shih Ssu-ming may be regarded as one of the great turning points in the history of the Chinese world, for it was accompanied and followed by a clear change of direction in every domain. The crisis seems to have hastened changes which were only just beginning in the first half of the eighth century. External relations, policy, the economy and society, and intellectual life all changed rapidly from the terrible years 755–63 onwards.

The tide of expansion ebbs

During the course of the crisis the whole defence system protecting the empire's frontiers disintegrated. Control of the Pamirs had been lost ever since the Arabs had occupied the Kashgar region a few years before the rebellion. The Uighurs, the principal allies of the legitimate government, spread to Kansu in 757 and thus dominated the whole area between Wu-wei, in the centre of Kansu, and Turfan. The Tibetans asserted their power and made incursions into the central Asian oases, Tsinghai and Kansu. In 763 they settled at Ning-hsia, on the upper reaches of the Yellow River, seized the horses on the imperial stud-farms in eastern Kansu, and advanced as far as Ch'ang-an. From 790 onwards all the territories west of the Yü-men Pass were finally lost to China. When we think of the Chinese lands' constant relations since the Han age with central Asia and the regions beyond the Pamirs, it becomes clear that this event was one with extremely important consequences for the history of Chinese civilization.

In the north-east, the kingdom of Silla, which had dominated Korea since the end of the seventh century, declared itself independent of the T'ang. Finally, in the regions between Szechwan and Burma, sinicized principalities permeated by Chinese, Indian, and Tibetan influences, and allied now to China, now to Tibet, had grown up since the middle of the seventh century. The most powerful of these kingdoms, that of the 'prince of the south' (Nan-chao) had swallowed up its rivals and from 750 onwards began to expand, in spite of the Chinese expeditions sent to bring it to heel. Nan-chao was to become an even greater threat in the ninth century, launching attacks up to the Ch'eng-tu region and seizing the Red River basin and Hanoi in 827. After the defeat of a Chinese expedition in 865–67 it even succeeded for a time in occupying the capital of Szechwan. Known from 902 onwards as the kingdom of Ta-li (a locality on the western shore of Lake Erh-hai in the west of Yunnan), this south-western kingdom was to exist until it was conquered by the Mongols in the middle of the thirteenth century.

This general retreat after the great expansion of the seventh century and the first half of the eighth was to become even more marked in the tenth century, with the formation of the sinicized Khitan empire in the north-east and the loss of Chinese control over the Red River basin. Deeply marked by more than a thousand years of Chinese colonization and administration, Vietnam shook off in 939 the tutelage of the Southern Han kingdom centred on Canton and thereafter always remained independent, if we except the epoch of the Mongol occupation and the short period at the beginning of the fifteenth century when Vietnam formed part of the Ming empire.

The changes in the fiscal system and the evolution of society

The changes were no less sweeping in a quite different field, that of fiscal organization, which was closely connected with the political constitution, the economy, and the structure of society.

The system of distribution of 'life' plots of the arable land intended to provide the tax in grain was fragile, in so far as it depended on accurate censuses and land surveys kept regularly up-to-date. Moreover it was impossible to apply uniform legislation everywhere because of the diversity of the geographical conditions and the varying density of the population. Where there was not enough land it was permissible to emigrate. In addition, wherever hemp growing was replacing patches planted with mulberry trees, as was the case in the whole of north-western China, there was a great temptation to include 'life' plots in family properties. Finally, the numerous derogations provided for in the regulations furnished opportunities to get round the law. By the end of the seventh century the class of small farmers endowed with 'life' plots was beginning to break up and the falsification of census registers was becoming general.

There were no doubt many different reasons for this phenomenon — voluntary emigrations caused by the incursions of nomads or Tibetans into the frontier regions, the attractions of the Huai and Yangtze areas, where rice growing and trade were developing, the pressure exerted by rich landowners in a position to make loans to peasants in difficulties. But probably this exploitation of the poorest people by the richest and most powerful was the main cause of the rapid fall in the number of taxable families during the course of the eighth century. In the seventh century and the first half of the eighth the great north-western families who dominated political life, the imperial nobility (blood relations and relations by marriage of the emperors, the families of imperial concubines), generals and high officials, and big monasteries owned private domains known by various different names, the commonest of which was *chuang-yuan* ('garden farm'). This kind of estate — a sort of country house in a park — would include a farm on the fringe of those of the peasantry. This farm would comprise mountain or hill land and orchards as well as fields growing cereals. The mills erected on water-courses by the owners of these estates were sometimes the cause of confrontations with peasants deprived of water for irrigation. These private estates expanded during the first half of the dynasty by swallowing up peasant land, to such an extent that their character changed and the term *chuang-yuan* came to denote large agricultural enterprises worked by tenant farmers and wage-earning labourers. Like Roman villas, these big domains were to give rise in later times to small agglomerations: numerous towns of the Sung age retain in their very name (*chuang*) the memory of this kind of origin. These changes are doubtless explained by the commercial development which the Chinese world experienced from the eighth century onwards.

The efforts made in the first half of the eighth century to reregister the families and lands which had disappeared from the census returns turned out to be unsuccessful. For this reason the government started to turn to a new kind of tax which was no longer based on the families of the farmers but on the lands (*ti-t'ou-ch'ien*) and the harvests (*ch'ing-miao-ch'ien*). This is the practice that was systematized and generalized by Yang Yen's famous reform of direct taxation in 780 — the *liang-shui-fa* or summer and autumn 'method of taxation'.

However, the reform of the agrarian taxes, part of which served to supply funds for the provincial budgets, was not sufficient. New sources of revenue had to be found, for numerous regions escaped the authority of the central government. State monopolies, which made it possible to tax consumable goods either at the point of production or at the point of distribution, enabled the government to make good the deficit with regular revenues which were independent of the political situation. The economic upsurge which had taken place in the Yangtze valley and in Szechwan during the eighth century was to ensure the success of these new taxes inspired by the memory of the famous iron and salt monopolies established in the reign of the Han emperor Wu Ti in 117 B.C. The salt monopoly — the most reliable and most profitable insofar as the state controlled the producing areas (the salt marshes of the maritime provinces from Hopei to the Canton area, the salt lakes of southern Shansi and the salt mines of Szechwan) — was created in 759, the alcohol monopoly in 764 and the monopoly in tea, the consumption of which was spreading rapidly, in 793. By 780 the salt monopoly was producing half the state's revenue. In 866 it reached 6 million bundles of 1000 coins and in 868 8.8 million. Thus the fiscal system and the relative importance of the different kinds of taxes changed radically between 760 and 800. Not only did the agrarian taxes change in nature, no longer being based on the cultivators but on the land, but taxes on commerce tended to assume more importance than the direct taxes levied on the small farmers. This tendency was to grow even more marked in the Sung period (960–1279).

The state's action in the fiscal domain resulted in favouring the rich merchants who took on the job of collecting the taxes on salt. In any case, it gave them the chance to handle large sums of capital and to increase their economic power. By about 800 trade between the Yangtze valley and North China, and between Szechwan and Che-hsi (southern Kiangsu and northern Chekiang), was in the hands of very rich merchants who had become the government's authorized agents — for example, the big salt merchants of Yangchow, the large commercial city on the Grand Canal twenty kilometres north of the Yangtze, and the rich business men of Ch'eng-tu in Szechwan. It is interesting to note the extraordinary growth of the tea trade during the course of the eighth century (the use of tea as a drink began to spread under the T'ang). By the end of the eighth century the revenue from the taxes on the tea trade — tea was grown in Anhwei, Chekiang, and Fukien as well as in Szechwan — reached 400,000 bundles of 1000 copper coins, that is, nearly 12 percent of the huge income from the salt tax.

The tea merchants played a considerable part in the invention of new methods of transferring credit. In the years 806–20 the first bills of exchange appeared, under the name of *fei-ch'ien* ('flying money'). The tea merchants who came to sell their cargoes in the capital handed over their profits to the offices in Ch'ang-an representing their provincial administrations (the *chin-tsou-yuan*) and received in return I.O.U.'s which enabled them, when they returned to their provinces, to receive payment in currency after deduction of the taxes levied in the capital. At the end of the ninth century and the beginning of the tenth, warehouses, pawnbrokers, money-changers and, later on, business firms in Ch'eng-tu (Szechwan) began to issue negotiable certificates of deposit which were the ancestors of the banknote. The first paper money issued by the state appeared in Szechwan in 1024. The shortage of means of payment at a time when commercial transactions were developing rapidly was the root cause of these innovations in the procedures for transferring credit.

The first great expansion of rice growing

In the eighth century the Chinese world's centre of gravity was tending to move from the Wei valley and the central plain, where it had remained fixed since antiquity, indeed since Neolithic times, towards the plains of the lower Yangtze basin. This extremely important historical phenomenon was no doubt connected both with the progress of 'wet' rice-growing and with the commercial development of the Yangtze area, which produced silks, tea, and salt (Huai salt-pans). While the method of cultivation used up to the sixth century consisted of harvesting the rice from the actual fields in which it had been sown, which made fallows indispensable, the practice of planting out seedlings permitted a rapid increase in yield in the T'ang period. In the eleventh century yields were to increase even more rapidly, thanks to the introduction of early ripening varieties of rice and later to the systematic selection of species. All these improvements made wet rice-growing one of the most skilled agricultural techniques in the world and one which was to provide the highest yields per acre down to our own day. It was also the T'ang period that saw the appearance of tools adapted to this kind of cultivation and already very similar in pattern to those used in our day. These tools were the chain with paddles (*lung-ku-ch'e*), which makes it possible to lift water from one level to another by means of crank gear, the harrow (*p'a*) and the rice-field plough. The progress in rice growing was to favour not only the peopling of the Yangtze valley but also, thanks to the system of canals built for political and strategic purposes about 600, to ensure additional supplies for North China, where production remained subject to climatic hazards. According to the censuses of this period, the population of the areas to the south of the middle and lower Yangtze increased from three million taxable individuals to ten million between about 600 and the year 742. In North China, on the other hand, where the majority of the roughly fifty million people of T'ang China were concentrated, there was a slight drop in the population, which fell in the northern provinces from 75 percent of the total to 53 percent between these two dates. The increase in the amount of rice carried on the Grand Canal at the time when P'ei Yao-ch'ing (681–743) reformed the water transport system by establishing relay-stations and granaries almost certainly enables us to pinpoint the moment when the agricultural upsurge of the lower Yangtze began to show results: seven million *shih*—more than eleven million bushels—of rice were transported to North China during the course of the years 734–36.

This expansion in rice growing did a great deal to help re-establish the dynasty after the great crisis of the years 756–63. The rice granary of the Huai and the lower Yangtze had been spared by the wars and from the end of the eighth century onwards the whole economy of the empire rested on this area.

The crumbling of the empire

Political developments

While the central government was able to give proof of a remarkable capacity for adaptation in the fiscal domain—between 780 and about 850 there was a real restoration of T'ang power—it failed however to regain all over the empire the political control which it had exercised before the rebellion.

An Lu-shan's exceptional power on the eve of the rebellion was due to his combining the command of the military regions of Fan-yang (Peking area), Ho-tung (Shansi), and P'ing-lu (Shantung). He had at his disposal nearly 200,000 men and 30,000 horses, apart from the help that he could be given by the nomadic tribes of eastern Mongolia and southern Manchuria. But the very cause of the rebellion, namely the *de facto* independence of the imperial commissioners (*chieh-tu-shih*) in command of military regions, was not removed. On the contrary, the constitutional authority was led to multiply the military regions in the provinces and to increase the powers of the *chieh-tu-shih* in order to combat the insurgents. At the end of the T'ang period there were forty to fifty military regions of varying importance, and the institution was to continue under the Five Dynasties (907–60), when there were still thirty to forty *fanchen*.

Table 12. Ten military regions (*fan-chen*) existing about 742

Name	Seat	Strength in soldiers	and	horses
An-hsi	Kucha (Tarim basin)	24,000		2,700
Pei-t'ing	Beshbalik (near the modern Urumchi)	20,000		5,000
Ho-hsi	Liang-chou (central Kansu)	73,000		7,900
Shuo-fang	Ling-chou (upper reaches of the Yellow River)	64,700		13,300
Ho-tung	T'ai-yuan (Shansi)	55,000		14,800
Fan-yang	Yu-chou (area of modern Peking)	91,400		6,500
P'ing-lu	Ying-chou (Shantung)	37,500		5,500
Lung-yu	Shan-chou (Kokonor)	75,000		10,000
Chien-nan	Ch'eng-tu (Szechwan)	30,900		2,000
Ling-nan	Canton	15,400		0

The *de facto* autonomy which the central government had been forced to grant to the imperial commissioners was to cause the division of the empire and the fall of the dynasty. However, this development seems to have been accelerated by a curious itinerant rebellion.

As a result of famines in North China, bands of robbers grew up in 874 on the borders of Shantung, Honan, and Kiangsu. In the following year they found leaders in the persons of two salt smugglers, the first of whom, Wang Hsien-chih, was to be executed in 878 after going over to the T'ang, and the second of whom, Huang Ch'ao, was to give his name to this rebellion. Starting out from south-western Shantung, the bands of insurgents travelled all the main roads of China, pillaging the richest towns and ravaging everything as they passed. They began by attacking the townships on the Yellow River. In 878 they left the area south of Loyang for the middle Yangtze and reached Lake P'o-yang. They then travelled round Anhwei and Chekiang, reaching Foochow and in 879 Canton, where they massacred the rich foreign merchants. They then took the road for Kwangsi and Hunan, occupying Loyang at the end of 880. The wave of insurgents, 600,000 strong, reached Ch'ang-an the next year. The capital and the surrounding area were put to the sword and set aflame. Driven out of Ch'ang-an by government troops, which took in their turn to pillaging, Huang Ch'ao returned five days later and subjected the unfortunate city to what he himself called 'a blood bath'. Only ruins were recaptured in 883 by the Sha-t'o Tatar troops commanded by Li K'o-yung (856–908), a sinicized Turk in the service of the T'ang. In the period of chaos that marked the end of the dynasty Li K'o-yung was to be one of the aspirants to the imperial power and succeeded in his aim by founding the Later T'ang dynasty in 923. The T'ang emperors had now become the playthings of the most powerful war-lords and after 885 no longer resided, except for short periods, in Ch'ang-an, the huge metropolis which in the seventh and eighth centuries had symbolized the glory and splendour of the T'ang, but at Loyang.

A former lieutanant of Huang Ch'ao's who had been induced to support the legitimate government, a man called Chu Wen (Chu Ch'üan-chung) (852–912), who occupied the strategic point of K'ai-feng in eastern Honan, founded the new empire of the Liang (Hou Liang, Later Liang) in 907. This date marks the nominal end of a dynasty which had lost any real power by 885.

A new form of power

The men directly responsible for the decline and fall of the T'ang dynasty were the *chieh-tu-shih,* the imperial commissioners in command of military regions (*fan-chen*); it was they and their armies who robbed the central government of its control over the provinces and put an end to the T'ang by causing a breakup of China which was to last for nearly a century.

The first military commissioners were members of the aristocracy or of the scholarly class, the literati, but the weakening of the imperial power after the rebellion of Wang Hsien-chih and Huang Ch'ao (874–83) led to the elimination of the old administrative staff in the military regions. Through a sort of democratic choice which often operates in armies which have made themselves independent of the central government, it was the troops who appointed their own generals and raised them to the dignity of 'imperial commissioners'. This choice was inspired solely by popularity, military ability, and personal authority; thus it was that men from the lowest strata of society were raised to power in the provinces. Chu Ch'üan-chung (Chu Wen), founder of the first of the five dynasties which succeeded each other at K'ai-feng between 907 and 960, was the son of a ruined country gentleman. Starting as an agricultural labourer, then becoming a section-leader in the army, he owed his appointment as imperial commissioner to his feats of arms in the campaigns against Huang Ch'ao. Wang Chien, who carved himself out a kingdom in Szechwan, was a former brigand who opted for a soldier's life; Ch'ien Liu, first prince of the kingdom of Wu and Yueh (southern Kiangsu and northern Chekiang), was an uprooted peasant who enrolled in the private militias of the great families of Hangchow; and the Wang brothers, who were to reign in Fukien, were former Honan bandits. One founder of a kingdom — Ching-nan on the middle Yangtze — was a former slave of a K'ai-feng merchant; another — Ma Yin, prince of Ch'u — was a carpenter who had taken to brigandage. Li K'o-yung, founder of the Later T'ang dynasty was, as we have seen, a leader of the Sha-t'o Turkish tribes who

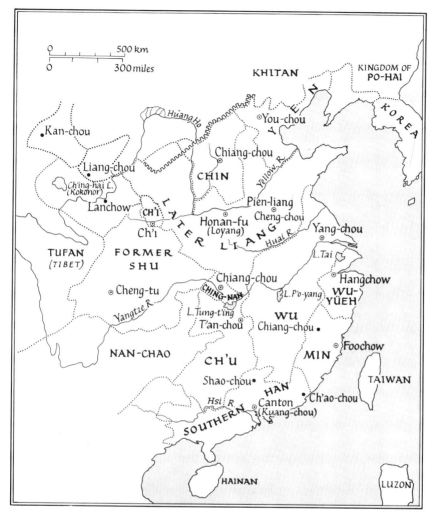

Map 16   The political breakup of China under the Five Dynasties (tenth century)

Table 13. The partition of the T'ang empire and the transformation
of the military regions into kingdoms and empires

Regions (*Fan-chen*)	Kingdoms (*Kuo*)	Empires
Northern Shansi 883	Chin 895	Hou T'ang 923
Eastern Honan and upper reaches of the Huai 883	Hou Liang 901	Hou Liang 907
Northern Anhwei and northern Kiangsu 892	Wu 902	Wu 927
Northern Hopei 894	Yen 909	Yen 911
Western basin of the Wei 887	Ch'i 901	Hou T'ang 927
Fukien 896	Min 909	Min 945
Szechwan 891		Ch'ien Shu 907
Hunan 891	Ch'u 907	
Chekiang 898	Yueh 902	Wu-Yueh 907

This table shows that the *de facto* independence of the future kingdoms of the Five
Dynasties had been gained by the end of the ninth century.

had put himself at the service of the T'ang emperor at the time of Huang
Ch'ao's rebellion.

There thus arose a new governing class in which the habits of the
lawless days remained very much alive: close ties bound the regional
satraps to their generals. It was the custom among brigands and rebels to
swear fraternity, and this oath implied even more duties than were required by ties of blood. We also find the practice of adoption developing
in the independent armies of the end of the T'ang period; the generals
who were heads of states took as their adoptive sons (*i-erh*) their
lieutenants and ministers. These ties of fictional relationship explain the
cohesion of the private guards and personal armies of mercenaries that
formed the most solid foundations of the new powers which in all the
regions replaced the authority of the central government by eliminating
its civil officials. The concentration of armed force in the hands of the
head of state was characteristic of the period of the Five Dynasties and of
the early Sung period. From this point of view, the process of evolution
which led from the autonomous military regions of the end of the ninth
century to the reunification of the Chinese lands by the founder of the
Sung dynasty was continuous: the Sung empire issued directly from the
independent commanderies of the end of the T'ang period.

To start with, the imperial commissioners designated their own successors—the imperial court only ratified the choice, trying at least to
sanction with its own authority what it could not prevent—and their
power soon became hereditary. Later on, round about 900, the independent regions assumed the name of kingdoms (*kuo*), and a few years after
that their leaders did not hesitate to usurp the title of emperor and to
found dynasties. The only differences between the 'Five Dynasties' which

followed each other at K'ai-feng and the 'Ten Kingdoms' which shared the rest of the former T'ang empire were that the K'ai-feng governments controlled a more extensive area, in North China, and that they were regarded as the successors of the T'ang.

Regional autonomy and economic expansion in the tenth century

The weakness of the central government at the end of the T'ang period favoured the awakening of regionalist tendencies: most of the kingdoms which arose out of the military regions corresponded with big natural areas. Such was the case with the kingdoms of Shu in Szechwan, of the Southern Han centred on Canton, of Min in Fukien, of Ch'u in Hunan, and of Wu-Yueh in Chekiang. Their independence allowed these regions to assert their natural vocations, to develop their economies autonomously, and to enter into relations with foreign countries. Some modern historians have seen in the revolt of the Szechwan brocade-makers headed by Wang Hsiao-po and Li Shun from 993 to 995 an autonomist movement which sought to prolong the economic and political independence of Szechwan at a time when the province was in the process of being annexed to the Sung empire: the rebellious craftsmen were threatened by the production of brocades in the K'ai-feng area. In the Yangtze basin and parts of the maritime provinces the economic boom which had become evident in the eighth century does not seem to have slowed down. The kingdom of Min in Fukien, whose land communications with the inland provinces were difficult, grew rich by developing its maritime relations and by exporting the silks and ceramics manufactured in Fukien, Chekiang, and Anhwei. The real expansion of Canton occurred at the beginning of the tenth century. The kingdom of Ch'u centred on Ch'ang-sha increased its production of silk and cloth, and drew a substantial income from its exports of tea to the North. But while Szechwan, the Yangtze basin, and the maritime provinces of the South seem to have experienced in the tenth century a period of prosperity which lasted through the eleventh, twelfth, and thirteenth centuries up to the Mongol conquest (1273–79), the North suffered considerably from the wars which ravaged it continuously between 890 and 923. Ch'ang-an was in ruins and Loyang was depopulated, so that we can understand why the governments which succeeded the T'ang from 907 onwards established their capital more to the east, right at the mouth of the Grand Canal. The North was short of soldiers for its armies and sometimes all able-bodied men were conscripted, whatever their age. Desertions were numerous—to eliminate them, men were branded—and continued to pose a serious problem until the end of the tenth century. As a result of the breaches made in order to flood territory occupied by enemy troops, the dykes of the Yellow River had lost some of their strength. In 931 they gave way and caused a catastrophe. In addition, the attacks of the Khitan, a Turco-Mongolian people of the regions to the north of Peking, contributed to the general insecurity and to the instability of the K'ai-feng governments.

Conclusion

The dawn of a new world

Certain new factors which made their appearance during the course of the T'ang age and at the end of it were to modify considerably the physiognomy of the Chinese world. First signs of the changes to come, they make it possible already to draw in outline the picture of a China very different from that of the seventh century, which had received from the medieval age the social and political traditions of the North and the literary and artistic legacy of the Six Dynasties.

In essentials, the new factors were these.

1. The decline and disappearance of the old north-western aristocracy and, more generally, the elimination of the old governing classes of the seventh and eighth centuries. The society of the Sung age was to be a society of new men, unconnected with the great families of aristocrats or literati of the first part of the T'ang age.

2. The formation in the ninth and tenth centuries of professional armies of mercenaries which were going to replace the conscript armies traditional since the Ch'in and Han ages. Hence a new definition of political power: the head of state was no longer supported by a number of powerful families who had put him on the throne, but by a body of picked troops who were personally devoted to him.

3. An apparently not very far-reaching change in the fiscal system which in fact had very important consequences. Whereas since the end of antiquity the state's main demand had been on men and their capacity for work — which made the sharing-out of cultivable land and the elimination of estates essential — Yang Yen's reforms of 780, necessitated by movements of population and the difficulty of carrying out checks, resulted in the transfer of this demand to cultivated areas, thus reinforcing a concept of property alien to the tradition. The recourse to armies of mercenaries, though explained by certain political circumstances, was also connected with this relaxation of the state's control over individuals.

4. The inability to use the roads to central Asia—a particular cause of the decline of the Buddhist church—and also, from the early years of the tenth century, the renewal of nomad pressure, which ended in the formation of big sinicized empires, of which there had not been any examples in the past. The closure of the northern frontiers caused a shift in the centre of economic and political gravity towards the east and south-east, a phenomenon which was accelerated and accentuated by the more and more marked upsurge of lower-Yangtze China. Unlike seventh-century China, which faced the interior of Asia, the China that started to come into being from the middle of the T'ang age onwards faced the oceans.

5. The agricultural, commercial, and urban expansion of lower-Yangtze China. This was due to progress in wet rice-growing; to the development of new commercial routes (tea, salt, the provision of forage and grain for the armies of the north) which bound Yangtze China and Szechwan closely to North China; and to the development of new commercial techniques (the negotiable certificate of deposit which was to give birth to the banknote). In this context, the institution of state monopolies favoured the rise of a new class of big merchants, who however could not escape the tutelage of the political authority.

6. The appearance of a technical innovation—the reproduction of texts and drawings by wood engraving—which, by causing a sudden diffusion of knowledge, led to the enlargement of the social base of the governing classes and also gave birth to a popular literature that was no longer transmitted orally, but in writing.

Chapter 13

From the Opening-up to the World to the Return to the Sources of the Classical Tradition

The intellectual history of the seventh to tenth centuries offers a remarkable parallel with the political evolution of the same period. Heir to the traditions of the medieval period, seventh- and eighth-century China carried Buddhist studies and poetry of regular form to their zenith. Loyal to the 'aestheticism' of the third to sixth centuries, it made few innovations except in the field of history, where an early effort at reflection made its appearance. It welcomed everything that came from abroad and exerted a profound effect on most of Asia. China's influence was almost certainly never so dazzling. But the ebb of Chinese expansion after the middle of the eighth century provoked a reaction of withdrawal into self, of hostility to foreign cultures and of return towards the sources of the Chinese tradition as it was before the medieval period. It was still only a question of tendencies, but these tendencies were to become dominant at the time of the great Chinese 'Renaissance' of the eleventh century.

The zenith of medieval culture

History and poetry

The traditions of the period of the northern and southern dynasties (fourth to sixth centuries) lasted into the Sui and T'ang periods and remained dominant until the middle of the eighth century.

The studied prose style, with its paired phrases, and the brand of courtly poetry which were in favour in Yangtze China in the sixth century were still cultivated at the beginning of the T'ang age, and literary criticism remained based on a purely aesthetic appreciation of works of literature. Witness to this is the interest still shown in the *Wen-hsuan,* an anthology of the best pieces of literature. In 658 Li Shan published his famous commentary on it which was to be included in 719 in the *Wen-hsuan with Five Commentators* (*Wu-ch'en-chu Wen-hsuan*). Similarly the *Notes by Periods on the Famous Painters* (*Li-tai ming-hua-chi*), in which Chang Yen-yuan assembled his critical notes on 371 painters and calligraphers from the Ch'in age to the year 841, continued the tradition of the works of pictorial criticism of the southern dynasties.

The T'ang period was the golden age of classical poetry, of the regular poem that combined alternating tones and rhymes in accordance with strict rules. The poetry of this period draws on the rich legacy formed by the long tradition which stretched from the lyric poetry of the Han age, moving in its simplicity, to the decadent and over-subtle poets of the last of the southern dynasties. But at the same time a refreshing wind came to renew the sources of inspiration in a China open to the steppes, the oases of central Asia and distant civilizations and also, from the social point of view, less compartmented. Poetry was no longer the perquisite of an exclusive aristocracy as it had remained under the southern dynasties, and from the end of the seventh century onwards the examination system had the effect of favouring the rise of new social strata. The idea, so strange to us, but in harmony with the moral and practical facts of the Chinese world of those days, that one could only be an accomplished man if one possessed a poetical culture had imposed a poetry test in the most highly esteemed of the competitions for recruiting civil servants. This stipulation was doubtless not unconnected with the astonishing upsurge of this kind of literature from the seventh to the tenth century. One must also take into account the role of Maecenas played by the emperors — the great Hsüan-tsung (712–56) was poet, musician, and actor — and the important part played by the circles of singing prostitutes frequented by the gilded youth of Ch'ang-an and by the candidates for the official competitions.

Some of the best poems of the T'ang age were to be collected and published at the beginning of the eighteenth century in the *Complete Collection of the T'ang Poets* (*Ch'üan-t'ang-shih*) (1705), which contains 48,900 poems by 2300 writers. Among the greatest of these poets were Ch'en Tzu-ang (661–702), Sung Chih-wen (died *c.* 710) and Shen Ch'üanch'i (died *c.* 713) at the beginning of the dynasty; and Meng Hao-jan (689–740), Wang Ch'ang-ling (?–755), Wang Wei (701?–16), Li Pai (701–62), Kao Shih (*c.* 702–65) and Tu Fu (712–70) in the brilliant reign of Hsüan-tsung and in that of Su-tsung. In the first half of the ninth century, when the new reforming tendencies made themselves felt, came Pai Chü-i (772–846) and his friend Yüan Chen (779–831), and finally Tu Mu (803–53) — known as 'little Tu' to distinguish him from his illustrious predecessor the great Tu Fu — Li Shang-Yin (812–59) and Wen T'ing-yun (812–70?). All these writers were original, personal poets who at the same time reflect the very dissimilar times in which they lived.

The state of classical studies was hardly any brighter under the Sui and T'ang than it had been since the period of chaos in which the Han dynasty ended. The *Wu-ching cheng-i* (*Correct Meaning of the Five Classics*), written by K'ung Ying-ta (574–648) and Yen Shih-Ku (581–645) and published in 653, is in fact only a compilation of the earlier commentaries of K'ung An-Kuo (end of the second century B.C.), Cheng Hsüan (127–200) and Tu Yü (222–84) on the *Tso-chuan,* and of Wang Pi (226–49) on the *I-ching.* In another commentator on the classics, Lu Yüan-lang (Lu Te-ming) (*c.* 581–630), we find a continuing interest in the works favoured by the School of Mysteries (*hsuan-hsueh*) in the third and fourth centuries. He wrote commentaries on the *Lao-tzu* and the *I-ching.*

On the other hand, new tendencies are apparent in history in the seventh and eighth centuries. Historiography developed considerably at the beginning of the T'ang period and started down a road the dangers of which were soon to be pointed out: apart from the histories of the northern dynasties (*Pei-shih*) (645) and of the southern dynasties (*Nan-shih*) (659) by Li Yen-shou (dates unknown), five dynastic histories were compiled by teams of official historiographers. The different parts of the *Suishu* (*History of the Sui*) were completed in 622 and 656, the *History of the Liang* (*Liang-shu*) and the *History of the Ch'en* (*Ch'en-shu*) about 629, the *History of the Northern Chou* (*Chou-shu*) in 636 and that of the Chin (*Chin-shu*) in 645. The mechanical character of these compilations, the control exercised by the political authorities over their drafting, the silences and distortions imposed on the authors by the men in power, and their lack of reflection and coordination were to be criticized by a writer of independent mind as early as the beginning of the eighth century. The *Generalities on History* (*Shih-t'ung*) by Liu Chih-chi (661–721), which appeared in 710 and was the first work of this kind in the history of the world, marks the start of a tendency to reflect on the problems of history and historiography which was to develop considerably in the eleventh century and to result much later, with Chang Hsüeh-ch'eng (1738–1801), in a philosophy of history which calls to mind Vico and Hegel. In fact Liu Chih-chi already heralds the historians of the Sung period and the philosophers of the seventeenth and eighteenth centuries in his rejection of any irrational interpretation (for example, the relation of the dynastic cycles to the succession of the five elementary virtues, *wu-hsing*), in his wish to retain in history only human factors, his view of the necessity for monographs on cities, clans, and the flora and fauna of different regions, his interest in recording words accurately in the form in which they were uttered (because they echo the man himself and retain the mark of his personality), his critical attitude to the Classics, his primordial concern for objectivity, and his quest for criteria of historical truth.

Just at the time when these first stirrings of the critical spirit were making themselves evident — and no doubt in conjunction with them — historical works of a new kind began to appear. Responding to the needs of the age and to a new interest in institutions, they testify at the same time to the reaction provoked by the routine character of the official compilations. These new works were political and historical encyclopaedias which no longer confined themselves to the traditional framework of dynasties but embraced more extensive periods, in order to be able to pick out the changes made to institutions down the years. Examples of such works are the *Cheng-tien* (740) by Liu Chih, the son of Liu Chih-chi, and the famous *T'ung-tien* by Tu Yu (732–812), a history of political institutions from antiquity down to the year 800, in which we find a note on the great Muslim centre of Kufa in Mesopotamia. These first encyclopaedias were the direct ancestors of the great historical works of the Sung age (twelfth and thirteenth centuries).

The zenith of Chinese Buddhism

Sui and T'ang China, from the end of the sixth century to the middle of the ninth, was the most brilliant centre of Buddhism, the universal religion for most of the peoples of Asia. It was to this fact even more than to the victorious campaigns waged from Korea to Iran that China owed its widespread influence. For Japan and Korea, T'ang China was a sort of second home of Buddhism, nearer than India but enjoying just as high a reputation for its remains, its legends, its sanctuaries, its famous places of pilgrimage, and its illustrious masters. Manifestations of the Bodhisattva Manjusri took place in the Wu-t'ai Mountains (north-eastern Shansi), and P'u-hsien (Samantabhadra), mounted on his elephant, haunted the mists of Mount Emei in Szechwan. Buddhism formed an integral part of the civilization, society, and political system of the Chinese world in the Sui and T'ang periods. The monasteries were centres of a culture both lay and religious, Chinese and Buddhist. The scholarly monk — poet, painter and calligrapher — was paralleled by the pious layman, interested in Buddhist philosophy, practising techniques of concentration, and capable of debating points of doctrine with the priests in monasteries or mountain hermitages.

We can follow the blossoming of a typically Chinese brand of Buddhism which made various innovations in the field of interpretation and doctrine. It was the age that produced the great sects that were to be perpetuated in Japan, and also the age in which Buddhism was enriched in China by new contributions from India and the Buddhist countries and by a considerable number of new traditions.

The history of the Chinese Buddhist sects is complex and cannot be dealt with in detail here. It should simply be noted that, contrary to the traditions established by their devotees, who sought to date the origins of their sects as far back as possible, their formation was relatively late. Only the principal one will be mentioned here. Some sects were very successful and spread to the laity, others never passed the narrow bounds of the religious communities. Such was the case with the eclectic school of T'ien-t'ai (a mountain in north-western Chekiang), which was founded by the monk Chih-i (538–97) and according to which the different sutras of the Greater Vehicle are arranged in chronological order and are addressed to different audiences, the text which contains the very essence of Buddhism being the famous *Lotus of the True Law* (*Fa-hua-ching*). Such was the case too with the school of Hua-yen, known as the 'school of ornamentation'. It was founded by the monk Fa-tsang (643–712), scion of a Sogdian family of Ch'ang-an, who took as his basic text the *Avatamsakasutra* (*Hua-yen-ching*).

The wide popular success of the Pure Land (*Ching-t'u*) sect, whose first patriarch was Shan-tao (613–81), is explained by the progress made since the time of Hui-yuan at the beginning of the sixth century by the great tide of devotion to the Buddha of Infinite Light (Amitabha) and also by the simplicity of its ritual: the vow to be reborn in the Pure Land, coupled with incessant homage to the Buddha Amitabha.

The typically Chinese *ch'an* sect (the Japanese *zen*), which took shape in the eighth century and was to remain one of the most long-lived, met an enthusiastic welcome among the literati. Unlike the Indian *dhyana,* of which the term *ch'an* is the Chinese transliteration, the school rejected the long ascetic training which made it possible, through the mastery of more and more difficult kinds of concentration, to attain the 'extremity of being'. Iconoclastic, hostile to all systems, dogmas, scriptures, and rites, this sect, founded about 700 by the Cantonese monk Hui-neng, a semi-barbarian, aimed at sudden illumination. In order to detach the mind from any discursive thought and from the notion of self, recourse was had to paradoxes, to meditation on absurd subjects ('cases', *kung-an*), to baffling responses, shouts, and sometimes even blows of a stick.

However, it was also the T'ang period's pilgrims and translators that made it one of the greatest in the history of Buddhism in East Asia. The two most famous pilgrims of the seventh century were Hsüan-tsang (602–64) and I-ching (635–713).

When Hsüan-tsang set off alone across the deserts of central Asia in 629 he was already one of the best authorities on Buddhist philosophy, insofar as it was accessible in Chinese translations. His aim was to procure a manuscript of the great treatise on metaphysics called *Lands of the Masters of Yoga* (*Yogacaryabhumisastra*; in Chinese, *Yu-ch'ieh shih-ti lun*) and to enlarge his knowledge in order to be able to resolve the contradictions between the different philosophical schools of Buddhism. After spending two years in Kashmir he reached the holy ground of primitive Buddhism in Magadha (the Patna and Gaya area in Bihar) and spent five years studying in the famous Buddhist monastery of Nalanda, near Rajagrha (the modern Rajgir). He then toured the whole of India, from north to south and from east to west, listening to the most celebrated teachers. But he was already their equal through his complete mastery of Sanskrit – a language into which he was to translate, in 647 after his return to China, the text of the *Lao-tzu tao-te-ching* for the King of Kamarupa (a kingdom in what is now Assam) – and through his detailed knowledge of Buddhist metaphysics and its immensely long and difficult treatises. Returning to Ch'ang-an in 645, after being away for sixteen years, Hsüan-tsang directed until his death the most prolific translating teams in the whole history of Chinese Buddhism. In the course of these eighteen years of work he was responsible for about a quarter of all the translations of Indian texts into Chinese (1338 chapters out of a total of 5084 chapters translated in six centuries by 185 teams of translators).

A year after the Master's return, one of his disciples used his travel notes to compile a general work on the countries that he had visited, from central Asia to the southern Deccan and from the Kabul area to Assam. This work was the *Ta-t'ang hsi-yü-chi* (*Treatise on the Western*

Regions in the Days of the Great T'ang). It provides information about climate, produce, manners and customs, political systems and history, as well as about the state of Buddhism in these various regions of Asia. The biography of Hsüan-tsang (the *Ta-tz'u-en-ssu san-tsang-fa-shih chuan*), which was begun as soon as he had died and was to be revised in 688, is devoted more particularly to a detailed account of his journeys.

The second most famous pilgrim of the seventh century, I-ching, embarked in 671 on an Iranian merchant ship with the intention of sailing to India. After a stay on the eastern coast of Sumatra, at the great Buddhist centre of Sri Vijaya (modern Palembang), he landed in 673 at Tamralipti on the coast of Bengal, near present-day Calcutta. From there he went to Magadha and resided for nearly ten years at Nalanda, the very spot to which Hsüan-tsang had come to learn thirty years earlier. He left India in 685 and went back, again by sea, to Sri Vijaya, where he remained until his return to China in 695. He was welcomed in Loyang by the empress Tse-t'ien in person. It was at Palembang that I-ching wrote his two famous historical works, the manuscripts of which he sent to Canton in 692. One deals with the state of Buddhism in India and South-East Asia (*Report on Buddhism sent from the South Seas, Nan-hai chi-kuei nei-fa chuan*); the other is a series of notes about the Chinese pilgrims who travelled to the Buddhist countries in the seventh century (*Report on the Eminent Monks who went to seek the Law in the Western Regions in the Days of the Great T'ang, Ta-t'ang hsi-yü ch'iu-fa kao-seng chuan*).

Only two other pilgrims' accounts of their journeys have survived from the T'ang age: that of the Korean monk Hui-ch'ao, who went to India by sea and returned to China through central Asia in 729, and that of the monk Wu-k'ung, who travelled to the north of present-day Afghanistan and the Ganges valley. Leaving Ch'ang-an in 751, Wu-k'ung returned to China in 790 via the oases of Kashgar and Kucha.

The closure of the central Asian routes, which were occupied by the Tibetans and the Arabs, and the dispersal of the Buddhist communities in China at the time of the great proscription of 842–45 were to cause the decline of pilgrimages to India. The last big pilgrimage was to be organized, in an official way, in 966. Over one hundred and fifty monks took part in it. A small number of them reached India (Gandhara, Nepal, and Magadha) via the central Asian oases. They returned to China in 976.

Through his teaching and translations—he translated the great *summa* of the *Lands of the Masters of Yoga* as soon as he returned to Ch'ang-an, in 646–48—Hsüan-tsang made known in China the extremely learned and elaborate philosophy of the Vijnanavada epistemological school, according to which the world perceived by the senses is a creation of the mind. But his influence, which had a great effect on his disciples and was to make itself felt in Japan, was restricted to monastic circles. A remarkable Indian scholar and an exacting philologian (he was responsible for the institution of extremely strict rules for translating), Hsüan-tsang seems to have been an exceptional figure in the history of Buddhism in China: he was the only Chinese who succeeded in mastering the huge field of Buddhist philosophy in all its breadth and complexity.

The introduction in the T'ang age of the esoteric Buddhism known as Tantrism was to have much wider effects. This kind of Buddhism, based on magic formulas and circles and best known in a purified form associated with symbolical speculations, seems to have developed considerably in India from the middle of the seventh century onwards—masters of the Tantra were teaching in Nalanda by this time—and to have spread rapidly to Ceylon and South-East Asia. It soon reached China and Tibet. Chinese translations of Tantrist texts multiplied in the eighth century. The most famous master and translator, Amoghavajra (in Chinese, Pu-k'ung) (705–44) had had two Indian predecessors who had arrived in China in 716 and 719. Almost certainly born in Ceylon, Amoghavajra spent his youth in China and was back in Ceylon between 741 and 746. From 756 onwards he translated a large number of Tantrist texts in Ch'ang-an and scored a great success at the T'ang court.

Tantrism was Indian Buddhism's last contribution to China. Very soon afterwards came the great changes which were to set the Chinese world on new paths and bring about the decline of the big monastic communities. With Tantrism the long period of intensive relations between the 'Indianized' lands and China came to an end. The death of Amoghavajra in 774 symbolizes in its way the end of the Chinese Middle Ages.

However, it should be noted that contacts between the Indian and Chinese civilizations were not limited to the field of Buddhism, rich and varied though that field was. The secular learning of India also found its way to China. We hear of the presence of scholars from the Indian world in Ch'ang-an and Loyang in the first half of the T'ang period, and translations of 'brahminical' texts dealing with astronomy, astrology, mathematics, and medicine seem to have been numerous in the seventh and eighth centuries. But Chinese mathematics also influenced in their turn Indian mathematics.

Foreign influences

In the first half of the T'ang period the upper classes were enamoured of anything 'barbarian'—dances, music, games, cooking, clothes, houses. It is true that the influence of the steppes and of central Asia had had all the time in the world to make itself felt in North China since Han days, but after the big offensives of the early seventh century contacts between China of the Wei and Yellow River valleys and Mongolia, the Tarim basin and the regions beyond the Pamirs became close, multiplied as they were by embassies, delegations bringing tribute, missions, caravans of merchants, and bands of religious pilgrims. Even more foreign colonies than under the Han emperors became established in the commercial cities of Kansu, Shensi, and Honan, on the Grand Canal and in Canton. One may say that the Chinese civilization of that time was cosmopolitan. The capital, Ch'ang-an, was the meeting-place of all the peoples of Asia — Turks, Uighurs, Tibetans, Koreans, people from Khotan and Kucha, Sogdians, Kashmiris, Persians, Arabs, Indians, Cingalese. Paintings and funerary statuettes of the seventh and eighth centuries bear witness to the interest which the Chinese of those days felt in the most distant of these foreigners, who usually had dark complexions and prominent noses. These paintings and figurines give us, with a touch of irony and a slight tendency to caricature, a very vivid picture of these strangers. This invasion of foreigners, of elements of distant cultures, of exotic products (slaves, animals, plants, foods, perfumes, medicines, textiles, and jewels) could not fail to affect the sensibilities of the age and to enrich the T'ang civilization with its new contributions. This is how the dances and music of central Asia and India came to change the taste of Chinese society. Indian music found its way into China via central Asia (Kucha) and later via Cambodia and Champa. Some elements in it were to be preserved in the court music of Japan. Everything that came from central Asia found favour with the upper classes — the dances and music of Turfan, Kashgar, Bukhara, and especially Kucha. A distinctive synthesis — and one much appreciated in China — of this music from Kucha and Chinese music was achieved in the trading city of Liang-chou (Wu-Wei, in Kansu), which seems to have been one of the most important centres for the diffusion of central Asian and Indo-Iranian influences in China.

Iranian influences

The two big currents of civilization flowing from Persia and India mingled and mutually enriched each other in the whole area extending from Afghanistan to the valley of the Amu-Darya and the oases of the Tarim basin. The most active merchants in central Asia and North China came from Samarkand (K'ang to the Chinese), Maimargh (Mi), Kish (Shih), and Bukhara (An). Their language, Sogdian, an eastern Iranian dialect spoken on all the roads from the Amu-Darya basin to the Wei valley, was the great medium of communication in central Asia. Since the trade routes continued from Bukhara on to Merv and from Balkh on to Herat, it is not surprising that Iranian influences penetrated fairly widely into China. By pushing on beyond the Pamirs the T'ang emperors had been led to interfere in Iranian politics. The presence of an embassy from Sassanid Persia in Ch'ang-an is mentioned as early as 638, and the Arab incursions which began in 642 were to tighten the links between the Iranian court and that of the emperor Kao-tsung. Even distant Byzantium had considered the idea of an alliance with China: a Byzantine embassy is reported to have been in Ch'ang-an in 643. In 661 Peroz, the last Sassanid sovereign, who had taken refuge in Tokhara (in the Balkh area), demanded China's help against the Arab attacks. An expedition was organized the following year which advanced as far as Ctesiphon, on the banks of the Tigris, and put Peroz back on his throne. Forced into exile once again, the unhappy monarch arrived in 674 at Ch'ang-an, where he was welcomed with much pomp by the emperor Kao-tsung and given the post of officer in the palace guards. He went back to the west in 674, then returned to Ch'ang-an again in 708 and died there shortly after his arrival.

The influence of Iran is perceptible in Chinese art and craftsmanship of the seventh and eighth centuries. For example, a new method of hammering and chiselling gold and silver objects spread in China at this time; it was of Persian origin. Similarly the game of polo, which seems to have certainly come from Persia, became one of the favourite pastimes of Chinese high society. But it was particularly in the religious field that Iranian influences made themselves felt, with the introduction of new foreign cults in the towns of Kansu, at Ch'ang-an, and at Loyang.

The Nestorian Christianity which had spread over Sassanid Iran in the fifth and sixth centuries had reached Herat, Balkh, and Samarkand, and infiltrated the western oases of the modern province of Sinkiang. It seems to have been introduced into the commercial cities of Kansu and into the Wei valley soon after the big offensives which had opened the roads of central Asia to China. A famous bilingual stele in Syriac and Chinese erected in the Nestorian church in the I-ning district of Ch'ang-an and dated 781 — its discovery in 1625 was to cause a sensation among the Jesuit missionaries — tells the story of the then quite recent evangelization of China. The Scriptures had been brought to Ch'ang-an in 631 by a Persian known in Chinese as A-lo-pen. Seven years later the T'ang court authorized the preaching of the Gospel and the construction of Christian churches. A prey to the hostility of the Buddhists during the reign of the empress Tse-t'ien (690–705), the new religion once again enjoyed imperial protection under Hsüan-tsung (712–56). It was a Christianity heavily tinged with Iranian influences in its dogma, its liturgy, and its vocabulary. Known in China as 'the religion of the sacred texts of Persia' (*po-ssu ching-chiao*) and as 'the religion of the great Ch'in' — a

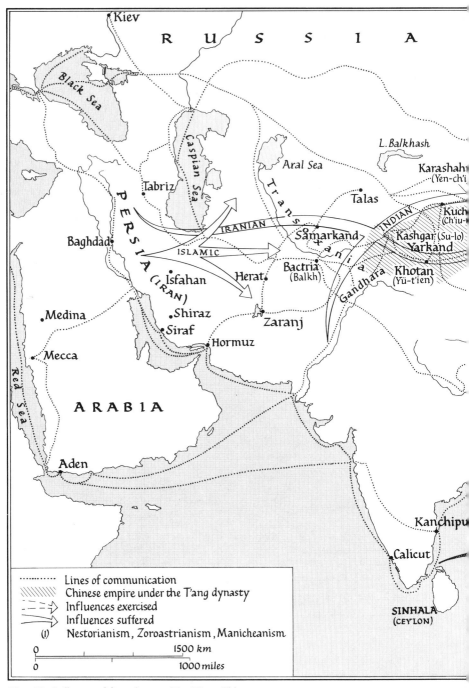

Map 17 Influences felt and exerted by T'ang China

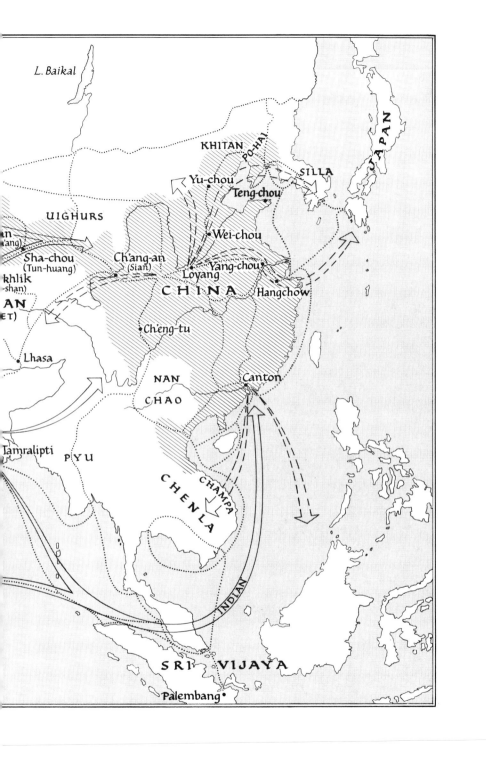

phrase which recalls the origin of this Christian heresy, condemned at the Council of Ephesus in 431, in the Byzantine empire – or again as 'the religion of light', Nestorianism scarcely had time to secure devotees in East Asia. Forbidden at the time of the great proscription of foreign religions in the years 842–45, it seems subsequently to have disappeared completely. It had made its converts mainly among the Sogdian merchants and western Turks (the gospels were also translated into Sogdian and Turkish), and it later made some progress among the Kereit Mongols of the Tchou Valley, to the south-west of Lake Balkhash, and among the Ongut of the Ordos. It was this steppe Christianity which was to provide the basis in the Mongol age for our medieval legend of the Christian Kingdom of Prester John. Its reintroduction into China by the Mongols – in the Yuan period there were Nestorian churches at Chenchiang and Yangchow in the lower Yangtze area and also at Hangchow – was to lead to nothing.

Another religion from Iran was to have a deeper influence. This was Manicheism (Mo-ni-chiao), the practice of which was authorized under the empress Tse-t'ien in 694. It seems to have been fairly firmly implanted among the Uighurs, sedentary Turks who played a big political and economic role in Turfan, Kansu, and Shensi from the middle of the eighth century onwards. The influence of the Manichean priests was to make itself felt in the realms of astrology and astronomy. It was they who introduced into China for the first time the week of days associated with the sun, the moon, and the five planets. The Chinese tradition, faithful to the division of space and time into four and five, had a week of ten days. Proscribed like the other foreign religions in the middle of the ninth century, Manicheism reappeared, strangely enough, on the coasts of Fukien and Chekiang in the eleventh and twelfth centuries, and also in the interior of these provinces, but amalgamated with a stock of Buddhist and partly Taoist traditions. This distinctive cult animated secret societies in rebellion in those regions against the established authorities. However, it could be that the influence of Manicheism was perpetuated in China until the fourteenth century: the name of the Ming dynasty (Ming = light) (1368–1644) may have been suggested to its founder by the persistent memory of Manichean traditions in the secret societies of the Mongol age.

As for the Mazdaism of Zarathustra, which was to disappear from Iran as a result of the Arab conquest, it seems to have penetrated into northern China by the second half of the sixth century, under the Chou and Ch'i dynasties. The military expansion of the Sui and T'ang doubtless increased the number of fire worshippers; in the seventh century there were Mazdaist temples in Tun-huang (Sha-chou), Wu-wei (Liang-chou), Ch'ang-an (temple founded in 631) and Loyang. Displays by magicians in those at Wu-wei and Loyang seem to have scored a certain success. There remained but few traces of this religion, which the Chinese christened *hsien-chiao* (religion of the god of fire), in the tenth to thirteenth centuries.

China and Islam from the seventh to the ninth centuries

During the whole period from the seventh to thirteenth centuries the two great civilizations of Eurasia were those of Islam and China. The T'ang expansion into central Asia and Transoxiania coincided with the great Arab conquests which were to extend the Islamic empire to Spain at one end and Russian Turkestan at the other. The Chinese T'ang and Sung empires, the former continental and warlike, the latter maritime and commercial, were contemporaneous with the Ommayad and Abbassid empires, and belong to the same period of Eurasian history. East Asia and the Islamic world even seem to have evolved in the same way, military conquest giving way to mercantile activities, literature, science, and technology in a world in which urban centres were expanding rapidly. China and Islam both experienced at the same time the terrible trial of the Mongol conquest: it was in 1258 that the armies of the khan Hulagu (1218–65) took possession of Baghdad, and in 1276 that the troops of Bayan (1236–94) entered Hangchow, capital of the Southern Sung.

Thus contacts between the Islamic world and the Chinese world began in the T'ang age and went on up to the Mongol age (thirteenth to fourteenth centuries), in the great political unit created by the successors of Ghengis Khan.

The first contacts took place at the time of the Arab expansion in the area between Mesopotamia and Lake Balkhash, from about 650 to about 750. The whole policy of the T'ang in this part of the world aimed at opposing the victorious advance of the Arab armies, but China's various alliances with the victims of the Ommayad conquest were unable to hold up their progress. Sassanid Persia was conquered between 642 and 652, the oases of Transoxiania were occupied from 704 onwards and the Arabs took possession of Khorezm, Ferghana, and Kashgar in the following years. The Chinese counter-offensive of 745–51 was halted south of Lake Balkhash at the famous battle of the river Talas which, eighteen or nineteen years after Charles Martel's victory over the Arabs at Poitiers, marked the end of Chinese ambitions in Transoxiania and the Kashgar region. The ebb of Chinese influence in the lands on each side of the Pamirs was accelerated by the great crisis caused by An Lu-shan's rebellion in 755–63.

Sino-Islamic contacts were to permit the transmission of certain techniques from East Asia to the Islamic world and thence to Europe.

The best known example is that of paper. The processes for manufacturing paper, developed and perfected in China from the first century A.D. onwards, spread from Samarkand to Baghdad and Damascus; from there they reached Egypt, the Maaghreb, and then Muslim Spain in the tenth to eleventh centuries. The first paper made in Italy dates from the end of the thirteenth century. But for the long journey thus made by a technique invented in northern China twelve centuries earlier, the Western world would not have come to know printing and modern times. According to tradition, it was the prisoners taken by the Arabs at the battle of Talas in 751 who taught them how to manufacture paper. In fact Chinese influences were at work in Transoxiania and Persia before the middle of the eighth century; Chinese paper manufacturers, weavers, goldsmiths, and painters were already settled in Kufa (the present Karbala, to the south-west of Baghdad) and Samarkand at the time of the Arab conquest.

The warfare between the Chinese armies and the Arab horsemen in Transoxiania and south of Lake Balkhash was not to prevent the establishment of political links between Chinese and Muslims: a contingent consisting probably of Persians and Iraqis was sent to Kansu in 756 to help the emperor Su-tsung in his struggle against the rebellion of An Lu-shan. Less than fifty years later an alliance was concluded between the T'ang and the Abbassids against Tibetan attacks in central Asia. A mission from the caliph Harun al-Rashid (766–809) arrived at Ch'ang-an in 798.

These diplomatic relations across central Asia were contemporaneous with the maritime expansion of the Islamic world into the Indian Ocean and as far as East Asia after the foundation of Baghdad in 762. It was after the transfer of the capital from Damascus to Baghdad that ships began to sail from Siraf, the port of Basra on the Persian Gulf, to India, the Malacca Straits, and South China. The trade between the Indian Ocean and the Chinese coast was concerned with luxury goods. Ivory, incense, rhinoceros horns, copper, and black slaves were carried on the outward voyage and silks, spices, and porcelain—most of it made in Fukien—on the return voyage.

In the middle of the eighth century the great port of Canton—the Khanfu of the Arab traders—a colonial city whose hinterland was still inhabited by aboriginal tribes, counted among its population (reckoned at 200,000) a certain number of foreign merchants with dusky faces. These merchants included K'un-lun (Malays), Po-ssu (Iranians, unless this term denotes a country of South-East Asia), P'o-lo-men (Brahmins, that is, Indian merchants), Chams from the east coast of Vietnam, Vietnamese, Khmers, and Sumatrans. The orthodox and Shiite Moslems had their mosques in the foreign quarter on the south bank of the Canton river.

The oldest foreign evidence about Canton we owe to a Moslem. This is the *Account of China and India* (*Akhbar al-Shin wal Hind*), which is attributed to the merchant Suleyman and dated 851.

The pillage of the city in 758 by Iranian and Arab pirates who seem to have had their base in a port on the island of Hainan, and afterwards the rapacity of the eunuchs appointed to the post of 'commissioner for merchant ships' (*shih-po-ssu*), had diverted some of the trade to northern Vietnam and the Ch'ao-chou area, near the Fukien border. But Suleyman's account dates from a time when more honest administrative practices had permitted – since the beginning of the ninth century – a resumption of trading activities in Canton. The sack of the city by Huang Ch'ao's troops in 879, the revolts of black slaves in Basra a few years earlier and then the earthquake which destroyed Siraf in 977 were once again to slow down trade between the Persian Gulf and the big port of tropical China. In the Sung age and after the Mongol occupation of South China, from the eleventh to the fourteenth century, the most active port was no longer Canton, but Ch'üan-chou – the Moslem merchants' 'Zaytun' – on the coast of Fukien.

The radiation of T'ang civilization

The Chinese expansion in Asia in the seventh and eighth centuries resulted in increasing the influence of T'ang civilization in all the neighbouring lands: central Asia, Tibet, Transoxiania, Korea and Japan, and the countries of South-East Asia. Certain elements of Chinese culture spread to the Turks of the Orkhon (the calendar, the cycle of twelve animals, etc.), and the Turkish vocabulary has retained to this day borrowings from Chinese which go back to this epoch. Chinese princesses married to Turkish and Uighur khans or Tibetan bTsan-pos introduced the Chinese classics into the nomads' tents and the stone palaces of Lhasa. The opening of the road to Tibet as a result of the alliance concluded between the T'ang court and the Tibetan royal family a few years before the middle of the century – the first Chinese princess given in marriage to the bTsan-pos arrived in Lhasa in 641 – enabled Chinese pilgrims to travel to the Buddhist holy places via the Tibetan capital and Nepal. This is how the monk Hsüan-chao in 651 and the monk Hsüan-t'ai in the second half of the seventh century made the journey to India. No doubt the same route was taken by many others whose names are now forgotten. Curiously enough, it was from China and not from India – which is relatively nearer – that the first Buddhist influences penetrated into Tibet in the second half of the eighth century.

Moreover, it should not be forgotten that what gave the T'ang empire part of its immense prestige all over Asia was that, with its great sanctuaries, its famous pilgrimages, and its eminent 'Masters of the Law', it was one of the great centres of Buddhism. The T'ang emperors' favours to this great religion and to other foreign cults were doubtless not always devoid of political considerations.

Chinese influences in Japan

In Japan the spread of Chinese influence assumed exceptional proportions during the T'ang age. As early as the first few years of the seventh century it caused a sudden upsurge of political centralization which in turn accelerated the process of borrowing.

No doubt the Chinese influence had never ceased to make itself felt in the Japanese islands and more particularly in Kyushu. The Japanese principalities had entered into relations with the Han empire as early as the time of the Chinese commanderies in Korea, and relations had been maintained with both North and lower-Yangtze China after the formation of the three Korean kingdoms at the beginning of the fourth century. But Chinese prestige in East Asia had never been so great as it became in the seventh and eighth centuries, and Chinese influence on Japan was never so general and so deep as in the T'ang age. Arriving in successive waves, first in 602-22, then in 646-71, it extended to every field—political and administrative institutions, language, literature, technology, religion—and rapidly transformed Japan into a land of Chinese civilization.

In the Nara (710-84) and Heian (794-1068) periods it was no longer even a matter of spontaneous borrowings but rather a policy of deliberate and systematic imitation. Thus Japan, better protected against aggression from outside, has been able to preserve down to our own day many Chinese traditions that go back to the T'ang age.

The Taiho Code, published in 701, and many other Japanese juridical and administrative compilations of the eighth century were closely modelled on the T'ang Code and contemporary Chinese legislation. The plans of the new capital, Heijo (Nara), founded in 710, and of Heian (Kyoto) (793) were both modelled on the plan of Ch'ang-an. The first official histories of Japan, the *Kojiki* (712) and the *Nihonshoki* (720), were compiled on the same lines as the Chinese dynastic histories. All the big Buddhist sects of Japan (Jodo, Tendai, Shingon, Zen, and so on) are offshoots on Japanese soil of the Chinese Buddhist sects of the T'ang period, the doctrines and sacred texts of which were brought to Japan by Japanese, and sometimes Chinese, monks. For example, Chien-chen (688-763), a medical monk from Yangchow in Kiangsu, went to Japan in 753 with four other Chinese monks and ended his days at Nara in 763.

Among the most famous Japanese monks who went to China to study with the great masters of the law and to visit the most celebrated Buddhist centres and holy places (Ch'ang-an, Loyang, T'ien-t'ai-shan in Shansi, and so on) was the monk Gembo (?–746), who set off with an embassy for Ch'ang-an in 716 and brought back to Japan, after an absence of eighteen years, five thousand Buddhist texts in Chinese and various objects of piety. Another was Kukai (774–835) (Kobo daishi), the celebrated founder of the Shingon sect, who travelled in China from 804 to 806; he was accompanied by Saicho (Dengyo daishi) (767–822), who returned home in 805. The monks Jogyo and Engyo (born at Kyoto in 799) were in China from 838 to 839, as was also Ennin, who left a detailed account of his travels, which were often hindered by the Chinese administration, and of the anti-Buddhist measures of 842–45. Between 838 and 847 Ennin visited Yangchow, the Huai valley, the coast of Shantung, the Wu-t'ai Mountains in northern Shansi, and Ch'ang-an and Loyang, returning to Japan via Shantung and the Korean coast. Finally, after Ennin, the following monks – among others – also travelled in China: Eun from 842 to 847, Enchin (Chisho daishi) (814–91) from 853 to 858, and Shuei from 862 to 866. As well as pilgrimages and embassies there were also commercial relations: we are told that at the end of the T'ang period numerous Chinese merchant vessels were to be seen in Japanese ports.

Korea, where Chinese influence was older and deeper, did not escape the powerful attraction of T'ang civilization either. When in 668 Silla swallowed up the kingdoms of Paekche and Koguryo, certain regions where there had been many Chinese colonists were incorporated in the new empire. For about fifty years, at the end of the seventh century and the beginning of the eighth, contacts between the T'ang and Silla became more frequent, thanks to the numerous embassies and to the journeys of Korean monks and students to China. Moreover, at that time Korea held a dominant position in the north-eastern seas. There were Korean colonies on the coast of Shantung and in the commercial towns situated on the Grand Canal between the lower Yangtze and the borders of Honan and Shantung.

The 'nationalist' reaction and the return to the sources of the Chinese tradition

A big change of direction in the intellectual life of China began round about the year 800. In essentials this change consisted of a deep desire on the part of some people to go back to the ancient sources of the Chinese tradition combined with an attitude of hostility to the foreign influences which had permeated China so widely since the end of the Han period. This reaction, which followed a period when the court and the upper classes had been particularly friendly to foreigners and to exotic fashions and products, seems to be largely explained by the aspect of a national defeat assumed by the rebellion of An Lu-shan and by the change of atmosphere which followed those tragic events. It was the culpable indulgence displayed by Hsüan-tsung's government towards the army leaders in general and towards the commanders of foreign descent in particular — An Lu-shan himself was the son of a Sogdian married to a Turkish wife — which had nearly swept away the empire and had left it so much weakened. The barbarians whom the dynasty had had to call on for assistance had settled in the north-west and were laying down the law in Kansu and Shensi. Plundering Tibetans who stole the horses from the imperial stud-farms — one of their raids reached Ch'ang-an in 763 — settled in the towns of Kansu between about 770 and 850, and Uighurs monopolized the horse trade, drawing large profits from it, or lent money on security in the capital and behaved like pitiless usurers. The wealth of the foreign merchants established in the big cities may have provoked the xenophobia that became apparent during rebellions. In 760 several thousand Arab and Persian merchants were massacred at Yangchow by insurgent bands led by T'ien Shen-kung, and a century later, in 879, it was also the foreign merchants who were attacked at Canton by the troops of Huang Ch'ao. But certain political attitudes in the upper classes corresponded with these popular reactions. The aristocracy of mixed blood which had stayed in power so long seems to have retained from its barbarian ancestors a greater aptitude for welcoming what came from outside China and also the taste for military adventures. There gradually grew among the literati and the officials recruited by competition, most of whom came from south-east China, the idea that the intrusion of the barbarians since the fourth century had slowly impaired Chinese purity, corrupted ancient moral standards, and thus brought about the decadence of China. These people, who had little interest in military affairs, thought that the military power should be strictly subordinated to the civil authority. On top of this there was the insolent wealth of the Buddhist church, the power of the monks, and the close and secret links which they maintained with the imperial ladies and the eunuchs. Now it happened that the eunuchs, whose power was on the increase round about the year 800, succeeded in controlling the government under Hsien-tsung (the Yüan-ho era, 806–20), themselves taking the decisions about the investiture and deposition of emperors. Everything led those who regarded themselves as the repositories of Chinese orthodoxy to react: the very excesses of the period, the decline of the aristocracy of Shensi and eastern Kansu since 'the land between the passes' (*kuan-nei*) had lost its economic and political predominance, and the closure of the roads to central Asia along which flowed the biggest wave of foreign influences. Foreign religions, and first and foremost Buddhism, were now cut off from their birthplaces – the oases of the Tarim basin, Kashmir, the borders of India and Iran, and India itself. China was ready to withdraw and turn in upon herself.

The term 'nationalism' would be an anachronism, yet it was certainly reactions analogous to those of nationalism that took vague shape after An Lu-shan's rebellion and that were to become evident again on other occasions in China's history. This attachment to an authentic tradition supposed to have been corrupted by foreign elements, this desire to return to the pure – and imaginary – sources of orthodox thought and morality are difficult to sum up, since they do not relate to the quite recent idea of a nation, but to the idea of culture. If we wanted one word for them, we should have to invent the barbarous term 'culturalism'.

The 'ancient style' movement

Curiously enough, the desire for a return to antiquity first asserted itself in the literary and stylistic field. The idea was to give back to Chinese prose the simplicity, conciseness, and vigour which it had possessed in Han days and at the end of antiquity. The first to show the way, by writing in the 'antique style' (*ku-wen*) was Liu Tsung-yüan (773–819). But according to Chinese notions form cannot be separated from content; the stylistic researches of the age of the Six Dynasties corresponded to a complete indifference to morality. Now literature is not just a kind of aesthetic relaxation. If it does not express sound and strong ideas, it is no longer anything but a contemptible exercise in virtuosity. The educational, moral, and political function which it had possessed in antiquity was inseparable from its form. Such were the themes which were to be elaborated by Han Yü (768–824), the greatest Chinese prose writer after Ssu-ma Ch'ien. Han Yü was an orthodox member of the literati and a notorious anti-Buddhist; his diatribe in 819 against the scenes of mass hysteria which accompanied the moving of a relic of the Buddha has remained famous. Doubtless Liu Tsung-yüan and Han Yü had had predecessors in certain historians and poets since the beginning of the T'ang age; among others, Liu Mien, prefect of Foochow in the Chen-kuan era (627–49), who took the view that since the end of the Han age the *tao* – wisdom and truth – of the ancients had been lost. But it was with Han Yü and Liu Tsung-yüan that the *ku-wen* movement acquired its patent of nobility. They set afoot the process of radical evolution which was to end, in the eleventh and twelfth centuries, in the sort of renaissance constituted by 'neo-Confucianism'. Indeed we already find in one of Han Yü's immediate successors a philosophical tendency which heralds the first neo-Confucians of the Sung age. In order the better to refute Buddhism, Li Ao (*c.* 772–836) studied Buddhist philosophy and soaked himself in the thought of the *ch'an* school. These studies led him to new conceptions of the classical ideas of *hsin* (mind) the *hsing* (hsian) which were to guide the whole philosophy of the Sung age. According to this philosophy, the basic nature of the Wise Man is disturbed by the passions (*ch'ing*) yet the nature of the Wise Man and his passions are as inseparable as the light and the dark. Truth — which is perfect sincerity (and impassibility), *ch'eng* — is beyond all distinction, beyond any opposition between basic nature and passions. Here we have the basic dialectical approach of the *ch'an* school transposed into the vocabulary of the Classics and of the *Mencius*.

The repression and decline of Buddhism

The xenophobic and 'nationalistic' character of the movement which was to end, in 842–45, in the great proscription of foreign religions and of the foremost among them, Buddhism, is quite clear from the reasons invoked at the time. As early as 836 a decree forbade Chinese to have any relations with 'people of colour', a term that denoted foreigners from the regions beyond the Pamirs or from South-East Asia—Iranians, Sogdians, Arabs, Indians, Malays, Sumatrans, and so on. The proscription decree, which was published after the event in 845, at a time when all the practical measures had been taken, accused Buddhism, a foreigners' religion, of having been the cause of the moral and economic enfeeblement of the brief southern dynasties—Chin, Sung, Liang in particular, and Ch'en. More precisely, it indicated that the reason why Nestorian and Mazdaist monks were being returned to secular life was 'in order that they may no longer corrupt Chinese manners'; and the decree proceeded to speak of the simplicity and moral purity which were to reign henceforth. The whole reaction was both emotional—a general hostility to all foreigners and the religious prerogatives which they had acquired before 755—and premeditated, to the extent that it corresponded with real political and economic facts: the power of the eunuchs, who were uneducated, superstitious, grasping devotees of Buddhism, and the Buddhist monasteries' scandalous wealth in land, men and metal coinage, at a time when the state was in financial difficulties and lacked copper for casting coins. The Buddhist church held most of the empire's stock of precious metals in the form of objects of piety, bells, and statues, and one of the measures adopted was to melt down bells and statues into coins—coins which were to be rejected in popular circles from fear of sacrilege.

However, it would be wrong to suppose that the proscription of foreign religions was sudden and brutal. The most radical measures were arrived at only by a series of progressions. At first it was only a question, in accordance with a usage that may be regarded as traditional, of purging the Buddhist priesthood, in order to rid it of uneducated monks and hypocrites. The next steps were the confiscation of the bonzes' private possessions, in accordance with a restrictive interpretation of the treatises on Buddhist discipline (monks made a vow of poverty), the suppression of Buddhist ceremonies in official worship, and more and more massive doses of secularization (three hundred a day in 845). Finally, the authorities proceeded to make a general inventory of the sacred property of monasteries and then to confiscate the estates, the families of slaves, the money, and the metals. Two hundred and sixty thousand Buddhist monks and nuns were secularized and reregistered as taxable; 150,000 dependants of monasteries who escaped taxation and forced labour for the state were also inscribed on the census lists; 4600 monasteries were knocked down or converted into public buildings, and 40,000 small places of worship demolished or converted to other uses. Only a few official temples served by a small number of monks were preserved. Religions of Iranian origin – Mazdaism, Manicheism, Nestorianism – suffered a far more drastic fate: they were totally forbidden and their monks – only a few thousand in number – were all laicized.

These severe measures were to do grave damage to Buddhism in China, even though, soon after the proscription, the successor of the emperor Wu-tsung (841–46) eased the rigour of the steps taken in the years 843–45, allowed a considerable number of unfrocked monks to return to the religious life, and authorized the reconstruction of certain monasteries. In any case the decrees were probably not fully applied except in the capital. Everywhere, even among the officials responsible for enforcing them, there was a quiet resistance which doubtless made it possible in some regions far removed from Ch'ang-an to spare the monks and their places of worship. T'ang China was as extensive as medieval Europe. Thus the power of the Buddhist communities was preserved and even strengthened in the tenth century in the kingdom of Min in Fukien and in that of Wu-Yüeh. Monasticism regained considerable strength in the Sung period and the Buddhist church recovered a large part of its power. But it was a church that had outlived itself and that seems to have lost its soul, for its bodies of learned monks had been dispersed and the traditions of its schools had been interrupted by the great proscription of 845.

Since the end of the eighth century Chinese Buddhism had been cut off from the great religious centres of Asia which had been its sources of inspiration for over five centuries. It no longer had access to the holy places, and Buddhism itself was threatened on the borders of India and Iran by the expansion of Islam. One single sect was to remain really active in China after the end of the T'ang age, and that was the *ch'an* sect (*zen* in Japanese), which was in fact more Chinese than Buddhist. Translations of Indian texts became rarer and rarer; the great translators, commentators, and exegetes were all dead. In the Sung age the historians of Buddhism were to draw up a balance sheet of the past. The *Ching-te ch'uan-teng lu* (*Collection of Writings on the Transmission of the Lamp Compiled in the Ching-te Era*), which appeared in 1004 and contains the biographies of 1701 *ch'an* monks, no longer shows any sign of the naïve fervour of the first Buddhist hagiographies, and the *Fo-tsu-t'ung-chi* (*General Annals of the Patriarchs of Buddhism*), a huge compilation inspired by the methods of the secular historians, seems to put a full stop in 1269 to general histories of Buddhism.

To sum up, it looks as if the great religious enthusiasm which animated the men of the sixth and seventh centuries had declined. There were doubtless many reasons for this phenomenon, but perhaps the principal and deepest one was the changes that had taken place in society. Buddhism probably lost its hold when the social forms to which it had adapted itself and which were those of the third to eighth centuries (endogamous aristocracies, the system of manors and dependants, urban and peasant parishes) had been affected by the general upsurge of the urban, monetary economy which occurred between the eighth and ninth centuries. The great monastery, a self-supporting economic unit with its estates, its families of serfs (*ssu-hu*), its mills, its oil-presses and its pawnshops, had been a sort of symbol of the moral, religious, and economic authority of Buddhism in China. Between the great monasteries and the lay aristocracy of the age of the Six Dynasties and the T'ang there seems to have been not only an analogy and a community of lot, but close ties. It is true that the proscription of 845 dealt a very severe blow to the Buddhist church, but the evolution of society was to complete the job of destroying the foundations which had already been so badly shaken. There is no religion which is not rooted in the social fabric in which it has developed.

Part 5

The Chinese 'Renaissance'

Prologue

The moralizing orthodoxy which has coloured the whole conception of the history of China from the twelfth century onwards and the framework of traditional historiography which reduces the past to events devoid of any temporal dimension—they concern only the central authority and governmental administration—have so firmly convinced us of the perennial nature of the social and political forms, the institutions, the economy, the ideas, and the technology of the Chinese world that the most profound changes and the most startling innovations pass almost unnoticed. What was regarded, in the history of Europe, as the advent of a new world is no more, according to the traditional view taken by Chinese history, than a change of 'dynasty'. If the past of the Chinese world differs so radically from that of Europe, it is primarily in the picture which we have drawn of it. This is certainly not without significance, since our whole world history is based on the primacy of the Occident, on the evolutionary nature of its history, and on the relative stagnation of the other civilizations.

But the innovations which make their appearance in East Asia round about the year 1000, once grouped together, form such a coherent and extensive whole that we have to yield to the evidence: at this period the Chinese world experienced a real transformation, the range of which was no less great than that of the changes which had occurred in it at the end of antiquity.

In this book the term 'Renaissance' has been adopted. It is no doubt open to criticism, even though the analogies are numerous—the return to the classical tradition, the diffusion of knowledge, the upsurge of science and technology (printing, explosives, advance in seafaring techniques, the clock with escapement, and so on), a new philosophy, and a new view of the world. When all is said and done, the Chinese world, like the West, has its own distinctive characteristics. But this allusion to European history should be taken simply for what it is—a mere reminder of the very general parallelism of the history of civilizations and the long-term fellowship which has united them during the course of their development.

Table 14.   Chronological table of the tenth to fourteenth centuries

Outer Mongolia	North-western borders	North-eastern borders	North China	South China
			Shansi Kingdom of Chin (895–923)	
			FIVE DYNASTIES (at Kai-feng)	Kingdoms of
			Later Liang (907–923)	Shu (907–923) in Szechwan
			Later T'ang (923–936)	Ch'u (907–951) and Ching-nan (907–963) in Hunan
		Empire of the LIAO (Khitan) (946–1125)	Later Chin (936–946)	Southern Han (911–971) at Canton
			Later Han (947–950)	Min (909–978) in Fukien Wu-Yüeh (907–978) in Chekiang
			Later Chou (951–960)	Wu and Southern T'ang (902–975) in Kiangsi
			Kingdom of northern Han (951–979)	
	Empire of the Western HSIA (1038–1227)	Empire of the CHIN (Jürchen) (1115–1234) annexes North China in 1126	NORTHERN SUNG (960–1126) at Kaifeng	
			SOUTHERN SUNG (1127–1279) at Hangchow	
Empire of the Mongols 1206, accession of Genghis Khan annexes Hsia empire in 1227; annexes Chin empire in 1234; adopts the dynastic name of YÜAN in 1271; annexes Southern Sung empire in 1276–1279.				
The Mongols are pushed back into Mongolia after 1368.			1368, foundation at Nanking of the Chinese Empire of the MING	

Chapter 14

The New World

There is not a single sector of political, social, or economic life in the eleventh to thirteenth centuries which does not show evidence of radical changes in comparison with earlier ages. It is not simply a matter of a change of scale (increase in population, general expansion of production, development of internal and external trade) but of a change of character. Political habits, society, the relations between classes, the armies, the relations between town and country, and economic patterns are quite different from what they had been in the aristocratic, still half-medieval T'ang empire. A new world had been born whose basic characteristics are already those of the China of modern times.

However, this new world lived under the threat of successive invasions which were finally successful, cutting off all of the empire's northern provinces at the beginning of the twelfth century and overrunning it entirely during the years 1273–79. This external threat was not without effect on the social and economic history of the Sung age. It determined the whole of Chinese policy from the end of the tenth century to the end of the thirteenth century.

History and political institutions

The events

In 951 General Kuo Wei founded at K'ai-feng the brief dynasty of the Later Chou and unified all North China except for the T'ai-yüan region, in northern Shansi, which was occupied by the little Turkish kingdom of the Northern Han, protected by the Khitan Tartars. But the work carried out by the Later Chou of 951–60 already heralded the great effort at economic reconstruction and political unification of the early days of the Sung dynasty. Abandoned land was brought back into cultivation, military colonies were established, taxes were lightened and imposed more equitably, the canals and dykes were repaired, the possessions of the Buddhist monasteries were confiscated in 955 (bells and statues were melted down once again, as in 845, to make coins), and victorious campaigns were fought against the kingdoms of Shu and of the Southern T'ang. Northern Szechwan and the area between the Huai and the Yangtze were annexed. Thus when General Chao K'uang-yin, raised to power by his troops, founded the new Sung dynasty at K'ai-feng in 960, he found himself at the head of a restored empire whose power was to permit him to consolidate and extend the work of his predecessors.

The new Sung government needed only twenty years to complete the conquest of the independent kingdoms and to unite under its authority territories seven times the size of modern France. The stages in the reunification were these:

963   Middle Yangtze (kingdom of Ch'u)
965   Szechwan (Later Shu)
971   Kwangtung (Southern Han)
975   Anhwei, Kiangsi and Hunan (Chiang-nan)
978   Kiangsu and Chekiang (Wu-Yüeh)
979   Shansi (Northern Han)

This succession of victories is doubtless partly explained by the worth of the institutions established by the Later Chou and by the quality of the armies of which the founder of the Sung had assumed command in 960. However, in contrast with what had happened in the seventh century, the military expansion remained confined to the Chinese lands and did not carry on outside them towards Manchuria, Korea, Mongolia, and central Asia. It was in fact halted to the north-east by the powerful Khitan empire, which had been built up in the course of the tenth century, and to the north-west by the Tibetans, who had spread to Tsinghai, Kansu, and Shensi. Finally, in the south-west the expansion was blocked by the kingdom of Ta-li, Nan-chao's successor state in Yunnan, which was not destroyed until the arrival of the Mongol armies in 1253. As for Vietnam, it had succeeded in freeing itself from the Chinese hold—in the shape of the Southern Han of Canton—in 939, and had made itself into a unified and independent empire in 968 (Dinh dynasty). The first of these two dates marked the end of the long hegemony which the Chinese empires and the kingdoms of South China had exercised almost uninterruptedly since the second century B.C. in the basin of the Red River and on the coast of Annam. In 981 Vietnam succeeded in repelling a Sung expedition. The year 1009 saw the foundation of 'great Viet' (Dai Viet) by the new Ly dynasty (1009–1225), which from 1073 to 1077 waged war against the Chinese armies and fleets in Kwangsi, in northern Vietnam, and along the coast, causing the Sung empire many difficulties in these unhealthy tropical regions, where the situation was complicated by the presence of numerous aboriginal groups.

In the reign of the third Sung emperor, Cheng-tsung (997–1022), the Khitan empire of the Liao, then at the height of its power, launched victorious offensives in Hopei and Shansi which forced the Sung to sign a treaty (Peace of Shan-yüan, in the Yellow River valley, 1004) by which they undertook to pay the Liao a heavy annual tribute. But neither this treaty nor the one which complemented it in 1042, increasing the charges on the Sung empire, sufficed to guarantee China perfect tranquillity on its new frontiers, while a still graver threat hung over the north-western provinces. In this area, inhabited by a mixture of Tibetan, Chinese, Turkish, and Mongol peoples, a huge political unit came into existence in the first half of the eleventh century under the leadership of a formerly nomadic people, the Tangut. This kingdom, known as the Western Hsia empire (1038–1227), extended from southern Mongolia to Tsinghai (Kokonor) and encroached on the predominantly Han provinces of Shansi, Shensi, and Kansu. With this empire, too, the Sung were obliged in 1044 to sign a burdensome peace which gave no immunity from new attacks.

The Hsia threat grew worse in the second half of the eleventh century, as did also economic difficulties. The central government called on a minister called Wang An-shih (1021–86), who, endowed with plenary powers, put into effect a whole series of reforms which called into question social, economic, and military structures and provoked in the long run a violent reaction on the part of the big land-owners and rich merchants. Wang An-shih was removed from power on the death of his patron, the emperor Shen-tsung, in 1085. The leader of the conservative party, Ssu-ma Kuang (1019–86), took over the reins of government and abolished the reforms. These party struggles, which weakened the empire, went on up to the sudden invasion of the Jürchen, a sinicized people from Manchuria, who overturned the Liao empire and occupied the whole of North China in 1126.

The Sung, who had sought refuge south of the lower Yangtze, ended by establishing their provisional capital at Hangchow. This was the Southern Sung period (1127–1279), so called in contrast to the first period of Sung history (960–1126). The conservatives had returned to power for good, but a new conflict made its appearance between those who advocated reconquest and those who favoured seeking a *modus vivendi* with the Jürchen Chin empire. Counter-offensives towards the north failed before the military power of the Jürchen. The Sung armies lacked fighting spirit and had no cavalry. The empire therefore moved towards a policy of appeasement directed by the prime minister, Ch'in Kuei (1090–1155). However, the peace concluded with the Chin had no effect because of a change of government. The treaties were broken repeatedly and the continual wars caused a rise in prices and taxes. Economic difficulties led in turn to social unrest. Political centralization gave almost absolute power to the various prime ministers who succeeded each other during the course of the twelfth and thirteenth centuries—Ch'in Kuei, Han T'o-chou (1151–1202), Shih Mi-yüan (?–1233), Chia Ssu-tao (1213–75). But the decline of the empire grew more and more marked down to the time of the Mongol invasion, which for all practical purposes had put an end to the dynasty by 1276 (the date of the fall of Hangchow).

The new state

It was under the second Sung emperor, T'ai-tsung (976–97), when the empire was being consolidated, that the basic institutions of the new state were adopted or perfected. A whole nervous system of information, control, and command was installed; it extended to the most remote parts of the empire and ensured that the central government had a more complete hold than ever before on the whole land. The centralization was increased at the time of the reforms of the Yüan-feng era (1078–85) and allowed the prime minister to play a part that in fact was to eclipse that of the emperors.

General policy was the responsibility of a Council of State consisting of five to nine members and chaired by the emperor. An office for drawing up official documents was associated with it; this was the Court of Academicians (*hsüeh-shih-yüan*), certain members of which sometimes served as councillors. But in every case the government heard numerous opinions, and decisions were taken only after discussions in which differing opinions were expressed. The emperor only ratified the proposals adopted or in the last resort gave the casting vote. Three services had the task of listening to the opinions, suggestions, or complaints of civil servants or ordinary private citizens. They were independent of each other and their members enjoyed a complete immunity which even the emperor himself could not question. Thus a certain objectivity was guaranteed. It is a fact that plans and proposals of every kind, emanating from people of very different classes, flowed under the Sung (more especially in the eleventh century) into the offices of the civil service and right up to the government.

The central administration, somewhat simpler in organization than the heavy edifice of the T'ang age, seems to have become more functional. It was divided into three big departments:

1. Economy and finance (the 'Three Services', *san-ssu:* service of state monopolies, budget service, population service).
2. The armies (*shu-mi-yüan*).
3. Secretariat (*chung-shu-men-hsia*), responsible for the administration of justice and personnel (recruitment competitions, appointments, promotions).

In the provinces, where the districts (*hsien*) were grouped in prefectures, some of which were more specifically military (the *chün* prefectures) or industrial (the *chien* prefectures) in character, imperial commissioners were responsible for particular tasks and supervised, according to their special responsibilities, judicial, fiscal, economic, or military affairs.

Besides the existence of organs of information and control independent of each other, and the extremely strict separation of powers and fields of competence, two characteristics of the political system of the Sung age deserve to be emphasized. The first of these characteristics is the multiplication of services dealing with economic questions; this was because the largest revenues of the state were commercial or industrial in origin. The second characteristic is the efficiency of the system for the recruitment and promotion of civil servants, thanks to mechanisms which favoured the selection of the best candidates.

It was in the Sung age that the system of recruitment competitions reached its greatest perfection. It subsequently degenerated, becoming in the authoritarian Ming and Ch'ing empires a heavy apparatus which retarded rather than assisted social advancement. Created to cut down the excessive power of the military aristocracy, the institution had taken shape under the T'ang emperors in the seventh and eighth centuries (the first competition is supposed to have been held in the year 606, under the Sui emperor Yang Ti). The candidates were put forward in very small numbers – one to three from each prefecture until 737 – or came from the state schools set up in the capital. There were various different sorts of competition in the T'ang period (classical scholarship, law, history of writing, mathematics, military ability, with tests of shooting and physical strength), but the one with the most prestige and the largest number of candidates was an examination in general knowledge and literary ability, including a poetry test. The reforms adopted in the Sung period, at the end of the tenth century and during the course of the eleventh, consisted in creating three different levels, so as to enlarge the field of recruitment (competitions in the prefectures, competitions supervised in the capital by the imperial secretariat, and competitions in the palace in the presence of the emperor), in finally retaining only one kind of competition, and in guaranteeing the objectivity of the tests by various measures such as making the scripts anonymous.

As in the T'ang age and other periods of history, success in the competitions was not necessarily followed – except for those at the top of the list, who obtained rapid advancement – by appointment to a post on the staff of the imperial administration. Other procedures were also used for the promotion of officials, including a system of recommendation, which made the author of the recommendation jointly responsible for the faults and errors of his protégé, and the use of reports framed as objectively as possible.

The development of the civil service in the eleventh to thirteenth centuries was to give it considerable weight in the political system and in the society of this epoch. In no other period of history did the 'mandarins' exercise such effective control over the management of the state. Favourites, empresses and their families, eunuchs, and all the people close to the sovereign and hence in touch with palace intrigues, who in other ages succeeded in affecting or even actually directing affairs of state, seem to have had no influence in the Sung period. The emperors themselves played only a secondary role, leaving the limelight to their ministers.

Political life, too, testifies to the power and guiding role of the civil service. The eleventh century saw the development for the first time of big political parties of opposing tendencies, the confrontation between which reflected certain social cleavages. Doubtless the situation was very different from that prevailing in the parliamentary democracies of today (the present regimes in the Eastern European States would provide a better analogy), but the bitterness of the conflicts in which the opponents risked their whole careers – for changes of policy involved a very extensive replacement of political personnel – reveals the intensity of political life in the Sung age.

The reform movement

In the history of China the eleventh century was the epoch of big attempts to reform the political and social system. The reform movement, though inseparable from the currents of thought of the period, was nevertheless bound up more closely than philosophy with the contingencies of history. It was the difficulties caused by the Liao and Hsia attacks that were at the root of attempts to remedy the deficiencies of the defence system. But since military problems can hardly be separated from their economic, social, and political context, the reforms—the work of clear-sighted men who took a comprehensive view of the state and society—finally affected all the institutions.

The threat posed by the Tangut, who had just founded in 1038 the empire of the Western Hsia, stimulated the government to call on the advice of a provincial official called Fan Chung-yen (989–1052), who suggested a plan intended to contain the new power in the north-west. The peace signed with the Hsia in 1044 was to seem like a partial success, which was put down to the credit of Fan Chung-yen. Summoned to join the government, Fan Chung-yen and his associates had in fact put into effect a ten-point reform plan dealing with the system of recruitment and promotion of civil servants and the agrarian and fiscal institutions.

With Fan Chung-yen it had been simply a matter of modifications to existing institutions, but the reforms introduced in the second half of the eleventh century look much bolder and more radical in character. It is not surprising that they aroused violent opposition and caused the division of the governing circles into two rival clans.

Modern scholars have used the word 'socialism' in connection with the 'new laws' of Wang An-shih (1021–86), and it is certain that an ideal of social justice and sometimes even egalitarian tendencies actuated certain sections of the intelligentsia and of the peasantry in the eleventh and twelfth centuries. But it is just as clear that Wang An-shih's aims were certainly not to call into question the foundations of society and political authority. He was inspired by liberal views and by the practical preoccupations of the administrator. Hostile to despotism and persuaded of the regulative function of the laws in the political and social field, Wang An-shih seems to have been endowed with a sort of sociological intuition. In his view the *de facto* discrimination from which the small farmers suffered, supporting alone the burden of direct taxation and corvées, was the deep-seated reason for the state's weakness; he thought that it was possible, by improving their situation and restoring a certain justice in the distribution of burdens, to induce them to cooperate more effectively in the struggle against the encroachments of the northern empires. Just as poor peasants were subject to the exploitation of those in a position to lend them money on interest at difficult moments, so the small craftsmen and traders suffered from the subjection in which they were kept by the corporations (*hang*) dominated by the rich merchants.

The reformers came from one of the regions of China, the south-east, where economic expansion had caused the intensive circulation of goods and money—Fan Chung-yen was a native of Suchow, Wang An-shih a native of Fuchow in Kiangsi—and their origin doubtless explains some of their convictions: for example, that what made possible the exploitation of the poor by the rich were the obstacles still impeding the circulation of wealth and the practice of hoarding. Not sharing the static conception of the economy which seems to have been much more common, Wang An-shih thought that it was possible to increase simultaneously, by developing production, both everyone's means of livelihood and the revenues of the state.

Wang An-shih, who had made his mark as early as 1056 by a plan for reforms intended to restore the situation in the north-west, was called upon to govern in 1068. He remained in power until 1076, when he was forced to give up his position under pressure from the conservative party. He was recalled in 1078, but forced out of power again in 1085 by Ssu-ma Kuang, his principal opponent, who in the same year secured the abolition of the 'new laws'.

Wang An-shih's reforms, adopted for the most part between 1069 and 1073, were very diverse in nature. They dealt with fiscal policy, the economy, the armies, and the business of administration. One of Wang An-shih's first concerns was to lighten the burdens of the farmers by fighting against the practices of making massive purchases and of stockpiling, by introducing control of the price of cereals and by reforming the fiscal system so as to make fraud more difficult. He changed the rules governing the transfer of taxes, authorized the conversion of corvées into taxes, instituted state loans at moderate interest, and set up official offices for loans on security in order to combat usurious practices. A great effort was made to improve irrigation and to disseminate knowledge of rural economy. At the same time attempts were made to find new sources of revenue less burdensome to the small farmers, and the state began to participate in big business. These measures made it possible both to increase perceptibly the state's income and to reduce by half the tax on land.

Another ambition of Wang An-shih's was to provide the state with administrative personnel devoted to it and with no other concern but the public good. This was his aim when he decided on a substantial increase in the salaries of state officials – Chinese civil servants were probably never better paid than in the Sung age, with the possible exception of the middle of the eighteenth century – and when he changed the too formalized pattern of the recruitment competitions, in which practical subjects (economics, law, geography) now at last gained a larger place. Public schools, their upkeep ensured by special estates, were established in prefectures and sub-prefectures in order to enlarge the field of recruitment.

However, it was above all in the military field that the most important innovations were made. At a time when the inflation of the armies of mercenaries only increased the charges on the state without securing an efficient defence, Wang An-shih decided to give back to the people the task of ensuring its own security by creating peasant militias. These militias (*pao-chia*), organized in units of ten families and regularly trained and supplied with arms, made it possible to reduce the swollen numbers of the regular armies.

The very lively opposition which Wang An-shih's 'new laws' met no doubt had economic and social causes: the reforms called into question too many privileges and acquired positions. But more than a mere difference of interests was involved in this obstinate struggle — which lasted over twenty years and went on even after the death of the two principal adversaries — between Wang An-shih's reform party and the conservative party led by the historian Ssu-ma Kuang and the mathematician Shao Yung. Personal antagonism and differences of temperament and education seem to have played a large part. There is no reason to exclude disinterested behaviour; the birth of the reform movement may well have been due to the typically eleventh-century attitude which gave everyone the right, whatever his position, to take his suggestions to the highest quarters.

It was no doubt this movement that was responsible for the foundation of public welfare institutes: orphanages, hospices, hospitals, dispensaries, public cemeteries, reserve granaries. More numerous in urban areas where the influx of people without resources and the sheer concentration of numbers posed difficult problems, these institutes were modelled on the charitable foundations created by the Buddhist monasteries in the sixth and seventh centuries. Inalienable estates — sources of permanent income — were assigned to them, and in the Sung age this kind of foundation became much more common. Not only did the state turn to them in order to guarantee some of its income; so did the great families for purposes of mutual assistance within the clan, following the example set by Fan Chung-yen with his 'estates of equity' (*i-chuang*). This secularization of a Buddhist institution, and the assumption by the state of the medical and charitable functions fulfilled by the monasteries, was one of the distant consequences of the proscription of the Buddhist church in 845.

The armies

From conscription to mercenaries

Although the Sung empire took an extreme interest in its own defence, inventing new machines, increasing the strength of its armies, creating a navy at the time of the Jürchen invasion and devoting most of its resources to the war from the end of the tenth century to the end of the thirteenth, it never ceased to maintain and assert the absolute supremacy of the civil power over the military power. The spirit which animated it was the opposite of that of its northern enemies. The exaltation of brute violence, the thirst for conquest and domination which mark the true warrior were entirely absent from it, while they were characteristic of its most redoubtable adversaries, the Jürchen and the Mongols. However, this lack of pugnacity with which Sung China has often been reproached is perfectly explicable; there is no need to look for any innate and permanent characteristics.

The system of employing mercenaries which was inherited and adopted by the Sung empire tended to make the profession of arms a specialized activity instead of everyone's business, as it had once been. For since the Ch'in dynasty the power of the Chinese armies had been based on conscription. Conscription furnished the main body of the forces, which were conveniently complemented by contingents of barbarians, nomads and mountaineers esteemed for their powers of endurance and pugnacity. But the Sung lacked the valuable assistance of barbarian auxiliaries and suffered from all the drawbacks of mercenary armies: increased expenditure, long periods of inactivity during which discipline is relaxed, and the tendency to behave like a foreign body in the state. The recruiting officers were the scourge of the countryside, and if soldiers were discharged they soon formed bands of brigands. Moreover, so as not to damage the rural economy, recruits were drawn for preference from the ranks of the rootless, of those on the loose, and of convicts granted a conditional amnesty, or else from the aboriginal tribes of the South reduced to seeking mercy after a rebellion. The civil authority thus felt more than ever the need to protect itself against any attempt at autonomy on the part of the military power. It sought to achieve this end by splitting up units, by dividing responsibilities, and by multiplying the sort of controls which deprive army commanders of any initiative. Bureaucratic habits also helped to weaken the defence system: official inventories were more important than the facts of the situation. Right from the beginning of the empire its founder had taken care to divide the élite troops of the palace armies (*chin-chün*) into three distinct units under the control of the *shu-mi-yüan*. From the end of the tenth century to the great Jürchen offensive of 1126, the effectiveness of the Sung armies (*chin-chün* near the capital and *hsiang-chün* in the provinces) never stopped declining, although their strength increased enormously. Restricted to 378,000 in 975, numbers had risen to 1, 259,000 in 1045. The reforms carried out by Wang An-shih between 1068 and 1085 — discharges, the creation of peasant militias (*hsiang-ping*) and of special frontier units (*fan-ping*), permanent training of the armies — made it possible to restore the situation, but by the beginning of the twelfth century the Sung armies were once again overmanned and inefficient, although military expenditure absorbed most of the budget and caused economic difficulties. While the armies which had taken part in the campaigns of 963–79 included numerous contingents of former nomads and mountaineers, the Sung empire could no longer recruit any of these valuable auxiliaries. In addition, the Chinese armies had been short of horses ever since the occupation of the breeding areas by the Hsia empire, and Wang An-shih's attempts to develop horse-breeding right in the middle of the agricultural zone (mainly in the lower valley of the Yellow River) ended in failure.

Yet in the Chinese world the eleventh to thirteenth centuries was a period of remarkable progress in military techniques. This progress was to change the very nature of warfare and in the long run to have profound repercussions on world history. It is to be connected with the spirit of research, invention, and experimentation characteristic of the age.

Even in recruitment, certain objective principles of selection were followed. The future soldiers were chosen after a series of tests of physical aptitude — running, jumping, eyesight, skill in shooting — and classed according to height, the tallest being posted to crack units, while the specialized corps for which this type of classification was not used — troops equipped with incendiary weapons, sappers, catapult personnel — began to multiply. The theory and technology of siege warfare developed considerably and at the same time, from the end of the tenth century onwards, there was a lively interest in questions of armament. New kinds of weapons were invented and perfected: *ballistae,* repeating crossbows, a sort of tank. Inventions were encouraged by rewards and the new weapons were tried out before being ordered in quantity from the arsenals. A treatise on the military art which appeared in 1044, the *General Principles of the Classic on War* (*Wu-ching tsung-yao*) by Tseng Kung-liang, mentions among other novelties a paraffin flamethrower with a mechanism consisting of a double-acting piston which made it possible to produce a continuous jet of flame.

The Sung retreat towards the Yangtze valley from 1126–27 onwards led to the development of a substantial navy, with bases on the great river and on the coast. It is worth mentioning that at this period boats with paddles actuated by a crank or by a system of connecting-rods were employed. Some of them had as many as twenty-five paddle wheels. They are mentioned in connection with naval battles against the Jürchen in 1130 and 1161. This very fast kind of boat is in fact attested as early as the eighth century and its history may go even further back than that. The first experiments with paddle-boats in Europe were to take place in 1543.

But it is above all through the discovery and perfecting of the use of explosives for military purposes that Sung China occupies an extremely important place in the general history of the human race.

Firearms

The first mention of the formula for gunpowder (coal, saltpetre and sulphur) occurs in the *Wu-ching tsung-yao* of 1044. We have to wait for the year 1285 to find the same mention in a European text (the first allusion to the powder is made by Roger Bacon in 1267). The discovery originated from the alchemical researches made in the Taoist circles of the T'ang age, but was soon put to military use in the years 904–6. It was a matter at that time of incendiary projectiles called 'flying fires' (*fei-huo*). By the time of the *Wu-ching tsung-yao* firearms had been diversified. This work in fact mentions smoke-producing and incendiary grenades, catapults for launching incendiary projectiles, and even explosive grenades (*p'i-li huo-ch'iu*). At the battle of Ts'ai-shih, in Anhwei, in 1161, catapults hurling explosive grenades (*p'i-li-p'ao*) were employed and secured the victory of the Sung armies over the Jürchen. At the beginning of the thirteenth century the Mongols were to make great use of exploding projectiles with a metal envelope (*chen-t'ien-lei*, 'thunderbolt that shakes the sky', and *t'ieh-huo-pa'o*, 'bombards with iron grenades'). They used these weapons in their attempts to invade Japan at the end of the thirteenth century; the Japanese called them *teppo* (in Chinese, *t'ieh-p'ao*). Thus the history of the first uses of gunpowder reveals that, although the initial step consisted in taking advantage of its incendiary or smoke-producing qualities, people soon came to exploit its capacity to burst. The third step was to lead to the use of the powder as a propellant in a guiding tube. The first experiments of this sort known to us date from 1132. These experiments employed a sort of mortar or rocket consisting of a tube of thick bamboo or wood (the bursting power of the powder was reduced by the use of a bigger proportion of saltpetre). The Chinese were the first to discover the principle of the rocket by adapting incendiary arrows to guide-tubes of bamboo. The first mortars with a metal tube of iron or bronze made their appearance about 1280 in the wars between the Sung and the Mongols, and a new term, *ch'ung*, was coined to denote this kind of weapon.

Thus what was passed on to Europe at the end of the thirteenth century was not only the formula for the powder but also the idea—the fruit of a long period of groping and of numerous experiments in East Asia—that this explosive could be used as a propellant inside a tube. The knowledge seems to have been transmitted via the Islamic countries (in the works of the Andalusian botanist Ibn al-Baytar, who died at Damascus in 1248, the Arabic term for saltpetre is 'Chinese snow', and the Persian term is 'China salt'). Tradition also maintains that the Mongols used firearms at the battle of Sajo in Hungary in 1241. The repercussions which the development of firearms in the fourteenth and fifteenth centuries were to have on the evolution of European history are well known—it contributed to the downfall of the warrior aristocracies of the Middle Ages. On the other hand, the invention of these new weapons could exert no influence on the political and social organization of the Chinese world; they simply formed an addition, in the context of state-controlled armies, to a series of different weapons which were perfected at much the same time. And it is doubtless the general conditions of warfare in East Asia (particularly in Mongolia in the Ming period) that explain why firearms were not developed more systematically in China.

It should also be noted that even before the appearance of firearms in Europe the adoption of the counter-weighted trebuchet was to revolutionize the art of siege warfare. This weapon, which was almost as dangerous to fortifications as gunfire, was an Arab adaptation of a weapon long in use in the Chinese world, the *p'ao*. The *p'ao*'s power and speed of propulsion were not achieved by twisting a rope or by tension on a spring, as in Alexandrine or Byzantine catapults, but by pulling down the short arm of a lever mounted on an upright post.

The new society

A class living on unearned income

In the eleventh century a series of different factors—the growth of agricultural production, the rise in incomes from land, the spread of education, the state's need for civil servants—caused an increase in the number of well-educated and relatively comfortable or very rich families. This period saw the advent of a new kind of man, of a new mentality, of a social and political system based on a class of *rentiers* living on the income from their land. From the Han age to the T'ang period, the great families with influence in their region·or at court tended to form more or less closed aristocracies, who took great care of their genealogies. Some of these families, in North China, owed their prestige to their military traditions and to the martial exploits by which certain of their members had gained fame. Their estates, when they were not merely pleasure parks or country houses, could be self-supporting and produced a range of different things. They included orchards, mills, fishponds, workshops, oil-presses, and so on. When occasion demanded, as it had at the end of the Han period and in the southern empires, these estates could be fortified and defended against brigandage, rebellions, and even at times the demands of the state. As for the relations of these 'country gentlemen' with their people ('guests', *k'o*, guards, *pu-ch'ü*, servants, *nu-pi*), they were patriarchal in nature. These patron–client and master–servant ties were recognized by custom and sanctioned by law.

The collapse of the system of allocating plots of land for life in the eighth century, the transfer to cultivated land of the bulk of taxation – whereas up to this time taxes had been calculated according to the number of individuals of working age (hence the limitations on the size of estates and the allocations of land to small farmers) – the expansion of rice growing (the new taxation system seems to have been based on the conditions peculiar to the areas of the Huai valley growing mixed crops, wheat and rice) – and, above all, the commercialization of agricultural produce were to involve profound changes. The tendency of the private estates (*chuang-yüan*) of the great families and of the monasteries to expand and encroach on the peasants' plots had grown more marked during the second half of the T'ang age. But the whole process, assisted by the change from conscripted to mercenary armies, had been completed by the tenth to eleventh centuries. From then on there was no further question of self-supporting domains, of closed aristocracies, or of patron–client relationships of the medieval kind. It was quite simply a matter of tenancy, of working for wages and of income from land, that is, of regular revenues which allowed some families to live in towns in comfortable circumstances. However, even though the new society, like preceding ones, remained based on the exploitation of the weakest, the mentality and machinery of subjection were different. Moreover, the governing class, the class which, through education, could attain political power and exercise domination at the local level, had considerably expanded. The families belonging to it usually included a principal wife, a concubine, and about ten children. In addition, big landowners seldom lived in the coutnry; they had their stewards or managers (*chien-chuang, kan-jen, kan-p'u*) who dealt with the farmers and agricultural labourers and managed their estates, which were sometimes continuous blocks, embracing several villages, and sometimes separate parcels of land. The farmers were often provided with board and lodging and furnished with tools, seeds, and animals for ploughing; their landlord would even arrange their marriages. However, all the advances were made on interest, at rates varying according to the nature of the loan: a tenth of the harvest for a plough-ox, a fifth for board and lodging and the loan of tools and 10 percent per month for loans of cash, seeds, or cereals. Country markets and the inhabited centres of the big estates often coincided and gave birth, thanks to the economic boom, to big townships (*chen* or *shih*, though many retained the name *chuang*) which completed the network formed by the big mercantile agglomerations.

Agrarian problems

In the rural cantons (*li* and *hsiang*), which comprised several villages (*ts'un* or *chuang*), the state made a distinction between resident families (*chu-hu*) and families alien to the canton (*k'o-hu*). The former owned small plots of land; they were divided into five categories according to the area of the plots (the middle category, the third, owning 100 *mu* of land, the fourth 50 and the fifth 20 to 30, much less than was needed to support a peasant family) and were taxable. The latter (the 'aliens') did not own any land, consisted solely of tenant farmers and agricultural labourers, and paid no taxes. The most comfortable peasant families, those in categories one and two, provided the guards (*kung-shu*, 'archers'), whose task it was to ensure order, and the canton's representatives on the governing body of the district (*hsien*). These were the *san-i*—heads of cantons, supervisors of the taxes and in charge of the police. But the big landowners escaped the classification, the responsibilities, and the taxes, which rested only on the small farmers.

No doubt this picture is not true of all regions (large estates were much more numerous in the big rice-producing area south of the lower Yangtze than in North China) or of all eras of Sung history. But there can be little doubt that the free play of economic forces increased the gap between rich and poor in the eleventh to thirteenth centuries and aggravated social tension in the country districts. Some of the reforms introduced from 1069 onwards were inspired by the disproportion, which had become more evident than ever, between the burdens imposed on the small farmers and the privileges of the great landowners. It has been estimated that in 1064–67 out of a cultivated area of 24 million hectares only 30 per cent were liable to tax. The measures in favour of the peasantry and the fight against tax evasion brought a relative improvement at the time of the great reforms of 1068–85, during Wang An-shih's ministry, but the situation deteriorated again in the reign of Hui-tsung (1101–25).

A brief but serious rebellion broke out during this period in the interior of Chekiang, in a region which produced tea, lacquer, mulberry trees for paper, and fir-wood, and through which trade between Kiangsi and Fukien passed. Provoked by requisitions for the imperial palace in

K'ai-feng, this rebellion was engineered by a secret society whose doctrines, basically Buddhist, were tinged with Manichean influences. Its members were strict vegetarians and worshipped devils. Very poorly armed, the insurgents, who were led by one Fang La, massacred the distinguished, the rich, and government officials. The capture of Fang La a year after the beginning of the rebellion brought the rising to an end and provoked a wave of suicides among the members of the sect.

During the breakdown of the years 1126–38, the region round Lake Tung-t'ing in Hunan suffered simultaneously from Jürchen incursions, the exactions of a corrupt administration, and the pillaging of a local semi-official army which had been created to fight the invaders and which recalls the 'great companies' of the European Middle Ages. A peasant rising broke out in 1130, led by a certain Chung Hsiang, who was a talented military leader, magician, and healer. Chung Hsiang is alleged to have remarked, 'The law separates the high and the low, the rich man and the poor man. I shall publish a law ordering that the high and the low, the rich man and the poor man shall be equal'. He was soon captured and executed, but his troops increased in number and built themselves defences in the marshes of the lake. Chung Hsiang's rebellion, which had started out by being destructive and egalitarian, turned into mere brigandage. In order to eliminate this abscess, which interfered with the organization of the defences against the Jürchen, a vast repressive operation was mounted. It went on until 1135 and was directed in its final year by the famous general Yüeh Fei.

The situation in the countryside was to continue to deteriorate during the whole Southern Sung period as a result of the concentration of land in the hands of a small number of privileged persons. After the treaty between the Sung and the Chin, which finally fixed the frontier between the two states, the whole rice zone south of the Huai, which had suffered a great deal from the fighting of the years 1130–40, was brought back into cultivation. But the operation was carried out to the profit of the big landowners, who were the only people with the necessary capital. By the middle of the thirteenth century the situation in the area south of the Yangtze, in the big productive region round Lake T'ai-hu, had become so explosive, and the collection of taxes had grown so difficult, that radical reforms were attempted by the great minister Chia Ssu-tao (1213–75). They met bitter opposition in the central government and in the Council of State, in which representatives of the big landowners sat. Chia Ssu-tao's plan was to limit properties to 500 *mu* (about 27 hectares) and to buy with state funds a third of the surplus, in order to establish 'public lands' (*kuan-t'ien*), the income from which would be allocated to military expenditure. The reforms were partially applied from 1263 until the death of Chia Ssu-tao. By the end of the dynasty 20 per cent of the lower Yangtze area was to have been converted into 'public lands'. The Mongols took possession of these estates and either handed them over to princes of the khan's family or kept the income from them to pay for the maintenance of their garrisons.

To sum up, social and economic conditions thus caused the development, from the end of the T'ang age onwards, of a class of tenant-farmers and agricultural labourers which was already much closer to that of today than to that of the dependants of earlier ages.

While the rural world, more sensitive than in days gone by to fluctuations in prices now that it was traversed by the great economic currents connecting towns and villages, provinces and regions, saw an increase in the number of its inhabitants deprived of land or without resources, at the same time new means of livelihood were available for the most wretched among them. The armies, consisting since the tenth century of mercenaries, recruited a large number of them. The various crafts, which in some sectors were beginning to look like industries because of the size of the workshops, the number of men employed, and the level of technology involved, attracted a labouring class far more numerous than the salt-mine workers and state craftsmen of the T'ang age had been. The need for labour was particularly marked in the mines, in metallurgy, ceramics, the paper factories, printing, and the salt-works. But the surplus country people went mainly to the big commercial agglomerations. These welcomed a whole floating population which made a living out of the small urban trades as shop assistants, employees of inns, taverns and tea-houses, door-to-door salesmen and public entertainers – not to mention pickpockets, crooks, thieves, and prostitutes of both sexes. Finally, the private mansions of the rich families and the big merchants, numerous in K'ai-feng and Hang-chow, gave shelter to abundant domestic servants, whose tasks, directed by stewards, were both very diverse and very specialized. All this was certainly new and is explained by the changes in the rural economy, by commercial and urban development and by the increase in the number of rich or simply comfortable families.

The urban expansion

The appearance of an extremely diversified class of big and small merchants, who were much more numerous than in the T'ang age, and the development of very large commercial centres were in fact characteristic of the Sung epoch. Heavily populated and very busy towns multiplied not only in the interior, especially along the course of the Yangtze, but also on the frontiers (Hsiung-chou near the modern Pao-ting in Hopei, Ch'in-chou near T'ien-shui in eastern Kansu) and on the coast (Hangchow, Wen-chou in Chekiang, Foochow and Ch'üan-chou in Fukien).

K'ai-feng, capital of the Five Dynasties, which reigned in succession there from 907 onwards, and capital of the Northern Sung from 960 to 1126, can serve as an example to illustrate the history of urban development between the ninth and eleventh centuries.

The first ring of walls dates from 781, but by the ninth century the approaches to the main roads leading out of the principal gates to the south and east were occupied by merchants' shops, craftsmen's workshops, and inns. Markets grew up there spontaneously and this commerical activity escaped the control exercised by the administration over the sites reserved for craftsmen and merchants inside the city, as in Ch'ang-an in the seventh century. These outside markets which multiplied on the outskirts of the towns at the end of the T'ang age were known as 'forage markets' (*ts'ao-shih*). Becoming the capital in 918, K'ai-feng soon became too cramped inside its ring of walls, and outer walls were built in 954. This did not prevent outer districts (*hsiang*, 'wings of a building', so called by analogy with additions made to an existing building) from forming quickly outside this second circle of ramparts. But the development of the town around its original nucleus would possess only a relative interest had it not been accompanied by a change which affected the very nature of the city. Whereas Ch'ang-an and the other important towns of the seventh and eighth centuries were primarily aristocratic and administrative cities in which the public authorities sought to keep all mercantile activities strictly under control, K'ai-feng provides the first example of a popular agglomeration in which commercial life and amusements were predominant. The political organs and their staff found themselves from this time onwards in direct contact with a typically urban population consisting mainly of the lower classes, while the commercial upsurge broke all the old rules which tended to preserve the aristocratic character of the city. The curfew was abolished at K'ai-feng in 1063 and from then onwards people could move about freely during the night. Businesses and places of entertainment (the *wa-tzu*, amusement quarters, which expanded greatly in Hangchow) remained open until dawn. But the regulation which confined mercantile and craft activities to definite districts seems to have disappeared even earlier: shops and workshops were set up all over the city and the separate districts lost their original walls. People no longer found their way about the town by the names of the districts, but by the names of the streets. The former were of official origin, the latter of popular origin. The street became one of the typical characteristics of the new Chinese towns. Whereas formerly nothing distinguished urban districts from the sections of a village (they were denoted by the same term, *li*, until the T'ang age), the urban agglomeration henceforth differed very sharply from the countryside in its mode of life and in its human denizens.

A more mobile society

The men of the eleventh to thirteenth centuries travelled about more often and more willingly than those of the T'ang, Six Dynasties, and Han periods. The fact is that the big commercial currents carried men along with them — boatmen, carters, sailors and merchants, some of whom regularly covered very long distances. Civil servants, whose numbers had risen, were professionally obliged to move about: they could not serve in their home district or remain in the same post for more than three or four years. Finally, the difficulties of rural life, the number and diversity of the small urban trades, and the attraction of the towns, centres of wealth and entertainment, caused a flow of vagabonds and impoverished peasants toward the big agglomerations. Means of transport were convenient and cheap; carts or boats could be hired cheaply everywhere.

It is comprehensible that in this society, which was more mobile than that of the preceding centuries and in which reverses of fortune were frequent, new kinds of relationships developed. The tendency to regroup, to form associations, among the upper classes as well as among ordinary people in the urban environment, was all the stronger since the risk of isolation was greater and mutual help more necessary. In the civil service, where party conflicts and the system of recommendation binding the sponsor to his protégé could lead unforeseeably, thanks to the principle of joint responsibility, to the ruin of anyone, solid and durable ties were formed between fellow students, between those successful in the examinations in the same year, between examiners and candidates, and between masters and pupils. In all classes — ordinary people, literati, itinerant merchants — there was a general tendency to form associations (*hui*) of people from the same region or the same canton. This explains the spread of certain local cults far from their places of origin. Finally, since the collapse of the system of markets controlled by the state and the dispersal of shops and workshops all over the town, the development of the corporations (*hang*) of merchants and craftsmen corresponded to the need for mutual understanding and common defence among the members of each profession. The amazing specialization of these 'guilds' is explained by the multiplication of 'tertiary' activities.

This need for mutual help also helps to explain the consolidation among the literati of the big family clan, which in its constitution, its principles, and its code of conduct constitutes one of the novelties of the

Sung epoch. One of the first to fix special rules for the family clans was the reformer Fan Chung-yen, who was responsible for a collection of family precepts and also for the creation of 'estates of equity' (*i-chuang*) that is, the establishment of special, inalienable lands, the income from which was to be used to look after the common needs of the clan — especially the education of the children — and to give help to its most underprivileged members. The term *i*, which can be translated approximately by 'equity', is in fact applied to all relationships involving mutual help and free assistance.

The economic expansion

The growth in food production

The development of the rice-growing areas of the Yangtze basin and South China had begun to gather impetus in the eighth century with the adoption of planting out seedlings and the appearance of new tools for tilling and irrigating the soil. This upsurge of rice growing continued and expanded during the course of the following centuries and was undoubtedly one of the great events in this period of the history of East Asia. The civilizations of East Asia were indebted to it for a sort of second wind. It was in the eleventh to thirteenth centuries that the kingdom of Ankor, which was contemporaneous with Sung China, reached its zenith. Before permitting the high densities of population that we find today in Java, in the Red River basin in Vietnam, or in some parts of eastern China, rice growing made it possible to release a large number of people from working the soil. It provided the reserves which have always proved indispensable since the Neolithic Age for the upsurge of civilizations, that is, for the development of the political and social organization, of the arts, of technology, and of thought. Of all the great cultivated plants, the paddy is in fact the one with the greatest yield per acre. The surplus production of the plains to the south of the lower Yangtze — 'when the harvest of Su(-chow) and Ch'ang(-chou) are ripe', says a proverb of the Sung age, 'the world is satiated', *Su-ch'ang shu t'ien-hsia tsu* — favoured the development of interregional trade, the commercialization of agricultural produce, the upsurge of the craftsman and the growth of the big towns. In the course of the tenth to thirteenth centuries the population of China experienced the second big increase in its history, for it grew from about fifty-three million in the middle of the eighth century to a figure which seems to have been in the neighbourhood of a hundred million.

Progress in methods of rice cultivation continued in the eleventh century. After 1012, varieties of early ripening rice which reach maturity in winter and make two harvests possible were imported from Champa (on the south-east coast of Vietnam) and were distributed systematically by the Chinese government. Known as *hsien*, they reached the region of Lake T'ai-hu, Fukien, and Kiangsi, and soon made it possible to double the area of land under cultivation. They continued to spread in the Ming age (1368–1644). At the same time new varieties obtained by selection from the Sung period onwards were to complete the range of early ripening, resistant rices. In the eleventh century 7 million *shi* (42 million hundredweight) were carried annually on the big canal connecting the Hangchow and Suchow region with that of K'ai-feng in Honan. The only effect of the tragic events of the first half of the twelfth century was to stimulate the agricultural development of Yangtze China. A big effort was made to extend the area under cultivation by reclaiming the land on the edge of lakes and marshes. These were known as *wei-t'ien* ('paddocks' enclosed by little dykes). In addition, the immigrants from the north introduced the cultivation of wheat and forage plants in the dry parts of the Yangtze basin.

Expansion of handicrafts and trade

Thus the agricultural upsurge of China in the eleventh to thirteenth centuries can be seen to have been the foundation of its economic expansion, insofar as it made a larger fraction of the population available for other tasks than the production of food (the annual harvest of rice and cereals reached about 300 million hundredweight).

The textile-producing plants gained ground (hemp; the mulberry tree for breeding silk-worms; cotton, which began to spread in several regions in the thirteenth century). The cultivation of the tea-bush developed in the hilly region south of the Huai and in Szechwan, and that of lacquer-producing trees in Hupei, Hunan, and northern Chekiang. All manufactures expanded rapidly. Such was the case with metallurgy under the Northern Sung. It was given fresh life by injections of capital from rich landowning families and by improvements in technology: pit coal was substituted for charcoal, hydraulic machinery was used for working the bellows, explosives were employed in the mines, and so on. The quantity of cast iron produced in 1078 exceeded 114,000 tonnes (it reached only 68,000 tonnes in England in 1788). Alongside small enterprises which recruited peasants in the dead season, there existed in southern Hopei, central Shantung, and northern Kiangsu substantial factories which employed a permanent and specialized labour force. Thus at Likuo, in Kiangsu, there were 3600 wage-earning workers. These big enterprises worked for the state.

In a general way, all mining production increased rapidly in the eleventh century—iron, copper (essential for casting coins), lead, tin. Numerous new mines were opened, especially in the southernmost regions of the empire.

Similarly, the production of ceramics experienced an unprecedented expansion. There were kilns and workshops in very many areas, but the most famous eleventh-century pieces came from the imperial kilns at K'ai-feng and other towns in Honan, and also from Ting-hsien in Hopei. In the twelfth and thirteenth centuries the best pieces came from Hangchow, from Ch'üan-lung and Chien-yang in Fukien, from Chi-an and from Ching-te-chen in Kiangsi. The technique of making porcelain, one of China's glories, reached perfection in the twelfth century.

Almost every region was famous for some product or other: southern Hopei for iron, the neighbourhood of Lake T'ai-hu for rice, Fukien for cane sugar, Szechwan and Chekiang for paper, Ch'eng-tu, Hangchow and the towns on the lower Yangtze for printed books, and so on. The development of trade allowed products to circulate on a vast scale. The appearance of big mercantile agglomerations in the empire as a whole, and more especially in the Yangtze basin, in Szechwan and on the coasts of Fukien and Chekiang, led to a general reorganization of trade routes in terms of the big towns and a development of exchanges inside the regions and between the regions themselves. Whereas in the eighth century the biggest trade was in taxable commodities (cloth and grain), private trade was now far larger in volume than trade in materials subject to a levy by the exchequer. Above all, for the first time in its history China took full advantage of the immense network—unique in the world—of navigable waterways formed by the Yangtze and its tributaries and extended towards the centre of North China by the canals connecting Hangchow to Chen-chiang and Yangchow to K'ai-feng. This network, more than 50,000 kilometres long, was traversed by the biggest and most various collection of boats that the world had ever seen until then. At certain points on the Yangtze the traffic was so dense that it led to the formation of positive floating towns. Sung China also profited from the facilities for coastal shipping presented by the uninterrupted length of indented coastline, full of good anchorages, extending from the northeastern tip of Chekiang to the frontier with Vietnam.

But the basic reason for the economic expansion of China in the eleventh to thirteenth centuries must be sought in the development of an urban bourgeoisie consisting of landowners and rich merchants and in the growth of internal demand. It was no longer only a question of supplying the imperial palace with luxury objects, for luxury had become the privilege of a larger part of the population. The number of rich families had increased. Wealthy buildings and furnishings, the art of laying out gardens, refinements in dress and cooking were characteristic of urban circles in the Sung age. It was not by chance that the art and technology of ceramics, architecture, weaving and, generally, all products affecting the comfort of daily life made such rapid progress in the eleventh to thirteenth centuries.

Foreign trade, with imports consisting mainly of luxury products — incense, rare stones (cornelian, agate, amber, camphor), ivory, coral, rhinoceros horns, ebony, sandalwood — produced a deficit for China, which had to pay for part of its purchases in copper coin and metals (lead, tin, gold, and silver). The copper coins issued in the Sung age spread over every country in Asia — the Hsia, Liao, and Chin empires, the lands of South-East Asia and the Indian Ocean. They were so plentiful in Japan that they were used as local currencies.

For outside, too, China was regarded as the land of luxury crafts, the land which produced the most coveted goods and provided the most profitable opportunities for trade. The northern empires, which in exchange for Chinese goods could furnish only horses, sheep, hides and wool, imported tea, salt (a large proportion of which was smuggled into the north-west), cloth, and metals. Accordingly, when the Hsia and Liao imposed treaties on the Sung in the first half of the eleventh century, they demanded the delivery of products essential to the development of their trade with central Asia and the Middle East — tea, silks, and silver. Silks and ceramics also formed the bulk of exports by sea from the ports of Chekiang and Fukien. Chinese porcelain was exported in such quantities to all the countries of East Asia and the Indian Ocean (it has even been found in Africa) that it is possible to trace the history of Chinese ceramics with the help of the specimens preserved in Japan, the Philippines, or Borneo.

The mercantile state

Adapting itself to the evolution of the economy, the Sung state substituted the more flexible system of commercial taxes on shops, products, and trade for the control of prices and markets and the requisitioning of craftsmen to which the political authority had had recourse throughout the medieval period. The movement was analogous and parallel to what had happened in the realm of agrarian taxation, where the dues, often payable in kind, and compulsory labour based on the individual's capacity for work, the control of families, and the distribution of land to the cultivators had given way to more impersonal impositions based on the yield of the land. Doubtless the actual situation was more complex, and varied from one locality to another. The corvée and the capitation tax still existed in the Sung age. There were traditional taxes peculiar to certain regions, rates of commutation dependent on local usage, and additional taxes. The complexity of the fiscal system and local or regional variations of it make it impossible to do more than indicate a general tendency to evolve in a certain direction. But there can be little doubt about the existence of the tendency; it was bound up with the commercialization of agricultural produce, the extension of the monetary economy, and a general upsurge of trade and commercial currents. In the Sung epoch the state not only drew a substantial portion of its receipts from the taxes on manufactures and commerce; it also turned itself into a merchant and producer, by creating workshops and commercial enterprises run by civil servants and by systematically developing the state monopolies in order to provide for the maintenance of its armies and to meet the rapid increase in military expenditure.

In fact the whole political history of the Sung age was dominated by this close relationship between defence problems and economic problems, which combined to form a sort of vicious circle. The establishment of the monopolies provoked cross-border smuggling which enriched and strengthened the Hsia, Liao, and Chin empires, while the economic privileges of the state encouraged fraud inside the country, and the heavier and heavier weight of taxation aggravated the difficulties and instability of the rural world.

Although there is a widespread notion that China has always been a country with an essentially agrarian economy, in fact its principal wealth in the Sung age—even more than in the Han period, at the end of the Ming period, and in the eighteenth century—came from commerce and craftsmanship. Ceramics, silks, iron and other metals, salt, tea, alcohol, paper, and printed books were the objects of intense commercial activity in which the whole empire was involved and of which the state was the principal beneficiary. In the eleventh century and in the early years of the twelfth the revenues from commercial taxes and monopolies already equalled the yield of the agrarian taxes; under the Southern Sung, in the twelfth and thirteenth centuries, they far exceeded it.

The state's receipts comprised:

1. the income from the monopolies in salt, tea, alcohol, and perfume;
2. the internal commerical taxes and the customs duties levied at the frontiers and at the commercial ports;
3. the corvées, a substantial quantity of which were commuted into taxes payable in money;
4. the capitation tax;
5. the taxes on land.

For the year 1077, these receipts broke down into:

1. 60,000 ounces of silver, each ounce weighing about 37 grammes (the annual production of the state mines attained 215,400 ounces);
2. 5,585,000 strings of a thousand copper coins;
3. 17,887,000 *shih* (a *shih* was about 60 litres) of rice and cereals (or nearly eleven million hundredweight);
4. 2,672,000 rolls of silk.

The revenue from maritime customs duties, which consisted of only half a million strings of a thousand coins at the beginning of the dynasty, rose to 65 million strings in 1189. 'Offices for merchant ships' (*shih-po-ssu*), which acted as both police and customs offfices, were set up at Chiao-chou, in the Ch'ing-tao area in Shantung, at Hangchow, Ning-po, Ch'üan-chou, and Canton. When ships arrived, the government operated a levy varying from 10 percent to 40 percent according to the nature of the merchandise imported. The rest of the cargo could be sold freely subject to the payment of a regular tax.

Extension of the monetary economy

One of the prerequisites for the economic upsurge of the eleventh to thirteenth centuries was a very considerable increase in the means of payment and the spread of the monetary economy. At the time of the Five Dynasties, from the early years of the tenth century to the unification of 963–79, the ten or so independent states which had divided up China among themselves had each issued their own coinage. North China had remained the domain of copper coins, whereas iron and lead coins had made their appearance in numerous parts of South China (Fukien, Kwangtung, Hunan, Kiangsi). This was in imitation of Szechwan, where, owing to the scarcity of copper, heavy and cumbersome iron coins had always circulated and were to remain in use under the Sung. The new empire succeeded about 960–1000 in restoring throughout its territory the use of one single type of copper coin. But the war effort was to prompt the state to increase the volume of this coinage to an unprecedented extent between the serious military difficulties in the north-west of 1038–55 (new coins of ten units — subsequently withdrawn from circulation — were issued at this point) and the Jürchen invasion of 1126. The record for casting was reached in the year 1073, with six million strings of a thousand coins, and the total of all issues under the Northern Sung is reckoned at 200 million strings.

In spite of this huge output, copper coins did not suffice for all the

Table 15. Figures for issues of coins in the ninth to twelfth centuries
(in strings of 1000 coins)

804	135,000
820	150,000
834	100,000
995–997	270,000 (average over three years)
1000	1,350,000
1007	1,850,000
1016	1,230,000
1021	1,050,000
1073	6,000,000
1080	5,949,000
1106	2,890,000
1124	3,000,000

needs provoked by economic development and by the growth of military expenditure. The use of unminted silver, which had begun to be employed south of the lower Yangtze and in Szechwan at the time of the Five Dynasties, spread in the eleventh century to North China, where the Uighurs of central Asia, who traded with the countries of the Middle East, contributed to the extension of this new method of payment by their imports of silver.

The certificates of deposit issued in favour of merchants in the ninth century by the representatives of their provincial governments in the capital—what was called at the time 'flying money' (*fei-ch'ien*)—and those issued privately a little later—from the end of the ninth century onwards—by the rich merchants and financiers of Ch'eng-tu in Szechwan were the precursors of banknotes, the first state printings of which were made in Szechwan in 1024. This institution, which was to spread widely in the Chinese world in the eleventh to fourteenth centuries but later fell into discredit and was only employed occasionally, gave powerful assistance to the expansion of both the private and the state economy during the Sung period. It made possible the reduction of issues of copper coin under the Southern Sung, although the misuse of this new money with a compulsory rate of exchange ended by aggravating the disorder in the economy just before the Mongol invasion.

Known variously as *chiao-tzu, ch'ien-yin, k'uai-tzu* or *kuan-tzu,* paper money became the principal kind of money in the twelfth and thirteenth centuries and remained so until the end of the Mongol period, spreading also into the Liao and Chin empires. Under the Southern Sung, issues reached the equivalent of 400 million strings. But alongside paper money commercial circles began to use negotiable instruments; the cheque, the promissory note, and the bill of exchange made their appearance in the eleventh century. The financial activities controlled by the proprietors of exchange offices (*chi-fu-p'u, chin-yin-p'u, tui-fang, chiao-tzu-p'u, chiao-yin-p'u, chih-p'u, fang-chai-hu, ch'ien-hu,* etc.) became one of the most important sectors of the mercantile economy in the Sung epoch.

The maritime expansion

The development of Chinese seafaring activities from the eleventh century onwards was without doubt one of the most important phenomena in the history of Asia. The testimony of European and Arab travellers in the thirteenth and fourteenth centuries leaves no doubt on this point: the activity of the big ports of Fukien, Chekiang, and Kwangtung at that time was on a far larger scale than that of European countries. The size of river and seagoing traffic in the Sung and Yüan periods, the role of the naval fleets in the defence of the Southern Sung in the twelfth and thirteenth centuries and during the Mongol attempts to invade Japan and Java at the end of the thirteenth century, and the great maritime expeditions of the Ming period in the years 1405–33, which ventured as far as the Red Sea and the east coast of Africa, all show quite clearly that in the four and a half centuries from the consolidation of the Sung empire to the great period of expansion of the Ming empire China was the greatest maritime power in the world. The phenomenon is explained by a number of circumstances connected as much with the political and economic context as with the history of seafaring techniques.

In Neolithic times and up to the vicinity of the Christian era, sea voyages were made, it seems, along the coast, advantage being taken of nearby islands. Thus even in prehistoric days the islands of Tsushima and Iki assisted relations between the coast of Korea and the Japanese island of Kyushu, just as the islands between the P'eng-lai area, in north-eastern Shantung, and the Lü-shun (Port Arthur) area doubtless made it possible to sail between Manchuria and eastern China. But the pattern of constant, regular winds which characterizes monsoon Asia was put to good use as early as the first few centuries of the Christian era in the oceans which wash the shores of the eastern and southern parts of the continent. Unexpected changes of wind and flat calms are less to be feared in these seas than in the Mediterranean. Consequently it was a sailing fleet, devoid of the benches of slave rowers of the Mediterranean world of antiquity and the Renaissance, that developed in this part of the world. Progress was made very early in the art of sailing. The fore-and-aft sail typical of Chinese ships is described as early as the third century A.D.

The monsoon pattern favoured long voyages without any ports of call, imposing on them an annual rhythm which had an effect on the history of civilizations: the north-east monsoon in winter and the south-west monsoon in summer made long-haul navigation in Asia a periodical activity which resulted in the formation of substantial foreign colonies on the coast of India, in South-East Asia, and in the Chinese ports from the mouth of the Yangtze to the Canton area. In the first few centuries of our era the coasts of southern India and Ceylon were already connected to Sumatra by non-stop voyages, and the long trip between Palembang and Canton seems to have been made regularly as early as the seventh century.

It looks as if one can distinguish two great geographical areas in the history of maritime technology in East Asia, one extending from the coast of Chekiang to Korea and Japan, the other covering all South-East Asia and South China. The former was the domain of shipping which owed its development to the inhabitants of the coasts of Liaotung, Korea, Shantung, and, at a later date, Japan. The latter, the scene in ancient times of the diaspora of the seafaring peoples speaking 'Malayo-Polynesian' tongues from southern China to Melanesia and Madagascar, was the meeting-place, from the start of the Christian era onwards, of boats which doubtless differed not only in place of origin but also in their technology. A kind of sail used on the boats of Lake Tung-t'ing right in the centre of China spread as far as Zanzibar, on the east coast of Africa, while marked differences distinguished Arab ships from the Chinese ships of Kwangtung and Fukien. Malays, Sumatrans, and Javanese were in contact with Arab and Indo-Iranian shipping before they came to know, much later, from the early years of the sixteenth century onwards, that of the western European countries.

Thus various different influences may have contributed to the apearance of the big Chinese high-seas junk towards the tenth or eleventh century. Its place of birth certainly seems to have been the great estuary of the Yangtze, where the transition from river to high-seas navigation takes place imperceptibly. The main stream and arms of the river reach a width of ten to twenty kilometres up to about 150 kilometres inland.

Like all Chinese boats since antiquity, the junk consists of a rectangular hull with its hold divided up by partitions which form a number of watertight compartments (this arrangement was to be consciously adopted by Westerners at the beginning of the nineteenth century). The vertical wall of the stern-post makes it possible to fit a rudder to it, and the first evidence of this invention, of such great importance in the history of navigation, dates from the end of the fourth century A.D. The stern-post rudder was to appear in Europe about 1180, at much the same time as the mariner's compass. The junks of the Sung age—big sailing ships with four or six masts, twelve big sails and four decks, capable of carrying about a thousand men—were the fruit of a long series of inventions and experiments. Anchors, rudder, drop-keel, capstans, canvas sails and rigid matting sails, used according to whether the wind blew from astern or ahead, pivoting sails which avoided the need to alter the rigging and aroused the admiration of Arab seafarers (the Chinese technique was the only one which made it possible to sail very close to the wind), oars with an automatic angle of attack which pivoted of their own accord in their fore-and-aft movements, watertight compartments, mariner's compass—all these improvements, some centuries old, others quite recent, contributed to the astonishing success of Chinese seamen. The application of the compass—long used for calculations by the geomancers—to maritime needs made ocean voyages safer. A work with a preface dating from 1119, the *P'ing-chou k'o-t'an* by Chu Yü, first records its use in Cantonese ships at the end of the eleventh century. Mentioned in Europe by Guyot de Salins in 1190, it was not generally used on board ships until after 1280.

But many other improvements were necessary for the progress of Chinese seafaring in the tenth and eleventh centuries. They concerned not only direction finding and the measurement of distances but also the knowledge of depths of water and currents. Chinese cartography, based since the third century on a system of equidistant north-south and east-west parallels, made remarkable progress in the Sung period. Ahead of medieval European cartography, which was still dominated by religious considerations, and even of Arab cartography, it was the most precise and accurate in the world at that time, as is shown by the maps engraved on stelae which have been preserved.

Progress in navigational techniques made the expansion of maritime activity possible, but the underlying reasons for this expansion were connected with political circumstances and the development of the mercantile economy. Cut off from access to central Asia, blocked in its expansion towards the north and north-west by the great empires which had arisen on its frontiers, the Chinese world turned resolutely to the sea. Its centre of gravity shifted towards the trading and maritime regions of the south-east, which were extended inland by the enormous network of the Yangtze and its tributaries. The sea routes starting from the Abbasid empire and connecting the Persian Gulf with India, South-East Asia, and the Chinese coast no doubt also played a part in this call of the sea. Piracy, practised in every age down to our own by the maritime peoples of East Asia from Java to Korea and Japan, was on the wane during the whole period in which the great upsurge of Chinese seafaring activity occurred. The maritime empire of Sri Vijaya on the south-east coast of Sumatra, so powerful in the eighth century, was in decline in the eleventh. The thalassocracies of Majapahit in central Java in the fourteenth and fifteenth centuries, of the kingdom of Malacca in the fifteenth century, and of Atjeh on the north-east coast of Sumatra in the sixteenth and seventeenth centuries came later.

The expansion of sea-borne trade in the Sung period led to the composition of works devoted to the description of the lands of South-East Asia and the Indian Ocean. Unlike accounts of travels written in earlier ages by civil servants on official journeys and by pilgrims, these notes on foreign countries record the information obtained from Chinese or foreign merchants used to making long sea voyages from the Chinese coast, the Philippines and Borneo to the Red Sea. We even find in them, as in Han days, information about the Mediterranean lands. The two most important works of this kind are the *Answers to Questions about the Regions to the South of the Mountain Ranges* (*Ling-wai tai-ta*) by Chou Ch'ü-fei, which appeared in 1178, and the *Accounts of Foreign Countries* (*Chu-fan-chih*) by Chao Ju-kua, the preface of which is dated 1225.

Chapter 15

The Civilization
of the Chinese 'Renaissance'

The changes which were taking place, or had already taken place, round about the year 1000 were not confined to social and political forms, the economy, and technical innovations. They were concerned with a deeper and less visible reality — man, his conception of the world, and his picture of time, space, and the individual. The eleventh century, which was distinguished by a return to the classical tradition, marked the end of the domination which Buddhism had exercised over the Chinese world since the fifth century A.D. The immeasurable times and spaces, the intermingling of living beings — demons, animals, infernal beings, men, and gods, through their transmigrations — this whole cosmic phantasmagoria disappeared, leaving in its place only the visible world. Man became man again in a limited, comprehensible universe which he had only to examine if he wished to understand it. One has the impression that a whole series of psychological changes took place, which an analysis of the literature of the time would doubtless reveal. The educated Chinese of the eleventh century was as different from his T'ang predecessors as Renaissance man from medieval man.

What is strikingly manifest is the advent of a practical rationalism based on experiment, the putting of inventions, ideas, and theories to the test. We also find curiosity at work in every realm of knowledge — arts, technology, natural sciences, mathematics, society, institutions, politics. There was a desire to take stock of all previous acquisitions and to construct a synthesis of all human knowledge. A naturalist philosophy which was to dominate Chinese thinking in the following ages developed in the eleventh century and attained its definitive expression in the twelfth.

This complete renewal of intellectual life was partly the result of social and economic changes, of the increase in the number of well-to-do families and of the growth of the towns, but another reason for it was also the more and more extensive use of a rapid and cheap means of reproducing written texts.

The background to the renewal

Learned culture and popular culture

The Sung age illustrates, possibly better than many others, the relationship between arts and letters and the facts of the social situation. Whereas in the seventh and eighth centuries an aristocracy in which there was a good deal of 'barbarian' blood had imposed its love of violent games (polo, riding, hunting), the governing class of the eleventh to thirteenth centuries, consisting of rich, educated families usually living in an urban environment on the income from their estates, despised physical effort and wished to stand aloof from the traditions of the steppe and from popular amusements. The profession of arms, so highly regarded at the beginning of the T'ang age, had lost its prestige ever since the armies had consisted of mercenaries recruited from the dregs of society. The intellectual, contemplative, learned, sometimes even esoteric, aspect of arts and letters among the Chinese upper classes asserted itself in the Sung period and was to remain dominant under the Ming and Ch'ing dynasties, in spite of reactions tending towards a return to practical knowledge and physical activities in original and isolated thinkers in the sixteenth and seventeenth centuries. Henceforth the lettered Chinese, apart from exceptions, was to be a pure intellectual who thought that games of skill and athletic competitions were things for the lower classes. This deeply rooted contempt in the governing classes for physical effort and aptitude was to persist down to our own day; sports were reintroduced into China only in fairly recent years, under the influence of the Anglo-Saxon countries. From the Sung period onwards only learned literature, painting, calligraphy, the collection of books and works of art, and the designing of gardens found favour with the educated classes.

However, while these literati cultivated classical poetry and the new, difficult genre of the poem to be sung, set to musical airs (*tz'u*) – a genre in which high officials like Su Shih (Su Tung-p'o) (1036–1101) or Huang T'ing chien (1045–1105) gained fame – devoted themselves to the academic painting which triumphed in the imperial palace under Hui-tsung (1101–25), or gave themselves like Mi Fu (1051–1107) to pictorial research, the expansion of amusements in the towns carried the seed of a popular literature which was to be one of the most fertile and life-giving elements in the whole literary history of China.

With its 'middle class' of shopkeepers and craftsmen and all its casual labourers, clerks, servants and shop assistants, the big commercial agglomeration of the Sung age created a new sector of society whose tastes and requirements were quite different from those of the upper classes. Urban life tended to take away from diversions and amusements their periodical character, their connection with fairs and country markets; it also dissolved their links with feasts and religious activities. It gave a specific, independent character to the efforts of the story-teller and the jester and made them into a professional activity. The towns of the Sung period, especially the capitals — K'ai-feng, Hangchow, Peking under the Chin and the Mongols — became permanent centres of entertainment. Amusement districts (*wa-tzu* or *wa-shih*), different from the districts inhabited by actors and musicians (*chiao-fang*) who, under the T'ang, were closely dependent on the imperial administration, served as popular meeting-places where all the professional showmen were to be found: story-tellers specializing in different kinds of stories (historical, sentimental, criminal, religious), actors of short, mimed plays with musical accompaniment, musicians and singers, puppeteers, animal trainers, specialists in the shadow-theatre, animal imitators, and so on. The city was the centre that gave birth to new literary forms which were to develop in parallel with learned literature from the thirteenth and fourteenth centuries onwards. With their everyday language abounding in regional variations, their style, and their tone, these tales, novels, and plays retained all the life and savour which they drew from their origins.

Wood-block printing and typography

In the West, possession of the capacity, from the middle of the fifteenth century onwards, to print texts on paper marked a decisive step forward in comparison with the manuscript copy on parchment. With printing, Europe emerged from the Middle Ages. The situation was quite different in the Chinese world. The spread during the ninth and tenth centuries of a means of reproducing written texts and drawings rapidly and cheaply was not felt as an event of a revolutionary nature, although, all things considered, its consequences were scarcely less important than those of the spread of printing in Europe. But this difference in reaction is easily explained. While Europe moved in a relatively brief space of time from the medieval copy on a rare and costly material to the printed book (Europe became acquainted in the twelfth century with paper imported

from the Islamic countries, began itself to make paper in Italy at the end
of the thirteenth century, welcomed wood-block printing enthusiastically
about 1380 and succeeded in perfecting between 1430 and 1460 the first
typographical techniques), the Chinese world experienced a process of
development which was both much more gradual and different in nature.
Paper, which was to prove indispensable for the reproduction of texts,
became the ordinary material for writing on from the end of the Han age
onwards (the first Chinese papers, discovered on the ancient Han *limes,*
date from the second century A.D.). The practice of using stelae bearing
texts or drawings as stamps or blocks (with a coat of damp paper, drying,
inking, and reproduction on paper with the help of a pad), which made it
possible down to our own day in all countries of Chinese civilization to
obtain cheap, faithful reproductions of engraved pictures or famous
pieces of calligraphy, was developed between the Han period and the
beginnings of wood engraving. Seals also made it possible to produce impressions of written characters, drawings, or religious pictures. Wood-
block printing, which made its appearance during the course of the
eighth century, was a sort of combination of these two processes (stamping and seal). The first known examples date from the end of the eighth
century; they consist of Buddhist pictures, accompanied by short texts,
which were found at Tun-huang (western Kansu) and of a Buddhist
magic formula preserved in Japan and probably printed in China between 764 and 770. In the collection of manuscripts from Tun-huang,
which includes several texts printed in the ninth and tenth centuries, the
first important document reproduced by wood-block printing is a text
from the 'Diamond Sutra' (*Chin-kang-ching*) dated 868. Other printed
texts have been discovered fairly recently; two came from the kingdom of
Wu-Yüeh (lower Yangtze and Chekiang) and bear the dates 953 and 974.
Another, dated 975, was found at Hangchow. By this time wood-block
printing was already in general use in the commercially busy and densely
populated towns of the Min River valley in Szechwan and of the plains
extending from Hangchow to the lower Yangtze. We are informed that
little works on the occult sciences, almanacs, Buddhist texts, lexicons,
short popular encyclopaedias, manuals of elementary education, collections of model compositions for the official competitions, historical
works, and so on were printed by the wood-block system in these areas as
early as the ninth century. It is worth emphasizing the popular and commercial character of these first applications of a technique which in all
probability was suggested by the need to reproduce religious texts.
However, the governing circles and the literati were not slow to take advantage of this new method of reproduction: at the suggestion of one
Feng Tao (882–954) the Nine Classics were printed at K'ai-feng by im-

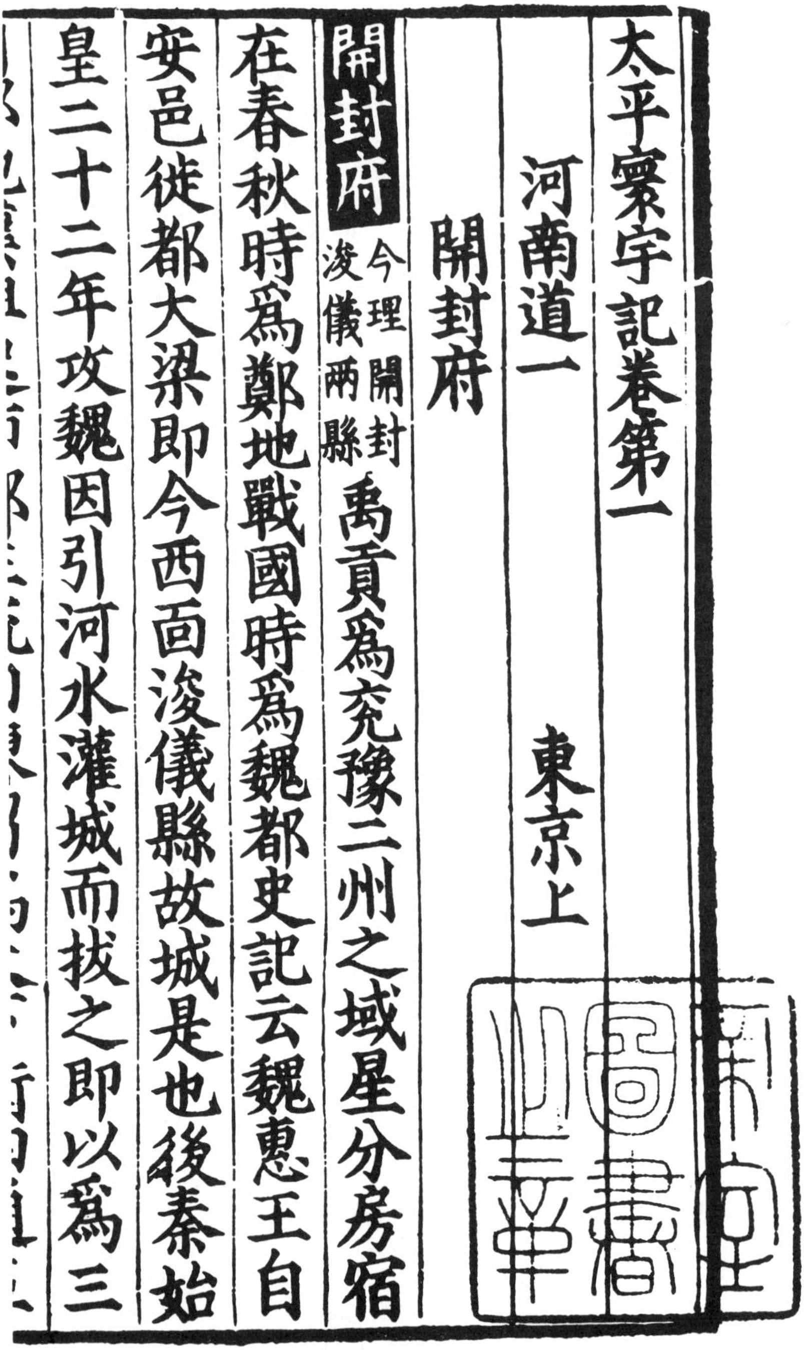

開封府 今理開封浚儀兩縣

太平寰宇記卷第一

河南道一　　　東京上

開封府

禹貢爲兗豫二州之域星分房宿

在春秋時爲鄭地戰國時爲魏都史記云魏惠王自

安邑徙都大梁即今西面浚儀縣故城是也後秦始

皇二十二年攻魏因引河水灌城而拔之即以爲三

Figure 10 Printed text of the Sung period (using the wood-block system). This is the first chapter of the *T'ai-p'ing huan-yü chi*, a geography of China and foreign countries that was completed in 979

perial command between 932 and 952. They were also printed in Szechwan between 944 and 951. Finally, the Buddhist canon was printed at Ch'eng-tu between 972 and 983. The whole work comprised 1076 headings in 5048 chapters and was engraved on 130,000 two-page blocks. From 1042 onwards wood-block printing was employed for the issue of the first promissory notes in Szechwan and for the publication of official decrees and ordinances. In 1027 the works on medicine and pharmacy were revised and printed so that they could reach a wider public.

Thus wood-block engraving, which made it possible to reproduce accurately the calligraphy and illustrations of texts, became part of ordinary life in the course of the tenth century. It was to retain a dominant position in all the countries of Chinese civilization (China, Japan, Korea, Vietnam) down to the spread of the mechanized, movable-type printing perfected in the West during the nineteenth century.

However, the invention of movable characters came earlier in China than in Europe, and the lands of East Asia employed typography at the same time as wood engraving. The first allusion to the use of movable type in China occurs in a collection of notes (*pi-chi*) mostly concerned with the history of science and technology, the *Meng-ch'i pi-t'an,* by Shen Kua, which appeared in 1086. The invention was due to one of the protégés of this Shen Kua, a certain Pi Shang, and dates from the years 1041–48. At the time of the occupation of South China by the Mongols, Wang Chen mentions in his *Treatise on Agriculture (Nung-shu),* published in 1313, the use of movable tin characters and suggests employing a turning case with the characters classified in it by rhymes. But the first big printings in movable type known to us were executed in Korea on the initiative of the central government, between 1403 and 1484. One hundred thousand Chinese characters were cast in 1403 and other founts were produced successively during the course of the fifteenth century. Two great families of printers of Wu-hsi in Kiangsu, the An and the Hua, used movable type made of copper. The big collection of tales of the *T'ai-p'ing kuang-chi,* first reproduced by the wood-block process at the end of the tenth century, was published in a typographical edition in 1574. At a more recent date, the huge illustrated encyclopaedia of the K'ang-hsi era, the *T'u-shu chi-ch'eng,* which contains nearly ten million characters, was printed in movable type between 1713 and 1722.

Thus from the eleventh century to the eighteenth, that part of East Asia which owed its civilization to China (and also, under its influence, its neighbours—Uighurs, Tibetans, Mongols, Manchus, who used alphabetical scripts) possessed a typographical tradition independent of the European one and also different in technique, for it did not involve a press. To judge by the size of editions, this tradition was far from negligible; but movable type had little chance of supplanting wood-block printing in countries of Chinese culture before the arrival of mechanized printing. For although the invention of typography was clearly an event of capital importance in a Europe where a few hundred letters sufficed for the printing of any possible text, it could not have the same significance in a world one of whose riches was precisely the wealth and diversity of the signs used for writing.

Contrary to what one is tempted to think, since in the West typography marked a decisive step forward in comparison with wood-block printing, the more complex and skilled system does not possess all the advantages. The superiority of Western printing only asserted itself slowly and did not become incontestable until mechanized methods were developed in the nineteenth century. Until then it remained a fairly slow and expensive way of reproducing written texts. At the beginning of the seventeenth century Matteo Ricci noticed that wood-block printers in China took no more time to engrave their blocks than European typographers took to compose their pages. Engraved blocks can be re-engraved, corrected and, unlike the printer's forms, can be kept in stock for new printings. While the spread of printing in Europe resulted in the impoverishment of the written tradition, because publishers could not take the risk of bringing out works which were not assured of a fairly large sale, Chinese wood-block printing, which was much superior in technique to European wood engraving of the fifteenth century (because of its experience with seals and stamping, and thanks to the use of special papers which allowed the text being reproduced to appear reversed on the back) had the great advantage of being a fairly inexpensive and very flexible procedure which did not require a large capital outlay. It thus made possible, from the tenth century onwards, an extraordinary multiplication of private and public editions, even if the number of copies of each was limited. Moreover—and this is extremely important—illustration was able to develop in 'Chinese' lands on parallel lines to the engraving of the texts, whereas in works printed in the West pictures only became common in comparatively recent years. Right from the start of wood-block printing, the majority of Chinese books—herbals, technical treatises, works on archaeology or architecture, novels, religious texts—were provided with illustrations, which were sometimes of remarkably high quality. Wood-block printing of texts and illustrations, which made great progress in the eleventh to thirteenth centuries, was to reach its zenith in the Wan-li era (1573–1619), a period when blocks were printed in three, four, and sometimes even five colours.

In spite of differences springing from particular technical and intellectual traditions, particular social and economic backgrounds, which explain why the routes followed in East Asia and in Europe were not the same, the fact remains that China made considerable progress in the reproduction and diffusion of texts. Our tradition goes back in essentials to the time of the Renaissance, but the written tradition in China goes back to the time of the Five Dynasties and the Sung. There was thus a time lag of some five hundred years between the Chinese world and Europe. There has been no other civilization in which the written tradition — in the form of inscriptions, manuscripts, and xylographs — played such an early importance.

Science and philosophy

The new technique rapidly gave birth to a very lively book trade. It caused a swift increase in the number of books written and made possible a much wider diffusion of knowledge than in the past. Whereas in the T'ang age the principal centres of learning had been the Buddhist monasteries, together with the state schools in the capital, in the eleventh to thirteenth centuries public and private schools and libraries multiplied. The private academies (*shu-yüan*) which came into being in the Sung period in all areas, but especially on the lower Yangtze, to the south of the river, were to play a very important role in the intellectual history of China down to the middle of the seventeenth century. One of the biggest libraries was that of the imperial palace, founded in 978 and containing eighty thousand volumes. Its catalogue was drawn up by the reformer Fan Chung-yen and the historian Ou-yang Hsiu between 1034 and 1036.

*Literary output in the Sung age
and the development of the sciences*

The eleventh to thirteenth centuries were the age of the first big collections of texts, of big encyclopaedias, and of inventories. By the end of the tenth century four famous collections (the four great Sung books, *Sung ssu ta-shu*) had been compiled and printed. The *Wen-yüan ying-hua,* a literary anthology which forms a continuation of the *Wen-hsüan* and covers the period from the middle of the sixth century to the beginning of the tenth, was put together between 982 and 986; the *T'ai-p'ing yü-lan,* an encyclopaedia in a thousand chapters completed in 983, and the huge collection of strange tales and stories in five hundred chapters called the *T'ai-p'ing kuang-chi* and first printed in 981, were both produced on official orders by Li Fang (925–95) in 977; and finally the *Ts'e-fu yüan-kuei,* a collection of political texts and essays with a thousand chapters, was compiled between 1005 and 1013.

But it was particularly the works produced by private enterprise, independently of any official command, that multiplied in the Sung age — historical works, collections of notes, treatises of a scientific character, local monographs, literary works, and so on.

Some aspects of this output, which was more abundant than that of previous ages, can be connected with the extraordinary fashion in the eleventh to thirteenth centuries for collections — collections of paintings and calligraphy, the richest and most famous of which, assembled by the aesthete emperor Hui-tsung (1101–25), were to be destroyed by the Jürchen invasion, collections of curious stones, of ancient coins, inks, jades. . . . Treatises on the natural sciences were numerous and, when they have survived, are very valuable for the history of plants and animals — treatises on mushrooms, bamboos, chrysanthemums, peonies, fruit-trees, birds. Two examples are the *Manual of Crabs* (*Hsieh-p'u*) by Fu Kung (1059) and the *Treatise on Citrus Fruit* (*Chü-lu*) by Han Yen-chih (1178).

There was also a fashion for various notes of a scientific, technical, literary, or artistic character. They were known as *pi-chi* or *sui-pi* (*notes jotted down with the brush*). One of the most important for the history of science and technology in China is the *Meng-ch'i pi-t'an* by Shen Kua (1031–94), an astronomer and physicist with an amazingly modern mind, in whose work we find the first allusion to the invention of movable type.

The oldest and most accurate of the documents that we possess on Chinese architecture dates from the Sung period. It was an admirably printed and illustrated treatise which appeared in 1103, the *Ying-tsao fa-shih,* the work of one Li Chieh, who was himself an architect and the constructor of temples and official buildings in K'ai-feng.

In the realms of medicine, geography, mathematics, and astronomy remarkable progress was made in the Sung age. Among the numerous medical works of the eleventh to thirteenth centuries it is worth noting the publication of the first known treatise on forensic medicine, the *Hsi-yüan-lu* by Sung Tz'u, which appeared in 1242. A universal geographical encyclopaedia in 200 chapters, the *T'ai-p'ing huan-yü chi* by Yüeh Shih, was published in 979. It was followed by an illustrated geography of the Sung empire in 1566 chapters, the *Chu-tao t'u-ching,* which was completed in 1010. Chinese cartography of the Sung epoch achieved a precision and accuracy never attained before. Shen Kua had the idea of making maps in relief. A vehicle for measuring distance travelled by road was designed and built in 1027.

The eleventh to thirteenth centuries, together with the Mongol epoch (late thirteenth century to mid-fourteenth century), formed one of the greatest periods in the history of mathematics in China, a period note-

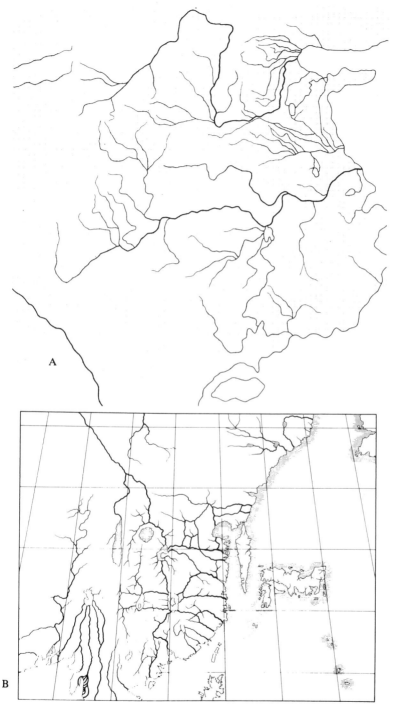

A

B

Figure 11 **A.** Chinese stone-engraved map, 1137. The north-south and east-west coordinates, which have been in use since the time of P'ei Hsiu (224–271), are worth noting. Each division represents 100 *li*, i.e. about 50 km. **B.** For comparison, an eighteenth-century English map

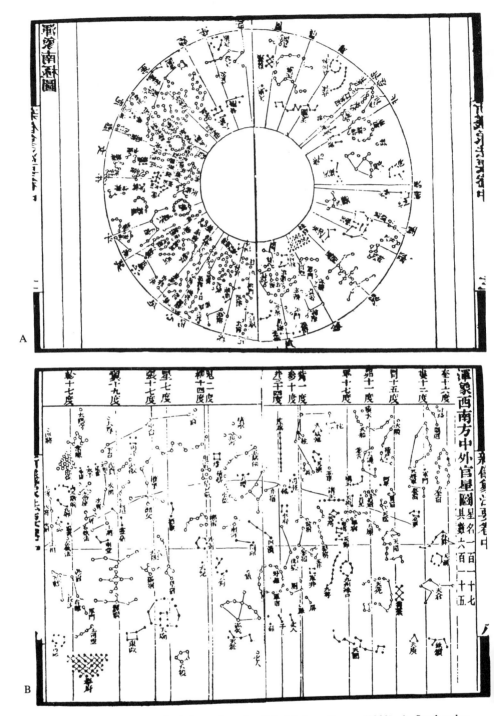

Figure 12 Astronomical charts from the *Hsin I-hsiang Fa-yao* (1092). **A.** South-polar projection of the sky. **B.** Regions of the sky corresponding to 14 of the Lunar Mansions. The Equator (centre) and the Ecliptic are both shown. The projection is Mercator

worthy for the development of algebra. The greatest names are Shao Yung (1011-77), to whom we owe a calculation of the tropical year accurate to within four seconds, Li Yeh (1192-1279) and Ch'in Chiu-shao (died 1262), author of an important mathematical work, the *Shu-shu chiu-chang*. Ch'in Chiu-shao was the first Chinese mathematician to use the nought, at the very time when it appeared—at the same time as Arabic numerals—in Italy.

One of the most important enterprises in the history of the astronomy and mathematics of the age was the construction at K'ai-feng in 1090 of an astronomical machine actuated by an escapement system and by cogs and transmission chains. If not the first, for there was a similar machine in China in the eighth century, it was at any rate one of the most perfect and one of the oldest mechanisms in the history of the world, with a slow, regular, continuous rotation. The astronomical machine of Su Sung (1020-1101) was worked by a wheel turned by the successive filling of pivoting cups fed by a tank with a constant level. This piece of clockwork was the most accurate so far developed.

The beginnings of scientific archaeology

The scientific tendencies characteristic of the Sung age also made themselves apparent in the field of archaeology. Discoveries aroused the enthusiasm of scholars and art-lovers. Certain antique objects—bronzes and jades—dating from the end of the second millennium B.C. were discovered during the reign of Hui-tsung (1101-25) in the region of Anyang, on the site which was to be identified at the beginning of the twentieth century as that of the last capital of the Shang dynasty. The taste for antiquities had two parallel consequences: on the one hand it enriched artistic traditions (fashion for antiques and imitations of antiques—forgers' techniques improved in time with the development of the market in *objets d'art*—influence of archaic styles of writing on calligraphy) and on the other it led to an upsurge of critical archaeology and epigraphy, which from the eleventh century onwards became sciences in the service of history. The first work on ancient bells and tripods dates from the Sung age, as do the first books with illustrations showing them. In 1092 Lü Ta-lin published his *Archaeological Plates* (*K'ao-ku t'u*), the first attempt at a scientific classification and dating of the bronzes of the second and first millennia B.C. At the end of the twelfth century Hung Tsun (1120-74), the brother of Hung Mai (1123-1202, author of a famous collection of strange or extraordinary stories, the *I-chien chih*), brought out his *Ancient Coins* (*Ku-ch'üan*), the first book on numismatics in the history of China.

But it was in the field of epigraphy that the most remarkable progress was made; this is doubtless explained by the passionate interest that the Chinese have always taken in the history of their writing. The most famous study was the one accomplished at the cost of long years of research by Chao Ming-ch'eng (1081–1129) and his wife, the great poetess Li Ch'ing-chao (1084–1141?). Their *Catalogue of the Inscriptions on Stone and Bronze* (*Chin-shih lu*) records two thousand ancient documents and corrects the errors in the catalogue of ancient inscriptions produced by the historian Ou-yang Hsiu in 1063, the *Chi-ku lu.*

Archaeology, like the history of institutions, which had also developed since the eighth century, invited people to look at the past as a continuous process of evolution which had gone on since remote antiquity down to the present.

New tendencies in history

The movement towards critical reflection inaugurated by Liu Chih-chi at the beginning of the eighth century had been provoked by the routine, mechanical way in which the numerous official histories produced at the beginning of the T'ang age had been compiled. At the same time the first historical encyclopaedias indicated a new approach: without worrying about the traditional frameworks and divisions, the historian should both embrace long periods of time and aim at producing a personal work. The many anonymous compilations had demonstrated that they could be only works devoid of any deep significance. The movement initiated in the eighth and ninth centuries resulted in the eleventh in a positive renewal of historical studies. We see at this period the assertion of a concern for greater scientific rigour and at the same time for moral considerations.

But first of all history had to rediscover the literary quality inherent in the first historical works — Ssu-ma Ch'ien's *Historical Records* (*c.* 90 B.C.), Pan Ku's *History of the Han* (*c.* A.D. 82), Ch'en Shou's *History of the Three Kingdoms* (end of third century). The 'ancient style' (*ku-wen*), the first devotees of which round 800 had looked like eccentrics, triumphed at the beginning of the Sung period. It was adopted by poets like Su Shih and Huang T'ing-chien and by politicians like Wang An-shih. It was in the 'ancient style' that Ou-yang Hsiu (1007–72) rewrote the *History of the T'ang,* suppressing most of the passages which indicated a certain degree of friendliness towards Buddhism. He did the same with the history of the Five Dynasties. The results were the *Hsin-t'ang shu* (*New History of the T'ang*) (1060) and the *Hsin-wu-tai shih* (*New History of the Five Dynasties*) (*c.* 1070), two works much prized down to our own day for their literary value. The second of them was modelled by its author on the ancient Annals of the kingdom of Lu, the *Ch'un-ch'iu* (722–481 B.C.): the mere choice of terms was intended to make an implicit judgement on the period of disturbances and divisions between the end of the T'ang and the accession of the Sung. These moralizing tendencies, the emphasis laid on the problem of dynastic legitimacy, and the search for an ethical significance in history were typical of the Sung age and in harmony with the new directions being taken by Chinese philosophy.

The biggest and most famous of the historical works of the eleventh century, the one which was to exert the deepest influence, was a general history of China from 403 B.C. to A.D. 959 written between 1072 and 1084. The *Complete Mirror for the Illustration of Government (Tzu-chih t'ung-chien)* by Ssu-ma Kuang, whose only predecessor was Ssu-ma Ch'ien in his admirable *Historical Records,* remains faithful, in spite of its author's concern to connect facts with each other, to the traditional division by years, months, and days. But the work is distinguished by two remarkable characteristics: its concern with the exhaustive search for sources of every kind (including literary works and inscriptions) and with a critical approach to the documents that can already be described as scientific. Of the *Tzu-chih t'ung-chien*'s 354 chapters, thirty consist of critical notes (*k'ao-i,* 'examination of divergences') discussing the reasons which have guided the author through the different or contradictory traditions concerning the same event.

Ssu-ma Kuang's magistral work was so unanimously admired that it inspired the composition of several similar works in the twelfth and thirteenth centuries. The philosopher Chu Hsi (1130–1200) produced a summary of it which was to enjoy great success in later ages. This was the *T'ung-chien kang-mu,* which adopts a moralizing conception of history. Continuations of Ssu-ma Kuang's great work were published: the *Hsü tzu-chih t'ung-chien ch'ang-pien* by Li T'ao (1115–84) and the *Résumé of Events by Years Since the Chien-yen Era* (1127–30) (*Chien-yen-i-lai hsi-nien yao-lu*) by Li Hsin-ch'uan (1166–1243). Finally, to remedy the drawbacks of the year-by-year cuts, Yüan Shu (1131–1205) divided up the content of the *Complete Mirror* by subjects in *Full Details of the 'Complete Mirror' Classified under Headings (T'ung-chien chi-shih pen-mo*), written between 1173 and 1175. He thus provided the model for a new kind of work which was subsequently to be imitated frequently.

The Sung age is also famous for its historical encyclopaedias. Cheng Ch'iao (1104–62) was the author of a collection of monographs, the *T'ung-chih,* dealing with the genealogy of great families, philology, phonetics, historical geography, botany and zoology, bibliography, archaeology, and other subjects. Contemptuous of the book-learning of the literati and very keen on the natural sciences, Cheng Ch'iao was too original a thinker to be appreciated by his own age. His historical work was rehabilitated only at the end of the eighteenth century before attracting the attention of modern scholars. Another historical encyclopaedia deals with the history of institutions. This is the *Wen-hsien t'ung-k'ao* by Ma Tuan-lin, who lived at the end of the Southern Sung period and the beginning of the Mongol occupation. Not completed until 1317, it formed a continuation to the *T'ung-tien* of Tu Yu (732–812).

Cosmology and ethics:
the construction of a naturalist philosophy

Just as history is not made by the brute facts but by the natural dynamism immanent in them which the historian must seek to grasp by intuition, so the true object of painting does not reside in the concrete representation of the visible but in the apprehension of the metamorphoses of being. Chapter 17 of the *Meng-ch'i pi-t'an,* devoted to painting and calligraphy, contains a famous passage in which Shen Kua goes so far as to proclaim the independence of the pictorial creation of the vulgar requirements of resemblance. What constitutes the value of the work of art is in fact the intuition which goes beyond the things, and finally all that the work reveals of the mind, culture, and human quality of its creator.

It would doubtless be possible to find antecedents, analogous tendencies in the history of Chinese thought before the Sung period, but the immanence of mind in the world had never been expressed before in such an explicit and clearly conceived way. It was the eleventh and twelfth centuries that saw the definition of the first philosophical system to take account of the solidarity or, to put it better, the basic identity of the natural order and the human order, of the moral and the cosmic. With the formulation of this universal, naturalist, rational philosophy we reach one of the peaks in the history of Chinese thought. We have reached the classical age, the age of maturity. This philosophy, which was to prove an obstacle to the first Jesuit missionaries and which was quite new to Europeans of the seventeenth century, was to become the foundation and the moral and natural justification of the authoritarian empire of the Ming and Ch'ing periods.

Hostile to Buddhism yet nevertheless influenced by Buddhist methods of teaching and monastic traditions of asceticism, the scholars of the eleventh century thought they were returning to the true Confucian tradition that they judged to have been interrupted since Mencius (*c.* 372–289).

This renewal was ultimately derived from the 'nationalist' reaction which had followed An Lu-shan's rebellion and from what was called the 'ancient style' (*ku-wen*) movement. The idea that it was necessary to go back to the living sources of the Chinese tradition and that the Classics, abandoned since the triumph of Buddhism, contained an implicit philosophy which, once extracted, would make it possible to ensure social harmony and public order, had already been expressed by Han Yü, and some of the orientations which were going to be defined in the eleventh and twelfth centuries had been dimly perceived by men like Li Ao, who died about fifteen years after Han Yü. What the eleventh century contributed to this current of thought was an illumination peculiar to this age of optimism and of faith in universal reason: the belief in the benefits of education, in the possibility of improving society and the political system, in the primacy of the mind. There was also a desire for systematization, the search for a total explanation of the universe which could be substituted for the explanation provided by the Buddhist religion and philosophy. Ou-yang Hsiu denounces the divorce which had occurred since the Six Dynasties between the political function (*chih*) and culture (*chiao*): the former, he says, without the latter is bound to be devoid of soul and corrupted; the latter without the former loses all touch with reality and any deep meaning. For Ou-yang Hsiu, as for his contemporaries, the great task of his age was to bring to life again the ideal of antiquity, when state and society, government and education formed one (we shall find these notions developed much later in Chang Hsüeh-ch'eng, the historian and philosopher of the late eighteenth century).

However, the great question for the thinkers of the eleventh century was that of the integration of man in the cosmos, of the identification of human nature and the universal order. Many of them were passionately interested in the problem of cosmic evolution, of temporal cycles and universal harmony, and they strove to translate it into graphic terms. Chou Tun-i (1017–73), Shao Yung (Shao K'ang-chieh) (1012–77) and Chang Tsai (1020–77) went for their inspiration to the *Book of Changes* (*I-ching*), the esoteric classic which had been immensely popular in the third and fourth centuries, and to the School of Mysteries (*hsüan-hsüeh*). In Shao Yung, cosmological preoccupations were based on a numerology with claims to universality. As for Ch'eng I (1033–1108), a disciple — like his brother Ch'eng Hao (1032–85) — of Chou Tun-i, he combined study of the *I-ching* with that of the Analects of Confucius (*Lun-yü*), of the *Mencius* (*Meng-tzu*) and of two small works drawn from the *Treatises on the Rites* (*Li-chi*): the *Great Learning* (*Ta-hsüeh*) and the *Doctrine of the Mean* (*Chung-yung*). These four works, which were to be more highly valued than the Classics proper from the Sung age onwards and were to be known as the Four Books (*Ssu-shu*), constituted the basic texts of the simultaneously rationalist, moralizing, and metaphysically based school in process of formation in the eleventh century. After the Sung withdrawal south of the Yangtze, Chu Hsi (1130–1200) made a synthesis of the very diverse and fruitful ideas which had found expression in the intellectual ferment of the eleventh century. He took over and applied to the Four Books a new method of explaining the Classics. Boldly rejecting the crutches of philology, he substituted for the phrase-by-phrase explanation practised since the Han age a philosophical commentary which sought to reach the deep meaning of the text.

Known in China as *hsing-li-hsüeh* (school of human nature and universal order), *li-hsüeh,* or *li-ch'i-hsüeh* (school of universal order and cosmic energy), Chu Hsi's school was to be known in the West by the much vaguer name of neo-Confucianism. Challenged in their time by other philosophical currents — mainly the one represented by Lu Chiu-yüan (1140–92), for whom, in accordance with a view reminiscent of that of the Buddhist Vijnanavada school, the world was a spatial and temporal extension of the mind (*hsin*) — Chu Hsi's ideas crystallized into orthodoxy in the fourteenth and fifteenth centuries and had a sterilizing effect on Chinese thought comparable with that exerted in the West by the philosophy of Aristotle and Thomas Aquinas.

Chinese philosophy is difficult to approach, since any translation of its terms at once evokes all the notions and concepts of Western philosophy. Some modern critics, by defining the line of thought represented by Chu Hsi as rationalist and the opposing line of Lu Chiu-yüan and Wang Shou-jen (1472–1529) as idealist, immediately introduce into Chinese philosophy an opposition peculiar to Western philosophy. But this distinction makes no more sense than that made by the Chinese Marxists between materialists and idealists, because the originality of Chinese thought resides precisely in the fact that it refuses all clear-cut distinctions between the sensible and the intelligible, matter and spirit, theory and practice. Therefore, Chinese thinkers more often manifest oppositions in practice — which at times can be very animated — rather than in theory. For some, like Lu Chiu-yüan, who was influenced by the Buddhist notion of the non-reality of the world, nothing exists outside of the spirit, and therefore only moral improvement is important (these subjective ideas were to dominate from the thirteenth century and once again from the Mongol occupation). To the contrary, others, like the utilitarians of the Wen-chou school in Chekiang, affirmed the primacy of action and the reality of the objective world. The question is therefore one of equilibrium between positive knowledge on the one hand and moral improvement and intuition on the other. These problems undoubtedly are of philosophical interest, but in China they do not assume forms that are familiar to Western philosophers.

Conclusion

After a general survey of eleventh- to thirteenth-century China, one is left with the impression of an amazing economic and intellectual up-surge. Marco Polo's surprise at the end of the thirteenth century was not simulated. The time lag between East Asia and the Christian West is striking, and we have only to compare the Chinese world with the Christian world of this period in each domain – volume of trade, level of technology, political organization, scientific knowledge, arts and letters – to be convinced of Europe's very considerable 'backwardness'. The two great civilizations of the eleventh to thirteenth centuries were incontestably those of China and Islam.

There is nothing surprising about this Western backwardness: the Italian cities which took on a new life at the end of the Middle Ages were at the terminus of the great commercial routes of Asia. Situated at the end of the Eurasian continent, Europe was at a distance from the great currents of civilization and the great trade routes. But its situation also explains its immunity, at any rate in its western areas, from the most serious invasions; it was making progress at the very time when the Mongol occupation, from Mesopotamia to the Bay of Bengal, was leading to the decline of the Islamic world. It profited from the new waves of trade and borrowings set in motion by the creation of a vast Mongol empire extending from Korea to the Danube. What we have acquired the habit of regarding – according to a history of the world that is in fact no more than a history of the West – as the beginning of modern times was only the repercussion of the upsurge of the urban, mercantile civilizations whose realm extended, before the Mongol invasion, from the Near-East to the Sea of China. The West gathered up part of this legacy and received from it the leaven which was to make possible its own development. The transmission was favoured by the crusades of the twelfth and thirteenth centuries and by the expansion of the Mongol empire in the thirteenth and fourteenth centuries. The mere enumeration of East Asia's contributions to medieval Europe at this time – indirect borrowings or inventions suggested by Chinese techniques – is sufficient to indicate their importance: paper, compass, and stern-post rudder at the end of the twelfth century, the application of the water-mill to looms, the counterweight trap, which was to revolutionize warfare before the development of firearms, then the wheelbarrow at the beginning of the thirteenth century, explosives at the end of the same century, the spinning-wheel about 1300, wood-block printing, which was to give rise, as in China, to printing with movable type, and cast iron (end of the fourteenth century). There we have, together with innovations of lesser importance, all the great inventions which were to make possible the advent of modern times in the West.

The upsurge of the West, which was only to emerge from its relative isolation thanks to its maritime expansion, occurred at a time when the two great civilizations of Asia were threatened. China, much weakened in the fourteenth century by the Mongol exploitation and by a long period of rebellions and wars, had to make a tremendous effort to restore its agrarian economy and to find its equilibrium again. The social redistribution and the new autocratic tendencies of the political authority were hardly favourable during most of the Ming period (1368–1644) to rapid development in the Chinese world.

Part 6

From the Sinicized Empires
to the Mongol Occupation

Prologue: Nomads and mountain dwellers in the tenth to fourteenth centuries

If one examines its evolution over the course of some centuries, the world of the cattle-raising nomads begins to look a good deal more complex and unstable than one might at first imagine. The continual changes that it underwent resulted from the multiplicity of ethnic groups involved, from differences in the types of breeding practised and in modes of life, from the varying proximity and depth of the influence exerted by the sedentary peoples, from political splits and regroupings and so on. The T'u-yü-hun, troublesome neighbours of T'ang China in the north-west during the sixth and seventh centuries, were the descendants of horse-breeders living in southern Manchuria in the fourth century. These ancient tribes gradually moved westward and finally settled in the Kokonor region in Tsinghai, where they mingled with the other peoples and became breeders of yaks, sheep, horses, and camels. At this stage they were no longer nomadic but semi-sedentary. The ancestors of the Jürchen, Tungus tribes of horse-breeders living in eastern Manchuria who were to take possession of the Liao empire at the beginning of the twelfth century, seem to have been hunters from the Siberian forests of the Amur valley. However, it is important when speaking of these peoples to make a distinction between those who were in contact with sedentary populations — neighbours of the Chinese in southern Manchuria, in Inner Mongolia, on the borders of China's northern provinces and in the Ordos bend — and the more distant peoples of Outer Mongolia and the valleys of the Altai. The former were affected by Chinese influences as a result of commercial exchanges, political relations, the presence of tillers of the soil in the territories which they controlled, and the influx of Chinese literati, administrators, and craftsmen. The latter, further away, were less easily permeated by these influences and were to preserve their primitive traditions and manners longer.

Among the former peoples were the Khitan, Jürchen, and Tangut cattle-breeders who were to found sinicized empires between the tenth and twelfth centuries on the north-eastern and north-western borders of the Chinese world. The Mongols belonged to the second category and in that respect were the successors, so to speak, of the Hsiung-nu of the second century B.C. and the Turks of the sixth and seventh centuries A.D.; established like them in the basin of the Orkhon, to the south of Lake Baikal, they were able, like the Hsiung-nu and the Turks, to create to their own advantage a great confederation of nomad tribes.

In the tenth century East Asia was on the eve of a new thrust by the steppe peoples, and a more formidable one than those of the past. From the Hsiung-nu to the Turks and from the Turks to the Khitan and Jürchen of the Sung age, noticeable progress was made by these people and one could distinguish three generations of nomads. The first, down to the fourth century A.D., was unfamiliar with the stirrup which was to give a firmer seat to mounted bowmen and thus increase the power of their attacks. Thus the Turks may have been more fearsome than the Hsiung-nu. As for the third generation, that of the Khitan and Jürchen and subsequently of the Mongols, it made decisive progress in its methods of making war thanks to the combination of the warrior traditions of the steppe with the skilled procedures of the armies of the sedentary peoples. In particular, it employed experts in siege warfare. The Khitan, Jürchen, and Mongol warriors were much better armed and more heavily equipped than their predecessors of the T'ang age. Each of them carried on him or with him a helmet, coat of mail, bows and arrows, axe, club, tent, and dried milk, and the horses were protected by a covering of leather or metal. Such heavy equipment demanded plenty of animals and means of transport. Thus the baggage-train assumed great importance, and carts, of which the Mongols made great use for the transport of arms and provisions, played a part in the success of these extraordinary conquerors. Each horseman had four to eight mounts and did not ride the same animal two days running. He jumped into the saddle only at the moment of battle, when the troops had converged by separate routes and were quite near their objective. The procedure was then to exhaust the enemy by successive waves of attack, each of them more heavily armed than the previous one. The duration of these assaults and their succession were carefully calculated.

Together with the techniques, the objects of war had changed. It was no longer a question of incursions to open up markets or of raids launched in autumn and winter when cereals and forage were becoming scarce, but of wars of conquest. Whereas down to the tenth century the men of the steppes had only founded states in North China after slow infiltration during the course of which they had become progressively sinicized, so that they were able to seize power on the spot, the Khitan, Jürchen, and Mongols turned to siege warfare and undertook the conquest of the agricultural lands with a view to exploiting them systematically. A principal factor in this historical evolution was certainly the economic and demographic decline of North China after the An Lu-shan rebellion (755–63) and the consequential weakening of Chinese continental defenses from the ninth to the fourteenth century.

This strengthening of the power of the steppe peoples was paralleled by progress in strategy and armaments among the sedentary populations. New kinds of weapons were invented in the eleventh century and means of defence were improved. When the Sung were forced to withdraw, in the early twelfth century, south of the Yangtze, one result was the development of a strong navy.

Chapter 16

The Sinicized Empires

The Khitan empire of the Liao

Various different peoples shared the northern borders of the Chinese world in the ninth century (Uighurs of Turfan in western Kansu, Tibetans and T'u-yü-hun in Tsinghai, Tangut in the Ordos bend, Shato Turks in northern Shansi, Khitan in northern Hopei, people of the kingdom of Po-hai in Manchuria), but it soon became clear that the Khitan were the most dangerous adversaries of the dynasties installed in K'ai-feng from 907 onwards, and it was not long before they set up a state.

These Khitan, distant descendants of the Hsien-pei of the fourth century, were nomadic cattle-breeders of the Siramuren valley (western Liao), a region where pastoral and agricultural modes of life were both practised. Numerous Chinese farmers lived there with the tribes of Turkish or Mongol stock, and the proximity of the Chinese lands explains the rapidity with which the Khitan were to adopt the culture and institutions of their neighbours. As early as 924 the Khitan launched an offensive towards the west in order to secure the adhesion of the Tangut and the T'u-yü-hun, and in the following year they destroyed the kingdom of Po-hai. At the time of their victorious attacks in the area of Peking, which they made into one of their capitals (calling it Nanking, 'southern capital'),[1] they gave their budding empire the name of Liao, the Chinese term for the Siramuren. In 946 they caused the fall of the Later Chin by penetrating as far as K'ai-feng, where they seized the courtiers and craftsmen and stole maps, official archives, the stelae on which the

1. In Chinese, Peking = 'northern capital' and Nanking = 'southern capital.'

Classics were engraved, water-clocks and musical instruments. Encroaching further on the present-day provinces of Hopei and Shansi and spreading in 986 into Manchuria, they soon touched the zenith of their power. In the first few years of the eleventh century their incursions reached the Yellow River valley and in 1004 the Sung were forced to sign a peace treaty at Shan-yüan, on the lower reaches of the Yellow River. At that time the Liao empire covered the major part of Manchuria and eastern Mongolia as well as the areas of Ta-t'ung, in northern Shansi, and Peking.

In fact its sway extended to the whole steppe zone from Manchuria and Korea to the T'ien-shan. The Jürchen tribes of northern Manchuria, Korea, the Tangut of the Ordos, and the Sung themselves were all constrained to recognize their suzerainty. The Liao were in contact with Japan and the Abassid empire, and the court of Baghdad asked for a Khitan princess in marriage. The relations thus established across the whole steppe zone, even before the Mongol expansion, no doubt explains why the name 'Khitan' (singular form; plural, 'Khitat'), popularized in the thirteenth and fourteenth centuries by the Mongols, became in the form 'Kitai' or 'Khitai' the word for China in Persian, West Turkish and the East Slavonic languages. It is well known that the term was thrust on the Europeans who visited the Mongol empire of East Asia. For Marco Polo, North China was Cathay.

It was doubtless even more the commercial role of the Khitan than their political importance in the steppe zone that helped to make their name known beyond the Pamirs and in Europe; the annual tribute paid by Sung China from 1004 onwards must have been used by the Liao empire for those semi-commercial, semi-diplomatic activities intended, in accordance with Chinese ideas, to strengthen the prestige of a dynasty. The tributes imposed on the Sung were fixed by the Peace of Shan-yüan (1004) at 100,000 ounces of silver and 200,000 rolls of silk per year. These figures were raised to 200,000 ounces of silver and 300,000 rolls of silk in 1042, in consideration of the help given by the Liao empire to Sung China in its struggle against the Tangut. It would not be surprising if part of this great wealth found its way across Asia. Thus the economic expansion of the Sung empire probably had repercussions among its neighbours and even further afield.

In fact the influence of China seems to have been the decisive factor in the creation, rise, and decline of Khitan power. By the beginning of the tenth century these peoples were already thoroughly enough sinicized to possess an agriculture, iron foundries, weaving-shops, and fortified towns. By 920 they felt the need to create a script close to the Chinese one in order to be able to write down their language; later they adopted a system based on the Uighur script. The institutions of the Liao empire were copied from those of China. In proportion as the political institutions were consolidated and society was transformed, so their culture tended to merge with that of China. All intellectual activity under the Liao was concentrated in the Peking area, as it was after them under the Chin. And although Peking may have been a city very much open to the influences of the steppes, it was also and primarily a Chinese city.

There were various different reasons for the gradual decline of the Liao empire. By the middle of the eleventh century the Khitan had lost their combative spirit and adopted a defensive attitude to their neighbours, building walls, ramparts for their towns, and fortified posts. The influence of Buddhism, the religion of non-harmfulness (*ahimsa*), and that of China's wealth and culture seem to have had a disintegrating effect on their manners. The empire's decline gathered speed at the beginning of the twelfth century as a result of a disastrous succession of droughts and floods, of dissensions in the ruling family, and of the progress made in the north-east by the Tungus tribes known by the name of Jürchen. The pressure of these Jürchen from the present province of Heilungkiang, with whom the Sung had made an alliance against the Liao, grew sharper from 1114 onwards and it finally caused the collapse of the Khitan empire in the years 1124-25.

Part of the Khitan nobility was to emigrate to the Uighurs of Sinkiang and to found with their help between 1128 and 1133, in the valley of the Ili, a kingdom known as the kingdom of the Karakhitan ('black Khitan') or, in Chinese terminology, of the Western Liao. This Turko-Mongol kingdom, very deeply sinicized—but also very Buddhist and permeated by Nestorian Christianity—had its capital at Balasaghun, to the south of Lake Balkhash, and was to extend to the areas of Kashgar and Samarkand. Thanks to its intermediary position, Chinese influences spread once again into the regions on each side of the Pamirs. Its victory over the Seljuk Turks near Samarkand in 1141 no doubt contributed to the formation of the medieval European legend of the kingdom of Prester John, perhaps already suggesting to the Christian world that it might have allies in Asia against Islam. The kingdom of the Western Liao was to be destroyed by Genghis Khan in 1218.

The Western Hsia, an empire
of cattle-breeders and caravaneers

In the north-west, the Sung empire's main worry up to about 1036 was the incursions of the Tibetans, but in fact it was other peoples who were to set up a big political unit in these regions. The Tangut, herdsmen of the Ordos area related to the Ch'iang of the T'ang age, spread towards western Mongolia and Kansu in 1002. In 1028, already enriched by commerce, they took possession of the two big trading centres of Wuwei – hitherto dominated by the Tibetans – and Chang-yeh, controlled by the Uighurs. In 1038 they founded an empire to which they gave the old Chinese name of Hsia, establishing their capital at present-day Yinch'uan (the ancient Ning-hsia) near the course of the Yellow River, downstream from Lan-chou. This was the empire of the 'Great Hsia' or, to give them their Chinese name, the Western Hsia (Hsi Hsia). Their governing class consisted of Tangut who had intermarried with Hsienpei, descendants of the Tabgatch (Toba) founders of the Northern Wei empire in the fifth and sixth centuries and of T'u-yü-hun. Themselves the products of a racial mixture, these rulers headed an empire whose population was heterogeneous – Tangut, Chinese, Uighur Turks, Tibetans – and in which the most various modes of life were mingled: farmers, caravaneers, nomadic cattle-breeders, semi-sedentary herdsmen, and so on. This was because, in spreading from the Ordos to Kansu, Shensi and the borders of western Mongolia, the Hsia empire had come to embrace steppe, desert, oases and agricultural territory. Even if the economy was based mainly on the rearing of horses, sheep, and camels and on the cultivation of wheat, barley, and millet generally practised by the Chinese, commercial activity nevertheless played a central role in this empire, for the Hsia controlled exchanges between the Sung empire and central Asia and also, further north, all the traffic on the route connecting south-eastern Mongolia, across the Ordos, with Kansu, Tsinghai, and Tibet. The biggest trade was obviously that with Sung China. At the markets set up on the frontiers, the exports consisted of horses, camels, oxen, sheep, beeswax, carpets, and forage; the imports were silks, incense, medicines, ceramics, and lacquer. But large-scale smuggling, mainly of Chinese salt, helped to enrich the Hsia empire; moreover, powerless to put a stop to Hsia incursions, the Sung were forced in 1044 to sign a peace treaty which obliged them to deliver as tribute every year 135,000 rolls of silk, 72,000 ounces of silver and 30,000 pounds of tea. As with the tribute paid by the Sung to the Khitan, some of these goods were probably to be re-exported by the Hsia and to serve as a means of exchange. In any case the mention of tea is worth noting, for it confirms that since the T'ang age the use of tea had spread to all the cattle-raisers of the steppes and to the mountaineers of Tibet.

Sung efforts to rid themselves of the embarassing Hsia presence in the north-west were unsuccessful, and the only effect of the offensives launched in 1081 was to weaken China. However, at the beginning of the thirteenth century the Hsia empire began to experience the first Mongol incursions. Its alliance with the Mongols against the Chin empire in 1225 did not prevent its being destroyed by the troops of Genghis Khan in 1227.

So ended this empire of caravaneers and cattle-breeders whose population consisted for the most part of Chinese farmers and townspeople. This composite character of the Hsia empire was also reflected in its institutions, which imitated both China and Tibet. The language spoken by the governing class — we now know that it was a Tibeto-Burman language fairly close to that of the Yi (Lolo) of south-west China — had never been written; experiments were at first made, as in Tibet, with a script based on those of India, then recourse was had to characters conceived on the same lines as Chinese characters. It must be supposed that this very complex system of notation was better adapted to the Hsia language than a phonetic notation of the Indian type, for it was adopted and generalized. We still possess numerous texts in this script — dictionaries, Buddhist and Taoist works, classical Chinese texts translated into Hsia and printed.

The Jürchen empire of the Chin

The Jürchen (or Jürchet; in Chinese, Ju-chen), the Tungus tribes of the modern province of Heilungkiang who were to put an end to the Liao empire, were the ancestors of the tribes who at the beginning of the seventeenth century adopted the name 'Manchu', conquered the Chinese provinces of Manchuria and in 1644 took Peking. The Jürchen language of the twelfth century was an old form of Manchu.

The rise of these tribes was extremely rapid. The first mention of them that we possess dates from 1069, but by 1115 their chief, Aguta, who resided to the north-east of modern Harbin, took the title of emperor and gave his dynasty the name 'Chin' (Kin, 'gold') — an allusion, so it is said, to the gold-bearing sands of that area. It was about this time that their attacks on the Liao began, and their warlike qualities were evident from the start. They needed only ten years to put an end to this weakened empire, undermined as it was by economic difficulties and internal dissensions. In 1120 the Jürchen made an alliance with the Sung; and in 1122 the Sung and Chin armies combined in offensives against the Liao empire. The Jürchen were recognized as the great power of the north-east by the Hsia in 1124 and by Korea in 1126. However, soon after the collapse of the Liao, in 1125, the Jürchen broke their treaty of friendship with the Sung and resumed their attacks towards Honan and Shantung. K'ai-feng fell in 1126. The emperor Hui-tsung, the crown prince, and three thousand members of the imperial family were led off into captivity in the Harbin area. Whereas the Khitan incursions in the early eleventh

THE EMPEROR WEI-T-SOONG AND HIS COURT, TAKEN PRISONERS BY THE TARTARS

Plate 38. The Emperor Hui-tsung (1101–25 A.D.) and his court being deported
by the Mongols: from a Western reconstruction of a painting by Fo-shang

century had not penetrated further than the valley of the Yellow River,
the Jürchen horsemen rode as far as the Yangtze and northern Chekiang,
where part of the imperial family and of the old Sung administration had
taken refuge. Between 1126 and 1135 most of the towns in these south-
eastern areas were put to the sword and burnt. Nanking and Hangchow
were taken by assault in 1129 and in 1130 the Jürchen ventured as far as
Ning-po, in the north-eastern tip of Chekiang. A first agreement between
the Chin and the Sung was made in 1138, the year in which the Sung
established their provisional capital at Hangchow, but in 1142 a more
durable peace was signed which fixed the frontier between the two states
on the Huai River and obliged the Sung to pay an annual tribute similar
to the one which they had paid the Liao. The territory occupied by the
Jürchen was never reconquered, in spite of offensives which were
sometimes victorious and in spite of the aid given by the Sung to the peasant resistance in Shantung.

Since the Jürchen offensives against North China and Yangtze China
had been accompanied by expansion in Manchuria and Mongolia, their
empire had reached its final limits before the middle of the twelfth century. It embraced Hopei, Shantung, the northern parts of the present-

day provinces of Kiangsu and Anhwei, Honan, southern Shensi and, further north, eastern Mongolia and Manchuria. Distrusting their own ability to administer the numerous sedentary populations which they had annexed to their empire, the Chin at first created political units at the head of which they placed Chinese who had joined them, former Sung officials. Their fear of rebellions also led them to maintain armed detachments everywhere to control the local inhabitants. But they soon suppressed these fictitious empires. The Ch'u 'empire' (to the south of the Yellow River), which they had entrusted to one Chang Pang-ch'ang, lasted only for a few months of the year 1127; the Ch'i 'empire', which covered the modern provinces of Shantung, Honan, and southern Shensi and was governed by Liu Yü (1078–1143), existed from 1130 to 1137.

The political history of the Chin after their conquest of North China can be summed up in a few dates. After the transfer of the capital from the Harbin area to Peking in 1153 new offensives were launched against the Southern Sung, but an internal crisis ended in 1161 in a usurpation. This was followed by a 'good neighbour' policy towards the Sung. Just before the big Mongol offensives of the early thirteenth century, in the reign of Chang-tsung (1189–1208), the expenditure consequent on the flooding of the Yellow River, on the attacks launched by the Sung, and on the efforts made by the Chin to maintain their position in eastern Mongolia in spite of the Mongol attacks caused economic difficulties. During the next few years the Chin were obliged to evacuate Manchuria as the Mongol troops advanced and in 1214 to transfer their capital to K'ai-feng, which was less exposed than Peking. The course of events accelerated at the time of the Mongol offensives of fifteen years later; in 1232 the Chin court, harried by the invading forces, moved from town to town in Honan until the emperor, surrounded by the allied Sung and Mongol armies, committed suicide in 1234.

The Jürchen displayed the same mixture of warlike qualities and capacity for adaptation as their Manchu descendants. Moreover the presence of sinicized Khitan and of large Chinese populations in the Chin empire explain the rapidity with which Chinese influences made themselves felt. The political and administrative organization, the economy and the culture of the Chin were Chinese. But the sinicization of their aristocracy gathered speed from 1132 onwards, after which date there were more and more Chinese in the upper ranks of the administration, and also after the transfer of the capital to Peking (1153). In fact this sinicization was so rapid that it provoked a 'nationalist' reaction; the emperor Shih-tsung (1161–89) tried to resurrect Jürchen manners, the Jürchen language, and Jürchen traditions. In 1173 the Jürchen language was made compulsory in the recruitment competitions held for descendants of the old tribes of Heilungkiang. But in spite of these efforts the language tended more and more to fall into disuse. Transcribed at first in 1120 in a script probably based on the Khitan script (the 'big characters', *ta-tzu*), it was written in 1138 in a new script, the 'little characters' (*hsiao-tzu*), which was generally employed from 1145 onwards. Stelae and printed works have preserved a considerable number of examples of this script. In fact the official texts of the Chin were drafted in Jürchen before being translated into Chinese (and into Khitan down to 1191), just as the Manchu texts of the Ch'ing dynasty were to be translated into Chinese and Tibetan in the seventeenth and eighteenth centuries.

Chapter 17

The Mongol Invasion and Occupation

The appearance upon the scene of the Mongols in the early years of the thirteenth century was to change completely the political map in the north-eastern part of the Asiatic continent. The Chin empire began to experience the assaults of these new conquerors from the Orkhon valley from 1211 onwards. It very soon lost Manchuria and the Peking area, which was occupied in 1215. The Hsia were destroyed in a campaign of brief duration (1225–27). Finally, twenty-three years after the start of the first attacks, the Chin empire collapsed completely and the whole of North China was under the sway of the Mongols. They needed another thirteen years to acquire a permanent footing in Szechwan and about forty to gain possession of Yangtze China and the southern provinces. The Mongol expansion into Burma and Vietnam came up against great difficulties, and their sea-borne expeditions against Japan and Java at the end of the thirteenth century were failures. The slow advance of the Mongols in East Asia forms a contrast to the lightning speed of their progress in the western parts of Asia and in Europe. Doubtless the swift incursions of Genghis Khan's troops into the northern Caucasus, the Ukraine, the Crimea, and even southern Poland during the years 1221–24 should be regarded simply as reconnaissance operations. It was only later that territories were conquered and empires set up — the empire of Ogodei (1224–1310) in the Altai and Dzungaria, the empire of Chagatai (1227–1338) in central Asia, the Pamirs and Transoxiania, the empire of the Il-khan (1259–1411) in Iran, Afghanistan, and western Pakistan, the empire of the Golden Horde (1243–1502) in European Russia up to the Yenisei. Nevertheless the conquest of territory and the

Table 16. The stages of the Mongol advance in Eurasia

1206: Temüjin proclaimed 'emperor of the seas': Genghis Khan (1167–1227)	
WESTERN PARTS OF EURASIA	EAST ASIA
1211–1224 1211, conquest of the kingdom of the Karakhitan (Hsi Liao) 1218, conquest of the kingdom of the western Uighurs in Hsin-chiang 1218–1223, conquest of Khorezm (Khwarizm) and first offensive in Russia 1224, advance into the north- western borders of India	*1210–1215* First offensive against the Chin (North China) 1215, capture of Peking *1225–1227* Offensive against Kansu and end of the kingdom of the Hsi-Hsia

1227: death of Genghis Khan and partition of the Mongol empire	
	Ogodei (1229-1241)
Batu Khan (1207–1255) leaves Karakorum in 1236 to found kingdom of the Golden Horde 1237–1239, second offensive towards Russia 1240, capture of Kiev, entry into Poland 1241–1242, advance into Bo- hemia, Hungary, Austria, Serbia, and Dalmatia	*1231–1234* Second offensive against the Chin 1231, start of attacks on Korea 1233, sieges of Kai-feng and Loyang 1234, end of the Chin
Hulagu-Khan (1218–1265) leaves Karakorum in 1253, to found kingdom of the Il-Khan 1258, capture of Baghdad and end of the Abbasids 1259, conquest of Iran	*1236–1239* First offensive in Szechwan Guyuk (Ting-tsung) (1246–1248) Mongke (Hsien-tsung) (1251–1259) Kublai (Shih-tsu) (1260–1294)
	1253–1259 Second offensive in Szechwan advance into Yunnan, northern Burma and Vietnam 1253, end of the kingdom of Dali 1257, occupation of Hanoi
	1257, first siege of Hsiang-yang
	1274, first expedition to Japan

	1281, second expedition to
	  Japan
	1282–1283, offensive against
	  Vietnam and Champa, raids
	  into Cambodia
	1287–1288, new expedition to
	  Vietnam
	1292–1293, expedition to Java
	1300, failure of the campaigns
	  in Burma

	1272–1279
	Conquest of South China
	1272–1273, second siege
	  of Hsiang-yang and
	  capture of Hsiang-yang
	1276, capture of Hang-
	  chow
	1277, capture of Canton
	1279, end of the
	  Southern Sung

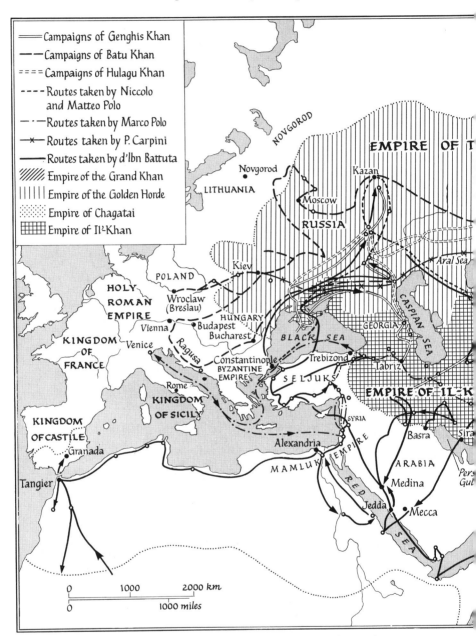

Map 18   The Mongol empires and offensives across the Eurasian continent

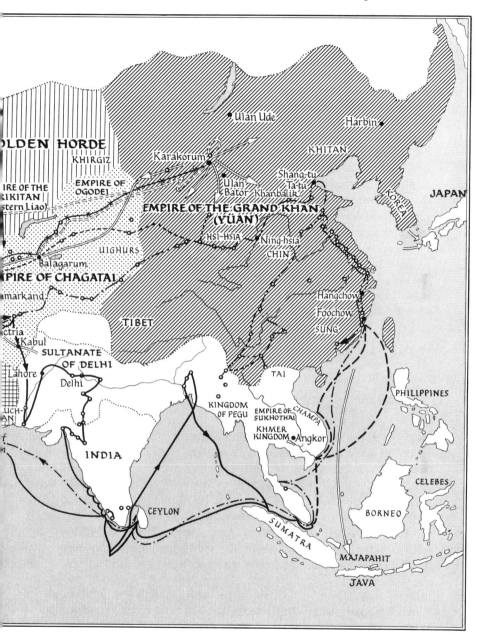

establishment of Mongol authority was in the last analysis accomplished more easily in the western part than in the eastern part of the Eurasian continent. In 1236 the Mongols were in the Kazan area; in 1237 they were marching on Moscow; in the next year they reached the Novgorod area and turned towards the lower Don valley. Kiev was threatened in 1239 and captured in 1240. Before returning to the lower Volga valley in 1242, the Mongols rode through Galicia, Hungary, Austria, Serbia, and Dalmatia. They needed only a few years to gain possession of the Abbasid empire (1258). The dry, thinly populated plains of western Asia and eastern Europe no doubt lent themselves better to penetration by the kind of army that had grown up on the steppes of Outer Mongolia than the mountainous regions of Szechwan and the densely populated plains, intersected by lakes and rivers, of the Huai valley and Yangtze basin. But the settled peoples of East Asia had also had long experience of the men of the steppe and in the course of incessant attacks since the end of the tenth century had been obliged to improve their means of defence. Guerilla bands had grown up in the rear of the Jürchen and Mongol armies. In the western parts of Eurasia, on the other hand, surprise seems to have had its full effect.

The Mongol regime

The installation of the Mongol system of exploitation

In the time of Genghis Khan, between 1210 and 1227, the Mongols still had no proper administrative organization at all. The people surviving after the massacres, in which craftsmen and priests were usually spared, were split up like slaves among the members of the Mongol aristocracy and a good deal of tilled land was converted into pastures. The various territories were cut up into independent districts, forming numerous private domains governed by feudal chiefs who had full power over their subjects. A tribal, military organization did duty for government and provided the general framework for the Mongol empire in East Asia. Unlike the Khitan and the Jürchen, the Mongols had scarcely felt the influence of China before the start of their career of conquest, and this influence was always to remain superficial (though the importance of Chinese propellent artillery among the Mongols from the beginning of the thirteenth century onwards should be noted). Down to the death of Genghis Khan their contacts with the peoples of North China were very limited, and it was only in the reign of Ogodei (1229–41) that, with the occupation completed, the wealth of North China began to be exploited methodically. In order to form durable political units and to continue their expansion, the Mongols had first to associate with themselves and employ in their service the peoples whom they had conquered, for they themselves were only a small minority in the midst of the very numerous and very different peoples which they united under their yoke. The conquest of South China, the expeditions against Japan, Burma, Vietnam, and Java were organized by the Mongols with troops raised in China itself and with Korean and Chinese fleets. In order to exploit the peoples and wealth of China, these conquerors with little aptitude for peace-time activities and little trust in the sedentary inhabitants were obliged both to copy Chinese institutions and to call preferably on the former Khitan and Jürchen subjects of the Chin empire and also on foreigners from central Asia, the Middle East or Europe. The need to turn to these intermediaries made itself felt as the conquest of North China progressed. The main architect of the Mongols' conversion to the administrative methods of the Chinese was Yeh-lü Chu-ts'ai (1190–1244), a descendant of the Khitan aristocracy (it was the Yeh-lü who had founded the Liao dynasty) and former official of the Chin empire who had moved over to the service of Genghis Khan when Peking was captured in 1215. On the accession of Ogodei in 1229, Yeh-lü Chu-ts'ai demonstrated to the new sovereign the usefulness of a regular fiscal system (he reckoned that requisitions and taxes could bring in annually 500,000 ounces of silver, 80,000 rolls of silk and over 20,000 tons of cereals) and he was appointed general administrator of North China. Under the influence of the conquered peoples the policy of the Mongols became less harsh and certain institutions of Chinese origin were gradually adopted. In 1229 postal relays were established for the first time, a system of property taxes was set up, and public granaries were built. In 1236 the first issue of paper money was made. In the same year translation offices were opened, with a view to the production of Mongol versions of the Chinese Classics and official histories. The first competitions for the recruitment of civil servants were organized in 1237 and an imperial library was created in Peking in the following year. In the reign of Kublai a *History of the Liao and Chin* (*Liao-chin shih*) was compiled at the Academy of History (*Han-lin kuo-shih-yüan*), founded in 1261. It was not until later — 1344 and 1345 — that the three official histories of the Sung, the Liao, and the Chin were completed, under the direction of the minister Toktogha (in Chinese, T'o-t'o).

Another adviser whose influence was preponderant after the death of Yeh-lü Chu-ts'ai was Liu Ping-chung (1216–74), an unfrocked monk of the Buddhist *ch'an* sect with a good classical education. Summoned to Kublai's court at Karakorum in 1249, Liu Ping-chung addressed to the

Plate 39. The inhabitants of Balkh leaving the city after the Mongol attack of 1221

Plate 40. Mongol siege of a Chinese city

Plate 41.   Mongol armies besieging the Fortress of Jundu, 1213
(from the Genghis Khan Miniatures from the Court of Akbar the Great)

khan of the Mongols a memorandum of ten thousand characters, the *Wan-yen shu,* on policy and administration, quoting the famous saying from a text of the Han age, 'one can conquer the world on horseback; one cannot govern it on horseback' (*i ma-shang ch'ü t'ien-hsia, pu k'o i ma-shang chih*). But the great programme of reforms advocated by Liu Ping-chung was not inaugurated until 1252. In 1267 Liu Ping-chung was entrusted with the construction of the new capital, Khanbalik, at Peking, and this transfer of the central government from distant Karakorum (Helin), which lay west of present-day Ulan Bator (Urga) and over 1500 kilometres from Peking, to the area which had been the centre of the Liao and Chin empires is an indication of a change of political viewpoint on the part of the Mongols: China, already half conquered, had come to look like an inexhaustible reservoir of men and wealth. The principal architect of the new capital was a Moslem; he was assisted by Chinese. The construction of the walls began in 1267 and was completed in 1292, while the imperial palace was built from 1274 onwards. Meanwhile, in 1271, the Mongols had adopted a dynastic name in the Chinese style—that of Yüan.

This progressive adaptation to Chinese institutions did not prevent the Mongols from remaining distrustful of former Chinese officials. Posts of command were kept for Mongols and the administration of the finances was entrusted to men from the Islamic areas of central Asia and the Middle East. Moslem merchants, grouped in associations known as *ortaq,* practically acquired a monopoly in the profitable business of collecting the taxes, in which they were assisted by Mongol military detachments. Marco Polo, a Venetian merchant, himself worked for the occupiers, and one can cite the case of a Russian who was appointed to an important post in Chekiang in 1341, after coming first in the doctorate examination in Peking in 1321.

Racial discrimination

One of the fundamental features of the system established by the Mongols in East Asia was in fact the discrimination practised between the various different peoples who had joined or been conquered by the Mongols. It was based not on racial criteria proper but on the date at which the subject peoples had been incorporated in the empire. Our main source of information on the discrimination introduced into China by the Mongols is the *Interrupted Labours* (*Ch'o-keng-lu*) by T'ao Tsung-i, a collection of different notes completed in 1366. This work, which contains in particular information about the popular revolts in south-eastern China in the middle of the fourteenth century, enumerates the various ethnic categories distinguished by the Mongols. The population was classified in three main groups: Mongols; various races (*se-mu-jen*), i.e. those who were neither Mongols nor Chinese and were not sinicized; and *Han-jen* (Chinese and sinicized peoples of North China). Seventy-two different groups of tribes were distinguished among the nomadic cattle-raising peoples, where there was also a clear distinction between military aristocracy and common people. There were thirty-one different groups of 'various races', which comprised peoples of Turkish origin (Uighurs, Qarluqs, Naimans, Tuvas . . .), Tibetans, Tanguts, Iranian merchants from the Amu-Darya basin known as Sartauls, Russians, and so on. As for the term 'Chinese' (*Han-jen*), it had a very wide meaning for the Mongols, for it applied to the Khitan, the Jürchen, and the sinicized Koreans living in northern and north-eastern China as well as to the Chinese themselves. By and large the term denoted the former subjects of the Liao and Chin kingdoms. From 1273–75 onwards these northern Chinese were to be joined by those of the south, who were christened 'new subjects' (*hsin fu-jen*) and had the lowest status in the whole empire.

This classification served as the basis for administrative, juridical, and fiscal discrimination. Key governing posts could be occupied only by Mongols, who held them on a hereditary basis. The civil governors of the administrative districts were either Mongols or, more rarely, foreigners (*se-mu-jen*), and the post of deputy governor was usually allocated to a Moslem.

In the penal code the most severe punishments were kept for the Chinese. For example, they were the only people to be tattooed for the crime of theft. Any murder of a Mongol by a Chinese involved the death penalty and the obligatory payment of a contribution to the funeral expenses (*shao-mai-yin*), while the murder of a Chinese by a Mongol was punished by a mere fine. The Mongols were allowed to possess arms; the Chinese were not. It was the Mongols who introduced into Chinese law, which they changed to make it comply with their need to dominate and with the authoritarian character of their empire, the sentence of slow death (*ling-ch'ih*) for hardened criminals.

When the first doctoral examinations were organized in the Chinese style in 1315, quotas were reserved for different nationalities: of a total of 300 appointments, a quarter were reserved for Mongols, a quarter for foreigners (*se-mu-jen*), a quarter for candidates from North China and a quarter for southern Chinese. The operation was a parody of the Chinese competitions, for the Mongols and various foreigners were uneducated and most of the families of literati lived in the lower Yangtze towns, in South China.

The Mongols thus instituted a strict social barrier in China, forbidding any intermarriage between the groups which they had defined. But these

barriers were general; they applied just as much to the Mongol aristocracy, whose posts of command were hereditary, as to the lower
classes, who were kept where they were by force. The state craftsmen—those who had been taken prisoner at the time of the conquest—could not change their profession, either themselves or their
children. The Mongol authorities gave them everything necessary for
subsistence and for their trade, but kept them well guarded in special
buildings. The situation was the same for the labourers in the salt-works,
whose conditions were so intolerable that there were mass escapes and a
number of rebellions. In 1342 their numbers declined rapidly in southern
Kiangsu and northern Chekiang from 17,000 to 7000. These salt-
workers, from the Huai to Chekiang, were to be among the most valiant
fighters in the insurrections which swept away the dynasty between 1357
and 1368.

Taxation and exploitation of the wealth of China

Once the administration of the conquered territories had been organized,
the peasantry in the north was subjected to a poll-tax and a fiscal system
which recalls that of the early T'ang age (the *tsu-yung-tiao*), although the
control of private properties and the distribution of land had not been
practised for a long time. Besides forced labour, those liable to tax had to
provide every year a certain amount of grain and a certain amount of
cloth. The quantities were fixed according to the number of men of
working age. In the south, on the other hand, the system was that of the
two annual taxes in force at the end of the T'ang period (the *liang-shui*).
There was a summer tax paid in cloth and an autumn tax paid in grain;
the amounts were fixed according to the area of land cultivated and the
taxation class of the family. On top of these obligations came the heavy
and barely tolerated burden, both in the north and in the south, of the
unpaid periods of service required by the government. The Mongols had
large needs in the way of workers for their postal system, which was
highly developed in China itself, for their big public works, and for their
armies.

But the fiscal pressure seems to have been stronger in South China,
whence the Mongols drew nearly half their revenues. It became intolerable on the lower Yangtze—the area which was to be the biggest seat
of rebellion in 1351–68—and in certain thickly populated plains in the
maritime provinces. The critical situation in these regions is explained by
the very small number of taxable citizens and by the policy adopted by
the Mongols immediately after the conquest. Having confiscated for
their own profit the 'public lands' (*kuan-t'ien*) created by Chia Ssu-tao at
the end of the Southern Sung period, they had taken care not to touch

the big private estates which were the very cause of the bad social imbalance from which the big rice-growing zones suffered. This caution, this unwillingness to make any changes in the social order of the conquered regions was to win for the new regime the neutrality or sympathy of the property-owning classes in the south, whereas hostility to the invaders had been more general in the north, a land of small farmers and civil servants who had found themselves deprived by the conquest of their land and their jobs. The maintenance of the big estates in the south, their extension to the whole empire—domains of the Mongol nobility, monastery lands, rich merchants' estates—and the aggravation of the peasants' condition were to lend the revolts of the end of the Yüan period all the greater strength in that hatred of the occupying power was joined by hatred of the rich.

After the conquest of Yangtze China the Mongols suddenly had resources twice as big at their disposal. However, it was not easy to transport this wealth towards the north. The canals which had still been in use at the beginning of the twelfth century were no longer navigable since their abandonment, and a shorter route was envisaged than the one established by the Sui about A.D. 600. This new route was to connect the big rice-growing zone round Lake T'ai-hu directly to the area of Peking, which had become the capital of the empire a few years before the conquest of the south. For the time being, the Yüan organized sea transport from the mouth of the Yangtze to the Tientsin area. A *Classic of the Sea Routes* (*Hai-tao-ching*), which dates from the beginning of the Ming period (end of the fourteenth century) and gives details of the route linking Nanking to Tientsin round the Shantung peninsula, is doubtless based on earlier manuals of the Mongol era. But at the same time work proceeded on the construction of the Grand Canal—the future Imperial Canal of the Ming and Ch'ing periods—which was to be completed at the beginning of the fourteenth century. The northern section was built between 1279 and 1294, not without difficulty owing to the nature of the terrain and differences in levels which necessitated the provision of locks. However, the putting into service of the Grand Canal was not to interrupt sea transport; the bulk of the traffic continued to go by sea until the end of the dynasty.

The Mongols seized possession of China at a time when it was in full economic expansion, and they were to profit by this expansion. But their domination accentuated the effects of the commercial development and of the spread of the monetary economy on society; under their sway the gap between rich and poor grew wider. Whereas the paper money issued in the Sung empire was only valid in certain areas and for limited periods of time, in 1260 the Mongols created a positively 'national' currency, valid in all regions and for an unlimited period. The issues of 1260, the

Chung-t'ung yüan-pao chiao-ch'ao, the value of which had dropped when it was forbidden to convert them into gold or silver, were succeeded by the issues of 1287, the *Chih-yüan t'ung-hsing pao-ch'ao,* which remained relatively stable in value until the great inflation at the end of the dynasty.

The Mongols also favoured the merchants of central Asia and the Middle East. These men, usually of Iranian origin, converts to Islam, familiar with the banking practices of the Moslem world, sometimes entrusted with farming the taxes in China, were in contact with the Mongol aristocracy, which often lent them money at high rates of interest. Thus China, exploited by her new masters, participated through the caravans that travelled the old silk roads and steppe roads in a world economic circuit without receiving any of the profits. The situation had certain analogies with the one which the Manchu empire was to experience in the nineteenth century. While the Mongols allowed only paper money to circulate in China, Chinese silver was drained, according to some historians, to the western parts of the continent. We can agree, in a general way, that an impoverishment of Chinese society occurred under the Yüan. These transfers of Chinese money to the Middle East and Europe would explain the great shortage of metal experienced by the Ming empire in its early days, at the end of the fourteenth century.

Revolts and resistance to the occupiers

Disputes over the succession weakened the central government from the beginning of the fourteenth century onwards, while the Mongol nobility demonstrated its indiscipline more and more openly. Reigns succeeded each other rapidly in the midst of internal troubles, plots, and usurpations. There were four sovereigns between the years 1320 and 1329 alone. Great ministers and high officials were the masters in Peking, while in the provinces the civil service and local authorities, which became more and more corrupt, acted as they pleased. But the dynasty had to face not only the insubordination of its own nobility but at the same time the growing hostility of the Chinese masses.

Rebellions multiplied from about 1300 onwards. They are sufficiently explained by the harshness of the Mongol exploitation, the corruption of state officials, hatred of foreigners, and the privileges enjoyed by the rich. But more immediate causes may have been at work – the rise in prices, already noticeable from 1276 onwards and caused no doubt by speculation, or else clumsy authoritarian measures which offended the peasant mentality. For example, the decision taken in 1315 to level tombs in the fields in order to increase the cultivated area set off riots. Opposition to the regime crystallized in secret societies, which were always being forbidden and persecuted but always sprang up again. Some of these societies were more distinctly religious than political in their aims. Such was the case with the White Lotus (*Pai-lien*), a sect dedicated to the worship of the Buddha Amitabha and founded a little before 1133 by one Mao Tzu-yüan of Suchow under the Southern Sung. It drew its recruits mainly from the ranks of poor peasants, and its devotees, who were strict vegetarians, refused to pay taxes or to carry out compulsory labour. The same was true of the sect of the White Cloud (*Pai-yün*), which was founded about 1100 by a monk of Hangchow called K'ung Ch'ing-chiao (1043–1121) and was rooted mainly to the south of the lower Yangtze. There were also millenary movements that awaited the coming of the Buddhist messiah Maitreya (Mi-le). There were risings of Maitreya sectaries in Honan in 1335, in Hunan in 1337, and in Kwangtung and Szechwan in the following years. But the most important of these secret organizations was the Red Turbans (*Hung-chin*) (1351–66), so called from the head-dress adopted by its members and already traditional in rebel movements of the Sung period. The Red Turbans played the main part in the big insurrections which began in 1351 on the lower Yellow River as a result of floods, spread in the next few years to Anhwei and ended in the collapse of the dynasty. Religious and political aspirations were closely intermingled in the revolts of the end of the Yüan dynasty and it looks as if, under the effect of persecution, a syncretism of various different influences occurred, most of them Buddhist—the cult of Amitabha and the millenary cult of Maitreya—but some of them Manichean and possibly Mazdaist.

Relations between East Asia, Christendom, and the Islamic countries

Up to the twelfth century the lands of East Asia had been in touch with the Hellenized Indo-Iranian world, and later with Islam, via the chain of oases of the Tarim basin and of Transoxiania, and also by the sea route, but the effect of the Mongol expansion was to lend a new importance in the thirteenth and fourteenth centuries to the old steppe route which had linked Mongolia to the lower Volga valley via Dzungaria and Kazakhstan since Neolithic times. This route, which leads straight out on to the plains of eastern Europe, was systematically organized by the Mongols, who extended to it the Chinese institution of postal relays. This system, adopted in 1229, was improved and made uniform in 1237. Granaries, pastures, remounts, and garrisons turned the stages which marked out the steppe routes into a remarkable organization which doubtless had something to do with the increase in contacts between Outer Mongolia and the Peking area on the one hand and Russia, Iran, and the Mediterranean on the other. The Mongol domain was traversed by men of every nation – Moslems of central Asia and the Middle East, Russian Orthodox subjects of the Chagatai, Il-Khan and Golden Horde empires, subjects of the former Liao and Chin empires of North China, and Genoese and Venetian merchants whose commercial relations with Russia and the Near East involved journeys to Mongolia and even Peking. Because of the links between business and administration in the Mongols' political system, certain foreigners were even led to serve as officials in the Yüan empire. Although Mongolian, transcribed in an adaptation of the Uighur alphabet (the quadrangular script created by the Tibetan lama 'Phags-pa and adopted in 1269 was to be little used), became the language of administration in China, Persian was the language most often employed in business circles, on the caravan route linking Tabriz to Peking. However, Russian seems to have made a certain amount of progress on the steppe route, and the unification of Asia by the Mongols seems to have encouraged quite a few Russians to venture into Mongolia and even into China. Some historians have taken the view that the Mongol conquest was at the root of the first Russian thrust towards Siberia.

Envoys and merchants from Christendom

Diplomatic and religious reasons made the countries of western Europe decide to send Franciscan missionaries to Karakorum and Peking: the kings and popes of the time of Saint Louis and of the last crusades had hopes of making converts and allies of the Mongols.

Giovanni dal Piano dei Carpini (1182?-1252), an Italian Franciscan born at Perugia, sent by Pope Innocent IV to Karakorum, left Lyons in 1245 and returned two years later. We possess notes which he wrote on the manners and customs of the Mongols, the *Ystoria Mongalorum*.

In 1253 William of Rubruck, a native of Flanders, was dispatched to Mongolia by the king of France, Louis IX, and Innocent IV at the time of the Sixth Crusade to seek the alliance of the Mongols against the Moslems. He crossed the Black Sea and the Crimea, and reached the steppe route by going up the Don. He had an interview with the khan Mongke in Karakorum, where he stayed in 1253-54.

After reaching Iran, the Italian Franciscan Giovanni di Monte Corvino (1247-1328) took ship in 1291 at Ormuz, which was then the point of departure of the sea routes to East Asia, and landed at Ch'üan-chou in Fukien. He was appointed Archbishop of Peking (Khanbalik) by Pope Clement V in 1307 as a result of the success of his mission. A coadjutor was sent to him a few years later. After his death in Peking in 1328 all traces of Roman Christianity were to disappear from China, so completely that the Jesuit missionaries of the end of the Ming period were quite unaware that they had had Franciscan predecessors.

Another Italian Franciscan, Odoric of Pordenone, set out for East Asia in 1314 or 1315. He visited Constantinople, crossed the Black Sea and arrived in Iran. From there he went by sea first to India and then to South-East Asia, arriving eventually at Canton, whence he took ship again for Foochow. After travelling from Foochow to Hangchow by the inland roads, he went to Peking by the Grand Canal and stayed there for three years. He returned to Europe through the interior of Asia and was in Italy in 1330. The story of his journey was written down by his friend Guglielmo di Soragna.

To the names of these Catholic missionaries must be added those of the famous Venetian merchants Niccolò, Maffeo, and Marco Polo. After leaving Venice in 1254 on a journey that took them as far as North China, the brothers Niccolò and Maffeo returned to Italy in 1269. They set off again in 1271 with their son and nephew Marco (1254–1324), travelled via the Pamirs, the oasis road, Kansu – where they stopped for a year at Kan-chou (Chang-yeh) to trade – crossed North China and saw Kublai Khan first at his summer capital of Shang-tu, 270 kilometres north of Peking, then in Peking in 1275. Marco Polo was given the task of governing the big commercial city of Yangchow and found himself entrusted with various different missions by the Mongols. He took ship at Ch'üan-chou in 1292, visited Vietnam, Java, Malaya, Ceylon, the Malabar coast, Mekran, and the south-east coast of Iran. He arrived at Ormuz in 1294 and returned to Venice the following year, after spending about a quarter of a century in East Asia. Taken prisoner by the Genoese, he dictated his memoirs in French to Rustichello da Pisa. These memoirs are the famous *Travels* (*Il Milione*).

These Europeans brushed shoulders in the Mongol empire of East Asia with numerous merchants, administrators, and envoys from the various parts of Asia. For example, at the time when William of Rubruck was in Karakorum an Armenian prince by the name of Hayton was also residing at Mongke's court. Most of these foreign travellers did not leave any memoirs, but one exception was Ibn Battuta. Born in Tangiers, Ibn Battuta (1304–77) started out in 1325 on a journey which took him to Egypt, Mecca, Iran, Arabia, Syria, the Black Sea, central Asia, and northern India. After eight years in Delhi he took ship for East Asia, made stops in Sumatra and Java, disembarked at Ch'üan-chou, visited Kwangtung, and finally reached Peking via the Grand Canal from Hangchow. On the return journey he set sail from Ch'üan-chou, reached the Persian Gulf again, went through Baghdad, Mecca and Egypt and was back in Tangiers in 1349. Unlike Marco Polo, Ibn Battuta was an excellent observer and describes in his travel notes on China hydraulic machines, paper money, the use of coal, the construction of boats, the manufacture of porcelain, and many other things.

Foreigners left traces of their sojourns in China, and if the Mongol domination had not been so brief their influence would not have failed to make itself felt more deeply. Two Christian tombstones (those of the Genoese Caterina and Antonio de' Vilioni, dated 1342) and a Moslem tombstone have been found at Yangchow, and a large number of Moslem, Nestorian, Catholic, Manichean, and Hindu inscriptions from the Ch'üan-chou area have recently formed the subject of archaeological reports. These inscriptions are in Arabic, Syriac, 'Phags-pa (especially in the case of the Nestorian stelae), and Tamil. All the evidence seems to indicate that the activity of the great port of Fukien did not slow down after the Mongol conquest of 1276; in fact it may even have increased from that date onwards. However, attention should also be drawn to the exceptional role of Peking—terminal of the roads across the steppe and capital of the Yüan empire from about 1274—as the meeting-place of all the foreign influences in China.

The Chinese diaspora over the Eurasian continent

While numerous foreigners came to China in the Mongol era, there was also a movement in the opposite direction. This has obviously attracted less interest in the West.

Some of those who went from North China to the Middle East or even to Europe are known to us. Such is the case with the Taoist monk Ch'ang-ch'un (lay name, Ch'iu Ch'u-chi) (1148–1227), patriarch of the Ch'üan-chen sect. Already in favour with the Chin emperor Chih-tsung, who had called him to Peking, he was summoned by Genghis Khan to Afghanistan in 1219. Starting from Shantung, whither he had retired, Ch'ang-ch'un set off in 1220 with eighteen of his disciples, crossed Outer Mongolia and the Altai, passed through Samarkand, went round the south of the Hindu Kush and arrived in 1222 at Genghis Khan's encampment in the Kabul area. Returning to Peking in 1224, after leaving Genghis Khan near Tashkent in 1223, Ch'ang-ch'un left an account of his journey, the *Ch'ang-ch'un chen-jen hsi-yu lu*.

Another Chinese, called Ch'ang Te, was sent on a mission to Iran in 1259 by the khan Mongke. He set out from Karakorum, travelled via the north of the T'ien-shan, Samarkand and Tabriz, visited Hulagu's camp and returned in 1263. The account of his journey, entitled *Record of a Mission to the West* (*Hsi-shih-chi*) was written down by one Liu Yü.

About 1275 the Chinese Nestorian monk Rabban Bar Sauma (?–1294), born in Peking, and his disciple Mark decided to set out for the Holy Land. They paid a visit to the Nestorian pope in the main city of north-western Iran, to the south of Tabriz. From there Sauma was sent on a mission to Rome and the kings of France and England by the khan Argun. After visiting Constantinople and Rome in 1287–88 he saw the king of England in Gascony and Philip the Fair in Paris. He was to leave a description of the Abbey of Saint-Denis and of the Sainte-Chapelle. It was his visit to Rome which was to cause Pope Clement III to send Giovanni di Monte Corvino to Peking.

But besides these famous personages a host of unknown people travelled as far as Iran and Russia and settled down far from their native country. When travelling from Peking to Kabul in 1221–22, the monk Ch'ang-ch'un had noted the presence of Chinese craftsmen in Outer Mongolia and in the Samarkand area. He had also learnt that Chinese weavers had settled in the upper Yenisei valley.

It is said that in the fourteenth century there were Chinese quarters in Tabriz and even in Moscow and Novgorod.

A Chinese general was in command of the khan Hulagu's armies at the siege of Baghdad in 1258, and Chinese hydraulic engineers were employed on the irrigation of the Tigris and Euphrates basins. The Mongol policy was to transfer the best qualified technicians from one end of the Eurasian continent to the other.

Thus the Mongol domination ensured the diffusion of certain Chinese techniques in the empires of the Il-Khan and the Golden Horde. Chinese influence is perceptible in Persian miniatures, and also in Iranian ceramics, music, and architecture of the Mongol epoch. Some people — but this is conjectural — have even thought that they could see traces of Chinese influence in Italian painting of the fourteenth century, and more particularly in Lorenzetti's *Massacre of the Franciscans at Ceuta* (*c.* 1340). But it is above all in connection with the two great inventions of modern times in Europe that the question of stimuli and contributions from East Asia arises.

The introduction in the fourteenth century in the western Mongol empires of playing-cards, printed fabrics, and paper money was obviously connected with the appearance of wood engraving in Europe and consequently of printing with movable type. Paper money was printed at Tabriz, a great cosmopolitan centre where Genoese, Venetians, Uighurs, Mongols, and Chinese met, in the last few years of the thirteenth century, and the Iranian historian Rashid al-Din (*c.* 1247–1318), who had made Chinese medicine known in his *Treasure of the Il-Khan on the Sciences of Cathay* (1313), is the first to mention the Chinese invention of wood engraving. Wood engraving, known in Europe thirty or forty years before the invention of printing, was immensely successful there. Holy pictures, playing-cards, and little books with text and illustrations were printed. As for the idea of using movable type, it is to be supposed

Table 17.   Technical inventions in China and in medieval Europe

CHINA	EUROPE
Age of the last crusades	
Maritime techniques	
Mariner's compass; attested by 1090, but doubtless in use	
in the 10th century	c.1180
Movable rudder: end of 1st century; fixed to the sternpost:	
end of 4th century	c.1190
Rational harnessing of the horse	
Breast-strap: 3rd–2nd century B.C. Horse collar: between	
5th and 10th century (borders of China and central Asia?)	c.1200
Wheelbarrow	
1st–2nd century	c.1250
Age of the Mongol expansion	
Arms	
Counter-balanced trap 5th–4th century B.C.	14th century
Gunpowder: discovered in 11th century	
First mention of the formula of gun powder: 1044	1285
First military uses of the powder: 904–906	second half of 14th century
Bridges with segmented arches	
610 at least	1340
Paper, wood engraving, printing	
Paper: 1st–2nd century	First papers imported from the Islamic world: 12th century
	First papers made in Italy: end of 13th century
First engraved texts: 8th century	c.1375 (valley of the Rhine)
First use of movable type: 1041–1048. Big Korean editions from 1403 onwards	development of printing with movable type: 1430–1460
Lock gates	
11th–13th century	c.1375
Cast iron, iron and steel metallurgy	
First mention of cast iron: 513 B.C. Attested by archaeological finds: 4th century B.C.	c.1380 (valley of the Rhine)
Improvement of metallurgical techniques (use of hydraulic power, bellows, production of steel): 2nd century B.C.–1st century A.D.	
Co-fusion process: 6th century	

that it was a quite natural one, since the Chinese, whose script did not lend itself very well to this invention, had thought of it by the beginning of the eleventh century.

As for the other great invention of modern times, the firearm, we know that it had been developed in China at the time of the battles between the Sung, the Chin, and the Mongols at the beginning of the thirteenth century and that the Mongols used this new kind of weapon for the first time in Europe at the battle of Sajo in Hungary in 1241.

We should have only an incomplete view of the effects of the Mongol expansion if we omitted to mention the phenomenon of the Chinese diaspora which it also caused in East Asia.

The maritime trade of the Sung age no doubt explains the presence of Chinese merchants in South-East Asia, in Ceylon and on the coast of Malabar; and the ones mentioned as being at Angkor about 1297 by Chou Ta-kuan in his *Treatise on the Customs of Cambodia* (*Chen-la feng-t'u-chi*) were no doubt settled there before the conquest of South China by the Mongols. However, there is nothing to suggest that the commercial relations of the big ports of Fukien and of Canton with the countries of South-East Asia and the Indian Ocean suffered from the occupation; evidence dating from 1349 mentions the existence of a Chinese colony at Tomasik, on the very spot where the great Chinese city of Singapore was to develop in the twentieth century. The conquest of the Southern Sung empire in 1273–79 even seems to have accelerated Chinese colonization in South-East Asia by causing the emigration of Chinese to Vietnam at the same time as to Japan. The Mongol expeditions of the end of the thirteenth century to Vietnam, Cambodia, Burma, and Java probably had the same effect, for the expeditionary forces consisted mainly of Chinese recruited in the former Southern Sung empire—'the army of new subjects' (*hsin-fu-chün*)—and some of the soldiers must have stayed on the spot. Thus the Mongol enterprises in South-East Asia probably prepared the way for the big maritime expeditions of the Ming period in the early fifteenth century.

Literature, science, and religion under the Mongol occupation

In an empire in which the Mongols reigned as absolute masters, entrusting to the Chinese only subordinate functions, it was natural that the conquerors should show little interest in the culture of their subjects. The first Mongol khan to have enquired into it a little was Tuq Temur (1328–39). So the favours accorded to the Sung 'neo-Confucian' school should not be taken too seriously. They came late, at the beginning of the fourteenth century. In 1313 the doctrines of Chu Hsi were declared orthodox; in 1315 the system of recruitment competitions was extended. Some works of the school of Chu Hsi, including the *Developments on the Ta-hsüeh (Ta-hsüeh yen-i)*, a work written in 1229 under the Southern Sung, were translated into Mongolian. This does not make up for the absence of classical studies and of Chinese philosophy under the Mongols. The situation was the same in the Liao and Chin empires, not to speak of the Hsia empire, where there was no big intellectual centre comparable with Peking. The Mongol regime was even less favourable to the progress of thought in China that that of the autocratic Ming was to be until the beginning of the sixteenth century.

However, science and technology suffered less from the foreign domination. One element of nomad mentality which the Mongols had retained was a respectful admiration for craftsmen and technicians as well as for priests. This accounts for the honours which they accorded to a man like Kuo Shou-ching (1231–1316), the engineer, hydrographer, mathematician, and astronomer. Introduced to Kublai Khan in 1263, he was entrusted in 1271 with all questions of irrigation and regulation of water-courses, and afterwards, in 1276, with a reform of the calendar, the calculations for which he completed in 1280. The upsurge which Chinese mathematics had experienced in the Sung empire continued under the Yüan. Two famous mathematical works appeared about 1300, the *Initiation into Mathematics (Suan-hsüeh ch'i-meng)* (1299) and the *Jade Mirror of the Four Principles (Ssu-yüan yü-chien)* (1303), both of them written by Chu Shih-chieh. The Taoist monk and geographer Chu Ssu-pen (1273–1337) published a big atlas, the Yü-ti-t'u, to which he devoted nine years of work, from 1311 to 1320. About 1350 Wang Ta-yüan wrote his valuable *Account of the Barbarians of the Isles (Tao-i chih-lueh)*, based on the notes which he had made during the course of numerous journeys in South-East Asia between 1330 and 1344, and we are indebted to Wang Chen (dates unknown) for some important treatises on agronomy, including the *Nung-shu* (1313). The great encyclopaedia in two hundred chapters by Wang Ying-lin (1223–96), the *Yü-hai,* lost at the time of the wars between the Yüan and the Sung, was found again and printed between 1341 and 1368.

The reign of the Mongols favoured the entry of Islam into China. The Yüan epoch saw the formation of Moslem communities in North China and Yunnan, a province entrusted from 1274 onwards to a Moslem governor from Bukhara by the name of Sayyid Ajall. The descendants of these communities, who were to merge completely with the local Chinese, nevertheless sought down to our own day to preserve their own personality and were to show a marked tendency to autonomy. The total number of Chinese converts to Islam, very numerous in eastern Kansu,

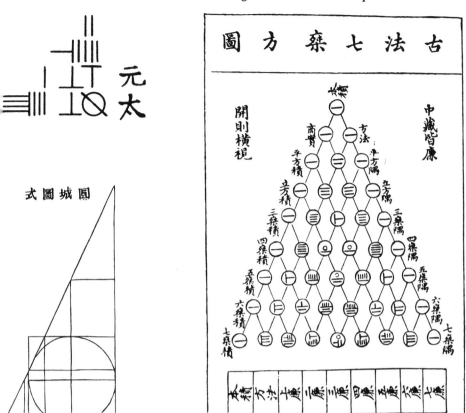

Figure 13 Sung and Yüan mathematics. From top to bottom and left to right (1) Notation for the equation + 2x³ + 15x² + 166x¹ – 4460 = 0 as given by Li Yeh (or Li Chih) 1192–1279). The equation is arranged as follows:

$$2x^3$$
$$15x^2$$
$$166x^1$$
$$4460x^0$$

The numerical symbol II at the top of this array should be read as $2x^3$ by virtue of its position: it is in the last column of the powers of 10 and the first row of the 4 powers of x. Other features worth noting are: (i) that position is significant in the representation of powers of 10 (from right to left) and of x (from bottom to top); the distinct rows of symbols rule out ambiguity; (ii) that a transverse stroke is used to show that a number is negative (in this case, the stroke across the zero of the bottom number). The economy of means, elegance, and convenience of this notation are obvious. (2) Figure from the *Ts'e-yüan hai-ching* (1248) illustrating the properties of circles inscribed in right-angled triangles. (3) Pascal's Triangle, as given in the *Ssu-yüan yü-chien* (1303), an algebraic treatise by Chu Shih-chieh.

North China (there are 250,000 Moslems in Peking today) and Yunnan, when combined with that of the Moslem inhabitants of Sinkiang, was estimated before the Second World War at fifty million. The jealous particularism of these peoples and their marginal situation, together with the clumsiness and exacting attitude of the Chinese government, were to lead to big and bloody rebellions in the eighteenth and nineteenth centuries.

The influence of Islam, and more particularly that of Moslem Iran, could not fail to make itself felt in the Chinese world during the Mongol epoch. The Mongols had entrusted the construction of their palace in Peking (Khanbalik) to a Moslem, and there were numerous examples of Moslem architecture in Mongolia and China. Mosques were erected in Yunnan, Szechwan, and Kansu, and at Hsi'an, Ch'üan-chou, and Canton.

Translations of Arabic texts were undertaken at the Islamic Academy (*hui-hui kuo-tzu hsüeh*) set up in the reign of Kublai Khan at the suggestion of Moiz al-Din, a high official in the imperial secretariat. It was doubtless in the domain of mathematics and astronomy that the influence of Moslem Iran was most perceptible. Shortly after the sack of Baghdad in 1258, an astronomical observatory was set up at Maragha, to the south of Tabriz, whither astronomers from every land were summoned; there were obviously Chinese among them. A new calendar was established in 1267 by the Persian astronomer and geographer Jamal al-Din (?–*c*. 1301), who in 1286 presented to the Mongol court an illustrated geographical work in Chinese. The Mongols instituted in Peking a Moslem observatory (*hui-hui ssu-t'ien t'ai*), in imitation of which the first Ming emperor was to create in Nanking, in the very first year (1368) of his reign, a Moslem astronomical office (*hui-hui ssu-t'ien chien*). In 1362 an astronomical treatise with lunar tables was written by Ata ibn Ahmad for a Mongol prince of China. In fact it is very probable that the development of Chinese astronomy and the algebraic bias of Chinese mathematics, whose most illustrious representatives in the Mongol age were Kuo Shou-ching (1231–1316) and Chu Shih-chieh, were encouraged by the contributions of Moslem Iran.

Even if the Mongol domination was not very favourable to the learned and serious literature which in China was the prerogative of the literati and politicians, it seems to have stimulated, by way of compensation, as it were, all forms of popular expression: first of all the realistic and satirical song, often inspired by hatred of the Mongols and of the groups favoured by the occupying power (central Asian Moslems, Tibetan monks, Chinese 'quislings'), but also the short story, the novel, and above all the theatre; in a word, a whole literature in vernacular dialects, most of which has not been preserved. This literature that arose in the popular quarters of the big cities was centred on the one hand on the commercial agglomerations of south-eastern China and on the other on the cosmopolitan city of Peking. Since its beginnings under the Sung — it is from the eleventh century onwards that we start to find more documents in the vernacular — this literature shows a continuous development unaffected by the political upheavals that occurred between the end of the eleventh century and the middle of the fourteenth — occupation of the north of Hopei by the Khitan, the Jürchen invasion of 1126, the capture of Peking by the Mongols in 1215, the occupation of Yangtze China in 1275–76, the rebellions of the end of the Yüan period. The Peking drama, the *tsa-chü,* the rise of which began under the Chin dynasty (1115–1234), a play with several characters consisting of a combination of sung sections (*ch'u*), dances and recitatives, with a musical accompaniment, was to be the greatest literary glory of the Mongol age. Usually written by anonymous authors, it has largely disappeared; out of a thousand plays whose titles are known to us, only 167 have survived to our day. The most famous are those of Ma Chih-yuan (middle of the twelfth century), the author of the *Han-kung-ch'iu* and the *Huang-liang-meng,* and Kuan Han-ch'ing (second half of the thirteenth century). We are indebted to the Pekingese Wang Shih-fu (*c.* 1300) for the immortal *Hsi-hsiang-chi* (*The Pavilion of the West*), a sentimental, romantic work. After the conquest of Sung China by the Mongols numerous dramatists settled in the lower Yangtze region, whose dramatic traditions were different from those of Peking. Among the writers established in this region at the end of the Yüan period was Kao Ming (Kao Tse-ch'eng), the author of the *P'i-p'a-chi* (*The Guitar*).

The religious policy of the Mongols consisted in successively favouring different sects, following the interests of the moment, and in entrusting to them the general direction of the religious affairs of the empire. Its inconsistencies are explained by the personal nature of the political power and by the attitude of the Mongols to religion — their indifference to philosophical questions, their weakness for magic, and their belief in miracles. When Genghis Khan sent for the Taoist monk Ch'ang-ch'un in 1219, it was not out of curiosity about the intellectual and ascetic aspects of the Ch'üan-chen sect to which he belonged and which had been founded in Shantung by Wang Ch'ung-yang (1112–70) — the founder had wanted to purify Taoism of all its occult practices and to effect a synthesis of the philosophy of the *Lao-tzu,* the Buddhism of the *Prajnaparamita* and the *Classic of Filial Piety* (*Hsiao-ching*). It was simply because of the fame of Ch'ang-ch'un, already much in favour with the Jürchen aristocracy of Peking under the Chin, and because the Mongol autocrat could not conceive that a famous priest did not possess thaumaturgic powers. After granting the Taoist church control of all religious questions in 1223, from 1242 onwards the Mongol emperors transferred their favour to the Buddhists of the *ch'an* school, under the influence of the monk Hai-yün (1202–57) and of Liu Ping-chung. Buddhism had in fact enjoyed a dominant position in the Khitan, Tangut, and Jürchen empires and it was natural that its influence should make itself felt in the Mongol empire. The Chinese Buddhist canon had been printed by the Liao, at P'ing-yang, in southern Shansi, between 1148 and 1173, and it had been printed again by the Chin. Under the Mongols a general history of Buddhism was to appear, from the origins to the year 1333. This was the *Fo-tsu li-tai t'ung-tsai*, an imitation of the *Fo-tsu t'ung-chi* of 1269. But after the Mongols had penetrated into Tibet (from 1252 onwards), this interest in Chinese Buddhism soon gave way to a lively interest in Tibetan Buddhism, whose magico-religious aspects and recourse to formulas (*mantra* and *dharani*) and magic circles (*mandala*) corresponded better to the religious sensibilities of the Mongols. From the accession of Kublai (1260) onwards, all the government's favours went to the Church of the Lamas.

The Tibetan lama 'Phags-pa (1239–80), who arrived in Peking in 1253, found the general direction of all the religious communities in the empire entrusted to him in 1260. After him it was a polyglot Uighur lama called Senge (?–1291) who became Kublai's all-powerful favourite. The lamas' power in China enabled them to exploit the religious communities. Senge took to financial speculation and exaction, and made himself guilty of plundering and of numerous murders. After the conquest of South China a new office of religious affairs was created at Hangchow. From 1277 onwards it was entrusted to a Tibetan monk called Yang-lien-chen-chia; he too became notorious for his misdemeanours. His most horrible crime in the eyes of the Chinese consisted in violating the tombs of the Southern Sung emperors near Shao-hsing in 1278 in order to gain possession of their treasure.

Thus the favours which the Mongols granted to the Church of the Lamas helped to increase the hatred of the Chinese for their masters. They also had other effects: on the one hand, the infiltration of Tibetan influences into Chinese Buddhist art, influences perceptible in sculpture and architecture, and on the other — something which was to have more important consequences — the spread of 'lamaism' to the steppe zone.

Part 7

The Reign of the Autocrats and Eunuchs

Prologue

A historical analysis of the long period of the Ming dynasty (1368–1644) makes it possible to distinguish three fairly clearly defined epochs. First of all, in the Hung-wu (1368–98) and Yung-le (1403–24) eras, came a period of economic reconstruction, of the installation of new institutions of a very original character, of diplomatic and military expansion not only in Mongolia, South-East Asia, and the Indian Ocean but also in central Asia. This movement of expansion, of which the campaigns in the north to reduce and push back the former Mongol occupiers and the steppe tribes were one of the most important aspects, was slowed down and then halted in the middle of the fifteenth century as a result of defeats in Mongolia. The second half of the fifteenth century and the first few years of the sixteenth were an era of withdrawal and defence. Finally, from about 1520 onwards, there was a second Chinese 'Renaissance', which was marked by a whole series of economic, social, and intellectual changes. This process of evolution ended, doubtless as a result of the rigidity of the political institutions, in a series of crises which succeeded each other from the last few years of the sixteenth century onwards – a crisis in commerce and in the urban work-force, a profound political crisis and then generalized revolts which went on up to the Manchu invasion.

Chapter 18

Reconstruction and Expansion

Dissolution of the Mongol empire and foundation of the Ming dynasty

The causes which were to lead to the collapse of the Yüan empire were many and, as so often happens, mutually related to each other: disorder in the administration, where innumerable contradictory regulations were in force, the rapacity of the Mongol and Moslem officials, an extremely rapid inflation of the paper money, the corruption of the Tibetan 'lamaist' monks who controlled all the Chinese clergy and interfered in political affairs, the oppression suffered every day by the Chinese population and the growing poverty of the peasantry. In the last analysis, the duration of Mongol rule in China had been brief; it was only in 1234 that they occupied the whole of North China and they did not complete the conquest of the South until 1279, while the revolts which were to put an end to their empire began in 1351 and a large part of China was lost to them by 1355. By this time centres of rebellion had been created in most of the provinces and the liberated areas extended to Honan, Shensi, Hopei, Shansi, and Szechwan.

The liberation of Chinese territory

Even if members of the educated classes joined them once they had started, all these patriotic rebellions were of popular origin. There were two big areas where the insurrection spread widely. One was in the provinces bordering on Shantung, where millenary movements proclaiming the impending coming of Maitreya (Mi-le), the redemptive Bodhisattva, were very active and people believed in the imminent restoration of the

Sung. The bulk of the rebels were of peasant origin. The Yellow River floods which explain the chronic instability of this part of China had grown worse since 1327 and were causing deadly famines almost every year. In 1344 the dykes broke downstream from K'ai-feng after continuous rain. The river flooded huge areas and it was not until five years later, after eight months' work, that the breaches could be filled. But the great task of repairing the dykes for which crowds of peasants were assembled favoured revolutionary propaganda. This whole region of the central plain and of Anhwei, further south, was dominated by the secret society of the Red Turbans (*Hung-chin*), whose supreme leader was Han Shan-t'ung, regarded as a reincarnation of Maitreya. In 1355 his son Han Lin-er proclaimed himself the first emperor of a new Sung dynasty.

The other great seat of insurrection was among the salt-workers, boatmen, and salt-smugglers of the lower Yangtze, where the rebels' leader was a man called Chang Shih-ch'eng. It extended to the seamen and pirates of the coast of Chekiang, where the rebel troops were led by Fang Kuo-chen.

Another less important centre of rebellion existed in the middle Yangtze area, where a heterodox religious movement resembling that of the Red Turbans developed; it was led successively by Hsü Shou-hui and Ch'en Yu-liang. As for Szechwan, which succeeded fairly quickly in escaping the control of the Mongol government, it formed a special case, for it was a relatively isolated province where there was a lively tradition of independence.

This situation was to give birth to a new empire, and for the first time in history movements of popular origin were to end in the foundation of a dynasty without any break between the period of insurrection and the one that was to follow it. The facility with which the liberation movements were able to adapt themselves would be difficult to explain had they not been extremely well organized: the economy, the administration, and the army all functioned normally both in the areas liberated by the Red Turban forces and in those which they controlled even before the Yüan administration had been expelled from them.

The man who was to found the Ming empire makes his first appearance as the leader of a secondary rebellion in the area in which the Red Turban risings had spread. Chu Yüan-chang, born in 1328, who was to adopt the reign-name of Hung-wu (1368–98), was the grandson of a Kiangsu goldwasher. His father was an itinerant agricultural worker in Anhwei and his mother was the daughter of a master sorcerer. At the time of the famines of 1344 Chu Yüan-chang had become a monk in order to make a living and from then onwards he had been influenced by the messianic traditions current in his province. In 1348 he put himself at the head of a band

Plate 42. Yüan bowl

Plate 43. Sung vase, black floral design on white

Plate 44. Sung vase, grey on white

Plate 45. Sung bowl, lotus design

of rebels which became strong enough to capture a small town in north-eastern Anhwei in 1352. In alliance with the Red Turban troops he won victory after victory; in 1359 he occupied Nanking and the surrounding region, and in 1360–62 the provinces of Kiangsi and Hupei. In the following year he was master of central China and in 1364 he proclaimed himself prince of the kingdom of Wu (*Wu-kuo wang*). During the course of the years 1365 to 1367 he eliminated his rivals in the lower Yangtze valley and Chekiang, Chang Shih-ch'eng and Fang Kuo-chen, and in 1368 founded the great Ming dynasty at Nanking. The offensive was continued in China itself and outside China, overflowing the limits of the Chinese provinces by its own impetus, so to speak. In 1368, the very year of the foundation of the new empire, came the capture of Peking, the main capital of the Yüan; in 1369 Shang-tu (K'ai-ping) in eastern Mongolia was taken; in 1370 the Mongol armies in Mongolia were encircled; in 1371 Szechwan was reconquered, and in 1372 and 1382 respectively Kansu and Yunnan, where there was still a nucleus of Mongol troops. At last, in 1387, the whole of China was reunified. The expansion abroad was confirmed by the great victory of Buinor (1388) in north-eastern Mongolia, by the adhesion to China of the Korean I dynasty, founded in 1392, and by expeditions to central Asia and South-East Asia. This policy, which aimed at re-establishing the prestige and security of China in East Asia, was to be pursued until the middle of the fifteenth century.

Reconstruction of the agrarian economy

However, the most serious problem was the economic chaos in which the empire found itself at the very moment of its foundation: China had been ruined by the Mongol exploitation and by the destruction involved in the war. The whole valley of the Huai had suffered terribly from the insurrections and some parts of Anhwei were completely depopulated. Land, dykes, and canals were in a state of abandonment almost everywhere. A huge effort at economic reconstruction had to be made and was in fact undertaken between 1370 and 1398.

The effort to restore agriculture in the reign of Hung-wu may seem comparable, for the China of those days, with that undertaken by the People's Republic of China after the Liberation of 1949. The work accomplished in some twenty years in the domains of irrigation, of the restoration of land, and of the planting of trees was impressive. Innumerable projects, great and small, for irrigation and the control of water-courses were put into effect in most of the provinces. In 1395, 40,987 reservoirs were repaired or built in the whole of China. Large areas of land were restored to cultivation and the devastated regions were systematically repopulated by transfers of population. The immigrants received extensive plots and benefited from state aid and from tax exemption for many years. The area of land reclaimed grew rapidly. The highest figures of the years 1370–80 bear witness to this:

1371	575,965 hectares
1373	1,911,692 hectares
1374	4,974,069 hectares
1379	1,485,572 hectares

The progression in the grain taxes tells the same story. These taxes amounted to 12 million *shih* (or about 7 million hundredweight) under the Mongol occupation. They reached almost 33 million *shih* (nearly 20 million hundredweight) in 1393, six years after the completion of the reconquest.

But the most astonishing thing was the effort made to reafforest China at this time. Over 50 million sterculia trees, palm trees, and varnish trees were planted in the Nanking area in 1391 with a view to the construction of a high seas fleet, which was in fact to be used for the maritime expeditions of the beginning of the fifteenth century. In 1392 each family holding colonized land in Anhwei was obliged to plant 200 mulberry trees, 200 jujube trees and 200 persimmon trees. Two years later the obligation to plant 200 mulberry trees and 200 jujube trees was extended to the whole empire. In 1396 over 84 million fruit trees were planted in the present-day provinces of Hunan and Hupei. According to the estimates of some historians, the total number of trees planted in the Hung-wu era amounted to about 1000 million.

The priority accorded to the agrarian economy at the beginning of the Ming period seems to have been both a necessity and a deliberate choice. In a devastated China the most urgent thing was to ensure a food supply for the population. But at the same time a new direction was taken for the future: the Ming and Ch'ing empires were to be mainly based on agriculture. There was thus a clear change in the economy of the state in the fourteenth century. Whereas in the Sung period the treasury was largely fed by commercial taxes and the mercantile economy still retained an important role under the Mongols, the essential portion of the state's resources was henceforth to be provided by the farmers.

The importance attributed to agrarian taxation explains the extreme care devoted in the Hung-wu era to the drawing-up of the general survey of all the lands in the empire and to the population registers. The first of these enterprises took twenty years and was completed in 1387: it was the *Registers Accompanied by Maps in the Shape of Fish Scales (Yü-lin t'u-ts'e*). As for the census registers or *Yellow Registers* (*Huang-ts'e*), they were compiled in the years 1381 and 1382, and revised in 1391.

Control of the population

Another remarkable characteristic of the institutions set up by the founder of the Ming dynasty consisted in a functional division of the population. It was understood in Hung-wu China that one was peasant, soldier, or craftsman by birth and destined always to remain so, from father to son. The families of peasants, soldiers, and artisans were dependent on three ministries, which acquired great importance at that time, for they each controlled part of the empire's population, had their own fiscal and administrative autonomy, and their own treasuries, warehouses, granaries, and arsenals. These three ministries were the Ministry of Finance (*hu-pu*), which dealt with the peasant families who furnished the bulk of the taxes, the Ministry of the Army (*ping-pu*), and the Ministry of Public Works (*kung-pu*). This functional division of the population was linked to a geographical distribution: the army families (*chün-hu*) were more numerous in the frontier regions and on the coast; the families of craftsmen (*chiang-hu*) were to be found mainly in the neighbourhood of the capitals, where they were obliged to reside or to betake themselves in order to do periods of compulsory service in the imperial workshops; and the families of peasants (*min-hu*) were to be found in all regions with a big agricultural production.

It could be that the founder of the Ming dynasty was influenced by the example of Mongol institutions, for the hereditary character of professions was one of the principles of the political and social system of the Mongols. But this social system, which was conceivable in an empire directed and exploited by a class of conquerors, was to begin to break up rapidly from internal causes by the beginning of the fifteenth century. Changes of status became more and more frequent, and the army families, whose position was regarded as one of the worst, declined in numbers so quickly that it became necessary to recruit mercenaries. However, the registers compiled in the Hung-wu era were to remain in existence and reference continued to be made to them in the following periods in spite of the changes in society, so that by the fifteenth century the population figures no longer corresponded with reality and the real taxes differed from the taxes calculated in theory. The censuses of the Ming period from the fifteenth century onwards are reckoned to be the least trustworthy in the whole of Chinese history. They indicate a general drop in the population from the fifteenth to the seventeenth century at the very time when there was in fact a regular increase.

At the base of the fiscal organization was the system known as that of the *li-chia,* groups of ten families responsible to the administration and entrusted with the task of sharing out equitably taxes and corvées among their members and of collectively ensuring the maintenance of order. This system of self-management was to be rapidly turned to their own profit by the richest and most influential members, who served as intermediaries between the local population and the services of the imperial government. The inadequacy of the administrative framework and the relative freedom left to the rural communities was to end in causing the poorest families to become dependent on the country gentry and the rich peasants. From the beginning of the fifteenth century the class of small working landowners was to disappear progressively, while there was an increase in the number of tenant farmers, wandering peasants (*t'ao-min*), and people who had come down in the world. These last were partly absorbed by the recruitment of mercenaries for the armies, if they did not find a livelihood in the clandestine operation of mines, brigandage, or piracy. The importance acquired by local customs in the field of finance and administration was characteristic of the Ming period. The civil servants were too few in number to ensure effective control of the population which they administered, and, even more than in earlier epochs, they had to adapt themselves to local usages and to rely on the country gentry for the execution of their directives. In the sixteenth century and the first half of the seventeenth there were ten to fifteen thousand officials for the whole of the empire, and an average of fifty thousand inhabitants per sub-prefecture (*hsien*). The sub-prefecture was the smallest administrative district; it was headed by an imperial official, who was assisted by locally recruited staff (*li*).

Absolutist tendencies

The Ming empire was founded by a peasant who seems to have felt an instinctive mistrust of the literati. This impelled him to control the government and the civil service very closely. His own origin perhaps explains why Hung-wu made a great effort to favour the recruitment and promotion of officials from the lower classes. Suspicious, and jealous of his own authority, Hung-wu soon turned against those who had helped him to attain supreme power. In 1380—Hung-wu was sixty-two at the time—there was the great trial of Hu Wei-yung, his old companion in arms and a native himself of Anhwei. Becoming too powerful, he was accused of planning a rebellion and was suspected of being in contact with the Mongols and the Japanese. Fifteen thousand persons were involved in this enormous trial, which ended in the execution of Hu Wei-yung. It

Plate 46. Hu Ta-hai, early years of the Ming dynasty, late fourteenth century

Plate 47. Statue of warrior, one of the many lining the
roads to the Ming Tombs near Peking

was the opportunity for Hung-wu to concentrate all power in his own hands. He suppressed the imperial Grand Secretariat (*Chung-shu-sheng*) and placed the six ministries (Public Administration, Finance, Rites, Armies, Justice, and Public Works) directly under his own authority. He proceeded at the same time to carry out a reform of the military administration which ensured that he had a closer control of the armies thanks to the creation of a General Direction of the five armies (*Wu-chün tu-tu-fu*), on which he kept a firm hand.

New purges took place in 1385, in the course of which a number of officials were executed. They were accused of irregularities or crimes of high treason (Hung-wu was morbidly sensitive and saw even in the use of certain written characters veiled criticism of his person and his origins). In 1390 the case of Hu Wei-yung, his friends, and associates was reopened; once again, over fifteen thousand people were involved in this trial.

Right from the start the Ming empire carried in embryo the absolutist tendencies which were to assert themselves in the fifteenth and sixteenth centuries. Whereas the political system of the Sung was based on the co-existence of independent organisms which checked each other and of various different sources of information, and whereas political decisions in that empire were the subject of discussions in which contradictory opinions could be freely expressed, the Ming government was characterized, as early as the end of the fourteenth century, by a tendency to the complete centralization of all powers in the hands of the emperor, to government by means of restricted, secret councils, by the isolation of the imperial authority, and by the development of secret police forces entrusted with the task of supervising the administration at its various different levels. The 'Guards with Brocade Uniforms' (*chin-i-wei*), a sort of political police for spying on high officials, were created in 1382 by Hung-wu, who thus set his successors a hateful example.

It may be that the example of the Mongol empire had something to do with the autocratic character of the new Ming empire. There is a good deal of evidence for this view; it should be noted, for example, that the Ming Code (*Ming-lü*) (1367, revised in 1374, 1389, and 1397) is marked by the influence of Mongol legislation.

The work of the founder of the Ming dynasty can be seen to be crucial for the history of the two centuries and a half that followed his death, and homage was rightly paid to him until the end of the dynasty as to a sort of hero. By means of a tremendous collective effort Hung-wu restored China's material prosperity, and he also gave it back its power and its prestige abroad, imparting to Chinese policy an impulse which made itself felt until the middle of the fifteenth century. Finally, he created the basic institutions of a new empire. But it is also clear that the founder was at the root of the political and social vices from which Ming China was to suffer. The climate of mistrust established in his reign was never dissipated; the misunderstanding and suspicion between the central government and its agents only grew worse with time. The tendency to centralization, to authoritarian, secret government was accentuated under Hung-wu's successors. Moreover the utopian constitution which he meant to impose on Chinese society and the institutions established in his reign were to remain the objects of a sort of veneration; people continued to refer to them in spite of the changes in the economy and in society. The result was a greater and greater disparity between the realities of the situation and the administrative theory based on censuses and tax quotas fixed at the end of the fourteenth century. Hence the triumph of compromises and expedients, the importance acquired by local customs and the accumulation of detailed regulations. Finally, the faults of the fiscal system and the real power left to rich and influential families at the local level were very quickly to aggravate the oppression suffered by the least favoured classes and therefore their instability.

The pursuit of expansion

Mongolia, Manchuria, and Vietnam

A year after Hung-wu's death the second Ming emperor, on the advice of his entourage, had sought to reduce the power of the princes of the imperial family, some of whom held commands in frontier regions. These measures were the ultimate cause of the rebellion of one of the emperor's uncles, the prince of Yen, Chu Ti, who commanded the armies in the Peking region. Chu Ti marched on Nanking in 1401, gained control of it in the following year with the help of the eunuchs, who favoured him, and adopted the dynastic name of Yung-le (1403–24). His reign was to be one of the most brilliant in the history of the empire. The efforts made to restore the economy in the Hung-wu era bore their fruit in the first quarter of the fifteenth century, which was a period of general prosperity. Abroad, the power of the empire continued to assert itself and the desire for diplomatic and military expansion did not weaken. In spite of the violent crisis of the years 1401–3, China did not seem to have lost its impetus.

After the Mongols' retreat to the north in the Hung-wu era, two groups of powerful tribes were to be left throughout the dynasty: the Oirats, a collection of different peoples, in the north-west and the Tatars in the north-east. This latter name was to be distorted into Tartars by Europeans, who applied it wrongly to the Manchus, a people of Tungusic, not Mongol, origin and also unconnected with the Tatars of Soviet Russia, who are of Turkish origin. At the time of the civil war unleashed by the prince of Yen under Hung-wu's successor, the Oirats showed signs of renewed activity, but the emperor Yung-le successfully resumed the offensive against the Mongol tribes and led five big expeditions in person, winning a great victory on the river Onon to the north-east of Ulan Bator in 1410. During his reign Manchuria was occupied up to the mouth of the Amur. A government-general of this region of taiga was established at Nurgan, to the south of the mouth of the Amur, by 1404.

Nearly 5000 kilometres to the south a Chinese army of 200,000 men intervened in 1406 in Dai Viet, in the north of Vietnam, and put an end to the kingdom of the Tran. However, this military occupation and the *de facto* annexation of the Red River basin and central Vietnam were not maintained without difficulty. A liberation movement which began in 1418 finally drove out the occupiers in 1427. Its leader, Le Loi, founded the new Vietnamese dynasty of the Le.

These big military offensives, which gave back to the China of the Yung-le era the frontiers of the Yüan empire and even extended them southward to include Vietnam, were accompanied by intense diplomatic activity from Japan to Java and from Indo-China to the Middle East. Emissaries were sent to central Asia. In Hung-wu's reign a Buddhist monk called Tsung-lei had been entrusted with a mission that was doubtless both diplomatic and religious in character: he was supposed to bring back sacred texts from the western regions and travelled in the interior of Asia from 1382 to 1386. Under Yung-le, one Ch'en Ch'eng was sent to central Asia on three occasions, in 1413, 1416, and 1420. He travelled as far as Transoxiania in the empire of Timur (Tamerlane) and on returning from his first mission wrote *Notes on the Stages of a Journey to Serindia* (*Hsi-yü hsing-ch'eng chi*) and *Treatise on the Barbarian Kingdoms of Serindia* (*Hsi-yü fan-kuo chih*). At roughly the same period a palace eunuch, Hou Hsien, went to Tibet and India between 1403 and 1406, to Nepal in 1413, and to Bengal in 1415 and 1420 by sea. He went back to Tibet for one last time in 1427, two years after the death of Yung-le.

The big maritime expeditions

The Yung-le epoch is famous for its big maritime expeditions which revealed, at the beginning of the fifteenth century, the technical superiority of China and her lead over Spain and Portugal, whose ships did not undertake long voyages on the high seas until the very end of this same century. China's lead is explained by the continuity of maritime traditions which went back to the eleventh century and were almost certainly never interrupted; the fleets which the Mongols caused to be built for the invasion of Java at the end of the thirteenth century were put on the stocks on the lower Yangtze, no doubt in the very same yards that had built the warships and merchant ships of the Sung age. The age of the big high-seas junk covers the whole period from the eleventh century to the big expeditions of the early fifteenth century. Thus these expeditions were not a transitory, exceptional affair, but should be placed in a more general context — that of the maritime side of the Chinese world. The dynastic histories made a fuss of the maritime expeditions of the Yung-le era because they were official enterprises. They would be incomprehensible if we forgot that, contrary to received ideas, China, as well as being one of the great powers of the steppe and the high plateaux of central Asia, was also a land of sailors and explorers.

Various different opinions have been expressed about the causes of the maritime expeditions of the early fifteenth century. Were they military and diplomatic expeditions, prestige operations, or enterprises intended to provide the imperial court with luxury objects and exotic curiosities? They probably had all these aspects to them. It is as well to note that they corresponded to a plan that had already taken shape in Hung-wu's reign and that they were already preceded in those days by intense diplomatic activity in overseas countries. It was with a view to long-distance maritime expeditions and to the construction of a high-seas fleet that more than fifty million trees were planted in the Nanking area in 1391. Right from its advent Ming China began to attract foreign embassies, and missions from all the lands of East Asia arrived in Nanking — in 1369 from Korea, Japan, Vietnam, and Champa; in 1371 from Cambodia and Siam; in 1370 and 1390 from the kingdoms of the Malayan peninsula and even from the coast of Coromandel. It is still possible today to see in the suburbs of Nanking the tomb of a king of Borneo who came with his family and a large retinue to the Ming capital and died there in 1408. Fragments of the funerary stelae making the identification possible were found recently.

Chinese missions led by eunuchs went in 1403 to Java and Sumatra, to Malacca, and even to Cochin, on the west coast of southern India. It may be supposed that the big ports of Canton, Ch'üan-chou, and Foochow had never stopped trading with these distant lands since the thirteenth century, for it would be difficult to explain the renewal of diplomatic relations in any other way. It is also clear that the Ming emperors had expansionist ideas very similar to those of the Mongols, even though the

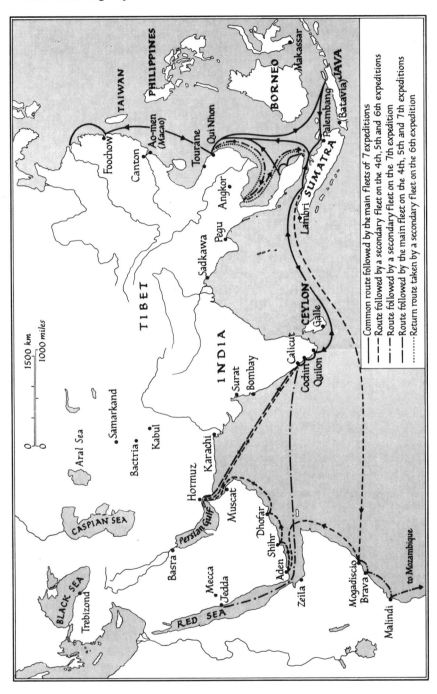

Map 19   The maritime expeditions of Cheng Ho (1405–1433)

style had changed: it was no longer a question of undertaking mere conquests for the sake of economic exploitation but of securing the recognition of the power and prestige of the Ming empire in South-East Asia and the Indian Ocean. The big maritime expeditions of the Yung-le era were contemporaneous with the military operations in Vietnam and its occupation from 1406 to 1427.

These expeditions were organized by a eunuch called Cheng Ho (1371–1433), a Moslem from Yunnan whose father was a hadji, having made the pilgrimage to Mecca.

He had entered the gynaeceum of the prince of Yen, the future emperor Yung-le, in Peking, after the conquest of Yunnan by Hung-wu in 1382. His family name was Ma (the first syllable of Mahomet), but he took that of Cheng in 1404. Appointed to some important military posts, he was put in charge of the seven maritime expeditions which took place in the reigns of Yung-le (1403–24) and Hsüan-te (1425–35). Here are their dates and routes:

1. 1405–7: Champa (south-east coast of Vietnam), Java, Sumatra, Malacca, Ceylon, Calicut (west coast of southern India). In Majapahit, a Javanese kingdom, Cheng Ho intervened in an affair of the succession to the throne, and in Palembang (south-eastern Sumatra) in a conflict between the local government and the Chinese colony.

2. 1407–9: Calicut, Cochin (also on the Malabar coast), and Ceylon. In these three places Cheng Ho put up stelae proclaiming that the kingdoms of Calicut, Cochin, and Ceylon were vassals of the Ming empire.

3. 1409–11: Siam, Malacca, Malabar coast, Ceylon. Cheng Ho opposed the claims of Majapahit to Malacca and erected a stele there. He inflicted a defeat on the royal army in the island of Ceylon.

4. 1413–15: Calicut and Ormuz, at the entrance to the Persian Gulf. After leaving Sumatra part of the fleet sailed direct, without a stop, to Aden and the east coast of Africa, which it reached in the neighbourhood of Mogadishu, in Somalia. This was a voyage of about 6,000 kilometres. On this expedition, the Chinese troops intervened in the internal affairs of the sultanate of Samudra-Pasai, in north-western Sumatra.

5. 1417–19: Ormuz again. Part of the fleet sailed from Sumatra to the coast of Somaliland and Aden. It returned in 1420 after accomplishing the longest round voyage of all those undertaken at this period and after calling again at Aden and Ormuz.

6. 1421–22: Cheng Ho's fleet went to Sumatra, while another fleet sailed towards East Africa and the Persian gulf.

7. 1431–33: Champa, Java, Palembang (south-eastern Sumatra), Malacca, Malabar coast, Ormuz. Some of the ships sailed from Calicut

to Jeddah, the port of Mecca, and rejoined the main body of the fleet via Aden and the south coast of Arabia.

In 1424, in the interval between the fifth and sixth expeditions, a small fleet sailed to Palembang.

These expeditions, which comprised several dozen very large junks carrying over twenty thousand men on each voyage, seem to have obtained all the results desired: China acquired great prestige in all the seas of East Asia and in the islands and peninsulas of South-East Asia, and trade in the shape of tribute from all the states of those areas expanded rapidly. The contacts made in the Near East on Cheng Ho's fourth expedition were no doubt at the root of two embassies to Nanking from Mameluke Egypt, one in the first quarter of the fifteenth century, the other in 1441. The superiority of the Chinese fleet explains the almost total disappearance in the first half of the fifteenth century of the Japanese pirates who had begun to appear on the Chinese coast at the beginning of the dynasty. It looks as if the choice of a Moslem—no doubt remarkable for his personality and knowledge—as commander-in-chief and chief ambassador to lands where Islam had long been established, or was beginning to make headway, was particularly judicious. Cheng Ho's successes in South-East Asia left such lively memories that he was deified there and his cult has not yet disappeared even today. The temples in which he is venerated bear the name of San-pao, an allusion to the official title held by Cheng Ho, that of *San-pao t'ai-chien*. As was the case with other embassies to distant countries, the sea voyages of 1405–33 were followed by the publication of geographical works which enlarged Chinese knowledge of the oceans and overseas countries and made it more precise. The most famous of these works are the *Treatise on the Barbarian Kingdoms of the Western Oceans* (*Hsi-yang fan-kuo chih*), which appeared in 1434, the *Marvels Discovered by the Boat Bound for the Galaxy* (*Hsing-ch'a sheng-lan*) of 1436 and the *Marvels of the Oceans* (*Ying-ya sheng-lan*), published in 1451 by one of Cheng Ho's companions, the eunuch Ma Huan, who had taken part in the first, fourth, and seventh expeditions.

The effect of Cheng Ho's expeditions was to strengthen the old currents of trade and Chinese emigration towards the lands of South-East Asia and the ports of southern India.

The start of the withdrawal

One may say that the return of Cheng Ho's last expedition in 1433 marked the end of an era, the era in which for four centuries China had been the great sea power of Asia. The decline of the Chinese navy in the sixteenth century, at the very time when the attacks of pirates were reaching their greatest intensity, is attested by the Europeans who were beginning to venture into the East Asian seas and is demonstrated by the difficulties encountered in suppressing piracy. The weakness of the Chinese fleets did not hinder trade and smuggling; trade between the Chinese coast, Japan, the Philippines, Siam, and other South-East Asian countries never seems to have been busier than in the sixteenth century. But by that time China was no longer the great maritime power that it had been at the beginning of the fifteenth century; after the end of Cheng Ho's expeditions it gave up the idea of pursuing a policy of prestige on the oceans.

This retirement on the maritime side was paralleled in the middle of the fifteenth century by a withdrawal on the steppes. After Yung-le's reign (1403–24) the Ming offensives in Mongolia met stiffer resistance from the nomads, who in their turn passed to the attack. As was so often the case in Chinese history, the restrictions imposed on trade with the people of the steppe were at the root of the difficulties and of the recrudescence of incursions. To prevent the Oirats from growing stronger, and perhaps to restrict to the indispensable minimum the purchases of horses, of which the Mongols were the main suppliers, the Ming government maintained the embargo on the trade in arms, copper, and iron, and was reluctant to open new horse fairs on its frontiers. During the Cheng-t'ung period (1436–49) the Oirat tribes were unified by Esen Khan (?–1454) and penetrated into eastern Mongolia. From then on incursions into North China became more and more frequent, and in 1449 came the famous incident of the fortress of T'u-mu in northern Hopei, when the emperor Cheng-t'ung was taken prisoner by the Mongols. He was not released until 1457, and only then for a ransom. Apart from the serious political repercussions that it had in Peking, the T'u-mu affair marked, abroad, the end of the period of expansion and the transition to a defensive policy.

The Mongol attacks of 1438–49 were in fact disastrous for the Chinese defence system, since they enforced a substantial withdrawal towards the south. The Great Walls which had been built between 1403 and 1435 in northern Hopei and northern Shansi followed approximately the line of the old fortifications erected by the Northern Ch'i in the middle of the sixth century and by the Sui in 585. The advance of the Mongol tribes made it necessary to construct a second line of defence (the 'inner great wall', *nei-ch'ang-ch'eng*) in the Cheng-t'ung period (1436–49) and a new line of fortifications to the south of the Ordos in the course of the Ch'eng-hua period (1465–87). The total length of these walls, double or triple in some places, is nearly 5000 kilometres. It is these walls of which

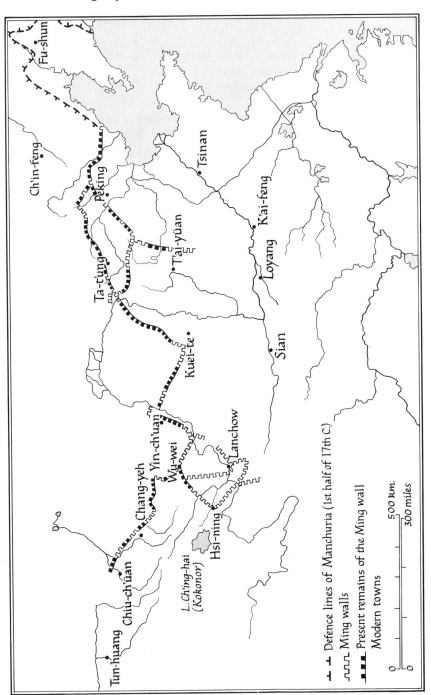

Map 20   The Great Walls of the Ming epoch

one can still see substantial stretches in North China and even near Peking.

After the middle of the fifteenth century no further large-scale effort was ever made to free the northern provinces from pressure and threats from the steppe. After the compromise period of the years 1449–57, during the captivity of the emperor Ying-tsung (Cheng-t'ung), the Ming confined themselves to ensuring — at great expense — the defence of their frontiers. This policy of passivity was to lead in the middle of the sixteenth century to a critical situation from which the empire was only just saved.

Chapter 19

Political, Social, and Economic Changes

The epoch that followed the great period of expansion of the Hung-wu and Yung-le eras at the end of the fourteenth and the beginning of the fifteenth century was marked on the one hand by a strengthening of the tendencies to secret, autocratic government which were so clearly defined in the dynasty's founder and on the other by a series of changes which altered in a more and more pronounced way the institutions set up in the Hung-wu era.

Political evolution

Eunuchs and secret police

One of the peculiarities of the Ming empire was the great influence — even at certain periods the omnipotence — acquired by the eunuchs. This situation was the natural result of an authoritarian government that was excessively centralized and secret. The root of the eunuchs' power and hidden influence was the domestic nature of their functions. They were entrusted with matters that concerned the very person of the emperor and those of the members of the imperial family. This was why they were given command of the palace guards, a position which enabled them to reach high military posts. This was also why they were entrusted with the management of the workshops which supplied the court with luxury products, why they checked the tribute (*kung*) sent by the provinces and foreign countries, and why they were appointed heads of missions to the interior of Asia or across the seas of South-East Asia and the Indian Ocean. The management of the imperial workshops and the supervision of trade and foreign relations provided them with an easy opportunity to enrich themselves. They were thus at the source of military power and commercial wealth. In contact with the emperors, abreast of palace plots, they were to acquire decisive influence over autocrats who distrusted the legitimate representatives of the imperial government in the provinces. The autocratic tendencies of the Ming regime made the rapid rise of these insinuating, clever, flexible, and devoted servants inevitable.

The founder of the dynasty had forbidden eunuchs to learn to read and had stipulated that they should suffer the death penalty if they interfered in politics; half a century later the eunuchs were controlling practically the whole administration, deciding on the appointment and promotion of officials in the central government and in the provinces. By strengthening centralization and by creating a Privy Council (the 'Pavilion of the Interior', *nei-ko*), which from 1426 onwards was gradually to replace the regular organs of government, the emperors had acted to the advantage of the eunuchs, who were finally to insinuate themselves into the very centre of power. The extraordinary ascendancy of these palace servants proceeded from the fact they were able to gain control of the secret police, one of the most fearsome weapons of the Ming autocracy. The men of the Eastern Esplanade (*tung-ch'ang*) who under Yung-le succeeded the Brocaded Guards (*chin-i-wei*) created by Hung-wu soon passed under the control of the eunuchs. In the years 1465–87 it was the Red Horsemen of the Western Esplanade (*hsi-ch'ang*) who fulfilled on behalf of the eunuchs the same function of acting as secret envoys, spies, and *agents provocateurs,* taking advantage of their limitless and secret powers to blackmail and corrupt people. The emperor, deprived of any means of obtaining information or checking it, condemned all those who were denounced to him without even giving them a hearing.

The eunuchs' power increased the imperial civil servants' feeling of insecurity with regard to the arbitrary authority on which they were dependent. It corrupted them and aggravated their disaffection to the central government. The most honest of them, and those most devoted to the emperor, found themselves faced by tragic contradictions. As well as these political reasons for their hostility to the eunuchs, there were also conflicts due to differences of origin and education. Most of the eunuchs were lower-class northerners, while the civil servants usually came from the families of literati of the lower Yangtze and northern Chekiang.

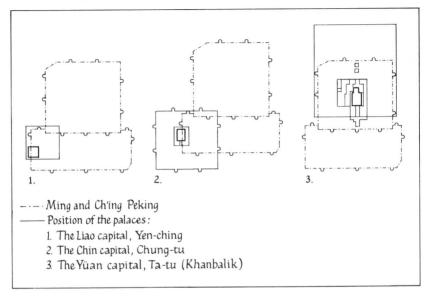

—·— Ming and Ch'ing Peking
——— Position of the palaces:
1. The Liao capital, Yen-ching
2. The Chin capital, Chung-tu
3. The Yüan capital, Ta-tu (Khanbalik)

Map 21   The successive positions of the Liao, Chin, and Yüan capitals on the site of Peking

The transfer of the capital

A decision fraught with consequences was to accentuate the divorce between the central government and its officials and, in a more general way, between the court and the literati as a whole. In 1421 Peking was raised to the rank of main capital, whereas until then Nanking had served as the seat of the central government and of the court. But the transfer, made possible by the restoration of the Grand Canal between 1411 and 1415, was carried out gradually, with part of the government service remaining in Nanking, and it was not completed until about 1450. This decision may seem rather surprising. Peking was in fact a peripheral city, where the influences of the steppe have always made themselves felt. Moreover it was relatively exposed to Mongol incursions and was to be seriously threatened by their attacks in the middle of the sixteenth century. The Mongol Yüan dynasty had made Peking its capital in 1271 and before that the Khitan and Jürchen empires had taken up residence there, but it was the first time that an empire of Chinese origin had established its capital in such a northerly area. It may be that the emperor Yung-le felt some attachment to the places where he had been prince and where he had found support at the time of his expedition towards the south. It may be, too, that he felt nothing but distrust and antipathy for the people of the lower Yangtze. But there may have been another reason for the decision — the strategic importance of the Peking area, for the control both of eastern Mongolia and of the north-eastern territories. It was in fact in Yung-le's reign that the frontiers of the empire were pushed up to the distant valley of the Amur. The transfer of the capital would in that case reflect the desire to expand towards the steppe zone and Manchuria, and finally the ambition to reassume in Asia the dominant position held by the Yüan empire between the end of the thirteenth century and the middle of the fourteenth.

But by settling in Peking the imperial government put itself at a distance from the highly-populated, industrious, commercial, and intellectual China of the lower Yangtze and northern Chekiang. It thus condemned itself to losing contact more easily with the élites of these areas.

Social and economic evolution

To obtain a general view of the social and economic changes of the fifteenth and sixteenth centuries it would be necessary to be able to follow all the details of them in each sector and in each region. This immense task remains to be carried out and we must still content ourselves with a few scattered facts and a general impression — that of a much more radical evolution than the mere recital of the events would lead us to suppose.

Some of the changes concerned the rural world, whose activities and products seem to have grown wider in range, while at the same time certain improvements in technique and certain economic changes occurred. However, this general enrichment of the country districts was accompanied by a rapid deterioration in the condition of the poorest and weakest. Extensive changes in people's circumstances seem to have begun to take place by the early fifteenth century: the transformation of the small landowners of the Hung-wu era into tenant farmers, changes of status in the three types of family instituted by the founder of the Ming dynasty, and a general search for new means of livelihood. The point of departure of all this was doubtless the slow acquisition of the poor peasants' land by the richer ones — that constant economic pressure at the rural level which governments are not in a position to check. The economic expansion and the generalization of the use of silver ingots and coins in the Chinese economy as a whole did the rest and accelerated the process of evolution. Such at any rate is the general impression which we gain at the moment.

The question of the army families

The founder of the Ming dynasty had wished to make the armies into a sort of autonomous organism, whose members and income were to be provided, from generation to generation, by families with a special status — the army families (*chün-hu*), settled on the lands of military colonies (*chün-t'un*). Out of each ten men, three were to be assigned to military tasks (*shou-ch'eng*) and seven to agricultural work. This combination of the activities of defence and food production was an ancient one and was justified by the difficulties of supplying armies in the regions most exposed to nomad incursions. What, on the other hand, constituted a novelty was the extension of the system to the whole of the empire and the decision to reserve the revenues from certain lands for military expenses. In this the Chinese were following the example of the Mongols who, the better to keep the population in hand, had distributed their armies over the whole territory of the empire, in which they occupied a sort of series of enclaves. But another inspiration for this system was a principle analogous to that of the Buddhist foundations, which assigned the interest on an inalienable estate to the permanent upkeep of a temple or hospice. This kind of foundation had grown so common in the secular world since the eleventh century that its religious origin had been forgotten. The military colonies of the Hung-wu era were created out of the 'public lands' (*kuan-t'ien*) taken back from the Mongols or confiscated from the leaders and partisans of movements in rivalry with that of Chu Yüan-chang, out of land restored in the devastated areas, or else out of land cleared in the northern provinces, in Shansi, in the Ta-t'ung area, or in Liaotung, in southern Manchuria. It looks as if the institution took root fairly quickly in Chinese society of that time: by the end of the fourteenth century the army colonies (*chün-t'un*) were exercising enough attraction on the rural world for poor peasants to have attached themselves to them voluntarily, thus forming a sort of labour force of inferior status which took the name of 'extra army (families)' (*chün-yu*).

The greatest concentrations of military colonies lay in the Nanking and Peking areas, in Liaoning, along the northern frontier, and finally in the south-west, in the provinces of Yunnan and Kweichow. A living, autonomous organism, spread all over the empire, the armies were naturally to acquire in time a sort of regional specialization, unless their distribution from the middle of the fifteenth century onwards was the result of directives issued at the beginning of the dynasty by its founder. Five groups of armies can be distinguished at that period.

   1. Those which, from Liaoning to Chekiang, defended the empire

against threats from the sea and ensured the protection of these regions both by sea and on land.

2. Those which, from areas lying from immediately north of Peking to Kansu, on both sides of the Great Walls, were entrusted with the task of defending the northern provinces against incursions from the steppe.

3. Those which in the south-western provinces, where non-Chinese inhabitants were numerous (Kwangtung, Kwangsi, Yunnan, Kweichow, Hunan), dealt with risings by these tribes, who were jealous of their independence.

4. Those entrusted with the defence of the two capitals and massed round the outskirts of Peking and Nanking.

5. Last, those which, in all the big agricultural areas and along the Grand Canal linking Hangchow to Peking, were allotted the task of dealing with supplies and transport.

Certain changes were gradually to take place in the system established in the Hung-wu era. The army families, whose original nucleus of old companions-in-arms of the dynasty's founder had been enlarged by the adhesion of certain elements among the Mongol troops and by the addition of convicts and peasants, began to decrease at the beginning of the fifteenth century as a result of desertions, for from every point of view the position of these families was regarded as the least enviable. But there was more to it than that: in parallel with this reduction in the number of personnel, the area of the lands assigned to the military colonies began to shrink rapidly in the middle of the fifteenth century, as a result of illicit purchases of them by rich landowners. Thus serious questions which had been resolved by the institution of the army families and the military colonies began to worry the government again — the questions of recruitment, of the financing of military expenditure, and of supplies. The Ming emperors were thus forced to return to the practice of the Sung age and to turn more and more to the recruitment of mercenaries. This was the case in particular after the disaster of 1449, when in Hopei and Honan units of mercenaries known as *min-chuang* ('brave men recruited from the population') were created. But it was seldom that local defence militias were formed, like the *t'u-ping* ('local troops') created at the end of the fifteenth century, or like the peasant militias formed at the time of the most serious attacks by Japanese pirates in the middle of the following century. In spite of the effectiveness of such troops, the central government distrusted them because they could always form the nucleus of a rebellion. As for the deficit caused by the disappearance of the military colonies, it was made good partly from taxes and partly by the creation of domains assigned in the northern provinces to rich merchants who were given the task of exploiting them. These were the *shang-t'un* or 'merchants' colonies'. In exchange for their development by wage-earning labourers and for deliveries to the armies, the merchants of the *shang-t'un* received licences to trade in salt. This institution was no doubt at the root of the rapid rise of the merchants and bankers of Shansi from the end of the Ming period onwards.

The progressive disappearance of the families of craftsmen

A process of evolution similar to the one which had led to the disappearance of the army families was to occur in the case of the families of craftsmen. In imposing a special status on craftsmen, the Ming dynasty's founder had followed the example set by the Mongols, who had kept the best of them — some 260,000 — for their own service and had separated them from the rest of the population. However, this special status was to be extended at the beginning of the Ming period to cover all craftsmen, while at the same time two categories of families were distinguished: those who resided in the workshops attached to the Ministry of Public Works — the *chu-tso* — and those who were obliged to spend a certain number of working days every year in these workshops, which were sometimes quite a long way from their homes. These families were known as the *lun-pan*. The unfavourable conditions imposed on the craftsmen (payments below current prices, the sometimes tiresome obligation of having to make long journeys to Nanking or Peking, reduction of their free time, and so on) and on the other hand the economic upsurge of the lower Yangtze and maritime provinces, where demand was strong and payment was made in silver, were bound to act jointly and to cause a constant reduction in the number of families dependent on the Ministry of Public Works. At the same time the progress of the monetary economy prompted the state gradually to replace the corvées by taxes; as early as 1485 craftsmen living in the provinces could redeem their turns of compulsory labour in the capitals by payments of money, and this practice grew so general that it was sanctioned by law in 1562. At that date all the services of craftsmen subject to periods of compulsory labour were replaced by taxes in money and this particular class of craftsmen therefore disappeared completely. But the number of craftsmen who 'lived on the job' also continued to decrease during the course of the dynasty. Under Yung-le, between 1403 and 1424, there were about 27,000 master craftsmen in the imperial workshops, each with, on average, three to five workmen under his orders. In 1615 there were only 15,139. By the time of the Manchu invasion the registers of craftsmen's families had practically disappeared and the new Ch'ing empire suppressed them completely in 1645.

Thus during the course of the fifteenth and sixteenth centuries, as a result of economic changes and of the evolution of society, there was a progressive liberation of the craftsman class, which had been at first more or less closely dependent on the state.

Social disturbances

The three classes of family with a hereditary profession instituted by Hung-wu thus began to break up by the beginning of the fifteenth century. The phenomenon was not confined to the army families and the much less numerous craftsmen families; the peasant families (*min-hu*), too, were not slow in escaping from their original status. Crushed by taxation and all kinds of burdens, robbed of his land by the rich, the former small landowner became a wandering peasant (*t'ao-min*), ready to turn to smuggling, the clandestine working of mines or piracy, unless he tilled the land of others. In some regions most peasant families sought to supplement their meagre resources with neighbouring activities — small trading, peddling, handicrafts.

The social troubles of the fifteenth and sixteenth centuries seem to have been caused mainly by the general instability in the professions and the multiplication of the number of uprooted people seeking new means of livelihood — particularly mining, smuggling, and piracy. There were doubtless a number of rebellions of a more traditional type: for example, the insurrections directed at I-tu, in Shantung, in 1420 by a sort of visionary called T'ang Sai-erh who claimed to be 'mother of the Buddha' (*fo-mu*) and whose troops attacked the towns of south-eastern Shantung. One could also mention the numerous risings of non-Chinese peoples — Thais, Tibeto-Burmese, Miao and Yao — in the south-western provinces since the beginning of the dynasty. There was sometimes a connection between these risings and rebellions led by the Chinese peasantry: in 1516 one P'u Fa-e roused the Tibeto-Burmese minorities of Szechwan by proclaiming the coming of Maitreya, the Bodhisattva-Messiah. There was nothing very new in all this. On the other hand, the advance of piracy on the coast and the insurrections provoked by the government's hesitant policy in the field of mining were typical of the Ming period and bear witness to the economic changes that occurred in the fifteenth and sixteenth centuries, as do the revolts by craftsmen in the towns from the end of the sixteenth century onwards. In order to prevent the working of iron and copper mines and the clandestine manufacture of arms, the Mongols had forbidden entry into certain mountainous regions. This policy was continued by the Ming dynasty's founder, but it was not applied everywhere or always with the same firmness. Sometimes the mines were open to private development, at others it was forbidden to work them, and in the latter case the government might use troops to enforce its decision. Threatened with expulsion, the miners would band together in the mountains to resist the government troops.

It could happen that the recalcitrant miners would join forces with a peasant revolt, as for example at the time of the big rebellion of Teng Mao-ch'i in 1448–49, on the borders of Chekiang and Fukien. The over-population of the plains and valleys of northern Fukien, where waves of immigrants had succeeded each other since the eleventh century, and the shortage of land, had encouraged the development of craft activities on the fringe of the traditional rice-growing: sugar-cane, indigo, tea, lichees, paper, grass-cloth, and iron enriched business men who acquired the peasant lands. The contrast between a class of rich landowners who lived in town and a class of wretched tenant farmers, overwhelmed by public and private burdens, created the explosive situation which was at the root of the rebellion. Teng Mao-ch'i's forces soon joined up with those of the rebellious miners of the silver mines on the border between Chekiang and Fukien. The miners were led by Yeh Tsung-liu. The insurrections spread and grew stronger, thanks to the conquest of townships and cities and to the capture of arms depots. They were not a mere explosion of despair but a revolutionary movement whose leaders were very much aware of the links between the economic and social situation in their region, the centralized, authoritarian political system of the dynasty and the inevitable complicity of the government with the local gentry.

During the course of the years 1450–58 the veto on the clandestine development of the mining areas became less strict, particularly in the upper Han valley, where immigrants were numerous. Finally the government tried to react and repression unleashed a series of insurrections. A million and a half people were expelled or killed. The same phenomenon recurred in 1476. Another example of these rebellions by clandestine miners is provided by the insurrections which occurred in 1565 in the mountainous regions between Chekiang, Anhwei, and Kiangsi, which had already suffered from the incursions of pirates in the middle of the sixteenth century.

Changes in the economy

At the end of the fourteenth century, when the Chinese economy was still suffering from the destruction caused by the fighting against the Mongols and by the civil wars, most transactions were carried out in kind and the bulk of the state's resources came from the deliveries of cereals required of the peasantry. However, Ming China still went on issuing paper money, as had been the practice since the eleventh century, and the state sought to impose the use of promissory notes by various different measures: the redemption of copper coins with notes in 1394, a veto on the use of silver and gold in business transactions in 1403, the payment of civil servants in promissory notes, and so on. But all these efforts turned out to be ineffective. The paper money, which was not convertible, depreciated in value as quickly as it had done under the Mongols. The promissory note with a nominal value in 1375 of one thousand copper coins or a *liang* of silver was worth three to four times less a few years later and a thousand times less than a *liang* of silver in 1445. The use of paper money could only be enforced at the price of injustices and arbitrary acts on the part of the state and its agents. So although the notes remained in circulation until about 1573 the issues had to be suspended in 1450 and afterwards were seldom resumed. Finally, when the very existence of the empire was threatened by popular rebellions and its economy was in danger of collapsing, the state had recourse on one last occasion to promissory notes. Notes – the last to be printed in China before the bank notes of the modern period – were to be issued between 1643 and the capture of Peking by Li Tzu-ch'eng in the following year. From the start of the Manchu empire it was to be an established dogma that recourse to paper money was the sign of a bad administration. So ended in China an institution that China had been the first country in the world to adopt. Its history in that country reveals a fundamental contradiction: the contradiction between a state economy and a commercial activity which it could not control and which overflowed it everywhere. The belief in the effectiveness of authoritarian measures for fixing the value of means of payment, a belief imposed by a long tradition of state economic activity, was to be completely contradicted by the general triumph of silver money.

By the beginning of the fifteenth century the use of ingots of silver began to be adopted in certain commercial regions that imported silver, such as Kwangtung, where taxes were already paid in this currency. By 1423 this method of payment had evidently spread to the lower Yangtze, for in that year the government decided that for the purpose of paying taxes a *liang* (or *tael* – a Malay term adopted by Europeans) of thirty-six grammes of silver was equivalent to four *shih* (or about two hundred and forty litres) of cereals. The use of silver gained ground everywhere during the second half of the fifteenth century. The following items were paid in silver: tribute from the provinces from 1465 onwards, the taxes of the salt producers from 1475, and the taxes exempting craftsmen from their periods of compulsory labour in 1485. From 1486–1500 onwards it was also agreed that the peasantry could be exempted from certain corvées by the payment of taxes in silver.

It must therefore be accepted that the amount of silver in circulation increased considerably during the course of the fifteenth century. This is probably explained by the clandestine trade with Japan, the main exporter of silver, and by the progress in local production. But this transformation of the economy was to be accentuated at the end of the sixteenth century with the influx of silver from America after the establishment of the Spaniards in the Philippines in 1564–65 and after the foundation of Manila in 1571. Increasing imports were to be joined towards the same time by the effects of the 'mining fever' of 1590–1605, when for some time the fixed tax on mines was replaced by a tax on production.

This process of evolution in the monetary economy seems to have had important consequences and its effects made themselves fully felt in the sixteenth century. First of all, it was at the root of the fiscal reforms carried out between 1530 and 1581 and systematized round about 1570–80 under the name of the 'single lash-of-the-whip method' (*i-t'iao pien-fa*). These reforms aimed at simplifying fiscal practices the complexities of which had become the source of innumerable abuses, but they also sanctioned the general use in the Chinese economy of the ingot and of silver coins imported from America. After their adoption almost all duties and taxes were to be paid in silver. We can glimpse the many consequences of this liberation of the economy on society.

External dangers

In the middle of the sixteenth century, from about 1540 to about 1560, China suffered the combined attacks of the Mongols on her northern frontiers and of pirates on all her coasts. These external pressures, which endangered her independence, seem to have been caused by a policy of restrictions on trade which, in the case of maritime relations, seems to be in contradiction with a big expansion of commercial activity.

The Mongol offensives

The Mongol thrust of 1438–49 had put an end to the period of Chinese expansion towards the north and ended in a sort of *status quo*. The thrust which started about 1540 and attained its greatest intensity in 1550–52 was much more serious and revealed the progress made by the steppe tribes towards unification. A new nomad empire threatened to come into existence and the Manchus were to have to struggle hard in the seventeenth century and the first half of the eighteenth to remove this ever-present danger. The offensives of the middle of the sixteenth century were led by a Mongol chief who seems to have been made of the stuff of the great conquerors. This leader was Altan Khan (or Anda Khan) (1507–82), whose grandfather, Dayan Khan (*c.* 1464–*c.* 1532), had succeeded in uniting under his authority the Tatar tribes and in dominating Mongolia from 1482 to about 1525. At the beginning of the Chia-ching era (1522–66) Altan Khan increased his incursions into Shansi and the Peking area. In one single month in 1542 he massacred or took prisoner 200,000 men, captured a million head of cattle and horses, burnt down several thousand dwellings, and devastated vast areas of cultivated land. In 1550 he besieged Peking for three days and in the following year obtained the opening of horse-fairs at Ta-t'ung, in the extreme north of Shansi, and at Hsüan-hua, to the north-east of Peking. In 1552, with the help of Chinese rebels, he seized control of part of Shansi and in Outer Mongolia occupied the old capital, Karakorum. In an effort to extend his authority to the whole of central Asia, Altan Khan gained control of Tsinghai in 1559–60, crushed the Kirghiz and Kazakhs in 1572 and penetrated into Tibet in 1573–78. He accepted a peace treaty with the Ming emperor in 1570 and a *modus vivendi* between the Mongols and the Chinese was established from 1573 onwards. But fresh dangers were soon to make their appearance in the north-east: the Japanese penetrated Korea at the end of the sixteenth century, and a new power came into being at the beginning of the seventeenth in the regions north of Peking. This new power was the Jürchen, who were soon to take the name of Manchus.

Piracy

In the middle of the sixteenth century China had to face a grave danger from the sea: the attacks of Japanese pirates, known by the name of Wokou (*wo,* 'dwarf', was an old term used to denote the Japanese), reached their greatest intensity between 1540 and 1565, and the most critical period fell in the years 1553–55, immediately after the most dangerous Mongol attacks led by Altan Khan. Piracy was doubtless not a novelty at that time; it seems to have flourished almost uninterruptedly throughout Chinese history and was practised by all the maritime peoples of South-East Asia—Koreans, Chinese from the coastal provinces, Vietnamese, Malays, Sumatrans, Japanese. Thus the term 'Wokou' should not be taken too literally, even if from the end of the fourteenth century to the beginning of the sixteenth Japanese may have formed the bulk of the pirates. The truth is that the general term 'Japanese pirates' covered a cosmopolitan collection of people whose activities were extremely varied. Among them were *ronin* (sort of mercenary knights), dependants of the daimio Matsudaira, and former traders and sailors of the Chinese coast. One of the Wokou leaders in the middle of the sixteenth century was a Chinese from Anhwei by the name of Wang Chih. A big merchant as well as a pirate, he traded with Japan, Luzon, Vietnam, Siam, and Malacca, devoting himself to smuggling sulphur (used for the manufacture of explosives), silks, and brocades. Installed in the islands off the south of Kyushu, he was so much feared that he was nicknamed 'the king who purges the seas' (*Ching-hai-wang*). Drawn by a trick to Hangchow, he was executed there in 1557. But humbler people were also to be found in the ranks of the pirates – smugglers on a smaller scale, sea captains of Chinese or foreign origin, boatmen, and sailors (*ch'uan-min*) who plied between the coast and the almost desert islands which served as ports of call, stores, or lairs. Finally, this piracy, which was closely associated with the trade in contraband goods, found numerous accomplices on the mainland – shipowners and merchants, gentry, and sometimes even officials of the imperial civil service.

But there had been a perceptible process of evolution since the end of the fourteenth century, when piratical activities seem to have been mainly connected with the struggles between the founder of the Ming dynasty and his rivals. Some of Hung-wu's opponents probably took refuge in the Japanese islands and there joined up with Japanese pirates. Among them there may have been former supporters of Fang Kuo-chen (1319–74), a dubious character who put his money simultaneously on the Mongol occupiers and the resistance movements, and whose troops were smugglers and pirates of the coast of Chekiang. Japanese pirates (Wokou) are reported in Korea in 1367 and 1371. Some of them ventured as early as this as far as the Yangtze estuary and pillaged the towns and countryside of the island of Ch'ung-ming, the Soochow area or, further south, the coast of Chekiang and Fukien. Thus the threat made itself felt right from the early days of the dynasty and the first defence measures were taken at that same time. A navy was formed, the naval command was unified, and the coasts of Shantung, Kiangsu, and Chekiang were fortified. Thanks to these arrangements, to Ming diplomatic activity in Japan, and to the Ming supremacy at sea, the pirates' attacks seem to have been reduced in the first decades of the fourteenth century. However, they never ceased completely, and one of the proofs of the importance attached to them by the Ming government is the actual organization of the armies: one of their main tasks was the defence of the coastal regions from the peninsula of Liaotung to Kwangtung. It was not

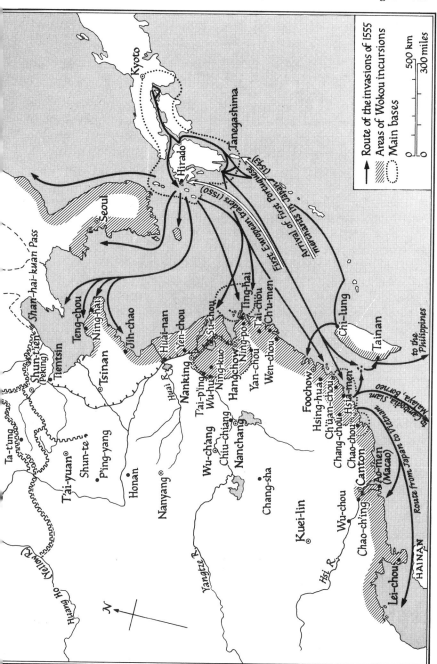

Map 22 Wokou incursions into eastern China

a matter simply of defending the strategic areas of Peking and Manchuria but of hunting the pirates down and of defending inland areas against their raids.

Nevertheless piracy was to expand on an unprecedented scale in the sixteenth century and it seems possible to detect the causes of this phenomenon. It seems basically to have been linked to a clear increase at this period in maritime trade on all the seas of East Asia, from Japan to Indonesia. The Ming emperors met this increase with a policy of restriction which lacked continuity and firmness and was based no doubt in principle on strategic as well as economic considerations. A planned state economy necessarily leads to such complications abroad when the controls cannot be sufficiently effective. It was almost impossible to watch the two or three thousand miles of coastline where clandestine trading was going on with the help of the islands and with the complicity of a large number of people at different levels of society. The same difficulties were to recur with the contraband activities of the Europeans in the first half of the nineteenth century. There was a big gap between the official regulations and the reality of the commercial situation; the restrictions imposed on trade might lead us to suppose that China was isolated at the very time when maritime trade was most intense.

Official relations with Japan could only be conducted through the port of Ning-po, at the north-eastern tip of Chekiang; Foochow was reserved for trade with the Philippines (a similar role had been assumed by Ch'üan-chou between 1368 and 1374 and again after 1403 in the Yung-le era); and Canton, the third port to possess an Office of Merchant Shipping (*shih-po-ssu*), was singled out for links with the Indo-Chinese peninsula and Indonesia. However, private trading went on all along the Chinese coast, openly or clandestinely according to the prevailing regulations. For example, the very busy port of Hai-ch'eng, near Hsia-men (Amoy) traded with Japan and the Ryukyu Islands as well as with Malacca and the Moluccas (between Celebes and New Guinea). Of all the trades which intensified in the seas of East Asia in the sixteenth century, possibly the most important was that between Japan and the Chinese coast; it dealt mainly in gold, silver, copper, and silks. This would be one explanation of the renewed activity of the 'Japanese pirates' at this period.

However, another factor seems to have contributed to the development of piracy. This was the economic and social changes in China itself and the aggravation of the situation of the least favoured classes. Smuggling and piracy looked all the more attractive because the poverty was so great and the possible profits so big. As we have seen, they formed activities of the same order as the more or less clandestine exploitation of the mines, and the hesitations of the imperial government, alternately tolerant and intransigent, did as much to expand piracy as it did to provoke miners' rebellions.

The immediate causes of the increase in attacks by the Wokou in the middle of the sixteenth century were the deterioration in official relations with Japan and the efforts of the Ming government at that time to put a brake on clandestine trade. From the Yung-le era (1403–24) onwards, Japanese embassies had been very strictly regulated; one single embassy every ten years was permitted, the number of ships being limited to two and the number of envoys to two hundred persons. These figures had been raised to three ships and three hundred persons after 1432, but they were in fact often exceeded, the embassies being more frequent than the regulations allowed. In spite of the suspensions decreed by the Ming, there were seventeen Japanese embassies in the years following 1432 and the volume of official trade seems to have been fairly considerable. On the occasion of these embassies the goods imported from Japan included tens of thousands of sabres on each voyage, sulphur, copper to the tune of hundreds of thousands of Chinese pounds, wood for dyes, fans, and so on. As for the return cargo, it consisted of silks, books, paintings, and copper coins.

It is worth pointing out the importance of these embassies for the history of Chinese influences in Japan during the Ming period. These missions included numerous Japanese Buddhist monks who were sometimes entrusted with official duties. Often cultivated men, these priests were interested not only in Buddhism but in the arts and in Chinese secular literature and philosophy. Up to 1403 they were allowed complete freedom to travel about China and to stay there, and even in the Yung-le era they were still authorized to remain for a whole year. Thanks to the embassies, over a hundred known Japanese monks were thus able to come to China in the fifteenth and sixteenth centuries, visiting, on the way from Ning-po to Peking, Hangchow, Soochow, Nanking, the valley of the Huai and Tientsin, and making contact with Chinese literati. Chinese Buddhist monks were also often sent to Japan with Chinese embassies, and they helped to spread the influence of contemporary Chinese culture in Japan. There was the case of a rich Chinese merchant by the name of Sung Su-ch'ing (1496–1523), a native of Chekiang, who, after trading with Japan and settling down there in 1510, formed part of the Japanese embassy which arrived in Ning-po in 1523. It was partly thanks to these official relations and through Buddhist monks that Chinese books, calligraphy, and paintings were preserved in Japan.

However, relations between Ming China and Japan were to deteriorate from 1522 onwards, the year in which the central government, faced with a recrudescence of attacks by pirates, decided to end the tolerant attitude which it had adopted during most of the fifteenth century. In the following year a dispute broke out at Ning-po between two Japanese embassies which both claimed official status. The one which the Chinese authorities refused to recognize pillaged the town, and these riots strengthened the hand of those in favour of firmness. In 1530 permission for the Japanese to send missions to Ning-po was withdrawn. From that moment onwards piracy made rapid progress, and more and more recruits began to come from China itself. The pirates' principal bases were in the Chou-shan (Chusan) Islands off the north-east coast of Chekiang, in the Hsia-men (Amoy) and Ch'üan-chou area, in the Ch'ao-chou area (north-east Kwangtung), and in the southern islands of the Japanese archipelago. The whole Chinese coast from northern Shantung to western Kwangtung was ravaged to a distance of sixty miles inland. In the rich and thickly populated area south of the Yangtze the pirates penetrated as far as Nanking and the southern part of the province of Anhwei. Coastal defence was so badly organized that the government was reduced to requisitioning fishing boats. It was only after the devastations and massacres of 1553–55 that the counter-offensive began to take shape. Relative calm was restored on the coast of Chekiang in 1556, and in Fukien in the following year, as a result of the offensive launched by the general Hu Tsung-hsien. But the Chinese coast was not more or less freed from piracy until after the operations led by Yü Ta-yu (1503–79) and Ch'i Chi-kuang (1528–88) in the years 1560–70.

The destruction caused by the pirates' attacks in the middle of the sixteenth century seems to have been very considerable. But the memory of the dangers incurred at that time also strengthened an old tendency to supervise foreigners and to restrict private trade.

Chapter 20

The Beginnings of Modern China and the Crisis at the End of the Ming Dynasty

Before the upheavals of the twentieth century, the three great turning points in the history of the Chinese world were situated at the junction of the Neolithic and Bronze ages, with the appearance of writing, the discovery of alloys, and the use of the cart with a shaft; at the time of the 'state' revolution of the third century B.C. — the age of the spread of iron casting and of armies of peasant infantry; and finally round about A.D. 1000, a time particularly fruitful in technical progress which saw the start of skilled rice-growing, the big junk, and the mariner's compass, the appearance of new weapons, printing, and so on — and also a kind of empire in which centralization met no further obstacle, in which the imperial authority could count on a very extensive class of literati and in which the profession of arms and agricultural activity were henceforth separated. As the social and political system of this 'mandarin' empire became consolidated, it looks as if the Chinese world did not experience any further notable changes; at the most, autocratic tendencies were accentuated after the Mongol interlude. In spite of the disturbances which accompanied the collapse of the Ming dynasty and the establishment of the new Manchu rulers in the middle of the seventeenth century, one may say that it was almost the same kind of state and society which lasted from the end of the eleventh century to the disappearance of the Manchu empire in 1911. But history is not made only of big changes like those which resulted in the ancient monarchy, the unification of the Chinese kingdoms by the state of Ch'in, and the mandarin empire. The changes which occurred in the course of the sixteenth century were clear enough and numerous enough for us to be able to speak of the beginning of a new age at this period. Perhaps one of the most important of these changes, from the point of view of its effects on society, was the generalization of silver as a means of payment. Not only did the quantity of silver in circulation in China increase rapidly during the course of the sixteenth century; it also continued to increase under the Manchus until round about 1820, and silver was to remain, alongside the copper coins which were used for small purchases, the only means of payment in important transactions until the beginning of the twentieth century. The generalization of silver in the sixteenth century coincided with an expansion of seaborne traffic (commerce and piracy) in all the seas of East Asia and with a revival of the towns and of urban activities. The techniques of certain crafts (weaving, porcelain manufacture, and printing in particular) were perfected, and these improvements were to enable China to reassert her position, after the depression of the middle of the seventeenth century, as the biggest exporter of luxury products. It was against this background of economic expansion and urban revival that the first modern European venturers appeared in the seas of East Asia – first the Portuguese and Spaniards, then the Dutch from the beginning of the seventeenth century. It was a phenomenon of no great importance for East Asia, since these newcomers simply joined in the commercial exchanges of the Far East and profited from the prosperity that this part of the world was experiencing; however, it was a phenomenon heralding times to come. Nevertheless China owed these newcomers the first contributions from Europe and America: more efficient firearms, the sweet potato, the ground-nut, tobacco (maize was to come later), and the first pieces of silver brought to the Far East from Manila by the Acapulco galleon. When one adds to all this the new tendencies which began to take shape in intellectual life and were to be confirmed in the seventeenth and eighteenth centuries, and also, secondarily, the first contacts with the science, technology, and religion of Europe round about 1600, we shall perhaps take the view that it is permissible to speak of the beginnings of a modern period in China and East Asia (in Japan, too, the end of the sixteenth century marked a turning point in history). It is true that historians of twentieth century China have acquired the habit of calling it 'modern' as opposed to a 'traditional' China corresponding vaguely to all the previous periods. But this terminology conceals certain value judgements; it implies a more radical break than in fact exists between the present and past of China and it seems to deny, in comparison with the historical evolution of the West, any significance to the evolution of the Chinese world up to our own day.

The urban revival

The generalization of the monetary economy with silver ingots seems to have wrecked the institutional framework erected by the founder of the Ming dynasty, insofar as it caused general mobility in society. It was at the root of the more and more radical changes which occurred from the beginning of the sixteenth century and gathered speed as a result of various different factors.

The upsurge of big business and craft industry

From about 1520 capital, which until then had been attracted to the land, moved away from it towards commercial and craft enterprises. Land prices continued to fall and were to collapse quite suddenly in the last few years of the sixteenth century. The phenomenon was particularly noticeable in the maritime provinces of the south and in the area from Hangchow to north-eastern Kiangsi — everywhere in fact where the monetary economy based on ingots and imported silver coins was in the ascendant. In these regions the agrarian economy declined in proportion to the upsurge of mercantile and craft activities. These areas, which were ones subject to the incursions of the Japanese pirates, were also those where the contraband trade with Japan, the Philippines, Siam, Indonesia, and other places flourished. Now it seems that this trade continued to develop during the sixteenth century, in spite of official vetoes and of the insecurity which prevailed on the coast. Controls and dangers in fact increased the value of the contraband goods. Some merchant ships were equipped to resist the attacks of the imperial navy. Inland, the difficulties of traditional agriculture explain the proliferation of small trades such as peddling, the manufacture of lacquer and bamboo objects, inks, and paint-brushes, and also the commercialization of agricultural produce and the development of industrial crops — cotton, vegetable oils, indigo, sugar-cane, tobacco. The lowest strata of the peasantry, who in some regions emigrated to the mines or joined the piracy and smuggling rings, also moved to the towns, seeking employment in small businesses and handicrafts, working as servants for rich families or as employees of a bureaucracy whose staff was growing continually. Small workshops grew into big enterprises, some of which employed several hundred workers. Peasant women took jobs at Sungchiang, south-west of Shanghai, in the cotton mills. According to contemporary descriptions, in the big workshops the employees were already the anonymous labour force that we regard as characteristic of the industrial age. There was a labour market, differing from one trade to another, in which skilful workers were hired at a high price while the rest formed a mass of wretched labourers who hung around the big workshops waiting to be engaged. In fact by the second half of the sixteenth century some sectors of Chinese craft work already had an industrial character. Such was the case with silk and cotton weaving, porcelain manufacture, and iron and steel production. Among the principal private or public enterprises were those of Ching-te-chen, to the east of Lake P'o-yang, where there were numerous porcelain ovens; Sung-chiang, a big cotton-weaving centre, which could not obtain sufficient cotton locally (huge areas round Sung-chiang and to the north of Hangchow were planted with cotton) but had to obtain part of its raw materials from Honan and Hopei; Soochow, famous for its luxury silks; Wu-hu, upstream from Nanking on the Yangtze, a town which specialized in dyeing; and Ts'u-hsien, in southern Hopei, which had a big concentration of iron foundries. At the end of the sixteenth century there were 50,000 workers in thirty paper factories in Kiangsi.

Chinese silk was sold in Japan at five or six times the price obtainable in China; this explains the size of the trade with the archipelago. Ceramics went off by the boatload to Nagasaki. Tea, bought in Fukien and Chekiang by the Dutch at the beginning of the seventeenth century, began to be exported to northern Europe. If we are to believe Ku Yen-wu (1613–82), the tax of 20 to 30 percent on sea-borne goods covered up to half the expenditure of the state at the end of the sixteenth century.

Technical progress

The numerous technical treatises which appeared at the end of the Ming period reveal the clear progress made in the procedures employed in certain crafts: silk looms with three or four shuttle-winders, improvements in cotton looms (cotton garments had come to be generally worn since the fourteenth century), procedures for printing wood blocks in three and four colours, and five in the Wan-li era (1573–1619), remarkable progress in publishing, the invention at Sung-chiang of an alloy of copper and lead for casting movable characters, procedures for manufacturing white sugar and icing sugar. We are all familiar with the astonishing results obtained in ceramics in the Ming period and especially in the Hsüan-te and Ch'eng-hua eras (1426–87), before the requirements of mass production, partly exported by sea, led to a certain decline in the quality and beauty of the pieces.

But technical progress was not limited to handicrafts; it also extended to agriculture, which was thereby led to diversify itself. The treatises on

Plate 48.   Ming wine ewer, blue and
white, Chia-ching, 1522–66

Plate 49.   Ming dish, sixteenth century

agricultural techniques which appeared at the end of the Ming period describe new machines for working the soil, for irrigation, sowing seed, and the treatment of agricultural products. Methods of improving the soil, the selection of new strains, and above all the introduction of new crops caused general progress in agriculture at the end of the Ming epoch. First the Portuguese, then the Spaniards, who traded in the ports of the southern coast during the sixteenth century, introduced plants from the New World. One of these, the ground-nut, was cultivated as early as 1530–40 in the sandy soils of the Shanghai area. In the nineteenth century it was to become one of the basic foods of the inhabitants of Shantung. The sweet potato, mentioned for the first time in Yunnan in 1563, seems to have reached China both by the south-west and by sea. It was adopted enthusiastically at the end of the sixteenth century and the beginning of the seventeenth, for it was an improvement on the Chinese taro. Satisfied, like the ground-nut, with poor and badly irrigated soil, in the eighteenth century it was to become a food equal in importance to rice for the inhabitants of Fukien and Kwangtung. Another plant which was known in earlier days and seems to have reached China by the road from Burma, sorghum, also spread widely in the fifteenth and sixteenth centuries. Maize, the only American plant, apart from tobacco, whose spread seems to have been less rapid than that of the ground-nut and the sweet potato, began to become more popular from the early seventeenth century onwards. It was to have a big future in China.

Complementary crops which could be grown on poor, undeveloped land, these new plants, the harvests from which helped to bridge the winter gap and to enrich the diet, did not yet cause the big agricultural revolution which was to occur in the eighteenth century, but it is reasonable to suppose that the effects of their introduction already began to make themselves felt at the end of the Ming period.

Finally, it should be noted that a sort of regional economic specialization made itself apparent in the sixteenth century. From the end of the Neolithic Age down to the seventh and eighth centuries the great productive region had been the wheat- and millet-growing area which extended in a circular arc from the valley of the Wei to the lower reaches of the Yellow River and spread out eastward into the whole of the central plain. From the ninth or tenth century pre-eminence passed to the rice-growing regions of the lower Yangtze, of the Huai valley, and of northern Chekiang. Capable of feeding a more and more numerous population and at the same time of furnishing North China with part of its surplus, these regions played a cardinal role under the Sung dynasty, in the period of the Mongol empire and down to the first half of the Ming period. However, during the course of the fifteenth and sixteenth centuries the role of great productive and rice-exporting region was to pass to the two provinces of the middle Yangtze, Hunan and Hupei, while the areas south of the lower Yangtze turned more and more to commerce and manufacturing.

Contrary to the indications of the Ming censuses, which after the Hung-wu era (1368–98) were the worst in Chinese history, all the evidence leads us to think that the population of China increased constantly between the end of the fourteenth century and the middle of the seventeenth. Some historians have felt justified in putting forward the figures of about 70 million for the beginning of the dynasty and of 130 for the end. These figures are not improbable and the increase seems to fit in with the economic expansion and agricultural progress of the sixteenth century.

A new urban, mercantile society

The epoch from 1560 onwards which succeeded the period of the Mongol offensives and the attacks of the Japanese pirates was one of the most fruitful in the history of the Ming dynasty. The whole first part of the Wan-li era (1573–1619), from 1573 to 1582, was particularly prosperous, but the vitality and contradictions of the society of the end of the dynasty also give the whole final period, down to the Manchu invasion, a singular interest. The rapid process of evolution which set in at this point in the history of the Chinese world was reflected in social changes: the formation of a proletariat and of an urban middle class, the transformation of rural life, which was permeated by the influence of the towns, and the rise of a class of important merchants and business men. The money-changers and bankers of Shansi, who had branches in Peking, the rich traders of Lake Tung-t'ing in Hunan, the shipowners, enriched by sea-borne trade, of Ch'üan-chou and Chang-chou in southern Fukien, and above all the great merchants of Hsin-an (the present She-hsien, in southern Anhwei) formed a new class calling to mind the business men of the early days of capitalism in Europe—although the mentalities and social and political conditions were different. The richest owed their wealth to their involvement in a state economy and played the part of suppliers to the armies. They dealt in products consumed on a large scale—rice, salt, cereals, cloth. In the Manchu epoch the bankers of Shansi were to extend their activities to Outer Mongolia and central Asia, sharing the trade and financial operations with the merchants of Hsin-an who were to dominate the whole Yangtze basin.

However, this process of evolution was also reflected in the upsurge and renewal of the various literary genres, of thought, and of knowledge.

From the end of the sixteenth century onwards it was accompanied by a series of political crises, and in the end it was to be compromised by the Manchu invasion and the occupation of the country.

The crisis period of the last fifty years

After the alert caused by the Mongol offensives and the attacks of the Japanese pirates in the middle of the sixteenth century, a relative improvement made itself felt as the external dangers faded away. The emperor who reigned under the reign-name of Lung-ch'ing (1567–73) was an enlightened autocrat, concerned about social justice and reforms. The policy inaugurated during his reign was continued at the beginning of the Wan-li era (1573–1619) — reduction of court expenses, defence of the small farmers exploited by the big landowners, regulation of the course of the Yellow River and the Huai. An honest and effective administrator, P'an Chi-hsün (1521–95), was in charge of the river's dykes and of those of the Grand Canal for twenty-nine years. All the measures of economic restoration taken at this time were mainly inspired by a high official called Chang Chü-cheng (1525–82), who in fact governed the country during the minority of Wan-li. But on the death of Chang Chü-cheng in 1582 the eunuchs regained the power which they had lost and once again there was no proper control and a rapid decline in the state's finances.

Financial crisis

The imperial palace spent money like water. One single example will suffice to illustrate the ostentation of the court: the construction of the emperor Wan-li's tomb between 1584 and 1590 — the tomb was discovered by chance and excavated in 1956–59 — cost eight million *liang*. The bricks were brought from Lin-ch'ing in north-western Shantung by the Grand Canal, the stones came from a mountain in the same province, and the trees used for the framework were cedars from Szechwan and the south-western provinces. But on top of the court's sumptuary expenses soon came those caused by the appearance of new dangers from outside. During one and the same year — 1592 — Po-p'ai, a Mongol chief of the Ning-hsia region, near the upper reaches of the Yellow River, seceded, the ethnic minorities of the Tsun-i region in Kweichow revolted, and the Japanese landed in Korea under the command of the shogun Hideyoshi Toyotomi (1536–98). The long operations conducted by the Ming regime against the Japanese troops between 1595 and 1598 ended in China's favour, but they completely exhausted the treasury. When, twenty years later, the Jürchen prince Nurhaci, who had assisted the Chinese armies in their struggle against the Japanese invasion, turned against the Ming, China was no longer in a position to offer effective resistance in the north-eastern provinces.

The war in Korea, from 1593 to 1598, cost the treasury twenty-six million *liang*. Yet the end of this war did not lighten the burden of military expenditure at the beginning of the seventeenth century, for the army of the late Ming period was a mercenary army with the double disadvantage of being overblown and ineffective. Its numbers had doubled since the end of the fourteenth century, but the increase corresponded to a decline in the quality of the troops. Matteo Ricci, in his account of China, written at the beginning of the seventeenth century, took a severe view of the soldiery of the time. 'All those under arms', he writes, 'lead a despicable life, for they have not embraced this profession out of love of their country or devotion to their king or love of honour and glory, but as men in the service of a provider of employment.' According to Ricci, the horses of the imperial army were poor nags which the mere whinnying of the steppe horses was sufficient to put to flight. The armies were the refuse dump of society and consisted of idlers, rascals, jailbirds, and highwaymen.

Another cause of the financial deficit was the allowances paid to relatives of the imperial family. Hung-wu's twenty-four sons had been deprived of all power in order to reduce to the minimum the risk of usurpation, but in return they had been endowed with extensive estates, owned pasturages in the northern provinces, had personal guards of 3000 to 19,000 men and received large salaries. This imperial nobility had grown from generation to generation, so much so that by the end of the Ming period it was a heavy charge on the budget. The Prince of Ch'ing-ch'eng alone had had ninety-four direct descendants. Under Wan-li (1573–1619) there were 45 princes of the first rank receiving annual incomes of 10,000 *shih* (the equivalent in money of about 600 tonnes of cereals), and also 23,000 nobles of lesser rank. Of the tax revenue from Shansi and Honan (7,400,000 *shih*), more than half (4,040,000) was devoted to paying these allowances. During the course of the years 1573–1628 this situation was to lead to a suspension of marriage permits for the princes and of grants of titles of nobility.

The financial difficulties encountered by the Ming government from the end of the sixteenth century onwards led it to take measures which for the most part only aggravated the social malaise. In order to compensate for a deficit due to a desertion of the land which seems to have grown extensive at this period, it raised commercial taxes, established customs posts on the Yangtze and the Grand Canal and made the taxes on the peasantry still more crushing. The scandalous exactions of the palace eunuchs, appointed commissioners of mines and commercial taxes from 1596 onwards, provoked here and there explosions of anger. At Lin-ch'ing, in Shantung, 45 drapers out of 73 and 21 satin shops out of 33 were forced to shut at the beginning of the seventeenth century. Revolts by workmen in the towns multiplied. Between 1596 and 1626 there were urban riots—sometimes caused by the arrest of honest officials—almost every year in the regions which until then had been the busiest: Soochow, Sung-chiang, Hangchow, Peking, and all the big centres of craftsmanship. In 1603 the miners of the private mines of Men-t'ou-kou, thirty kilometres east of Peking, made a protest march to the capital. The discontent, which was aggravated by economy measures and the dismissal of state employees as well as by the rise in taxes and duties, was to end in the big insurrections of 1627–44. These were preceded in 1621–29 by rebellions of the non-Chinese population, caused on the borders of Yunnan, Szechwan, and Kweichow by forced recruitment to the armies.

Political crisis

The years 1615–27 were marked by the serious conflict between a group of upright civil servants and loyalist intellectuals on the one hand and the insolent power of the eunuchs on the other, a power based on their familiarity with the emperor, on complicities gained inside and outside the palace, and on the passivity of an administration rendered docile by corruption and fear. The party which united these men of very different origins formed round one of the numerous private academies (*shu-yüan*) which at the end of the Ming period were often centres of free literary and political discussion. The academy of Tung-lin at Wu-hsi, in Kiangsu, went back to the twelfth century and had been founded by a scholar–civil servant of Fukien called Yang Shih (1053–1135). Revived in 1604, it had become one of the principal centres of the opposition. Its members, for the most part independent literati or former civil servants who had been dismissed, cultivated the anti-absolutist ideas of the *Meng-tzu* and turned against the court and the government the political and moral principles of the Confucian tradition. This approach was constantly adopted in Chinese history down to the Manchu epoch. One would be wrong to see in Confucianism only an official ideology in the service of the government; it was just as often a weapon in the hand of the opposition. The adherents of the Tung-lin took their stand first of all on the ground of the legitimacy and regularity of certain practices.

At the end of the Wan-li era three affairs closely concerning the imperial palace roused passions and provoked a crisis. In 1615 there was an incident which was seen as an unsuccessful attempt on the life of the crown prince; in 1620 there was the suspicious death of the emperor T'ai-ch'ang, who was thought to have been poisoned by the eunuchs; and in the same year there was the resistance of the eunuchs to the removal of a former favourite. Some people already see in these affairs the hand of the formidable eunuch Wei Chung-hsien. History recounts that this Wei Chung-hsien (1568–1627) was a good-for-nothing who, to pay his gambling debts, had had himself castrated, sure of finding a job in the palace. Although illiterate, he was appointed to the Office of Rites thanks to the support of the lady Ko, nurse of the future emperor T'ien-ch'i (1621–27). In 1621, on the accession of the new emperor, he was put in charge of the imperial tombs. The members of the Tung-lin, whose authority had asserted itself for some time during the Wan-li era, returned to power at the beginning of the T'ien-ch'i era, but their influence did not last long. Wei Chung-hsien organized his network of accomplices and soon controlled the whole adminstration, thanks to his secret police. From 1625 until the death of the emperor T'ien-ch'i there was a terrible repression of the members and supporters of the Tung-lin, many of whom were executed in prison. A list of over seven hundred 'conspirators'—high and middle-rank officials—was published, which made it possible to carry out a general persecution. The academies which served as centres for the opposition were closed. Meanwhile Wei Chung-hsien had the idea of putting up temples everywhere in his own honour and in that of his accomplices. These were the 'temples to the living' (*sheng-tz'u*). Each of these buildings, the first of which was erected on the shores of the Western Lake at Hangchow in honour of the governor of Chekiang, P'an Ju-chen, was the occasion of fabulous expenditure. To increase his own power, Wei Chung-hsien multiplied the number of complimentary appointments and fictitious posts, while corruption spread like a plague. This terrible eunuch was assassinated on the accession of the last Ming emperor (1628–44) and the Tung-lin was rehabilitated. There was to be a resurgence of the Tung-lin at Soochow in the shape of the 'Party of Renewal' (*Fu-she*), also known as the 'Little Tung-lin', which presented itself as a politico-literary circle. It was to number over two thousand members, about a quarter of them civil servants, but after exerting some influence its members were in their turn kept out of power.

The crisis of the years 1615–27 had profound political, moral, and intellectual repercussions on the generations of that epoch. It led to the rejection of a dominant philosophy—that of Wang Yang-ming (1472–1528)—which was too detached from concrete political problems, encouraged people to question an absolutist regime which was in contradiction with the tradition of the literati, and finally created a moral disarray which was the prelude to the even deeper one to be caused by the Manchu invasion.

Popular insurrections

On top of the political crisis and the dramatic financial deficit there came, from 1627 onwards, the threat of the Jürchen in Mongolia and Liaoning and the popular rebellions whose spread was to cause the fall of the dynasty.

In 1627–28 a series of bad harvests due to persistent droughts caused a serious famine in northern Shensi. Peasant troops, joined first by deserters from Manchuria and then by the soldiers of the staging posts discharged for economy reasons in 1629, ravaged the countryside and attacked the towns. Opposed in Shensi, the insurgents moved in 1632 to the neighbouring province of Shansi and went on pillaging into Hopei. Soon other provinces were affected — Honan, Anhwei, southern Shensi — the rebel troops withdrawing or spreading out as circumstances dictated. In spite of momentary successes, the government armies turned out to be incapable of putting an end to this endemic rebellion, which as the years went by increased in numbers of adherents, in power, and in organization. The multitude of leaders of small bands, the rivalries and anarchy of the early days were replaced in 1636 by a certain unity of command under the aegis of two men who were to remain at the head of the insurgents until the Manchu invasion. These two were Li Tzu-ch'eng (1606–45), a former shepherd who had entered the postal relay service and who directed the rebellion in North China, and Chang Hsien-chung (1606–47), a soldier from Yenan who controlled the areas north of the Yangtze.

After 1641 the rebellion's significance changed; firmly entrenched in Honan, Li Tzu-ch'eng now dreamed of overturning the Ming regime. These dynastic ambitions were demonstrated by a first effort at administrative organization. Li Yen, an erstwhile graduate from a rich family of literati, and Niu Chin-hsing, a former candidate in the official competitions, became his political councillors. In 1643 the centre of the rebellion in the north moved to the valley of the Wei in Shensi. In his capital of Hsi-an, rechristened Ch'ang-an, Li Tzu-ch'eng proclaimed in February 1644 the accession of the new dynasty of Ta Shun. In the spring he occupied Ta-t'ung, in northern Shansi. Resistance collapsed everywhere and Li Tzu-ch'eng's armies entered Peking on 24 April. The emperor Ch'ung-chen, abandoned by everyone, strangled himself in the morning of the 25th on the Coal Hill, to the north of the palace. However, a month later Li Tzu-ch'eng was defeated by the Manchu troops, which had been joined by Wu San-kuei, the general entrusted by the Ming with the defence of Peking, in the Shan-hai-kuan area. Retreating across Shansi, Shensi, and the valley of the Han, after losing almost all his troops Li Tzu-ch'eng was finally killed by peasants on the borders of Hupei and Kiangsi.

As for Chang Hsien-chung, after a period of great activity in the provinces of Hupei and Hunan, he had settled in Szechwan. After establishing his capital at Ch'eng-tu, on 9 September 1644 he had proclaimed the foundation of the Great Kingdom of the West. With little talent for acting as head of state, and ruling by means of a reign of terror, he was to meet his end on 2 January 1647 (if we are to believe the most reliable source) to the west of Ch'eng-tu, after being surrounded by the Manchu troops.

The Manchu threat

The situation of the Ming empire just before the invasion explains how it was that the Manchus had little difficulty in entering China and seizing power. Everything favoured them: the general anarchy, the collapse of the public finances, the central government's panic, raised to the highest pitch by the emperor's suicide, the weakness of the armies stationed in Hopei to defend the capital, and finally the divisions among the Chinese themselves and the complicity which the invaders found in part of the population. Many members of the upper classes preferred an alliance — which they hoped would be provisional — with the external enemy to the triumph of the popular rebellions. Some people, long in contact with the future conquerors of China, were even ready to collaborate. The case of Wu San-kuei was not unique, as is shown by the example of another Ming general, Hung Ch'eng-ch'ou (1593–1665). Hung had taken an active part in the struggle against Li Tzu-ch'eng's troops between 1634 and 1638, and had been summoned to defend the capital against the Jürchen threat in 1639. Captured in 1642, he enrolled under the Manchu flag.

In any case, from the strategic point of view, the Manchus had gained the essential ground between the capture of Shenyang (Mukden) and Liaoyang in 1621 and the occupation of the whole of Manchuria as far as Shan-hai-kuan in 1642. In fact the Ming empire's defence system in the north-east was constituted by the three provinces of Hopei, Liaoning, and Shantung (the Liaotung peninsula could be reached by sea from the northern coast of Shantung in twenty-four hours). The alliance with Korea contributed to the security of this region. But this defence system

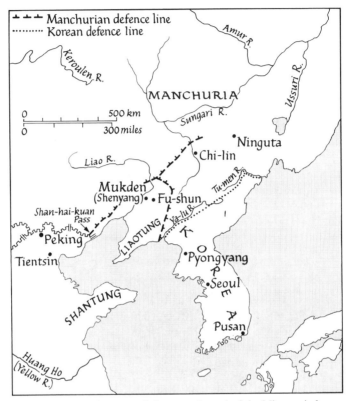

Map 23   The north-eastern defences at the end of the Ming period

was fragile, for no natural barrier blocked the plains of Manchuria, and
the Shan-hai-kuan pass was the only good means of communication between Hopei and Liaoning. To make up for the absence of a natural barrier the Ming had built a defence line which ran from west of the mouth
of the Yalu at K'ai-p'ing, 300 kilometres north of Peking, and another
from Shan-hai-kuan to Chi-lin (Kirin). These 'frontier walls with rows of
willows' (*Liu-t'iao pien-ch'iang*) were formed of ditches and banks
planted with willows intended to stop the Jürchen cavalry. The fall of
these defences and the occupation of the Liao-ho basin put Peking within
the immediate range of the invaders.

Chapter 21

Intellectual Life
in the Ming Age

Prologue

Half a century ago, at a time when research was less advanced, it was considered that the Ming dynasty had been a period of sterility and servile imitation. It is true that the disturbances which occupied most of the fourteenth century led to a serious decline aggravated by the advent of a dynasty whose founder, and most of whose ruling class, came from the people. In the domain of philosophy and the sciences—algebra, astronomy, geography, archaeology, and so on—there was a clear recession from the high levels reached from the eleventh to the thirteenth centuries. Similarly, the fifteenth century was certainly not one of the most innovative and brilliant in the history of China. Learned traditions are the most fragile ones. However, from the beginning of the sixteenth century onwards there was a reawakening of philosophical thinking which grew continually wider in step with the urban revival. The terms 'individualism' and 'anarchism' would doubtless be inadequate to the extent that they make us think of European history, but they give some idea—*mutatis mutandis*—of the innovations of an era in which new tendencies and more traditional currents of thought mingle and clash. Moreover, the end of the sixteenth century and the first half of the seventeenth were marked by a remarkable development of the theatre, the short story, and the novel, and by the upsurge of a semi-learned, semi-popular culture. It was the culture of an urban middle class eager for reading-matter and entertainment, but its influence extended to the lettered classes. Never had the book industry been so prosperous or its products of such good quality. Many of the features regarded as typical of the Manchu epoch appear already: a revival of interest in technical and scientific knowledge (a revival stimulated from the early years of the seventeenth century by the contributions of the first Jesuit missionaries), a passion for rare books and the collection of well-stocked libraries, research into historical phonology, and an interest in textual criticism. Above all, late Ming China rediscovered the importance of the political, social, and economic realities too long neglected by the devotees of a quietist philosophy and of withdrawal into oneself. The continuity through the change of dynasty is quite perceptible.

Thus not only was the Ming epoch far from being a period of stagnation, but the tendencies which made themselves apparent in its last part already herald a China nearer to ourselves. The history of learning, arts, and letters confirms what social and economic history suggests: the modern period in China begins at the end of the Ming age.

Philosophy, science, and literature

The evolution of currents of thought

The period of economic reconstruction and of military and diplomatic expansion that marked the early days of the Ming dynasty was at the same time a period of reinforcement of the neo-Confucian orthodoxy inherited from the eleventh and twelfth centuries and given an honoured position by the Mongol dynasty from 1313 onwards. From this point of view the publication in 1415 of an anthology of the philosophers of the Sung period (the *Hsing-li ta-ch'üan* or *Summa of the Philosophers of Human Nature and of the Principle of Order*) and of two school manuals giving the official interpretations of the Five Classics and of the Four Books (the *Wu-ching ta-ch'üan* and the *Ssu-shu ta-ch'üan*) constituted an important event. These works were to serve as a basis for classical studies and to remain in use until the beginning of the eighteenth century. However, the official interpretations were not always respected in the mandarin competitions. Under the influence of new philosophical currents of thought a clear relaxation occurred during the course of the sixteenth century, and round about 1600 there was often no longer anything orthodox in the scripts of the examination candidates. One must therefore take care not to form a simplistic notion of what is called Confucianism. Moreover, the term 'orthodoxy' does not entirely suit it, for in reality the classics and the commentaries on them do not refer to any dogma, and outside the official competitions, which were tests of an extremely formal character, important divergences are expressed among the literati.

Like their predecessors, the most famous philosophers of the fifteenth and sixteenth centuries had in mind a wisdom which, in principle, was completely disinterested. Moreover a considerable number of them refrained from embarking on the administrative career and may have been put off it by the compromises which it involved and by the autocratic nature of the imperial government, dominated as it was by cliques and by the eunuchs. The tendencies which developed at this time put much less stress on the reading and interpretation of the texts, to which Chu Hsi, the great master of the twelfth century, had attached such importance, than on conduct and moral reform. Such was the case, apart from certain idiosyncrasies of their own, with Wu Yü-pi (1392–1469) and his disciple Hu Chü-jen (1434–84). A strengthening of these tendencies came at the end of the fifteenth century with the Cantonese master Ch'en Hsien-chang (1428–1500), who gave a large place to exercises in quietism. The object was to arrive at absolute spontaneity and perfect accord between the mind and the world, an accord which was the principle of all moral action. From then onwards the influence of Ch'an (Zen) Buddhism, already perceptible in the first neo-Confucian thinkers of the eleventh century, grew stronger and stronger, in spite of more traditional tendencies. Wang Shou-jen (Wang Yang-ming) (1472–1528), who was to exert considerable influence on the whole sixteenth century in China, and also on Japan and Korea, inherited on one side the conceptions of Ch'en Hsien-chang, and defined a new anti-intellectualist philosophy which 'interiorized' the *li,* the principle of order in society and the universe, and rejected any separation between action and knowledge. The central notion of his philosophy is that of 'innate moral knowledge' (*liang-chih*) (the term is borrowed from Mencius), a principle of good which is inherent in the mind before any contamination by egoistic thoughts and desires, and which one must try to rediscover in oneself. It was Wang Yang-ming's teachings that formed the basis for the development of most of the schools of the sixteenth century, though there were many variations in the tendencies of these schools, which consisted of a few dozen, or sometimes several hundred, disciples grouped round one of a large number of masters. The fashion for academic discussions (*chiang-hsüeh*) and the multiplicity of centres of studies endowed with libraries (*shu-yüan* or academies) were characteristic of the age. Some people saw in this multiplication of schools a worrying sign of division; the general harmony of minds was threatened by profound divergences which concerned in particular the most venerable traditions. The further we advance in the sixteenth century, the more independence of mind there is, and the more classical traditions are affected by Buddhist and Taoist influences.

One school in particular is noteworthy for the emphasis which it put on spontaneity and on the rejection of social constraints. Its basic thesis was that no effort is required to attain 'innate knowledge', since this is embodied and present in every man. It was to this school, known as the school of T'ai-chou, founded by a self-educated former salt-worker by the name of Wang Ken (1483–1541), a disciple of Wang Yang-ming, that one of the most famous literati of the end of the sixteenth century belonged. Spurned by some of his contemporaries and an object of opprobrium for posterity, Li Chih (1527–1602) has been rehabilitated in the People's Republic of China because of his denunciation of Confucianism. The author of works which caused a scandal, and in which he called into question the verdicts on historical characters and accused his own age of hypocrisy, Li Chih drew attention to himself by the violence of his attacks and by the eccentricity of his conduct. At the same time he was very representative of his age. He was not alone in his sympathy for Buddhism, his lively interest in the vernacular literature which flourished at the time—he annotated two novels, the *Water Margin* (the *Shui-hu chuan*) and the *Three Kingdoms* (the *San-kuo chih yen-i*)—his defence of the oppressed (the lower classes, women, ethnic minorities), his taste for heroic characters and exceptional individuals, and his attacks on traditional morality. We find similar attitudes among his contemporaries, attitudes which reflect an evolution in thought which it seems legitimate to connect with the social changes of the end of the sixteenth century and with the development of an urban culture in which learned and popular traditions mingled. However, the crisis which began in the last few years of the sixteenth century with the war in Korea and the dispatch into the provinces of palace eunuchs as supervisors of mines and of the commercial taxes was not long in causing a 'rigorist' reaction and the return to a certain degree of orthodoxy.

The deterioration in manners and in the political climate, the advance of corruption, and the irresponsibility of the imperial authority were in fact keenly felt by some of the literati. An attempt at moral reform seemed indispensable to them. Quietism, introspection, withdrawal into oneself, the borrowings from Buddhism, and the syncretist tendencies of the age were in opposition to the true Confucian tradition, which insisted on the social responsibilities of the educated classes. The wise man had to be useful to the world and take everyday realities as the starting-point of his reflections, not walk about with his head in the clouds. Doubtless the break with the sixteenth century was not complete; the fashion for philosophical discussion, the role of the private academies, and the importance of the 'intuitionist' current of thought did not disappear, but the climate was quite different. There was an awakening of conscience on the part of a large portion of the intelligentsia; it wished to exert an effect on political evolution (this was particularly true of the Tung-lin Academy and all the movements connected with it), and it called into question a philosophy which had no end outside itself. There was also a revival of interest in all branches of practical knowledge: agronomy, military techniques, hydraulics, astronomy, mathematics, and so on. This combination of a certain moral strictness with a more scientific turn of mind was to be characteristic of the Manchu epoch, but it already appeared at the end of the Ming dynasty.

The progress of practical knowledge

Ku Yen-wu (1613–82) and the great philologists of the eighteenth century are usually given the credit for having developed a scientific method of textual and historical criticism. In fact this method had antecedents in the sixteenth and at the beginning of the seventeenth century with Mei Cho, who as early as 1543 denounced the apocryphal nature of the version of the *Shang-shu* or Classic of History in ancient characters, and particularly with Ch'en Ti (1541–1617), who was the first to establish rigorous criteria in the field of historical phonetics in his *Researches into the Ancient Rhymes of the Book of Odes* (*Mao-shih ku-yin k'ao*) (1606).

We are indebted to another philologist, Mei Ying-tsu, for the first classification of Chinese characters under 214 radicals — a classification which has remained traditional since his time — in his dictionary, the *Tzu-hui* (1615), which deals with 33,179 written characters. Mathematics suffered a grave decline from the fourteenth century onwards, the learned traditions of North China being completely forgotten, while the popular traditions of the South persisted in the Ming age. It was the translations of Western mathematical works at the beginning of the seventeenth century that reawoke Chinese interest in the science of numbers and brought about the rediscovery of the ancient Chinese mathematical traditions. However, we cannot pass over in silence a discovery which owed nothing to the influence of the Jesuits, since it predated these translations. The imperial prince Chu Tsai-yü (1536–1611), who was passionately interested in mathematics and musicology, was the first person in the world to define the equally tempered scale. He described the principles of it in his *Essence of Music* (*Lü-hsüeh ching-i*), which was probably written between 1584 and 1596, some years before the equally tempered scale appeared in Europe, between 1605 and 1608.

But it was above all in the domain of practical knowledge that the spirit of the age made itself apparent. Numerous works of a scientific or technical character were published at the end of the Ming period. They dealt with almost every branch of knowledge (the pharmacopoeia, medicine, botany, agriculture, craft procedures, geography, and so on) and doubtless bear witness to the progress which had been made in the sixteenth century.

The *Kung-pu ch'ang-ku hsü-chih* (*What Everyone Should Know about the Workshops and Stores of the Ministry of Public Works*) (1615), one of the richest mines of information about Chinese technology, was followed in 1637 by the publication of the *T'ien-kung k'ai-wu,* another illustrated work dealing with agricultural techniques as a whole, weaving, ceramics, iron and steel, river transport, armaments, inks and papers, and so on. Wang Cheng (1571–1644) describes in one of his works numerous agricultural, hydraulic, and military machines of his own invention. He also compiled, in collaboration with the German Jesuit Johann Schreck, *Illustrated Explanations of the Strange Machines of the Far West* (*Yüan-hsi ch'i-ch'i t'u-shuo*). Numerous treatises on agriculture appeared at the end of the Ming period: *Nung-shuo* by Ma I-lung (1490–1571), *Shen-shih nung-shu,* on the agricultural methods of the plains of northern Chekiang (end of Ming period), *Nung-p'u liu-shu* (agriculture and gardening) (1636), and above all the famous work produced by Hsü Kuang-ch'i (1562–1633), the disciple of Matteo Ricci and the translator of European scientific works, the *Nung-cheng ch'üan-shu* (1639), a veritable encyclopaedia of Chinese agricultural techniques. It also contains information about Western hydraulic techniques.

Among the works on medicine (hygiene, dietetics, acupuncture and moxibustion, gynaecology, and so on) and pharmacy published between the beginning of the sixteenth century and the middle of the seventeenth, special mention must be made of the big treatise on botany and on the pharmacopoeia by Li Shih-chen (1518–98), the *Pen-ts'ao kang-mu.* Begun in 1552 and completed after sixteen years of assiduous work in 1578, this vast work, which contains notes on nearly a thousand plants and a thousand animals with medicinal uses, was printed with magnificent plates in 1596. In it is mentioned for the first time a method of smallpox injection which does not differ in principle from the one which was to give birth in the West to the science of immunology.

Military science, on the other hand, did not make much progress. A big treatise on the military art — a sort of seventeenth-century pendant to the famous *Wu-ching tsung-yao,* which appeared under the Sung in the middle of the eleventh century — was published in 1621. This was the *Wu-pei-chih,* by Mao Yuan-i; it is not a very good book. The information

Figure 14 Ming technology. **A.** Sowing machine; **B.** Mill; **C.** Machine for reeling off thread; **D.** Pottery workshop. The pictures are taken from the *T'ien-kung k'ai-wu* (1637)

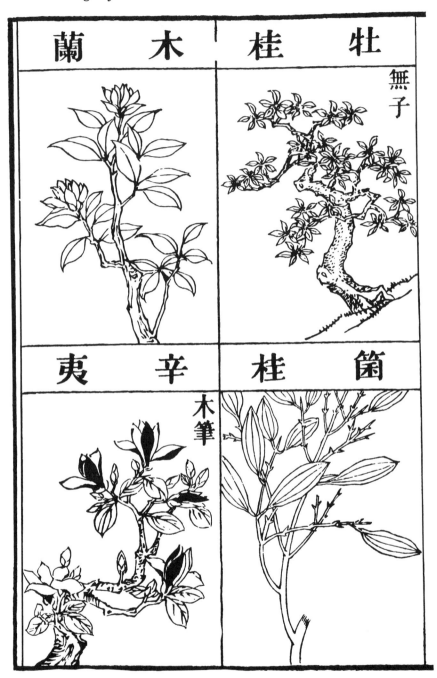

Figure 15   Plate from the *Pen-ts'ao kang-mu*. **Right:** two species of cinnamon. **Left:** two species of magnolia

which it contains on firearms provides the occasion to recall here the history of this kind of weapon since the time when it had started to develop in China (tenth to thirteenth centuries). Retaining an important role in the Ming period, cannon of the Chinese type had been widely employed in the events of 1407 in Vietnam. Perfected in Europe as a result of experiments by the German monk Berthold Schwarz (1310–84), new, more effective firearms (cannon and portable weapons) were to be introduced into East Asia by the Portuguese in the course of the sixteenth century. They were not much appreciated in China, where the military remained attached to bombards of the traditional type, but they were a great success in Japan. The Japanese pirates who ravaged the Chinese coast in the middle of the sixteenth century were already using the harquebus, a weapon imported into the island of Tanegashima, the name of which became the common term for the arm in Japan. These new weapons had something to do with the difficulties of the Ming armies in Korea, in their battles against the troops of the shogun Hideyoshi in 1593–98. From then onwards the Ming sought to adopt cannon of the European type, known in China as 'Frankish bombards' (*Fo-lang-chi ch'ung*). In order to combat the Manchu attacks the Ming asked the Jesuits to arrange for the purchase of cannon from Macao.

But it is possible that the Chinese learnt about European firearms in the sixteenth century by other channels than the Portuguese. A work that appeared in the Chia-ching era (1522–66), the *Hsi-yü t'u-ti jen-wu lüe,* which deals with the oro-hydrographic system, the products and peoples of central Asia, Iran, Iraq, and Turkey up to Constantinople, seems to prove that there were relations between Ming China and the Mediterranean Near East at that time.

Other geographical works reveal the progress of knowledge about foreign countries at the end of the Ming epoch. The *Shu-yü chou tzu lu* (preface dated 1574, printed in 1583) deals with Korea, Japan, the Ryukyu Islands, Vietnam, Tibet, central Asia, and Mongolia. The *Tung-hsi-yang-k'ao* (*Study of the Eastern and Western Oceans*) by the Fukienese Chang Hsieh (completed in 1617, printed in 1618) is devoted mainly to the lands of South-East Asia, but gives valuable information about Japan, the Dutch, and the techniques of navigation. One of the most remarkable geographers in the history of China lived in this first half of the seventeenth century, which was so fruitful in publications. This was Hsü Hung-tsu (Hsu Hsia-k'o), the first person to take such a lively interest in relief and geology. His works were the fruit of direct observation and of notes made during thirty years of travelling through the whole of southern and western China. Hsü Hsia-k'o traced the source of the Hsi-chiang, the big Cantonese river, and also that of the Yangtze.

During his explorations of the upper valleys of the big Indo-Chinese rivers he recognized that, contrary to the general view, the Salwen and the Mekong are separate in their upper reaches. But this geographer's great talent is revealed above all by the value of his descriptions and geological observations.

An urban literature

The literature of leisure, written in a language much closer to the spoken dialects than to classical Chinese, expanded in an unprecedented way at the end of the Ming period. It was addressed to an urban public avid for entertainment and not very well educated, but free of the intellectual constraints inculcated by a classical training. We have indirect proof of the size of this public in the large number of popular editions. The progress of printing and wood engraving in the Wan-li era (1573–1619) was accompanied by a rapid increase in the number of cheap publications. The printing houses of northern Fukien, which published a number of popular encyclopaedias, were one of the main centres of this trade from about 1571 onwards.

Springing from the long tradition which went back to the amusement quarters of K'ai-feng and Hangchow in the eleventh to thirteenth centuries (the oldest written versions of the great novels date from the fourteenth century), the romantic literature of the end of the Ming period had broken away from its origins and displays certain novel features which can really only be explained by a profound evolution in manners; imagination, invention, psychological analysis, and plot play a much bigger part than they do in the works of the fourteenth century, the *San-kuo-chih yen-i* and the *Shui-hu-chuan*. The subjects themselves are enriched and developed. The authors, though sometimes civil servants, belonged most often to that numerous class of jobless literati who existed by means of various expedients, trying to make a living from the orders of well-placed people or from the slender income which they drew from the profession of tutor or schoolmaster.

The two most remarkable novels of the end of the Ming period are the *Voyage to the West* (*Hsi-yu-chi*), published about 1570, which recounts the adventures of the monk Hsüan-tsang and the monkey Sun Wu-k'ung in the course of their pilgrimage to the Indies, and the *Chin-p'ing-mei* (*Flowers of the Peach Tree in a Golden Vase*), which describes the life of a rich merchant of Shantung and dates from about 1619. They bear witness to the transformation of manners and the progress of the literary art. The former is a mixture of humour and fantasy, drawing abundantly

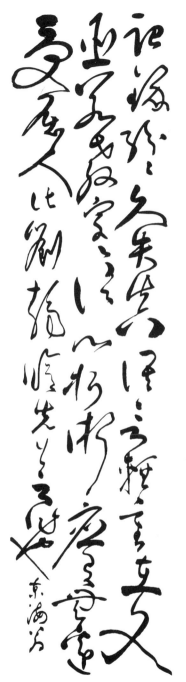

Figure 16 Ming calligraphy. A linked cursive style, written by Chang Pi (1425–1487)

on the most varied sources of inspiration; the second is psychological and realistic, the first novel of manners in history. As well as novels—the developed form of the shorter tale—there was a series of sentimental, criminal, satirical, erotic, heroic, or edifying stories, which usually combined these different features. Large collections of them were published between 1623 and 1632—the *P'ai-an ching-ch'i* (*Tales Which Make One Exclaim in Surprise and Strike the Table*) and the *San-yen* (*Three Collections of Stories*). An anthology of these stories, many of which are real masterpieces, was printed between 1632 and the year of the Manchu invasion (1644) and bears the title *Chin-ku ch'i-kuan* (*Extraordinary Scenes of Yesterday and Today*). It was the *Chin-ku ch'i-kuan* that inspired in Japan Rinrashi's *Pure Conversations by Moonlight* (*Gekka seidan*), published in 1790. In China itself the tales of the end of the Ming period were to exert great influence on the more learned literature in the classical language of the eighteenth and nineteenth centuries.

As well as this literature intended for a new urban public, the theatre, favoured by the imperial princes and the rich families, experienced a decided increase in popularity. Several examples of the plays written for it have been discovered recently. The most illustrious dramatists of the time were T'ang Hsien-tsu (1550–1616) and Juan Ta-ch'eng (1587–1646), a high official in contact with the eunuch party. The former, who gave up his official career to devote himself to the theatre, was responsible for various masterpieces including a romantic piece, the *Pavilion of the Peonies* (*Mu-tan-t'ing*), the theme of which is an ideal love whose power succeeds in bringing back a young woman to life.

The first influences from modern Europe

The events which occurred round about 1500 in the Near East and the Mediterranean basin had a decisive effect on Portuguese expansion towards the Indian Ocean and the seas of East Asia. The fall of the Frankish colonies in Syria and the victories of the Turks in Venetia set the seal on the decline of Venice and Europe's traditional trade with the Islamic world. The control of the trade routes by the Mamelukes of Egypt prompted the circumnavigation of the Cape of Good Hope. In the wake of Vasco da Gama, who, guided by the Arab pilot Ahmad ibn Majin, sailed from Malindi (in Kenya) to Calicut, on the Malabar coast, in 1498, the Portuguese were the first to venture into the East Asian seas at the beginning of the sixteenth century. They then sought to worm their way into the extensive trade—combined with piracy—which was to expand so much during the sixteenth century and in which all the countries of East Asia were concerned — China, Japan, the Philippines, Indonesia, and the Indo-Chinese peninsula. Like the Malays, the Portuguese traded in pepper between South-East Asia and South China. They soon tried to rob the Javanese and Sumatrans of control of the maritime routes and trade, and made contact with the Japanese in the southern part of their archipelago and at Ning-po.

The Portuguese galleons first approached the coast of Kwangtung in the years 1514–16. We are informed of their presence in Fukien from 1540 and in Japan from 1542. The Spaniards reached the seas of East Asia in 1543, and the Dutch, whose power was beginning to grow, round about 1600. These newcomers to the trade routes of the Far East and South-East Asia, christened Fo-lan-chi ('Franks' — the Portuguese and Spanish) and Hung-mao-i ('Barbarians with red hair' — the Dutch), came to form part of the human scene in those parts of the world and were connected by the Chinese with the lands of South-East Asia in which they had established their trading-posts. It is not impossible that certain European influences began to penetrate through these traders into the maritime regions of southern and south-eastern China, in the same way that Indian, Iranian, and Islamic influences had affected the same areas in days gone by. However, it is only from the arrival in China of the first Jesuit missionaries during the last few years of the sixteenth century that we begin to have reliable information at our disposal.

The arrival of the first Catholic missionaries in East Asia

Western Christendom had had its first contacts with East Asia, or, to be more precise, with Mongolia and the Peking region, between the middle of the thirteenth century and the year 1338, the date of the death of Giovanni di Monte Corvino, the first archbishop of Mongol Peking, which at that time was called Khanbalik. In those days what most interested the papacy and the kings of France was obtaining the alliance — against Islam — of a cosmopolitan empire which seemed to welcome all religions. When the first Catholic missionaries landed in the countries of East Asia in the middle of the sixteenth century in the wake of the Portuguese adventurers, all trace of these medieval Christian missions had disappeared. Moreover, the European state of mind had changed. It was the age of the conquistadores and of the Counter-Reformation. Sixteenth-century Europe was animated by a will to conquer and to proselytize unknown to medieval Europe. The main object of the creation of the Jesuit order by Ignatius Loyola in 1534 was the conversion of the pagans.

Seven years after the arrival of the first Portuguese merchants in Tanegashima, the island to the south of Kyushu, St. Francis Xavier, a Spanish Jesuit, landed in the archipelago (1549) and began his preaching activities in western Japan and at Kyoto. He died near Canton in 1552 without having been able to make his way into China.

It was a period when piracy was raging and all foreigners were suspect. The Portuguese, buccaneers and adventurers, were unfavourably regarded by the Chinese authorities, but they succeeded in setting up a small depot for the profitable trade between China and Japan, at the spot called Macao, to the west of the Pearl River estuary. It was the only point on the Chinese coast where the missions were to be able to gain a permanent foothold, and it became their principal base for operations in the Far East. Where all his predecessors had failed, the Italian Jesuit Matteo Ricci (1552–1610) was to succeed by dint of perseverance and the spirit of adaptation. Having managed to enter Kwangtung in 1583, he was at Nan-ch'ang, the capital of Kiangsi, in 1595, then in Nanking, and finally settled in Peking from 1601 onwards. Dressed until 1595 in a Buddhist monk's robe, as was the custom with the missionaries in Japan and the Philippines, Ricci realized that to win over the most highly educated Chinese he would have to adopt their dress and manners and serve a long and difficult apprenticeship in the classical culture of China. He thus gradually succeeded in defining a method of evangelization which consisted in emphasizing the—at any rate apparent—analogies between Chinese classical traditions and Christianity, in siding with orthodoxy against Buddhism, Taoism, and popular beliefs, and in flattering the taste of the literati for the science, technology, and arts of Europe. The missionaries also introduced into China a few mechanical curiosities such as clocks (Ricci was to become the tutelary deity of Chinese clockmakers, venerated in Shanghai in the nineteenth century in the shape of the 'Bodhisattva Ricci', Li Ma-tou p'u-sa). But it was not so much for these curiosities, which were regarded as pointless, as for their scientific and technical knowledge that the Jesuits were appreciated at the court and among high-ranking civil servants. The services that they rendered to the emperors as mathematicians, astronomers, cartographers, interpreters, painters, and musicians were to enable them to retain their position in Peking until the dissolution of their order at the end of the eighteenth century.

The first Jesuit missions were to be established along the road that Matteo Ricci had followed from Macao to Peking, at Chao-ch'ing, Shaochou and Nan-hsiung in Kwangtung; at Kan-chou and Nan-ch'ang in Kiangsi; and at Nanking, Huai-an and Tsinan. They were to spread from

Plate 50.   The reception of the Dutch ambassador on his embassy to Peking for the Dutch East India Company, by Jan Nieuhoff, 1669

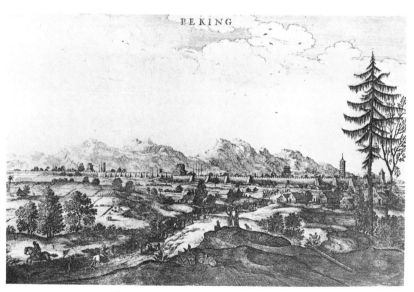

Plate 51.   Peking, 1671, by Jan Nieuhoff

Plate 52. Dutch cargo ships at Macao, guarded by man-of-war, by Jan Nieuhoff, 1669

Plate 53.   Dutch ships at Canton, by Jan Nieuhoff, 1669

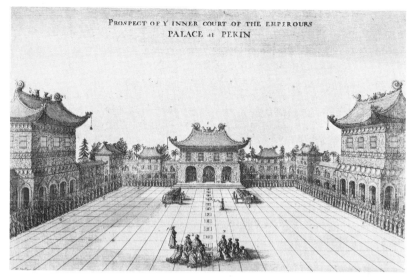

Plate 54. The inner court of the Emperor's Summer Palace in Peking, with the Emperor welcoming the Dutch ambassador, by Jan Nieuhoff, 1669

Plate 55. Temple of the Five Hundred Buddhas, near Peking

there to most of the provinces at the end of the Ming period, but were more numerous in the lower Yangtze area and in Fukien, where Dominicans and Franciscans from Manila were also active.

A very small number of missionaries arrived by the Burma road or through central Asia; for example, the Portuguese brother Benedict of Goez, who set out from Agra, the capital of the Mogul dynasty, in the reign of Akbar (1556–1605), in 1602, to see whether Marco Polo's Cathay was really China. He passed through Kabul, Samarkand, and the oases of the Tarim basin, and arrived at Chiu-ch'üan, in Kansu, in 1605. From there he wrote to Father Ricci, who sent a Chinese convert from Macao, Brother Sebastian Fernandez, to meet him. Fernandez arrived in Chiu-ch'üan in 1607, just before the death of Goez. Finally, it should be noted that in 1661–62 two missionaries made the same journey in the opposite direction, from Peking to Agra, but via Tibet and Nepal. Here we have the proof of the astonishing permanence of certain routes down the centuries, for these same roads of central Asia and Tibet had been traversed and explored by a large number of Buddhist pilgrims in the fourth to ninth centuries.

The difficulties of dialogue

Points of view on each side differed radically: what, in the eyes of the missionaries and of the Catholic hierarchy, was a mere means of making converts formed, for most of the governing class, the only advantage in the presence of the Jesuits at the court. By showing the excellence and superiority of the sciences and inventions of Europe, the missionaries thought that they were simultaneously demonstrating the preeminence of the religion which had been revealed to that part of the world. But apart from a small number of literati and high-ranking civil servants in close relations with the Jesuits and convinced of the relationship between the ancient Chinese traditions and Christianity, the lettered classes as a whole were hostile to the new religion. The development of the Christian communities among the ordinary people seemed to them to threaten public order, and they saw in Christianity only a tissue of extravagant and contradictory ideas. The fact is that in China Christianity was to come up against obstacles that were difficult to surmount, springing as they did from the differences between societies and civilizations whose historical antecedents, mental attitudes, behaviour and manners displayed no similarity. The Chinese world offered no easy point of approach to a religion which required total commitment and implied the existence of an absolute. Religious fervour was not unknown to the Chinese, but on the other hand they were unfamiliar with the category of the transcendent because of their basic concept of an immanent order that was at the same time cosmic and human, natural and social.

Thus the dialogue between Christians and Chinese was based from the start on profound misunderstandings which were to grow worse in the eighteenth and nineteenth centuries. The Christians were soon accused: (1) of wishing to corrupt Chinese morals, since they forbade people to honour their ancestors (after a period of relative tolerance in the seventeenth century, the Vatican directives became intransigent on this point in the eighteenth; but the 'quarrel over rites' reflects a conflict which had broken out much earlier among the missionaries themselves, immediately after the death of Matteo Ricci in 1610); (2) of destroying the statues and sanctuaries belonging to Chinese cults; (3) of doing homage to a man who had suffered the extreme penalty; (4) of plotting and spying on behalf of the Japanese and the coastal pirates and smugglers; (5) of placing seven spheres in the heavens and of proposing an oblique ecliptic mounting instead of the equatorial mounting traditional in China (it was Aristotle's cosmology as revised by Tycho Brahe that the Jesuits taught the Chinese; the heliocentric system, condemned by the Church, was not introduced in China before 1760); (6) of creating secret associations (just as the members of secret societies were obliged not to disclose their affiliation in any circumstances, so it was in the interest of neophytes not to reveal that they belonged to the Church); (7) and finally of secretly indulging in operations to transmute metals and in maleficent incantations.

Right from the early seventeenth century these criticisms all formed the subject of pamphlets which reached a very wide public. One of the first of this long line of anti-Christian treatises was the *P'o-hsieh-chi* (*Collection in which the Heresies are Refuted*), which appeared in 1639. Unlike the missionaries, who thought they could perceive the traces of a very ancient Christian revelation in the old beliefs in the 'Lord from on high' (Shang-ti), the Chinese literati hostile to the missionaries saw in Christianity only a bastard form of Buddhism sometimes mixed with borrowings from Islam. This argument was often to be employed and appears in particular in a *Short Account of Macao* (*Ao-men chi-lueh*) published in 1751.

No doubt Chinese reactions varied according to milieu. In the countryside it seems that the missionaries aroused right at the start an interest caused by curiosity. Their strange manners and practices provoked amazement. The funeral of a Christian would draw a large crowd. The missionary might seem like a variety of Buddhist priest, and doubtless Christianity took root in the rural areas to the extent that a sort of syncretism occured between the foreign religion and Chinese traditions concerning holiness and the sacred. Thus in the biography of Father Étienne Faber, a missionary in Shansi at the end of the Ming period, we meet again several of the themes of Buddhist and Taoist hagiography. This Christian priest is credited with having been able to approach fierce animals without being devoured by them; he possessed the gift of healing; succeeded in warding off an invasion of grasshoppers by sprinkling them with holy water; exorcised haunted houses; foresaw the precise date of his own death; his corpse did not decay, his tomb was spared by a river in flood and after his death he was transformed into the god of the Local Soil (*Fang-t'u-ti*).

At the beginning of the eighteenth century Father Louis Le Comte (1655–1728), a missionary from the Bordeaux area, suggested the following methods for converting the common people:

1. The use of stories and parables.
2. The attribution of great importance to 'ornaments, processions, chants, the noise of bells, ceremonies'.
3. The inculcation of respect for 'images, relics, medals, holy water'.
4. Concentrating on the instruction of children.

In essentials, these were the procedures adopted by Buddhist priests in China fifteen hundred years earlier.

The most eminent converts

However, in the upper classes the Jesuits were to obtain splendid results with a small number of literati. The most famous of these literati converted to Christianity were the three called the 'three pillars of the evangelization' (*K'ai-chiao san ta chu-shih*): Hsü Kuang-ch'i, Li Chih-tsao and Yang T'ing-yun.

Hsü Kuang-ch'i (1562–1633), born in Shanghai and successful in the doctoral examination in 1604, was one of the first to make contact with the Jesuit missionaries. Engaged as tutor by a rich family of Shao-chou, he met first Father Lazare Cattaneo there, then Matteo Ricci in Nanking in 1600. Another missionary, Jean de Rocha, baptized him and christened him Paul. From 1604 to 1607 Hsü Kuang-ch'i lived in Peking and there received instruction from Ricci alongside Li Chih-tsao. From then onwards he started to translate European manuals on mathematics, astronomy, geography, and hydraulics. He was responsible in particular for the translation, between 1606 and 1608, of a work on trigonometry, the *Ts'e-liang fa-i* (Hsü Kuang-ch'i discovered that Chinese and Western trigonometrical methods were identical), of the *Elements of Euclid* (*Chi-ho yüan-pen,* 1611) and of a treatise on hydraulics (the *T'ai-hsi shui-fa,* 1612). After returning in 1607 to the lower Yangtze, where he had fresh contacts with the Jesuits, he retired for good in 1621 to Shanghai, where he translated a *Treatise on the Soul.* In 1630 he recommended to the court Adam Schall for the establishment of a new calendar and father Longobardo for negotiations to buy cannon at Macao. A small church was built near his home in the suburbs of Shanghai, in the family township of Hsü (Hsü-chia-hui; in Shanghaiese, Zikkawei). It was round this church that the important Catholic mission of Zikkawei grew up in the nineteenth century. Hsü Kuang-ch'i's famous treatise on agriculture, the *Nung-chen ch'üan-shu,* was published after his death, in 1639.

A scholar and civil servant like Hsü Kuang-ch'i, Yang T'ing-yun (1557–1627) was born in Hangchow. Appointed censor at Peking in 1600, he dealt with transport on the Grand Canal and the administration of the Soochow region. At first attracted by *ch'an* Buddhism during a period of retirement at Hangchow in 1609, he met Lazare Cattaneo at Li Chih-tsao's house in 1611. He also met Father Nicolas Trigault. Converted by them to Christianity, he was baptized the following year under the name of Michael. With his relations and friends, he founded an Association of the Holy Water (*sheng-shui-hui*) and wrote a book on Christian doctrine. In 1615 he brought out miscellanies on the sciences, geography, European philosophy, and Christianity, and in 1621 an essay in which he sought to demonstrate the superiority of his adopted religion to Buddhism. He collaborated in the writing of explanatory notes for the *Atlas of the World* published in 1602 by Matteo Ricci under the title of *K'un-yü wan-kuo ch'üan-t'u.* These notes formed the *Chih-fang wai-chi,* printed in 1623. In the year of his death, 1627, Yang T'ing-yun had a Christian church built in Hangchow.

Li Chih-tsao (?–1630) was a native of Hangchow, like Yang T'ing-yun. He met Ricci shortly after the latter's arrival there in 1601 and saw in his house the map from the *Atlas of the World.* Passionately interested in geographical questions, Li Chih-tsao set about studying Western sciences and cartographical procedures. He studied with Ricci from 1604 to 1610 and acted as the translator of various scientific and religious works. Returning to Hangchow in 1611, he invited Fathers Cattaneo, Sebastian Fernandez and Nicolas Trigault to preach in the city. At the time of the first 'persecution' of the Christians launched by Shen Ch'üeh in 1616, and during the second in 1622, Li Chih-tsao protected the Christians of Hangchow. In 1625 he wrote a note on the Nestorian stele which had just been discovered at Hsi'an in Shensi (this bilingual stele retraces in Chinese and Syriac the history of Nestorianism in the T'ang capital since its introduction in 631; it is dated 781), and identified Nestorianism with Christianity. Another work on this famous stele was to appear in Hangchow in 1664 under the title of *Treatise on the Nestorian Stele* (*Ching-chiao-pei-ch'üan*); it is attributed to Father Emmanuel Diaz and contains illustrations of two Nestorian crosses discovered near the big port of Ch'üan-chou in 1638. In 1629, a year before his death, Li Chih-tsao was entrusted, together with Hsü Kuang-ch'i and Father Longo-bardo, with the establishment of a new calendar.

Reciprocal influences

It is not very easy to do full justice to the consequences of these contacts between cultivated Europeans and members of the Chinese élite in the first half of the seventeenth century, for, over and above the list of works translated and the clear cases of transmission, all kinds of influences, taking paths which cannot be precisely traced, spread through both the Chinese world and Europe like shock waves. In the three main fields where the Jesuits' knowledge had found employment — and went on finding it up to the end of the eighteenth century — namely astronomy, mathematics, and cartography, the contribution made by Europe is incontestable, but the stimulus which it provided was also, and possibly still more, important. It was almost certainly the Jesuits who were mainly responsible for the rebirth of Chinese mathematics in the seventeenth and eighteenth centuries. One may say, in a general way, that the scientific tendencies of seventeenth- and eighteenth-century China were reinforced by the contributions of the West.

However, we must take care not to attribute to early seventeenth-century Europe a general superiority; the Christian West and the Chinese world had very much the same amount to learn from each other at that point in history.

Curiously enough, the astronomical traditions of the Chinese were more 'modern' — as Joseph Needham has pointed out — than those of the Jesuit missionaries. Far from foreseeing the coming revolution in Western astronomy, the latter taught the old principles — celestial spheres and ecliptic coordinates — which contradicted Chinese ideas and habits. The cosmological theory most current in China, the *hsüan-yeh*, regarded the stars and planets as lights of unknown composition floating in an infinite space. This theory of infinite space was in harmony with the Indian and Buddhist concept of the infinity of times and spaces (calculations of the T'ang age put certain astronomical events a hundred million years in the past). Not only the ancient conception of the crystalline spheres but also the ecliptic coordinates and axes of the instruments shocked the Chinese, accustomed as they were since the Han age to the equatorial system, which was to be adopted generally in modern astronomy.

In the West, neither Marco Polo's *Il Milione* or *Travels* (1298), the exaggerations and apparently fabulous details of which had reduced its effect, nor the brief accounts produced by the Franciscan friars sent to the court of the Mongol Khans of China could have any perceptible repercussions on a medieval conception of the world which gave much room to the marvellous and to Christian revelation. It was not the same in a Europe which had become much more sensitive to the diversity of peoples and manners and was becoming aware of that series of reflections on human societies which leads from Montaigne to Montesquieu. Even before the reports, letters, and books of the Jesuits, the accounts produced by the first sixteenth-century travellers to southern China contributed the first elements of that knowledge of China which was to have such profound consequences in the seventeenth and eighteenth centuries.

These accounts of travels, and in particular the *Relation* of Martin de Rada (1533–78), a Spanish Augustinian who arrived in China via Mexico and the Philippines, and the *Treatise* by Gaspar da Cruz, a Portuguese Dominican, which was printed in 1569, served as a basis for the composition of the *Historia de las cosas mas notables, ritos y costumbres del gran Reyno de la China* by Gonzalez de Mendoza, published in Rome in 1585. There were thirty editions of this book in the various European languages between that date and the end of the sixteenth century. The work was tremendously successful and was to be read by all educated people until 1656, when it was supplanted by the book of the Flemish Jesuit Nicolas Trigault (1577–1628), the *De Christiana Expeditione apud Sinas* (1615; French translation, 1617), and by the *De Bello Tartarico* (Antwerp, 1654) written by the Italian Jesuit Martino Martini, who died at Hangchow in 1661.

These first books on China were at the root of various borrowings, of which two at least are known for certain.

The idea of building bridges suspended on iron chains dates in Europe from 1595 and was very probably suggested by the accounts of Portuguese travellers who had seen constructions of this kind in Kwangtung or Fukien. This type of bridge, doubtless originating from Szechwan and the Sino-Tibetan borders, had been in use in China since about 600. However, the first example in Europe dates only from 1741 and was the result of a suggestion by the Austrian architect Fischer von Erlach (1656–1723), who expressly declared that he had been inspired by Chinese models.

The other borrowing was a curious adaptation of a Chinese practice attested at various epochs and in different regions of China—the addition of a mast and sail to wheelbarrows. The Dutch engineer Simon Stevin (1540–1620), who seems to have been inspired by reading Mendoza's *Historia* or *Itinerary of the New World* (1585), or more probably by reading the *Itinerario* by Jan Huyghen van Linschoten (1596), had the idea of building carts with sails. These vehicles were successfully tried out about 1600 on the beaches of the northern Netherlands and continued to arouse lively interest during most of the seventeenth century. They were the first vehicles to demonstrate that one could move on land at hitherto unknown speeds.

It is noteworthy that the first studies and theories of magnetism were purely Chinese. Polarity, induction, retentivity, and variation were known much earlier in China than in Europe, where the first experiments relating to electrostatics and magnetism go back to W. Gilbert (1544–1603) and were developed in the seventeenth century. Even supposing that no link should be established between the development of this new sector of physical science and the contributions of China, it remains true that Chinese notions about magnetic phenomena were connected with cosmic theories which probably made their influence felt in Europe in the eighteenth century. Similarly, the political and social ideas of the Chinese, their institutions, their arts, and their techniques were to exert an influence which was not without effect on the formation of modern Europe.

General conclusion to the history of the late Ming

The changes that were products of the sixteenth century are so clear and so numerous that one can place the beginning of a new period by them. One of the most important, perhaps by virtue of its effects on the society, was the general use of silver as a means of payment. Not only did the amount of silver in circulation rapidly increase over the course of the seventeenth century, but it continued to grow under the Manchus until about 1820; and silver remained, along with bronze coins for small purchases, the sole means of payment for major transactions until the beginning of the twentieth century. The general use of silver in the sixteenth and seventeenth centuries coincided with a huge increase in maritime traffic (both commercial and pirate) in all the seas of East Asia and with a rebirth of villages and urban activity. Certain handicraft techniques (especially weaving, porcelain, and printing) were perfected, and these improvements allowed China to solidify its position, after the depression in the middle of the seventeenth century, as the greatest exporter of luxury products. It was in this context of economic expansion and urban renewal that the first modern European adventurers appeared in the seas of East

Asia: first Portuguese and Spaniards, then, at the beginning of the seventeenth century, the Dutch. This was a phenomenon of no great importance for East Asia, since these new arrivals simply inserted themselves into the commercial circuits of the Far East and profited from the prosperity that this part of the world was experiencing. But the phenomenon was a harbinger of times to come.

China owed these adventurers its first imports from Europe and America: more effective firearms, the sweet potato, the peanut, tobacco – maize was to come later – and its first silver coins, introduced in Manila by a galleon from Acapulco. When one adds to this the new orientations that took shape in intellectual life during the seventeenth century as well as, secondarily, the first contacts with European science, technology, and religion (from *c.* 1,600), then it is perhaps valid to speak of the beginnings of the modern period in China and East Asia. In Japan also, the end of the sixteenth century marked one of the great turning points of history. It is true that twentieth-century Chinese historians have adopted the custom of describing it as 'modern' by placing it in opposition to a 'traditional' China that corresponds in a vague way to all earlier periods. But this terminology conceals certain value judgments: it implies a more radical break than there really was between the Chinese past and present and at the same time, by comparison with the history of the West, it seems to deny any significance to the transformation of the Chinese world until our own times.

Part 8

Authoritarian Paternalism

Prologue

The new Manchu power, which relied at first in its conquest of China on the collaboration of the Chinese of the present-day north-eastern provinces (Manchuria) and profited everywhere from the general anarchy, soon came up against difficulties which delayed the definitive installation of the new regime. The Southern Ming offered considerable resistance, which was assisted by a big new outbreak of piracy, and the southern provinces seceded immediately after they had been conquered. However, this period of uncertainty, which lasted down to the complete recapture of the south-western regions in 1681 and the conquest of Taiwan (Formosa) two years later, was followed by a rapid consolidation of the Manchu power. This consolidation was helped by the greater mildness of the regime, the more pronounced sinicization of the Manchu upper classes and the emperors' efforts to gain the sympathy and collaboration of the Chinese literati. An unprecedented expansion of agricultural and craft production, as also of trade, was reflected during the eighteenth century in general prosperity accompanied by a rapid increase in the population. Simultaneously the new empire's policy of diplomatic and military intervention in Mongolia, central Asia, and Tibet obtained brilliant results: from the middle of the eighteenth century onwards the Sino-Manchu empire covered nearly twelve million square kilometres and its influence extended far beyond its frontiers. At that time China was the richest and biggest state in the world.

But as this period of exceptional well-being went on, the first signs of a decline began to appear: frontier conflicts and rebellions by colonized peoples grew more frequent, the defects in the political system, not very noticeable in a period of prosperity, grew more marked, and the first big peasant revolts broke out in North China in the last few years of the eighteenth century. A train of events had started which the government was never to succeed in halting. The immense size of the empire, the growth of its population, an economy whose yield could scarcely be increased, an excessive centralization, and an ineffective administration were to constitute grave handicaps at a time when the Chinese world was entering a period of decline and economic recession.

Chapter 22

The Conquest
and the Foundation
of the Manchu Regime

The rise of the Manchus

The period of formation

The people who in 1635 were to assume the name of Manchus (Man-chou) were Jürchen, descendants of the Tungus tribes who in the twelfth century had founded the Chin empire (1115-1234) in the north-eastern territories and North China. Allies of the Chinese from 1589, they had assisted the Ming armies in their fight against the Japanese invasion in Korea during the years 1592-98. United by a leader callèd Nurhaci, the Jürchen tribes of eastern Manchuria owed their power to their military organization and to their wealth; they had gained control of the trade in pearls, furs, and mining products in the north-east and drew large profits from the cultivation of ginseng (*jen-shen*), the root of which was valued for its medicinal properties and sold for a very high price. Nurhaci's ascent had been made possible by the 'sedentarization' of the Tungus and Mongol tribes of the region to the north-east of Shenyang, in Liaoning, where the steppe empires of the eleventh to fourteenth centuries — Liao, Chin, and Yüan — had set up prefectures in the Chinese style which were replaced in the Ming epoch by military garrisons (*wei*). Surrounded by Chinese advisers — the Chinese population was relatively large in this part of the north-eastern provinces — Nurhaci had been able to create a feudal and military organization in this area. It consisted of a collection of domains governed by leaders of the Jürchen aristocracy and military units modelled on Chinese garrisons. These units, which were called Banners (*ch'i*) and were distinguished by the colours of their flags, were created in 1601. They were to multiply during the course of the Manchu conquests thanks to the adhesion of Mongol units and to the incorporation of Chinese units. They were divided into Inner Banners, consisting of the Manchus and their dependants, and Outer Banners, kept for auxiliary troops. Until the end of the eighteenth century they were to be one of the most effective military organizations that East Asia had ever known.

After gaining the alliance of the eastern Mongols against those of Chahar, a province lying to the west of Jehol and to the north of Shansi, the Jürchen adopted a hostile attitude to China from 1609 onwards. In 1616 Nurhaci proclaimed himself Khan of the Jürchen and founded the dynasty of the Later Chin (*Hou Chin*). In 1618 he seized Fushun, to the east of Shenyang, and from that year onwards began to direct attacks against North China. In 1621 he took Shenyang and Liaoyang and four years later set up his capital in Shenyang, rechristened Mukden. After his death in 1626 he was succeeded by Abahai (1627–43), who indulged in great military and political activity and pursued the work of his predecessor; in the absence of genius or originality, perseverance was to be one of the main qualities of the Manchus. Abahai undertook the long conquest of Chahar, imposed his will on Korea in 1638 and finished by occupying the whole of Manchuria down to the Shan-hai-kuan Pass in 1642, and the whole Amur region (the province of Heilungkiang) between 1636 and 1644. Abahai's entire policy aimed at the imitation of Chinese institutions. His advisers and generals were Chinese and the modern arms which he possessed were furnished from China by deserters. In 1635 Abahai replaced the name 'Jürchen' by 'Manchus' and in the following year changed the dynastic name of Chin into Ta-ch'ing (great Ch'ing).

Thus on the eve of the capture of Peking in 1644 the Manchus had acquired the military strength, the political cohesion, the administrative organization, and the strategic bases which were to enable them to seize power in China and to subject this huge country to their domination. It took them less than half a century to do this.

The installation of the invaders in China

Having conquered the old Chinese colonial territory of Manchuria, the Manchus were to find there valuable assistants for the conquest and administration of China. Some of their high officials, especially at the end of Abahai's reign (1627–43) and in that of Shun-chih (1643–61) were men from the Liao-ho basin and often natives of Shenyang (Mukden) or the surrounding area. Such was the case, as early as 1618, with Fan Wen-ch'eng (1597–1666), one of the four great dignitaries of the Nurhaci epoch. Fan Wen-ch'eng belonged to a family of Ming civil servants and one of his ancestors had been head of the Army Ministry in Peking. At the time of the capture of Fushun in 1618, Fan Wen-ch'eng had moved into Nurhaci's service and in 1636 had been appointed Grand Secretary in the capital, which was then Mukden. Like him, the generals who helped the Manchus to conquer North and South China—K'ung Yu-te (?–1652), Wu San-kuei, Shang K'o-hsi (1604–76), Keng Chang-ming (?–1649), Sun Yen-ling (?–1677)—were natives of Liaoning and had in some cases been recruited by the Manchus at the time when they seized control of this region.

These early collaborators, representatives of a genuinely Chinese administrative tradition, literati who knew both Chinese and Manchu, were enrolled in the Inner Banners and sometimes attached to the family of the Ch'ing emperors. The Manchus called these close retainers 'people of the house', *booi* (in Chinese, *pao-i*), and kept them in their service from father to son. In the seventeenth century and even at the beginning of the eighteenth, these *booi* played the part of informants with the Manchus and intermediaries with the Chinese élite. Entrusted with the internal administration of the palace and with the control of the big workshops which supplied the court with luxury products (porcelain from Ching-te-chen, silks from Nanking, Soochow, Hangchow, and so on), confidants, and advisers of the imperial family, they were to occupy a position similar to that of the eunuchs, without acquiring, however, the excessive power which the latter had gained in the Ming epoch.

The Manchus settled in China like a race of lords destined to reign over a population of slaves, just as the Mongols had done. From 1668 they banned the Han from Manchuria, that old Chinese colonial territory, in order to keep an area free from all foreign influence and to preserve a monopoly in the exploitation of ginseng. They forbade mixed marriages. The principle of segregation was applied in Peking and the other big cities: the capital was divided into a Manchu city to the north, from which all the former inhabitants were expelled, and a Chinese city to the south. In 1645 all Chinese affected by smallpox—in fact all those with skin diseases—were expelled from Peking. Alarmist rumours ran through the city; people thought that the occupying power was going to exterminate the whole Chinese population. The fact is that the conquest was carried out with extreme savagery. An inhabitant of Yangchow who miraculously escaped the general massacre of the population left an account of the horrors which he witnessed when the Manchu troops entered this rich commercial city on the lower Yangtze in 1645. The manuscript of this account, the *Journal of the Ten Days of Yangchow* (*Yang-chou shih-jih-chi*) was to be preserved in Japan. The change in dress and hair-style—the wearing of the pigtail (*pien-tzu*)—which was imposed on pain of death in 1645 on the whole Chinese population caused riots, some of which were repressed by massacres—at Chiang-yin and Chia-hsing in Kiangsu, for example. It should be remembered that the Jürchen, the ancestors of the Manchus, had also imposed the wearing of the pigtail on their subjects in the Chin empire and that the pigtail was a traditional hair-style among the steppe people; the Manchus braided their own hair in several tresses, and much earlier, in the fifth century, the Tabgatch were described by the Chinese as 'corded heads' (*so-t'ou*).

From the beginning of the conquest the Manchus expropriated the peasants and constituted estates from which Chinese were excluded. These Manchu enclaves (*ch'üan*), created between 1645 and 1647, were numerous all over North China—especially in the neighbourhood of Peking—and eastern Mongolia.

The Manchus made the labour force which cultivated their estates (prisoners of war and peasants deprived of their property who, to retain a strip of land, agreed to work in the enclaves) into positive slaves. Liable to be bought and sold like animals, subject to numerous corvées, very harshly treated and condemned to stay where they were, these labourers sought any means of escaping, in spite of the whipping or death penalty which they incurred and caused their relatives and neighbours to incur. The Chinese supporters of the Manchus, enrolled in the Banners, played the part of prison guards and police spies. The effects of this system, which created an atmosphere of terror and encouraged corruption, soon turned out to be disastrous. Realizing that moderate, uniform taxation was more profitable than direct exploitation, and that free men work better than those who have been reduced to slavery, the Manchus gradually gave up their enclaves and the free peasants regained possession of their land. From 1685 onwards the Banners were forbidden to confiscate any fresh land and round about 1700 the question of the enclaves and of fugitive slaves was practically settled. Doubtless all the sufferings imposed on the Chinese peasantry were pointless; the Manchus' mistake is explained by their wish to apply in China ideas and practices which could only be justified in the context of steppe societies. However, if the change of policy was only gradual it was on the other hand fairly radical, since China was indebted to the Ch'ing for experiencing in the eighteenth century the mildest agrarian taxation it had ever known in the whole of its history. This fiscal system almost certainly played a considerable part in winning over the majority of the population to its new rulers.

Delays and difficulties

The resistance of the Southern Ming

The invaders had seized possession of North China almost without a fight, but in the south they were to meet a long resistance which was continually weakened by a general lack of cohesion and by the struggles between patriots who favoured resistance and pacifists inclined to collaborate with the enemy. The fact is that the Ming, who had lost the goodwill of the people, were doomed in any case to disappear. However, the memory of this period of some fifteen years when the descendants of the Ming emperors, harried from province to province by the advance of the Manchu armies, tried to maintain a semblance of legitimate authority, was to be exalted by the great patriotic literati of the early Ch'ing dynasty.

After the fall of Peking and the installation of a new emperor in Nanking, peace talks were started with the Manchus, who were still regarded by part of the ruling classes as their allies against rebel movements. But these negotiations were broken off through the efforts of a patriotic minister called Shih K'o-fa (?–1645). After six successive assaults on Yangchow, defended by Shih K'o-fa, the city was captured. A month later Nanking fell. The emperor was handed over to the Manchus by a disloyal general. This was the start of a period of wandering which was to take the descendants of the Ming from Chekiang and Fukien to Kwangtung and Kwangsi, and finally to the most distant province in the whole empire, Yunnan. One ephemeral emperor succeeded the other as the Manchu troops advanced. Chekiang and Fukien, where two emperors had been proclaimed simultaneously, were occupied in 1646 at the same time as Szechwan, where the Manchus got rid of Chang Hsien-chung, the former rebel leader of the end of the Ming period. The year 1647 saw the capture of Canton by the invaders and a new sovereign was proclaimed at Kweilin, in north-eastern Kwangsi. This was Prince Chu Yu-lang, who adopted the reign-name of Yung-li (1647–60), the only emperor whose reign had any importance during the Southern Ming (Nan Ming) period. After recapturing Canton and reconquering a large part of South China in 1648, Yung-li was forced to withdraw to Yunnan. Weakened by dissensions among their generals in 1656, the Southern Ming were unable to resist the attacks of the armies led by Wu San-kuei in 1658–59.

Yung-li was obliged to seek refuge at Bhamo, over five hundred kilometres west of K'un-ming, on the Irrawaddy, in north-eastern Burma. He was taken prisoner there in 1661 and strangled in K'un-ming the following year. Yung-li's court had welcomed at Kweilin and in Yunnan some Jesuit missionaries (among others Father André-Xavier Koffler), who asserted that they had converted some ladies in the emperor's entourage and in particular Yung-li's own mother. On their advice she sent an embassy to the Vatican. This delegation returned to K'un-ming in 1659.

Major new outbreak of piracy

This resistance to the invaders, which was based on attachment to the persons of the last representatives of the imperial Ming family and on an upsurge of Han patriotism, found valuable assistance in the recrudescence of piracy. The Southern Ming had more or less secret links with the pirates of the south-east coasts.

A half-Chinese, half-Japanese born on Hirado, an island in the neighbourhood of the present port of Sasebo, in Kyushu, in fact ruled the coast of Fukien from about 1650 onwards. This pirate chieftain, by the name of Cheng Ch'eng-kung (1624–62), was to remain down to our own day a sort of national hero in Taiwan. His activities, like those of the Wokou in the sixteenth century, were a mixture of piracy and commerce, but at the same time they had obvious political implications. Installed near Hsia-men (Amoy), in southern Fukien, he pillaged the rich maritime cities of the coast, extending his raids as far as southern Chekiang and north-eastern Kwangtung. However, at the same time he traded with Japan, the Ryukyu Islands, Vietnam, Siam, and the Philippines, was in contact with the Europeans who frequented the East Asian seas and sought to increase his political influence by taking the Southern Ming side against the Manchus. His good relations with the survivors of the fallen dynasty won him the signal favour of the right to bear the name of the imperial family, Chu; hence his nickname of Kuo-hsing-yeh ('excellency with the royal family's name'), which was recorded by the Dutch as 'Coxinga', or in other similar forms. He served as intermediary between the Southern Ming and Japan, where he went on several occasions (in 1648, 1651, 1658, and 1660) to ask for help which never came. In 1658–59 he repeated the exploits of the Japanese pirates, the Wokou, in 1553–55 by venturing as far as Nanking, right in the occupied zone, but he had to retreat and content himself from then onwards with harassing activities on the coast. To combat Coxinga and to put an end to the complicity from which he benefited in the maritime provinces, the Ch'ing decreed in 1662 that all the coastal regions from Shantung to Kwangtung should be evacuated. This was a tragedy for the local inhabitants, who saw their towns and villages systematically razed to the ground and were forced to leave the area. The effects of these barbarous measures on China's trade and foreign relations have probably never been fully evaluated. They almost certainly halted or seriously slowed down China's trading activities at the end of the seventeenth century and thus encouraged the intrusion of the Europeans — Portuguese, Spanish, and Dutch — into the seas of East Asia.

Forced to find a refuge outside China, during 1661 Coxinga attacked the shores of the big island of Taiwan, where the Dutch had been installed since 1624. He forced them out of it with his fleet of 900 ships and 25,000 men. On his death in 1662 he was succeeded by his son Cheng Ching, who supported the governor-general of Fukien, Keng Ching-chung, in his rebellion against the Manchus. Cheng Ching held out in Taiwan until 1683, when the Ch'ing organized a big expedition which put an end to this independent kingdom and annexed to China for the first time this island with a bigger area than Belgium and still inhabited by numerous Malayo-Polynesian tribes.

Just as the pirates of Fukien in Coxinga's time were in contact with the Southern Ming, so the activities of the Tanka on the coast of Kwangtung seem to have had links with the loyalist resistance. The Tanka were an aboriginal population of fishermen who lived permanently in their boats (hence the name *ch'uan-min,* 'boat people', sometimes given to them). They were famous pearl fishermen. Their piratical activities caused many difficulties to Shang K'o-hsi, the first military governor appointed to Kwangtung by the Ch'ing, and thus indirectly helped the Southern Ming resistance and the attempts at secession.

The rebellion of the 'Three Feudatories', 1674–81

It is known that in their conquest of China the invaders had employed the services of some of the old political, administrative, and military personnel of the Ming empire, the men who were called the *chiu-ch'en* ('ancient servants or officers') or *erh-ch'en* ('those who had been successively in the service of the two dynasties'). But there were legitimate suspicions about these officials who had joined the new regime. Arrests had taken place in 1656 and a considerable proportion of the old personnel had been progressively replaced from that date onwards by new officials recruited by competition, the Han-ch'en ('Han officers'). However, it had not been possible to extend this purge to the southern provinces, more distant and less well controlled, where the Ch'ing had been forced to allow fairly wide autonomy to the army leaders from the north-east who had participated in the conquest and reduced the resistance of the Southern Ming.

In granting extensive powers to the generals who had helped them in the conquest of South China, the Manchus had embarked on a dangerous course which led to the formation of governments that were almost independent of Peking. They ran the risk of losing control of their empire. Raised to the dignity of 'princes', the military governors of the coastal provinces and south-west China were to retain and hand on to their descendants the armed forces which had been placed under their orders at the time of the campaigns against the Southern Ming. They were to take advantage of the tendencies to autonomy of the areas which they governed and to find on the spot the resources essential for independence. Thus the most powerful of them, Wu San-kuei (1612–78), after annihilating Li Tzu-ch'eng's armies in 1644 and 1645 alongside the Manchu forces and heading campaigns from 1657 to 1661 to exterminate the Ming loyalists who had taken refuge in Yunnan, had never demobilized his troops. Reigning over Yunnan and Kweichow, he also in fact controlled the neighbouring provinces of Hunan, Shensi, and Kansu. He drew his resources from the subsidies with which the Peking government continued to furnish him (in 1667 he received thirty million *liang* of silver for the upkeep of his armies) as well as from the monopolies which he had instituted in the products of the salt mines of Szechwan, the copper and gold mines, and the trade in ginseng and rhubarb, not counting the profits from the trade with Tibet (sale of tea and purchase of horses). When, taking advantage of the absence of authority at Canton, where the local governor Shang K'o-hsi (1604?–76) had renounced his functions, the court decided to suppress the autonomous governments of the 'princes', Wu San-kuei rebelled openly at the same time as Keng Ching-chung (?–1682), the governor of Fukien, and founded the ephemeral Chou empire (1673–81). They were followed by Sun Yen-ling (?–1677), military governor of Kweilin, in Kwangsi. In 1674 Wu San-kuei won over to his cause Wang Fu-ch'en (?–1681), governor of Shensi and Kansu since 1670, and then, in 1676, Shang Chih-hsin (1636?–80), the son of Shang Ko-hsi, who reigned over Kwangtung and Kwangsi. In that year Wu San-kuei was on the point of reconquering the whole of China and of putting an end to the power of the Manchus. But the wind changed: in 1676 Wang Fu-ch'en and Keng Ching-chung made their submission to the Ch'ing, and Shang Chih-hsin did the same in 1677. Wu San-kuei died in the following year and his grandson, Wu Shih-fan, succeeded him on the Chou throne. In 1679 the Ch'ing armies recaptured Kiangsi, in 1680 Szechwan and in 1681 Kweichow. Besieged in his capital, K'un-ming, Wu Shih-fan committed suicide. Thus ended the 'Rebellion of the Three Feudatories' (*san-fan chih luan*) (Wu San-kuei, Keng Ching-chung, and Shang Chih-hsin), the most serious crisis that the new Manchu dynasty had experienced.

The liquidation of the tendencies to autonomy south of the Yangtze marked the general strengthening of the central government's hold on the empire as a whole, the end of the period of adaptation and the consolidation of the new regime. Thus one may say that the long period of internal stability which was to last until the end of the eighteenth century began in 1681, two years before the final conquest of the island of Formosa.

Chapter 23

The Enlightened Despots

The great emperors K'ang-hsi (1661–1722), Yung-cheng (1723–36) and Ch'ien-lung (1736–96) showed a sense of adaptation, an openness of mind, and, in short, a degree of intelligence which makes them deserve the description 'enlightened despots', all the more since their reigns, from the end of the seventeenth century until about 1775, seem to have been a sort of concrete application of the moralizing, rationalist philosophy of 'neo-Confucianism'.

The reign of the moral order

The winning-over of the educated classes

From the capture of Peking to the elimination of the regional power created by Wu San-kuei in the south-west, nearly forty years elapsed, years marked by the invasion of the North, the wars against the Southern Ming, the difficulties caused by piracy, and finally the secession of the southern provinces. Most of the intelligentsia refused to collaborate with the invaders. They went to earth and hid their dangerous writings. However, with the gradual disappearance of the generations which had lived through the last Ming reigns and the period of resistance, the assumption of control by the new regime became more noticeable. The new masters, who adopted the autocratic, centralized institutions of the defunct empire without making any great changes, while systematically favouring their own aristocracy and thus ensuring for themselves control of all the positions of command, soon realized that it was essential to win over the old governing classes and at the same time to foster a spirit of submission to the new dynasty.

The resumption of the official competitions in 1646 was to do much to secure a return to normality by providing the empire with young civil servants devoted to the new regime and by directing all the activity of the literati towards this sole means of access to honours and social prestige. By closely associating the former governing classes of the Ming period with their own authority, the enlightened despots of the Ch'ing dynasty fulfilled their dearest wishes and put an end to the atmosphere of suspicion and serious divorce between the central authority and its agents from which the defunct dynasty had suffered so severely. Under the Ch'ing, there were to be no further conflicts like the one between the eunuchs and the Tung-lin party in the years 1615–27. On the contrary, there was to be a good understanding between the imperial throne and the Chinese educated classes during most of the Sino-Manchu dynasty. The antagonism between Chinese and Manchus tended to die down in the course of the eighteenth century and only flared up again as a result of the social and political crises of the late nineteenth and early twentieth centuries.

Moreover, the mildness of the Ch'ing government from the end of the seventeenth century onwards, its anxiety to spare the peasantry (which explains the calm that prevailed in the countryside), and the advantages accorded to the agents of the state resulted in making the new dynasty seem like the one most in conformity with the ideals of the literati, the one closest to the humanitarian, paternalist ideal of an orthodox work like the *Mencius*. The high salaries of civil servants in the K'ang-hsi era had put a brake on corruption, and the emperor Yung-cheng (1723–36) even went so far as to institute a very substantial bonus, the *yang-lien*, intended to 'maintain probity'.

But there was more to it than that: K'ang-hsi and his successors made themselves the patrons of classical studies and Chinese culture, adopting with regard to cultivated Chinese circles a policy similar to the one which they followed to win over the Buddhist peoples of Mongolia and central Asia. They wished to seem the most enthusiastic devotees of Chinese culture as well as the best defenders of lamaism. The emperor K'ang-hsi travelled personally, at great expense, to the cities of the lower Yangtze, the centres of the Chinese intelligentsia, on six occasions – in 1684, 1689, 1699, 1703, 1705, and 1707. Ch'ien-lung was to follow his example in 1751, 1757, 1762, 1765, 1780, and 1784. But flattery and ulterior political motives were accompanied by real sympathy in these emperors, who were completely converted to Chinese culture. K'ang-hsi, who was interested in science, a good mathematician, and a skilful musician, was also, like Ch'ien-lung, something of a poet and calligrapher. But what revealed most clearly these enlightened sovereigns' interest in the immense intellectual wealth of China were the great publishing enterprises which they sponsored – the writing of the *History of the Ming,* the compilation of catalogues of paintings and calligraphy, of dictionaries, of a big anthology of the T'ang poets, and above all the big collection of works in Chinese made between 1772 and 1782. These official commissions gave numerous literati jobs which freed them for several years from the worry of earning a living. For many they provided the opportunity to reveal their talents and their inexhaustible erudition. They also had another merit – that of disarming the very circles which in the seventeenth century had produced the most resolute opponents of the Manchu domination.

All these things – the relative mildness of the political climate, the adoption by the emperors themselves and by the Manchu aristocracy of Chinese culture, the expansion of the empire abroad, the internal peace, and the general prosperity – were to help to assuage the bitterness of the most intransigent patriots.

A 'Confucian' empire

But we should possess only a false and incomplete idea of the position of the Chinese élite if we confined ourselves to underlining the paternalistic policy of the three great emperors of the eighteenth century. This paternalism was in reality only the other side of a fundamentally authoritarian conception of the imperial power. If the Manchus did not have any declared enemies inside China, it was not solely because Chinese society as a whole and in general was satisfied with the regime and with conditions of life; it was also because opponents were pitilessly pursued. The Ch'ing emperors required of each one of their subjects respectful submission to their power and unfailing loyalty to their person. They considered one of their essential tasks to be the inauguration everywhere – through its diffusion in all strata of society – of neo-Confucian orthodoxy, of the reign of moral order. This indoctrination, which was rendered easier by the proliferation of schools, even in the rural areas, seemed to them all the more essential in that the foreign origin of the dynasty could raise questions about its legitimacy. Thus in the official code of morality the accent was placed on the principle of authority and the virtues of obedience. Orthodoxy declined into a doctrine of submission. It is true that this development, which was bound up with the advance of the authoritarian empire since the foundation of the Ming dynasty, went back beyond the advent of the Ch'ing. But if there was ever a 'Confucian' empire, in which the links between moral orthodoxy and the political system were clearly evident, it was certainly the Manchu empire. The desire to impose the reign of moral order and at the same time to justify their own power was very much in evidence in the three emperors of the eighteenth century. Yung-cheng revised and enlarged the *Holy Instructions* (*Sheng-yü*), which his predecessor had published in 1681. He ordered that they should be read aloud in public. He required every candidate in the official competitions to read the work which he himself had written to justify the Manchu domination—the *Ta-i chüeh-mi lu* (1730). As early as the reign of K'ang-hsi there had been signs of a reaction against unorthodox works and corrupting novels, which were put on the index of proscribed books in 1687. Censorship became more severe in 1714. Under Ch'ien-lung all writings, both ancient and modern, in which the 'Barbarians' were criticized, even by allusion, and all works not strictly orthodox in inspiration, were systematically sought out so that they could be censored or destroyed. This was the famous 'literary inquisition' of 1774–89, which was carried out in conjunction with the compilation of the huge collection of works in Chinese, one of the greatest glories of Ch'ien-lung's reign, and was continued after its completion. The regime did not confine itself to censoring and destroying works which could injure the moral order; it persecuted the authors and their relatives.

These odious acts of tyranny—the Manchu princes who had been converted to Christianity were the victims of similar persecutions under Yung-cheng, not so much because of their faith as because of their attitude at K'ang-hsi's accession—betrayed the nature of the political system. If the Manchu regime usually seemed very mild, that was because it applied itself to the task of spreading a spirit of submission and obedience, and because it made moral order the foundation of its power and stability.

The most extensive empire in the world

It was on the steppes that the destiny of the Manchus had been shaped and in eastern Mongolia that they had won their first decisive success by gaining the support of the Mongol tribes of that area. The almost unexpected void which had opened before their eyes in China after their conquest of the north-eastern territories had drawn them on, so to speak, to advance further and further. But the origins of the Manchu power were to continue to guide the destiny of the new empire: the Ch'ing were called to become the great power of the steppe zone and of central Asia.

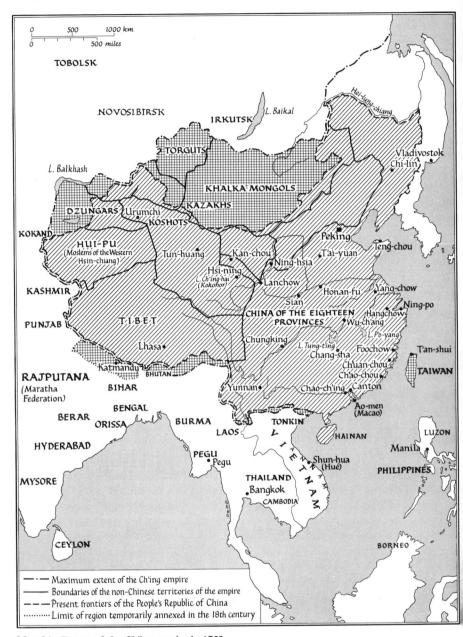

Map 24   Extent of the Ch'ing empire in 1759

Mongolia, Central Asia, and Tibet:
war, religion, and diplomacy

The Manchu expansion into the interior of Asia was bound up from the start with the military and religious (or, if you like, diplomatic) problem posed by the steppe peoples. The Mongols' alliance with the Ch'ing had aroused the anxiety and hostility of the powerful western tribes known by the general term of Oirats and comprising the Koshots, the Dzungars, the Torguts and the Borbets. At the time when the Manchu power was developing in the north-east, the Koshots controlled the whole area between Urumchi, the present-day capital of Sinkiang, and Kokonor (Tsinghai). By 1640 they were practically masters of Tibet. Now this dominant position in Tibet possessed, in the eyes of the steppe tribes, a crucial political significance. To appear as the protectors of the Dalai Lama was to acquire immense prestige with them. Lamaism had made considerable progress among the nomadic herdsmen since the time of the great Yüan empire, whose solicitude for the Tibetan monks had been made plain by about 1280, and the influence of Lamaism had increased since the end of the sixteenth century all over the steppe zone. The Koshot domination of Tibet was to be succeeded by that of the Dzungars, who in 1678–79 conquered the whole of western Sinkiang, where they put an end to the Islamic principalities of the oases. Their leader was Galdan (1644–97), a great figure in the history of central Asia at the end of the seventeenth century. In 1686 Galdan attacked Outer Mongolia and threatened the Khalkha, eastern Mongols who put themselves under the protection of the Ch'ing and were to remain their faithful subjects throughout the dynasty. The Ch'ing response to this attempt by the Dzungars to re-establish a big nomad empire in the centre of Asia was to be both military and diplomatic. In 1696 and 1697 they occupied the regions to the south of Lake Baikal, a strategic area from which the eastern Turks in the sixth to seventh centuries and the Mongols in the thirteenth had directed their big offensives. The first Ch'ing victory over the Dzungars was to be followed during the first half of the eighteenth century by a series of campaigns which led to an extension of the Sino-Manchu empire to the region south of Lake Balkhash and even to Nepal.

For the Ch'ing, diplomacy consisted in refining on the favours bestowed by the Mongols on the religious authorities of Tibet and of making the Tibetans feel the superiority of China. In 1652 the Dalai Lama was invited to Peking, where he was received with great pomp. By the second half of the seventeenth century the capital of the Ch'ing empire had become the great centre for the printing of Tibetan and Mongol Buddhist works, and in the eighteenth century the Ch'ing encouraged the

Plate 56. Mandala in gilded bronze, from
Tibet in the Ch'ing era

Plate 57. The Potala Palace, Lhasa, Tibet

translation of Lamaist texts into Mongol and Manchu. Nine years after his accession, in 1732, the emperor Yung-cheng converted his palace in Peking, the Yung-ho-kung, into a Lamaist temple. It was to be one of the high places of Tibetan Buddhism in the capital. When the Ch'ing succeeded in gaining a firm foothold in Tibet in 1751, they took good care not to display their power too openly; as a Chinese protectorate, Tibet was to retain a large measure of internal autonomy. The essential point was in fact that the great religious centre of Lhasa should not fall into the hands of the Mongols again.

In spite of their defeat the following year, the Dzungars' power did not decline in the least. In the reign of Tsewang Rabtan, or Araptan, Galdan's nephew, they succeeded in creating a vast empire which stretched from southern Siberia to the frontiers of Tibet and embraced the valley of the Ili, south of Lake Balkhash, and the western part of Mongolia. The first attempt of the Ch'ing to gain a foothold in Tibet, in 1705–6, was frustrated by the Dzungars, who occupied Lhasa and the main Tibetan centres in 1717 and 1718. However, a Sino-Manchu army which started out from Szechwan advanced into the high Tibetan plateaux in 1720 and after expelling the Dzungars from Lhasa left a fixed garrison there. From 1751 onwards Chinese control over Tibet became permanent and remained so more or less ever after, in spite of British efforts to seize possession of this Chinese protectorate at the beginning of the twentieth century.

The creation of the 'New Territories'

However, the Dzungar problem was not resolved until 1757. After a period of relative understanding between the Ch'ing and the Dzungars from 1728 onwards, and after the treaty fixing the frontier at the Altai range, relations deteriorated and Peking decided to send an expedition into the Ili territory, the strategic base of this formidable foe. This was the campaign of extermination of 1756–57. Most of the Dzungars were massacred and their very name was abolished. Henceforth they were known only by the name of Ölöths. The conquest of the Ili valley was followed in 1758 and 1759 by that of the Islamic oases of the Tarim basin. The Ch'ing Banners entered Aksu, Kashgar, and Yarkand. All the conquered areas, from the Altai to K'un-lun and from Tun-huang to the Pamirs, were put under military command and administered by the army. They received the name of 'New Territories' (Sinkiang) — the Chinese Turkestan of Western geographers. It was only much later, in 1884, after a long period of Chinese colonization, that these territories, where since the dawn of history Indo-Iranian, Islamic, Turkish, Mongol, Tibetan, and Chinese influences had all mingled, were to be promoted to the rank of province. Right from their inclusion in the Sino-Manchu empire they were a land of exile for political and common criminals.

A continental, cosmopolitan empire

The Ch'ing empire thus reached its greatest extent in 1759. It controlled territories covering thirteen million square kilometres. The Chinese empire had never attained before, and was never to attain again, such a size. The area of the People's Republic of China is today only 9,736,0000 square kilometres, for the Ch'ing empire embraced not only Outer Mongolia and Taiwan but also regions since occupied by Russia to the south of Lake Balkhash and to the east of the lower reaches of the Heilungkiang (Amur) and of the Ussuri (region of the Sikhota Alin range). About 1665 the Ch'ing armies had even ventured as far as the outer Khingan, north of the Amur, which the Russians were to call the Stanovoi Mountains and which today form part of the territory of the Soviet Union. But the influence of the Sino-Manchu empire made itself felt even beyond its frontiers: most of the Asian countries (Nepal, Burma, Siam, Vietnam, the Philippines, the Ryukyu, Korea) recognized its sovereignty and were more or less dependent on it.

Like the present-day People's Republic of China, the Ch'ing empire consisted of a number of very different peoples. Administrative documents were usually drawn up in Manchu and Chinese, but sometimes also in Kalmuk (western Mongol), in eastern Turkish and Arabic script, and in Tibetan. The administration was constrained to publish polyglot dictionaries which today constitute valuable documents for the history of languages, thus continuing a tradition which went back to the beginning of the Ming dynasty — that of the dictionaries of the interpreting offices, the *Hua-i i-yü.*

It should also be noted that this empire consisting of provinces, colonies, and protectorates was far from uniform in its administrative arrangements. Manchuria, which was reserved for Manchus, enjoyed a special status which distinguished it from the Chinese provinces; in Mongolia, it was personal bonds of loyalty between heads of tribes and Ch'ing emperors that ensured the adhesion of the inhabitants to the empire; Tibet was subject to a fairly liberal protectorate régime; and the New Territories of Sinkiang were occupied and administered by the army.

A country where moral order reigned, eighteenth-century China was also the greatest imperialist power in Asia. Its domination of the major part of the continent, its uncontested power and the preponderant interest for it of central Asian questions were to be among the decisive factors in its attitude to Western enterprises in the nineteenth century.

An era of prosperity

This empire, which covered a large part of the Asiatic continent, was also the country, of all those in the world, where the increase in wealth and population was the most rapid. In the eighteenth century China entered an era of prosperity due to an unprecedented upsurge in agriculture, manufacturing, and commerce. It was in the front rank of nations for the volume of its production and of its internal trade.

High watermark of agricultural techniques

Chinese agriculture reached the highest point in its development in the eighteenth century. Its techniques, the variety of species cultivated, and its yield made it the most skilled and highly developed in history before the appearance of modern agronomy. On top of the traditional crops (wheat, barley, millet, rice, the varieties of which had multiplied since the eleventh century) came new ones—the sweet potato, the ground nut, sorghum (*kao-liang*), maize—which made it possible to spread the harvests over the whole year, were content with poor or badly irrigated land, and solved the problem of bridging the winter gap. The consequences of the introduction of American plants from the sixteenth century on made themselves fully felt and caused a positive revolution in agriculture. In addition, vegetables and fruit came to play a large part in people's diet, not to mention the additional resources provided by the rearing of pigs and poultry and by the skilful fish-farming which was widespread in all areas where irrigation was employed. Industrial crops (cotton, tea, sugar cane) were expanding rapidly.

In comparison, the agriculture of many areas of Europe at the same period looks singularly backward. The Chinese peasant of the Yung-cheng era and the first half of the Ch'ien-lung era was, in general, much better and much happier than his equivalent in the France of Louis XV. He was usually better educated. Public and private schools were so numerous that comfortably-off peasants could easily pay for the education of their children. Some great literati of the eighteenth century were of quite humble origin.

Moreover, the agrarian policy of the Ch'ing favoured the small farmers. They were very moderately taxed and an ordinance of 1711 went so far as to forbid any increase in quotas, even in the case of a growth in the population. The Chinese rural areas thus seem to have experienced general prosperity during the major part of the eighteenth century. It was only in the last twenty years of Ch'ien-lung's reign that the situation started to deteriorate as a result of the sudden aggravation of the burdens imposed on the peasantry and of the pressure exerted in such cases by the richest landowners, who were the only people in a position to lend at interest.

The remarkable upsurge in Chinese agriculture in the eighteenth century, stimulated in addition by the concomitant expansion in craft production and trade, suggests that we should perhaps revise certain modern judgements.

The very dense populations of certain plains and deltas in East Asia (the central plain in North China, the lower Yangtze valley, the Red River delta in Vietnam, the coastal plains of South China and Java) are very often mentioned as being characteristic of monsoon Asia, and people see in them one of the elements of a vicious circle typical of these old lands: a high birth rate, backwardness of techniques which remain essentially manual ones, and extreme general poverty, aggravated in the nineteenth and twentieth centuries by social conditions accentuating the inequalities and preventing any radical reform. But what the layman tends to regard as the visible proofs of 'backwardness' or 'under-development', in comparison with the situation of the rich, industrialized countries, is in fact the culminating point of a history marked by remarkable progress. If the 'developed' countries eat their fill, they owe this much less to their own genius than to the circumstances of their history and in particular to the fact that the clearest progress in their agriculture was made only in quite recent times. Europe, a region of meadows, fallow land and forest, has never been short of cultivable soil.

The eighteenth century is the moment in history that best reveals the difference in rates of evolution. It was then that the mediocre agriculture (so far as yield was concerned) of a thinly populated Europe, whose population was nevertheless growing, was faced with the skilful, diversified agriculture of a China experiencing an extraordinary demographic expansion. It was at this point that, thanks to an accumulation of technical progress which had gone on since the ninth to eleventh centuries, the population of China and East Asia as a whole registered a clear advance on that of Europe. The societies of the Far East have not been 'behind' those of the West; they have simply followed another route.

Craftsmanship on an 'industrial' scale
and unprecedented commercial expansion

What is true of subsistence is also true of craft production and mercantile activities: in the eighteenth century the Chinese world succeeded in making the best possible use of the techniques of the pre-industrial age. The

Plate 58.   Extract from a manual on painting, 1679

Plate 59.   Porcelain bowl, early eighteenth century, showing
a scholar reading in a pavilion

conjunction of these three domains—agriculture, crafts, and commerce—should moreover be underlined, for the relations between them were extremely close. The economic development of China in the eighteenth century may seem like the resumption, after a century of wars and internal troubles, of that of the Wan-li era (1573–1620), but it outstripped the earlier period in extent.

The textile industry, the largest and most productive of all Chinese manufacturing activities, supplied a market which never stopped growing and provided the peasantry with a supplementary source of income, thanks to the possibility of working at home. By the end of the seventeenth century the cotton goods industry of Sung-chiang, to the southwest of Shanghai, gave permanent employment to 200,000 workers, not counting bespoke work.

The tea plantations had spread over the whole Yangtze basin and were very numerous in Fukien and Chekiang. Exports of tea by sea (it should be noted that the western European word for tea is of Fukienese origin, while the term adopted by some of the Slav languages is close to the pronunciation of the Chinese term in the northern dialects) rose from 2.6 million English pounds in 1762 to 23.3 million at the end of the eighteenth century and continued to grow in the nineteenth. Harvested by the planters (*shan-hu*, 'mountain families'), the tea was prepared in big workshops (*ch'a-chuang*) employing several hundred wage-earning workers and then taken over by wealthy corporations of merchants, who dealt in Canton with the East India Company.

The porcelain ovens of Ching-te-chen, to the east of Lake Po-yang in Kiangsi, where tens of thousands of ceramic craftsmen worked to fulfil orders from the court and wealthy families as well as for export, and those of the less important centre of Li-chiang in Hunan, near Ch'ang-sha, held the records for the production of ceramics. Celadon and porcelain were exported in growing quantities to Japan, Korea, the Philippines, the Indo-Chinese peninsula, Indonesia, and even Europe.

We must also take into account the paper and sugar manufactured in Fukien, the hempen cloth of Hsin-hui in Kwangtung, the steel of Wu-hu on the Yangtze, upstream from Nanking, and the ironmongery produced since the Ming period at Fatshan (Foshan), near Canton, and exported all over South-East Asia. Certain famed kinds of cloth such as the fine cottons of Nanking, the silks of Soochow and Hangchow and the raw silk of Huchow, to the north of Hangchow, figured alongside tea, ceramics and lacquer-ware among the products exported even to Europe. The extraordinary vogue for Chinese furniture in eighteenth-century Europe is well known. In 1703 the French ship *Amphitrite* sailed back from Nanking with a cargo consisting entirely of Chinese lacquer work.

Table 18. The revenues of the State under the first Ch'ing emperors
(in millions of liang)

Year	Land and capitation tax	Taxes on salt	Commercial taxes
1653	21.28 (87%)	2.13 (9%)	0.1 (4%)
1685	27.27 (88%)	2.76 (9%)	0.12 (4%)
1725	30.07 (85%)	4.43 (12%)	1.35 (4%)
1753	29.38 (73%)	7.01 (17%)	4.30 (10%)
1766	29.91 (73%)	5.74 (14%)	5.40 (13%)

These figures show not only the growth but also the relatively modest proportion formed by the fiscal revenues of commercial origin. And the receipts from customs dues on maritime trade were only a very small percentage of this total income from commercial taxes. One can understand the lack of interest in the British proposals at the end of the eighteenth century for an increase in trade.

China traded with the whole world – Japan, South-East Asia, Europe, and America (via Manila) – and this trade, which had developed since the abolition of the restrictions on foreign trade after the conquest of Taiwan in 1683, was beneficial to China. It encouraged the various crafts and agricultural production and caused silver money to flow into the country. It has been estimated that of the 400 million silver dollars imported from South America and Mexico into Europe between 1571 and 1821 half was used for the purchase of Chinese products by the western countries. If the estimate is accurate, it would tend to prove that China, which owed to the New World plants which eventually caused a sort of agricultural revolution, was one of the countries which profited most from the discovery of America.

No doubt in the Ch'ien-lung era the part played by this sea-borne trade in the Chinese economy as a whole was still small: at the end of the eighteenth century commercial taxes on internal trade reached four million *liang* against 650,000 *liang* for the revenue from the maritime customs. The empire's extent, the number of its inhabitants, and the scale of their activities suffice to explain this difference. This foreign trade concerned above all the maritime provinces, to which, in order to satisfy demand, the tea plantations were extended. An exporter of finished products, China reached the point as early as the eighteenth century of importing rice from South-East Asia – mainly from Siam and the Philippines – into the provinces of Fukien and Kwangtung, which lived mainly on commerce and craftsmanship and grew insufficient agricultural produce. Some thousands of junks, large ships of a thousand tons with a crew of a hundred and eighty men, arrived every year at Amoy. Canton and Amoy were in touch with the coasts of Vietnam and Cambodia, with Luzon, Malacca, Song Khla in Siam, and Johore in the Malay peninsula. This trend in the economy of these maritime provinces enables us to understand their apparent 'over-population' and poverty in the nineteenth century, which was to be a period of recession.

The most remarkable thing about the economic upsurge of China in the eighteenth century was the size of the commercial streams and the extent of the regions controlled by certain corporations of merchants. Not only the Chinese provinces but also Mongolia, central Asia, and the whole of South-East Asia were caught up in the Chinese commercial network. The links were obviously tighter in China itself. Each big corporation (the bankers of Shansi, the merchants of Hsin-an in Anhwei, whose power went back to the Ming period, the salt merchants of Yangchow, whose activities consisted of combined operations in the salt of the Huai and in the rice of Hunan and Hupei) possessed in all the big towns a sort of local seat (*hui-kuan*) which served as a meeting-place, hotel for members passing through, depot, branch, and bank.

These rich merchants, who sometimes formed famous 'dynasties', played a political role thanks to the mere size of their fortunes and to the extent of their influence at the local level. They were also often men of taste and patrons of the arts, and this fact alone entitles them to a place in the intellectual history of the Ch'ing epoch.

Population explosion and colonization

Internal peace, the mildness of the political climate, and above all the progress of agriculture and the general prosperity were doubtless the main reasons for the growth of China's population in the eighteenth century. This demographic expansion had no parallel in the other countries of the world at that time. While the population of Europe rose from 144 million in 1750 to 193 million in 1800, in China—if the censuses are reliable—there were 143 million people in 1741, 200 million in 1762 and 360 million in 1812.

Chinese colonization developed in the New Territories of Sinkiang, which absorbed part of the growth in the population. Military colonies were established there whose lands covered 300,000 *ch'ing* (nearly a million and a half hectares) in 1765. Emigration to South-East Asia also increased considerably. Such was the case in particular in Borneo, where the sultanates founded as a result of the conversion of Indonesia to Islam by Indian Moslems left part of the trading activities to Chinese colonists of Hakka origin. As is still the case today, emigrants from the same canton were all specialists in the same profession—development of auriferous sands, agriculture, cattle rearing, fishing, or commerce. One important colony, in the sultanate of Pontianak, on the west coast of Borneo, was organized as a sort of republic independent of the Ch'ing

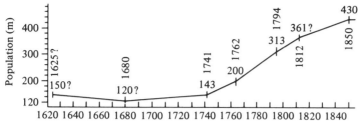

Rough graph of the growth of the Chinese population from the beginning of the seventeenth century to the middle of the nineteenth century (in millions). The demographic increase, which according to the census figures would have been 14.85 per 1000 between 1741 and 1794 declined to 5.66 between 1794 and 1850. It came to a halt after the middle of the nineteenth century.

empire, although it remained in constant touch with its native district, the region of Ch'ao-chou, in the north-east of Kwangtung. There were 200,000 Chinese living in it at the end of the eighteenth century. Founded in 1777 by a man called Lo Fang-pai, this little state, the Lan-fang Kung-ssu ('the Lanfang Company') was to last until 1884.

But Chinese colonization also went on in China proper, in the southern provinces – Kweichow, Yunnan, and Kwangsi. The immigrants came either from Kwangtung or the northern provinces, as is proved by the present distribution of dialects. The growth of the Chinese (Han) population was also almost certainly connected with the conflicts, which became more and more frequent, with the Thai, Miao and Yao or Tibeto-Burmese inhabitants of these regions. The plundering of land, the usurious practices of the Chinese business men and the attempts of the Chinese administration to extend and strengthen its control over the territories of the ethnic minorities were at the root of numerous rebellions, which were to become still more widespread in the nineteenth century.

Frontier conflicts

The expansion of their empire put the Ch'ing into direct contact with distant countries and caused tensions and conflicts. Complications on the frontier between Yunnan and Burma led to the dispatch of Chinese armies into the upper Irrawaddy valley in 1767, and the difficult war which the Ch'ing banners had to wage in this hot, unhealthy region lasted until 1771. From that time onwards Burma recognized the suzerainty of China. But the last big military exploit of Ch'ien-lung's reign was really the amazing expedition which, after crossing the high Tibetan plateaux, entered Nepal in 1791 to punish the Gurkha tribes for the raids which they were accustomed to make into southern Tibet.

Table 19.   Embassies from European countries to China,
from the discovery of the Cape route to 1820

	Portugal	Netherlands	Russia	Vatican	England
1521	*				
1655		*			
1656			*		
1661		*			
1664		*			
1670	*				
1676			*		
1689			*		
1693			*		
1705				*	
1715			*		
1719			*		
1720				*	
1725				*	
1726	*				
1753	*				
1767			*		
1793					*
					(Macartney mission)
1794		*			
1805			*		
1808			*		
1816					*
					(Amherst mission)
1820			*		

First clashes with Russian colonization in East Asia

Contacts with Russia went further back and dated from the early days of the dynasty. Between 1650 and 1820 Russia was to send more embassies to Peking than any other European country—eleven, as opposed to the thirteen sent by Portugal, the Netherlands, the Vatican, and England together. The fact was that from the middle of the seventeenth century onwards eastern Siberia began to be explored by groups of Cossacks, who held the local hunting peoples to ransom, sought to acquire a monopoly in the fur trade and built fortified posts. Okhotsk, on the Pacific, was founded in 1649 and Irkutsk, south-west of Lake Baikal, in 1652. Russian incursions into the valley of the Heilungkiang (Amur) brought riposts from the Sino-Manchu troops. The Russian prisoners were enrolled in the Banners. The little post of Albazin (Yaksa) in particular, founded by Khabarov in 1651, was the stake in numerous battles in the area of the river Zeya between Russian colonists and Chinese troops, who occupied the post in turn. The Ch'ing even organized a maritime expedition in 1661 to recapture Albazin. However, the Russians entered into negotiations with the Ch'ing in 1686, the Dutch acting as intermediaries, and three years later the first treaty between Russia and China was signed at Nerchinsk, 1300 kilometres north of Peking. The Jesuits Gerbillon and Pereira took part in the talks as interpreters, and the resulting document, drawn up in Latin, Manchu, Chinese, Mongol, and Russian, fixed the frontier between the Ch'ing empire and the Russian zone of influence. A new treaty was to be concluded during the reign of Yung-cheng, in 1727. It was signed at Kiakhta, a small town 150 kilometres south of Lake Baikal through which most of the trade between China and Russia in the eighteenth century was to pass. This trade consisted mainly in the exchange of furs for cotton goods and silks; tea was to become more important from the end of the eighteenth century onwards. (the value of the tea sold to Russia was 1.4 million roubles in 1760 and 8 million in 1800). The treaty of Kiakhta established new frontiers and fixed the size and frequency of Russian trade missions to Peking.

Revolts of colonized peoples

The treatment accorded to ethnic minorities was possibly a little less tyrannical than the Tsarist regime at the same period, since in 1770–71 170,000 Kalmuks from Tarbagatay (in north-western Dzungaria) took refuge in Sinkiang. But, generally speaking, it seems to have grown harsher during the course of the eighteenth century, perhaps because the demographic expansion of the Han (people of Chinese language and culture) led the Ch'ing government to practise a more and more interventionist policy. Still rare in the reign of Yung-cheng (1723–36), rebellions and campaigns of repression multiplied at the end of Ch'ien-lung's reign at the same time as police action on the frontiers of the empire. This stiffening of attitude, which grew more marked at the end of Ch'ien-lung's reign and coincided with the great 'literary inquisition' of 1774–89, is also partly explained by the initiatives taken by the governors and generals responsible for maintaining order on the frontiers and in the areas inhabited by non-Chinese peoples: the political climate favoured adventurism and encouraged corrupt practices at the end of the eighteenth century.

As early as 1726–29 the governors-general of Yunnan and Kweichow tried to rob the ethnic minority leaders responsible to the Chinese authorities (the *t'u-ssu*) of their powers and to subject the aborigines to the regular administration of the Chinese districts. This caused extensive disturbances which spread and were savagely repressed. The Ch'ing also had difficulties in the Chin-ch'uan, a very mountainous region in north-western Szechwan, where the local inhabitants, whose culture was Tibetan, rebelled from 1746–49 onwards. Order was re-established only after long and costly campaigns, the last of which, in 1771–76, was to cost the treasury 70 million *liang* of silver, more than twice the cost of the conquest of the Ili valley and western Sinkiang. Cannon made by the Portuguese of Macao were employed in these last operations.

Revolts by the Moslem peoples of Sinkiang and by Chinese Moslems of Kansu became more numerous after the conquest of the Ili valley. They occurred first of all in western Sinkiang in 1758–59, then in the oasis of Ush to the south of Lake Balkhash in 1765. Another took place in Kansu, where the suppression lasted from 1781 to 1784. A rising by the aborigines of Taiwan was crushed amid rivers of blood in 1787–88 by an expeditionary force from the mainland. Finally, in the last few years of Ch'ien-lung's reign, in 1795–97, there were serious new rebellions of the ethnic minorities of Hunan and Kweichow.

Vietnamese piracy

There was a recrudescence of piracy on the south and south-east coast round about 1800 as a result of a *coup d'état* in 1787 in Vietnam, a country which, though independent, paid tribute to the Ch'ing. Vietnamese generals occupied the capital, Hanoi. In the following year the Ch'ing sent an expeditionary force to the assistance of the legal Le government (the Le dynasty had been founded in 1428 by Le Loi). But the Sino-Manchu armies, which came by land from Kwangsi and by sea from Kwangtung, suffered a defeat and withdrew in 1789. A new dynasty was proclaimed, the Nguyen dynasty, which was to last up to the occupation of the country by the French. The name 'Dai Viet' ('Great Land of Viet') was replaced by 'Vietnam' (Viet of the South). As a result of the change of regime, numerous Vietnamese loyal to the old dynasty went into exile in China; some settled in Nanking, others as far away as Kalgan (Chang-chia-k'ou, north-west of Peking), and they were even to be found in central Asia, in the colonial lands of the Ili valley, to the south of Lake Balkhash. But the events in Vietnam had more distant consequences in China. They were at the root of the piratical activities conducted by Viet-namese and Chinese from 1795 onwards on the coasts of Kwangtung, Fukien, and Chekiang. The suppression of these activities, at first directed by the Fukienese admiral Li Ch'ang-keng (1750–1808), took from 1800 to 1809. The fleet of the Vietnamese pirates was destroyed by a typhoon off the coast of Chekiang in 1800, but the Chinese pirates continued to harry the maritime provinces of south and south-east China and in 1806 they launched a successful attack on the coast of Taiwan.

Deterioration of the political and social climate

The advance of corruption and the first peasant revolts

The end of Ch'ien-lung's reign was a period of improvidence and waste. The distant and difficult wars in central Asia, Nepal, Burma, and western Szechwan, the pensions and salaries for favoured persons, and the upkeep of a large and demanding court absorbed a considerable proportion of the state's resources. To these burdens, whose weight began to make itself felt on the taxable population, were added those resulting from the parallel advance of malpractices. Even if it must be admitted that corruption was a vice inherent in the political system, on the other hand it is certain that there were lulls in the incidence of the evil and that it was effectively restrained by the controls effected and by the action taken against guilty officials. The general prosperity and the moral atmosphere which had prevailed under the first Ch'ing emperors and during the first half of Ch'ien-lung's reign had contributed to reducing its effects. In the last quarter of the eighteenth century, on the other hand, corruption seems to have made rapid progress in the whole of the Chinese administration. The example set by the emperor and the court seems to have caused a taste for wealth and luxury to spread through the upper classes.

But the change is also explained by the increasingly autocratic character of Ch'ien-lung's policy. From 1775 onwards the ageing emperor took a fancy to a young general of the Banners called Ho-shen (1750–99), who was to exert a hidden but all-powerful influence in the government and on the administration of the empire. Sent to Kansu in 1781 to suppress a Moslem rising, he showed himself to be so incompetent that he was immediately recalled. But Ho-shen, who held a number of different offices, soon appointed men in his own pay and organized a vast network of corruption. He made himself particularly notorious at the time of the repression of the revolts by poor people of central and western China who had banded together in the secret society of the White Lotus. These revolts were partly due precisely to Ho-shen's exactions. Ho-shen and his minions—Fu-k'ang-an, Ho-lin, Sun Shih-i—dragged out the campaigns, inflating their expenses to enrich themselves and presenting massacres of innocent people as victories.

These first big peasant revolts of the Ch'ing epoch are thus explained both by the increase of the burdens laid on the rural population and by the exactions of Ho-shen. Poverty and injustice suddenly gave fresh life to the ancient organization of the White Lotus (*Pai-lien-chiao*), which had played a big role during the rebellions of the end of the Mongol era, in the middle of the fourteenth century, then again at the end of the Ming period; like most of these forbidden confraternities, it had continued to exist in secret. The White Lotus rebellions were not effectively quelled until after the elimination of Ho-shen in 1799, and in fact they went on until 1803, increasing the deficit of the public finances; the cost of the operations for the years 1798–1801 alone reached one hundred million *liang*.

The effects of the corruption which Ho-shen's sway had helped to spread from the end of the Ch'ien-lung era onwards were to make themselves felt in a vital sector – the maintenance of the dykes and of the works regulating watercourses. The officials in charge of these tasks embezzled state funds and seven big floods of the Yellow River occurred during the Chia-ch'ing era (1798–1820), in spite of the considerable funds allocated to the repair of breaches in the dykes. These criminal malpractices ended in the terrible catastrophe of 1855, when the course of the Yellow River, the flow of which can reach 20,000 cubic metres per second when it is in full flood, moved from the north to the south of the Shantung peninsula – a distance as great as that between London and Newcastle (the last change of course of a similar size had occurred in 1324, under the Mongols). The next cataclysm of the same kind was to take place in 1938.

The vices of the political system

The manners and spirit of the governing class were the product of a political system first analysed and criticized by the philosophers of the seventeenth century and subjected later to the same process by the political thinkers of the nineteenth century: China suffered from an unhealthy degree of centralization. Peking expected to settle all questions, even in their smallest details, all over this immense empire which its conquests had extended to the major part of the Asiatic continent and which was a whole world in itself. Situations varied according to locality, population, natural conditions, and local usage. But a proliferation of regulations, a tyrannous mass of legislation tied the emperor's representatives in the provinces hand and foot. The disproportionate importance enjoyed by paper work of an extremely formalist character, the threat of unexpected visits by inspectors from the censor's office (*tu-ch'a-yüan*), the innumerable traps into which the local official was liable to fall and which could only be avoided by relying on secretaries with a perfect knowledge of the regulations, the multiplicity of his tasks, his ignorance of the area which he administered – an ignorance which forced him to trust locally recruited clerks and to seek the good offices and advice of the gentry – all these factors would suffice to account for an attitude of timorous caution in the civil servants *en poste*. But this attitude was reinforced by an education which, since the advent of the 'neo-Confucianism' of the Sung epoch, strengthened inhibitions.

Moreover, in the state of permanent insecurity in which the literati lived, the exceptional fortune of success in the three series of triennial competitions (*sheng-yüan, chü-jen* and *chin-shih* were the titles acquired in the competitions held in the prefectures, in the provinces and then in the empire at Peking) and entry upon the mandarin's career constituted a piece of good luck from which it was necessary to profit as quickly as possible. The chosen person was indebted for his success to his parents, to his friends, and sometimes to those who had betted on his success and financed his studies. It was accepted that civil servants should take advantage of the time when they were occupying a post to acquire a certain amount of money and to discharge their obligations. They were very badly paid from the Ch'ien-lung era onwards and the heavy public and private burdens incumbent on them forced them to raise taxes and duties which were only recognized by usage and varied according to district, so much so that the boundary between the legal and the illegal was not very well defined. It was difficult to say where misappropriation began, for from the start the resources for which civil servants had a perfectly legitimate need were provided irregularly and the distinction between public expenses and private expenses was not always clear. Finally, civil servants found themselves caught in a system of social relations in which exchanges of courtesies were indispensable to the conduct of affairs. But here again it is risky to try to draw a clear line between what was permitted and what was not permitted: the gift demanded by usage and politeness could change into a bribe, offered or solicited, without its being possible to say precisely where corruption started. To sum up, it looks as if the political system of the great authoritarian Ming and Ch'ing empires combined what China owed to its Legalist and humanist – i.e. 'Confucian' – traditions, while preserving only vitiated and harmful forms of them: hypertrophy of the centralized bureaucracy on the one hand and a system of human relations which looks like a trade in influence on the other. We cannot accuse the men involved, for many of them had a clear awareness of the faults in the administrative machine of which they formed one of the cogs and of the nature of the society in which they lived. Many had a sense of integrity and of the public interest, but they came up against a system which was bigger than they were and of which they found themselves prisoners.

The advance of corruption and the very noticeable reduction in official salaries brought out clearly at the end of the Ch'ien-lung era the faults of a system which was acceptable in a period of prosperity. The nineteenth century promised to start badly: the crisis in the public finances, the progress of corruption, and the peasant agitation were signs that were all the more disquieting in that the political conscience of the ruling classes had been lulled to sleep by the reign of moral order and by the years of euphoria. The emperor was isolated by the respect and veneration which surrounded him and which he had wished to inculcate in each of his subjects.

Chapter 24

Intellectual Life from the Middle of the Seventeenth Century to the End of the Eighteenth Century

Dominated in the long period of humiliation, uncertainty, and troubles which lasted until about 1683 by the problem of the state and society, Chinese thought was to become more serene in the eighteenth century, that epoch of political and social consolidation and of economic expansion. Without making a radical break with the tendencies which had come to the fore in the preceding period, it was to take a different direction. The eighteenth century saw the triumph of a scientific spirit which applied itself to the whole field of written tradition and had remarkable philosophical implications.

The philosophers of the seventeenth century

The invasion which followed and ended the great rebellions of the last twenty years of the Ming epoch, the resistance, the secession of the South, which for a short time had made it seem likely that the new dynasty was going to crumble, in short the whole period of struggle which began with the entry of the Manchu troops into Peking in 1644 and ended with the suicide of Wu San-kuei at K'un-ming in 1681 was also a period of free thought and of radical criticism of the institutions and intellectual foundations of the authoritarian empire. At that time the vices of absolutism were analysed in a penetrating fashion, philosophical traditions and the traditional methods of teaching were criticized, and a Chinese 'nationalism' based on the notion of belonging to a community and a culture was defined more clearly. The Manchu occupation seems to have precipitated a moral crisis which the most eminent thinkers of that epoch, one of the richest in free-ranging, fertile, and original minds, succeeded in surmounting by the process of reflection. Besides, for these men, work in the study was a sort of continuation of, or substitute for, the direct action which circumstances one day forced them to renounce.

Continuity of intellectual trends in the seventeenth century

But these men were at the same time successors. From the atmosphere of renewal and of social and economic change which had made itself felt in the Wan-li era (1573–1619) they inherited an absence of conformism, an openness of mind and an intellectual curiosity which were characteristic of the whole seventeenth century. Their tendencies to social and political criticism prolonged a current of thought which had been set in motion by the decadence of the state and the omnipotence of the eunuchs. The links between the reformist movement of the late Ming period and the upsurge of political philosophy at the time of the Manchu conquest are obvious. The great thinkers of the early Ch'ing period sprang from the opposition circles of the late Ming period; they belonged for the most part to the 'Society of Renewal' (*fu-she*), the literary and political club which formed a sort of revival of the Tung-lin party in the Ch'ung-chen era (1628–44). The Manchu conquest seemed to them like the consequence of the political and social vices of the old empire now defunct, and their first aim was to put on trial an epoch which had lost all contact with reality and when most of the intelligentsia had been satisfied with abstraction or subjectivist theories.

The continuity is also apparent, in spite of the invasion, in the field of literature. Although part of his work belongs to the years after the disaster of 1644–45, Chin Sheng-t'an, born in 1610, still belongs to the period of intellectual renewal of the end of the Ming dynasty. We meet again in his work the same interest in unorthodox literature as we saw in Li Chih. He was sick of the Classics and his favourite reading was the great Buddhist Sutra, *The Lotus of the True Law* (*Fa-hua-ching*) and, besides Ch'ü Yuan's *Li-sao* and Ssu-ma Ch'ien's *Historical Records*, *The Water Margin* (*Shui-hu-chuan*). In 1641 he published some studies in literary criticism on this novel, and these were followed in 1656 by other studies of a famous play of the Mongol epoch, *The Romance of the*

Western Chamber (Hsi-hsiang-chi), a sentimental, romantic work. Chin Sheng-t'an had his head cut off in 1661 for taking the side of students who protested on the occasion of a ceremony organized at the death of the emperor Shun-chih.

In the second half of the seventeenth century novelists and dramatists continued to follow earlier traditions typical of the late Ming period. It was at this time that the famous *Palace of Long Life (Ch'ang-sheng-tian)* by Hung Sheng (1645–1704) appeared; its theme is the love affair between the concubine Yang and the emperor Hsüan-tsung. *The Fan with the Peach Flowers (T'ao-hua-shan)*, by K'ung Shang-jen (1648–1718), also belongs to this period. Li Yü (1611–80?), an unsuccessful candidate in the doctoral examination, who decided to devote his life to the theatre and the novel, remained, like his contemporary Chin Sheng-t'an, a man of the late Ming period. He wrote among other things a famous erotic novel, *The Cushion of Flesh (Jou-p'u-t'uan)*.

Similarly, painting continued to show a remarkable vitality and originality in the circle of the 'mad monks', the most famous of whom are Pa-ta shan-jen (late Ming–early Ch'ing) and Shih-t'ao (second half of the seventeenth century). These independent painters were the spiritual ancestors of the most original contemporary artists — Chao Chih-ch'ien (1829–84), Jen I (Jen Po-nien) (1840–95), Wu Ch'ang-shih (1844–1927) and Ch'i Pai-shih (1862–1957).

At the beginning of the Manchu dynasty literature, art, and philosophy had not yet suffered the effects to be produced in the following century by the establishment of moral order.

Criticism of absolutism and the first researches into the intellectual history of China

The best way to illustrate the flowering of political philosophy at the beginning of the Manchu dynasty is probably to describe, at least briefly, the figures of the most famous thinkers of that generation. Although they share certain general tendencies, each of them is so original as to demand individual treatment. They all had a decisive effect on contemporary thought. They inspired the reformers and revolutionaries of the late nineteenth century and the first half of the twentieth.

Huang Tsung-hsi (Huang Li-chou) (1610–95), the oldest of his generation, came from a civil service family of Ning-po, in Chekiang. Brought up in circles opposed to the rule of the eunuchs, he witnessed in his youth the clandestine struggle of the Tung-lin party. His father, an adherent of this party, was executed in prison on the orders of Wei Chung-hsien in 1626. Four years later Huang Tsung-hsi joined the Society of Renewal (*fu-she*) in Nanking. He incurred the lasting enmity of Juan Ta-ch'eng (1587–1646), a corrupt high official (also a talented dramatist and scholarly sybarite) who had come back into favour after the execution of Wei Chung-hsien, one of whose most faithful allies he had been. Huang Tsung-hsi owed his last-minute salvation only to the advance of the Manchu troops on Nanking, but he immediately joined the struggle against the invaders. In 1649 he went to Nagasaki with other resistance leaders to ask help of the Japanese. Finding that his efforts were vain, he gave up the struggle and retired to his native district, there devoting himself to research into history, philosophy, astronomy, and mathematics. His first work, the *Ming-i tai-fang lu* (1662), is a general criticism of the absolutist institutions of the late Ming period. His political ideas are liberal: according to him, the prince and his ministers should be at the service of the people and not the other way round. Violently opposed to the Manchus, he refused the offers of an official post made to him in 1678 and 1679 and also the opportunity to collaborate in the plan for a *History of the Ming* launched by the emperor K'ang-hsi. A specialist in the history of the Southern Ming and of the leading figures of this period of resistance, Huang Tsung-hsi was to remain famous above all as the first person to undertake research into the intellectual history of China. His two best-known works are a collection of studies of the philosophical schools of the Ming period, the *Ming-ju hsüeh-an* (1676) and a general history of the Chinese philosophy of the Sung and Yüan ages (eleventh to fourteenth centuries) which he was to leave unfinished at his death. This was the famous *Sung-yüan hsüeh'an*.

These researches were inspired by reflection on the crisis that led to the end of the Ming dynasty and on the basic reasons for China's defeat by foreign invaders. They are explained by Huang Tsung-hsi's passionate interest in the problem of the moulding of men and by the importance that he attributes to education. His work as a whole, in which bold, sometimes even revolutionary, ideas are often expressed, gives the impression of being a critique of the state and of the society of his time.

An evolutionary brand of sociology

Wang Fu-chih (Wang Ch'uan-shan) (1619–92), who was born at Hengyang in Hunan and was nine years younger than Huang Tsung-hsi, had also belonged to the Society of Renewal. Summoned to Kwangtung, to the court of the prince of Kuei, the future Southern Ming emperor Yung-li (1647–60), he had taken part in the struggle against the invaders and then had suddenly decided – like so many others at that time – to seek in studious retreat what was probably both an escape and a new kind of action. Little known during his lifetime—his complete works were not published for the first time until the first half of the nineteenth century, and the plates of this first edition were to be destroyed during the T'ai P'ing Rebellion (1851–64)—Wang Fu-chih is close in many respects to Huang Tsung-hsi. They are both critical of the intuitive, subjectivist philosophy of the end of the Ming period, they both have liberal, anti-absolutist ideas and they are both interested in the history of the resistance to the Manchus. But historical reflection is carried much further by Wang Fu-chih than it had been by Huang Tsung-hsi; a whole philosophy (which looks like a naturalist and 'materialist' one) is implicit in his ideas about historical evolution. According to Wang Fu-chih, the transformation of human societies is the product of natural forces. Thus the transition from fief to administrative district which characterized the great revolution of the end of antiquity was an ineluctable phenomenon. For the same reason the traditional picture of ancient times as a golden age is contrary to what can be rationally deduced about the past; the history of man has been marked by the uninterrupted evolution and constant progress of societies. The sovereigns of remote antiquity remind him of the Miao and Yao chiefs of Hunan among whom he had come to reside. A sacrilegious comparison inspired by love not of scandal but of the truth! What is more, we find in Wang Fu-chih what we should call today a 'structuralist' conception of history which is probably less surprising in a world in which the notion of totality was always fundamental than it might be in the West. According to Wang Fu-chih, the institutions of any given age form a coherent whole from which this or that practice cannot be isolated; there is not only necessity in evolution, but congruence between society and institutions at each stage in this evolution. Thus the old system of local selection and recommendation of civil servants in use during the Han age could no longer be resurrected, because all the conditions which made it viable had disappeared. Similarly, says Wang Fu-chih, it is illusory to try to go back to the division of land into equal plots, for since then the notion of private property has developed. Those who are full of nostalgia for the past and seek remedies for present ills in a return to ancient institutions base their hopes on a fundamental error in historical perspective.

To this keen sense of the evolution of human societies in time, Wang Fu-chih adds a penetrating sociological intuition which makes him sensitive to the multiple differences between different cultures. Thus there are hardly any human societies more dissimilar in their modes of life and traditions than those of the Han and of the steppe people. That is what, in Wang Fu-chih's eyes, condemns the Manchu invasion and justifies resistance to the new power. Wang Fu-chih, whose writings were to be read with passionate enthusiasm by the men of the late Ch'ing period and the early days of the 'republic' (it is known that Mao Tse-tung was a member of the society for the study of Wang Fu-chih's writings, the *Ch'uan-shan hsüeh-she*, founded at Ch'ang-sha in about 1915), seems to have been the first theorist of a Chinese 'nationalism' based on the community of culture and mode of life. He points out that animal societies — those of ants, for example — are organized to attain two primary objectives, the preservation of the species (*pao-lei*) and the safety of the group (*wei-ch'ün*). It should be the same in human societies: the state has no function more important than that of preserving a certain type of civilization and of defending its subjects against attacks from outside.

*Ku yen-wu, the father of scientific criticism
in history and philology*

Ku Yen-wu (Ku T'ing-lin) (1613–82) is often regarded as the most important historian and scholar of his generation. Born at K'un-shan, near Soochow, he belonged in his youth to opposition circles and joined the Society of Renewal in 1642. For a short time he was in the service of Prince T'ang of the Southern Ming in Fukien. Passionately interested in economics, military defence, and administration, from the middle of the seventeenth century onwards he made a number of journeys through North China. His secret aim was to visit the areas occupied by the guerrillas and to examine the advantages offered by different regions and localities for a war of resistance. These numerous journeys — he was to make his sixth and last visit to the tombs of the Ming emperors, north of Peking, in 1677 — also provided him with the opportunity to add continually to his knowledge of geography, epigraphy, history, and economics, and to carry his thinking further. One of his first works, the *T'ien-hsia chün-kuo li-ping-shu,* was the fruit of his geographical researches, which were dominated by economic and defence problems. Its value lies in the fact that Ku Yen-wu compares his personal knowledge of the ground with the information provided by the local Ming age monographs, which he had studied exhaustively. What characterizes Ku Yen-wu is his constant concern for effectiveness; according to him, knowledge cannot be separated from action. He interlards his reflections with concrete suggestions of an economic or administrative character.

His most famous work is the *Jih-chih-lu,* a collection of the notes which he made day by day in the course of his vast reading. Containing a preface dated 1676 and printed after his death, in 1695, this work is extremely rich in content and touches on a wide variety of subjects — the

Classics, history, politics, society, geography, psychology, morality, and so on.

Ku Yen-wu is regarded as the founder of the new school of textual and historical criticism which was to triumph in the eighteenth century. He enlarged the field of history and, put forward for the first time a conception of it that can be termed scientific, calling on the auxiliary sciences of epigraphy (we are indebted to him for some *Notes on the Writing Employed in the Inscriptions on Bronze and Stone, Chin-shih wen-tzu chi*), archaeology, phonology (in 1677 Ku Yen-wu published his *Five Writings on Phonetics, Yin-hsüeh wu-shu*) and geography. He proposed the same methods of rigorous, rational analysis for the study of the Classics, inaugurating a return to the most ancient commentators, those of the Han age, and in particular to the great Cheng Hsüan (A.D. 127–200).

Ku Yen-wu's philosophical and political ideas are in harmony with his scientific concepts. He attacks the vague and abstract character of the notions of *hsing* (human nature) and *hsin* (mind) which had become the sole subject of moral and philosophical discussions since the Sung age. In his view the 'neo-Confucian' school of the natural order (*li-hsüeh*) was only a mediocre avatar of Buddhist philosophy. It is high time, he says, to replace these sterile academic controversies on nature and mind with a realistic attitude. One must return to the real man, to the concrete, and open one's mind to all forms of knowledge. And Ku Yen-wu did a great deal more than indicate the way to his successors.

In the field of politics, we find in the writings of Ku Yen-wu a penetrating analysis of the causes of the state's decadence. He passes an extremely severe judgement on the political and administrative system of the late Ming period – a system which was to be preserved without any big changes by the new Manchu dynasty. We meet again the idea, already formulated by Huang Tsung-hsi, that sovereigns, formerly at the service of the people, have ended by regarding the empire as their own property. But the fundamental causes of the defects in the political system, according to Ku Yen-wu, was the divorce that had occurred on the one hand between the central authority and its agents in the provinces and on the other between rulers and people. The suspicion with which civil servants were regarded from above, the proliferation of regulations and the multiplication of checks and of levels of supervision reduced the authority of magistrates to very little and forced them to rely on a small bureaucracy of clerks familiar with local conditions and with the complexities of a body of legislation that paralysed all initiative. As a result, 'The authority of the Son of Heaven has come to reside not in the civil servants appointed by the government but in their clerks and junior officials'. This theme was subsequently to be taken up again very frequently, especially in the nineteenth century. For this excessive absolutism and concentration of authority there was only one remedy — the reintroduction into the political system of a certain degree of local autonomy. Provincial officials had to be given back the authority which they had lost and encouraged to develop a taste for taking the initiative and an awareness of their responsibilities.

The return to the concrete; the new style of education

The general tendency of the second half of the seventeenth century was to criticize the intellectual traditions of the Ming age and to return to the concrete. The thinkers of this period all show a lively interest in practical and scientific knowledge. Ku Yen-wu was a geographer, economist, and strategist, and he checked his enormous book-learning by going over the ground in person. But he was not the only man of his time to do this. Ku Tsu-yu (1631–92), who was eighteen years younger, wrote an important work of historical geography, the *Tu-shih fang-yü chi-yao,* which was the fruit of his reflections, of his reading, and of the incessant travels which he made in China between the ages of twenty-eight and fifty. And Huang Tsung-hsi was not only the first historian of Chinese thought; he was to leave behind him eight books on mathematics, astronomy, and musical theory. A little later Mei Wen-ting (1632–1721), who was very well informed on Western mathematics as revealed to China by Matteo Ricci and his successors, compared them with Chinese mathematics and rehabilitated the latter.

One of the most consistent defenders of practical knowledge (*shih-hsüeh*) was Yen Yüan (1635–1704). Trained in his youth in the traditions of the school of Chu Hsi — he devoted himself to the study of the *Hsing-li ta-ch'üan,* the great summary, compiled in 1415, of the philosophers of human nature and the natural order — he was suddenly put off it by the profound crisis which shook him when he discovered that he was his grandfather's grandson by adoption. From this time onwards he became one of the harshest critics of 'neo-Confucian' traditions and tended to reject classical culture in its entirety as false in its principles and harmful in its consequences. His researches into antiquity led him to the conviction that ancient culture had been essentially practical in character: it made room for archery, chariot-driving and the science of numbers. Yen Yüan rehabilitated physical effort and manual dexterity. He wished to replace the bookish education that produced only timorous, introverted individuals unsuited to action and incapable of taking decisions with a training that would call on the whole man and give a proper place to practical skills. In 1696 Yen Yüan became head of an academy in Hopei and included in the timetable military training, strategy, archery, riding, boxing, mechanics, mathematics, astronomy, and history.

This amounted to a total rejection of classical studies which, in Yen Yüan's view, had perished under the jumble of commentaries and commentaries on commentaries. But Yen Yüan based his anti-intellectualism on philosophical concepts; manual work and contact with concrete realities, he says, are themselves a form of knowledge. What is more, there can be no real knowledge without action and practical application. 'What *li* (order, structure, reason for things and beings) could there be,' he asks, 'outside facts and things?'

No doubt we should not regard Yen Yüan as a sort of exception; his philosophy is in harmony with the dominant tendencies of his age. However, he was to remain practically unknown to his contemporaries; his ideas were to be revealed mainly after his death, by his disciple Li Kung (1659-1733).

Politics, society, and intellectual life under the enlightened despots

As the authority of the Manchu dynasty grew more firmly established, the whole moral atmosphere changed. Attachment to the defunct dynasty, Chinese patriotism, hatred of the invaders, the ardour displayed in the criticism of the empire's institutions, in short all the effervescence of the years following the invasion gradually tended to subside. The educated classes rallied to the support of the new regime, and the enlightened despots who headed it seemed simultaneously to be anxious to demonstrate in a dazzling fashion the virtues of the autocracy and of the social traditions which had been the target of the seventeenth-century philosophers. Their rule was to see the last and most brilliant upsurge of the authoritarian empire and moral orthodoxy — an upsurge which was subsequently to reveal itself as fatal to the Chinese world, although it was favoured by historical circumstances.

In the field of literature and thought the state's activities were to have both harmful and beneficent aspects. On the one hand, the pitiless warfare against all forms of opposition and the establishment of the moral order resulted in the repression of the great current of social and political criticism of the seventeenth century and in hastening the disappearance

Figure 17   Scenes of daily life from the end of the eighteenth century (The pictures are from the *Shinzoku kibun*, a Japanese work of 1799)

of the urban, 'bourgeois' literature typical of the end of the Ming period. On the other hand, the good general understanding which the emperor K'ang-hsi and his successors succeeded in establishing with the old lettered classes, the prosperity and internal peace, the encouragement given by the state and the very substantial works that it commissioned were to make the eighteenth century one of the happiest in the intellectual history of China. Probably never did the Chinese literati sum up better in themselves the aesthetic, literary, and philosophical traditions of their own civilization. Men of encyclopaedic interests and enormous erudition, but also men of taste who liked simplicity and moderation, the Chinese literati of the eighteenth century, or at any rate the best of them, were – though certainly in a very different human context – the real contemporaries of the European writers and the 'philosophers' of the Age of Enlightenment.

The moral order

The institutions inherited from the Ming empire, and above all the resumption of the official competitions from 1646 onwards, were of tremendous assistance in consolidating the new Manchu regime. The immediate object of restarting the examinations was to renew the political and administrative personnel; but by giving direction to the old governing classes and mobilizing all their activities, from cantonal to central government level, the competitions made it possible in the long run to associate them closely in the exercise of power. As the sole means of access to political honours and responsibilities, the examinations served to inculcate in those who sat for them the virtues of devotion and submission indispensable to the autocratic empire. At the same time they also drained the energies of generations of literati. The artificial character of the tests had been clear since the institution of the composition in eight parts (*pa-ku*), which, according to Ku Yen-wu, had been made obligatory in 1487. These sterile, empty stylistic exercises consisted in developing in eight paragraphs the meaning of a sentence, or of part of a sentence, drawn from a Classic, after the style of the French dissertation with introduction, thesis, antithesis, synthesis, and conclusion.

The numerous private academies (*shu-yüan*), equipped with good libraries, which had been set up under the Ming from the middle of the sixteenth century onwards had quickly become centres of free discussion and opposition to the government. Most of them had been closed after the defeat of the Tung-lin party in 1625–27. Better advised and more inflexible towards all forms of criticism, the Manchus took care to exercise very strict control over teaching and the academies. The ones which they set up in 1657 were run by the state and the teaching henceforth dealt only with compositions in eight parts.

On top of the new regime's abundant efforts to develop an official educational system, and to increase the number of schools, came the censoring and persecution of writers convicted, or even only suspected, of hostility to the foreign dynasty or of lack of good will. This policy became harsher under Yung-cheng (1723–35) and ended in the great literary inquisition of 1774–89 in the reign of Ch'ien-lung: 10,231 works in 171,000 chapters were put on the index of prohibited books and over 2320 of them were completely destroyed. At the same time brutal measures were taken against the authors and their relations – execution, exile, forced labour, confiscation of property, and so on. For some twenty years a hunt went on throughout the empire for books deserving condemnation because they displayed a lack of respect for the Ch'ing – if only through the presence of forbidden characters (e.g., those appearing in the emperor's personal name) – because they criticized the barbarians of the past, seemed to be heterodox in inspiration, or contained information of strategic interest. Informing was encouraged by large rewards, and the possession of suspect works and guilty silence about them were punished with the most serious penalties. The result was a vile or stupid rivalry to serve the government.

If the great literary inquisition of the Ch'ien-lung era has remained famous, it owed its wide scope and its effectiveness to its being associated with the great compilation of all the written works known at that period, the *Ssu-k'u ch'üan-shu.* But it reflected preoccupations that seem to have been constant in the three great emperors of the eighteenth century. As early as the reign of K'ang-hsi the same concern for moral orthodoxy, the same susceptibility on the part of the imperial authority to the smallest signs of disrespect or opposition, had made themselves clearly apparent. For example, in Chekiang in 1663 the numerous relatives and friends of the author of a *Short History of the Ming,* printed in 1660 and considered subversive, had been condemned to death or exile.

The reaction against licentious works began to take shape by the end of the seventeenth century. Novels likely to corrupt their readers were put on the index in 1687 and the censorship became even more strict in 1714. The new Manchu dynasty was puritanical, and hostile to the literature of entertainment written in a language close to the spoken tongue. Under K'ang-hsi this literature disappeared almost completely and gave way to more elaborate and learned forms. It may be that in this field the state was moving in a direction desired by educated circles themselves; it may be, too, that it was acting in harmony with changes in society and with the disappearance of a certain class of readers – the not very cultivated urban bourgeoisie which had come into existence at the end of the Ming period. In any case, insofar as the literature of entertainment survived, it changed its nature and its readership. The famous collections of stories by P'u Sung-ling (1640–1715) (*Liao-chai, c.* 1700), by Yüan Mei (1716–98) (*Tzu-pu-yü,* 1788), and by the great scholar Chi Yün (*Yüeh-wei-ts'ao-t'ang pi-chi,* between 1789 and 1798) are written in a classical style more difficult of access, full of literary reminiscences and allusions. Similarly, the age of the great popular novels of the fourteenth century, such as the *Tale of the Three Kingdoms* or the *Water Margin,* or of the seventeenth century, such as the *Pilgrimage to the West,* seemed to have passed away. The novel became subtly ironical—like the *Ju-lin wai-shih,* the *Unofficial History of the Forest of Literati,* by Wu Ching-tzu (1701–54) (*c.* 1745)—psychological, like the admirable *Dream of the Red Chamber* (*Hung-lou-meng*) which Ts'ao Hsüeh-ch'in left unfinished at his death in 1763, or erudite, like the *Conversations of an Old Countryman Warming Himself in the Sun* (*Yeh-sou-pu-yen*) by Hsia Ching-ch'ü (1705–87).

While the reign of moral order seems to have put an end to the upsurge of political philosophy and vernacular literature characteristic of the late Ming and early Ch'ing periods, the pressure of moral and political constraints does not seem to have stifled reflection, the critical spirit, or even imagination. In spite of the persecution suffered by those guilty of treason and in spite of the authoritarian nature of the Manchu regime, the eighteenth century gives the appearance, all things considered, of having been a period of equilibrium. Although they did not abandon in the least their critical attitude, highly intelligent men like Tai Chen (1723–77) and Chang Hsüeh-ch'eng (1736–96) were in perfect harmony with their age; and so was an eccentric like Yüan Mei (1716–98), a free-thinking poet who was not frightened by fear of scandal. An advocate of freedom of expression in literature—far from attributing to poetry a moral aim, Yüan Mei grants it no other object but the expression of the poet's sentiments and personality—he made himself the apostle of the emancipation of women, proclaiming his hostility to polygamy and to the binding of little girls' feet, a fashion which had spread since the Sung age. The same feminist tendencies were to appear again at the beginning of the nineteenth century in the Pekinese Li Ju-chen (*c.* 1763–1830), a linguist and the author of a famous novel in a hundred chapters, the *Ching-hua-yüan,* which he wrote between 1810 and 1820 and which was to be printed in 1828. Following a procedure which was very fashionable for a time in European literature and is also to be found in Japan, Li Ju-chen draws satirical effects from the depiction of an imaginary country, a kingdom of women (an ancient myth in China) in which the situation of the sexes is the opposite of that to be found in the Ch'ing empire.

But these veiled or direct criticisms are of no significance. We are far from the social and political criticism of the thinkers of the seventeenth century. On the whole, the intelligentsia was content with its lot under the enlightened despots. The correspondence of the eighteenth-century literati perhaps bears witness in its way to this feeling: this epistolary literature, as rich as that of France or England in the Age of Enlightenment, is intimate, simple, direct, sometimes familiar in tone. Such is the case, for example, with the work of Cheng Hsieh (Cheng Pan-ch'iao) (1693–1765) – to name one of many – an eccentric of knightly generosity, an imaginative calligrapher and the author of a collection of *Family Letters*. This simple, intimate style is still to be found in a charming autobiography written at the beginning of the nineteenth century by an unlucky scholar, the *Six Stories of a Wandering Life* (*Fu-sheng liu-chi*) by Shen Fu.

The patronage of the emperors and the rich merchants

The system of official competitions in use since the Sung age resulted, with its successive stages and numerous candidates, in multiplying the number of holders of degrees who never reached the enviable position of imperial civil servant. These penniless literati, constrained to live an unstable life, were obliged to seek protectors and to earn their living as tutors in rich families, as private secretaries of officials, or as ordinary schoolmasters, and sometimes even to follow less brilliant professions. For these men the writing of composition manuals for the competitions, of biographies, epitaphs, novels, stories, or plays, either to order or for the commercial market, were a valuable additional source of income. These economic facts are thus not unconnected with the history of literary production in China since the Sung age, particularly in the Ming and Ch'ing periods. It certainly seems as if the general prosperity and the important state commissions ensured greater stability in the eighteenth century for the large proportion of literati who had no regular income.

In fact, from the K'ang-hsi era (1662–1723) onwards, official commissions kept a large number of literati busy on vast enterprises – editions of texts, compilations, and works of criticism and scholarship. The first big publishing enterprise of K'ang-hsi's reign was the *Official History of the Ming Dynasty* (*Ming-shih*). The project was conceived in 1679 and its direction was confided to Hsü Ch'ien-hsüeh (1631–94), a nephew of Ku Yen-wu, in 1682. A large team of historians devoted itself to the composition of this voluminous dynastic history, which was more extensive and more precise than any previous one. Work began in 1679 and went on for over half a century, until 1735. The complete history contains 366 chapters.

It was also in the reign of K'ang-hsi that the compilation of an enormous illustrated encyclopaedia, the *Ku-chin t'u-shu chi-ch'eng,* was undertaken. Begun privately by a certain Ch'en Meng-lei in 1706, it was not completed until 1725. Involved in a matter of rebellion at Foochow, Ch'en Meng-lei was condemned to death; however, the sentence was commuted and he was deported to Mukden (Shenyang). He came back into favour before the death of the emperor K'ang-hsi, but was to be exiled once again by K'ang-hsi's successor, who demanded that his name should be expunged from the book which had been his life's work. This encyclopaedia in 10,000 chapters contains the following headings: (1) the calendar, astronomy, mathematics; (2) geography; (3) history; (4) technology, fine arts, zoology, botany; (5) philosophy and literature; (6) laws and institutions. It was printed in movable copper type in 1728 and contains altogether nearly ten million characters.

Another undertaking of the K'ang-hsi era was the great compilation of poets of the T'ang age, the *Ch'üan-t'ang-shih,* an enterprise which was supervised by one of the old servants of the Manchu court known as *booi* (*pao-i*), namely Ts'ao Yin, grandfather of the author of the famous *Hung-lou-meng* (*Dream of the Red Chamber*). Completed in 1703, the *Ch'üan-t'ang-shih* gathered together over 48,900 poems by 2200 different writers of the T'ang age.

The *P'ei-wen yün-fu,* a dictionary of expressions of two or three characters classified by rhymes, which quoted examples drawn from various different works, from the Classics to the seventeenth century, was finished in 1716 and contains 558 chapters. The same year saw the appearance of the famous dictionary of characters of the K'ang-hsi era, the *K'ang-hsi tzu-tien,* which was to serve as the basis of Western sinologists' work from its publication down to the beginning of the twentieth century. The work of a team of thirty philologists, who devoted five years to the task, it gives the meanings and uses of 42,000 characters classified according to the system of 214 radicals instituted at the end of the Ming age.

Altogether there were fifty-seven big official publications patronized and subsidized by the state in the course of the K'ang-hsi era. But by far the most important work was to be the compilation made in Ch'ien-lung's reign and known as the *Ssu-k'u ch'üan-shu* (*Complete Collection of Written Works Divided into Four Stores*). Collecting together all the printed and manuscript works preserved in the public libraries or by private individuals, it demanded ten years' work by a team of 360 literati, from 1772 to 1782. The search for the books and manuscripts, which were obtained with or without the owner's consent, went on for many years and seems to have been fairly exhaustive. The whole work numbered 79,582 volumes (the similar enterprise of the beginning of the fifteenth century, the *Yung-le ta-tien,* numbered only 11,095), divided up according to the system of the 'four classes' (*ssu-pu*: canonical, historical, philosophical, and literary works). Fifteen thousand copyists were employed to reproduce this huge collection, which it would have been impossible to print by the means available at that time. A catalogue of notes giving information on authors, editions, and the value of the texts was added to the collection and printed in 1782. This work, bearing the title of *Ssu-k'u ch'üan-shu tsung-mu t'i-yao,* is the most valuable and most complete of all Chinese bibliographical treatises.

On top of all this state activity, which was so encouraging to literature, the arts, and scholarship, there were the effects of the patronage of rich merchants, collectors of rare books, paintings, and calligraphy, who acted as patrons of the literati and the scholars. The salt merchants of Yangchow, in Kiangsu, whose ancestry went back to the end of the Ming period, were among the most famous Maecenases of the eighteenth century. Among them were the brothers Ma — Ma Yüeh-kuan (1688–1755), poet and bibliophile, and Ma Yüeh-lu (1697–?), and also the latter's son, Ma Yü. The poet and philologist Hang Shih-chün (1698–1733) and Ch'üan Tsu-wang, a specialist in historical geography, were guests of the brothers Ma in Yangchow. Other famous literati to profit from the patronage of the rich merchants were Ch'i Chao-nan (1706–68), the author of works on the history of rivers and canals, of studies in historical chronology and of a monograph on the great port of Wenchou and its surrounding area in Chekiang (the *Wen-chou fu-chih*); Ch'ien Ta-hsin (1728–1804), the historian and epigraphist; and the great Tai Chen. Some of them, such as Yen Jo-ch'ü (1636–1704), a mathematician, geographer, and specialist in the Classics, even belonged themselves to these rich merchant families. This was also the case with Juan Yüan (1784–1849), a man with an encyclopaedic mind to whom we owe works on the history of painting, mathematics and astronomy, classical philology, epigraphy, and regional history (he wrote a monograph on Kwangtung, the *Kwangtung t'ung-chih*). However, he is famous above all for his great collection of critical commentaries on the Classics (*Huang-ch'ing ching-chieh,* 1829).

The decline of the great families of rich merchants, ruined by the depreciation of the copper currency from about 1800 onwards, was to coincide with a very swift reduction in official commissions and with the end of the big publishing enterprises. Hence there were profound changes in the circumstances of intellectual circles in the nineteenth century.

The upsurge of textual criticism
and the philosophers of the eighteenth century

Formation of the school of critical studies

The application of the scientific principles of textual and historical criticism defined by Ku Yen-wu and the men of his generation was to lead to the questioning of the most venerable of written traditions, that of the Classics, and it played in the Chinese world, over a century in advance, a role similar to the one that was to be played in the West by Hebrew philology in the field of biblical studies. One may thus compare Ku Yen-wu, or better still, one of his most illustrious successors, Tai Chen, with Ernest Renan; the same scientific rigour and the same concern for truth inspire both Tai Chen and the founder of biblical studies.

At the end of the seventeenth century Wan Ssu-ta (1633–83), a disciple – like his brother Wan Ssu-t'ung (1638–1702), who collaborated in the *History of the Ming* from 1679 to 1692 – of Huang Tsung-hsi, demonstrated that the *Chou-li* (*The Rites of the Chou*) was not, as had hitherto been believed, a work of the early Chou period, but a late compilation dating from the age of the Warring States (fifth to third centuries B.C.). Yen Jo-ch'ü (1636–1704) resumed the work started on the *Shang-shu* (the *Classic of History*) by Mei Cho, whose book had been published in 1543, and adduced fresh proofs of the apocryphal nature of the tradition in ancient characters in his *Critical Commentary on the Shang-shu in Ancient Characters* (*Shang-shu ku-wen shu-cheng*). He also refuted the attribution of the *Ta-hsüeh,* one of the Four Books of the school of Chu Hsi, to Tseng Ts'an, a disciple of Confucius. Hu Wei (1633–1714) denounced as creations of the early Sung period the famous diagrams which had played a leading role in the cosmological theories of neo-Confucianism enshrined in the *Writing of the Lo* (*Lo-shu*) and the *Table of the River* (*Ho-t'u*).

But the philologists of the eighteenth century were to go still further in their criticism of traditions held in the highest respect since the Sung age, not hesitating to commit what may be regarded as terrible blasphemies. Yüan Mei (1716–98), the free-thinking, baroque, mannered poet who from love of scandal paraded feminist ideas and surrounded himself with a court of female disciples, was the first to see that the *Songs of the Principalities* (*Kuo-feng*) in the venerable *Book of Odes* (*Shih-ching*) were mere love songs, a theory which was to be adopted and expounded in detail by the French sinologist Marcel Granet (1884–1940). Wang Chung (1745–94) dared to dethrone Confucius, who had been promoted since the Sung age to the position of patron of orthodoxy, and to put him back in the place which he had occupied in the fourth to third centuries B.C., by the side of Mo-tzu, just as famous as Confucius in those days, if not more so. Ts'ui Shu (1740–1816) was to refuse to allow any value to the traditions about the sovereigns of remote antiquity (Yao, Shun, Yü and so on), allegedly paragons of virtue, basing himself on the fact that traditions develop and are enriched with fresh details as time goes on. All the myths on which the Chinese tradition had lived were gradually questioned and destroyed.

The great movement of philological criticism which was one of the principal glories of the eighteenth century started in the second half of the seventeenth century and gives the impression of having been primarily a reaction against the philosophy of the school of Chu Hsi and that of the intuitionist school of Wang Yang-ming. Without worrying about basing their interpretations on a rigorous analysis of the texts and documents of the past, the thinkers of the Sung and Ming ages let themselves be carried away into speculations which distorted the true teaching of the ancients. Very soon after the Manchu invasion some scholars even denounced the Buddhist influences which had crept into the work of philosophers and commentators on the Classics. The dualist concepts of the school of Chu Hsi, and the subjectivist and intuitionist theories of Wang Yang-ming and his successors, drew their origin, so these scholars said, partly from Buddhist metaphysics and partly from the thinking of the *ch'an* school. It was therefore necessary to go back to the most ancient traditions, to break away from the jumble of interpretations accumulated since the Sung age. Generally known as the *K'ao-cheng-hsüeh* ('school of verifications and proofs'), the new critical movement is sometimes called the *Han-hsüeh* ('Han school'). But strictly speaking, the name 'Han school' applies only to the philological traditions which had developed by the end of the seventeenth century in a family of literati in Soochow whose most eminent representative was Hui Tung (1697–1758). However, in that case it was a question only of a specialization confined to the commentators of the Han age. Making use of all the scientific methods of investigation known at that time (archaeology, epigraphy, historical phonology, historical geography, and so on) and of every possible kind of source, the critical movement of the eighteenth century was much more than a mere return to the commentators of the Han period. Its leading characteristic was its scientific bias. The scholars of the seventeenth and eighteenth centuries were almost all more or less versed in the sciences – mathematics, geometry, astronomy, mechanics, and so on. Huang Tung-hsi had busied himself with mathematics and astronomy; Tai Chen began his career with scientific studies.

Tai Chen: scientist, scholar, and philosopher

This school of critical studies which was responsible for such a substantial body of work in the fields of philology and archaeology reached its zenith in the second half of the eighteenth century. Its most eminent representative at that time was Tai Chen (1723–77), a cloth merchant's son from Anhwei who was not to reach the highest grades of the scholar's career until the end of his life. His ever watchful critical faculty, the rigour of his reasoning, his devotion to the truth, the diversity of his knowledge, the clarity of his writings, and the originality of his thinking entitle him to be regarded as one of the greatest geniuses of his epoch. Tai Chen, one of whose mottoes was, 'one must not let oneself be deceived either by others or by oneself', and for whom objective proofs were the only criterion of truth, distinguished between the certainties to which the combination of irrefutable proofs allowed one to attain and ideas in process of verification—what we should call hypotheses. With him we witness the advent of a truly scientific spirit, sure of its method and holding principles which hardly differ from those which in the West made possible the progress of the exact sciences. But this scientific spirit was applied almost exclusively to the investigation of the past.

Like many of his contemporaries, Tai Chen had a very inquisitive mind. Like his predecessor Mei Wen-ting (1632–1721), who had made a comparative study of Chinese and Western mathematics, he was passionately interested in the history of mathematics. Knowledge of the rules for calculating formulated by Napier (1550–1617) may have stimulated him to make a study of the ancient Chinese calculating rods which had made it possible, at least as early as the thirteenth century, to resolve equations with several unknown quantities. The result of this study was the *Ts'e-suan* (1744). He wrote a treatise on the measurement of the circle (the *Kou-ku ko-yüan-chi*, 1755) and researched into, and republished, the old works on mathematics of the Sung and Yüan periods. But it was above all in the domain of philological studies that Tai Chen revealed himself as one of the greatest masters. He annotated the poems of Ch'u Yüan, the great lyric poet of the third century B.C. (the *Ch'ü Yüan fu-chu*, 1752), worked on historical phonetics and wrote a commentary on the treatise on the techniques of antiquity which forms the last part of the *Treatise of the Chou Officials* (*Chou-kuan* or *Chou-li*) and probably dates from the fifth to third centuries B.C. (this commentary is the *K'ao-kung-chi t'u-chu, Illustrated Commentary on the Memorandum on Crafts*, 1746). But his efforts were largely devoted to the huge official compilation of texts from every source, the *Ssu-k'u ch'üan-shu,* a project of which he became one of the principal directors from 1773 onwards.

Tai Chen was not only one of the most eminent scholars in the history of China but also one of the greatest thinkers of his age. The fact is that the scientific attitudes which he adopted in the field of philology were inseparable from a certain philosophy. His most striking works in this domain were the *Yüan-shan (On the Origins of the Good)* (1776) and a study of Mencius *(Meng-tzu tzu-i shu-cheng, Critical Commentary on the Literal Meaning of Mencius)* (1772), in which, following an approach springing at the same time from methodical doubt and from an immense respect for antiquity, he reveals and denounces the distortions which the neo-Confucian philosophers of the Sung age had inflicted on Mencius's thinking. An enemy of neo-Confucian orthodoxy, for which nature was a composite of *li* (immanent order or natural reason) and *ch'i* ('breath' or energy), he retained only the latter term, which he considered sufficient to account for all phenomena. Faithful in this to the underlying tendencies of Chinese thought, he drew the consequences of this monistic conception on the level of practical life: even the most elevated morality, he maintains, is derived from our desires and our instincts, not because morality is based on egoism—that would be a simplistic explanation—but because it is connected with what is most deep-seated in man. The instinct for self-preservation, hunger, sexual desire, and so on are manifestations of the cosmic order *(tao).* There is no such thing as disembodied intelligence, independent of needs and passions, any more than there are abstract faculties (justice, equity, humanity, sense of ritual). 'To try to suppress desires,' says Tai Chen, 'is more dangerous than trying to stop the course of a river.' Virtue does not consist in bullying and curbing desires; it consists in using them harmoniously. We thus find in Tai Chen a radical criticism of the conformist morality which had been accepted since the Sung age and which, in the name of reason *(li),* prevented the humblest and youngest from expressing themselves and fulfilling their aspirations. In his view, this system of morality was the main source of crime and discord.

Although he found few followers for his philosophical concepts, which do not seem to have caused much of a stir in his own time, Tai Chen was on the other hand to have some eminent successors in the field of scholarly research. Three great philologists continued his work at the end of Ch'ien-lung's reign and into the early years of the nineteenth century. These three were Tuan Yü-ts'ai (1735–1815), a direct disciple of Tai Chen, Wang Nien-sun (1744–1832) and Wang Yin-chih (1766–1834); they were the last famous representatives of this school of 'critical studies' which had shone with such lustre in the eighteenth century. From the beginning of the nineteenth century it was to begin to lose its pre-eminent position.

A philosophy of history

Twelve years younger than Tai Chen, Chang Hsüeh-ch'eng (1736–1801) was, like Tai Chen, one of the most profound and original thinkers of the eighteenth century. However, in an age when the fashion was for erudition, textual criticism, and, above all, exegesis of the Classics, Chang Hsüeh-ch'eng was something of an exception in that he represented opposite tendencies. The main themes of his reflections were historiographical method and the philosophy of history. This is the reason for the lack of attention paid to him in his own day. However, Chang Hsüeh-ch'eng was to be rehabilitated in the twentieth century by Chinese and Japanese sinologists.

Sensitive, like Wang Fu-chih and Ku Yen-wu, to regional differences, Chang Hsüeh-ch'eng thought that it was essential first of all to know the history of the various parts of China. As extensive as Europe, China could not be treated in his view as a uniform whole. It was only through histories of the different regions, by recourse to local monographs (*fang-chih*) and by the composition of new monographs (Chang Hsüeh-cheng himself devoted his attention to writing a *fang-chih*, which has unfortunately been lost) that it would be possible to keep one's bearings in a history as complex as that of the Chinese world. It was therefore important to constitute local archives, to gather first-hand information by questioning old people, and to collect inscriptions, manuscripts, local traditions, and so on. Like Ku Yen-wu, Chang Hsüeh-ch'eng thought that the sources of history were encyclopaedic in nature. But he is more radical in this domain; in his view, all written works, of whatever nature, including the venerable Classics, were historical evidence. However, once this exhaustive documentation has been collected, it is not a matter, he says, of indulging in mechanical compilation, like the teams of historiographers of the seventh century. History, while remaining an accurate reflection of the past, must be a personal work. The best historical works have always been the accomplishment of isolated individuals; such is the case with the most admirable of them all, Ssu-ma Ch'ien's *Historical Records*.

The most curious thing is that these historiographical preoccupations ended in producing a philosophy; Chang Hsüeh-ch'eng's famous formula, 'everything is history, even the Classics', gave birth to the corollary that history had the same value as the Classics. It was asserted that history incorporated in itself a philosophical principle, that it included in itself the *Tao*, which is itself invisible and known to man only in its historical manifestations. Human societies obey the natural reason denoted by the *Tao*. The present itself is history. It bears witness to the universal reason and therefore possesses—contrary to what lovers of antiquity think—the same value and dignity as the past. Although the 'textual criticism movement' represented a healthy reaction against the excesses of the intellectualist philosophy of Chu Hsi and the intuitionist philosophy of Wang Yang-ming, it also had its negative side. The triumph of erudition often went hand in hand with the renunciation of any attempt at reflection and synthesis. Research into details became an end in itself and the most futile discovery satisfied a scholar's vanity. It was therefore important to return to the fundamental verity that the visible world is informed by an immanent *Tao*, a typically Chinese concept but one which from the historian's point of view—that of Chang Hsüeh-ch'eng—is not without Hegelian echoes: it is by direct contact with history, lived and past, that the philosophical sense is formed.

The work of the Jesuits and the influence of China on Europe

The dialogue initiated by Matteo Ricci and the first Jesuit missionaries who arrived in China at the end of the Ming period was not to be interrupted. On the contrary, the Jesuits established themselves more firmly in China under the first two Manchu emperors and their presence was tolerated in Peking all through the eighteenth century in spite of the intransigence displayed by the Vatican and the legitimate irritation of the emperors Yung-cheng and Ch'ien-lung. Thanks to the missionaries, the learned world of Europe was plentifully supplied with scientific information and data about China and about the Manchu empire at the time of its zenith, while China itself received certain new contributions from Europe. Full justice has almost certainly not yet been done to the important consequences of these exchanges, in spite of the numerous books which have already been devoted to them.

The scientific work and the influence of the Jesuits in China
Clever enough to maintain their position at the court and in the provinces in the midst of the insurrections and chaos which attended the end of the Ming dynasty, and afterwards during the period of conquest and repres-

sion of resistance movements, the Jesuit missionaries were to meet in the emperors Shun-chih and K'ang-hsi a sympathetic attitude which was limited only by fear of the political consequences of their proselytizing activities. Father Adam Schall von Bell (1592–1666), who was born in Cologne and arrived in Peking in 1622, was the director of the astronomical service in the capital at the time of the Manchu conquest. It was he who, thanks to his diplomacy, succeeded in safeguarding the interests of the missions in China under the new regime. In 1650 he obtained the authorization to build the first Catholic church in Peking, the Nan-t'ang, which was completed two years later. Put in a very difficult position by the attacks of Yang Kuang-hsien (1597–1669), a Chinese convert to Islam, the sworn enemy of the Jesuits and author of an anti-Christian pamphlet (the *Pu-te-i, The Intolerable,* 1659), he was condemned to death in 1665 and was saved only at the last moment by a providential earthquake. His successor was the Fleming Ferdinand Verbiest (1623–88), an eminent mathematician and astronomer, who triumphed over Yang Kuang-hsien and his allies in the years 1668–89 by demonstrating the superiority of European astronomy; he thus strengthened the position of the missionaries in the empire.

As in the last fifty years of the Ming period, conversions remained limited — both at the court and in the provinces — by the serious obstacles arising out of the differences between the two civilizations (unitary politico-social organization, local power of the Buddhist priests, Chinese manners and customs; radically opposed moral and religious traditions of Europe). The Manchu nobility may have been a little more open than the Chinese literati to the Christian truths because of the affinity of Christianity with the religious traditions of the steppes. But there is every reason to believe that the influence of the Jesuits would have grown deeper and wider if the conciliatory attitude adopted by Matteo Ricci to Chinese customs and usages had not provoked reactions among his colleagues as soon as the great missionary was dead and if it had not in the end been repudiated by the Church. This was the famous 'dispute over Chinese rites' which poisoned relations between China and Europe in the eighteenth century. The problem was to know whether the notion of Shang-ti ('The Lord on High' of the Classics) was to be regarded as the residue of a Revelation that had occurred in remote Chinese antiquity but had progressively been forgotten, or whether the concepts of the Chinese were to be considered basically atheistic and agnostic, and their cults and ceremonies heretical. It was thought absolutely essential that the Heaven of the Chinese (*t'ien*) should be either God or pure matter, when in fact it was neither, but immanent, universal order. The controversy was an old one, for it had been started by Father Longobardo soon after 1610. This opponent of Ricci had complained that the Chinese did not recognize any spiritual substance separate from matter and made no absolute distinction between the moral principles of human societies and the physical principles of the universe. However, it was only at the beginning of the eighteenth century that the conflict was to break out openly. The efforts of the Jesuits in China had already been compromised by the attacks to which they were subjected in Europe, where their sympathy for the Chinese had long been suspect, when in 1705 the Vatican decided to send Monsignor Charles de Tournon to China with orders to forbid the missionaries to show the slightest tolerance for the traditional usages of the Chinese – the homage paid to Confucius and the sages of antiquity, ceremonies in honour of the dead, and so on. Two years later, in Nanking, Monsignor de Tournon anathematized the superstitious practices of the Chinese. The result of this great dogmatic rigidity was to ruin in large part the work accomplished at the cost of so much effort since the beginning of the seventeenth century. Apostasies were numerous, conversions became rarer and hostility towards Christians, both foreign and Chinese, increased. K'ang-hsi, who had been well disposed towards the missionaries some years earlier, was irritated that the Jesuits, whom he regarded as in his own service, should take their orders from the Vatican. Moreover, the 'dispute over rites' ended in favour of the opponents of tolerance just at the very time when the intellectual climate and political circumstances were about to make the missionaries' position more difficult. The progress of orthodoxy and the importance assumed by central Asian questions in the general policy of the empire were to make the reign of Yung-cheng (1723–35) one of the least favourable periods for the extension of missionary activities. The Manchu princes who had been converted to Christianity were the victims of persecution. Yung-cheng himself was drawn towards lamaism, whose political importance at that time is well known, and, in a more general way, towards Buddhism. He turned his former palace of Yung-ho-kung into a lamaist temple (1732), encouraged new editions of Buddhist texts, and in his old age founded a society for Buddhist and Taoist religious studies. Father Gaubil reports the following remark made by the emperor on 21 July 1727, the day after a visit from a Portuguese embassy: 'If I sent bonzes to your European provinces, your princes would not allow it.'

The Society of Jesus was to be dissolved in 1773 by the brief *Dominus ac Redemptor* of Pope Clement XIV.

As at the end of the Ming period it was their knowledge and scientific work, and sometimes also their talents as painters and musicians, that gained the missionaries all their credit with the emperors. These men, almost all of them remarkable persons, accomplished in difficult conditions a tremendous task, simultaneously learning Chinese and Manchu, making astronomical observations and researches, preparing atlases, doing geographical work, making detailed studies of Chinese history and chronology—a chronology which called into question the date of the Flood—and producing translations, without forgetting their apostolate and their religious duties. In the seventeenth century they came from Italy, from Portugal, from Spain, from the Flemish lands, from Germany, from France, and sometimes even from central Europe; in the eighteenth century there were more Frenchmen among them. Louis XIV's policy, which favoured the Jesuits, had in fact gained them a predominant position after K'ang-hsi's edict of tolerance (1692). The first two official missions of Louis XIV's reign, the first leaving La Rochelle in 1687 with Fathers Fontaney, Le Comte, Gerbillon, and Visdelou the second in 1698 (first voyage of the *Amphitrite*), were to be followed by several others. France was the European country that maintained the closest relations with China in the eighteenth century and the one in which the philosophical arguments provoked by the discovery of China were the most passionate.

The Jesuits' work, which undoubtedly helped to accentuate the scientific tendencies of the *k'ao-cheng-hsüeh* school and stimulated research into the history of Chinese mathematics, was encouraged by the liberal patronage of the emperors in the same way as the parallel work of the Chinese literati in the field of publications and erudite research. Thus part of their accomplishments must be put down to the credit of the enlightened despots who reigned under the names of K'ang-hsi and Ch'ien-lung.

Apart from their work on astronomy and mathematics, it was in the field of cartography that the Jesuits most distinguished themselves, thus continuing a tradition that went back to Matteo Ricci. The *Atlas of K'ang-hsi,* the *Huang-yü chüan-lan-t'u,* an enterprise suggested by Father Gerbillon, was completed as a result of surveys and work which lasted from 1707 to 1717. Engraved on copper plates in 1718, it is better than contemporary maps of Europe. China was still ahead in cartographical techniques in the Ch'ien-lung era, thanks to imperial patronage and to the capacities of the Jesuits and of their excellent Chinese colleagues. The *Atlas of Ch'ien-lung* was published in 1769, on the basis of surveys made from 1756 to 1759.

An inquisitive and open-minded person, K'ang-hsi was interested in Western painting, architecture, and mechanics. It was at his request that in 1702 Father Antoine Thomas fixed the length of the *li* as a function of the calculation of the terrestrial meridian—ninety years before the defini-

Plate 60. Summer Palace of the Ch'ien-lung Emperor, built by Jesuit architects; it was razed by British and French forces in 1860 and later rebuilt by the Empress

tion of the kilometre. The Chinese painter Chiao Ping-chen, who was responsible for the forty-six famous engravings of the *Keng-chih-t'u* (pictures showing the various stages of work in the fields and of silk production) (1696) studied European perspective. In 1676 Father Pereira played the harpsichord in K'ang-hsi's presence and a few years later wrote, in collaboration with an Italian priest, the first treatise to appear in China on European music, the *Lü-lü cheng-i.*

Ch'ien-lung embellished his summer palace, the *Yüan-ming-yüan,* to the north-east of Peking, by building there in 1747, on the missionaries' advice, pavilions in the Italian style and by installing fountains. The paintings which adorned the palace were executed by Fathers Guiseppe Castiglione and Jean-Denis Attiret. This palace was to be sacked by French troops and burnt down by the English in 1860. Endowed with a certain talent for painting, Father Castiglione was to remain in the service of the imperial palace for nearly fifty years, until his death, painting landscapes, portraits, interior scenes, and palaces, and working with renowned Chinese painters. In collaboration with Jean-Denis Attiret and Jean-Damascene Sallusti he copied the sixteen famous pictures representing the main battles of the Ili campaign (*P'ing-ting-i-li*). Engravings of these pictures were made in Paris in 1774.

It is probable that China received far more from these intellectual, scientific, and artistic contacts than the best-known borrowings lead us to think.

The dissolution of the Society of Jesus and the death of Ch'ien-lung ended an era during which the learned and cultivated missionaries of the Peking court had played a predominant role in the relations between China and Europe. In subsequent periods missionary activities were to develop in a very different context.

Borrowings from China and European reactions

We are still far from having pin-pointed and accurately appreciated all the consequences of the discovery of China by Europe since the sixteenth century. It could be, in the final analysis, that it has contributed far more than we think to the formation of the modern world. The fact is that, with the age of decline and humiliation that the Chinese world has undergone, the passionate interest aroused in the eighteenth century by the social and political institutions, the thought, the technology and the art of China has been forgotten. The West has come to pride itself on its rapid progress, all the credit for which, it thinks, can be attributed to itself alone. But it may be that one day we shall pass a somewhat more qualified judgement on the rise of the West.

On 18 August 1705, Leibniz wrote in a letter to Father Verjus, 'I see that most of your missionaries tend to speak with disdain of the knowledge of the Chinese; nevertheless, since their language and character, their way of life, their artefacts and manufactures and even their games differ from ours almost as much as if they were people from another planet, it is impossible for even a bare but accurate description of their practices not to give us very considerable enlightenment, and one that is much more useful in my view than the knowledge of the rites and furniture of the Greeks and Romans to which so many scholars devote themselves.' Even if the programme sketched by Leibniz was carried out only very imperfectly and in a very incomplete way by the men of the eighteenth century, it seems that the philosopher had a very sound presentiment of the profound effects of these contacts between two worlds.

Several voluminous works based on the information collected by the missionaries were published in France during the course of the eighteenth century: *Lettres édifiantes et curieuses* . . . (Paris, 1703–76, 34 vols.), *Description . . . de la Chine et de la Tartarie chinoise* by J. B. du Halde (Paris, 1735, 4 vols.), *Description générale de la Chine* by J. B. Grosier (Paris, 1785), *Mémoires concernant l'histoire, les sciences, les arts, les moeurs et les usages des Chinois* (Paris, 1776–1814, 16 vols.). Philosophers like Leibniz, scholars like Nicolas Fréret (1688–1749), politicians like the minister Henri Bertin (1720–92), who organized a systematic enquiry into Chinese technology, kept up a voluminous correspondence with the

Jesuit missionaries in China. These numerous contacts were not without consequences.

Numerous plants, including rhubarb, and numerous trees still unknown in Europe were imported from China in the seventeenth and eighteenth centuries. We are indebted to G. J. Vogler (1747–1814), who had been able to examine in St. Petersburg a Chinese *sheng* – a musical instrument modelled on the mouth-organs of the Sino-Thai world – for the adoption in the West of the free reed, a device which forms the basis of harmoniums, harmonicas, and accordions. Among other borrowings were the winnowing machine, used in China since the Han age, the practice of providing ships with watertight compartments, the breeding of silkworms and the technique of making porcelain (the first attempts, by J. F. Böttger, 1682–1719, date from 1705). In 1675 a Russian embassy asked that Chinese engineers should be sent to Russia to build bridges there. Variolation, generally practised in China as early as the sixteenth century, consisted in inoculating the patient's nostril with a very small quantity of the contents of a smallpox pustule. This was the application of the principle of vaccination even before the discovery of this process in Europe; the Chinese had sought a means of reducing the virulence of the virus. The procedure, having spread to Turkey during the course of the seventeenth century, began to be known in Europe at the beginning of the eighteenth. Lady Montagu, the wife of the British ambassador in Constantinople, had her whole family inoculated. In 1796 Edward Jenner perfected vaccination against smallpox. But besides the certain borrowings, the list of which is not yet complete, there are also a number of probable ones.

Borrowings from different and original technical traditions can be surprisingly fertile, and this or that elementary device may turn out to be of fundamental importance. It is the same with intellectual traditions and institutions.

Although it may be true that eighteenth-century Europe enthused over a China of which it painted a false and often idealized picture – and this enthusiasm subsequently provoked, by a natural reaction, denigration – and although China may have served the French *philosophes* as a pretext for their attacks on the Church and the *ancien régime,* knowledge of China was nevertheless not devoid of any positive content.

Whatever judgement we may pass on the political and social system of eighteenth-century China – culture and political power were in fact the privilege of a mere fraction of the population, as in our bourgeois societies of the nineteenth and twentieth centuries – the enormous privileges granted to birth in pre-revolutionary Europe were unknown in China. It is a fact that 'manners and laws', a theme developed at such length by the Age of Enlightenment, were there the foundation of the political and social order. China furnished the first example of a disciplined, rich, and powerful state which owed nothing to Christianity and seemed to be based on reason and natural law. It thus made a powerful contribution to the formation of modern political thought, and even some of its basic institutions were imitated by Europe.

The Chinese 'system of examinations' was described for the first time by Mendoza in 1585, then by Nicolas Trigault in his *Recueil d'observations curieuses* (1615) and by Montfort de Feynes in his *Voyage fait par terre depuis Paris jusqu'à la Chine* (1615). But the idea of recruitment competitions for the public services really began to make progress from the end of the eighteenth century onwards. In his *Despotisme de la Chine* (1767), Francois Quesney suggested that the king should surround himself with a council of wise men recruited from all classes of society like the Chinese mandarins. The example of China must have played some part in the establishment of recruitment competitions by the French revolutionary regime in 1791. Applied in India by the East India Company in 1800, the same institution was to be extended to Great Britain in 1855 with the adoption of examinations for recruitment to the Civil Service.

Vauban advised Louis XIV to start making censuses of the population like the Chinese, who had employed them since the Han age. The first censuses known in Western countries took place in 1665 in French Canada and in 1749 in Sweden. The whole modern science of demography arose out of a practice which would doubtless have been adopted in any case sooner or later, but which was first suggested by China.

The importance attributed to agriculture in Ch'ing China inspired the thinking of the Physiocrats, F. Quesnay (1695–1774) and his friends the Marquis de Mirabeau (1715–89) and Dupont de Nemours (1739–1817), who introduced in the West the notion of 'natural order' and proclaimed the primacy of agricultural production over craft, industrial, and commercial activities, which they regarded as sterile from the point of view of the economy as a whole. Through the agency of the Physiocrats, Chinese concepts were to be at the root of the development of political economy.

The aesthetic feeling itself was influenced by China. The extraordinary popularity in eighteenth-century Europe of the blue and white porcelain of the K'ang-hsi period and of Chinese furniture and knick-knacks is well known. Chinese gardens and architecture were made fashionable at Kew by W. Chambers (1726–96) in 1763, and China helped to guide the feeling for nature in the direction which was developed by the Romantic movement.

All this has long been known. But research should be resumed, pursued, and extended to those diffuse influences, those hypotheses that only rigorous analysis would make it possible to convert into certainties. In reality, the ideas inspired by China were not confined to the realms of political and social thought, institutions, and technology; there is a strong possibility that they also affected the formation of modern scientific thought. If these Chinese influences were one day to be confirmed, this would be an important element to add to the already innumerable proofs of the solidarity of all civilizations.

The 'mathematical' quality of the Chinese script which had struck the Persians of the fourteenth century—in his *Treasures of the Il-khan on the Sciences of Cathay* (1313), Rashid al-Din takes the view that the Chinese script is superior to the Arabic script to the extent that it is independent of pronunciation—also attracted the attention of Leibniz (1646–1716), and may have stimulated the development of mathematical logic in Europe. Doubtless Leibniz was soon to note that the meaning of the Chinese characters is far from being unequivocal, thanks to the historical accumulation of significations, which vary according to the context. But it is a fact that one of the characteristics of Chinese thinking is to proceed by the manipulation of symbols; in one sense Leibniz's intuition was sound.

Another characteristic and basic feature of Chinese thinking is the predominance of the notion of general, spontaneous order over the notion of direct, mechanical action. It so happens that Leibniz, who followed with lively interest the reports furnished by the Jesuits in China and was in correspondence with Father Grimaldi, substituted for the idea that the world is a machine the idea of an organism consisting of an infinity of organisms. Far from linking up with earlier Western traditions, this final concept of the *Monadology*, with its hierarchy of monads and their pre-established harmony, cannot avoid calling to mind the neo-Confucian concept of the *li*, the immanent principle of general order which makes itself manifest at all levels of the cosmic whole and ensures in the grand ensemble that every being possesses its share of *li* and cooperates spontaneously, without direction or mechanical impulsion, in the universal order. It was through a concept that recalls those most generally accepted in the Chinese world that Leibniz succeeded in resolving the unyielding opposition between theological idealism and atomic materialism that until his time had dominated all Western thinking. To enable modern scientific thought to develop, it was in fact necessary for the West to give up seeking reality outside things, to abandon the idea, so deeply rooted in its intellectual traditions, that nature and beings consisted of a machine and its driver, of a body and a soul, and come to see, like the Chinese, that things contained in themselves all reality and its most subtle mysteries. Leibniz, the sinophile, is at one end of the chain that leads to the most recent developments in scientific thought. Such, at any rate, in brief, is the hypothesis of Joseph Needham, that eminent specialist in the history of science in China.

In any case, it is noteworthy that, in their specifically 'modern' aspects, the experimental sciences that developed from the sixteenth century onwards were in accord with Chinese concepts (magnetism, the notion of a field of force, the idea of corpuscular vortices, the idea of propagation by waves, the concept of an organic totality and of the self-regulation of organisms, and so on) which were absent from the Western tradition. It would be surprising if the conjunction were the effect of chance alone.

Part 9

From Decline to Takeover

Prologue

The first half of the nineteenth century was characterized by a constant deterioration of the social climate, the many causes of which have hardly yet been analysed. These causes included an imbalance in the state's finances which went back to the end of Ch'ien-lung's reign, a period of mad expenditure; the advance of corruption in the ruling circles and in the government service since the time of Ho-shen, the emperor Ch'ien-lung's favourite; the continuous growth in population up to the middle of the nineteenth century; the over-extension of an empire in which the colonized peoples were numerous and suffered from the stronger and stronger pressure of the colonizers; the unfavourable balance of trade from 1820–25 onwards; and an economic recession that was all the more perceptible in that it followed a period of prosperity and euphoria. About 1850 these various causes of tension and disequilibrium ended in the most serious social explosion that the Chinese world had ever experienced. The T'ai P'ing Rebellion (1851–64) and the series of risings that echoed it and went on until about 1875 constitute the most important fact in the history of the nineteenth century. The shock administered to the ruling classes by this great social and political crisis, the efforts necessary to overcome it, and the considerable losses and destruction that accompanied it were at the root of some important changes: the appearance of new political personnel trained in the course of the wars of repression, the weakening of the central government, the decline of the economy. The empire that was restored after the great civil war was no longer the same empire that had existed previously.

It was in this context of decline and crisis that the first intrusions of the Western powers into China took place, from 1840 onwards. But the British attacks of 1840–42, which were bound up with opium smuggling, were only to acquire their true historical significance in retrospect: they were the first manifestation of a policy of colonialist intervention, the nature and aims of which changed as the industrial power of the Western nations developed. The civil war, the strain of reconstruction, and China's difficulties in central Asia facilitated the West's new enterprises in 1857–60 and forced the rulers of China all the more into a policy of compromise since they badly needed foreign capital and engineers to help their military and industrial efforts. But external pressure grew sharper and sharper from 1870 onwards, accentuating the contradictions between those who favoured conciliation and those who favoured intransigence, between modernists in touch with the foreigners and traditionalists ignorant of the realities of the age. At the same time the backwardness of a China too vast and too highly populated to permit a radical, rapid transformation increased in comparison with the small nations whose industrial development was accelerating. Japan, which had profited from its relative isolation to model itself on the Western countries, crushed the Chinese army and navy in 1894. The Treaty of Shimonoseki opened a new period in the history of the Chinese world — that of its takeover by outsiders.

Chapter 25

The Great Recession

The internal causes of the decline

Worrying signs of a deterioration in the state and in the social equilibrium began to appear at the end of Ch'ien-lung's reign and at the beginning of the nineteenth century. The first great peasant revolts of the Ch'ing age began in the north-west and in Honan in 1795, the very year in which the aboriginal inhabitants of Hunan and Kweichow rebelled and piracy began again on the coasts of Kwangtung and Fukien. It became clear at the end of the eighteenth century that the glorious reign of Ch'ien-lung had been an age of unconcern, in which the public reserves had been squandered without counting the cost. The court and the state had lived above their means, and corruption, favoured by the centralization of power in the hands of the emperor and by the pernicious influence of his favourite, Ho-shen, had known no bounds from 1775 onwards. The government, deluded by false reports, was badly informed of the situation in the provinces and of the real progress of the military campaigns. While the first Ch'ing emperors had been particularly economical (K'ang-hsi, so it is said, spent no more on the court in thirty-six years than the last Ming sovereigns spent in one year), the expenses of the Manchu aristocracy and the court rose beyond measure in the second half of Ch'ien-lung's reign. Distant wars, the difficulties encountered in suppressing the revolts by aborigines and Moslems, and the emperor's largesses completed the process of exhausting the treasury in the last few years of the eighteenth century. Ch'ien-lung's successors, who confined themselves to making slight reductions in court expenditure, did not succeed in restoring the situation. In the reign of Yung-cheng (1723–35), the state's reserves amounted to sixty million *liang;* in 1850, on the eve of the terrible T'ai P'ing Rebellion, they were only nine million. Nor did Ch'ien-lung's successors succeed in eliminating corruption and weakness in the Manchu armies, the Banners, which at the height of their power had imposed Chinese sovereignty on such a large part of Asia.

The euphoria which seems to have taken hold of China during the major part of the eighteenth century doubtless had harmful effects in the long run. It looks as if it caused a sort of lethargy in the political field, where it allowed the paternalist authoritarianism of the Manchu power to grow more rigid, as well as in the social and economic domain. But there was an even more serious side to the situation: everything suggests that the political and administrative system, the techniques of production and the commercial practices which had corresponded to the needs of a less extensive and less highly populated empire had become inadequate in an empire which controlled vast territories and whose population seems to have more than doubled in a century. The demographic upsurge which in the eighteenth century had provoked such a remarkable expansion seems to have produced the reverse effect on China's economy in the first half of the nineteenth century. The economy ran out of steam while the population continued to increase rapidly. According to the census figures, the population of China increased by 100 million between 1802 and 1834, the date at which the finance ministry announced that the empire had over 400 million inhabitants. Such a rise is inconceivable. Nevertheless the census figures reflect a reality – the increasingly serious overpopulation of many Chinese provinces.

It was a difficult situation, aggravated by the deterioration in the state and the continual increase in the population, that Ch'ien-lung bequeathed to his successors Chia-ch'ing (1796–1820) and Tao-kuang (1821–50), whose two reigns covered the first half of the nineteenth century. The peasant revolts inspired by the White Lotus sect (*Pai-lien chiao*) were not repressed until 1803. And there was to be a resurgence of this movement a few years later: new troubles broke out in the lower Yellow River valley, in Honan, in Hopei and in Shantung from 1811 onwards. The insurgents, who belonged to the Society of the Celestial Order (*T'ien-li-chiao*), a reincarnation of the White Lotus, found accomplices at court among high officials dissatisfied with Chia-ch'ing's policy of austerity and used to living in the grand style under Ch'ien-lung. A plot organized in liaison with the rebels came into the open at Peking in 1813, but collapsed just when the imperial palace was about to be taken by storm. The rebellion in the provinces was crushed a year later.

However, although the *Pai-lien-chiao* rebellions were successfully dealt with, the actual causes of the peasant agitation were not eliminated.

These were the land shortage, which persisted in spite of clearances and the extension of new crops (maize, sweet potato, ground-nut), the increase in fiscal burdens of every sort, the depreciation of the copper coinage in relation to silver, which began to become rarer since imports of the American metal had declined, the fall in ground-rents tied up with the rapid rise in the price of land, the concentration of land in the hands of a few rich landowners (especially in the south), and the accompanying transformation of small farmers into agricultural labourers. All these factors led to permanent tension in the countryside.

Peasant agitation continued throughout the first half of the nineteenth century, although it did not provoke any insurrections as serious as those which north-western China had experienced in the years between 1796 and 1804. Revolts are recorded in almost all the provinces, including – for the first time – those of South China. One of the gravest occurred in 1832–33 in the mountainous region on the border between Hunan and Kwangsi. The atmosphere favoured the spread of brigandage and the development of secret societies, which were like religious confraternities, their members being bound by oath and regarding each other as close relations. It was during the first half of the nineteenth century that the secret society known as the Triad (*San-ho-hui* or *T'ien-ti-hui*) and its numerous ramifications took root in South China.

Meanwhile control of the aboriginal peoples of the south and of the territories with a Moslem majority in the west of Sinkiang continued to remain precarious and difficult. The Tibetans of Kokonor rebelled against the Sino-Manchu administration in 1807, and the Yao of Kweichow in 1833. The Moslems of western Sinkiang, led by a Kwadja Turk called Jehangir, seceded in 1825, and the oases of Kashgar and Yarkand were not recaptured until 1828, after a three-year campaign.

The unfavourable balance in foreign trade caused by the imports of opium was to add to the difficulties of an empire already threatened by so many weaknesses and hampered by divisions in the ruling circles.

Smuggling and piracy

The import of finished products into countries deprived of industries and in process of being colonized marked a turning point in the history of the subjection to the rich nations of the lands which today form the Third World. But this turning point occurred only at the end of the nineteenth century, with the development of mass production. About 1800 the East India Company, which in 1786 had obtained a monopoly in trade with Canton, imported a small quantity of cotton goods and some Yorkshire

Table 20.   Imports of opium into China during the nineteenth century

Years	Number of cases
1729	200
1790	400 +
1817–1819	4,228 (average)
	Start of the policy of importing
1820	4,244 (about 5,000?)
1821	5,959
1823	9,035
1826–1828	12,851 (average)
1829	16,257
1830	19,956
c.1836	30,000 (roughly)
1838	40,000 (at least)
c.1850	68,000
1873	96,000
1893	Imports begin to decline because of the rise in prices
1917	Imports stop completely; opium is produced in China itself in sufficient quantities to cover all needs

woollens into China. But the English cloth which found takers in India did not sell well in China, for the Chinese cotton industry was well developed and sufficed for all the country's needs. It was threatened only at the very end of the nineteenth century by massive imports of American cotton goods. Thus it was not from the sale of finished products that the British company drew most of its profits, but from the smuggling of a drug, the high value of which in relation to its small volume made the voyage to China – still an adventurous business – a highly profitable operation.

The deficit on the balance of trade

Opium, which was not cultivated on a large scale in China until the beginning of the twentieth century, had been known there since the end of the Ming period. Described by Li Shih-chen at the end of the sixteenth century in his famous treatise on pharmacology, under a transcription of the Arabic word *afyun,* it was imported into Fukien in the seventeenth century by the Portuguese. Imports, which had reached about two hundred cases a year by the beginning of the following century, were officially forbidden in 1729. This veto was extended to the whole empire in 1731. But opium growing made progress from the end of the eighteenth century onwards, after the occupation of India by the British. The East India Company acquired its first territorial rights in Bengal in 1757. It extended them to Bihar in 1765. In 1773 it gained possession of the monopoly in smuggling opium into China and developed the cultivation of the poppy, first in Bengal, then later in central India. By 1810 four to five thousand cases of opium (each containing 65 kilograms of the drug) were being imported every year into Canton, and imports were to increase rapidly in spite of all the vetoes issued by the Chinese government. Such vetoes were issued in 1796, 1813, 1814, 1839, and 1859.

It was in 1816 that the East India Company, whose monopoly soon had to compete with free trade (the company was to be wound up in 1833), took the decision to develop this lucrative trade systematically. Imports of opium from the British possessions in India (first from Bengal, then from Malwa), and to a much lesser extent from Turkey, were to continue to grow rapidly from about 1820 onwards and throughout the course of the nineteenth century. For more than sixty years the sale of this drug was to form the principal source of revenue for the British Indian empire in its relations with China. It was thanks to opium that British trade with China avoided falling into deficit during this period.

There is no doubt that there was a sudden increase in imports in the years preceding the 'Opium War' and this explains the agitation of the Chinese authorities and of the Peking government. The fact is that, apart from the physical and intellectual ravages caused by the use of the drug in its devotees, who were usually minor local officials, employees of the *ya-men,* opium smuggling had serious moral, political, and economic consequences. In Kwangtung, on the eve of the incidents of the Opium War (1839–42), it had created an inextricable situation which could only be clarified by draconian measures, owing to the network of collusion which had been woven at every level between boatmen, pirates engaged in smuggling, carriers, pedlars, government employees, and civil servants

Plate 61. Breaking bulk on a tea ship in London docks, from a nineteenth-century engraving

Plate 62. Opium smokers, nineteenth-century China, from an original photograph

of every grade. It extended and aggravated corruption. Moreover – and this is doubtless what finally induced the central government to react – this smuggling was undermining the Chinese economy, which was already weakened by the wars of the end of the eighteenth century and by demographic pressure. It was the imports of opium which between 1820 and 1825 caused the sudden imbalance in foreign trade. Hitherto favourable to China, from that time onwards the balance of payments showed a deficit.

The sale of opium in China could no longer be counterbalanced by the purchase of Chinese products, even though exports of the latter had continued to expand since the end of the eighteenth century. The principal product exported was tea, in which there had been a substantial trade in the interior of Asia since the Sung and Yüan periods. The spread of tea-drinking in Europe from about 1730 explains the continual growth in exports (especially from 1760–70 onwards), which rose from 12,700 tonnes a year about 1720 to 360,000 tonnes a year around 1830. This substantial commercial trend had repercussions in China: the tea plantations were extended, mainly in Kwangtung, Kiangsi, and Anhwei, but also in Fukien, Chekiang, Kiangsu, and Hunan, and the industry became more highly organized. Other products occupied a smaller place in exports to Europe, but made no less clear progress: purchases of silks rose from 1200 piculs round about 1750 to 6400 about 1830, and purchases of the fine cotton cloth known in Europe as 'nankeen' rose from 338,000 pieces in 1785–91 to 1,415,000 pieces in 1814–20.

However, this expansion of Chinese trade did not suffice to eliminate the deficit caused by opium smuggling.

Between 1800 and 1820 ten million *liang* of silver had entered China. Between 1831 and 1833 ten million *liang* left the country. Thanks to the various 'treaties' successively imposed on China, this flight of Chinese silver, which was essentially due to purchases of opium, never stopped throughout the nineteenth century (at the end of the century opium still formed 30 per cent of imports). During the T'ai P'ing War (1851–64), when most of the trade was concentrated in Shanghai, thirty million *liang* left the port of Canton alone. After reforms in the administration of the salt industry from 1832 onwards the budget deficit was reduced, but the growth of the population and the absence of new resources ended in a rise in prices and general impoverishment. The state could not help without attempting to prevent the drain on its currency.

The first opium 'war'

The ruling circles were aware both of the danger and of the difficulties implicit in a policy of systematic prohibition; hence the apparent indecision of the central government and the disagreement about the measures to be taken. Three tendencies came to the surface in Peking. Some advisers were in favour of radical measures of prohibition, others preached a sort of legalization of opium imports, and yet others, taking the view that legal restrictions could lead to evils worse than the original one, thought that the absence of any regulations would deprive the clandestine trade in opium of its main interest. In 1836, when imports were increasing rapidly, Hsü Nai-chi suggested that, to stop the flight of money out of China and to increase the state's revenues, a heavy tax should be imposed on imports of opium and foreigners should be obliged to buy Chinese products (silks, cotton goods, tea, porcelain) in return. However, it was the champions of total prohibition who triumphed three years later in the person of Lin Tse-hsü (1785–1850), perhaps because the danger was becoming more pressing. Despatched to Canton in 1839, Lin Tse-hsü caused 20,000 cases of opium to be seized and ordered the British merchants to decamp without delay. In the explosive atmosphere produced by these extreme measures the British responded with acts of piracy at the mouth of the Chu-chiang (the Pearl River) and then on the coast of Chekiang, where they occupied Ting-hai, a big island in the Chusan archipelago; further north, they threatened the port of Tientsin. But China did not give way. The British attacks were resumed in 1841 after the arrival of reinforcements: the foreigners again attacked the forts of Chu-chiang, occupied afresh Hsia-men (Amoy), Ning-po, and Ting-hai, and threatened Hangchow and the lower Yangtze valley, the British fleet sailing up river as far as Nanking. To put a stop to all this, the Chinese government agreed to open negotiations; the result was the famous Treaty of Nanking of 1842, the effects of which were to be much more serious in the long run than the Chinese negotiators had probably foreseen. From their point of view the British attacks obviously fell into the historical context of acts of piracy committed by foreign peoples and of incursions by nomads wanting markets to be opened at the gates to China. The attacks of the Japanese pirates and those of Coxinga had threatened the coastal provinces of the lower Yangtze much more seriously than the British attacks of 1840–42, and some of the incursions from the steppe had also been much more devastating. The English troops who attacked Canton in 1841 numbered only 2400, and the reinforcements which they received the following year did not exceed a few thousand men. In the last analysis the rights conceded to the aggressors were out of proportion to the risks incurred. The weakness of China at the time of the First Opium War was not so much the obsolete nature of its artillery and the lack of fighting spirit and discipline of the imperial troops as the country's political condition and the social malaise which was soon to erupt in the terrible T'ai P'ing Rebellion. The main causes of the empire's weakness were probably corruption, the powerlessness of a finicking administration suffering from a superfluity of regulations, excessive centralization combined with lack of coordination, and the enormous distances involved (Canton is over 2000 kilometres from Peking), which resulted in decisions being taken at Peking only after a long delay. If the Ch'ing government ended by capitulating, this was because it was already hesitant and divided about the line to follow even before the British attacks began. The emperor Tao-kuang himself was badly informed, indecisive, and miserly with public money. His envoy to Canton in 1841 agreed on his own responsibility, without waiting for Peking's approval, to the withdrawal of the Chinese troops and the payment of an indemnity of six million silver *liang* to the British. At first convinced by Lin Tse-hsü, the champion of firmness, Tao-kuang subsequently leaned towards a compromise and then decided in 1841 to resume the offensive. The efforts made to resist the foreigners were not negligible: cannon were cast, warships with paddle-wheels were built, in accordance with a tradition that went back to the Sung age, and the ports were blockaded. In addition, peasant militias were formed in 1841 in the Canton area and successfully checked the marauding of the British troops. But the militias, which could have been one of the most effective means of combating foreign incursions in the nineteenth century, were unfavourably regarded by the government and the administration, who feared that they might turn their weapons against the established authorities.

The Treaty of Nanking ended the difficulties for the time being. China ceded to Great Britain the rocky little island of Hong Kong, paid an 'indemnity' of twenty-one million silver dollars and agreed to open to trade, that is, mainly to imports of opium, the ports of Amoy, Shanghai, and Ning-po as well as Canton. She agreed at the same time to suppress the monopoly of the Cohong (Kung-hang), the offical association of the merchants of Canton since 1720. This association supervised, in accord with the administration, all trade with foreign countries (South-East Asia, the Indian Ocean, Europe), a considerable part of which was carried in Chinese ships. The additional treaty of 1843 granted the first extra-territorial rights (British subjects were exempted from Chinese jurisdiction) and contained the 'most favoured nation' clause (any advantage acquired by other nations was to be automatically extended to Great Britain). Consular jurisdiction and the creation of the first concessions (*tsu-chieh*) opened the first breaches, which were to enable the Western nations, thanks to the constant progress of their military and economic power, to exert a stronger and stronger hold on China and to limit more and more her independence and sovereignty.

Monetary problems

The conflicts caused by the smuggling of opium and the immediate effects of the imports of the drug, the volume of which never stopped growing from 1820 to the eve of the Sino-Japanese war of 1894, should not make us forget the less visible yet extremely profound effects on the Chinese economy and currency.

The history of silver in East Asia has not yet been studied in detail. However, the use of this metal as a means of payment, a use which persisted in China right into the republican era (1912–49), was almost certainly one of the important factors in the deterioration of the Chinese economy from the time when this economy found itself in competition with gold economies on which it became more and more dependent. While the attraction of gold seems to have been one of the decisive causes of the great maritime expansion from Europe to the Indies and America, the dearth of this metal in East Asia, except for Japan, and probably also traditions peculiar to the Chinese world – the predominance in China of the state economy over the mercantile economy – produced the result that gold did not play an important monetary role there. It was because it was relatively abundant and stable in value, unlike paper money, that silver was adopted in China as a means of payment in parallel with copper coins. Its use became general in the fifteenth and sixteenth centuries and imports from America increased the volume of silver in circulation in Kwangtung and Fukien in the second half of the sixteenth century. About 1564 the Mexican silver dollar or peso, produced in large quantities in Central and South America, appeared in Canton and Foochow, and it remained in use down to our own day.

However, at the same time as the amount of silver increased, thus bearing witness to the constant enrichment of China between the end of the sixteenth century and the end of the eighteenth, the value of silver also continually dropped in comparison with that of gold. While at the end of the sixteenth century silver still retained the high value which it seems to have had all through the period during which Japan had remained the principal exporter of precious metals in East Asia (at that time the relation of the value of gold to that of silver was 1 to 4), from around 1575 it started to depreciate. In 1635 the gold *liang* was already worth ten silver *liang*. The reversal in China's trade balance about 1820–25 coincided with the start of a fresh fall in the value of silver on the international market – a fall hastened by the adoption of the gold standard by the Western powers in the second half of the nineteenth century – just when the Chinese economy began to suffer from Western commercial competition as well as from the war indemnities imposed on the country by the aggressors. In 1887 the silver *liang* was worth 1.20 American dollars; in 1902 it was worth only .62 of a dollar.

At the same time as China's currency was depreciating on the world market, silver continued to leave the country in large quantities during the nineteenth century. In spite of a fall in the price of opium (a case fetching 1000 to 2000 Mexican dollars before 1821 was worth only 700 to 1000 dollars after 1838), the value of silver, exports of which did not slow down, rose in China to the detriment of copper money:

Before 1820 a *liang* (c.36g.) of silver was worth about 1000 copper coins
In 1827 it was worth	1300 " "
In 1838 "	1600 " "
In 1845 "	2200 or more

This rise in the price of silver did grave harm to the poorest classes who formed the great majority of the Chinese population, for it was they who held most of the copper coins, while their taxes were calculated on the basis of silver money.

From these very brief indications a general and provisional conclusion can be drawn: just as silver–copper bimetallism tended in China itself to aggravate the condition of the least favoured classes, so world gold–silver bimetallism helped to weaken the Chinese economy during the course of the nineteenth century. These monetary mechanisms aggravated the economic recession which characterized the first half of the nineteenth century.

China and the West

The activities of the West in China are usually presented in a favourable light to sooth the pride of the European countries and of America: the Westerners, so the story goes, led China to emerge from a thousand years of isolation, they awakened her to scientific and industrial civilization and forced her to open her doors to the rest of the world. A routine mentality, the corruption of the mandarins, the tyranny of the emperors, the naïve belief of the Chinese that they were at the centre of the universe, and the superstitions of a wretched populace are compared unfavourably with the spirit of enterprise, the notion of progress, science and technology, freedom, Western universalism, and Christianity.

Moreover, the intrusion of the Western countries into East Asia had, in this part of the world as elsewhere, such grave repercussions that the traditional view of the history of the Far East seems to change radically from the moment that it occurred: for most historians, Chinese as well as Western, the first cannonades of the British sailing ships in the Pearl

River mark the beginning of an entirely new epoch in the history of China. This new period seems to fit all the better into world history in that it becomes an integral part of the history of a West whose evolution from antiquity down to our own day is seen as the keystone of any universal history. By the same token, all the earlier periods in the history of the Chinese world which cannot be related to the history of the West tend to lose their intrinsic interest and significance.

But this is to fail to recognize the solidarity of civilizations, to ignore the world role of China in the past, its relations with central Asia, Iran, India, the Islamic world and South-East Asia, the continual coming and going of merchandise, techniques, and religions across the Eurasian continent, but for which the history of Europe itself would be scarcely comprehensible. It also means dismissing as negligible the specific structures and traditions of the Chinese world. Menacing as the dangers from outside were in the nineteenth century, and profound as the evolution of China may have been, internal problems have never ceased to be preponderant; it is in terms of these structures and these traditions that the Chinese world has changed. This accounts for certain attitudes and certain features that link the China of today to the China of yesterday.

Moreover, by comparing the two civilizations—the Chinese and the Western—globally, by reducing history to their confrontation, we neglect a fundamental element: time. We substitute a stereotype for a series of successive changes which have affected both China and the Western world. In the history of the relations between the Ch'ing empire and the industrialized nations of Europe and America, one must take account not only of the changes that have occurred in China, in society, the economy, the political system, intellectual life, but also of those experienced for their part by the Western countries. Their colonial expansion, the development of their industries, the strengthening of their armies and fleets, the evolution of their foreign policy were all marked by different stages. The England of the last few years of the nineteenth century was already quite different from the England of the First Opium War (1839–42). It is as well to remember that the clearest technical progress in Europe and the United States did not occur until the second half of the nineteenth century. In 1830 only three percent of the vessels of the Western navies were steamships, propelled by paddle-wheels; the steam navy did not really begin to develop until screw propulsion was adopted in the middle of the nineteenth century. The first ships with steel hulls were not built until 1880, ten years after the opening of the Suez Canal (1869), an important date in the colonial expansion of the European nations to the Indies and the Far East. Railways only expanded on a large scale after 1850.

Table 21.   Length of railway networks
(in km)

1840	7,700	1870	210,900
1850	38,700	1880	373,500
1860	108,100	1890	618,400

When the use of coal became general in Europe and America in the middle of the nineteenth century, only ninety million tons of it were being extracted, fifty-six million of them in Great Britain. The total was to rise to 1340 million tons in 1913, at the time when new sources of energy were discovered. Oil and electricity, the internal combustion engine and the electric motor began their career at the beginning of the century.

The invention of the Bessemer converter dates from 1855, that of the Martin furnace from 1864 and that of the Thomas process from 1878. In 1850 the total production of pig-iron was ten million tons; in 1913 it was to reach seventy-eight million.

The cost of English cotton goods fell by 80 percent between 1850 and 1870, thanks to the progress of mechanization. But it was only at the end of the nineteenth century that the combination of banking capital and industrial capital made possible the spectacular development of mechanized production; it was then that, through the increasingly rapid progress of technology, the economic and military power of the industrialized nations of Europe and America, soon to be joined by Japan, became really fearsome for China. This had not been the case fifty years earlier. Finally, it is perhaps worth remembering, since we tend to regard China as an essentially rural country, that in 1830 less than twenty percent of the inhabitants of Europe lived in towns and that only about twenty cities had populations of more than 100,000.

The real threat that England posed for the China of the first half of the nineteenth century was not nearly so much a military one as an economic one: the imports of opium helped to undermine the economy of an empire whose finances and political system had continuously deteriorated since the end of the eighteenth century. And that is the essential point, for this internal decline ended in the terrible social explosions and in the insurrections of colonized peoples that were to shake the empire between 1850 and 1878.

What changed the political conditions, the ruling circles, the economy and fiscal system and the intellectual life of China so perceptibly between 1850 and 1870 was not the activities of the Western powers but the great social and political crisis of the T'ai P'ing War. The almost exclusive attention devoted by Western historians to the history of the economic and military penetration by the nations of Europe and America has falsified the true picture.

The new foreign attacks on China between 1858 and 1860 were to take place in this context of internal crisis, and when the pressure of the industrialized nations grew fiercer at the end of the nineteenth century China had been left so short a breathing-space that she no longer had the time, the means, the peace or the autonomy necessary to recruit her strength and fight effectively against the onrush of imperialism.

It is the combined effect of the evolution of the industrialized nations and of internal developments in the Ch'ing empire, together with the concatenation of events, that account for the march of history and the tragic fate of China.

Chapter 26

The Social Expansion and Its Consequences

The underlying causes of the terrible insurrections which shook the empire to its foundations from 1850 to 1878 were already at work at the beginning of the nineteenth century and these great rebellions may be regarded as the outcome of the slow process of deterioration which had been going on for half a century. The growth of the population in a period of economic recession, the depreciation of the copper currency, which affected the most depressed classes, the defects of an ineffective and corrupt administration, and the financial difficulties which induced the state and its officials to increase the burdens of the poorest people – by 1843 the government was forced to reduce the salaries of its civil servants and the provincial budgets – all helped to bring about the terrible social explosion heralded for some fifty years by numerous harbingers such as the rebellions of the White Lotus and the Celestial Order in North China, the renewal of piracy on the coasts of Kwangtung, Fukien, and Chekiang, the sporadic risings of the peasantry and of the non-Chinese populations in South China and the proliferation of sects and secret societies.

The lower Yellow River valley, subject as it was to big floods, and the arid lands of North China, where, since the abandonment of the irrigation works in the ninth and tenth centuries, unexpected droughts could occur, had always been the scene of popular risings. But it was in tropical China, in areas which half a century earlier had been among the most prosperous, that the biggest insurrection in Chinese history was born and spread like a train of gunpowder. The provinces of South China, more sensitive to variations in the level of economic activity, probably felt the recession of the first half of the nineteenth century much more sharply than the northern provinces. The scarcity of silver and the rise in prices caused by the imports of opium, together with the diversion of the trade of Canton to Shanghai after the Treaty of Nanking (1842), accelerated the decline of the economy and the deterioration of the social atmosphere in Kwangtung, Kwangsi, and Hunan. Between 1845 and 1858 exports of tea from Canton fell from 76 to 24 million pounds, while at Shanghai they rose during the same period from 3.8 million pounds to 51.3 million pounds. The recession ruined a whole population of boatmen, carriers, and merchants who made a living out of the commercial activity in the Canton area and along the main roads that traversed the interior via the valleys of the Hsiang and the Kan. These people were to provide the great T'ai P'ing Rebellion with some of its first troops. In the same way, the complete stoppage of traffic on the Grand Canal from 1849 onwards, by reducing the families of boatmen to poverty, was to contribute to the extension of the rebellious areas.

The Kingdom of Heaven

The great rebellion which originated round about 1850 in tropical China had thus had the ground prepared for it by the establishment of secret societies with revolutionary tendencies and a religious tinge. Feelings of hostility towards the Manchus had probably remained alive there since the time of the Southern Ming resistance (1645–61) and the period of secession (1674–81). The speed with which the movement that was to give birth to the T'ai P'ing grew in the province of Kwangsi and spread to the provinces of Kwangtung and of the middle and lower Yangtze is explained not only by poverty and injustice but also by the underground work carried out by the clandestine organizations affiliated to the Society of the Triad (*San-ho-hui*), also known as the Society of Heaven and Earth (*T'ien-ti-hui*).

A revolutionary tradition

The man who was to become the head of the great rebel empire of the T'ai P'ing emerged from a despised Chinese minority, the Hakka (K'o-chia), former immigrants into South China. Hung Hsiu-ch'üan (1813–64) came from a poor family in eastern Kwangtung, but nevertheless received the rudiments of a classical education and took part, without success, in the official competitions. He was a visionary, predisposed to become one by his temperament, but also perhaps by his origins and the local religious traditions. The reading of tracts handed out by the Protestant missionaries established shortly before in Kwangtung decided him on his vocation of Messiah. The mystical egalitarianism which was to be one of the characteristic features of the T'ai P'ing movement sprang from these first contacts of Hung Hsiu-ch'üan's with the propaganda disseminated by the missions. In 1847 he made the acquaintance of an American missionary called Roberts and started to preach in eastern Kwangtung, a region where the economic depression had made itself felt with particular sharpness since the diversion of trade from Canton to Shanghai which followed the Treaty of Nanking. Emboldened by the success of his preaching, he founded an Association of the Worshippers of God (*Pai-shang-ti-hui*), whose very name recalls the translation adopted by the Protestant missionaries for the name of God (*Shang-ti*). In two or three years he recruited nearly thirty thousand members – unemployed boatmen and carriers in the port of Canton and on the commercial route linking Canton to the valley of the Hsiang in Hunan, miners, charcoal-burners, poor peasants, bandits, and deserters. The society also recruited among the Hakka and the aboriginal inhabitants of Kwangtung and Kwangsi.

The Worshippers of God, soon known as the T'ai P'ing, first eliminated a rival group in Kwangsi consisting of unions for defence against the banditry which flourished in the region, then merged with the anti-Manchu secret societies. The rebellion started in eastern Kwangsi, in the village of Chin-t'ien-ts'un, in 1850. The T'ai P'ing, who were distinguished by their hair-style – they abandoned the pigtail, the sign of enslavement to the Manchus, and were sometimes to be called 'bandits with long hair', *ch'ang-mao-fei* – destroyed dwellings and proceeded to the confiscation and sharing out of estates. Distributing land equally to those of an age to cultivate it, they followed a principle similar to that established by the agrarian laws of the T'ang age and drew their inspiration from the theory of the draught-board field (*ching-t'ien*) which figures in the *Chou-li* (*Rites of the Chou*), a work of dubious authenticity already invoked, in the Han age, by the usurper Wang Mang and, in the T'ang age, by the empress Wu Tse-t'ien. Similarly, the organization of individuals and families in paramilitary groups among the T'ai P'ing was in conformity with ancient administrative traditions as well as with the framework of the secret societies. Twenty-five families formed a *k'u* ('store'), with its church (*li-pai-t'ang*), five men formed a squad, five squads a patrol, four patrols a battalion, and so on up to divisions of 2,500 men (corresponding to groups of 13,156 families) and armies of 125,000 men. Military, religious, and administrative functions were not separated. The T'ai P'ing established a regime in which no one possessed

Plates 63–66. Nineteenth-century plates representing the daily life of an ethnic minority in South China, from a MS of 1840–50

any property of his own, in which the individual was very strictly supervised and in which, after the suppression of all private trade, each person's indispensable needs were satisfied by the collectivity, in which authority was basically theocratic. All this was not so new as it might seem: the system had its roots in ancient Chinese political and religious traditions, in which the myth of a vanished golden age joins up with the utopia to come. In a very different society and a very different historical context—the second century A.D.—the Yellow Turbans had created a hierarchical, theocratic society whose object was the establishment of the era of justice and purity bearing the name of Great Peace (*t'ai-p'ing*), a name taken up again by the Worshippers of God and called to mind in its own way by the new term of Kingdom of Heaven (*t'ien-kuo*). Although it is true that Christian influences were perceptible in the T'ai P'ing ('equality is the ideal of the all-powerful God who has sent Hung Hsiu-ch'üan to save the world'), and although its adherents were obliged to attend weekly religious services, other influences could also be noted and the new contributions of Christianity were forced into a typically Chinese mould. When Hung Hsiu-ch'üan, who governed by divine inspiration, proclaimed himself to be the younger brother of Jesus Christ, he was only following in the footsteps of other rebel leaders and usurpers who had been regarded as reincarnations of Maitreya, the saviour Buddha. Buddhism, Taoism, and the classical traditions of the *Meng-tzu* and the *Chou-li* all made their mark on the T'ai P'ing movement, and the Christian missionaries were struck by the profoundly heterodox aspects of the Christianity professed by these rebels with long hair.

The movement was not only egalitarian and revolutionary, but also puritan and feminist. It condemned concubinage and the practice—which had spread since the Sung age—of bandaging little girls' feet. It aimed at the absolute equality of the sexes in work and war. Women received equal shares of land with the men and formed exclusively female armies. The T'ai P'ing prohibited all useless luxury and forbade gambling for money, alcohol, tobacco and opium. But these puritan—and also iconoclastic—tendencies, which followed the same direction as the propaganda of the Protestant missionaries, were not a radical novelty. The rebellion led by Chang Hsien-chung at the end of the Ming period had also been animated by a destructive rage which attacked luxury goods and the rich. Chang Hsien-chung, too, had created female armies (*p'o-tzu chün*).

Rise and fall of the T'ai P'ing rebellion

In 1851 Hung Hsiu-ch'üan founded the Kingdom of the Heaven of the Great Peace and proclaimed himself King of Heaven (*t'ien-wang*). He

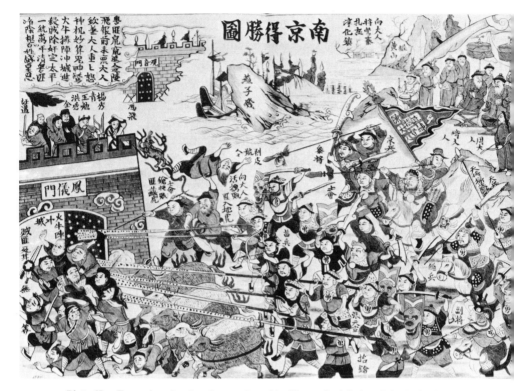

Plate 67. Engraving showing the attack on Nanking, celestial city of the T'ai P'ing, 1864

conferred this same title of King on his ministers and army commanders: deputy King (*i-wang*) and Kings of the east, west, south, and north. One of them, Yang Hsiu-ch'ing (*c.* 1817–56), was an organizer and strategist of genius; another, Shih Ta-k'ai, was an exceptionally talented general. In 1852 the T'ai P'ing occupied north-eastern Kwangsi (Kweilin area) and south-western Hunan and then advanced towards Ch'ang-sha and the towns on the middle Yangtze (Yüeh-yang, Han-yang), reaching the areas to the south-west of Nanking (Chiu-chiang in Kiangsi, An-ch'ing in Anhwei). The following year they captured Nanking, which they christened Capital of Heaven (*t'ien-ching*). Nanking was to remain the political and administrative centre of the *T'ai P'ing t'ien-kuo* until its fall in 1864. Then came the conquest of the lower Yangtze (Chen-chiang and Yangchow), where they cut communications on the Imperial Canal. In 1853–54 the new empire spread towards the north and west. The T'ai P'ing armies even ventured into the Tientsin area, threatening Peking, but were forced to retreat by cold and hunger; they were defeated in

Shantung in 1854. However, the gains of territory in the whole Yangtze valley remained substantial.

In the face of this sudden and triumphant expansion by the rebels the Ch'ing government was at first at a complete loss. The Banners were powerless to halt the wave of insurgents and in 1856 the government armies, led by Hsiang Jung, suffered a decisive defeat. The inflow of taxes dropped steeply and transport was disorganized as a result of the halting of traffic on the Yangtze and of the loss of the empire's richest territories. In 1855 there were big floods on the Yellow River, the course of which moved from the south to the north of the Shantung peninsula and was not stabilized until 1870. However, after the first few years of panic and powerlessness the defence was organized effectively, not under the guidance of the central government but on the initiative of the Chinese provincial administrations and the lettered class, which felt directly threatened by a rebellion that attacked the established order and all traditions. New leaders appeared and new, locally recruited armies were formed, sometimes with the financial help of rich merchants. In the west there was the army of the Hsiang, the literary name for Hunan, under the energetic leadership of the Hunanese Tseng Kuo-fan (1811–72), who created a navy for operations on the Yangtze, obtained the moral and material help of the Chinese upper classes and financed the war by issues of paper money and by the new internal toll on commercial traffic, the *li-chin,* instituted by the Ch'ing in 1853. This army recaptured Wu-ch'ang, on the right bank of the Yangtze, in 1854, reached Chen-chiang four years later, advanced to Chiu-chiang and threatened Nanking. But the systematic reconquest began only in 1860, with the three armies of Tseng Kuo-fan, Tso Tsung-t'ang (1812–85), another Hunanese (this was the army of Ch'u, the name of the ancient kingdom of the middle Yangtze), and Li Hung-chang (1823–1901), a native of Ho-fei in central Anhwei (army of the Huai).

However, the T'ai P'ing strove to modernize their armies and to reorganize their administration at the instigation of Hung Jen-kan (1822–64), the King of Heaven's cousin, who had received a Western education in Hong Kong and Shanghai and in 1859 published a political treatise (the *Tzu-cheng hsin-p'ien*) in which he advocated the adoption of American political institutions, the creation of railways and of mining and industrial enterprises, the establishment of banks, and the development of science and technology. But the *T'ai P'ing t'ien-kuo* was weakened by internal dissensions among its leaders which were only to grow worse with time. The distribution of land provoked the hostility of the middling and small landowners. The leaders did not respect the rules of austerity imposed on the generality of their followers, but on the contrary lived in luxury. The war and the frequent moves caused the modernization programme to remain a dead letter. The plans for building steamships, railways, and factories had to be abandoned. On the military plane, the T'ai P'ing had advanced too rapidly along the Yangtze valley and had neglected to gain a solid footing in the depths of the countryside. They did not try until 1856 to make an alliance with the Nien, another set of insurgents in North China, and refrained from occupying the Shanghai region in order not to upset the Western powers, whose support they hoped for in vain. Finally, they had no cavalry, a deficiency which robbed them of the ability to manoeuvre quickly. In 1862 the Westerners, who until then had preserved an attitude of relative neutrality, decided to support the Ch'ing, since they felt their interests threatened by the advance of the T'ai P'ing on Shanghai. A corps of mercenaries was formed which was to fight alongside the Chinese troops under the command of the famous British soldier C. J. Gordon (1833–85), the man who was later to meet his death at Khartoum.

In 1864 Tso Tsung-t'ang recaptured Hangchow and started to besiege Nanking. Nanking was taken and the King of Heaven poisoned himself. However, the fighting was to continue against certain elements of the T'ai P'ing armies in Fukien for another two years. Yet other elements crossed over to Formosa or moved down into Vietnam (Tonkin), where from 1867 onwards they were to form militias entrusted with the struggle against the former supporters of the Le and against banditry. Known as the Black Flags (*Hei-ch'i-chün*), they were to take an active part in the resistance to the French invasion.

The T'ai P'ing Rebellion provides a convenient opportunity to pose one or two questions about the other great insurrections of the past. The saying that Chinese dynasties lasted until peasant revolts caused the Mandate of Heaven (*t'ien-ming*) to pass into other hands, thus producing a return to the *status quo,* has little connection with reality. It takes no account of the great diversity of the insurrections (the social and professional origins of the rebels, the links of the insurgents with other social groups, the regional character and geographical spread of the risings, their organization, ideas, and goals), or of the evolution of the Chinese world and of the particular social and political conditions of the periods in which the insurrections occurred. The formation of armies independent of the central government, the secession of aristocratic families, the infiltrations and insurrections of former nomad tribes settled in China and the invasions from the steppes all played a larger part in the changes of 'dynasty' than the peasant revolts.

Moreover, the phrase 'peasant revolt', to the extent that it conjures up

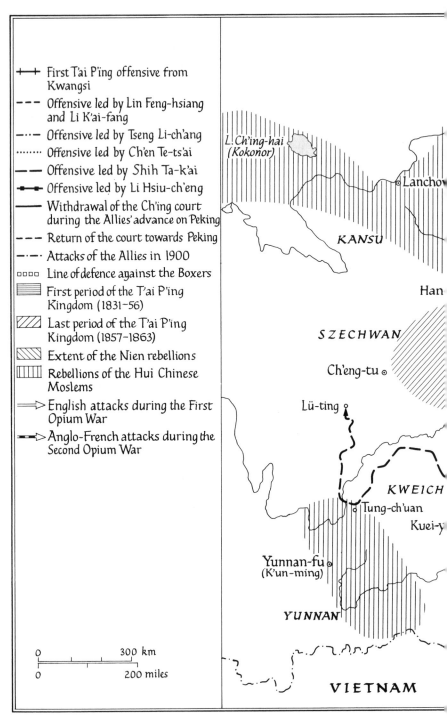

Map 25 Offensives mounted by the T'ai P'ing and other military operations in the
nineteenth century

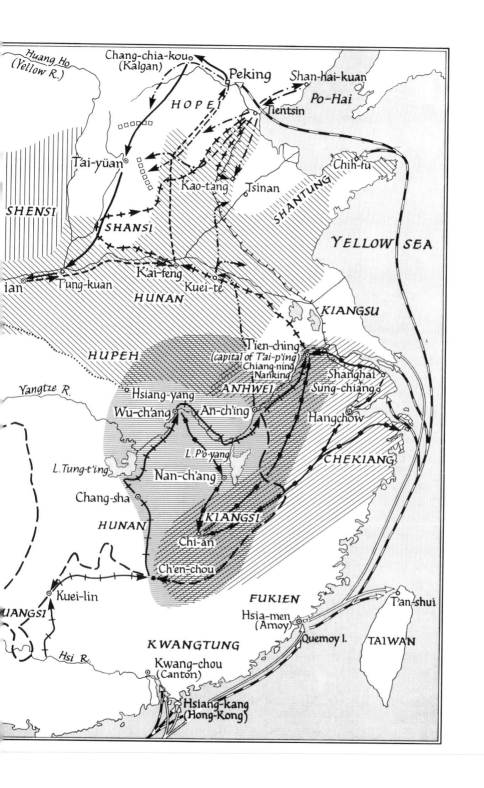

Table 22.   Rebellions and risings of the years 1850–1878

	1850	1860	1870
	I I I I I I I I I I I I I I I I I I I I I I I I I I I I I I I I I		
T'ai P'ing t'ien-kuo (1850–64)	·····——————————————··········		
Nien (1853–68)	········———————————————————————		
Miao of Kweichow (1854–72)	——————————————————————————————————········		
Hui of Yunnan (1855–73)	········———————————————————————————········		
Hui of Shensi-Kansu (1863–73)	········———————————————···············		
Hui of Sinkiang (1862–78)	————————————————————————————		

the anarchic, disorganized action of peasants pushed to the point of despair, is inaccurate. On the contrary, one of the most striking characteristics of Chinese insurrections was that in most cases they involved a disciplined framework and a hierarchy. An autonomous village administration set up in a clandestine fashion would take over from the official administration in the zones where the insurrection had succeeded in driving out the imperial officials. The big secret societies with their millenarian tendencies remained faithful to the basic principles of the rural or professional confraternities—subscriptions, internal rules, bonds of a more or less family character between the members, the duty of mutual help, a hierarchy of functions, and hereditary membership within families.

In addition, some people have seen in the large borrowings which the T'ai P'ing made from Christianity a sign of radical innovation and conclusive evidence of Western influence. This view fails to recognize the role played by heterodox religions in the big rebellions of Chinese history and the opposition—a basic factor in China—between the official cults, patronized by the legitimate authority, and the religious practices frowned on by the state (*yin-ssu*). Taoism, Buddhism, and Manicheism all provided popular risings with the messianic hope of a world of peace, harmony, and general prosperity; the Christianity of the T'ai P'ing comes into the same category.

Other insurrections

However, the T'ai P'ing Rebellion was no more than the most important rising in a whole series of insurrections. One may say that this great rebellion helped the Nien one in the north, which started later and lasted longer; there were links between the two movements. There were also links between the Nien and the Moslem insurgents of north-western China, who were themselves in contact with the Islamic rebels of western Sinkiang. But these insurrections were primarily the reflection of a political and social climate. The poverty of the times, the injustices suffered by the most underprivileged, and the corruption of their rulers suffice to account for the temporal conjunction of the troubles.

The Nien

In North China, the agitation which began in 1851 on the borders of Shantung, Honan, Anhwei, and Kiangsu is credited to a secret society, the Nien (a term which means 'pinch while turning' or 'twist' – perhaps it referred to the paper used for lighting fires), which was probably a recrudescence of the White Lotus Society (*Pai-lien-chiao*). Its adherents were poor peasants, salt-smugglers and deserters, who were joined by a few unsuccessful literati. The movement was revolutionary and anti-Manchu, but does not appear to have had any clearly defined objective; the redistribution of wealth by pillage, raids, or pressure on the rich seems to have formed the main activity of the Nien. The rebellion began to become dangerous to the central government from 1853 onwards, by which time it had spread towards Hopei and from Shantung to Honan. A few years later the great floods of 1855 added to the number of insurgents.

The fortified villages of the Nien, their small units of cavalry, their tactics of harrying and then of retreating in case of danger, and the collusion which the combatants enjoyed in the countryside rendered very difficult the task of the imperial Banners and 'Green Battalions' of Chinese troops dispatched against them. These slow-moving, ineffective forces, which had given proof of their incapacity in the first few years of the T'ai P'ing War, failed to prevent the rebellion from spreading. The Nien gave their assistance to the T'ai P'ing at the time of the latter's offensive in the direction of Peking in 1854–55, and tried to coordinate their activities with those of the armies of the Kingdom of Heaven from 1856 to 1863. But after the collapse of the T'ai P'ing in 1864 the central government, freed of the most serious threat, launched a series of big offensives against the Nien. After calling on the Mongol general Seng-ko-lin-ch'in, who succeeded in regaining control of Shantung but was killed in the big victorious Nien counter-offensive of 1865, the authorities turned to the new men who had succeeded in mastering the T'ai P'ing: just when the Nien were at the zenith of their power Tseng Kuo-fan was appointed commander-in-chief of the government forces. In 1866 the rebels controlled two big areas: one in Shantung–Honan–Hupei–Kiangsu, the other in Shensi, in liaison with the revolts of Chinese Moslems which had broken out three years earlier. In 1867 they marched on Peking, and Tseng Kuo-fan gave up his command to Li Hung-chang. In the following year the threat to Peking grew sharper with the combined advance of the insurgents of Shensi towards Shansi and Hopei, and of those of Shantung and Hopei towards the north. But Li Hung-chang ended the rebellion in that same year.

The colonized peoples

These events were contemporaneous with other troubles. From 1854 onwards there were the risings of aboriginal peoples in Kweichow, pushed to desperation by the thefts of land and the exactions of the Chinese administration (these risings were not to be completely repressed until 1872); while from 1855 in Yunnan, and from 1862–63 in the north-west and in Sinkiang, there were the insurrections of Chinese Moslems and of Islamized peoples of central Asia. Except for those in Sinkiang, which were encouraged by foreign powers, the fundamental cause of most of these risings was probably the pressure of peoples of Chinese language and culture, whose numbers had continued to increase since the middle of the eighteenth century.

The communities of Chinese Moslems, the result of intermarriage between foreign Moslems and Han, had developed since the Mongol age in Yunnan and the north-western provinces (Shensi and Kansu), and formed social groups who lived slightly apart from the Chinese population and wanted to preserve a personality based on their religious affiliation and on their more distant ethnic origins. Their very lively particularism explains why even today these people are counted among the 'ethnic minorities' (*shao-shu min-tsu*). The unfavourable discrimination with which they were treated by the Han and by the imperial administration was at the root of their rebellions in 1855–73. In Yunnan the difficulties arising in 1853 out of a conflict between Han and Moslem tin-miners degenerated in 1855 into a rebellion. In the following year a massacre of Moslems was organized by the officials responsible for suppressing the revolt. One of the leaders of the insurrection was an imam by the name of Ma Te-hsin who had made the pilgrimage to Mecca and had lived for two years in Constantinople. Anxious to increase his own influence, Ma Te-hsin finally agreed to submit to the Ch'ing in 1861. He was succeeded by a man called Tu Wen-hsiu, who had created in the Ta-li area, four hundred kilometres from the provincial capital (the present-day K'un-ming), an independent sultanate, the kingdom of P'ing-nan, and had adopted the name of Sultan Suleyman. The rebellion, which won followers among the Han and the aboriginal inhabitants of the province, also found support from Burma. It was finally suppressed only in 1873, after a slow reconquest accompanied by general destruction and massacres.

Among the Moslems of the provinces of Kansu and Shensi, who had last rebelled on a large scale in 1781–84, the agitation started again in 1862 in support of the T'ai P'ing War and as a result of a T'ai P'ing offensive towards Shensi in 1861–62. The movement's principal leader was a Moslem reformer called Ma Hua-lung (?–1871); it spread rapidly from the Wei valley to western Kansu and the borders of Mongolia north-east of Tsinghai.

At the end of 1868 the Peking government called on Tso Tsung-t'ang, one of the most capable leaders in the war against the T'ai P'ing, whose efficiency and talent for organization were to permit the slow but steady reconquest of the two north-western provinces. The westward march was accompanied by terrible destruction and massacres. Shensi was completely pacified by the end of 1869. In 1871 Tso Tsung-t'ang's armies advanced towards central Kansu. In 1872 Tso occupied Lan-chou, the provincial capital. Finally the capture of Suchow (the former and present Chiu-ch'üan, in western Kansu) after a long siege marked, if not a complete return to calm, for the agitation was to continue until 1877, at any rate the end of any serious threat in these areas.

From Suchow, where he established his headquarters, Tso Tsung-t'ang pursued his operations in the direction of Hami—where some of the former rebels of Kansu had taken refuge—and more generally towards the New Territories (Sinkiang) as a whole, which had seceded in 1862. The movement had started in the western oases of Sinkiang, where the Moslem inhabitants of Turkish and Iranian origin had shaken off the Sino-Manchu yoke, renewing the attempt which they had made in 1825–28. The T'ai P'ing War and the contemporaneous rebellions had caused a relaxation of the Ch'ing hold over central Asia, and by about 1873, on the eve of Tso Tsung-t'ang's campaigns, the whole of the New Territories had joined the rebellion. The leader of the insurgents, a man called Yakub Beg (*c.* 1820–77), a prince of the family that reigned at Kokand, in the upper valley of the Syr-Darya, made himself master of the whole Tarim basin from the Pamirs to the Lob-nor. The Turks, British, and Russians entered into relations with him in the hope of weakening China and of gaining a strong position for themselves in central Asia. However, in spite of the opposition of one section of the government, Tso Tsung-t'ang succeeded in obtaining a loan from foreign banks and in organizing an expedition. He mastered his redoubtable enemy during the course of the years 1876 and 1877. By the beginning of 1878 the whole of Sinkiang had been pacified, and this remarkable military exploit inspired confidence again in the extreme patriots who rejected any compromise with foreigners.

The consequences

The Ch'ing empire had very nearly disappeared. All the necessary conditions for this had been present, and the traditional idea of a restoration of this empire in the course of the reign of T'ung-chih (1862–75) corresponds in large measure with the reality; there was a profound break between pre- and post-T'ai P'ing China. The economy, the finances, the political personnel, the distribution of forces in the empire, and the moral and intellectual atmosphere were no longer the same after the T'ai P'ing Rebellion.

Among the most immediate effects was the enormous loss of material and wealth caused by the bitter fighting between the insurgents and the government forces, and by the generalized massacres and systematic destruction. The losses in human lives were unparalleled in history. The whole rich and densely populated area, famous for its industries and intellectual centres, which extended from the neighbourhood of Nanking to the region of Lake T'ai-hu and Hangchow had been ravaged. In many places the traces of the tragedy were still visible fifty years later. The exact figure of dead is unknown, but the most reasonable estimates vary between twenty and thirty million people. More than half the population of Yunnan is said to have disappeared during the suppression of the Moslem revolts. In Shensi and Kansu the number of victims is reckoned to have been several million; the figure for Kweichow is five million. In all the combat areas the vacuum was to be filled only slowly in the course of the second half of the nineteenth century. Thus on the middle and lower Yangtze it was immigrants from Honan, Hupei, Hunan, northern Kiangsu and the area between Shao-hsing and Ning-po in Chekiang who came to repopulate this part of China, formerly the most active and highly developed part.

Priority of agrarian reconstruction

This terrible blood-letting no doubt reduced the demographic pressure and for the moment relieved a peasant economy that suffered cruelly from shortage of land. However, once the massacres and destruction had stopped, the restoration of the peasant economy seemed the great priority; every possible effort had to be devoted to this before one could even think of modernizing industry. The first things that had to be done were to provide a wandering, starving peasantry and all the discharged soldiers with the means to feed themselves, to put the land back into shape, to rebuild the towns, the dykes, the reservoirs, and the granaries, to advance to the new colonists the essential agricultural capital (seeds, tools, plough animals), and to lighten as much as possible the burdens on the peasantry. It is estimated that the agrarian taxes in the T'ung-chih era were reduced on average by thirty per cent as compared with those of the years immediately preceding the great T'ai P'ing Rebellion. The general lassitude after the huge massacres and the efforts made to help the peasantry explain why there was no further peasant agitation before the end of the nineteenth century.

Thus a relative improvement made itself felt in the years following the collapse of the Kingdom of Heaven. Thanks to this instinctive reaction — the fruit of long historical experience — which led it to restore its agrarian economy first, the empire achieved a certain equilibrium again. But this effort at reconstruction, which extended to nearly half China proper, was to weigh heavily on the country's economy. New resources had to be found, and it was the commercial and industrial sector that provided them. On the other hand, although the massacres had brought some immediate relief to the rural world, the political and social system was once again to favour, as it had before the rebellions, the wealthy landowners and the gentry.

Aggravation of the burdens imposed on commerce

Not only had commerce and industry suffered very severely from the destruction of the years 1850–65; they also had to bear the main burden of reconstruction. China, which in the eighteenth century and the first half of the nineteenth had been a great producer of finished products, was to tend subsequently to become the almost exclusively agrarian land that modern geographers and historians have regarded as typical of the pre-industrial state; in fact, it was only the result of a relatively late development.

The extension to all the provinces, between 1853 and 1857, of a new tax intended to defray the expenses of the war against the T'ai P'ing changed the traditional balance of the empire's finances. This tax, the *li-chin* (*likin*), which exacted two to twenty per cent of the value (in theory, one copper coin per *liang*) of all goods in transit inside China, was never applied to imported merchandise and remained in force until 1930–31. It is very probable that by increasing the burdens on craftsmen and on Chinese industry, which was beginning to develop timidly from 1860 onwards, it helped to weaken them just at the time when they had to

Table 23.   Government revenues, 1850–1910
(in millions of *liang*)

Grain	Before 1850	c.1890–1895	c.1900–1910
Grain tax	30	32	33
Salt tax	5–6	13	13
Chinese external customs	4	1	4
Western customs	0	22	35
Lijin	0	15	14
Sales of titles and offices	1	5	4
Total	40	89	103

Table 24. Revenue from maritime customs, 1885–1894

	Lijin	Revenues of the maritime customs
1885	14	14
1889	c.14.9	21.8
1894	c.14.2	22.3

face foreign competition. The commercial taxes and the multiplication of customs dues accentuated the general tendency of the regions to live more and more on their own resources.

A table of the central government's revenues reveals the growth during the second half of the nineteenth century of the charges which weighed on commerce and the production of finished products – and hence, indirectly, on the whole population.

While the volume of taxes in grain scarcely varied between the period preceding the T'ai P'ing War and the beginning of the twentieth century, other kinds of resources multiplied sevenfold during the same period. The reform of the administration of salt and the sale of offices – two steps taken during the T'ai P'ing War – contributed at the same time as the creation of the *li-chin* to this development of indirect taxation.

The reorganization of the maritime customs by Robert Hart from 1863 onwards was to give the central government a substantial part of its resources between the end of the T'ai P'ing War and the Sino-Japanese War.

However, except for the revenues from the external customs service, which was directed from 1863 to 1911 by Robert Hart (from 1911 onwards these revenues were to be completely absorbed by the payment of indemnities for the Boxers), all forms of taxation remained subject to substantial misappropriations. This makes it almost impossible to evaluate the burdens actually imposed on the Chinese population. Not only did the yield from the regular duties and taxes not reach the Peking government and the provincial governments intact, but there was a whole system of customary taxation which escaped any proper accounting, quite apart from the various pressures exerted at all levels by the officials and agents of the administration.

Political changes

Through the terrible destruction which they wrought, the risings of 1850–73 seriously reduced China's capacity for resistance. They also resulted in changes in the general distribution of political power.

The first few years of the T'ai P'ing Rebellion revealed even more clearly than the localized attacks of the British men-of-war in the First Opium War had done the weak and decayed state of the traditional Chinese armies – the Banners of the Manchus and those assimilated to them on the one hand and the 'Green Battalions' (*lu-ying*) of Chinese troops on the other. However, when resistance to the T'ai P'ing collapsed, there was a general mobilization of energies in the Chinese upper classes. Only the individual efforts of the local officials and gentry and the financial aid of the merchants and rich landowners could remedy such a catastrophic situation. This was how first free corps, then divisions, and finally whole armies gradually came into being.

By making it necessary everywhere to seek out and promote the most capable men, the war revealed unknown talents. Around the big army commanders, whose authority was confirmed in the course of the fighting, there grew up a sort of retinue of able men consisting of all those – friends, relations, disciples or contacts – who had participated in the fighting and formed part of the numerous general staffs of the new armies. To the three greatest men of the period – Tseng Kuo-fan (1811–72), Tso Tsung-t'ang (1812–55) and Li Hung-chang (1823–1901) – can be added Hu Lin-i (1812–61), Li Han-chang (1821–99), the brother of Tseng Kuo-fan, and Liu K'un-i (1830–1902). But many others who played a lesser role in the fighting were to leave their names in the political and intellectual history of the second half of the nineteenth century. The T'ai P'ing War gave birth to new forces and to a new political personnel whose influence was to be preponderant in the period from the capture of Nanking in 1864 to the Chinese defeat of 1894. The men with the most influence round about 1870 were Li Hung-chang, whose armies had crushed the Nien two years earlier, and Tso Tsung-t'ang, the pacifier of the north-west and central Asia. They alone had at their disposal disciplined armies and troops used to fighting. The links which they retained with their former colleagues and subordinates, the support which they enjoyed in their own provinces, and the resources which they drew directly from the areas where they had established their bases of operations gave them a certain independence in regard to the central government. The fact is that the very circumstances in which the new armies for the suppression of the revolts had been formed explain their essentially regional character.

But the resistance to the T'ai P'ing was also to be marked by other features. The new impetus came from the old Chinese ruling classes: the triumph of the T'ai P'ing would have resulted in the destruction of the old political and social order and in the decline of all the classical traditions. The leaders of the new armies were civil servants and literati never intended for the profession of arms. But the peril which threatened the traditional order united them in the common defence of the empire and the dynasty. The T'ai P'ing was not only a political and military crisis; it was also a moral crisis. In the eyes of the empire's defenders, the success of the rebellion was the sign of a sort of perversion, an indication of the weakening of the ancient values. Devotion to the emperor, the feeling for social and family hierarchies had to be inculcated more firmly than ever in all the emperor's subjects. Thus the T'ai P'ing Rebellion provoked a reaction towards orthodoxy and aroused in the ruling classes a livelier attachment than ever to the traditional morality and values. This orthodox reaction arising out of the crisis of the years 1850–64 is an essential factor in the history of the second half of the nineteenth century, for up to the Sino-Japanese War of 1894 it was to inspire most Chinese reactions to foreign enterprises and Western innovations.

The most convinced advocates of modernization of the armies and industry were also the most ardent defenders of orthodoxy; almost all of them in fact came from the general staffs of the big armies formed to suppress the T'ai P'ing revolt. The needs of the war had led the commanders of these armies to make contact with the Westerners, for foreign dealers, business men, banks and governments could furnish arms, grant loans, and help them to create arsenals and factories. Of all the politicians of the period, it was the new men thrown up by the struggle against the T'ai P'ing who were the most open to the problems of the modernization of the army and the military industries, and the readiest, too, to make concessions to foreigners. However, for them modernization was bound up with the maintenance of the traditional political and social forms and with the reinforcement of orthodoxy.

The birth of the contradictions

The weakening of the central government was to be masked for a long time by the holy alliance brought into being among the ruling classes by the great T'ai P'ing Rebellion and the risings which prolonged it. But a political cleavage which was to deepen in the T'ung-chih (1862–75) and Kuang-hsü (1875–1908) periods began to appear as early as the crisis period of 1860–61. These two years brought the advance of the Franco-British colonial troops on Peking, the flight of most of the court to Jehol, the entry of the foreign troops into a capital left defenceless, the suspicious death of the emperor Hsien-feng and the *coup d'état* by the empress Hsiao-ch'in (Tz'u Hsi: Ts'eu-hi). The small group of new men (Tseng Kuo-fan, Li Hung-chang, Tso Tsung-t'ang, and their associates) was henceforth to be opposed by the majority of the great Manchu dignitaries and high Chinese officials, the party of conciliation with the foreigners by the most intransigent patriots. This cleavage roughly corresponded with the old division between northerners, people from regions with little economic activity and no contact with foreigners, and southerners, who were more open-minded, better informed, and less bellicose. The members of the central government as a whole regarded with a jaundiced eye the ascendancy gained by the leaders of the armies which had suppressed the T'ai P'ing and feared the development of tendencies to autonomy in the provinces. These tendencies were still latent, but did in fact assert themselves at the end of the nineteenth century. At the same time they deplored the policy of loans and compromise which these new men followed where foreigners were concerned. The fact is that, with the decline of the Manchu aristocracy and the development of the regional authorities directly supported by the yield of the land taxes, the court tended to become the scene of intrigues not directly related to the real situation of the empire. Thus among the supporters of the new men's policy there were only a few high Manchu dignitaries. Wen-hsiang (1818–76) and I-hsin (1833–98), Prince Kung, were among the most famous exceptions, and it is noteworthy that their attitude of systematic hostility to foreigners was radically modified from the time when they participated in the Peking negotiations of 1860. But the opposition between the two parties was to become sharper after the Tientsin incidents of 1870. Totally absorbed by her passion for power, Tz'u Hsi, who was to dominate the political life of China from 1875 to her death in 1908, was able to profit from the situation, manoeuvring between 'modernists' and 'conservatives', keeping herself in power by playing off one side against the other, and thus leaving the real problems of the age unsolved.

Chapter 27

The Failure of Modernization and the Advance of Foreign Intrusion

Nowhere in the world was the great transformation entailed by the arrival of the industrial age, the first signs of which appeared in England between the end of the eighteenth century and the years round about 1830, accomplished without crises and tragedies. This long-lasting phenomenon affected the different countries of Europe very locally and in a very unequal fashion. In Russia, a large agricultural country where slavery was abolished only in 1861, it was not until the 1880s that modern industry on a large scale was established. Everywhere the old political, social, and economic structures put a powerful brake on the successive changes involved in the progress of technology and of the means of production, communication, and transport. It was natural that the weight of the past should make itself felt more heavily than elsewhere in a land of ancient civilization like China.

However, one cannot pretend that, from the point of view of technology, China was very far behind many Western countries. The first modern armament factories and new shipyards for the construction of steamships had appeared there by 1865–70. Nor can one say that China was radically incapable of industrializing herself, since the Chinese industrial enterprises of the end of the nineteenth century are reckoned to have been as well equipped as their equivalents in Great Britain. The iron and steel complex of Han-yang was two years ahead of the steelworks created in 1896 at Yawata by the Japanese government. The railway line from Peking to Kalgan, built in 1909 by the Chinese engineer Chan T'ien-yu (1861–1919) with teams of Chinese foremen and workers at much lower cost than the lines built by foreign companies, was a real technical exploit when we take into account the difficulties of the terrain and the speed of execution.

Nor did China lack scientific traditions which were to enable her to assimilate the new developments of Western science in the nineteenth and twentieth centuries.

If the Chinese world did not succeed in entering the industrial age at the right moment – a failure which was at the root of its terrible fate from the end of the nineteenth century onwards – this was due not so much to a basic inaptitude as to a particularly unfavourable conjunction of historical circumstances. After the period of decline and recession which the Ch'ing empire had experienced in the first half of the nineteenth century, two concomitant phenomena occurred to reinforce the obstacles formed by the social and political traditions of the Chinese world: these phenomena were the great internal crisis of 1850–75 and the military and economic pressure of foreign imperialism. The privileges acquired in China by Western merchants helped to weaken the Chinese economy; and the encirclement of the empire by the Western nations, the incidents provoked by the presence of missionaries, and foreign demands and attacks provoked a 'traditionalist' reaction. The enfeeblement of the central government and the political divisions, the weakness of Chinese agriculture, the dramatic lack of capital, and the essentially military character of the new industries prevented any reform of administrative methods and practices and seriously limited the effort at modernization. The truth is that China had neither the leisure nor the means to adapt herself to the changes of the age.

The problems of modernization

The first attempts at industrialization

In East Asia the purchase of arms from Westerners is a tradition that goes back to the first Portuguese adventurers of the sixteenth century. The Ming used Western cannon – more effective than their own traditional artillery – at the time of their counter-attack on Pyong-yang in 1593, and also bought some from the Portuguese of Macao in 1622 for their armies engaged in fighting the Manchus. The Manchus in turn asked Father Verbiest in 1675 to arrange the casting of European-style cannon for their campaigns against Wu San-kuei. There is evidence that heavy artillery was used by the imperial armies in the wars of the eighteenth century, even in regions as difficult of access as the borders of Tibet or Burma, but the weak resistance encountered by the British troops in 1840–42 indicates that at this period the Chinese artillery was either obsolete or nonexistent. It was only from the T'ai P'ing War onwards that the situation began to change: both insurgent and government leaders bought arms from European dealers, strove to build navies, and sought to obtain both loans and technical aid in order to create armament industries. This was the background to the creation between 1853 and 1860 of small arsenals and shipyards in Hunan and Kiangsu on the initiative of Tseng Kuo-fan and Tso Tsung-t'ang. The same period saw the publication (in 1859) of the *Tsu-cheng hsin-p'ien* (*New Writings to Help the Government*) by Hung Ten-kai, the King of Heaven's cousin, who had frequented missionary circles in Shanghai and Hong Kong. But, as already indicated, the effort at modernization on the rebel side failed completely, owing to internal dissensions, attacks from outside and the disfavour into which the T'ai P'ing fell with foreigners from 1862 onwards. On the emperor's side, on the other hand, negotiations with the Westerners were to be facilitated from 1861–62 onwards by the policy of cooperation inaugurated by the foreigners after the conventions of Peking and by the creation of an office of external relations, the *Tsung-li ko-kuo shih-wu ya-men* or, in abbreviated form, the *Tsung-li-ya-men* (1861).

The three men mainly responsible for the suppression of the revolts of 1857–78 — Tseng Kuo-fan, Tso Tsung-t'ang and Li Hung-chang — were thus in a position to create new armament industries with the help of Western technicians. Towards the end of the T'ai P'ing War they even benefited from the support of small contingents of foreign mercenaries whose efficiency helped to bring about the collapse of the rebellion. The most important of the new industrial enterprises of this period were the arsenals and shipyards established in Shanghai by Li Hung-chang and Tseng Kuo-fan between 1865 and 1867 (*Chiang-nan chih-tsao-chü*) and the naval shipyards of Ma-wei near Foochow built by Tso Tsung-t'ang in 1866 with the help of French technicians. The first Chinese gunboat left the Mao-wei yards in 1868, and about 1870 the Shanghai arsenals were one of the biggest industrial enterprises in the world. Tso Tsung-t'ang for his part developed in the north-west, where he was charged with the task of putting down the Moslem revolts, mining prospection, arsenals, and cloth mills.

From 1872 onwards the industrialization movement, still directed by the small group of new men thrown up by the T'ai P'ing War, grew wider in scope and called on the financial aid and the experience of the merchants enriched by trading with foreigners — the men known by the Portuguese term of *compradores* (in Chinese, *mai-pan*). This was how Li Hung-chang created in 1872 the Chinese Steamship Company; in 1878 the K'ai-p'ing Mining Company (K'ai-p'ing is near T'ang-shan, between Tientsin and Shan-hai-kuan); in 1879 the K'ai-p'ing Mines Railway; in 1880 a telegraph company at Tientsin; and in 1882 a cloth mill in Shanghai which did not begin to function until 1890 and was to be destroyed by a fire in 1893.

After the defeat suffered by China in 1885 in the Franco-Chinese incidents, it became clear that the efforts made up to that point were inadequate. The internal difficulties and the threats from outside had encouraged the strengthening primarily of China's military potential, but it was now realized that the whole Chinese economy needed reinvigorating, just at the time when foreign pressure was making itself felt more sharply. A fresh effort was therefore made to build railway lines, open mines, set up steelworks and create technical schools, while at the same time the organization of a modern army and navy was taken in hand again. The disastrous defeat of 1894 and the Draconian conditions of the Treaty of Shimonoseki perceptibly reduced China's independence and powers of resistance. The destruction of her armies and of her fleet was followed by the imposition of a very heavy war indemnity and by the occupation of strategic areas by Japan. Recovery from this grave defeat was rendered all the more difficult by the fact that it was followed six years later by the crushing indemnity exacted from China after the Boxer movement. One may say that from 1895 onwards any hope of recovery was excluded for a long time. For more than half a century the Chinese world was to suffer terrible trials before winning back its independence.

The causes of the failure

In the short lapse of time granted to China to create a modern industry and to renovate her army and navy in order to fight against the growing economic and military power of her external enemies, that is, from the recapture of Nanking in 1864 to the disaster of 1894, she had simultaneously to end the revolts, re-establish her authority in central Asia, make good all the destruction, and struggle on all sides against attacks from outside. The Ch'ing government continually had to attend to what was most urgent—negotiate with the Western nations, contract loans with foreign banks (forty million *liang* were borrowed between the T'ai P'ing War and 1894)—in order to provide for immediate needs. And the fact is that at this period the central government had lost a large part of its authority and resources. It shared real power with the regional governors, who had made themselves indispensable in the campaigns

Table 25.   The efforts to industrialize between 1840 and 1894

1840–1842	Casting of cannon, construction of boats with paddles and crank-gear.
1853–1860	Arms factories and small shipyards in Hunan, Kiangsu, and Kiangsi.
1855	Armament factory in Kiangsi.
1861	Armament factory and naval shipyard at An-ch'ing (Anhwei).
	Creation of the *Tsung-li-ya-men*, the office for relations with foreigners.
1862	Big arsenal and naval shipyard at Shanghai (*Chiang-nan chih-tsao-chü*).
	Powder factories in the provinces.
	Creation of the *T'ung-wen-kuan*, the school of Western languages and sciences in Peking.
1863	Creation at Shanghai of a school like the *T'ung-wen-kuan* in Peking.
1864	*T'ung-wen-kuan* in Canton.
1865	Nanking arsenals.
1866	Naval shipyards of Ma-wei, near Foochow.
1867	Naval Academy of Foochow. Tientsin arsenals.
1868	The first Chinese steamship leaves the yards at Ma-wei.
1869	Arsenals in Sian and Foochow.
1870	The Shanghai arsenals are one of the biggest industrial enterprises in the world at this time.
1872	The Sian arsenal is transferred to Lan-chou.
	Creation of the Chinese Steamship Company.
	Thirty-two students from Shanghai are sent to the United States.
1876–1877	Naval cadets sent to Great Britain, France, and Germany.
1877	Opening of the K'ai-p'ing mines.
1879	K'ai-p'ing Mines Railway.
1880	Telegraph Company and School of Telegraphy in Tientsin.
	Beginning of the construction of the Northern Fleet.
1881	Telegraph line from Shanghai to Tientsin.
	Chi-lin factory in Manchuria.
1882	Shanghai Electricity Company.
1886	Tientsin School of Military Engineers.
1887	Canton Naval Academy, Canton arsenal.
	Tientsin Railway Company.
	Gold mines of Mo-lo in the Heilungkiang basin.
1888	The Northern Fleet is brought into being.
1889	Big arsenal of Han-yang.
	The Shanghai cloth mills begin to operate.
1890	Blast furnaces at Han-yang.
	Iron mines of Ta-yeh in Hupei.
	Hupei cloth mills.
1893	Peking–Shan-hai-kuan railway.
	Taiwan railway.

against the insurgents and who had their own armies and revenues. It actually received only about a fifth of the *li-chin,* the tax on commercial transits, and about a quarter of the other taxes. The court, jealous of the power acquired in the provinces by these new men, sensitive to the arguments of the most intransigent patriots and badly informed about the facts of the contemporary situation, lived withdrawn into itself. While one child or adolescent emperor succeeded another (T'ung-chih came to the throne at the age of six in 1862, Kuang-hsü at the age of four in 1875 and Hsüan-t'ung was to be named emperor at the age of three in 1908), it was dominated by a woman who used all her energy, intelligence, and cunning to keep herself in power. Thus in the second half of the nineteenth century China was governed in theory by a central authority which was not in a position to understand the necessity and urgency of modernization or to direct it. Not only was it passive; it even tended to oppose innovations. The foreign attacks in China itself and the threats which hung over the frontiers of the empire caused opinion to turn against those responsible for modernization. It was in fact these men who, having become arbiters of the situation, negotiated with the foreigners and continually found themselves obliged to grant them fresh privileges. Moreover public opinion was afraid that the creation of factories, mines, and railways would increase the hold of foreign capital on the Chinese economy, facilitate the penetration of the Westerners, increase unemployment, and strengthen the power of the regional governors at the expense of the central authority.

The two factors which made possible the industrial and military rise of Japan in the Meiji era were absent in China: there was neither a strong central government nor regular resources. It was thanks to the taxes levied on the peasantry that Japan was able to build up her industry and her army. Chinese agriculture was in no condition to support an increase in the burdens which it had to bear. The destruction caused by the civil war and the insurrections, the impoverishment due to the rise in the price of silver, and the frequent famines and floods resulted in the stagnation or regression of the agrarian economy in China in the second half of the nineteenth century. The high officials who governed the regions and who took the initiative in creating arsenals, factories, and shipyards had no alternative but to call on the capital of the merchants who had grown rich by trading with the foreigner. But the capital available turned out to be totally inadequate. Moreover, the *compradores* could find little enthusiasm for enterprises in which the interest rates of eight to ten percent were much less attractive than traditional investments (agricultural loans, Chinese banks of the old sort, pawnships giving loans against security, land), which brought in an annual profit of 20 to 50 per cent.

Like capital investment, the effort to provide technical and scientific education was much inferior to what it ought to have been in such a big country. While on the one hand the promoters of industrial projects were able to profit from the experience gained by the *compradores* with foreign countries, on the other hand they lacked Chinese technicians. The most technical aspects of the new enterprises had to be entrusted to foreigners.

On top of these handicaps, the most serious of which were probably the absence of any lead from the central government and the lack of capital, came the weight of an inefficient bureaucracy, the distribution of dividends that were too high, and the pressure of a state at the end of its resources. For example, in 1899 the Peking government succeeded in raising 2,800,000 *liang* from the provinces. The main victims of this piece of fiscal tapping were to be the Chinese Steamship Company and the Shanghai Telegraph Administration, enterprises linked financially to the iron and steel complex of Han-yang, the P'ing-hsiang coal-mines, and the Hua-sheng textile factory in Shanghai. Instead of protecting its budding industry, the state, following an ancient instinct, smote the most dynamic enterprises more heavily. This is why, after a fairly long period of initial success, most of the new enterprises turned out to be not very profitable when confronted with foreign competition or even began to show a loss.

It is astonishing that in spite of all these obstacles the promoters of modern industries, classically educated civil servants with no training at all for such a task, should have achieved tangible results in all sectors – heavy industry (iron- and coal-mines, blast furnaces, arsenals and shipyards), light industry (textiles and small arms), finance (modern banks) and communications (steamship company, telegraph lines, railways). Up to 1894 the level of industrial technology was much the same in China as in Japan, which was generally regarded as more advanced. The amount of capital invested was of the same order in both countries, but while the dispersal of the Chinese enterprises and their small number in relation to the size of the population diluted the effect of industrialization in China, their concentration had a decisive effect in Japan. Moreover, the internal wars and the foreign threat had led people in China to concentrate mainly on unproductive war industries, even before the infrastructure indispensable to the development of a modern economy had been created. In Japan, on the other hand, there was a better distribution of effort, thanks to the general policy adopted and implemented by the Meiji. All these circumstances and finally the crushing burdens imposed on the Chinese economy in 1895 and 1901 explain why the two countries evolved differently. Foreign merchants enjoyed the

Plate 68. Peking in the second half of the nineteenth century, from an original photograph in the London Missionary Society archives

Plate 69. Shanghai, a commercial street, *c.* 1880

same privileges in Japan as in China, but while 90 percent of foreign trade in Japan was still in the hands of British and American companies in 1880, the percentage had dropped to 80 by 1890 and to 60 by 1900. Japan won back her economic independence just at the very time when the foreign hold on China was growing tighter and turning the ancient Ch'ing empire into a sort of international colony.

In any case, the history of Japan in the Meiji era cannot be put on a parallel with that of China, as historians have so often done, comparing the talent for adaptation which the Japanese people displayed with the obtuse traditionalism of the Chinese. The two countries are simply not comparable, because of their vastly differing sizes and populations. One is scarcely bigger than the British Isles; the other, in its most densely populated parts, has the dimensions and almost the diversity of Europe up to the Russian frontier. The historical backgrounds were also very different. Japan did not experience the terrible civil war, the destruction, and the internal difficulties which were China's lot from the middle of the nineteenth century until about 1875. Nor did she experience the constant foreign pressure exerted without respite on the Ch'ing empire, a pressure which never stopped increasing from the time of the first massive imports of opium about 1830. While China seemed like a bottomless market for booming industries, Japan was less attractive to Western cupidity and was not slow in participating herself in the rush for the spoils. That she was able to borrow on a large scale from foreigners and lay the foundations of a modern industrial economy at a time when China was a prey to constant difficulties was due to the fact that she had remained more apart and better protected against the disintegrating effects of the economic, military, and political pressure of the Western nations.

It is true that the social peculiarities, the nationalism, and the warlike traditions of Japan favoured her adaptation to the modern world and the adoption of the conquering spirit typical of Western imperialism, but the disproportion between this little country and the huge Ch'ing empire, and the radical difference in historical conditions, operated even more to her advantage.

There would have still been time at the end of the nineteenth century for China to correct her initial mistakes and to make up the accumulated delay; the goals to attain were known, the reforms necessary had been defined and there was no lack of capable men. But to achieve this China would have had to be protected against the fearsome foreign economic pressure and to benefit from international aid. Quite the opposite occurred.

Free enterprise or state economy?

People have tried to find the reason for China's backwardness and for the failure of her attempts at industrialization in the absence of the factors which in the West made the development of free enterprise possible. It is certainly true that nothing comparable is to be found in the Chinese world. The spirit of enterprise and competition, the taste for saving, the notions of advantage and profitability were not only absent; they were in contradiction with the whole humanist tradition of China. In China social success could not be reduced to vulgar enrichment, but implied above all the acquisition of honours and offices which gave access to political power and prestige. Chinese ethics preached devotion to the state, personal culture, self-effacement, and modesty. Even in business, real capital was not economic in nature, but social; it consisted of moral credit, dignity, authority. It was on the basis of this credit bestowed by an acquired reputation, by blood relationships and by ties contracted that deals were negotiated.

There had existed in China since the end of the Ming period big merchants and rich bankers who dealt in bills of exchange and built up huge fortunes, but these men had nothing in common with the great entrepreneurs of the beginning of European capitalism. It looks as if their activities were more closely related to tax farming than to genuine private enterprise. Satisfied with the semi-official role which had devolved on them, they did not seek to oppose the administration of the state but on the contrary strove to be integrated as much as possible in it. They were greedy for titles and official positions – they made an important financial contribution to the empire when it was in difficulties – and their ideal was to be assimilated to the great scholarly civil servants. They collected books and paintings and acted as patrons of the arts. Living in luxury, they felt morally obliged to enrich their own relatives.

The predominance of the political factor over all others and the historical experience peculiar to the Chinese world explain these traditional attitudes. Every civilization has its own genius. That is what people forget when, to account for China's inability to modernize herself, they confine themselves to accusing her political system and her tradition of a planned economy. All in all, the imperial regime was no more detestable than many others. The administrators of the T'ung-chih era (1862–75) showed energy, initiative, and intelligence, and what they accomplished was by no means negligible. Their failure sprang more from contemporary conditions and from the lack of direction at the top than from radical incapacity. If they had been better protected the new

Chinese industrial enterprises would have been able to develop; and if they had been more numerous they would have modified the economy and traditional attitudes. The upsurge of free enterprise was not a condition necessary to the salvation of China; in turning in our day towards a collectivist, state economy nearer to its ancient traditions the Chinese world has remained faithful to its own genius.

Similarly the adoption of parliamentary institutions modelled on those of the Western nations was to turn out later to be a nonsense, not because China was not 'ripe' for liberal democracy, but because such borrowed institutions were profoundly alien to Chinese traditions. Free enterprise and liberal democracy are the result of a process of development peculiar to the Western nations; to believe that all societies must necessarily pass through the same stages of a linear evolution, the model for which has been provided once for all by the West, is to fail to recognize the diversity of civilizations and their specific characters.

The advance of foreign intrusion and its consequences

No doubt the repeated acts of aggression committed by the West in China and the exorbitant privileges exacted by foreign nations should not be regarded as the sole cause or even the main cause of the failure of modernization. But these acts of aggression and these privileges played a large part in it. The advantages acquired by the Westerners damaged an economy already much weakened by the civil war; and the attacks of England, France, and Russia had much more serious consequences on other levels. They confirmed the essentially military orientation of the effort to industrialize, thus denying China the leisure to provide herself with the infrastructure essential for the modernization of her economy; and they aroused a deeper feeling of hostility which soon became one of the principal obstacles to the necessary changes.

The history of the Western penetration of China is in the West the best known aspect of the whole history of China. Hence a distortion of the perspective: the slightest demonstrations of force by England or France draw more attention than the terrible internal wars which shook the Ch'ing empire and mobilized all China's energies for more than twenty years, completely changing the country's political conditions and economy. The history of the countries of East Asia fades away almost completely behind that of Western advances and conquests in this part of the world. But if we wish to understand how the intrusion of the Western countries into China occurred, then the situation actually existing in

China at that time becomes extremely important. It was at a time when over half the provinces were not under the control of the legitimate authorities, when civil war was raging, and even before the formation of the big armies that made it possible to suppress the rebellion, that England and, after her, the other Western nations snatched from China rights much more extensive than those which they had acquired after the First Opium War.

The advance of the process of subjection

From 1850 onwards, England had profited from China's internal difficulties to extend the opium traffic on the coasts of Kwangtung and Fukien. In 1856 the affair of the *Arrow*, a smugglers' ship stopped by the Chinese authorities, furnished the pretext for a fresh series of military incidents which Western historians have christened the 'Second Opium War'. In 1857 five thousand British soldiers laid siege to Canton. In the following year English and French ships destroyed the forts of Ta-ku, which defended the mouth of the Hai-ho (Pei-ho) not far from Tientsin, on the approaches to Peking. In the same year the Ch'ing government was forced, under pressure, to sign the Treaty of Tientsin (1858). Ten new cities were opened to foreigners, who acquired concessions in them; consulates were set up in Peking, and the Catholic and Protestant missions obtained the right to settle freely in the interior and to own land and buildings there. A fresh indemnity was inflicted on China, which had to pay four million *liang* of silver to Great Britain and two million to France. Rights similar to those gained by these two countries were conceded to Russia and the United States. However, in spite of the treaty, the fighting started again, and the Chinese resistance was effective enough to provoke a second expedition after the Anglo-French fleet had suffered heavy losses in 1859 before the forts of Ta-ku. In the next year came the march on Peking by an expeditionary force of about twenty thousand British and French colonial troops, the entrance into the city of this force, and the sack and burning of the Summer Palace, the famous *Yüan-ming-yüan* which the emperor Ch'ien-lung had embellished on the advice and with the help of the Jesuit missionaries.

The conventions signed in Peking in 1860 forced China to make fresh sacrifices: Tientsin was opened to foreigners and the peninsula of Chiu-lung (Kowloon), opposite Hong Kong, was ceded to Great Britain. A fresh indemnity of sixteen million *liang* was required of the Chinese government. Finally, these conventions were completed by two economic clauses: the textiles which the Western nations, especially England, were

Map 26 The hand-over of China to foreigners

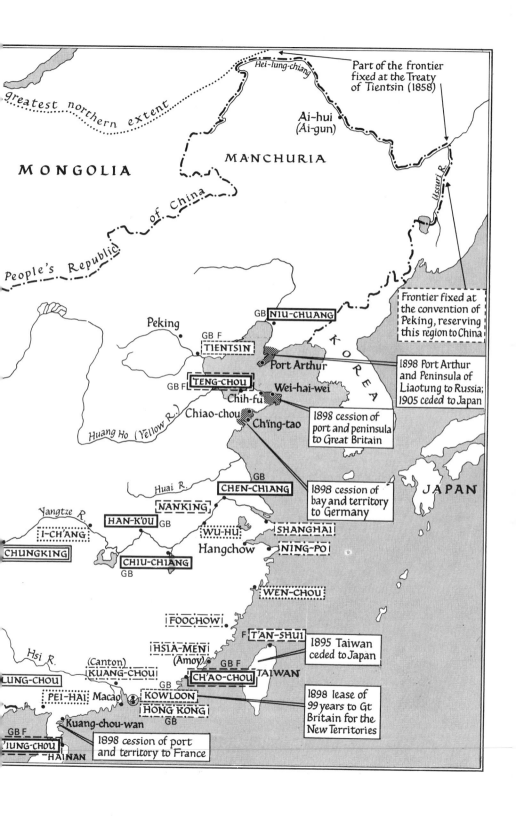

Part of the frontier fixed at the Treaty of Tientsin (1858)

greatest northern extent

Hei-lung-chiang

Ai-hui (Ai-gun)

MONGOLIA

MANCHURIA

of China

People's Republic

Ussuri R.

Peking

GB NIU-CHUANG

KOREA

GB F
TIENTSIN

Port Arthur

Frontier fixed at the convention of Peking, reserving this region to China

GB F TENG-CHOU

Wei-hai-wei

1898 Port Arthur and Peninsula of Liaotung to Russia; 1905 ceded to Japan

Chih-fu

Chiao-chou

Ch'ing-tao

1898 cession of port and peninsula to Great Britain

Huang Ho (Yellow R.)

Huai R.

GB
CHEN-CHIANG

1898 cession of bay and territory to Germany

JAPAN

Yangtze R.

NANKING

HAN-K'OU GB

WU-HU

SHANGHAI

I-CH'ANG

Hangchow

NING-PO

CHUNGKING

CHIU-CHIANG
GB

WEN-CHOU

FOOCHOW

F TAN-SHUI

1895 Taiwan ceded to Japan

Hsi R.

HSIA-MEN
(Amoy)

GB F

(Canton)
KUANG-CHOU

CH'AO-CHOU TAIWAN

LUNG-CHOU

GB

1898 lease of 99 years to Gt Britain for the New Territories

PEI-HAI Macao

KOWLOON

HONG KONG GB

Kuang-chou-wan

GB F

'IUNG-CHOU

1898 cession of port and territory to France

HAINAN

seeking to dump on the Chinese market were exempted from customs duties and foreign fleets gained the complete freedom of the Chinese river network. The Treaty of Tientsin and the Peking conventions were signed in a very different historical context from that of the Treaty of Nanking in 1842. The First Opium 'War' still belonged to the age of the sailing ship and the merchant venturer. In 1857–60, the period of the second series of foreign attacks, big industry was already in full swing in the most highly developed European countries. The agreements signed, which were to be scrupulously respected on the Chinese side, also had a much wider scope, and the effect of the privileges obtained by the foreigners soon made itself felt on the Chinese economy.

Finally, China lost not only her autonomy in the sphere of customs but also control of her own customs services. The British hold on the maritime customs, which were reorganized from 1863 onwards by the Scotsman Robert Hart (1835–1911), doubtless had happy effects in the short term, for it eliminated all embezzlement and provided the empire with a regular income. But it put the foreigners in a position to appropriate for themselves, when the moment came, the revenues of the Chinese customs. This is what happened when, from 1911 onwards, China was induced to guarantee with these revenues the crushing debt of the Boxer indemnity.

The treaty of 1858 and the Conventions of Peking in 1860 also cleared the way for further development of the concessions, positive enclaves on Chinese soil not subject to the authority of the Peking government, and the start of the incessant difficulties which were caused by the settlement of missionaries all over the empire.

Established in China in greater numbers from 1860 onwards, the foreigners were to be led by the pressure of their commercial, religious, and political interests, and as a result of conflicts with the authorities and the population, to intervene more and more frequently and to make larger and larger demands. The agreements of Tientsin and Peking were soon to be overtaken by other conventions, each Western nation—even small countries like Belgium—wanting to enjoy the same rights and constantly to extend its privileges. The smallest incidents were to serve as pretexts for demonstrations of force and for demands for indemnities and reparations which increased China's subjection. For example, in 1876 China was constrained to sign the Conventions of Chih-fu (near Yen-t'ai, in north-eastern Shantung) with Great Britain after the murder of an English interpreter on the borders of Yunnan and Burma; the result was five new 'open ports' on top of the fifteen or so already existing.

The encirclement

This constant pressure by the Western nations in China itself was accompanied by the encroachments of Great Britain, Russia, France, and soon Japan on the borders of the empire and in the lands which had formed part of the Chinese sphere of influence in the eighteenth century.

The Western nations now aimed not only at setting up commercial posts in East Asia in order to ensure control of the local trade, but also at occupying the countries of this part of the world and turning them into colonies.

As early as 1858 Russia had occupied the territory of the Sikhota Alin to the south of the lower reaches of the Amur and to the east of the Ussuri, a region which had been part of the Chinese empires since the thirteenth century. About ten years later the governor of Russian Turkestan had taken advantage of China's difficulties in the Tarim basin and of the secession of the New Territories (Sinkiang) under the leadership of Yakub Beg to invade the Ili valley in 1871 as far as the strategic town of Kulja (I-ning). Immediately after the reconquest of the Tarim basin, completed at the beginning of 1878 by Tso Tsung-t'ang, the Chinese court sent the Manchu Ch'ung-hou (1826–93) to St. Petersburg to demand the restitution of the conquered zones. Chosen for this mission because of his knowledge of foreigners—he had taken part in negotiating the various treaties and conventions signed at Tientsin between 1863 and 1869, then in the settlement of the Tientsin incidents, and in 1870–72 had led the embassy of expiation required by France—Ch'ung-hou accepted at Livadia (near Yalta, in the Crimea) conditions which were to be judged unacceptable both by the court and by public opinion: the Russians returned only a small part of the territories annexed and obtained fifty million roubles in compensation. Fresh discussions in 1881 allowed China to regain possession of a larger part of her territory in return for the payment of an indemnity of ninety million roubles and the cession of other territories in the upper Irtysh valley.

The first attacks by Japan, which was beginning to build up a modern industrial economy and a modern army, occurred in 1874. Taiwan was subjected to a raid which had no immediate consequences, but the Ryukyu Islands, tributaries of the Ch'ing empire, were occupied. China was obliged to recognize their annexation in 1881. Moreover, in 1876 Japan imposed on Korea a treaty similar to those exacted from China by the Western powers, obtaining the opening of certain ports to Japanese commerce and the recognition of economic privileges. This was the start of the long process which was to lead China to commit herself in Korea to counter Japanese pressure and which was to end in the conflict of 1894.

The foreign threat had made itself felt much earlier in Vietnam, another country that formed part of the Chinese sphere of influence and whose links with China were close and ancient. In 1862–67 Vietnam had been shorn of its southern provinces (Cochin China) as a result of the encroachments of France. But the advance of the French colonial troops up the valley of the Sung-cai (Red River) met much more serious resistance in 1881–82. The Vietnamese there had the assistance of the Black Flag army (*Hei-ch'i-chün*; literally, 'Black Banners'), which consisted of former T'ai P'ing soldiers who had taken refuge in northern Vietnam. They were commanded by Liu Yung-fu (1837–1917). Chinese contingents were sent from the neighbouring provinces of Kwangsi, Kwangtung, and Yunnan. In spite of the passions aroused in China by French activities in Vietnam, in 1884 Li Hung-chang, still an advocate of conciliation, obtained a provisional settlement which obliged the Chinese troops to withdraw. But the reaction of the intransigent patriots, who were very powerful at court, caused one of the reversals so frequent at that time in China's foreign policy and indicative of the division of powers and the hesitations of the central government. Tz'u Hsi recalled I-hsin, one of the principal engineers of the policy of conciliating foreigners and building up China internally. Appeals for resistance were launched and fresh troops were sent to the Red River valley. Defeated at Lang-son, the French decided to carry the war to the coast of China. Part of the Chinese fleet built in the shipyards of Ma-wei, near Foochow, was destroyed by Admiral Courbet, who at the same time organized a blockade of Taiwan. In the following year (1885) the French laid siege to Ning-po, occupied the P'eng-hu Islands (Pescadores) and tried to starve out Peking by stopping the seaborne convoys to North China. China was forced to sign a new treaty at Tientsin. This treaty, although it did not stipulate the usual 'war indemnities', was equivalent to a total capitulation: France was given a free hand in Vietnam and China renounced her traditional relations with this ancient land of Chinese civilization. In addition, three cities in south-west China had to be opened to French trade.

Economic effects

The privileges acquired in China by foreigners were to have two series of consequences, the effects of which were to grow more serious with the development of the foreigners' industrial power. The first series of conse-

Table 26.   The rise in imports

	1871-1873	*1881-1883*
Opium (in cwt)	37,408	42,777
Cotton yarn (in cwt)	37,791	118,020
Iron and copper (in cwt)	142,806	273,717
Kerosene (in gals)	0	176,513,915

quences was of an economic nature: these privileges probably weakened the Chinese economy, already seriously damaged by the great T'ai P'ing crisis, and in the long run caused a more and more perceptible imbalance between traditional sectors in decline and modern sectors dependent on and controlled by foreigners. This imbalance was to make itself manifest — at the expense of the interior — in the upsurge of the regions where the Western footing was strongest: the open ports were in fact magnets attracting capital and the Chinese population. At the same time the development of foreign commerce tended to make the Chinese economy more and more dependent on the world market and consequently more and more vulnerable to the uncontrollable fluctuations of this market.

On entry into China foreign products were subject only to a uniform tax of five percent; they were exempt from the transit tax, the *li-chin,* which hit Chinese products heavily. These very advantageous conditions allowed an increase in imports. Yet this increase was much less rapid than the foreign companies might have expected; the great mass of consumers was too poor to absorb the surplus industrial production of the rich nations. However, to the extent that imports affected the fragile equilibrium of the rural economy, they had repercussions on the traditional crafts and on agriculture; cotton, tobacco, and opium plantations were to expand at the expense of food crops.

In addition, from 1862 onwards the foreign shipping companies, mainly British and American, absorbed more and more of the trade carried until then by Chinese boats and sea-going junks on the Yangtze River system and the coast. The biggest profits from the river and sea traffic went to the foreign companies, while some of the Chinese carriers were put out of work. The Chinese Steamship Company, created by Li Hung-chang in 1872 to fight the Western hold, was to meet a savage response from the British and American companies, which suddenly lowered their prices.

The other series of consequences caused by the Western footing in China was of a political and moral nature — more and more frequent friction and conflicts between foreigners and the native population, growing hostility to the Westerners, and the formation of a huge body of reactionary opinion hostile to innovations.

Psychology and politics

The presence in China of foreigners was an element that cannot be ignored. Their modes of life and behaviour, their pretensions and wealth, and the humiliations which they inflicted on the empire and its inhabitants caused the birth and development of a hostility which often extended to the innovations which they introduced. Whereas many of the great Jesuit missionaries of the seventeenth century were cultivated, scholarly men anxious to make contact with the leading Chinese, the agents of the great colonial expansion of the nineteenth and twentieth centuries were for the most part men of little education. Having no contacts except with individuals on the edge of Chinese society – servants and commercial go-betweens – forming an international society shut in on itself, insulated from Chinese circles by the very facilities which they enjoyed, by a feeling of their own superiority, by the disdain inspired by Chinese manners, and by the daily spectacle of the poverty and vices from which China suffered, they generally felt little interest in a civilization which was profoundly alien to them, difficult of access, and apparently in complete decadence. Yet it was on their evidence that the Western countries formed their picture of contemporary China.

In their eyes, the science, technology, commercial practices, and political institutions of the West were a good in themselves and anything that helped to open China to their influence was bound in the end to be beneficial to it. However, the behaviour of the foreigners in China and the constant recourse to demonstrations of force or to the actual use of it were to have serious psychological consequences. They were at the root of an atmosphere of incomprehension, distrust, or hatred which affected all relations between China and her foreign occupiers. They created in the Chinese a sort of inferiority complex which was to harm gravely the process of adaptation to the great changes of the contemporary age.

A more particular cause of friction was to be furnished by the privileged position which the Christian missionaries enjoyed after the Treaty of Tientsin in 1858. Incidents arising out of incomprehension of certain Chinese customs, out of the intolerance of certain priests, out of conflicts of interest, or out of the suspicions aroused by the behaviour and practices of the missionaries, and fed since the beginning of the seventeenth century by widely diffused tracts, sometimes degenerated into disturbances involving bloodshed which were suppressed by force. The priests and their catechumens, sometimes low-class self-seeking Chinese unfavourably regarded by the population as a whole, were assured of the armed protection of the Great Powers. The foreigners, who enjoyed the privileges of extraterritoriality, obtained the infliction of severe penalties on their adversaries and the payment of heavy indemnities (400,000 *liang* for thirteen affairs between 1862 and 1869). One single example will suffice to illustrate the general mode of behaviour: at the beginning of 1870, before the famous Tientsin incidents, Count Julien de Rochechouart, a mere *chargé d'affaires,* sailed up the Yangtze with four gunboats to make the Chinese authorities, who were having difficulties with the missionaries, see reason. In the long list of incidents caused by the presence in China of Christian missionaries, those of June 1870 occupy a special place because of their gravity and consequences: they were at the root of a sudden fit of hatred for foreigners, especially the French, who officially had supreme control over the Catholic missions. They put the advocates of a policy of conciliation towards the Western nations in a difficult position and gave fresh strength to the call for systematic opposition to foreigners, thus compromising the attempts at modernization.

When the Sisters of Charity started offering rewards to people who brought them orphans, the population saw this move as a confirmation of the traditional belief that Christians indulged in magical practices with the eyes and hearts of children. The French consul, faced with a delegation led by a Chinese magistrate, lost his head and gave the order to fire on the demonstrators. The effect was immediate: the crowd ran amok, massacred about twenty foreigners, and destroyed the buildings of the Catholic mission. In compensation, the Chinese government was forced to have eighteen suspects executed, to demote the local officials, to pay France an indemnity of 490,000 *liang,* and to send an embassy of expiation.

As a result of these incidents a campaign to denigrate the advocates of conciliation was launched. One of its principal weapons was the circulation of pamphlets known as *ch'ing-i* ('pure or disinterested views'). Chinese who adopted foreign ways, were converted to Christianity, or made use of the Westerners' inventions were denounced as traitors. Grave suspicion rested on those who, like Li Hung-chang, sought to come to an understanding with China's enemies in order to build arsenals, factories, or railways. Tseng Kuo-fan's career was compromised from 1870 onwards by the complacency with which he seemed to have settled the Tientsin incidents with France. These pamphlets, which were the mouthpieces of a public opinion pushed towards a radical patriotism, played a large part in all the crises provoked by infringements

Table 27.   Acts of war and encroachments by the Western countries
and Japan in China from 1840 to 1894

1840	Occupation of the Chousan (Chusan) Islands in Chekiang and attack on Ning-po by the British.
1841	British attacks on Canton, Hsia-men (Amoy), Ning-po and Shanghai.
1842	British attacks on Shanghai and Nanking. Annexation of Hong Kong by Great Britain.
1844	British concession at Hsia-men (Amoy).
1845	British concession at Shanghai.
1850	Annexation of the mouth of the Amur (Heilungkiang) by the Russians in violation of the treaties of 1689 and 1727.
1854	Annexation of the north bank of the Amur by the Russians.
1856	Bombardment of Canton by the British.
1857	Bombardment of Canton and the Hai-ho forts by the British and French.
1858	Occupation of Canton and the mouth of the Hai-ho. The Russians occupy the territory to the south of the lower reaches of the Amur and to the east of the Ussuri.
1859	Fresh attack on the Hai-ho forts.
1860	Attack on the Hai-ho forts and incursion into Hopei. The British and French colonial troops enter Peking, and pillage and burn the summer palace. The British annex the peninsula of Chiu-lung (Kowloon). British concession in Tientsin.
1861	British concessions in Hankow and Canton. French concessions in Canton and Tientsin.
1862	British concession at Chiu-chiang (Kiangsi).
1863	International concession at Shanghai.
1868	The British bombard the port of An-p'ing in Taiwan.
1871	The Russians occupy the Ili territory.
1874	Japanese attack on Formosa and annexation of the Ryukyu Islands by Japan.
1881	The Russians finally annex part of the Ili territory occupied since 1871.
1884	The French Admiral Courbet bombards Foochow, sinks the Chinese Mawei fleet, and blockades the rice transports between Shanghai and North China in the hope of starving out Peking.
1885	The French occupy the P'eng-hu Islands and part of Taiwan.
1887	Final annexation of Macao by the Portuguese.

of China's sovereignty; for example, at the time of the Japanese intervention in the Ryukyu Islands in 1879 and, in the same year, on the occasion
of the Ili affair (the Treaty of Livadia, in which China's representative
had been too conciliatory), or again at the time of Li Hung-chang's
negotiations with France in 1883. These attacks by champions of
resistance at any price prevented the expression of more sophisticated
and realistic opinions, so much so that this jealous patriotism thwarted
its own aims. In the matter of modernization, China tended to reject
through a xenophobic reflex what she would have accepted had she been
more independent.

Foreign pressure did not act only as an incitement in China; it also
acted as a social, economic, and political brake, as well as a
psychological one. The desperate quest of certain intellectuals for a saving ideology in the Confucian tradition and the touchy conservatism of
numerous patriots illustrate this reaction of national pride, which was so
good in principle but so harmful in its effects. It was a China torn
apart — incapable of recognizing her own countenance, and soon led to
deny herself — that foreign nations quarrelled over from the last few
years of the nineteenth century onwards. The tragedy of all the colonized
countries was in China a tragedy in proportion to the greatness of her
civilization. China still bears today the marks of this profoundly
traumatic experience.

Conclusion

Up to the development, hand in hand with the arrival of foreign capital
and industries in the open ports, of a Chinese commercial middle class
round about 1900, the attempts at industrialization were promoted by
civil servants with a classical training who were given only very limited
support by the central government and who met — in spite of their attachment to traditional concepts of the state and society — a powerful current
of opposition. Forced of necessity to adopt a policy of conciliation and
understanding with the foreigners, these advocates of borrowing the
Westerners' methods and technology were the target of the most ardent
patriots, in whose eyes the defence of China and that of her traditions
were two sides of the same coin. The industrial development which
would have allowed China to grow stronger demanded that this overex-
tended empire exhausted by long and costly campaigns — the reconquest
of Sinkiang was not completed until 1878, and even then only thanks to
the very large loans that Tso Tsung-t'ang obtained from foreign
banks — should enjoy a certain respite. It was essential to avoid, by stick-

ing to the letter of the treaties, any conflict with the Westerners or Japan. China had the greatest need of capital, technicians, and experts, all things which could only be supplied by the authors of the acts of aggression against her. Yet at the same time there was a risk that accepting such assistance would strengthen the foreign hold on the country. This fear explains the growing mistrust which was to be aroused from the end of the nineteenth century onwards by plans for loans and industrialization. Finally, the unemployment which might be caused by the modernization of transport and production in a country in the depths of an economic recession represented a real danger.

If the position of the advocates of modernization was not to be compromised, attacks from outside had to stop. Unfortunately the respite which followed the Conventions of Peking in 1860 was of short duration. In the years 1870-90 pressure on China and countries in her sphere of influence became sharper than ever. The occupation of the Ili region by the Russians, the intervention of Japan in Korea, Taiwan, and the Ryukyu Islands, and the French attacks in northern Vietnam and on China herself all provoked crises which weakened the position of the innovators. The defeat of 1894 was the prelude to a vast attempt to dismember China by all the aggressors. By then it was too late for this great country, already gravely wounded, to be able to pull herself together again.

The event which was to rob China of any chance of recovery occurred in fact in the last few years of the nineteenth century. The Japanese penetration of Korea, perceptible since 1876, was—among many others—one of the Peking government's gravest worries. As in China, foreign pressure had led in Korea to the formation of a traditionalist, reactionary current of opinion which the Ch'ing had tried to support by sending General Yüan Shih-k'ai into the peninsula. But the insurrection launched at the beginning of 1894 by a secret society of religious and xenophobic tendencies provoked a serious crisis just when Japan's military potential had been powerfully strengthened. The conservative advocates of intervention, led by their main spokesman Weng T'ung-ho, who four years later was to appeal for help to the reformers, succeeded in making their point of view prevail over that of Li Hung-chang, who was conscious of the wretched state of the Chinese fleet, disorganized as it was by financial difficulties. During the brief conflict between China and Japan in Korea the Chinese armies suffered a grave defeat and the northern fleet was practically destroyed in the Gulf of Po-hai.

The results of the treaty concluded at Shimonoseki, on the strait dividing Hondo from Kyushu, were to be far-reaching: between 1895 and the first few years of the twentieth century China was in fact to lose her economic, territorial, political, and military independence. She entered the most tragic period in her whole history just when the economic expansion of the rich nations was accelerating.

The concatenation of events suffices to explain her failure without its being necessary to call into question her political, social, and intellectual traditions. In other circumstances China could have adapted herself to the great changes of the industrial age; she did not lack men with a sense of organization or scientific and technological traditions. The wastefulness and heedlessness of the court, the corruption, the attachment to the past and the anti-modernist reaction were doubtless much more the product of circumstances than of any elements inherent in the Chinese world.

Chapter 28

Intellectual Currents in the Nineteenth Century

The general atmosphere changed in the neighbourhood of 1800 and intellectual life began to take a new direction. These changes are explained by the weakening of the authority of a state which until then had made its omnipotence felt and had taken the Chinese intelligentsia under its protection as well as under its control. They are also explained by the deterioration of the social climate and of political life. The result was, if not disillusionment with the established order, at any rate a lively interest in the practical questions with which government and administration have to deal—finance, transport, production, commerce. This desire for improvements of a technical nature and for a renovation of the methods of government was paralleled by new tendencies in what were apparently the most disinterested branches of learning.

The school of critical studies (*K'ao-cheng-hsüeh*), which had shone with such lustre in the time of Tai Chen (1724–77) and produced work of remarkable quality and breadth, was linked to the political and social context of the eighteenth century, that of a powerful and prosperous China governed by cultivated emperors who were great patrons of the arts. The great publishing enterprises patronized by the state in the reigns of K'ang-hsi and Ch'ien-lung had given a decisive stimulus to the intellectual life of the age; they formed part of a policy which had disarmed the initial hostility of the Chinese educated classes to the Manchus. These enterprises ended with the reign of Ch'ien-lung, and the only big official compilation to appear after 1798 was the *Complete Collection of the Prose Writers of the T'ang Age and the Five Dynasties (Ch'üan-t'ang-wen)* (over 20,000 titles and over 3000 authors), which was completed in

1814 after six years' work. The salt merchants of Yangchow, who had formed rich libraries and art collections, subsidized publications, and entertained and helped numerous scholars of renown, were ruined round about 1800 by the depreciation of the copper currency. The only comparable people in the nineteenth century were men like Wu Ch'ung-yao (1810–63), a Cantonese merchant who had built up a big fortune in the opium trade and to whom we are indebted for an excellent collection of literary works from Kwangtung collected under the title of *Yüeh-ya-t'ang ts'ung-shu* (1853). It looks as if everything contributed at the beginning of the nineteenth century to a decline in the great tradition of philological and archaeological criticism of the *K'ao-cheng-hsüeh*. The disciples of Tai Chen and the great scholars of this school disappeared during the first thirty years of the nineteenth century. Ch'ien Ta-hsin died in 1804, Chi Yün in the following year, Tuan Yü-ts'ai in 1815, Wang Nien-sun in 1832 and his son Wang Yin-chih two years later. It was not that the tradition was interrupted from this time onwards; it continued into the first half of the twentieth century, and most of the great Chinese scholars of 1895–1949 belonged to this school of scientific rigour and rationalism. This renaissance of the school of critical studies was to be accompanied by a return to the liberal, patriotic philosophers of the early Manchu period (Ku Yen-wu, Wang Fu-chih and Huang Tsung-hsi, to mention only the most eminent).

Reformed Confucianism

The fading of the school of critical studies was accompanied by the upsurge of new tendencies provoked by the decline of the empire and the successive crises which the Chinese world went through: the White Lotus risings round about 1800, the deterioration of political life and the economic recession, the British attacks of the First Opium War and the great social explosion of the T'ai P'ing. A new and lively interest made itself apparent in a philosophical tradition which had been neglected and practically forgotten since the Han age — that of the texts in 'new script' (*chin-wen*). The most illustrious representatives of this tradition had been Tung Chung-shu (*c.* 175–105 B.C.) and Ho Hsiu (A.D. 129–82), the great interpreter of Kung-yang's commentary on the *Annals of Lu*. Thus a new school, known as that of the *Kung-yang* (*Kung-yang-hsüeh*) or of the texts in new characters (*chin-wen-hsüeh*) developed at the beginning of the nineteenth century. In the view of the members of this school, it was not from the Sung age onwards that the real meaning of the Classics had been falsified, but much earlier, at the time of their transmission at the beginning of the Han age after the collapse of the Ch'in empire. At that time, alongside the texts preserved by the oral tradition and noted down in new characters, documents written in ancient characters (*ku-wen*) had appeared and finally been accepted as authentic. This authenticity was contested by the new school, which also adopted again, in a modern light and with religious preoccupations, the theses of Tung Chung-shu and Ho Hsiu, namely that the Classics contained a deep, hidden meaning which had a practical value for the government of men and the organization of society. The *Annals of Lu* (*Ch'un-ch'iu*), so it was maintained, were written by Confucius not as a mere chronicle, but as a work aiming at a radical reform of manners and institutions. Confucius was virtually a sort of sovereign (*su-wang*), the equal of the saints of remote antiquity; and finally, according to the conceptions of the interpreters of the texts in new characters, humanity was called to pass through different stages, at the end of which it was to attain unity, harmony, and universal peace.

Thus with the radical reformism of the *Kung-yang-hsüeh* were associated mystical and eschatological tendencies, which were to be reinforced during the course of the nineteenth century by the trials and misfortunes of the Chinese world. Faced with the conquering Christianity of the Westerner, the Chinese literati felt prompted to sanctify the great sage and his writings. Faced with the threats from outside, they proclaimed the reformist and evolutionary character of what they regarded as the true classical tradition. For these reasons, most of the great scholars and reforming politicians of the nineteenth century were adherents of the school of texts in new characters. If we leave aside the precursor and pure philologian Chuang Ts'un-yü (1717–88), who had been one of the first to interest himself in the texts in *chin-wen,* it was Liu Feng-lu (1776–1829) who directed Chinese thought along the new path of reformism. Liu Feng-lu rehabilitated the two great works of the Han school of *chin-wen* — the *Ch'un-ch'iu fan-lu,* by Tung Chung-shu, which he regarded as a correct interpretation of the true thought of Confucius before it had been falsified at all, and Ho Hsiu's commentary on the *Kung-yang-chuan,* of which he made a systematic study in his *Kung-yang-ch'un-ch'in Ho-shih shih-li* (preface dated 1805).

Liu Feng-lu's two principal disciples, and the most famous thinkers of the first half of the nineteenth century, were Kung Tzu-chen (1792–1841) and Wei Yüan (1794–1856), who flourished respectively just before and during the incidents of the First Opium War. In 1839 Kung Tzu-chen wrote to Lin Tse-hsü, who had just arrived in Canton, to encourage him in his attitude of intransigence to foreigners. He said that the British trade in opium was ruining the Chinese economy and that it was essential to strengthen China's military power by setting up factories to produce modern weapons. An enemy of the traditional competitions, of the practice of bandaging little girls' feet and of all superstitions, Kung Tzu-chen was the author of social and political writings which were to have a great influence on the reformers of the late nineteenth century, particularly on K'ang Yu-wei. As for Wei Yüan, a historian and geographer whose concern for reform was also based on the new philosophy of the *Kung-yang-hsüeh,* his works were to win a very large readership round about 1850. At the time of his stay in Canton from 1838 to 1841, Lin Tse-hsü had enquired into the weapons, navy, and strategies of the Westerners and in his *Notes on the Four Continents* (*Ssu-chou-chih*) he complemented his findings with extracts from foreign publications. Wei Yüan, who had taken part in the struggle against the British in 1840–42 and was to organize militias to fight the T'ai P'ing in 1853, was inspired by Lin Tse-hsü's notes to write in 1842 his famous *Illustrated Treatise on Overseas Countries* (*Hai-kuo t'u-chih*). This work, first published in 1844 and reprinted with additions in 1847 and 1852, suggested using the foreigner's techniques and setting the nations which were attacking China against each other, on the old principle of 'overcoming the Barbarians by the Barbarians' (*i i chih i*). It was to score a great success not only in China but also in Japan, where it was translated in 1854–56 and probably influenced the movement for modernization which was to end in the reforms of the Meiji era.

The development of the school of texts in new characters was thus bound up with a very wide current of interest in practical problems (administration, social and political organization, economics, taxation, strategy and weapons, agriculture, and so on), and this movement had started by the early days of the nineteenth century, well before the first attacks of the British gunboats. It was in 1827 that Ho Ch'ang-ling (1785–1848), a politician in contact with Wei Yüan, collected essays by civil servants and literati of Kiangsu on social, political, and economic questions (what was called the *ching-shih,* the 'setting in order of the age') under the title of *Huang-ch'ao ching-shih wen-pien* (new editions of this work, augmented and brought up to date, and continuations of it, were to appear from 1882 onwards). Towards 1837 Ho Ch'ang-ling encouraged the manufacture of silk and cotton in Kweichow and forbade the cultivation of the poppy, which was beginning to spread there. Pao Shih-ch'en (1775–1855) was already interested as a young man in military, agricultural, and legal questions, as well as in the problem of transport, and served as technical adviser to high officials. And it was in 1834 that Ch'en Hung-ch'ih, who came from Hunan, started to write his official monograph on the defences of Kwangtung (*Kuang-tung hai-fang hui-lan*).

Nor did the interest in the Western countries and in their science and technology — or rather the renewal of this interest — date only from the Opium War either. The *Maritime Notes* (*Hai-lu*) of Wu Lan-hsiu were compiled at the beginning of the nineteenth century; they were based on information supplied by a Chinese sailor called Hsieh Ch'ing-kao (1765–1821), who had served as a young man in European ships and visited numerous European countries. The work written by Li Chao-lo (1769–1841) on the strength of enquiries among the Europeans of Canton, the *Hai-kuo chi-wen,* appeared in 1823.

Orthodox reaction and reformist revival

From the middle of the nineteenth century onwards the T'ai P'ing crisis was to cause a profound upheaval in Chinese intellectual life. Numerous libraries and art collections were destroyed, valuable ancient and modern manuscripts disappeared, and most of the literati were mobilized for the effort of reconquest and political recovery. It was from the general staffs of the anti-rebel leaders, in contact with the daily realities of the war, that the new Chinese governing class and intelligentsia were formed. One of the effects of the rebellion was to provoke an orthodox reaction and a revival of the ancient school of T'ung-ch'eng in Anhwei, a school made illustrious round about 1800 by Yao Nai (1731–1815), and in the years just before the rebellion by Fang Tung-shu (1772–1851). Faithful, like his predecessors, to the 'neo-Confucian' traditions of the Sung age, Fang Tung-shu reproached the adherents of the school of critical studies with sacrificing morality to erudition. After the middle of the nineteenth century it was Tseng Kuo-fan, the great vanquisher of the T'ai P'ing, who was to be the most eminent representative of these orthodox, moralizing tendencies. Li T'ang-chieh (1798–1865), who, at the level of the central government, was one of the main architects of the restoration of the T'ung-chih era in 1862–65, also preached moral integrity and control of the passions. He was a great admirer of T'ang Pin (1627–87), a philosopher in the 'neo-Confucian' tradition influenced by the 'intuitionism' of Wang Yang-ming. The current of the T'ung-ch'eng school was to flow on until the end of the Manchu epoch; two of its adherents were Lin Shu and Yen Fu, the two great translators into classical Chinese of Western literary and philosophical works.

By favouring a powerful orthodox reaction, the great social crisis of the years 1851–64 reduced the influence of the reformist tendencies which had found expression in the first half of the nineteenth century and compromised the attempts at modernization. Although the rulers who emerged from the war against the T'ai P'ing thought it necessary to strengthen China's military power by borrowing the Westerners' technology, they also thought that it was even more important to return to orthodoxy and to put the traditional morality back into force. In their view China had to draw the strength necessary for her salvation from an effort to restore morals and from a return to moral conformism. The question of political changes was scarcely even raised; the majority of the most convinced advocates of modernization regarded the maintenance of the traditional institutions as fundamental. The manners and behaviour of the Westerners were too profoundly different from those of the Chinese world, and the two civilizations were so clearly opposed to each other, that there could be no question of borrowing anything from the foreigners but their science and technology. Accordingly Feng Kuei-fen (1809–74), who may be regarded as the theorist of the modernizing movement that succeeded the T'ai P'ing War, took care to distinguish the fundamental from the subordinate; that is, Chinese traditions on the one hand from the practical knowledge of the Westerners on the other. Very open-minded where administrative and financial problems were concerned, a specialist in mathematics, cartography, and the history of writing, interested in Western science, Feng Kuei-fen, like the other supporters of modernization, was a conservative who was anxious to secure industrial progress and military reinforcement. The functioning of the existing institutions could be improved by reforms, but any change in manners or political organization was excluded. It was the same attitude that we find in the Slavophiles of the time of Kireyeski (1806–56) and Khomyakov (1804–60), who wanted 'Western machines, but not Western ideas', a phrase curiously similar to Feng Kuei-fen's, 'Chinese knowledge for foundation, Western knowledge for practice' (*chung-hsüeh wei t'i, hsi-hsüeh wei yung*).

But the successive humiliations suffered by the empire, the defeats inflicted by France in 1885, and still more the military disaster of 1894 gave fresh impetus to the movement for reform which, with the readership of the *Kung-yang-hsüeh* growing wider, triumphed in the person of K'ang Yu-wei (1858–1927) very soon after the Treaty of Shimonoseki. It was in fact from the scholars and philosophers of this school (mainly from Liao P'ing, 1852–1932) that the famous reformer borrowed most of his ideas, and his key work, the *Ta-t'ung-shu* (*Universal Harmony*), may be regarded as the final outcome of the tendencies of the school founded at the beginning of the nineteenth century by Liu Feng-lu. The three principal theses of K'ang Yu-wei each form the theme of one of his three main works:

1. Most of the texts in ancient characters (*ku-wen*) are forgeries produced by Liu Hsin, the imperial librarian at the end of the earlier Han dynasty. This thesis is developed in the *Researches into the Apocryphal*

Classics of the School of the Hsin Dynasty (Hsin-hsüeh wei-ching k'ao), published in 1891.

2. The concepts of Confucius, a sort of Chinese Christ, were completely misrepresented by Liu Hsin and the supporters of the school of texts in ancient characters. The real Confucius was a democratic reformer. This is the argument of the *Researches into the Reform of Institutions Undertaken by Confucius (K'ung-tzu kai-chih k'ao)*, which appeared in 1897.

3. In accordance with a scheme already outlined by Liu Feng-lu, who drew his inspiration from the chapter *Li-yün* in the *Treatise on Rites (Li-chi)* and from the *Kung-yang-chuan* (the world evolves from primitive disorder towards the great unity, *ta-t'ung*), humanity must experience in the course of its evolution three stages, the last of which will see the disappearance of frontiers and social classes, the formation of a universal civilization, and the inauguration of a definitive peace. Modern institutions (constitutional monarchy, parliament, and so on) and the development of commerce and industry respond to the needs of this process of evolution. Such are the ideas expressed in the *Ta-t'ung-shu,* written by K'ang Yu-wei in 1897 but kept secret and published only after his death, in 1935. In this socialist utopia the reformer envisages the abolition of the family, of nation states and of private property, and the establishment of a world government. He even goes to the length of planning the rules for living in this world of the future: communal dormitories and restaurants, collective nurseries, the rearing and education of children by the community, marriages lasting a year, cremation of the dead, and so on.

The return to forgotten traditions

K'ang Yu-wei's ideas call to mind the theories of the utopian socialists and the positivism of Auguste Comte (division of the history of humanity into successive stages and the desire to create a lay religion). However, this dogmatic system of thought with a mystical tendency did not undergo any direct influence from Western philosophy and drew its inspiration from purely Chinese traditions, if more or less heterodox ones. Nevertheless this convergence with Western currents of thought poses a general problem touching the whole history of Chinese thought since the arrival of the Europeans in East Asia. Up to about 1900 the influence of Western thinking was extremely diffuse and almost impossible to define. It had no immediate effect, but seems to have stimulated the Chinese world to seek in its own traditions the elements possessing some affinity with the foreign concepts which were infiltrating into China by the most diverse paths.

This — as well as the needs of the age — is the explanation of the renewed interest which arose after the T'ai P'ing Rebellion in the philosophers of the age of the Warring States, in the liberal, patriotic thinkers of the early days of the Manchu dynasty and in Buddhist traditions. Tai Wang (1837–73), a writer of the Kung-yang school, studied the works of the thinkers of the age of the Warring States and in 1869 published a work on Yen Yüan and Li Kung, the two philosophers of the K'ang-hsi era who had advocated a return to 'practical studies' (*shih-hsüeh*). Feng Kuei-fen, already mentioned earlier, was a great admirer of Ku Yen-wu, the liberal, patriotic scholar of the beginning of the Manchu occupation.

A scientific spirit and method in philology and history, positivism, criticism of absolutist institutions, definition of a Chinese 'nationalism' based on a type of culture, and the existence of a community which it was the state's function to defend against aggression from outside — such had been the contributions of the philologians, historians, and sociologists of the early days of the Manchu dynasty. Somewhat forgotten in the euphoria of the eighteenth century, these liberal, anti-Manchu thinkers had a profound influence on the orientation of Chinese thought from the last thirty years of the nineteenth century onwards.

Chinese intellectual life doubtless becomes more and more complex as we approach our own epoch. The most diverse currents mix and mingle and it is all the more difficult to retrace their history since we are dealing with a field which has not yet been studied in any detail. What China knew of the West in the nineteenth century was generally confined to technical innovations which the humanist tradition of the Chinese tended to regard as secondary to the moral rules which ensure the functioning of society. Only those who had had long and frequent contacts with the Western world were able to fathom certain fundamental differences and to attempt a comparison of a sociological character. Such was the case with Wang T'ao (1828–97). In touch with the British missionaries in Shanghai by 1848, attracted for a time by the T'ai P'ing, whose service he entered in 1861, and obliged for this reason to take refuge under a false name in Hong Kong, he there became the collaborator of the Scottish sinologist James Legge (1815–97) and remained with him until 1874, helping him to translate the Classics and the Four Books. From 1868–70 he stayed in Legge's house in Scotland. On his return to Hong Kong, Wang T'ao wrote a *Short History of France* (*Fa-kuo chih-lüeh*) in 1871 and, the following year, a remarkable history of the Franco-Prussian War of 1870, the *P'u-fa chan-chi,* and a treatise on artillery (*Huo-ch'i t'u-shuo*). One of the first Chinese journalists, he founded the daily paper *Evolution* (*Hsün-huan*) in Hong Kong and in 1884 became editor-in-chief of the great Shanghai paper *Shen-pao.*

His experience of the West led Wang T'ao to reflect on the causes of the relative strength and weakness of nations. Fascinated by the example of England, a small country which had become a great maritime industrial and commercial power, he saw her reserves of coal as one of the causes of her expansion, but asserted that in the last analysis wealth and power depend on a more general factor, the importance of which far exceeds that of economics and technology. This was the political factor. England's success sprang essentially from the fact that the same spirit animated her rulers and educated classes, from the fact that decisions were taken in common and thus everyone contributed willingly to the collective effort of the nation. Just as the British miracle was based on the country's political institutions and on the understanding between rulers and ruled, so the decline of China was mainly caused by the rift which had occurred between the central power and the educated classes. The ancient institution of the censorship, which had enabled the empires of days gone by to know the state of mind of the provinces, had disappeared with the advance of the authoritarian empire since the beginning of the Ming dynasty. For China to grow powerful again, the imperial government would have to seek the support of the influential families whose fate was bound up with its own. China was suffering precisely from the fact that the central government, which in principle took all the decisions, had lost all contact with those who could support it and collaborate with it. The harm was all the more serious since the empire was much vaster, and consequently formed a much looser whole, than the little countries of Europe which were shut in on themselves.

Wang T'ao was no doubt not a very original thinker; the ideas which he applied to the historical context of his own age are already to be found in Wang Fu-chih (1619–92) and his contemporaries. But the priority which he gave to the political factor was characteristic of all contemporary Chinese thought. It was no use adopting foreign technology if administrative methods were inadequate and if the very foundations of the state were in ruins. Reformers as well as conservatives took the view that ethics and politics came before the development of the economy and technology, which were mere means of wealth and power.

The scientific influences of the West

If in the domain of philosophy Western influences were thinly diffused and did not begin to have any direct effect until the publication of translations began about 1900, in the domain of science and technology the phenomenon of assimilation began much earlier. The long task of comparison and of integrating foreign contributions into the Chinese tradition started as early as the time of Matteo Ricci, that is, at the very beginning of the seventeenth century. But the current grew wider in the second half of the nineteenth century after the creation of the Institutes of Languages and Sciences in Peking, Shanghai, and Canton in 1862–64 and of the technical schools attached to the naval arsenals and shipyards built in the years 1865–70. The activity of the missionaries in the field of science and technology was not negligible either. Finally, Chinese students were sent to the Western countries for periods of instruction from 1872 onwards.

One hundred and twenty students were sent to the United States between 1872 and 1875. A smaller number set out from the naval college at Foochow in 1875 for Germany, to study artillery, the manufacture of armaments, strategy, and the techniques of naval warfare. In 1876 thirty students from the Foochow Arsenal went to France and England and spent periods in the naval shipyards, the mines, the iron- and steel-works and the mechanical industries. It is also worth noting that in 1881–82 four Chinese women students in the United States obtained medical qualifications and on their return became the first lady doctors in China. Further batches of students were sent to Europe and the United States in the years 1880–90, but financial difficulties and the very high cost of these missions made it necessary to reduce them substantially at the end of the nineteenth century.

The first visits of students to foreign countries were badly organized and produced only mediocre results. The young children sent to the United States soon became completely Americanized, while the students from the Foochow Naval Academy sent to Germany were too old and did not adapt themselves. On the other hand, the students and apprentices from the Foochow Arsenal who went to France and England in 1876 shared very effectively in the construction of the new Chinese fleet which was unfortunately to be annihilated by the Japanese in 1894.

The dialogue between the Chinese and Western mathematical traditions which had been initiated in the first few years of the seventeenth century went on in the nineteenth century. An important work of comparison and synthesis was accomplished in China with the rediscovery of Chinese mathematics of the eleventh to fourteenth centuries and with the seeking out and reprinting of the lost works which had interested men like Tai Chen and Juan Yüan—who wrote from 1797 to 1799 his collection of notes on the works of Chinese and foreign mathematicians and astronomers (*Ch'ou-jen-chuan*)—or Lo Shih-lin at the beginning of the nineteenth century (Lo Shih-lin died in the massacre of the population of Yangchow by the T'ai P'ing). Others concerned with the comparative study of the Western and Chinese traditions and with the translation of works on mathematics and physics in the nineteenth century were Li Shan-lan (1810–82; translator of mathematical works in conjunction with the British missionaries of the London Missionary Society of Shanghai), Cheng Fu-kuang, the author of a treatise on optics, the *Ching-ching ling-ch'ih,* published in 1835, and Hua Heng-fang (1833–1902).

Even the subjects in which Chinese traditions were perceptibly behind the West after the progress recently made there (chemistry, botany, geology, palaeontology, etc.) began to be absorbed into the body of Chinese science from the end of the nineteenth century onwards; and in the first half of the twentieth the contribution of Chinese scholars in most sectors of scientific research was to be far from negligible.

Part 10

China Crucified

Prologue: The beginning of the terrible years

The Sino-Japanese War of 1894 opened a new stage in the political, social, and economic disintegration of the Chinese world. The consequences of the defeat were so serious in every field that one may say that from this time onwards China was no longer mistress of her own fate. The fleet which she had tried to build up under difficult conditions was annihilated. By the treaty of 1895 she was required to pay reparations of 200 million *liang* — three times the annual income of the imperial government — and on top of that came the 30 million *liang* which were to allow her to retain the Liaotung peninsula for a few more years. The territorial ambitions of Japan, which annexed Taiwan and the P'eng-hu Islands (Pescadores) and gained a dominant position in the north-east (Manchuria), encouraged the Western powers to proceed in their turn to annexations of Chinese territory and to divide China up into 'spheres of influence', preserves, so to speak, for their exploitation of the ancient empire's wealth.

Germany seized the Ch'ing-tao and Chiao-chou areas in south-eastern Shantung in 1897, Great Britain occupied the region of Wei-hai (Wei-hai-wei) and the eastern extremity of the Shantung peninsula in 1898, and Russia took the southern part of the peninsula of Liaotung (the region of Ta-lian — 'Dairen' in Japanese — and Lü-shun, rechristened Port Arthur by the Westerners). France, whose ambitions were directed towards south-west China, followed their example in 1899 and took possession of the Chan-chiang (Kuang-chou-wan) area in western Kwangtung.

Moreover, what Li Hung-chang, a politician respected by his foreign interlocutors, had been able more or less to prevent before the defeat of 1894 could no longer be avoided in the years following the Treaty of Shimonoseki: foreign industries were installed in China itself, in the open ports, and the new 'leased territories'. The economic subjection of China to foreign nations swiftly increased. Foreign capital flowed in, and banks, factories, and mines swiftly grew in number, all managed by Western and Japanese firms which profited in the occupied towns and regions from the very low wages which they could pay to a poverty-stricken labour force.

What made this foreign hold on China so serious was that it occurred at the very time when the industrial and technological progress of the Western nations — and consequently of Japan — was at its most rapid and at the very time when the Chinese economy was in the process of collaps-

Table 28. The dismemberment of China

1895	Annexation of Taiwan and the P'eng-hu Islands (Pescadores) by Japan. German concessions at Hankow and Tientsin.
1896	Russian and French concessions at Hankow.
1897	Germany annexes the Ch'ing-tao and Chiao-chou areas in Shantung. Japanese concessions at Suchow (Kiangsu) and Hangchow (Chekiang).
1898	The British annex the Wei-hai region in Shantung, and the Russians that of Ta-lian and Lü-shun (Port Arthur) in the south of the Liaotung peninsula.
1898	Japanese concessions at Hankow and Sha-shih (Hupei), Tientsin and Foochow (Fukien).
1899	The French annex the region of Chan-chiang (Kuang-chou-wan). Japanese concession at Hsia-men (Amoy).
1900	Sack of Peking and the imperial palace by the colonial troops of the Allied nations. Punitive expeditions by General von Waldersee against numerous towns in North China. Russian concession at Tientsin.
1901	Japanese concession at Ch'ung-ch'ing (Chungking) (Szechwan).
1902	Belgian, Italian, and Austrian concessions at Tientsin.
1911	Outer Mongolia passes under Russian control.
1914	Central and western Tibet pass under British control The Japanese establish themselves in Shantung, in the territories previously occupied by Germany.
1931–32	Japan invades and annexes Manchuria.
1933	The Japanese penetrate into Jehol (south-eastern Mongolia) and into part of Hopei.
1937	Bombing of Shanghai and Nanking by the Japanese air force. Start of the general invasion of China by Japan.

ing. The reparations imposed on China in 1895 and 1901 (200 million *liang* and 450 million silver dollars) may not have been fabulous sums for the rich nations of that period; but they were a crushing burden for a country which was at the end of its resources, which saw foreign markets closing to its tea and silk, and which was powerless to halt the invasion of its towns and countryside by foreign products. It should be noted, by the way, that the Shimonoseki reparations enabled Japan to adopt the gold standard in 1897 and that they played a large part in the development of her economy round 1900.

This economic hold was accompanied by a military presence; the foreigners reached the point of keeping in China warships and troops ready to intervene at any moment. Unlike the concessions acquired in the big towns and utilized for commercial purposes, the leased territories were employed above all as military bases and strong points.

The moral and political consequences of the defeat were no less serious. Li Hung-chang, the only statesman who had any authority and who had dominated Chinese politics for nearly a quarter of a century, was removed from power after the Treaty of Shimonoseki. The result was a political vacuum that none of the most powerful figures of the time was capable of filling. Yüan Shih-k'ai, who succeeded Li Hung-chang as commander of the northern armies, was a purely military man without any breadth of vision, and the regional governors who ruled the middle and lower Yangtze (Chang Chih-tung and Liu K'un-i) were mainly concerned to keep their empires away from international eddies. Absence of any firm direction, divisions and disarray in the governing circles and among the intellectuals – such were the characteristics of political life in China at this crucial time round about 1900.

Demonstrations of disarray

From 11 June to 21 September 1898 a small group of intellectuals led by the great reforming scholar K'ang Yu-wei (1858–1927) succeeded in imposing their will on the Peking government, putting in train a whole series of institutional reforms inspired by Japanese and Russian models: modernization of the recruitment competitions, reform of the administration, publication of the state budget, creation of a ministry of the economy, and so on. This was the period known as the 'Hundred Days of Reform'. Supported at first by Yüan Shih-k'ai, commander of the armies of the northern zone, and by the governor of the provinces of Hupei and Honan, Chang Chih-tung, the reformers were finally abandoned by them as a result of an unfavourable reaction by conservative circles. Yüan Shih-k'ai took the side of the empress Tz'u Hsi, who regained control of the situation. Six of the reformers were executed, including the philosopher T'an Ssu-t'ung (1865–98), while K'ang Yu-wei and his disciple Liang Ch'i-ch'ao (1873–1929) fled to Japan, where they founded an Association for the Protection of the Emperor (*Pao-huang-hui*).

This episode in modern Chinese history, which is perhaps not devoid of interest in itself, reveals above all the uncertainty of the political situation and should be placed in the context of an epoch of humiliation and disarray. The reforms were obviously an illusory remedy at a time when Chinese territory was being shared out among foreign nations, the Chinese economy was collapsing and, as a result of the rapid upsurge of

Plate 70.   Li Hung-chang (1823–1901)

Plate 71.   Empress Tz'u-Hsi and
ladies in waiting

'late 72.   Sun Yat-sen (1866–1925)

Plate 73.   Yüan Shih-k'ai (1859–1916)

the Western nations and Japan, the gap between the industrialized countries and a huge empire which had remained essentially rural was growing wider every day.

It is the same disarray and the same basic impotence in face of the economic, political, and military grasp exerted by the industrialized nations that explain how it was that by a sort of impulse inspired by despair the Peking court decided to give its support to a popular rebellion. The aggravation of rural poverty, the unemployment caused by the importation of cloth and paraffin, as well as by the development of modern systems of transport (railways and steamships), and the hostility provoked by the behaviour of foreigners, especially the missionaries, were at the root of a general agitation among the peasantry in the last few years of the nineteenth century. The secret societies came to life again (Society of the elder Brothers, *Ko-lao-hui*; Society of the Big Sabre, *Ta-tao-hui*). The famines and floods which afflicted Shantung from 1898 onwards provoked the recrudescence there of one of the branches of the ancient Society of the White Lotus. This was the *I-ho-ch'üan,* the members of which practised Chinese boxing as a method of physical and moral training and for this reason were called Boxers by Westerners. Violently xenophobic, the Boxers were turned into fanatics by their faith in magical practices supposed to make them invulnerable. They attacked railways, factories, shops selling imported products, Chinese converted to Christianity, and missionaries. Driven out of Shantung by the energetic action of Yüan Shih-k'ai, at the beginning of 1900 the rising spread to Shansi and Hopei. The presence of the insurgents in the Tientsin–Peking–Pao-ting area, where foreigners were numerous, precipitated events: the threat to their own nationals led the foreign powers to intervene. Those in favour of supporting the Boxers then gained the upper hand at the court, and the Ch'ing empire officially declared war on the Western nations. But the principal men responsible for Chinese policy in the provinces, anxious to keep their regional powers intact and probably regarding the court's support for the Boxers simply as blind and unrealistic, stood aside from the conflict. Between June and August 1900 the Allied troops recaptured Tientsin and marched on Peking. The emperor and the empress Tz'u Hsi (who was not to return to the capital until 6 January 1902) fled to Sian in Shensi. Peking was sacked and punitive expeditions were organized by the German troops in the cities of North China. The protocol signed in Peking in 1901 imposed on China formidable reparations of 450 million silver dollars, a veto on all activities hostile to foreigners, the cessation of imports of arms, the dismantlement of the Ta-ku forts, the control by foreign troops of the

Tientsin–Peking railway, the execution of some high officials, and deputations of atonement to foreign countries.

The Boxer affair, which marked a further step in China's subjection to foreigners, had provided Russia with the opportunity to occupy Manchuria. The installation of the Russians in the north-east was to be at the root of the Russo-Japanese conflict of 1904–5, in the course of which the Tsar's armies were to be crushed by the new military might of Japan.

Chapter 29

The Disintegration of the Traditional Economy and Society*

The formation of a commercial middle class, the appearance of a proletariat, the new ideas that spread among the intelligentsia, the political
movements and parties — these are the factors which engage most attention in the China of 1895–1949. The fact is that these modern
developments call to mind those experienced by the Western countries;
China seems to have been involved in the same process which had caused
much earlier the evolution of the industrialized countries of Europe and
America. It looked as if China was drawing nearer to the West. But in according to these aspects of the recent history of China a special interest
and significance, one is liable to neglect certain fundamental facts which
exclude any parallel with the earlier history of the West. These facts are
the presence of a huge rural population, which often lived at bare subsistence level, the economic and political enfeeblement of China, her
dependence on foreigners, and the more and more decisive role played by
independent armies equipped by means of costly foreign loans. The very
context of the appearance and development of what people like to consider as proofs of the 'modernization' of China should forbid any
analogy with the history of the West. It is only by a misuse of language
that one can describe as 'social classes' corresponding to those of the
Western countries a sometimes rootless intelligentsia, a middle class

* For the whole contemporary part of this book, the valuable help and observations of M. Lucien Bianco have enabled me to improve my first version. I
should like here to express my grateful thanks to him.

which was a by-product of the foreign colonies in the open ports and in the lands of South-East Asia to which Chinese emigrated, and a wretched proletariat which could hardly be distinguished from the mass of people without resources impelled by poverty to move to the big cities. The growth of Shanghai with its American-style skyscrapers, its banks, and its foreign and Chinese factories was like the swelling of a cancerous tumour. It was not so much a proof of the progress made by the Chinese world as a symbol of its take-over by outsiders.

While in some parts of China the rural masses had no time to think of anything but their immediate survival, the new social groups that had arisen out of the breakup of Chinese society certainly experienced great accesses of patriotism which temporarily united these heterogeneous sections of society. But the weakness and impotence of the middle class, the intelligentsia, and the proletariat were obvious. Chinese business men, owners of banks, factories or import–export businesses, were torn between love of their country, the desire for economic independence, and their subjection in fact to the big foreign banks and businesses established in China. The conditions of life and the numerical weakness of the proletariat prevented it from playing any effective role. Moreover, the first working men's organizations were to be decapitated by Chiang Kai-shek (Chiang Chieh-shih) at the time of his *coup d'état* in 1927. The intelligentsia, disunited and riddled by contradictory ideas, was in deep disarray. But although decision-making power was in the hands of military leaders during the entire first half of the twentieth century, continual pressure exerted by the students and intellectuals was nevertheless in the long run not without effect on the evolution of politics. The movement of 4 May in particular marked the beginning of an awareness and a spiritual transformation that went far beyond the confined society of intellectuals, the universities, and the schools.

It is absurd to compare the ephemeral republican revolution of 1911–12 with a bourgeois revolution like the one that France had experienced at the end of the eighteenth century. Real power never belonged to the bourgeoisie; it was in the hands of those who had armies at their disposal. And it was thanks to the formation of a different sort of army, one that was no longer a parasitical growth but built up in symbiosis with the rural population, that China was to free herself both of the foreign invasion and of the military powers.

Thus Chinese political — and intellectual — life in the first half of the twentieth century has an artificial look which is reinforced by the marginal character of the political movements; they originated in Japan, in the Chinese colonies of South-East Asia and in the open ports, which formed, so to speak, Western enclaves in China. This political agitation, conducted mainly by students and the intelligentsia, was not in the long run without effect, but could not materially change a history which was in fact marked by the succession to power of different military leaders. The period can be divided into four stages:

1. The years 1895–1916, during which the *ancien régime* collapsed and disappeared, were dominated by the military supremacy of Yüan Shih-k'ai, commander of the armies of the northern zone (*Pei-yang lu-chün*).

2. The military governors whom Yüan Shih-k'ai had installed in the provinces before his death quarrelled in 1916 and shared out China between them with the support of the various foreign powers which possessed 'spheres of influence' in China (Japan, Great Britain, France, etc.). This was the period of the 'war-lords' (1916–28).

3. The advent of Chiang Kai-shek, favoured by the patriotic movement, which had grown stronger since 1919, marked a new stage in the history of contemporary China. Heir to the 'war-lords', Chiang Kai-shek, who was favourably regarded by the foreign powers in so far as he enforced order, imposed his dictatorship by obtaining willy-nilly the support of the Chinese commercial bourgeoisie. This was the 'Nanking decennium' (1928–37).

4. The Japanese invasion forced Chiang to take refuge in Szechwan. Cut off from Shanghai, the Nationalist government found its economy deteriorating rapidly, while the foreign occupation favoured the rise of the guerrilla movement under the control of the Communists. The final struggle, between the capitulation of Japan in 1945 and the last few months of 1949, naturally ended in favour of the popular militias; China had found the secret of her liberation in the formation of a peasant army animated by a deep-seated feeling of patriotism.

The ruin of the Chinese economy

The pressure of reparations

The depreciation of the Chinese currency in relation to the gold of the world trade dominated by the Western nations grew more marked at the end of the nineteenth century, just at the very time when China was going to be forced to pay crushing reparations to those who were attacking her. The *liang* of 38 grammes of silver, which was worth 1.20 American dollars in 1887, had lost half its value fifteen years later and was worth only .62 of an American dollar in 1902. This fall in the price of silver was to continue, in spite of a slight recovery towards the end of the First World War. The fundamental weakness of the Chinese currency was ag-

Table 29. Reparations imposed on China by foreign nations

1841	6 million *liang* by the British, who threatened Canton.
1842	21 million *liang* by Great Britain.
1858	4 million *liang* by Great Britain. 2 million *liang* by France.
1860	16 million *liang*, of which half went to Great Britain and half to France.
1862–69	Indemnities of some 400,000 *liang* as a result of incidents between missionaries and the Chinese population.
1870	Indemnity of 490,000 *liang* after the Tientsin incident.
1873	500,000 *liang* after the Japanese incursion into Taiwan.
1878	5 million *liang* to Russia (Treaty of Livadia).
1881	9 million *liang* paid to Russia, this indemnity allowing China to take possession again of part of her territories in the Ili valley.
1895	200 million *liang* paid to Japan after the Chinese defeat.
1897	30 million *liang* paid to Japan in exchange for the evacuation of the Liaotung peninsula by the Japanese troops.
1901	450 million silver dollars paid to the Western allies at the time of the invasion of Hopei (Boxer indemnity).
1922	66 million gold francs paid to Japan in exchange for the evacuation of the territory of Chiao-chou in Shantung. Numerous indemnities required of China after incidents between missionaries and the Chinese population are not mentioned in this list for the years after 1870.

gravated by the deficit in the balance of payments and by the losses involved in the payment of reparations. Still limited until the Treaty of Shimonoseki to sums that the Chinese economy could stand, from about 1900 onwards these indemnities could only be paid by recourse to loans from foreign banks. The payment imposed by Japan after her victory already represented three times the state's annual revenues. The Boxer indemnity six years later exceeded still further China's capacity to pay. The 450 million dollars demanded in fact constituted a charge of 982 million, if we add the very high interest which China was required to pay in order to liquidate her debts. In 1911 the Chinese National Debt amounted to 200 million silver dollars. It was to reach 800 million American dollars in 1924. It became clearer and clearer that this country in which so many people lived in profound poverty and which had experienced so many tragedies could never rid herself of the enormous burden imposed on her by the richest and most prosperous countries in the world.

Immediately after the Treaty of Shimonoseki China obtained a loan of

400 million francs from a Franco-Russian consortium, on the security of the revenues from the maritime customs. In 1896 and 1898 came two further loans of £16 million sterling from another consortium of foreign banks. Between 1902 and 1910 the Peking government was to succeed in paying 225 million *liang* of the Boxer indemnity by taking a levy on its revenues and by resorting in the provinces to threats of what the foreign nations would do in case of non-payment.

From 1895 onwards China was subjected to the triple burden of reparations, loans contracted with foreign banks, and expenditure destined to rebuild modern armed forces. On top of this massive load came the effect of more specific factors which helped both to change and to weaken the Chinese economy. This economy in fact became more and more dependent on the variations of the world market and consequently much more vulnerable. Agriculture and manufacturing industry adapted themselves to external demand by developing new crops, to the detriment of foodstuffs, or new kinds of work (for example, the weaving of imported cotton yarn). The result was periods of prosperity in certain sectors, followed by harsh recessions. Imports of cotton yarn, which had risen from 33,000 to 387,000 piculs (1 picul = *c.* 60 kg) during the years 1870–80, subsequently fell again because of the massive imports of cheap cotton goods. In some regions the Chinese cotton industry was ruined by the influx of European—especially British—textiles in 1893–99 and by that of American cotton goods in 1899–1900. Imports of cotton goods were to reach their highest figure in 1920, then to fall again as a result of poverty. Exports of tea had increased rapidly between 1830 and 1880, rising from 30 million pounds in weight to 150 million. But thanks to the plantation of tea bushes in India, Ceylon, and Japan, where there was a move towards industrial methods of production, the price of tea fell from 1880 onwards. Seven years later, in some provinces four-fifths of the tea hills were already lying untended; a whole sector of the Chinese economy, and one that until then had been prosperous, was ruined. A similar fate overtook the production of silk; exports of silks showed a clear recovery in 1885–87, but they soon suffered from the competition of silks produced in Japan, in Lyons and in Italy.

The economic takeover

After the Treaty of Shimonoseki, which opened China up to foreign industries, there was an influx of Western and Japanese capital into the open ports and leased territories; foreign countries hoped both to benefit from an impoverished, cheap labour force and to be in the best position to sell their products in China. According to some estimates, foreign capital in China rose from 787 million gold dollars in 1896 to 1610 million in 1914. In 1890 there were 499 foreign businesses on Chinese soil; in 1923 there were 6865.

The Chinese economy seemed to be reinvigorated by this inflow of money and this industrial development. The cities in which the foreigners had established their businesses—Shanghai above all, but also Tientsin, Ch'ing-tao, Wu-han, Hong Kong, etc.—were in full swing. The new industries provided work for a large number of people without resources and gave renewed life to the surrounding countryside; and the big city forms a favourable environment for the development of a host of small professions and trades. But this prosperity was artificial and deceptive. The effect of the influx of foreign capital was to aggravate the imbalance between the industrial centres on the coast and a huge hinterland where the conditions of life continued to deteriorate. The 300,000 foreigners resident in China about 1920 may have spent part of their income there, but the foreign companies sent a considerable proportion of their profits home, thus bleeding the slender resources of China yet again. Finally, the inflow of Western and Japanese capital increased the servitude of the Chinese economy to foreigners.

Round about 1920 the whole Chinese economy was dependent on the big foreign banks in Shanghai, Hong Kong, Ch'ing-tao, and Hankow, and on powerful companies such as the Kailan Mining Association, the capital of which was Japanese. The customs, the administration of the salt tax, and the postal services were run by foreigners, who kept all the profits. Western and Japanese warships and merchant shipping were everywhere—in the ports, on the coast, and on the Yangtze River network. Apart from a few Chinese firms which succeeded with difficulty in fighting the competition to which they were subjected, the whole modern sector of industry (cloth mills, tobacco factories, railways, shipping, cement works, soap factories, flour mills and, in the towns, the distribution of gas, water, and electricity, and public transport) was under the control of foreign companies. Chinese banking, industrial and commercial capital was much smaller than the British, American, Russian, Japanese, and French capital invested in China. The big Western banks in Shanghai controlled the essential part of Chinese revenues, in particular the maritime customs. In addition, they attracted all the private capital seeking reliable protection, which it could not find with the Chinese banks.

Exposed to very severe competition, Chinese firms experienced a relative improvement only at the time of the First World War. British imports fell by 51.5 per cent and French imports by 29.6 per cent between 1913 and 1918, and German imports stopped completely in 1917 after

China had entered the war on the Western Allies' side. Japan's position, the only one improving at that time, was jeopardized by numerous boycotts of Japanese products. The number of Chinese spindles increased by 125 per cent between 1914 and 1921. The relative improvement in the Chinese economy was reflected in 1918–19 by a business recovery and a rise in the value of the Chinese silver dollar. But the respite did not last long; competition made itself felt again after 1919 and caused the bankruptcy of numerous Chinese firms. Japanese spindles, which numbered 111,926 in 1913 and 621,828 in 1922, had risen to 1,268,176 three years later.

The case of textiles, one of the most important economic sectors, is in fact particularly instructive. While Chinese entrepreneurs had the greatest difficulty in finding funds in an extremely small market, Japanese industries could call on plenty of capital, which was lent to them at 3 per cent interest, a much lower rate than the 10 per cent charged by Chinese banks. Moreover, thanks to an agreement with the shipping companies, Japanese textile firms paid 30 per cent less for the transport of raw cotton from India. Finally, their products were exempt in China from the heavy transit tax — the *li-chin* — which was imposed on all Chinese products. Greater banking facilities, lower rate of interest, fiscal exemption, lower transport charges, and better organization — all these things explain the difference in cost of manufacture: Chinese cotton goods were 114 per cent dearer to produce than the cotton goods manufactured in China by Japanese firms.

A great exporter of finished products in the eighteenth century, China had remained for some time afterwards the land of fine cotton goods and also, up to about 1880, the country of silks and tea. From the end of the nineteenth century she was reduced to importing not only steel, machinery, railway material, arms, and so on, but even products for current consumption. Confined at first to the urban markets, American and British cotton goods imported *en masse* in the last few years of the nineteenth century were finally sold in all the rural areas as well. Even oil for lighting was imported: the small Chinese *t'ung* oil industry could not stand up to the imports of paraffin, which had already reached 7,309,000 hectolitres by 1910 and rose to 9,761,000 hectolitres in 1923. And this huge country, where the rural masses, forced to practise a very strict subsistence economy, suffered from endemic undernourishment, even had to import part of its food — sugar, rice, flour — from abroad. The big famines necessitated massive purchases: 5.3 million silver dollars' worth of rice from South-East Asia in 1920 and the enormous amount of 80 million dollars' worth in 1922.

The Western nations took a long time to see their mistake: China was not the inexhaustible source of wealth, the new Eldorado which they had imagined round about 1840 and which it could in fact have become if its economy had developed. At the end of the nineteenth century the total Western trade with the Chinese empire did not exceed £50 million sterling, that is, much less than the foreign trade of a small country. The fundamental reason for the low figure of this trade was the impoverishment of China. However, when the Chinese economy had been ruined between the last few years of the nineteenth century and the beginning of the First World War, the Western nations began to lose interest in China. The great hecatomb of 1914–18 and the difficulties which followed it in the West contributed to this loss of interest, as well as the chaos and poverty in which the Chinese world found itself plunged. After the great expansion of the years round 1900, investment slowed down. Some countries surrendered the privileges which they had acquired in China to Chiang Kai-shek's government in Nanking; others did the same during the Second World War. The West abandoned this wretched prey to Japan.

Natural calamities

As the end of the nineteenth century approached China seemed to become the plaything of a destiny which she could no longer ward off. Both mankind and the elements conspired against her. China of the years 1850–1950 — the China of the most terrible insurrections in her history, of foreign bombardments, of invasions and civil wars — was also the China of great natural cataclysms. Almost certainly the number of victims involved had never been so high in the history of the world.

From the middle of the seventeenth century to the end of the eighteenth China had experienced few famines and floods, but from the first half of the nineteenth century onwards natural disasters multiplied and, what is more, were on an unexampled scale. The fact is that the density of the population in the big agricultural regions, the fragility of the system of subsistence, the lack of foresight and the incapacity of a corrupt administration all combined to transform the slightest climatic disturbances into catastrophes. The absence of reserves, the poor organization of assistance and difficulties of transport explain the seriousness of the famines which followed the droughts in North China. The poor maintenance of the dykes and the rise in the level of the river beds were at the root of the great floods of the years 1850–1950. Hunger and poverty had driven a considerable number of poor peasants to exploit the high ground and in particular to extend the maize plantations to it. But the intensive deforestation in the nineteeth century caused the erosion of the soil, the alluvial deposits from which raised the beds of the rivers.

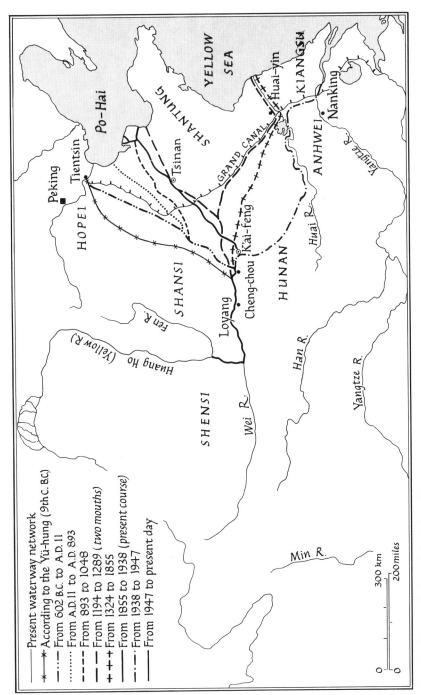

Map 27   The wanderings of the Yellow River

The dykes, badly maintained, were no longer strong enough to hold the mass of water when the rivers were in flood. This chain of causes, the first of which was the Chinese peasantry's hunger for land from the first half of the nineteenth century onwards, was understood by the historian Lin Tse-hsü (1785–1850), the geographer Wei Yüan (1794–1856) and the hydrographical expert Wang Shih-to (1802–89). It was at the root of the terrible floods which now affected not only the lower valley of the Yellow River but also, more frequently than in days gone by, the lower Han valley and the lower reaches of the Yangtze. These murderous floods were not only destructive in themselves but also gave rise to epidemics. The Yellow River burst its dykes to the west of K'ai-feng in 1855 and changed its course from the Huai area to the Tsinan area. In 1938 it was to carve itself a new course towards the north of Anhwei, which it was to abandon in 1947. Very serious floods were to occur in the lower valley of the Yangtze in 1931 and 1935.

But the great droughts in North China had still more terrible effects. The drought of 1876–79 in Shensi, Shansi, Hopei, Honan, and part of Shantung caused the death of nine to thirteen million people; while that of 1892–94 claimed roughly a million victims. However, the extension of the railway network from about 1900 onwards did make it possible to reduce the dramatic effects of the great famines in time of peace; only half a million people died in 1920–21. On the other hand, thanks to political circumstances, there were nearly three million deaths in the province of Shensi alone in 1928–31. During the Second World War, when most of the country was occupied by the Japanese armies, famine claimed nearly two million victims in Honan in 1942–43.

China of the years 1919–49 was a demoralized country which had lost all hope, a world in which pity and justice no longer had any meaning, where horror had become a daily event. To take just one example, in 1938 the Nationalist armies made breaches in the dykes of the Yellow River to hold up the Japanese advance; the resulting flood killed several hundred thousand Chinese peasants.

Movements of population and social changes

Doubtless care must be taken not to make any categorical judgement that could easily be proved false by this or that particular case; China is too vast and too diverse, and during the first half of the twentieth century she experienced too many changes of fortune, for it to be possible to make any general statements. Such is the case with peasant poverty. This was often dreadful; nevertheless in some regions and at certain times the

peasants did live in relative comfort. The same is true of the establishment of foreign industries. To see only the negative effects (the ruin of
certain crafts and of certain traditional products, the export of capital,
the unequal struggle in which the budding Chinese industries found
themselves involved, the inhuman conditions in which the proletariat
lived) is to leave out of account the development of new, more profitable
crops and the new jobs provided for a superabundant peasantry. However, in the absence of the innumerable monographs which will one day
provide the basis for a better synthesis, the author of a general history is
nevertheless obliged to give a general view, even if it is only a provisional
one.

The China of the first half of the twentieth century was a poor country, most of whose techniques of production had hardly made any progress since the beginning of the nineteenth century (some of them even
seem to have regressed). Most of her population were subjected to an exploitation which knew no bounds precisely because of the general poverty. On top of this exploitation there sometimes came, as the last straw,
natural catastrophes (floods, droughts, plagues of locusts, earthquakes)
and the plundering and destruction indulged in by Chinese or foreign armies. Doubtless none of this was new to China; the peasants had long
suffered usurious rates of interest, rents up to half the value of the
harvest, the exactions of the tax-collector, freaks of nature and the
violence of the soldiery. However, people had probably never experienced
before such an accumulation of misfortunes. It would almost certainly
be as unjust to ascribe all this to China's traditions and to her social and
political system as it would be to attribute the sole responsibility for it to
the imperialism of foreign countries. Let us simply say that it was a concatenation of historical events that had led to all these trials. A country
that had succeeded in feeding such a large number of people was bound
to suffer severely if there was the slightest imbalance in its economy.

Exodus and emigration

Demographic pressure explains certain movements of internal migration
and of emigration abroad which noticeably affected the distribution of
the population in China itself and of the Chinese population of East Asia
as a whole. On the one hand there was a concentration in the industrialized towns and the surrounding countryside, and on the other, in North
China and especially Shantung, an exodus towards the inhospitable lands
of the north-east (Manchuria) and considerable emigration from the
southern provinces of Kwangtung and Fukien to overseas countries.
These centrifugal tendencies caused by excessive poverty had in fact

begun much earlier, but they grew more marked in the first half of the twentieth century.

Even at the time of the Treaty of Nanking, China had seemed to the Western countries like an inexhaustible reservoir of cheap labour. From about 1845 a network for the export of coolies to America, especially to the silver mines of Peru and the sugar-cane plantations of Cuba, had been organized at Hsia-men (Amoy), a port in southern Fukien, and at Shan-tou (Swatow), a port in north-eastern Kwangtung. These sections of the Chinese coast, which lived in the eighteenth century on their hand-icrafts — their agricultural production was already inadequate — had been particularly affected by the economic recession in the middle of the nine-teenth century. Enticed by hopes of a better life, these wretched people were lodged in hutments before their departure and crowded into the holds of ships in such dreadful conditions that many died during the voyage. The cargo ships involved in this profitable slave trade were known as 'floating hells'. In 1866 the Chinese government had presented a draft convention. It was rejected by the Western powers. The great ex-pansion in gold production of the years 1850–73 had given fresh strength to the emigration movement and from 1867 onwards there was massive recruitment of Cantonese coolies for California (in Chinese, 'the old mountains of gold', *Chiu-chin-shan*), where gold had been discovered in 1848, and afterwards for Australia (the 'new mountains of gold', *Hsin-chin-shan*), where gold was found in 1851. However, this spontaneous or deliberately encouraged emigration provoked the hostility of the workers' trade unions in the United States, where racial hatred was mounting. In 1880 the American government, under pressure from the trade unions, had had to suspend the immigration of Chinese. Five years later, in 1885, the riots at Rock Springs (Wyoming) resulted in the death of twenty-nine Chinese miners. China made a fresh, but vain, protest against the cruelty of which her nationals were the victims. The treatment inflicted on Chinese immigrants in the United States and the banning of all immigration caused a widespread boycott of American goods in China in 1905. That year saw the appearance of a Chinese novel describ-ing the wretched life of the coolies in the southern states of North America (*The Society of Wretchedness, K'u-she-hui*).

Emigration to America and Australia therefore slowed down at the beginning of the twentieth century. The only notable example of Chinese emigration to the Western countries in the twentieth century was the dispatch of 140,000 Chinese workers to France in 1917–18. They were to help in the war effort there and subsequently returned to their own coun-try. The most important demographic phenomena in the history of China in the first half of the twentieth century were the settlement of

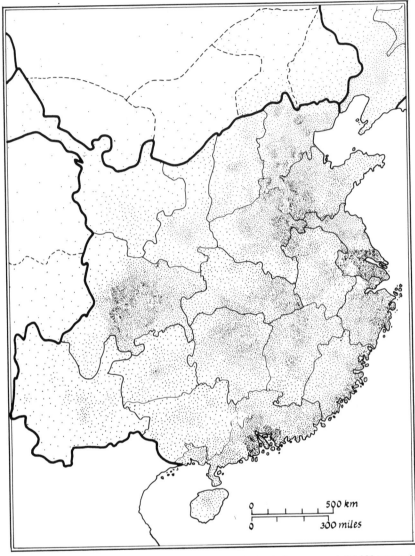

Map 28   Distribution of population in China in 1925 (each dot represents 25,000 persons)

peasants from Shantung and the lower reaches of the Yellow River in the north-east, where the population rose from fifteen million in 1910 to forty-four million in 1940, and the great exodus of Cantonese, Hakka, and Fukienese to the French, British, and Dutch colonies in South-East Asia. The Chinese population of Singapore rose from 54,000 in 1866 to 224,000 in 1911; and that of the Dutch East Indies from 175,000 to 295,000 at the same dates. But it was during the first half of the twentieth century that emigration to South-East Asia really grew sizeable. The general increase was of the order of 50 to 60 per cent between 1900 and 1930. This new influx swamped the old Chinese colonies, and it was at this time that Singapore, Malacca, Penang, and Cholon (a suburb of Saigon founded by exiles at the time of the Manchu invasion) became almost completely Chinese cities and that the Malay peninsula was largely peopled (nearly half the population is Chinese) by former peasants and coolies from Kwangtung and Fukien, people from Ch'ao-chou, Amoy, Foochow, Canton, or from the Hakka communities of South China.

Attracted by the economic activity arising out of the expansion of the colonial and capitalist system in South-East Asia, these immigrants joined in and acted as intermediaries. They were to be found in the tin mines, the rubber, tea, and pineapple plantations, the rice fields, market gardening, chemists' shops, the building industry, and banks. The majority of them had to be content with minor positions as small businessmen, craftsmen, farm labourers, or plantation workers. They were more active and enterprising than the peoples among whom they lived and some of them succeeded in making big fortunes. One could mention a number of big business men, equivalents of the American 'self-made men' of the early twentieth century, who came to occupy an important place in local economic life in Malaya, Thailand, Burma, and French Indo-China. About 1936 the capital held by the Chinese immigrants (*Hua-ch'iao*) in South-East Asia was estimated at 644 million American dollars.

There thus grew up overseas a sort of Chinese bourgeoisie resembling that of the open ports, tied to foreign interests and more or less converted to Western modes of life and ideas. Its influence and role in the vain attempt to set up a parliamentary democracy in China were far from negligible. It gave its moral and financial support to the republicans and to the Society of the Alliance (*T'ung-meng-hui*) founded in Tokyo in 1905 by Sun Yat-sen (Sun Wen) and Huang Hsing. More generally, the assistance given by overseas Chinese *émigrés* to their families in Kwangtung and Fukien helped to relieve to some extent the poverty of the latter.

Table 30.   The Chinese in South-East Asia
(1958 statistics from the *East Economic Review*, March 1958)

Country	Chinese population	% in relation to the total population
Thailand	3,500,000	18
Malaysia	3,013,000	44
Indonesia	1,598,000	2
Vietnam, Laos, and Cambodia	1,221,000	4
Singapore	861,000	77
Burma	400,000	2
Sarawak (N.W. Borneo)	164,000	27
Philippines	154,000	1
North Borneo	83,000	
Total	10,994,000	

(The figures given by V. Purcell for 1960 produce a slightly higher total: 11,227,000.)

The wealth and influence of some of the colonists and the practice of usury also explain the jealousy, mistrust, or hostility of the local populations; the granting of independence to the former British, French and Dutch colonies in South-East Asia after the Second World War, and the nationalist upheavals that accompanied it, were unfavourable to the local Chinese.

It should also be noted that the poverty of the maritime provinces of South China caused emigration to Madagascar, Africa, central Asia, India, Oceania, and elsewhere. The Chinese diaspora extended to the whole world.

Recent statistics about Chinese colonization in South-East Asia are difficult to interpret because of the rules adopted by the host countries, which often obliged the Chinese to change nationality, and also because of intermarriage and assimilation. Thus the official figures only provide an approximation.

The breakup of the traditional society

The centrifugal movement which emptied certain country areas to the advantage of the open ports, and the coastal provinces to the advantage of the peripheral regions (the north-east and South-East Asia), was accompanied by the breakup, so to speak, of Chinese society. Not only capital but also the men of worth deserted the big rural areas of the interior. With the development of the large cities, open to foreign influences, the opposition between town and country grew sharper. The old educated classes had had strong provincial ties and had retained in spite of everything some contact with the rural world. By tradition they had shown some concern for its well-being. It was not the same with the commercial bourgeoisie and the intelligentsia of the open ports; their mode of life, the circumstances of their existence, their profoundly Westernized ideas removed them further and further from the peasantry and made them blind to the problem — fundamental from every point of view — of the Chinese countryside and agriculture. Everything encouraged them to despise this world of poverty and superstition; for them it represented the past. After all, the West, which had become the model for most of them, appeared to them in the guise of industrial and commercial power.

But this gulf between the peasantry of the interior and the privileged people of the marginal China of the open ports was only one of the characteristics of the China of the first half of the twentieth century; it is legitimate to say that a sort of general atomization affected Chinese society of that period. Sun Yat-sen, the founder of the republic, was to say, 'We are like scattered grains of sand.' The new groups which made their appearance thanks to the political and economic take-over were heterogeneous, strangers to each other, and often divided into hostile sections. They sometimes had a narrower view of the situation and a less clearly developed national conscience than the old Chinese educated classes. While scholarly civil servants of the old school, such as Chang Chih-tung (1837–1909) in Hunan and Chang Chien (1853–1926) in the poverty-stricken area of Nan-t'ung to the north of the lower reaches of the Yangtze, had striven to fight against the foreign hold by developing steel production in their provinces and by creating textile factories and modern schools, the new Chinese bourgeoisie, which had sprung from mercantile circles devoid of general culture (former commercial agents — *compradores* — of the big foreign countries or merchants enriched in the trade with foreigners), pursued only selfish ends. It is true that it suffered from its lack of independence and from the competition of Japanese and Western firms, and that for this very reason it was capable of patriotism. But it was quite powerless to break away from the system of colonial exploitation established by the foreigners. In any case its activities made hardly any contribution to freeing the Chinese economy from its subjection; because of the small amount of capital available and of the harshness of the competition, industrial enterprises run by the Chinese bourgeoisie were not very numerous. The economic and political conditions of the time encouraged it to turn to banking and speculation.

More open-minded and more sensitive to the increasingly serious decline of their country, the men educated in Japan or the Western countries were in a position to make judgements and comparisons. Their patriotism was more lively and more generous than that of the commercial middle class. The sudden action by the intellectuals and young people of school age after the First World War — the famous movement of 4 May 1919 — surprised people by its violence and wide scope. But the intellectuals and the new trained personnel did not escape the general demoralization. Their conditions of life were extremely precarious (a fair number of Chinese engineers were unemployed) and they had no outlets but politics or teaching. Half rootless, partly strangers to their own country, they lived in a world where the law of the jungle reigned: to survive or succeed were the only goals of existence when social cohesion had disappeared. This is part of the explanation for the favour found with the Chinese intelligentsia by the themes of Western middle-class thinking — the romantic exaltation of the individual, the struggle for life, the survival of the fittest, and so on. From 1927 onwards Marxism was to look like the only doctrine leading to salvation.

There was also the new Chinese proletariat, the product of the invasion of foreign capital and of the pauperization of the countryside. Mines, railways, docks, the factories of the industrial centres attracted the surplus of a wretched peasantry. However, it is difficult to distinguish this proletariat from the mass of people with no fixed income who sought to find a livelihood in the most diverse occupations and sometimes the least honourable ones (begging, gambling, prostitution, racketeering, crime, the opium traffic, etc.). The number of unemployed was considerable. The mass of people who had come down in the world — former peasants or discharged soldiers — was estimated at some twenty million about 1926.

The conditions of life of the industrial proletariat in China were worse than those of European workers in the early days of industrialization — a twelve-hour day, no security of employment, no sickness or accident insurance, women and children working, and so on. Entirely dependent on the recruiting agents, until about 1920 this proletariat had no other forms of organization than the traditional mutual aid groupings — associations of people from the same village or the same area. Like the *émigré* coolies in South-East Asia, the workers maintained their links with their home district and sent their families part of their slender earnings. Workers' organizations only began to appear in the years 1919–21, thanks to the great patriotic, revolutionary movement which followed the Paris Peace Conference. But they were to be crushed by Chiang Kai-shek in 1927. Controlled by criminals and the police, the new official trade unions created by the Nationalist government were to prevent the weak Chinese proletariat from playing any political role in the years 1928–49.

To these disunited groups should be added a small number of military leaders and their subordinates, men of usually somewhat mediocre education who nevertheless played the principal role in the history of China during the first half of the twentieth century.

One of the fundamental reasons for China's impotence when confronted with foreign pressure, and afterwards one of the main causes of her misfortunes in the first half of the twentieth century, was the recourse—traditional since the tenth and eleventh centuries—to mercenaries and professional armies. The peasant militias which had been formed in Kwangtung at the time of the British attacks in 1840–42 were the expression of a spontaneous reaction which had had no lasting consequences because the political concepts of the Ch'ing empire, in which military questions were traditionally the responsibility of the Manchu aristocracy, excluded direct recourse to popular initiatives. For the same reason the formation of militias consisting of volunteers, and organized by the local officials in Hunan, Kiangsu, and Anhwei at the time of the T'ai P'ing Rebellion, had not brought about any change of attitude or practice. The armies recruited at that time had therefore become, with the weakening of the central government, independent forces under the direct control of their leaders. The results were the absence of any unity of command—the effects of this deficiency made themselves felt particularly during the French attacks of 1884–85—and the development of autonomic regional tendencies which prevented the Chinese armies from being the instrument of a general policy with the defence of the empire as its primary objective. Instead, they turned into relatively autonomous organisms independent of the central government. It was thus inevitable that with the decline of the state the armies and their commanders should come to be the real arbiters of Chinese political life. The disarray and political vacuum which followed the Treaty of Shimonoseki and the removal from power of Li Hung-chang explain the ascendancy gained by a mere soldier like Yüan Shih-k'ai, commander of the best-equipped and best-trained armies in existence round about 1900. Thus a process of evolution going back to the T'ai P'ing War was to end in making the Chinese armies in the first half of the twentieth century into alien, parasitical bodies, whose function was not to fight against foreign aggression and occupation, but on the contrary to assume in internal politics a role no longer filled by any other power.

The mechanism which would permit China to unify herself again and to free herself both from these parasitical bodies and from foreign invasion could only be fresh recourse to volunteers, and the formation, village by village and district by district, of peasant militias. This was the solution to the decline of national unity envisaged by men like Wang T'ao about 1870 in the framework of imperial institutions.

Chapter 30

Political Developments in the First Half of the Twentieth Century

The epoch of Yüan Shih-k'ai

The disappearance of the old regime

Much weakened by the defeat of 1894 and by the results of the Boxer adventure, from 1901–3 onwards the Ch'ing government turned to introducing a series of reforms reminiscent of those advocated by K'ang Yu-wei and his friends in 1898. These reforms included the creation of ministries between 1903 and 1906, the publication of the details of the budget from 1908 onwards, the abolition of the traditional competitions (1905) and the reform of the educational system, the creation of provincial assemblies (1909), and the proclamation of a new code of law (1910), the work of the eminent jurist Shen Chia-pen (1837–1910) and inspired by Western legislation. The moribund dynasty was conforming to the fashions of the time. It even displayed some sort of desire for centralization, a whim inspired by its urgent need of money. The Manchu aristocracy was staging a revival and trying to get its hands on the only profitable enterprises in the provinces. Yüan Shih-k'ai, whose power worried Peking, was relieved in 1907 of his post as commander of the armies of the northern zone (*Pei-yang lu-chün*) and appointed minister for foreign affairs. At the same time Chang Chih-tung, governor of the two Hu (Hunan and Hupei), was summoned to the capital and had to leave his middle Yangtze empire. Sheng Hsüan-huai (1849–1916), a corrupt civil servant and a former protégé first of Li Hung-chang, then of Chang

Chih-tung, secured in 1908, thanks to Japanese loans, control of the Chinese Steam Navigation Company and of the Han-yeh-p'ing Company (Han-yang steelworks, iron-mines of Ta-yeh in Hupei and coal-mines at P'ing-hsiang in Kiangsi — the work of Chang Chih-tung). The same Sheng Hsüan-huai reappeared in 1911 at the head of the vast operation of loans from foreign banks and of the purchase and nationalization of the railways which was to provoke a patriotic and regionalist reaction in the provinces and bring about the fall of the dynasty. The old regime was condemned to disappear not so much by its clumsiness and inconsistency as by the economic collapse and by its need to put pressure on the provinces and 'sell China to the foreigners' by borrowing from Western and Japanese banks. The result of this was the growing disaffection of both the old ruling classes and the bourgeoisie of the open ports, of the conservatives and the modernists.

On top of this basic cause of weakness came the secondary effect of anti-Manchu and anti-monarchist currents which had developed in various different circles — the students and intellectuals who had emigrated to Japan, the new Chinese bourgeoisie of South-East Asia, the secret societies of South China and Hunan, the officers of the new armies trained in military schools run by foreign instructors. Japan, taken as a model since 1896 and much admired since her victory over the Russian fleet at Tsushima in 1905, played a very important role in this process of evolution. Various associations in Japan in fact lent the different groups of political refugees a support which was not always disinterested. The most important current of thought among the *émigrés* was the one that favoured a constitutional monarchy on the Japanese model. Its mouthpiece, the erstwhile reformer Liang Ch'i-ch'ao, who wielded a lively pen, had a wide audience among the intellectual élite. Less traditional was the republican tendency represented by Sun Wen (1866–1925), better known in the West by his Cantonese name of Sun Yat-sen. Unlike Liang Ch'i-ch'ao, Sun Yat-sen had neither a classical training nor a historical and philosophical turn of mind. He was a man without roots who was to spend most of his life abroad seeking support and subsidies. Born near Macao and brought up in Honolulu, Sun Yat-sen studied medicine in Hong Kong and at first gave the impression of being a run-of-the-mill conspirator connected with the secret societies of Kwangtung. The associations which he founded in 1894 (the *Hsing-chung-hui,* Society for the Rebirth of China) and in 1905 in Tokyo (the *T'ung-meng-hui,* United League) were much more like associations of conspirators than real political parties. Their activities consisted of plots and surprise attacks which were all doomed to failure. The most famous attempt at rebellion was the one which took place in Canton on 27 April 1911 and claimed seventy-two victims (the 'seventy-two martyrs'). Sun Yat-sen's republican ideology was fairly summary; his three basic themes (the *San-min-chu-i*) put the accent on nationalism, liberal democracy and social justice. But the doctrines were of little importance as compared with action, and Sun Yat-sen's supporters (his friend Huang Hsing, a Hunanese connected with the secret societies of his province and in touch with revolutionary circles in the new armies; Wang Ching-wei, 1883–1944; Hu Han-Min, 1879–1936; and Chang Ping-lin, 1868–1936) naively believed that the salvation of China lay in their hands.

The old regime collapsed without any real contribution from the heterogeneous group of republican revolutionaries except that of a relatively negligible supporting factor. The 'revolution' of 1911 was not a 'bourgeois' revolution, as people have claimed in order to be able to insert it in a scheme of historical evolution furnished by Europe or by the Marxist theory of the five stages of humanity (primitive communism, slavery, feudalism, capitalism and socialism). It was a mere interlude in the breakup of political power in China. The success of the republicans was unexpected: a military revolt at Wu-ch'ang (Hupei) on 10 October 1911 unleashed a vast movement of secession which spread to most provinces. By the beginning of December south, central, and north-west China had broken with Peking, as a result of an alliance between the provincial assemblies and the military. Sun Yat-sen returned from the United States and Great Britain just in time to be elected President of the Republic at Nanking and took office on 1 January 1912. However, at the same time he offered Yüan Shih-k'ai the presidency of the Republic if he was ready to defend the new regime, and this in itself clearly reveals the extreme weakness of this republic without any armed forces or revenues. In the last analysis the Republic was only—with the addition of the various groups of political refugees—a continuation of the former provincial assemblies of gentry rid of the semblance of central authority constituted by the Peking government. In fact, although the gentry were willing that their provinces should be represented in a national parliament, all eyes were turned towards Yüan Shih-k'ai, the only man with a well-trained and well-equipped army and also the only man who could secure some attention from foreign countries. The revolution, which was practically bloodless, was primarily the result of the unavoidable disappearance of a dynasty which could only maintain its position by bleeding the provinces and borrowing from foreign banks.

The dictatorship of Yüan Shih-k'ai

Recalled by the court in October 1911, Yüan Shih-k'ai profited from the disturbances to secure very wide powers of decision which he employed in bargaining with the extremely weak Nanking government. Two days after the abdication of P'u-i (the emperor Hsüan-t'ung, aged six), on 14 February 1912, these negotiations succeeded: Yüan Shih-k'ai replaced Sun Yat-sen at the head of the Republic and the government was transferred to Peking. The abolition of the parliamentary institutions and the dictatorship of Yüan Shih-k'ai, which were to follow, were the inevitable result of the forces in play. The republican coalition which triumphed in South China and the Yangtze basin lacked in fact not only military support and finance, but also cohesion. It consisted of the provincial gentry, who belonged to the old ruling classes now in process of disappearing, of army officers converted to the new ideas, the republican intellectuals, and the constitutional monarchists who had decided to support the Republic. The already very extensive powers of Yüan Shih-k'ai grew even stronger as the months went by. On 22 March 1913 Sung Chia-jen, organizer of the Kuo-min-tang, the new nationalist, republican party, and a convinced defender of parliamentary institutions, was assassinated at Shanghai station. A few months later Huang Hsing and Sun Yat-sen were forced to return to Japan.

On 10 January 1914 Yüan Shih-k'ai dissolved the parliament. In May a constitution giving him practically full powers was proclaimed. On 1 January 1916 he re-established the monarchy for his own purposes. Obviously there was no question of a return to the old regime, for its institutions had disappeared for ever with the changes in Chinese society. Moreover regionalist tendencies and foreign pressure—mainly from Japan—were still as strong as ever, and this military dictatorship was just as weak and just as much threatened as the moribund dynasty of the years 1901–11. In July and August 1913 seven provincial governors of south and central China had rebelled against Yüan Shih-k'ai's efforts to extend his hold on the provinces. Supported by the little group of champions of parliamentary democracy disappointed by Yüan Shih-k'ai's authoritarian methods, this attempt at secession is known in the history books as the 'Second Revolution'. The men installed in the central provinces by Yüan Shih-k'ai when order was restored—Feng Kuo-chang at Nanking, Tuan Ch'i-jui at An-ch'ing (in Anhwei), Li Chun at Nan-ch'ang—were not slow to demonstrate in turn their own desire to be independent of their protector. Conditions tended all the more to favour a crumbling of authority in that Yüan Shih-k'ai was subject to pressure from Japan and, induced to yield to this pressure, *ipso facto* alienated a large part of public opinion. On the outbreak of the First World War Japan seized the railway lines, military bases, and territories which Germany had held until then in Shantung. In January 1915 the Japanese embassy in Peking presented Yüan Shih-k'ai with a list of twenty-one demands which aimed at making China into a Japanese protectorate. Yüan Shih-k'ai was obliged to recognize as a *fait accompli* the Japanese hold on Mongolia, Manchuria, and Shantung. He ceded to Japan the only Chinese industrial enterprise of any importance, the Han-yeh-p'ing Company, together with the blast furnaces of Han-yang and the iron- and coal-mines of Ta-yeh and P'ing-hsiang.

By the beginning of 1916, six months before his death, the dictator was beginning to encounter resistance from his minions. Tuan Ch'i-jui in North China and Feng Kuo-chang in Nanking were already looking like rivals. T'ang Chi-yao, governor of Yunnan, strengthened by Japanese support, proclaimed his independence, and soon eight provinces in the south and west seceded. It was the beginning of the period of the war-lords, during the course of which ten former officers of the northern armies, protégés of Yüan Shih-k'ai, became independent heads of armies.

The period of the war-lords

Internal policy and foreign presence

Like the moribund dynasty of 1901–11, Yüan Shih-k'ai and his successors of 1916–28 could only keep themselves in power by borrowing from consortiums of foreign banks. Control of the state's regular income (customs duties, duties on salt, profits from the post office) ensured that the banks would get their money back. But these loans could only be granted to the extent that the Chinese political authorities seemed to be reliable in the eyes of foreign nations. It was logical that they should refuse Sun Yat-sen's weak republican government the advances which they granted shortly afterwards to Yüan Shih-k'ai, who was regarded as the 'strong man' of China during the years 1912–16. The biggest loan had been granted in 1913 — £25 million sterling, with an initial deduction of £4 million and the repayment of nearly £68 million between 1913 and 1960. The consortium of German, British, French, Japanese, and Russian banks which advanced this sum of £21 million sterling was able in exchange to secure control of the revenue from salt and of capital deposited in Chinese banks. It was clearly out of the question that such loans should be granted to a political authority which had threatened, as the one headed by Sun Yat-sen in Canton from 1923 to 1925 was to attempt to do, to put an end to the exorbitant privileges acquired in China by foreign nations.

The end of the First World War was to resuscitate the rivalry between the nations which had divided up the old empire into spheres of influence and to favour the political breakup; hence the ascendancy of the men christened 'war-lords' by the Anglo-Saxon press — independent military governors with their own resources and their own armies – and hence also a complex game of alliances between war-lords and the formation of military cliques hostile to each other. These armies, swollen by peasants without any means of subsistence, resembled modern troops in their equipment (the Western nations were able to unload on China part of the stocks left unused at the end of the First World War) and in their means of transport (railways and steamships), but bands of brigands in their behaviour. Living on the countryside as they moved about, they resorted to pillage and to every kind of exaction. The political weapons of the war-lords were cunning and bargaining, with unexpected changes of external policy, and corruption – and sometimes terror – at home. During the whole period of the war-lords the internal situation of China grew continually worse. There was inflation, the growth of banditry, the disorganization of commerce, and a big increase in the planting of opium – a source of revenue for certain war-lords. The Chinese peasantry was sorely tried in some regions by exploitation, war, and pillage.

The political chess-board changed in accordance with the shifting combinations between the war-lords and their civil allies. Nor was the influence of the foreign powers negligible. In the years following the death of Yüan Shih-k'ai, Manchuria, the zone of Japanese influence, was the fief of Chang Tso-lin (1875–1928), head of the military clique of the Feng-t'ien (Liaoning). Tuan Ch'i-jui (1865–1936) and Hsü Shu-cheng (1880–1925) were dominant in central China and Fukien, again with the help of Japan, from whom Tuan Ch'i-jui obtained considerable assistance in 1918 (the Nishihara loans). This was the group known as the Anfu clique (Anhwei–Fukien). The Yangtze valley, the British zone, was held by the clique known as the Chih-li group (Ts'ao K'un, 1862–1938, and Wu P'ei-fu, 1872–1939). But Great Britain also kept an eye on South China, where the political situation could have an effect on the activities of Hong Kong. As for France, which had not abandoned its dream of penetrating the South-East, it supported T'ang Chi-yao (1882–1927), Japan's former client, in Yunnan.

In July 1920 the Anfu clique was defeated by the Feng-t'ien and Chih-li groups. In the winter of 1921–22 the Washington Conference, by calling a halt to Japanese expansion in East Asia, produced a new distribution of the political forces and an armed conflict between Chang Tso-lin, the representative of Japanese interests, and Wu P'ei-fu, the client of Great Britain. However, we cannot follow in detail these incessant changes in an extremely unstable situation, complicated by the rivalries between foreign nations and the pressure of their interests. The essential fact to grasp is the general relationship connecting Chinese political life in the first half of the twentieth century with the rivalries between foreign nations and the pressure of their economic, political, and military interests.

From the efforts of Sun Yat-sen
to the triumph of Chiang Kai-shek

It is clear that in these conditions the patriotic movements in the towns, the student demonstrations, the strikes by industrial workers and dockers, and the boycotts of foreign products could have no perceptible or lasting effects. For this reason the efforts of those who dreamed of saving China from chaos were doomed to failure, since these men were forced to seek abroad support which could not be disinterested and at home the always temporary alliance of the war-lords. This explains why the efforts of Sun Yat-sen came to nothing.

Obliged to go into exile again in Japan in August 1913, Sun Yat-sen returned to Shanghai during the summer of 1916, after the death of Yüan Shih-k'ai. In July of the following year, nursing the hope of winning over the military leaders of South China, he landed in Canton, but, soon disappointed, set out again in 1918 for Shanghai. On 4 May 1919 the schools, the intelligentsia and a large part of the bourgeoisie became extremely roused when they learnt of the terms of the Treaty of Versailles, which gave to Japan all the rights and territories acquired in China by Germany. At that time Japan seemed to the Western powers to be their best ally against the Bolshevik regime. This movement, which started at Peking university, spread to all the big cities. It was followed by a boycott of Japanese products and by strikes by the seamen, the railwaymen, the workers in the cotton mills and so on. In December 1920 Sun Yat-sen tried to take advantage of the events which had occurred two months earlier in South China, where a new military leader, Ch'en Chiung-ming (1875–1933) had succeeded in evicting from Canton the Kiangsi clique, which until then had been all-powerful there. Entering Canton in triumph, he was elected president of this local republic on 5 May 1921 and tried to inaugurate a regime in conformity with his democratic aspirations. But the hostility of Great Britain and the increasingly open conflict with Ch'en Chiung-ming forced him to leave his native province again; the redistribution of political forces that followed the Washington Conference worked against Sun Yat-sen. Back in Shanghai in June 1922, he awaited a new shift in the situation at Canton, and eventually returned there at the beginning of the following year. At that point he found a new ally abroad – the Soviet Union, which was interested in weakening the position of the Western nations in the Far East. In the summer of 1923 Sun Yat-sen's young brother-in-law, Chiang Chieh-shih (Chiang Kai-shek), a soldier trained in Japan, was sent to Moscow to spend a period of instruction with the Red Army. At the same time a Soviet mission (Borodine, a political adviser, and Galen, a military adviser) arrived in Canton. In January 1924 the Nationalist party (the Kuo-min-tang) was reorganized on the Soviet model and became a centralized, hierarchical, bureaucratic, omnipotent party called to extend its control over every part of the state and the army. In May 1924, with the help of Soviet advisers, the Military Academy of Huang-p'u (Whampoa) was created in the suburbs of Canton. It was to furnish the officer corps of a new army, which was gradually to develop and to be placed under the command of Chiang Kai-shek. In October 1924 an unexpected shift in the situation in Peking, where the 'Christian general' Feng Yü-hsiang (1880–1948) had succeeded in installing himself, encouraged Sun Yat-sen to seek once again an understanding with the new master of North China. Sun Yat-sen travelled to Peking to discuss an alliance and died there on 12 March 1925.

The Kuo-min-tang, which succeeded in maintaining its position at Canton thanks to the development of its army – which numbered 85,000 men and 6000 officers trained at the Huang-p'u Academy – finally attempted in July 1926 the expedition to the North (*pei-fa*) of which Sun Yat-sen had so often dreamed. In conjunction with large forces belonging to the war-lords (of the six armies commanded by Chiang Kai-shek, five consisted of reorganized troops of the war-lords; the sixth was formed of the new recruits of the Kuo-min-tang army), the expedition progressed without great difficulty towards the Yangtze valley, with some of the local armies joining it as it advanced. The whole of the lower Yangtze area was occupied in February–March 1927.

It was at this moment that Chiang Kai-shek took advantage of his place at the head of the armies to ensure himself a dominant position *vis-à-vis* the heterogeneous coalition of which the Nationalist government consisted. Sure of the support of the well-to-do Chinese business men of Shanghai, who were linked to foreign interests, he broke with the section of the Kuo-min-tang which had settled at Wu-han, on the middle Yangtze, and on 12 April 1927 crushed amid rivers of blood the popular insurrection which had broken out in Shanghai on the approach of the Kuo-min-tang armies. The foreign nations with interests in China could from then on be assured that there was no risk of revolution in China and were ready to support the new regime which Chiang Kai-shek established at Nanking on 18 April 1927.

The Nanking decennium

Chiang Kai-shek's success was partly due to his remarkable aptitude for profiting from circumstances, to a genius for tactics and bargaining which made him the equal of the most skilful war-lords. But the ultimate reasons for his victory were the weakness and disunity of his adversaries and the natural play of the economic and political forces on which China's fate in fact depended. By procuring through the criminal classes control of the Shanghai police and by crushing pitilessly the rebellion of the great Kiangsu metropolis, the real economic capital of China, Chiang Kai-shek had acquired at one blow the benevolent neutrality of the big foreign companies established in Shanghai and the sympathy of Chinese business circles, which were tired of the conflicts between war-lords and worried about the revolutionary tendencies which had begun to appear within the Kuo-min-tang. The new regime in Nanking soon acquired the support of most property-owners, insofar as it seemed capable of ensuring the order indispensable to the conduct of business. For its own part, the Nanking government was obliged to collaborate with the powers possessing important interests in China; it was forced into this position by its hostility to the revolutionaries and by the bonds which willy-nilly united the Chinese business class with the big foreign companies. Heir to the war-lords, whom it tried to win over or eliminate without entirely succeeding, it also owed much of its strength to the powerful centralized organization established by Soviet advisers during the years 1924–25. The one-party system ensured absolute control of the government, the civil service, the army, and the political police; and it enabled Chiang Kai-shek to keep firm hold of power. Foreign countries showed themselves ready to grant to this strong regime, which they had desired for so long, the means indispensable to its economic equilibrium. Between 1928 and 1931 Chiang Kai-shek's China was to win back some of the rights which the Manchu government had been forced to yield; the number of foreign concessions in the open ports was reduced and the receipts from the customs, the salt tax, and the post office reverted to the Nationalist government. The 'generalissimo' thus had at his disposal regular resources, of which the maritime customs formed nearly half.

Unification made rapid progress. By 1928 the Nationalist armies had occupied Peking, which was demoted from its status of capital and rechristened Pei-p'ing, while the master of the north-eastern provinces, Chang Hsüeh-liang, heir to his father Chang Tso-lin, joined Chiang Kai-shek. In 1930 Chiang Kai-shek had to reassert his authority, which was temporarily shaken in North China by a coalition led by the former war-lord of Shansi, Yen Hsi-shan, and by the 'Christian general', Feng Yü-hsiang.

Foundations and characteristics of the Nationalist regime

By the beginning of the Nanking period (1927–37) Chiang Kai-shek was thus the most powerful of the military leaders. He had the advantages

over his rivals of a solid political organization (a one-party system based
on the Soviet model), of a somewhat better financial foundation, which
he strove to consolidate by controlling banking circles, and of the
prestige lent to him by the official recognition of all foreign countries.
But for that very reason the Nanking regime differed from that of the
war-lords; it was much more closely tied than its predecessors had been
to the commercial middle class – which it was to exploit to its own advantage – and also much more open, of necessity, to Western influences.
Most of its officials and agents had been in contact with foreigners or
had been educated abroad. In spite of its own intentions, it was an
emanation of the Westernized middle classes of the open ports, and this
very fact explains why, in spite of its declared aim of encouraging
agriculture, it was to take practically no interest in the tragic fate of the
peasantry.

But the Nanking regime also owed its particular colouration to the circumstances of its time; it came into existence at the period when the
world was witnessing the upsurge of Italian Fascism, German National
Socialism, and Japanese militarism, while the parliamentary democracies
were hit by the great American economic depression, and the U.S.S.R.
was living under the bureaucratic police system directed by Stalin.
Violently hostile to revolutionary movements and a great admirer of
strong regimes, Chiang Kai-shek strove to imitate their methods of propaganda and to disseminate a 'Confucianism' modified to suit modern
taste. This was the 'New Life Movement' (*Hsin-sheng-huo yün-tung*), a
sort of moral order bound up with the cult of Confucius and the exaltation of the founder of the Chinese Republic. A political police, the 'Blue
Shirts', was entrusted with the task of hunting down liberals and revolutionaries.

Created by business men linked first to the imperial government and
later to Yüan Shih-k'ai's regime and to the governments dominated by
the war-lords, the Chinese banks had played a crucial part in financing
military expenditure. For that very reason they represented a sort of
relatively independent power which had acted in Chiang Kai-shek's
favour at the time of his *coup d'état*. At that time they were in a period of
rapid growth because of the drainage of capital from the interior to the
great economic centre of Shanghai, where bank deposits increased by 245
per cent between 1921 and 1932. The number of banks in the great
metropolis had risen from 20 in 1919 to 34 in 1923 and to 67 in 1927. It
was to reach the figure of 164 in 1937. But from the moment of its installation in Nanking the Kuo-min-tang insisted on closer and closer collaboration from the banking sector, granting it, in return for the support
required to guarantee the government's finances and make good its

deficit, big advantages and wider facilities for speculation. The result was a kind of state capitalism which enabled the Nationalist government to be sure of the support of business circles at all times and to control capitalists who showed signs of acting too independently. The regime's finances were soon dominated by a few families who owned big banks closely tied to the Nanking government. These families were the Sungs (T. V. Sung: Sung Tzu-wen, a Harvard graduate and Chiang Kai-shek's brother-in-law), the K'ungs (H. H. K'ung: K'ung Hsiang-hsi, descendant of a Shansi business family), and the Ch'ens (Ch'en Kuo-fu and his brother Ch'en Li-fu, men from the Kiangsu commercial middle class). In 1934–35 the Kuo-min-tang profited from numerous banking bankruptcies resulting from the massive purchases of silver made by the United States in the winter of 1933–34 to tighten its hold. Thanks to the nationalization of silver proclaimed on 3 November 1935, the Chinese dollar was stabilized, the banknotes issued by the Nationalist government were accepted everywhere and prices stopped rising. Four state banks dominated the money market at that time; their main function was to finance war expenses and the treasury deficit by issues of bonds with interest rates varying between 20 per cent and 40 per cent. The main beneficiaries were high officials in the government.

Even if they suffered by the regime, as was the case mainly with the new bourgeoisie that owned the banks and industrial enterprises, the propertied classes as a whole were satisfied with an order of things that did not question their privileges. In the countryside the Nanking government did not undertake any fundamental reform of the rent or tax system. The impoverished peasantry thus continued to be the victim of what, through a concatenation of causes and effects, might seem like a sort of inevitable curse. The excessive number of mouths to feed, the extremely small plots into which the land was divided (one and one-third hectares per family), its poor yield in spite of desperately hard work, and the burden of taxation ensured that the smallest inequality of wealth became the means of exploitation thanks to usury and rents. Everything helped to keep the majority of the population in abysmal poverty.

*The Japanese invasion of Manchuria and
the development of the Red Army*

The main objectives of Chiang Kai-shek were on the one hand the extension and maintenance of his control over the party and over the whole apparatus of the state—the army, the police, the finances—and on the other the foundation of a powerful military force for the new regime. Half the expenditure of the state was devoted to the equipment of the armies and to the struggle against the independent war-lords. However, other enemies soon appeared. These were the peasant unions, led by dissident Communists, which were formed south of the Yangtze and later on the rural soviets founded in the south of the province of Kiangsi, in the region of Jui-chin. From 1931 to 1934 Chiang Kai-shek was to direct a series of campaigns against the Soviet Republic of Jui-chin. The fifth and last campaign, which enjoyed the benefit of German advisers and foreign loans, made it possible to oust the Communists from the region.

During this period there occurred a crucial event in the history of contemporary China: the invasion and occupation of the north-eastern provinces by Japan in 1931–32. Completely taken up by the struggle against the 'Communist bandits', Chiang Kai-shek accepted the loss of these territories as inevitable; they had long been penetrated by Japanese capital and their war-lords had often had close links with Japan. Chang Hsüeh-liang's adhesion was in fact quite recent. But, above all, the Kuo-min-tang armies, which were in course of formation, could probably not have stood up to a direct confrontation with the well-trained and well-equipped troops of the invaders. A conflict would have been fatal to a regime which was only just beginning to consolidate its position. However, the occupation of these territories larger than France, with a population of nearly forty million, good ports, coal-mines and the densest railway network in the whole of East Asia, was bound to increase Japan's economic strength considerably. It gave her an excellent strategic base for her conquest of China and was to constrain the Nationalist government to temporize and withdraw before the advance of the Japanese invasion of North China.

Because of the threat that it caused to hang over Chiang Kai-shek's government and because of the effects that it was to have on Chinese political life, the invasion of Manchuria by the Japanese troops deserves to be regarded as the most important event in this period of Chinese history.

Led by the very logic of things to confirm its choice of a reactionary attitude, the Nationalist regime, by its attacks on liberals and revolutionaries, was to favour the success of the most radical tendencies. For it is noteworthy that the free play of the most diverse political and intellectual ideas, which had characterized the anarchic period of the war-lords, was succeeded from 1928 onwards by a period in which the predominance of the Communists in the political opposition and that of Marxism in intellectual life became more and more marked. The temporizing tactics adopted by the Nationalist government in face of the Japanese invasion, and, the patriotic struggle of the Red Army and the peasant militias, was finally to win over to the Communists a larger and larger majority of its opponents.

The final success of the Communists has led people to attribute to

Plate 74.   Mao Tse-tung in the 1930s

Plate 75.   Chou En-lai, in Paris, 1920, the year he
  joined the Chinese Communist Party in exile

Plate 76.   Lu Hsun in Shanghai, 1930, the year he founded the
League of Left-Wing Writers

Plate 77.   Chang Kai-shek, in London, 1942

them retrospectively an importance which they were far from possessing at the time of the party's foundation and during the Canton period, in 1923-26. A small political group founded in 1921 by a few intellectuals concerned to organize and develop working-class action in the open ports, the Communist party would never have triumphed if it had remained faithful to the norms imposed on it by its Soviet advisers and to the distant directives of Moscow, which knew absolutely nothing about the facts of life in China. This first period was dominated by *a priori* concepts and by the fixed idea that there was only one path that could lead to the revolution – the path that Russia had taken. Absolute faith in the revolutionary vocation of the proletariat and profound mistrust of the peasantry were the basis of Communist orthodoxy. Hence the need for a provisional alliance of the Communist party with the Nationalist bourgeoisie of the Kuo-min-tang until the bitter fruits of industrial capitalism ripened in China. This policy had led quite naturally to the crushing of the Communist party and to the massacre of the working-class leaders. It was in infringement of Soviet directives and in contradiction with received orthodoxy that a peasant revolutionary movement was to develop in the rural areas. Instead of the sudden urban rising, in conformity with an old Western tradition, which had secured all the levers of power for the October Revolution, what occurred in China was the long investment of the towns by the countryside.

The principal heads of the peasant unions and of the rural soviets which were formed from 1927 onwards differed little in origin and training from the first leaders of the Chinese Communist party. Ch'en Tu-hsiu (1879-1942), had studied in Japan and France; Li Ta-chao (1888-1927) had been educated first at a military academy run by the northern armies and later in Japan; Chou En-lai (1898?-1976), the son of a minor civil servant, had lived in Japan, France, and Germany; and Chu Te (1886-1976) had been a student in Göttingen and Berlin. The only one who had never left China was Mao Tse-tung (1893-1976), who came from a family of well-to-do peasants in the neighbourhood of Ch'angsha, in Hunan, and had lived throughout his youth in his native province. But, far from the artificial atmosphere of the big cities permeated by Western influences, the Communist movement was to link up with the most authentic revolutionary traditions of the Chinese world. Theory was replaced by practice, and reasoning by an intuitive understanding of the close links between the system of exploitation of the countryside and the political ascendancy of the bourgeoisie of the open ports, an ascendancy which was itself indissociable from the hold exerted by foreign capital. To break this vicious circle it was therefore necessary to ensure the triumph over the urban world of the rural world, the victim of the double pressure of foreign capital and the Chinese bourgeoisie. To arrive at this goal, firm direction and indomitable energy were required, whatever the tactical necessities imposed by circumstances might be; for example, the accent was put on social justice during the years of confrontation (1927–37) with the Nationalist regime, then afterwards on the patriotic struggle against the Japanese invader. The men most suited to leadership had gradually to be formed in the course of the fight. Instruction and indoctrination had to go on tirelessly. Hence – thanks to a typically Chinese aversion for abstractions and theories – the essentially practical character of Communist thinking in China and its apparent weakness in the eyes of Westerners.

<h2 style="text-align:center">From the Japanese invasion
to the advent of the People's Republic</h2>

The launching of the big Japanese invasion from the north-eastern provinces in July 1937 and the bombing without warning of Shanghai in August marked the opening of the last period – the decline of the Nationalist regime and the upsurge of the resistance to Japan.

The Chungking period

The Kuo-min-tang government withdrew to Hankow at the end of 1937, and then from Hankow to Chungking, in distant Szechwan, beyond the Yangtze gorges, while the Japanese armies occupied all the provinces to the east and north of the Yellow River, the whole of the Yangtze valley up to Lake Tung-t'ing and all the big towns to the east of a line running from Ch'eng-chou to Canton. The invasion and the campaigns that followed it caused panic and exoduses. Between the end of 1938 and the middle of 1939 the population of Chungking, an old provincial city which became the constant target of the Japanese air force, rose from 200,000 to over a million. For the regime the break was a brutal one; it was suddenly deprived of its main sources of revenue, the customs duties and taxes levied in the regions now occupied by Japan. It was cut off from the great economic metropolis of Shanghai, and from the banking and international circles which constituted its political base and its clientele. This withdrawal into the interior of China was to have very important effects on its evolution. Its only resources were the capital repatriated by the Chinese banks and the aid – at first limited – which foreign countries gave it. The main countries involved were – above all – the Soviet Union, which was to ignore the peasant Communists until their final victory (its aid amounted to 250 million American dollars between 1937 and 1939), the United States, Great Britain, and France. However, the Japanese attack on Pearl Harbour, on 7 December 1941, was to ensure it substantial support from the United States from that time onwards. Doubtless the American aid of more than two billion dollars which the Nationalist government received during the Second World War – to which must be added two billion more in the years 1945–49 – was relatively little in comparison with the fifty billion granted by the United States to the total of nations at war with Germany and her allies, but this quantity of money represented an enormous contribution to an economy as poverty-stricken as that of Nationalist China in the Chungking days. And, while ensuring the survival of the regime, it was to have profoundly corrupting effects on it.

The system displayed its parasitical nature in the development of a huge bureaucracy and an overblown army whose personnel was to rise at one point to five million men. It abandoned itself to the facile solutions of inflation, with the consequence that prices rose more and more rapidly and the Chinese dollar fell in value at an accelerated pace. By 1944 the dollar was worth five hundred times less than on the eve of the Japanese invasion. This monetary collapse, together with the external aid and a bigger American presence than ever, with its bases, its aircraft, its depots, its means of transport, and its radio stations, favoured speculation, the use of influence for private ends, and corruption. Some of the former privileged classes, the lowly officials of the regime, teachers – in a word, all those not enabled by their position to enrich themselves by illicit means – lived in poverty and felt more and more disaffected to the regime.

This disaffection was strengthened by the scant success of the military operations and Chiang Kai-shek's persistent hostility to the Communist partisans fighting the invader. Reduced by the campaigns of encirclement of 1931–34, the soldiers and leaders of the Chinese Soviet Republic of Kiangsi had withdrawn towards the west in October 1934 and had reached northern Shensi across the chains of mountains of western Szechwan. Pursued by the Nationalist armies, forced to find their way through the most inhospitable regions, those who undertook this 'Long March' (*ch'ang-cheng*) of 12,000 kilometres – the great epic of Chinese Communism – were nearly 100,000 when they set out; only seven or eight thousand reached their destination. Those who had escaped very soon made Yenan the centre of a new soviet base, organizing the struggle against the Japanese and continually recruiting new supporters from the peasantry. Forced in 1936 to combine his efforts with those of the Communists, two years later Chiang Kai-shek launched a big offensive

Plate 78.   Supply convoy en route to the forces encircling the
Soviet Republic of Jui-chin in Kiangsi (1931–4)

Plate 79.   Troops of the People's Liberation Army on the northern front, 1948

against the revolutionary bases in the north-west, and it was only with reluctance and reticence that he accepted the principle of the common front under pressure from the United States during the course of the Second World War.

The civil war of 1946–1949

However, the capitulation of Japan in August 1945 suddenly changed the whole basis of the problem and seemed to give new life to Chiang Kai-shek's regime. The reconquest of a considerable part of the territories evacuated by the Japanese armies, the return to Nanking, the official recognition of Nationalist China as one of the victors in the Second World War, invited to participate in international conferences, produced a moment of euphoria. It remained only for the regime, which possessed the support of all countries and large armies very well equipped by the United States, to rid itself once and for all of the 'Communist bandits'. So began in 1946 one of the biggest civil wars in contemporary history.

The two opposing sides were radically different from each other. Big armies of the classical kind which lived on the country like parasites, pillaging the countryside and holding it to ransom, were confronted by the three times smaller peasant militias, who mingled with the anonymous rural masses, waging a war of attrition, raids, and localized operations. The defeat of Japan had been relatively less favourable to them than to the Kuo-min-tang armies, which had extensive transport facilities at their disposal. Even in the north-east, where the Communists had obtained a strong foothold during the clandestine struggle against the Japanese occupying forces, the Nationalist troops had been able to seize control of the main centres at the time when the Soviet armies were withdrawing, after dismantling and sending westward piece by piece the factories of this industrial area. However, the advantages enjoyed by the Nationalists were more apparent than real; their lines of communication were too extended and their armies held only the towns. The regime had not cured itself of its vices. As the fighting went on and the tactical superiority of the partisans – popular in the countryside thanks to their policy of redistributing the land – became clear, it grew more and more demoralized. Thus when the Red armies won their first big victories, almost the whole of public opinion swung over to them. In the middle of 1947 the Red Army took the offensive in the north-east, isolating the Kuo-min-tang forces. In 1948 it captured Loyang and K'ai-feng in Honan, and then Tsinan in Shantung. It then went over to the last phase in its offensive – the deployment of large units, all of whose equipment had been captured in the fighting and part of whose personnel consisted of deserters who had come over from the enemy with weapons and baggage. During the offensive of September–October 1948 the whole of the north-east was conquered and the Nationalists lost 400,000 men, including some of their best troops. The decisive battle took place during the winter of 1948–49, in the area of Hsü-chou (northern Kiangsu). Five hundred and fifty thousand men of the Nationalist armies were put out of action. The Communist troops, who had already entered Peking and Tientsin, were in Shanghai in May, in Canton in October, and in Chungking in November. While the Nationalist government sought refuge in Taiwan, the People's Republic of China was proclaimed on 1 October 1949.

It has been said that national feeling was the great motive force of the history of contemporary China. The truth is that this pronouncement is only true of the last period, that of the struggle against the occupying power; Chinese patriotism remained an impotent aspiration, embodied above all in the young people of the schools and in the intelligentsia, so long as it was deprived of the only means by which it could be expressed – a people's army, independent of foreign interests. The alliance of the peasants and of the soldiers of the Red Army was forged during the course of the struggle against the Japanese invaders, in the territories occupied by Japan. Hence its strength, its success, and the very wide sympathy which the liberation movement encountered. There was a gulf between the political agitation of the first thirty years of the twentieth century and the organization of the peasant soviets of Kiangsu and of the Yenan period – the gulf that separated the dream from reality, and the disarray of intellectuals in search of theories of salvation amid the jumble of imported ideas from the assurance of fighters who had made contact again with the vast rural population, while retaining control of the situation.

Chapter 31

Philosophical and Literary Developments

While in the nineteenth century Western influences had acted in a diffused way, stimulating a sort of Confucian reform and an orthodox reaction, in the first half of the twentieth century the whole history of ideas was dominated by Western contributions. But we must not get the wrong idea about the significance of this phenomenon. This massive intrusion of traditions profoundly alien to those of China was only one aspect of the takeover of the Chinese world. Moreover, it is inseparable from the context of humiliation and disarray which characterized this whole period. The Chinese intelligentsia was the victim of an inferiority complex fed by all the insults inflicted on China—the Treaty of Shimonoseki, the occupation of the 'leased territories', the Boxer protocol, loans secured on the only regular resources of China, the concession of railway lines to foreigners, the granting to Japan of the former German possessions in Shantung by the Paris Peace Conference, the volleys fired by the Concession police on 30 May 1925 in Shanghai (13 dead) and on 23 June of the same year in Canton (52 dead), the occupation of the north-eastern provinces by Japan, and so on; not to speak of the daily humiliations endured by the Chinese in China itself and abroad. The intellectual life of this period was closely bound up with political history.

The intrusion of Western ideas, already perceptible in the field of philosophy at the beginning of the twentieth century, was aggravated by the disappearance of the literati of the old regime and the development of an intelligentsia educated in Japan, in the United States and Europe, and in China itself, in schools and institutions where the teachers were foreigners. More or less converted to the Western mode of life, living in the open ports where a prosperity maintained by the foreign presence reigned, numerous Chinese intellectuals, and with them the young people in the schools, came to think that the salvation of China lay in the total rejection of all her traditions and in the systematic imitation of the West. Hence a feverish thirst for knowledge and a wild ferment of ideas and theories. What arrived from the West, in bulk, as circumstances dictated and in the greatest confusion, was welcomed with enthusiasm. But one cannot absorb a whole intellectual heritage in a few decades; there was certainly rootlessness and infatuation with foreign fashions in China, but the final conclusion must be that the Chinese did their reading through the prism of autochthonous traditions. There was probably hardly any borrowing that could not be regarded as an extension of genuinely Chinese thinking.

Three periods, corresponding to three stages in political history, can be discerned in the intellectual history of the first half of the twentieth century. The first, from about 1900 to the disappearance of the old regime, was characterized by an attempt at adaptation which reflected the more or less radical reformist tendencies which enjoyed their greatest success at that time. The most famous intellectuals of that period still belonged to the old literati who were in process of disappearing. The second period, on the contrary, was one of total disarray and of a tidal wave of Western influences in the China of the open ports. This astonishing intellectual effervescence was gradually to die down during the last period, which corresponded to the dictatorship of Chiang Kai-shek: romantic individualism and blind imitation of the bourgeois West were to give way before the slow but sure progress of Marxism. Art and literature were to pass into the service of the Revolution.

The influence of Japan and the discovery of evolutionary philosophy

Tendencies to syncretism characterized the political, philosophical, and literary movement of the first ten years of the twentieth century. It was the period which witnessed the triumph of a more or less radical reformism whose supporters and interpreters still belonged to a class that was disappearing—the literati of the old regime. Unable to understand that since Shimonoseki, since the division of China into spheres of influence and since the Boxer affair the tragic fate of China was finally sealed, the best minds thought that the Japanese path—the path of compromise between tradition and modernization—was still possible. This illusion no doubt sprang from the fact that the political institutions had not yet crumbled. There was still an inland China. To the reformers of every hue and of every origin, Japan, a country close to China both geographically and culturally, then seemed like a model in every field—education, army, institutions, public morality. The Japanese influence was reinforced by the large number of Chinese students who went to Japan to complete their education in the universities, technical schools, and military academies (their number is estimated to have been 15,000 in 1906); by the welcome received by the political *émigrés* from various different Japanese associations and from the Meiji government—as early as 1898 the *Tôa dô bunkai,* the 'Cultural Association of East Asia', had been created to further Japanese influence in the Far East; and by the enhanced prestige of Japan after her victory over the Russian army and fleet in 1905. It was usually through Japanese translations that Chinese students made contact at that time with the literary and philosophical works of the West.

The republican revolutionaries and conspirators, who also found encouragement in Japan, represented only a marginal minority, a clandestine current. On the contrary it was the reformers, the advocates of a constitutional monarchy of the Japanese type, who had then the biggest audience among the intellectuals and the young. Their spokesman was Liang Ch'i-ch'ao, who revealed himself as a talented pamphleteer. A refugee in Japan since the failure of the 'Hundred Days of Reform' in 1898, he was tirelessly active there, seeking by his articles in the press, his pamphlets, his books, to galvanize his compatriots, analysing the causes of China's decline, assimilating and adapting to the Chinese tradition the new ideas of his time—evolutionism, liberalism, the spirit of enterprise, the worship of science, and so on. In his view it was a matter of forging a new sort of man, for the evil came from the fact that people had grown accustomed to humiliations. Mildness, submission, the spirit of tolerance, the traditional morality bound up with a type of civilization and a political system that had disappeared and had been overtaken by events had to be replaced by the spirit of competition, of struggle, by nationalism and intransigence—in short, all the qualities displayed by the Western nations and by Japan.

We also find this insistence on the need for a transformation in depth of the public ethos in a contemporary of Liang Ch'i-ch'ao's, Yen Fu (1853–1921), a Fukienese who, after receiving a classical education, had studied at the school attached to the Foochow Arsenal, where he had learnt English and acquired a technical and scientific background. During a period of training in Great Britain, with the Royal Navy, Yen Fu had discovered the works of Darwin and Spencer. He had also interested himself in British law and administration. On his return to China in the closing years of the nineteenth century he was to become one of the first translators of the English evolutionary philosophers. His translation of *Evolution and Ethics* (*T'ien-yen-lun*) by T. H. Huxley in 1898 had gained him sudden fame and had been followed by a whole series of other translations between 1900 and 1910 — *The Study of Sociology* (*Ch'ün-hsüeh ssu-yen*), by H. Spencer, *The Wealth of Nations* (*Yüan-fu*), by Adam Smith, *On Liberty* (*Ch'ün-chi-ch'üan chieh-lun*), by John Stuart Mill, and *L'Esprit des lois* (*Fa-i*), by Montesquieu.

Written in the classical language and in a refined style, full of literary and sometimes obscure allusions, Yen Fu's translations were accompanied by personal commentaries. They had considerable influence, inculcating the idea that natural selection and the struggle to live were laws which applied not only to the animal kingdom but also to nations. This interest of Yen Fu and his contemporaries in Darwinian evolution and Anglo-Saxon sociology had in fact a political motive behind it; these ideas formed a justification for the dissemination of a new ethos inspired by the West: individualism, liberty, and democracy had gradually to penetrate into Chinese manners and institutions.

It was not a question of copying the West, but of using it as an inspiration, and this intention was perceptible in the very form, which remained traditional. Yen Fu's translations were written in classical Chinese and interspersed with personal reflections. The first translations of Western literary works were also in the classical language and were really adaptations rather than translations properly so-called. They were the work of a contemporary of Yen Fu's, another Fukienese by the name of Lin Shu (1852–1924). Suddenly attaining celebrity in the last few years of the nineteenth century, thanks to a translation of Alexandre Dumas's *Dame aux camélias,* Lin Shu, who did not know any foreign language, was to adapt very freely, on the basis of translations made to him orally, more than one hundred and sixty Western novels by authors as different as Walter Scott, Defoe, Dickens, Cervantes, Ibsen, and Victor Hugo.

This combination of a fresh content with traditional forms, which is characteristic of the work of the two principal translators of the early years of the twentieth century, recurs in Chinese literature proper. More than a thousand novels appeared between 1900 and 1910. All of them were in sympathy with the reform movement, were inspired by national preoccupations, and aimed at political and social criticism. But they remained faithful to the great models of the Chinese novel of the eighteenth and nineteenth centuries through their division into episodes, the multiplicity of the characters, and their realism. The most famous are those of the great scholar Liu E (1857–1909) — the *Lao-ts'an yu-chi* (*Account of Master Ts'an's Journey*) (1902) — of Wu Wo-yao (Wu Chien-jen) (1866–10), who wrote more than thirty novels in the years

1900-10, and of Li Pao-chia (Li Po-yüan) (1867-1906), the author of the famous *Kuan-ch'ang hsien-hsing-chi,* which takes as its target the circles of corrupt officials of that time.

The Western invasion

The political and intellectual climate changed from 1915-17 onwards, and it was then that the first signs began to appear of the great period of moral confusion, intellectual ferment, and invasion by Western fashions and ideas. The phenomenon was to reach its climax from 1919 onwards. The causes of this change in intellectual life were no doubt many, and we must certainly give due weight to the after-effects of the disappearance of the dynasty and the old lettered classes, to the demonstrations of Japanese imperialism (the occupation of the Shantung territories, the twenty-one demands, the progress of Japan's economic hold on China), to the disappointments caused by the parodies of parliamentary democracy and the dictatorship of Yüan Shih-k'ai, who tried a restoration and sought to revive the cult of Confucius, and to the growth in the number of students educated abroad, especially in the Western countries. But it seems as if there was above all a deep break between the generations at this time. The movement was launched and led by the young people in the schools and by the students who had returned from abroad.

The ever more numerous Chinese who had studied in Japan, Europe, or the United States experienced a deep feeling of shame with regard to their own country and its traditions. In the state of decline into which China had fallen, traditional manners and customs, the literature and arts of the literati — all that remained of the old China — seemed to them like an odious caricature. Any compromise with the past had become impossible; it was necessary to break once for all with all the old Chinese traditions and, in order to lift China out of its state of prostration, to awaken people's consciences and reach the widest possible public.

The first activities of this radical movement, which was to attract the young people in the schools and the new, more or less Westernized intelligentsia of the open ports — the interior of China was hardly involved because of its poverty and isolation — were the foundation of reviews and literary societies. The oldest and most important review was founded at Shanghai in 1915 by Ch'en Tu-hsiu (1880-1942), a man who had held a scholarship in Japan and was to become in 1921 one of the founders of the Chinese Communist party. It bore the significant name of *Hsin-ch'ing-nien* and the French sub-title of *La Nouvelle Jeunesse.* Ch'en Tu-hsiu's first article was an 'Appeal to Youth' that resounded like a declaration of war on the moral traditions of China, which were systematically compared with the dynamism and spirit of enterprise of the West. Two years later there appeared the 'Suggestions for a Literary Reform' of a young Chinese educated in the United States, one Hu Shih (1891–1962). The article aimed at a radical reform of literary usages and advocated the abandonment of the classical language in fields where its use was traditional, the abolition of clichés and literary allusions, and the use of simple, direct language inspired by the spoken tongue (*pai-hua*). From this time onwards use of the *pai-hua* was to make very rapid progress. Ch'en Tu-hsiu for his part prayed for the development of a revolutionary, living, realistic literature.

The movement of 4 May 1919, launched by the students of Peking when it was announced that the former German possessions in China had been granted to Japan, gave a decisive impulse to the development of the most radical political and literary tendencies. Followed as it was by other demonstrations, by strikes and by boycotts which bore witness to the resentment caused by this fresh infringement of the rights of China, which had entered the war against Germany in 1917, the initiative taken by the Peking students marked the beginning of a period of political agitation aggravated by the repressive measures taken by the governments of the war-lords. Political and literary clubs multiplied, as did more or less ephemeral reviews. Western influences grew more and more perceptible. Translations became more numerous; there were controversies between the holders of opposing philosophical views; and a new kind of novel, based on European models, made its appearance and developed.

This intellectual ferment was in its depths much more turbid and complex than a superficial view of it might lead us to suppose; it cannot be summed up as a sudden patriotic reaction inspired by Western ideas (science, democracy, individualism, nationalism). Arising out of the take-over of the Chinese world, it reflected the rootlessness and maladjustment of a youth and an intelligentsia which felt very deeply the contradictions of which they were themselves the victims.

Quite as much as a desire for action, it was the attempt to escape from a situation without any outlet, it was despair, withdrawal into self, and a morbid romanticism which expressed themselves in philosophical debate and literary works. The diversity of temperaments and educational backgrounds involved—some consisting of ideas inherited from the Chinese tradition, others formed by foreign influences—explain the individual variations and the multiplicity of schools and tendencies.

The very conditions in which this invasion of Western fashions and ideas took place explain why, once the fever had subsided, no very profound traces were to remain. Many of the intellectual currents of the period 1917–28 were conspicuous for their ephemeral and artificial character. Their success was very often due to certain connections between Chinese and Western traditions. For example, it can be granted that there are certain affinities between the philosophy of Bergson and the 'intuitionism' of Wang Yang-ming, between the Anglo-Saxon theory of art for art's sake and certain attitudes typical of the Chinese literati, between Taoism and Darwinism; and these affinities were underlined by the writers themselves.

As in the first few years of the twentieth century, Anglo-Saxon influences predominated because of the British foothold in China and because of the large number of students educated in the United States. Hu Shih introduced the pragmatist philosophy of his teacher John Dewey (1859–1952), who was himself invited to China in 1919–21. The English neo-realist and logician Bertrand Russell also stayed in China in 1920–21. French and German influences were less noticeable. Ts'ai Yüan-p'ei (1868–1940), who had studied in Berlin and Leipzig, and in 1917 reformed Peking University, translated F. Paulsen's *System der Ethik* and wrote a *History of Chinese Ethics* (*Chung-kuo lun-li hsüeh-shih*) (1917). His efforts reinforced those of the scholar and historian Wang Kuo-wei, who at the beginning of the century had been one of the first to introduce Chinese readers to Nietzsche's and Schopenhauer's 'philosophy of will', with his *Essays on Ching-an* (*Ching-an wen-chi*) (1905). It should be noted that there was also an anarchist current of thought, which linked up with the egalitarian concepts of the secret societies. It had revealed itself at a very early stage among the Chinese students in Paris with the creation of a review, *Le Siècle nouveau* (*Hsin shih-chi*) (1907–8), one of the founders of which was a student of biology at Montpellier, Li Shih-tseng, born in 1882, the translator of Kropotkin. The writer Pa-chin, who came to Paris in 1922, was to be converted himself as a young man to the anarchist movement, adopting as his *nom de plume* the first and last syllables of the names of his favourite writers, Bakunin and Kropotkin.

The unanimity which had marked the start of the movement of 4 May 1919 was succeeded by a period of passionate discussions. Moralists and advocates of a purely scientific conception of society clashed. Criticisms of the mercantile, mechanical civilization of the West made themselves heard as a result of the disrepute into which Europe fell after the First World War. The first ones were formulated by Liang Ch'i-ch'ao after returning from Europe in 1919. They were taken up and carried further by Liang Shu-ming, born in 1893, in a comparative study of the civilizations of the East and the West and of their philosophies (*Tung-hsi wen-hua chi ch'i che-hsüeh*), in which the author sees in the Chinese tradition of the adaptation of desires to economic and social necessities a superior form of humanism, as compared with the exacerbation of desires which, according to him, characterizes Western civilization, and as compared with the opposite excess which he considers typical of Indian civilization, whose traditions, he says, aim at the annihilation of self and at the elimination of desires. However, these intellectual controversies soon gave way to a more fundamental opposition between revolutionaries and pure academics. By 1928 Hu Shih, whose influence had been so preponderant since 1917, had lost most of his audience. His place was taken by Kuo Mo-jo (born in 1892), one of the first converts to Marxism.

A parallel process of evolution occurred in the field of literature, which was also marked in the years 1917–28 by a proliferation of the most diverse tendencies. The greatest novelist of the period was Lu Hsün (1881–1936), critic, controversialist and translator of Gogol, Plekhanov, Lunacharsky and Jules Verne, as well as of Japanese, Polish, Hungarian, and other writers. But there were also other writers of merit; for example, Yeh Sheng-t'ao (born in 1892), Yü Ta-fu (1896–1945), Mao-tun (born in 1896), Pa-chin (born in 1904), and the woman novelist Ting-ling (born in 1907). The sombre and often melodramatic works of these writers express rebellion or despair.

The development of Marxism

The discovery which related the oppression suffered by China, a half-colonized country, to the capitalist system that had generated imperialism, took place in the years 1919–20. It was the work of a small group of intellectuals led by Ch'en Tu-hsiu and Li Ta-chao (1888–1927). The key to the special history of the Chinese world since the first attacks of the Opium War was provided by a general interpretation of the history of humanity. The characteristics of the capitalist, imperialist countries—the cult of the individual, religious intolerance, the pursuit of profit for its own sake, free enterprise—were suddenly put in a fresh light, together with the reasons for their conflict with the underlying tendencies of the Chinese world. Numerous affinities probably explain the attraction very quickly exerted in China by Marxism. In its negation of any transcendental reality it seemed to link up with one of the constants in Chinese thinking. The theory of the five stages, which, through the workings of a socio-economic dialectic, lead humanity from primitive communism to the socialism of the future, recalled the eschatological visions of the 'great harmony' (*ta-t'ung*) of the school of Kung-yang, given lustre by K'ang Yu-wei, whose epoch was not so far in the past. It also called to mind certain historical concepts of the seventeenth-century Chinese philosophers, whose influence had never ceased to make itself felt. The abolition of private property, put into practice by the T'ai P'ing in the middle of the nineteenth century, corresponded to one of the deepest aspirations of the Chinese revolutionary tradition and linked up with certain older 'statist' traditions. Marxism thus seems to be in harmony with certain tendencies of Chinese thought. For its part, communism indicated a possibility of action and furnished the model for a revolutionary organization similar to that of the secret societies of China. The Soviet Union's help seemed to confirm these hopes.

The fact remains that in China communism had to adapt itself to very special conditions—those of a huge rural country, deprived of its economic independence and the victim of terrible exploitation, those of a semi-colonized China where the industrial proletariat was too weak and too wretched to play any decisive role; and those of an armed conflict which was to go on continuously from 1927 until the final victory of 1949—against the Nationalist armies before and after the Japanese invasion, and against the forces of the occupying power. If Chinese communism looks primarily peasant, military, and patriotic, it is thanks to these special conditions.

Right at the start it was necessary to sacrifice the first devotees of the new faith—the men who, convinced of the possibility of action by the workers in the open ports, came up against the coalition of Chinese bourgeoisie and foreign capital and who, on orders from Moscow, had to accept willy-nilly an alliance with their natural enemies. Two years after the execution of Li Ta-chao in 1927 by the war-lord government of Peking, Ch'en Tu-hsiu, already held responsible for the policy imposed on him against his will by the Kremlin, was to be expelled from the party. The urban intellectuals had to make way for the obscure fighters of the rural areas, and daily practice had to be substituted for the theories of orthodox doctrine.

Everything was to favour the Communists from the advent of Chiang Kai-shek onwards—the Kuo-min-tang police's persecution of the liberals, the inertia of the Nationalist government in face of the Japanese invasion, the struggle against the resistance movement embodied by the Communists, and the ever more swiftly advancing corruption and decrepitude of Chiang Kai-shek's regime. As the years went by, more and more Chinese intellectuals were converted to Marxism. Marxist publications multiplied between 1935 and 1945; the authors most in demand were Marx, Engels, Lenin, and Bukharin. Literature shed the influences of the 'bourgeois' West: introspection, doubt, and the romantic exaltation of the individual were no longer fashionable. It tended to become a weapon in the service of the revolution and was encouraged to take this path by suggestions from Yenan. For example, in 1942 Mao Tse-tung defined the revolutionary functions of literary and artistic creation and proposed that writers should draw their inspiration, when the opportunity arose, from those aspects of the ancient Chinese traditions which could be adapted to the needs of the present struggle.

Historical sciences and exact sciences

It is noteworthy that in spite of the tragedies of the age and in spite of the extremely precarious conditions of life Chinese scholars and scientists pursued their researches and their efforts to develop scientific education in China. The vivifying contacts between Chinese and Western traditions and the links established with European and American scientists played some part in the surprising resistance offered by disinterested learning in the midst of chaos and destitution, but it was above all to the patriotism of her scientists and scholars that China was indebted for the preservation of her scientific traditions.

In the field of the historical (history, epigraphy, archaeology) and philological sciences, in which China had shown herself to be particularly advanced and had possessed a solid scientific tradition since the seventeenth and eighteenth centuries, some important discoveries were to give a new impulse to research. These discoveries were the disclosure, from 1899 onwards, of the inscriptions on bone and tortoise-shells dating from the end of the second millennium B.C.; the excavations from 1927 onwards at An-yang in Honan on the site of the last capital of the Yin (or Shang) (fourteenth to eleventh centuries B.C.); the discovery in 1900 of the rich hoard of paper manuscripts of the fifth to tenth centuries A.D. near Tun-huang in western Kansu; the bringing to light from 1906 onwards of the notes on wood and bamboo of the Han age in the regions of Tun-huang and of Chü-yen in western Mongolia (first century B.C. and first century A.D.); and the opening of the Ming and Ch'ing archives (fifteenth to nineteenth centuries) in the Imperial Palace at Peking. All these discoveries, which were to be followed by many others after 1950, contained enough material to modify radically all historical views about the most distant past of the Chinese world, about epigraphy and archaeology, and the history of literature, religion, and art.

The scholars who collaborated in working on these new documents and who strove to find in the extremely rich heritage of Chinese civilization certain neglected traditions which presented analogies with Western traditions (popular literature, the theatre, sophistics, logic, Buddhist metaphysics, etc.) came from every circle of society and belonged to

every political persuasion, but the most eminent among them were connected with the Chekiang school, the heir to the school of critical studies
(*k'ao-cheng-hsüeh*) of the eighteenth century. Round about 1900 this
school was represented by Yü Yüeh (1821–1907), a historian, man of letters, and specialist in the Chinese philosophers of the fourth and third
centuries B.C., whose fame had spread as far as Japan, and by Sun I-jang
(1848–1908), one of the first specialists in the inscriptions of the end of
the second millennium, a bibliographer in search of Chinese works
preserved in Japan, editor of the work of the philosopher Mo-tzu and
promoter of modern schools in Chekiang. The last and most famous
representative of the school of critical studies in the first half of the twentieth century was Chang Ping-lin (1869–1936). A native of Hangchow,
the friend and associate of Sun Yat-sen and Huang Hsing – the three of
them were regarded as the 'Three Patriarchs of the Revolution' (*Ko-ming
san-tsun*) – he had been the disciple of Yü Yüeh. Briefly attracted by the
reforming ideas of K'ang Yu-wei, he soon moved over to the anti-
monarchist opposition at the time of his stay in Japan, where he arrived
in 1899 and where he made the acquaintance of Sun Yat-sen.

Lo Chen-yü (1866–1940) and Wang Kuo-wei (1877–1927) can be linked
with the same Chekiang school. Preoccupied as a young man with questions of agronomy, which he regarded as fundamental, Lo Chen-yü had
created in Shanghai, after Shimonoseki, an Association for the Study of
the Civilizations of East Asia (*Tong-wen hsüeh-she*), which had practical
aims and to which he had invited Japanese professors. After becoming
Director of the Institute of Agronomy at Peking in 1909, he left China at
the time of the 1911 Revolution and took refuge in Japan from 1912 to
1919. Tutor to the former emperor Hsüan-t'ung, the young P'u-i, at
Tientsin from 1925 to 1929, Lo Chen-yü was to accept official posts in
the new state of Manchuria created by the Japanese. He was one of the
pioneers in the study of the Tun-huang manuscripts, of the inscriptions
on bone and shells, and of the archives of the Imperial Palace. Another
convinced monarchist, Wang Kuo-wei, had entered the *Tung-wen hsüeh-
she* at Shanghai in 1898 and had there learnt Japanese and English. After
studying physics in Japan in 1902, he had taught philosophy in the
teachers' training colleges of Nan-t'ung and Soochow in Kiangsu,
discovering during this period of his life the German philosophers – Kant, Schopenhauer, and Nietzsche. Much affected by the
fall of the dynasty in 1911, he took refuge in Japan, like his friend Lo
Chen-yü. He then gave up Western philosophy and returned to the tradition of critical studies, publishing works on the history of the theatre in
Sung and Yüan times (1915), on the Classics, on the historians and on the
inscriptions on bronze of the Chou age. We are also indebted to him for

studies of the Han documents found at Tun-huang and Chü-yen, the An-yang inscriptions and the Tun-huang manuscripts. Another historian who made an important contribution by his historiographical method to the renewal at that time of traditional ideas about the ancient history of China was Ku Chieh-kang (born in 1895), the friend of Chang Ping-ling and Hu Shih.

Less well known but probably still more remarkable was the development of teaching and research in the field of the exact sciences. This was due to the efforts of scientists trained partly in China and partly abroad (mainly in the United States after 1927), who strove to train disciples and to establish schools and laboratories. Thanks to these men Chinese science reached international standards in several departments. Men like Ting Wen-chiang (V. K. Ting, 1887–1936), the eminent geologist who founded the Chinese Geological Society in 1922 and the Chinese Palaeontological Society in 1929 (the year of the discovery of Peking Man), the mathematicians Ch'en Hsing-shen (Shiing-shen Chern, born in 1911) and Chou Wei-liang (Chow Wei-liang, born in 1911), one of the pioneers of algebraic geometry, the biochemist Hsien Wu (1893–1959), and the physicists Yen Chi-tz'u (Ny Tsi-ze, born in 1900) and Wu Ta-yu (born in 1907)—the teacher of Tsung-tao Lee, who won the Nobel prize for physics—made a contribution recognized by scientists all over the world to scientific progress. Some of them, such as the atomic physicist Ch'ien San-ch'iang (born in 1910), a disciple of Frédéric and Irène Joliot-Curie, today play a crucial part in the organization of research and in the military strengthening of the People's Republic of China.

Part 11

A New Chapter
in Chinese History:
The People's
Republic of China

Prologue

The quarter of a century that began with the proclamation in Peking on 1 October 1949 of the People's Republic of China and ended with the death of its founder and inspiration in September 1976 has every chance of remaining an exceptional period in history. It was marked by extraordinary excitement, by a profound evolution, by violent shocks, and by a very dangerous increase of population. However it is still too early to say what its place in history will be, since this history is still in the process

The clear break with the previous period is obvious and there can be no question of denying all that distinguishes present-day China from that of 1919–45 and even more from nineteenth-century China. But what seems new to the layman is sometimes not as new as he imagines. There are many links with the most recent past. The generation that lived through the 'Nanking decennium' and the Sino-Japanese War is only just disappearing at the end of the twentieth century. And the principal leaders of the years 1950–75 were all moulded in the time when Chiang Kai-shek presided over the destiny of China. Mao Tse-tung himself, born in 1893, remained until his death the man of the soviets of Kiangsi, of the Long March and of Yenan. But there are also links — subtler no doubt, but just as strong — with a more ancient past. The revolutionary, egalitarian, utopian aspirations of the Chinese tradition seem to have continued to inspire the leaders of the new China. Moreover, a sense of organization, collective discipline, indoctrination, public works of gigantic scope, and even the surprising transition from chaos and anarchy to order are not such new things in China. Certain 'statist' traditions and certain moral traditions seem to have been perpetuated — doubtless in a completely new framework — down to our own day. Although the terms of reference are quite different from those of days gone by and although the international context is also very different, it could be that with the passage of time what connects present-day China with her past will be more clearly apparent; we are still too sensitive to aspects of the present which may be purely ephemeral. And the most recent years still belong more to the realm of the journalist and the political commentator than to that of the historian.

The novel features of the new regime

The profound disagreement in every field between China and the Soviet Union after 1960 should not make us forget that all the institutions of the

Plate 80. Mao Tse-tung proclaiming the People's Republic of China, 1 October 1949, Tien An Men Square, Peking

Plate 81. Mao visiting steel plant in Anwei Province, 1959

Plate 82. Mao, as Chairman of the Central Committee of the Chinese Communist Party, and Chu Teh, Vice-Chairman of the Central Committee and commander-in-chief of the People's Liberation Army, taking the salute on National Day Parade, 1 October 1952, Tien An Men Square, Peking

Plate 83. Official portrait of Mao, 1959

new China were modelled on those of the U.S.S.R. and that the Chinese Communist party is a faithful replica of the Bolshevik party (the same was also true of the Nationalist party, the *Kuo-min-tang*). Soviet influence was extremely strong in China just at the time when the foundations of the new regime were installed. In China, as in the Soviet Union, state institutions are completely controlled by the party. The party is present everywhere and directs everything, even if it has no competence to do so – administrations, enterprises, rural communes, factories, hospitals, schools, universities, and so forth. Even if party members do not enjoy such big privileges as they did in the Soviet Union – and even if the life of the minor officials is fairly painful – membership of the party nevertheless brings with it numerous advantages. The governing élite is formed by the oldest members of the party, those who took part in the pre-liberation struggles. These elderly members (the same phenomenon of ageing leaders was to be found in the U.S.S.R.) are marked off from the mass of newcomers, who occupy only posts of lesser responsibility or carry out only executive tasks. The only criterion for promotion in this weighty hierarchy is devotion to the party and political orthodoxy. Thus there are fundamental analogies between the political systems of China and the U.S.S.R. That is what has led certain specialists in contemporary affairs to predict that China, once the eddies of the years 1950–75 have died away, might well develop in much the same way as the Soviet Union.

However, all through the most recent period, the new Chinese regime has given the impression of being quite original in the importance attributed to indoctrination and to the conversion of minds on the one hand and in a certain revolutionary romanticism on the other. From 1950 until the death of Mao in 1976 the life of the Chinese was continually shaken and sometimes turned upside down by a ceaseless series of 'movements' intended to mobilize the whole or part of the population by obsessive recourse to every conceivable means of communication – posters, newspapers, radio, explanations, and discussions. In the families and at the innumerable meetings organized at places of work, it has been everyone's patriotic duty to criticize and denounce those of his relatives and closest companions who are opposed to the regime, lukewarm, or too independently minded. It is also a duty to accuse oneself of one's own failings, even the most trifling ones, and of one's lack of devotion to the party. The study sessions, usually devoted to the works of Mao Tse-tung or to the editorials of the *People's Daily,* the examination of conscience, conversion and repentance and humiliation make it possible to maintain a high level of 'political' consciousness and to break down the resistance of troublemakers. In this way the population eliminates 'counter-revolutionary elements' of its own accord and reforms itself by means of continual emulation and refinement.

One may say that since 1950 the principal activities of the new China have been propaganda and indoctrination. It will probably never be possible to evaluate the material and human cost of these activities, but it must be very considerable. Ever since the foundation of the People's Republic of China the transformation of society has almost always taken precedence over economic development and problems of management. What is the explanation of this priority of 'politics' over the economy? The history of the Chinese Communist party possibly provides a clue: it was by practising what it preached, and by seeking to convince people that the Red Army established itself in the rural areas, and the village assemblies where the former rich peasants were tried probably provided the model for a more general practice, intended to promote the revolution under the control of the party and to change people's mentality. But other important factors were the temperament and preponderant influence of Mao Tse-tung and at the same time certain tendencies peculiar from the start to the Chinese Communist party. Right from its foundation the party nourished utopian aspirations which continued a very old popular tradition, that of the Great Unity (*ta-t'ung*) or Great Peace (*t'ai-p'ing*) which had originally inspired the T'ai P'ing Rebellion and which had been expressed in the *Ta-t'ung-shu* of K'ang Yu-wei at the end of the nineteenth century. The classless, unanimous society in which everything belongs to everyone — the reverse of the mandarin society — is an old myth which in time has assumed very modern colours. These aspirations are based on the conviction that everything is possible and that it is sufficient to will it. Faith takes precedence over knowledge and the judgement of the party over that of the experts. This belief in the power of the will was particularly marked in Li Ta-chao; it was also one of the basic elements in the temperament of Mao Tse-tung.

The conflicts and crises which the People's Republic of China has experienced since its foundation have usually been due to the difficulties encountered in trying to apply directives that were too ambitious. These difficulties have caused about-turns and changes in the 'political line', and have revealed divergences of ideas at the highest levels. The advocates of a rapid and radical transformation of society were very soon opposed by practical managers who were conscious of the dangers of improvisation and favoured a rhythm of development better suited to human capacities. The opposition between different tendencies ended in factional struggles inside the party, with each faction seeking to exploit to its own advantage the irritation provoked in the population by the authoritarianism and incompetence of the party officials. These conflicts degenerated into positive anarchy at the time of the Cultural Revolution, when the contradiction between the omnipotence of the party machine and the revolutionary aspirations of the young people became quite clear. In these conflicts, as in daily practice, extremely free use is made of the Marxist vocabulary, the terms employed being intended to express moral judgements on the adversary of the moment, not to reflect an objective analysis of society.

From the alliance to the rupture with the Soviet Union

The Civil War, which had lasted twelve years, ended quickly in victory for the Communists because of the vacuum created by the collapse of Chiang Kai-shek's regime and because of everyone's longing for peace after so many years of suffering. Moreover, part of the population and a fair number of intellectuals were prejudiced in favour of the Red Army. Far from pillaging and commandeering the peasants like the Nationalist troops, the Communists lived in close contact with the peasantry and organized the sharing out of the land, thus putting an end to the exploitation of the most deprived. In addition the Communist troops were the only ones who fought effectively against the Japanese occupier. Discipline, social justice, and patriotism gained them sympathy. However, it looks as if the corruption of the Nationalist regime, the inflation, and the general weariness played an even more decisive part in winning over almost the whole population to the new regime.

Although the Communist organization had had time to prepare for its new responsibilities, victory came almost too quickly for it. Its experience was limited to the rural world and to guerrilla actions. In the space of a few months it had to cope with the administration of vast territories and very large cities. It inherited a destitute China, suffering both from the lowest standards of living in the world and from serious industrial backwardness; civil war and the war against the Japanese had raged since 1937 and people were long accustomed to injustice and corruption. However, the new rulers very quickly succeeded in eliminating all opposition, in establishing order and discipline everywhere, in putting an end to inflation, in making sure that everyone had food and clothing, in restarting the factories, and in reopening all the railway lines. By 1952 the reconstruction was complete. What is the explanation of this rapid recovery and of the subsequent progress up to 1958, which form a contrast to the long difficulties of the U.S.S.R. after 1917? Certain Chinese qualities — perseverance, ingenuity, a sense of mutual help and of organization — had something to do with it, but other important factors were the enthusiasm for, and pride in, independence, the patriotism of a great people long and unjustly despised, the hopes placed by many people in the new regime, and finally the devotion and discipline of the party workers and the firmness – yet at the same time prudence – with which the situation was taken in hand.

Considering the size of the population (less than six hundred million in 1960), the Communist revolution was not as bloody as one might have expected. Although the repression of opponents was pitiless, the new regime seems to have been anxious not to alienate the former middle class which at the start was involved in the effort of reconstruction in semi-private and semi-public enterprises. On the other hand, the government extended to the whole of rural China the measures taken in the areas controlled by the Red Army before the Liberation. Artificially divided from 30 June 1950 into five categories (landed proprietors; rich, fairly rich, and poor peasants; agricultural workers), the villagers were encouraged everywhere to expose the injustices which they had suffered at the hands of the landowners and the money-lenders and to demand the punishment of the guilty during the course of stormy meetings which sometimes ended in violence and summary executions. But the redistribution of land, which made everyone a small landowner, seems to have been welcomed by the majority of people. This cautious approach in the early days has often been emphasized and bears witness to a certain Chinese flexibility. It was in fact imposed by circumstances; the People's China was soon to turn towards a pretty precise imitation of the Soviet model.

The Soviet model

By 1952 the generally undersized plots which had arisen out of the agrarian reform began to be regrouped. From 1954 onwards the first 'production cooperatives', the equivalents of the Soviet kolkhozes, began to appear. But at the same time as the collectivization of the land was progressively generalized a big effort was made, in 1955–57, to develop heavy industry – steel, coal, oil, electricity. In giving an absolute priority to the development of heavy industry, China was modelling herself on the Soviet Union. Advisers and technicians from the U.S.S.R. were at that time numerous in China. A tremendous effort was demanded of the peasantry, which had simultaneously to change its habits and feed towns with populations growing rapidly thanks to the emigration from the countryside, pay for the machinery sold by the U.S.S.R. and the eastern European countries, and provide certain factories with products of agricultural origin. But for the first time in her history China began to equip herself with the basic industries indispensable to her independence. It was a process of development that no longer affected simply the coast and the Shanghai region, as in the semi-colonial period, but the interior as well; nor was it limited, as in earlier times, to the consumer industries. The effort made to extend the railway network in the inland provinces had the same object.

However, tension in the years 1955–57 was excessive, and the need for a certain relaxation of constraints seems to have become apparent to the ruling circles. The disquiet caused in the countryside by the collectivization of the land had in fact been reflected in a drop in production. It was therefore decided to give more independence and to leave scope for more initiative to the peasants, who were often irritated by the incompetence and authoritarian attitude of the party officials sent from the towns. A free market was once again allowed to exist. A liberal wind had been blowing through all the Communist countries since the Twentieth Congress of the Russian Communist party; the China of those days was all the more sensitive to it since for her the relaxation of constraints had become a necessity. Everywhere people were allowed to express their basic complaints. Above all an effort was made to regain the support of the intellectuals, almost half of whom were either hostile to the regime or had considerable reservations about it. Rendered extremely cautious by the numerous sessions of 'thought reform' to which they had been subjected, they refused at first to criticize, as they were urgently invited to, what was wrong with the methods of the party. Numerous pressing exhortations were required to induce them to speak out. However, once launched, the movement of 'A Hundred Flowers', as it was called, ended in May 1957 in a positive condemnation of the regime. Students and intellectuals denounced the parody of democracy that was being enacted at every level: all power was held by the six members of the Permanent Committee and everything everywhere was decided in advance; the constant interference of the party in every domain prevented any serious work from being done; those who made the decisions were usually incompetents with no other merit than that of having managed to push themselves forward by giving proof of docility and by protesting their political orthodoxy; work and efficiency were not so well rewarded as hypocrisy. There were even attacks on the Soviet Union, which had dismantled the factories in the north-east and insisted on being paid down to the last copeck for the aid which it provided for one of the poorest countries in the world. The whole movement foreshadowed the period of the Cultural Revolution, when the young people were to break out in revolt against the stifling tyranny of the party. However, the rulers of China were taken by complete surprise; they had not imagined that there was such discontent and such a profound longing for freedom. The unrest among the students and the rioting in Wuhan at the end of June 1957 made it essential to regain control of the situation quickly. The party's authority was brutally reasserted and the experiment of the 'Hundred Flowers' was brought to an end. It had lasted altogether five weeks.

Thus the attempt at liberalization in intellectual circles had backfired against the regime. But it was the same in the countryside: the general relaxation of constraints and of centralization, and the revival of a free market, led the peasants to neglect the collectivized sector and to concentrate all their attention on the sources of individual profit. Here too it was essential to put a stop to the collapse of the system. The step taken was not a return to the previous situation but an extraordinarily bold experiment.

The Great Leap Forward

If intellectuals and peasants had taken advantage of the measures of liberalization to turn against the regime and to go back to traditional attitudes, it was because the reform of people's mentalities had not been deep enough; a fresh and vigorous effort was required to change radically the whole of Chinese society. Such were probably the considerations that led to the vast effort to recast both rural and urban communities completely which bears the name of the Great Leap Forward and which was a dazzling expression of Mao Tse-tung's revolutionary romanticism. In the years 1958 and 1959 there was an extraordinary mobilization of all energies. The propaganda and organization involved outstripped all previous efforts. The Soviet brand of kolkhoz was abandoned in favour of much vaster autonomous units known as People's Communes. These communes, each of which grouped together over twenty thousand people, had to administer themselves and settle all questions concerning them – agriculture, industry, commerce, social affairs, defence, and so on. Everything was collectivized, even the little individual plots which the peasants had been authorized to enlarge in 1957. All private property, even individual ownership of items of daily use, was abolished. Family life disappeared and was replaced by collective living. It was also considered desirable to abolish all distinctions between town and country, and to this end a great effort was made to industrialize the countryside by building small blast furnaces and by calling on everyone's inventive genius as well as on traditional techniques. There was also an effort to increase agricultural production very rapidly by utilizing every piece of land and by multiplying irrigation projects. Birds that damaged the harvest were systematically destroyed and in all districts the watchword was deep ploughing and closer sowing. The aim was to accomplish in two years everything proposed in the Second Five-Year Plan and to achieve at one blow the socialist society. Everything seemed possible.

Plate 84.   Traditional agriculture: rice growing

Plate 85.   New agriculture: lecture by agronomy student to members of an agricultural
school organized by a people's commune in Honan Province, 1959

The excellent harvest of 1958 appeared to confirm all hopes in the atmosphere of rivalry then prevailing; the statistics of increased figures at every level established by party officials anxious to win favour were more than encouraging. But the harvest in 1959 was mediocre and enthusiasm began to wane. The next two years were the darkest in the history of the People's Republic; as a result of the worst drought for a century, China became reacquainted with a scourge that she might have considered to have been banished for ever — certain regions were smitten by famine. The number of dead has been estimated at over thirteen million. The catastrophic harvests of 1960 and 1961 aggravated the consequences of errors committed during the Great Leap Forward; everywhere people had improvised, there had been no coordination and new methods of cultivation had been enforced in contempt of peasant experience. There had been a huge waste of goods and energy. Another factor helped to make the crisis worse: worried and irritated by the signs of independence which China was giving, the Soviet Union suddenly halted its aid in 1960, broke the contracts for technical and scientific cooperation, and recalled all its technicians. China then entered a long period of international isolation.

From the rupture with the U.S.S.R.
to the death of Mao Tse-tung

The scene differs according to the point of view from which one looks at the history of the People's Republic of China since its foundation, but it is perhaps in the continuous movement which has led China to free herself from the tutelage and imitation of the Soviet Union that one of the most illuminating elements in this history is to be found.

First of all, it was her alliance with the U.S.S.R. that involved China in spite of herself, immediately after the Liberation, just when reconstruction was most urgent, in the bloody Korean War. But this conflict, by aggravating the cold war, contributed effectively to tightening the bonds between the two nations and to pushing China back on to the side of the countries dominated by the Soviet Union. The immediate effect of the invasion of South Korea on 25 June 1950 was the neutralization of the Straits of Formosa by the United States. By granting massive military and financial help to the survivors of the Nationalist regime who had taken refuge in Taiwan, the United States was to prolong artificially Chiang Kai-shek's moribund regime on an island which for the past fifty years had formed part of the Japanese empire. It was the start of the fiction of the two Chinas, and twenty years had to pass before a country of eight hundred million inhabitants gained access (in 1971) to the United

Nations and the other international organizations. By outlawing China and organizing a vast blockade round her from Korea and Japan to South-East Asia, the United States strengthened Chinese tendencies to isolation, hardened the regime, and increased China's subjection to the U.S.S.R. In every field – industry, science, technology, teaching, foreign policy – China was during this period completely dependent on the Soviet Union, to which she had been bound since 1950 and for thirty years by a pact of 'friendship, alliance and mutual assistance'. It is true that the repayable advances of the U.S.S.R., and the cooperation of its technicians and of those of Eastern Europe, contributed to the reconstruction and economic recovery. But it is clear that the Soviet model was very ill-adapted to the Chinese case (costly investments in big industrial combines were hardly suited to a poor country with a surplus of manpower) and that China's dependence on the U.S.S.R. was in itself an aberration. It was inevitable that sooner or later this situation should come to an end. The great turning point arrived round about 1959. It is worth recalling that it was after the quarrel between China and the U.S.S.R. that the Maoist movements came into being in the West.

The first big demonstration of Chinese independence was in fact the Great Leap Forward. To decide to press on towards socialism and to try a whole series of experiments never made before (People's Communes, collectivization pushed to the extreme, industrialization of the countryside, and so on) was equivalent to rejecting the Soviet model and to becoming a dissident. The Twentieth Congress of the Russian Communist party, de-Stalinization, peaceful coexistence, the whole big thaw which began to make an appearance in the Soviet Union and the countries of Eastern Europe from 1956 onwards came at a particularly inopportune moment for the rulers of China; for them there could be no question of 'demobilizing' just when they were demanding a tremendous effort from China. Similarly, on the Soviet side, mistrust and irritation only grew. As early as 15 October 1957, even before the Great Leap Forward was launched, Khrushchev had denounced the secret agreement which bound the U.S.S.R. to provide China with the means necessary for the manufacture of nuclear weapons (a denunciation of which Peking was not notified until June 1959). To the Soviet leaders the Great Leap Forward seemed like madness. Moreover, they were worried by the aggressive mood of the Chinese, by their efforts to reconquer the island of Quemoy, off the coast of Fukien, and by their dispute with India, Russia's ally. Before the attacks on Quemoy, in 1959, there had been the big rising in Tibet, a rising which had been savagely crushed. It was this Tibetan affair which was to lead to the war with India in 1962. And soon China was to be in conflict with the U.S.S.R. itself, over the territories

taken from China by Tsarist Russia. Thus while the cold war had tight-
ened the bonds between the Soviet Union and China, 'peaceful coexistence' had the opposite effect. Both in internal policy—in connection
with the paths taken by the revolution and by socialism—and in international relations, the rulers of China could only dissociate themselves
from those whom they were soon to describe as 'revisionists' and new
tsars.

Interlude, 1960–1965

In 1960 China had simultaneously to draw the necessary conclusions
from the failure of the Great Leap Forward and to face the fresh
challenge of the sudden withdrawal, at the most critical moment, of all
aid from the socialist countries. More or less isolated, she was to prove
capable of confronting adversity without anyone's help and of once
again showing a right sense of proportion. In 1960 certain unpopular innovations were abandoned, the size of the communes was reduced and
there was a return to 'material stimulants', that is, a free market was once
again allowed to exist. Technicians and specialists were allowed to have
their say, and their views were taken into account. This change of direction was accompanied by changes in the composition of the ruling team
and by the removal from the scene in practice of Mao Tse-tung, who had
been replaced as President of the Republic since April 1959 by Liu Shao-
ch'i. In high places and among certain intellectuals there was covert
criticism of the reckless policy of Mao Tse-tung. It was this, people
thought, which had led to the catastrophe. It was time to put the rudder
amidships again and to give agriculture a priority which should never
have been contested. Henceforth attention was concentrated on agricultural development, on the creation of a fertilizer industry, on light industry, and on the mechanization of agriculture. However, all the in-
spirations of the Great Leap Forward had not been lost; workshops and
small rural factories still bear witness to the same concern for decentralization—the opposite of the Soviet tradition. By 1963 China had
emerged from famine, and the peasants, on whom until then the whole
weight of industrialization had rested, found their standard of living improving slightly. Finally, it was from 1962 onwards that a policy of
birth control began to be applied for the first time (although without
noticeable effects). We are thus bound to recognize the merits of the
rulers of this period, who were to be the object of the most violent attacks
at the time of the Cultural Revolution. They managed to rescue China
from a dramatic and dangerous situation.

However, the men in power did not rule in complete tranquillity.
Although pushed into the background, Mao Tse-tung retained immense

Plate 86. Control room of a 300,000 Kw generating system, fitted with automatic testing equipment, 1977

Plate 87. China's first four-roller rolling machine, Liaoning Province, 1975

prestige and he had solid support in the army, where one of his former companions-in-arms, Lin Piao, made it his task from the end of 1962 onwards to spread the study of the 'Thoughts of Mao Tse-tung'. It was in September 1962, at the Tenth Plenary Session of the Eighth Central Committee, that the Maoist counter-offensive began. The People's Liberation Army and its heroes were put forward as models, while the civil administration was infiltrated by soldiers who formed inside it a parallel hierarchy devoted to Mao Tse-tung. However, the 'movements' launched by Mao Tse-tung met the passive resistance of the party apparatus. But at the end of 1965 Mao directed his attacks against those who had criticized him at the time of the Great Leap Forward or who had displayed their disagreement by their attitude. These were first of all a number of intellectuals—mainly Wu Han, Teng T'o and Liao Mosha—and the students were invited to denounce the ideological deviations concealed in their works. This new 'movement', which might have failed like the previous ones by meeting the displeasure of the party, in fact found a big response in schools and universities; hence the name 'Cultural Revolution', a term which applies above all to its point of departure. It was because it appealed to young people, to their enthusiasm and emotions, that the Cultural Revolution ended in the tremendous explosion that it did. Soon incited to direct their attacks not merely against certain writers but against the whole party apparatus (the real target of Mao Tse-tung), and finding themselves in opposition alongside the most admired leader of the new China, the students and schoolchildren had the intoxicating feeling that they constituted one of the greatest forces in China and that they enjoyed real power.

The Cultural Revolution and its sequel

Inaugurated in November 1965 by attacks on certain writers, and subsequently by the dismissal of the mayor of Peking, of the minister of culture and of his deputy, the Cultural Revolution did not really begin to assume the aspect of a revolution until summer 1966. From that point onwards it was not just a few intellectuals or high officials who were the object of the campaigns of criticism and denigration, but the two main figures in the state and the party—Liu Shao-ch'i himself and Teng Hsiaop'ing, the secretary general of the party. In August 1966, at the Eleventh Plenary Session, skilful manoeuvres made it possible to demote Liu Shao-ch'i, while Lin Piao was proclaimed Mao Tse-tung's crown prince. At this same time, in response to an appeal from Mao Tse-tung, schoolboys and students all over China formed themselves into Red Guards. Entrusted with the fate of the revolution, they hunted down,

Plate 88.   Anti-American mass rally, Peking, 1964; the slogan reads: 'U.S. Imperialism
get out of the Congo! Get out of Taiwan! Get out of Africa!
Get out of Latin America!'

harried, maltreated and sometimes drove to suicide those whom they
regarded as counter-revolutionaries — local leaders, intellectuals, or erstwhile bourgeois — confusing in their zeal victims and beneficiaries of the
regime. During searches of people's homes they seized and destroyed old
books and works of art. Crowding into the free trains put at their disposal,
they came to Peking from all over China in millions, to see Mao Tse-tung
and march past him. The Cultural Revolution drew all its force and violence from the aspirations of Chinese youth, from its desire for purity and
emancipation, from its need for devotion and devotion to a personage
with great prestige. In the summer and autumn of 1966 the Cultural
Revolution was Chinese youth's great festival, its great opportunity to
express its feelings.

But by the end of 1966 things were starting to go wrong. The attacks of
the Red Guards very often forced local leaders to abandon their posts,
and in some places it was no longer clear who wielded the power. The
anarchy became general and roused people's hopes of making their complaints heard; the revolution snowballed. Exasperated by the excesses of
the Red Guards, some people formed rival groups, which also cited Mao
Tse-tung as their patron, and confrontations between the two sides
became more and more frequent. Street battles took place in Shanghai,

Plate 89.   The port of Shanghai, *c.* 1960

Plate 90.   New buildings in Peking, near the railway station, 1980

which was brought to a standstill by strikes, in December 1966 and January 1967. The threat of civil war and of the secession of whole provinces began to loom up; the only body which had escaped the general disintegration was the army. It was therefore to the army that Mao Tse-tung and Lin Piao were to appeal more and more often in order to restore order and to set up a new administration, both civil and military, which took the name of Revolutionary Committees. Requiring as it did everywhere a search for difficult compromises, the task of restoring order was to take a long time. First undertaken during the summer of 1967 after the serious rioting at Wu-han in July, it was not completed until the spring of 1969. Officially the Cultural Revolution was still in progress, but in fact there was no longer anything revolutionary about this long period. To reconstitute the state and the party, former party officials dismissed by the Red Guards but subsequently rehabilitated were called upon, while campaigns were launched against the 'ultra-leftists', that is, against all those who had hoped for a genuine revolution and were still trying to cause one. Many people were disappointed by this fresh triumph of the opportunists. The most indisciplined Red Guards were made to see reason and a small number of new leaders who had emerged from the Cultural Revolution were incorporated in the party apparatus. The state and the party nearly overthrown in 1967 were somehow reconstructed, with important changes in the managing team and — something quite new — the army playing a preponderant role. The Twelfth Plenary Session of October 1968 dismissed Liu Shao-ch'i and confirmed Lin Piao as Mao Tse-tung's successor. One of the principal aims of the Cultural Revolution had been attained: the authority of Mao Tse-tung had been restored and reasserted in striking fashion. From this moment the old sovereign would fall more and more under the control of a small group who would later come to be known as the Gang of Four and whose principal figures were his wife Chiang Ch'ing and Lin Piao.

However, the Cultural Revolution was not simply an operation designed to allow Mao Tse-tung to regain power; it was accompanied by a vast movement of political justification. One of the most frequently proclaimed aims was to prevent the revolution from drowsing off, to halt before it was too late the formation of a privileged class of bureaucrats, to forestall in short a process of evolution like the one that had taken place in the Soviet Union. Liu Shao-ch'i and the men who had succeeded in putting the Chinese economy on its feet again after the Great Leap Forward were represented as 'revisionists' in the attacks which were launched against them. Henceforth 'politics' once again took precedence over the economy. In the themes emphasized during the course of the Cultural Revolution the inspiration of Mao Tse-tung was clearly perceptible: the goal to attain was always a radical mutation of society and of its attitudes, the abolition of all distinctions between manual and intellectual work, and the disappearance of all privileges and of all class distinction. But ironically, distinctions based on family background enacted at the beginning of the regime were now strictly applied and created something like castes inside Chinese society. Those whose parents had a middle-class background became veritable pariahs. Another aspect of the Cultural Revolution, one that was just as important, was the cult of Mao Tse-tung. Organized by Lin Piao, this cult developed enormously and in the course of a few years rose to a sort of paroxysm. The number of copies printed of a collection of selected thoughts of Mao, the *Little Red Book*, broke all known records. But the figure of the 'Great Helmsman', the story of his life, and the books that he had written also became the object of positive worship.

The period from 1969 to the death of Mao Tse-tung in 1976 may be regarded as a prolongation of the Cultural Revolution. Its effects still made themselves felt in every field. The social and political crisis had been an extremely grave one and had left its mark on everyone. The repression which had descended on the most convinced revolutionaries left a great deal of bitterness behind. Weariness and disaffection to the regime spread considerably. The effects of the Cultural Revolution on the Chinese economy were also very noticeable. As a result of the disorganization of the railways, of the strikes, of the disturbances, and of the dismissal of the managers there was a tremendous fall in production. The total cost of the Cultural Revolution was certainly very high, and that China was able to withstand this new trial without too much damage is a proof of her extraordinary powers of resistance.

In the field of education, the arts, and literature, the purge was so radical that anything outside the limits of official propaganda was suppressed. Schools and universities were closed for years on end — it was a long time before the universities opened again — and numerous teachers were sent into the fields to reform their ideas by manual work. In the domain of music and the theatre, the only works allowed were a few extolled by Chiang Ch'ing, Mao's wife, who had been promoted to the direction of cultural affairs.

Nor was the Cultural Revolution without effect on the evolution of political power. Formerly an association of dignitaries, the ruling team became a small group of favourites and intimates centred round an ageing Mao Tse-tung in an atmosphere of suspicion and intrigue. The mysterious disappearance in 1971 of Lin Piao, accused of an attempt at usurpation, was one of the first signs of the way in which the regime had evolved.

From the death of Mao Tse-tung to the beginning of the 1990s

After the death of Mao Tse-tung in September of 1976 one might have expected a radical change in personnel and political orientation. But it was an obscure police authority linked to the radicals, Hua Kuo-feng, who succeeded him, and it was not until the end of 1978 that the prag-matists, headed by Teng Hsiao-p'ing, were able to establish themselves in power in a lasting fashion. De-Maoization could begin. The period that opened at this time resembles the New Political Economy of the Soviets, but also the years that followed the catastrophe of the Great Leap For-ward. The gradual return of family farming concerns, the authorization given to the creation of small private enterprises, and the restored link between remuneration and production produced an immediate and lively rebirth of activity in the countryside, where specialized farming for com-mercial purposes returned. Fish-culture, arboriculture, and animal breed-ing expanded. Agricultural revenue tripled between 1979 and 1985. Habitat, transportation, and energy were treated less badly than they had been up to that time. Preoccupied by the enormous delay that China had amassed, the new leaders decided to call in a big way upon Western and Japanese technology and capital. At the same time, the long isolation of the People's Republic ended in 1980. China reintegrated into the great international organizations, even though it still maintained cold relations with the Soviet Union and was in open conflict with Vietnam.

The loosening of constraints and the gradual disappearance of collec-tive structures created disparities between city and countryside, a large diversion of revenues, and new problems of management. The sharp rise in agricultural prices forced the state to soften the problems created in the cities by these rises with heavy subventions that aggravated the inflation and the deficit. In 1981 it became imperative to slow down the pace of investment. If the reforms were a success in the countryside, they ran aground to a certain extent in the industrial and urban sectors, where the old cadres remained in place. The operatives of state enterprises and the minor party cadres whose privileges were threatened by the new course of things were naturally hostile to the reforms.

But in 1984 a decisive acceleration of reform made the urgency of development indispensable. Management freedom and initiative were given to enterprises that now became autonomous and competitive. Almost half of all price restrictions were lifted. Specially regulated economic zones were created in Kwangtung, Fukien, and the lower Yangtze; fourteen coas-tal cities were opened to foreign investment. Bank loans supplanted state subventions. The following year these reforms translated into spectacular progress for light industry and for the production of consumer goods. But at the same time the absence of any coordination, the laxness of the banks, and inflation, as well as strangling bottlenecks in transportation, energy, and raw materials, forced a return to new controls on prices and on the autonomy allowed to enterprises and provinces. Thus, after the reformers came to power, measures to liberalize the economy were followed by the inevitable return to measures of control.

However, the opening to foreign products, technology, and capital, along with the resumption of dialogue with the outside world, even with the Soviet Union and its allies, were not accompanied by any real transformation of the government. The conduct of public affairs remains the exclusive prerogative of the party — that is to say, of a privileged caste. Coming unexpectedly after the terrible ordeals of the Cultural Revolution, the growth of large inequities in prosperity, the rapid progress of fraud and corruption, and the reign of money explain the grave moral crisis that has afflicted Chinese society since the end of the Maoist era. As had occurred during the short period that followed the Great Leap Forward (1961–64), the freedom that returned to the countryside caused a resurgence of forms of family solidarity as well as former social and religious practices that were believed to have been definitively eliminated by communist indoctrination. Even currently rather uninformed about the outside world, the Chinese have become more aware of the backwardness of their own country; and this has engendered a deep feeling of frustration. For many, an egocentric search for the good life by any means has become the only goal of existence. But also, for a long time, there have been many indications among the youth of deep dissatisfaction, of their thirst for freedom and independence. We should recall, among other signs, the 1974 manifesto of the students of Canton abused by the Cultural Revolution, the 'Peking spring' of 1978 with its posters on 'democracy wall' where the hopes of young people at the end of the Maoist period were expressed, the 1987 movement for political reform and, most recently, the large student demonstrations during the spring of 1989. One forgot for a moment that the system remained in place and that the modernization extolled by Teng Hsiao-p'ing totally excluded any liberalization of the government: the massacre of peaceful, unarmed students in T'ien-an men Square on 4 June 1989 revealed how deep was the separation between the political leaders and the most enlightened part of Chinese society — the students and intellectuals. Hopes to see China enter on the path towards a system of laws and respect for human rights were disappointed, the proponents of such an opening were eliminated, and, at the same time, certain tendencies towards a return to centralized economic decision making and to practices of the Maoist era manifested themselves again. But, in as much as it is no longer possible to return to the former state of affairs, the extraordinary economic development of the maritime provinces that the 1984 measures set in motion has not slackened and has even sharply accelerated following new encouragements from Teng Hsiao-p'ing during his trip to the South in 1992. A reservoir of cheap manual labor deprived of any rights, China has experienced a great influx of foreign capital, especially from Hong Kong and Taiwan. The maritime provinces from Shanghai to Canton have completely integrated themselves into the sphere of East Asian prosperity.

But we should not forget China's handicaps. Perhaps the most serious are the difficulties of reconstructing the education system following its ruin during the Cultural Revolution; overpopulation, which birth control restrictions imposed in 1970 has slowed but not entirely stopped; and finally and most important, the total inability on the part of the government to adapt to the new situation both within the country and internationally – an inability made most clear by its threats directed towards the future of Hong Kong. But there are also some reasons to have confidence in the future: the extraordinary dynamism that this vast country has shown allows us to think that these handicaps will one day be surmounted.

Final note

China has changed so profoundly during the last century that one may well ask of what interest a knowledge of its past may be, a past that for a majority of people seems no longer relevant.

But this would, first, show a strange contempt for all that Chinese civilization has produced in its long, remarkable history in all domains: art, literature, religion, thought, technology . . . forgetting that its innumerable masterpieces are part of the common inheritance of humanity. A true world history cannot exclude China, at the very least because its civilization has radiated over the countries that stretch from central Asia to the shores of the Pacific, from Siberia to the tropics. China has been, for close to three thousand years in this part of the world, *the* civilization *par excellence*, comparable for us in the West to that civilization which developed in the Middle East, in the Mediterranean basin, and in Europe, where close ties united what our scholarly traditions have taught us to separate: Greece and the Near East, Christianity, Judaism, and Islam. All of East Asia inherited the moral, artistic, and intellectual traditions of China. Even Japan, which economists sometimes classify alongside the West and which is a strongly original country with a distinct history and culture, nevertheless owes much more to China than it realizes and admits.

Moreover, the original character of a civilization that developed for such a long time without direct contact with the West furnishes inexhaustible material for the comparative history of humanity and its history. There survive from the Chinese past both a prodigious mass of precisely dated written documents and remains of material culture, of which great quantities are supplied each year by archaeological excavations. It can be said that a good part of the entire history of China remains yet to be discovered and understood.

Finally, the modern world owes much more to China in matters of technology, science, and institutions than most people imagine – from silk, paper, and firearms to the examination system. We would not be what we are without China.

It is true that the present transformations all seem to be headed in the same direction: towards a uniformalization of the world following Western standards. China itself, now situated in the middle of the most dynamic group of countries in the world, is transforming before our eyes much faster than anyone could have ever imagined. And nevertheless, China does not, any more than does the West, have reason to renounce a past that in spite of everything has left such deep marks on the behaviour and traditions of the Chinese of today. It is precisely by reclaiming its history and by seizing awareness of the originality of its traditions that China will be able to emerge from the demoralization that has resulted from the disastrous experiences of the Maoist period and from the memories of the humiliations formerly imposed by the Western nations and Japan. The West has been too quick to identify modernity with Westernization. Perhaps we shall yet become aware of the grave handicap for our future that our ignorance of this part of humanity, of its history and of its roots, presents.

Plate 91.   The destruction of the old order: two Chinese boys, watched by their grandmother, clamber over a pre-revolutionary street decoration

Plate 92.   Peking: organized parties of Chinese and foreign visitors now throng the former Imperial Palace; shown here is the Hall of Great Harmony, once an outer throne hall, now a picture gallery

General Chronology

Sui and T'ang

Sui	581–618	Reunification of China by the Sui in 589.
T'ang	618–907	In the seventh century, large expansion
Rebellion of An Lu-shan	755–764	across Asia. Growth of rice-producing area of China (Yangtze basin). Tax reform. Disappearance of the old aristocracy.
Five Dynasties	900–960	Subdivision of China in a dozen states.

The Mandarin state from its formation to the Mongol occupation

Northern Sung	960–1127	Eleventh century, spread of printing. Development of the scholar class. Urban and maritime economic take-off. Recruitment by competition for state officials. Professional military.
Liao	916–1127 in the Northeast	Encroachment of steppe empires into the northern provinces.
Hsia	1032–1227 in the Northwest	After 1127, all North China occupied by the Chin; after 1234, by the
Chin	1115–1234	Mongols.
Southern Sung	1127–1279	The Sung retreats to south of the Huai River in 1127.
Yuan (Mongols)	1271–1367	All China is integrated into the Eastern empire of the Mongols. Native insurrections after about 1350.

Restoration of the Mandarin state

Ming	1368–1644	1368–1420, the Mongols are driven back toward the North. Strengthening of absolutism. 1520–1644, spread of silver money, urban and commercial economic take-off. 1590–1644, political crisis, then large-scale insurrections. Manchu threat.

The Manchu empire

Ch'ing	1644–1911	1644–1663, establishment of the Manchus. In the eighteenth century, expansion into Mongolia, central Asia, and Tibet; general prosperity and rapid population growth. From the end of the eighteenth century, corruption, border conflicts, uprisings, and economic stagnation. After 1820, opium import causes economic deficits. After 1840,
T'ai-p'ing rebellion	1850–1864	attacks from the Western powers. 1850–1898, modernization checked. China gradually loses its independence.

From the end of the Manchu empire to the People's Republic of China

| Republic of China | 1912–
(on Taiwan
after 1949) | 1912–1927, warlord period. After 1927, Chiang Kai-shek's nationalist China. 1937–1949, Japanese invasion and civil war. |
| People's Republic of China | (on the continent after 1949) | 1950–1957, reconstruction. 1958–1959, Great Leap Forward. 1966–1969, Cultural Revolution. Anarchy and destruction. 1969–1977, sequel to the Cultural Revolution. 1978, return of the pragmatists to power. Opening to foreign capital. 1980, reforms accelerate. 1989, suppression of the democracy movement and halt to reforms. After 1991, unprecedented economic expansion. |

Chronological Tables

B.C.	History	B.C.	Civilization
XVIIc.	Foundation of the SHANG (or YIN) DYNASTY.	XVIIc.	Beginnings of bronze in the basin of the Yellow River (?).
1384	Establishment of the Shang in their last capital near An-yang, according to the chronology of Tung Tso-pin.	c.1384–1025	Inscriptions on bone and shells of the end of the Shang period at An-yang (Honan).
c.1025	Destruction of the Shang by the Chou; beginning of the WESTERN CHOU.		
c.1000	Development of the technique of horse-riding in the western parts of Asia.	X–IXc.	First inscriptions on bronze vessels. Most ancient religious hymns of the *Shih-ching*.
827–782	(Reign of King Hsüan.) Incursions by peoples of the North (first nomad horsemen?).	841	Beginning of dated history.
771	Barbarian invasions in Shensi. The Chou leave their capital in the valley of the Wei and make their principal residence at Loyang. Beginning of the EASTERN CHOU.		
		753	Beginning of the *Annals of Ch'in.*
722	First year of the *Ch'un-ch'iu period* ('*Springs and Autumns*').	722	Beginning of the *Annals of Lu,* the *Ch'un-ch'iu.*
704	The sinicized kingdom of Chu in Hupei and on the middle Yangtze spreads into southern Honan.		

Note: Items preceded by the sign † concern the history of religions, those preceded by the sign * concern the history of science or technology

B.C.	History	B.C.	Civilization
688	First appearance of the term *bsien* (district) as applied to a conquered territory.		
667	Solemn oath between principalities which makes Ch'i, a kingdom in Shantung, the head of the Chinese confederation against barbarian invasions. Start of the hegemony of Ch'i.		
632	Chin, a kingdom in Shansi, succeeds to the hegemony.		
606	Ch'u threatens the royal domain of the Chou in Honan.		
597	King Chuang of Ch'u is recognised as leader of the confederacy.		
594	Fiscal reform in the principality of Lu in Shantung.		
589	Big battle between Ch'i and Chin, the principal adversaries of the time.		
562	The prince of Lu is removed from power and retains only religious prerogatives.		
543	Fiscal reform in Cheng.	513	*First mention of the casting of iron (?).
506	Offensive by Wu (southern Kiangsu) against Ch'u. Wu occupies Ying, the capital of Ch'u.	501	*Mention of four procedures of medical diagnosis: examination of the complexion and tongue, primitive forms of auscultation, medical history of the patient, examination of the pulse.
494	The kingdom of Yüeh recognizes the kingdom of Wu as its overlord.		

B.C.	History
486–482	Wu connects the Yangtze to southern Shantung by a canal.
481	END OF THE CH'UN-CH'IU PERIOD.
473	Wu is crushed by Yüeh, its southern neighbour.
453	Division of the kingdom of Chin into three principalities (Han, Wei and Chao). Start of the period of the WARRING STATES (CHAN-KUO).
445	Expansion of Ch'u towards the east at the expense of Wu.
408	Wei pushes Ch'in back towards the west and spreads to the Northern Lo, where it builds a line of fortifications.
367	Division of the royal house of the Chou into two principalities: Western Chou and Eastern Chou.
361	Arrival in Ch'in of the legalist reformer Kung-sun Yang (Shang Yang).
358–352	Wei extends its defences to the Ordos bend.
c.356–348	Big reforms by Shang Yang in Ch'in.
354–351	Siege of Han-tan, capital of Chao in south-western Hopei.

B.C.	Civilization
479	Traditional date of the death of Confucius (K'ung-tzu).
467	*Observation of Halley's comet.
444	*Calculation of the solar year: 365 1/4 days.
c.395	Death of the Legalist Li K'uei (or Li K'e), minister of Wei.
c.381	Death of Mo-tzu.
c.350	*Oldest catalogue of the stars.

B.C.	History	B.C.	Civilization
		338	Execution of the Legalist Kung-sun Yang (Shang Yang), the reformer of the institutions of Ch'in.
334	Ch'u absorbs Yüeh (lower Yangtze and northern Chekiang).	c.335	Death of Yang Chu, pessimistic philosopher and apostle of egoism.
328	Institution of prime minister in Ch'in.		
325	The prince of Ch'in takes the title of king (*wang*).		
318–316	Ch'in advances into Szechwan.		
307	Chao creates a corps of cavalry against the nomads.		
c.300	Ch'in, Chao and Yen build walls against the nomads of Mongolia and Manchuria. Work on the course of the Min-chiang in Szechwan.	c.300	Death of the sophist Hui Shih and of the Taoist philosopher Chuang Chou, author of the Chuang-tzu.
c.298–280	Expedition by Ch'u into eastern Szechwan and Yunnan.	c.289	Death of Mencius (Meng-tzu), the successor of Confucius.
286	Ch'i puts an end to the principality of Sung in eastern Honan.		
280	Ch'in enters Kweichow.	c.277	Death of the great poet Ch'ü Yüan of Ch'u.
278–7	Ch'in expands at the expense of Ch'u in Hupei and Hunan.		
259–7	Ch'in besieges Han-tan, the capital of Chao.		
256	Ch'in puts an end to the royal house of the Chou.	c.250	Death of the sophist Kung-sun Lung.
249	Start of the ministry of Lü Pu-wei in Ch'in.		
246	Accession in Ch'in of King Cheng, the future First Emperor of the dynasty of the Ch'in. Construction in Ch'in of a canal 150 km long in Shensi.		

B.C.	Civilization
240	*Observation of Halley's comet. c.240, death of Tsou Yen of Ch'i, a specialist in the five elements (*wu-hsing*).
239	The *Lü-shih ch'un-ch'iu*, a summary of the knowledge of that time.
235	Death of the philosopher Hsün-tzu, a sociologist of Confucian inspiration influenced by Legalism.
213	The 'burning of the books'.

B.C.	History
239–235	Transfers of population in Ch'in to people the Wei valley.
237	Li Ssu succeeds Lü Pu-wei as minister of Ch'in.
230–221	Ch'in successively annexes the kingdoms of Han, Chao, Wei, Ch'u, Yen and Ch'i.
221	Foundation of the CH'IN EMPIRE.
221–214	Expeditions to Fukien, Kwangtung, Kwangsi and northern Vietnam.
220	Construction of a network of imperial roads. Reconstruction and prolongation of the Great Walls built about 300 B.C.
215	Campaign of Meng T'ien in Mongolia against the Hsiung-nu.
214	Expedition to Nan-yüeh (region of Canton and Hanoi). Transfer of 500,000 criminals to Nan-yüeh.
212	Construction of the imperial palaces.
210	Death of the First Emperor.
209	Beginning of the insurrections and of the civil war. Foundation of the first empire of the steppe by Mao-tun, leader of the Hsiung-nu tribes.
208	People's rebellion led by Ch'en She.
207	Assassination of the second emperor.

B.C.	History	B.C.	Civilization
206	END OF THE CH'IN DYNASTY.		
203	Hsiang Yü and Liu Pang divide the empire between them; Ch'u, the kingdom of Hsiang Yü, to the east; Han, the kingdom of Liu Pang, to the west.		
202	Liu Pang eliminates Hsiang Yü and proclaims himself emperor of the HAN.		
201	Liu Pang gives part of the territories of the empire to his old companions-in-arms as fiefs.		
200	Liu Pang sets up his capital at Ch'ang-an, the present Sian, in Shensi. About 200, general withdrawal of the Chinese defences to south of the Great Walls.		
198	Transfer of rich families of Ch'i (Shantung) and Ch'u (middle Yangtze) to the region of Ch'ang-an.		
191	The most rigorous laws of the Ch'in are abolished.		
188	The laws against merchants are made less severe.		
187	More penal laws of the Ch'in abolished.		
180	Death of the empress Lü. The members of her clan are exterminated.		
179	Nan-yüeh recognizes the overlordship of the Han.		
177	Advance of the Hsiung-nu into Honan.		
175	Authorization of the private casting of coins.		
174	Death of the *shan-yü* Mao-tun, founder of the Hsiung-nu empire.		
		168	Death of the scholar Chia I, the famous adviser of the emperor and the author of political essays and *fu* (poetic descriptions).

B.C.	History	B.C.	Civilization
167	Mutilation as a punishment disappears from the penal code. Creation of the sentence of hard labour.		
166	First mention of the system of signalling codes (fire and smoke) on the frontiers of the steppe.		
165	First official examinations for the selection of civil servants.		
158	First mention of military colonies (*t'un-t'ien*) on the northern frontiers.	157	Death of Lu Chia, the Taoist scholar and author of the *Hsin-yü*.
144	Incursion of the Hsiung-nu into Shansi and seizure of the horses of the imperial stud.	140	*First Chinese book on alchemy.
141	Accession of the Emperor Wu (Hsiao-wu-ti).		
139 or 135	Departure of Chang Ch'ien for central Asia in search of the great Yüeh-chih.	c.135	*First mention of the six-pointed shape of snow crystals in the *Han-shih Wai-chuan*.
136	Start of the exploration of the roads through Szechwan to Burma and India, on the initiative of T'ang Meng.	133	†Dispatch of magicians (*fang-shih*) in search of the Isles of the Immortals.
131	Attempt to advance into Yunnan and Kweichow.		
130	Construction of a road between Szechwan and Kweichow.		
129	Construction of a canal 150 km long between Shensi and Honan.		

B.C.	History	B.C.	Civilization
128	First campaigns in Manchuria and Korea.		
127	Law about the division of fiefs between sons.		
126	Chang Ch'ien returns from Ferghana and Bactriana.		
124	Attempt at rebellion by Prince Liu An of Huai-nan.	124	Creation of an office of fifty specialists in the Classics in new characters.
122–109	Expansion of the Han towards the south.	122	Suicide of Prince Liu An of Huai-nan, at whose court the *Huai-nan-tzu*, a work of Taoist philosophy, had been written.
121	The Han armies advance 1000 km into Mongolia.	120	Creation of the Yüeh-fu, the office of music, with the task of collecting popular and foreign songs.
120	Over 700,000 victims of disaster are transferred from Shantung to Shensi.	117	Death of Ssu-ma Hsiang-ju, famous author of *fu*.
117 and 115	Creation of commanderies in Kansu.		
115	Chang Ch'ien sets off again for central Asia, towards the land of the Wu-sun (valley of the Ili).		
113	Great effort to irrigate and exploit the north-western territories.		
108	Creation of four Han commanderies in Korea. First expeditions to central Asia.	109	†Search for the Isles of the Immortals.
105	Han embassy at Seleucia, on the Tigris.	105	Death of Tung-chung Shu, commentator on the Classics. As a result of embassies from the kingdoms of central Asia, the vine and lucerne are introduced into China.
102	Creation of fortified posts in Mongolia. Soldiers and convicts extend the Great Walls from Lan-chou to Yü-men-kuan.	104	†Basic reform of the calendar.

B.C.	History	B.C.	Civilization
101	Success of second expedition against Ferghana.		
99	Insurrections of the populace in the eastern parts of the empire.		
98	State monopoly in alcohol.		
95	Canal 100 km long connecting the Wei to the Ching, in Shensi.		
		93	Discovery of manuscripts of the classics in old characters.
		92	Start of the sorcery trials in the imperial palace. c.92, death of the great historian Ssu-ma Ch'ien, author of the *Historical Records, Shih-chi*.
87	Death of Emperor Wu.	89	*Chao Kuo invents new agricultural implements and a new system of rotation of crops, the *tai-t'ien*.
		81	Discussion on the maintenance or abandonment of the state monopolies in salt, iron and alcohol. The content of these discussions was to appear a few years later in the *Yen-t'ieh lun, Discussions about salt and iron*.
68	Garrisoning of forts beyond the Great Walls abandoned.		
64	The Han concentrate their efforts on the defence of the southern oasis route.	65	*Oldest water mills in the world, in Asia Minor.
60	Power of the Hsiung-nu begins to decline.		
		52	*Equatorial armilla of Kuo Shou-Ch'ang.
		51	Conference at the court on the interpretation of the classics.
		46	Recruitment of specialists in *yin-yang* and portents.

B.C.	History
18	Sales of official titles.
14	Peasant revolts.
7	Plan for the limitation of private properties.
3	Pao Hsüan's criticisms of contemporary policies and of the oppression of the peasantry.
1	Start of the power of Wang Mang.
A.D.	
2	First known census: 12,366,470 families and 57,671,400 individuals.

B.C.	Civilization
41	The number of students at the Academy is raised to 1000.
28	*Start of the systematic recording of sun spots.
26	Liu Hsiang, the imperial librarian, presents his *Commentary on the Five Elements* in the *Hung-fan*, *Hung-fan wu-hsing chuan*, Investigation of Lost Books.
15	The *Fang-yen*, first work on Chinese dialects.
8	The number of students at the Academy is raised to 3000.
7	Abolition of the Office of Music (Yüeh-fu-kuan). Liu Hsiang's bibliographical classification, the *Ch'i-lüeh*.
6	Death of Liu Hsiang, author of the *Hsin-hsü* and the *Shuo-yüan*.
3	*Amulets of the Queen Mother of the West (*Hsi-wang-mu*) circulate among the lower classes in Shantung.
2	Ban on suicide out of loyalty to someone who has died (*hsün-ssu*).
A.D.	
5	Death of K'ung Kuang, specialist in institutions and interpreter of the classics.

A.D.	History
6	Wang Mang, 'provisional emperor' on the death of the emperor P'ing, exercises a sort of regency.
7	Wang Mang's monetary reform. Rebellions against Wang Mang.
9	Wang Mang founds the Hsin dynasty. 'Nationalisation' of land.
10	The old Han nobility is reduced to the status of ordinary private citizens.
11	The Yellow River breaks its dykes and changes course.
17	Spread of peasant revolts as a result of natural calamities and of requisitioning for the army.
20	Wang Mang constructs ostentatious buildings in Ch'ang-an.
22	Expeditions against the insurgents of Shantung and Hupei, who adopt the name of *Red Eyebrows* (*Ch'ih-mei*).
23	The dynasty founded by Wang Mang is swept away by insurrections of the people and rebellions of the old imperial nobility.
25	The Red Eyebrows enter Ch'ang-an. Liu Hsiu proclaims himself emperor: beginning of the Later Han or EASTERN HAN. Loyang is made the capital.
27–28	The new emperor of the Han eliminates his rivals and puts down the Red Eyebrow risings.

A.D.	Civilization
8	Death of Yang Hsiung, rationalist, Taoist philosopher, supporter of the traditions in old characters, and author of the *Fa-yen* and the *T'ai-hsüan-ching*.
20	*First mention of batteries of pestles driven by water.
23	Death of Liu Hsin, the imperial librarian, editor of ancient texts, including the *Tso-chuan* and the *Chou-li*.
31	*First mention of the application of hydraulic power to the bellows of blast furnaces for casting iron.

A.D.	History	A.D.	Civilization
36	Reconquest of Szechwan and end of the independent empire of the Ch'eng-Han.		
40	Insurrection of the inhabitants of the Red River basin and western Kwangtung.		
42–43	Victorious expedition of Ma Yüan against the Vietnamese rebellion of the sisters Trung Thac and Trung Nhi.		
50	Settlement of those southern Hsiung-nu who had joined the Han in the commanderies of northern Shansi and of Shensi.		
		c.56	Death of the rationalist philosopher Huan T'an.
57	Embassy from a Japanese principality in northern Kyushu.		
		65	†First mention of a Buddhist community at P'eng-ch'eng, in northern Kiangsu.
69	Dykes of the Yellow River repaired over a distance of more than 500 km.		
70	Construction of the Pien Canal in Honan.		
73–94	General Pan Ch'ao regains control of the oases, which had been lost for over 60 years.		
77–91	Khotan becomes the seat of the Han government-general in central Asia.		
		78	Death of Tu Tu, author of *fu* (poetic descriptions) and of a political essay, the *Ming-shih-lun*.
		79	Conference at the court on the interpretation of the Classics. An account of this conference provides the material of the *Pai-hu-t'ung*.

A.D.	Civilization
c.82	The *History of the Han* (*Han-shu*) by Pan Ku and his sister Pan Chao.
83	The *Lun-heng*, by Wang Ch'ung: criticism of superstitions and received opinions; natural explanations of physical phenomena. Selection of specialists in the *Tso-chuan*, the *Ku-liang-chuan* and the *Shang-shu* in ancient characters and in the *Shih-ching* of Mao.
92	Death in prison of Pan Ku, author of the *History of the Han*.
100	The *Shuo-wen chieh-tzu*, the first dictionary of characters (9353 articles). First Chinese adaptation of an Indian Buddhist text.
101	Death of Chia K'uei, commentator on the Classics in ancient characters.
105	*The eunuch Ts'ai Lun presents the emperor with the first kinds of paper.
c.118	*The *Ling-hsien* by Chang Heng, a work of astronomy.

A.D.	History
87	Embassy from the Kushans arrives in Loyang.
88	Abolition of the monopolies in iron and salt.
89–105	Indian embassies in Loyang.
97	Kan Ying, sent by Pan Ch'ao to the Roman East, is held up at the western frontier of the Parthian empire.
101	Embassy from the Parthians.
106	Reduction of the court expenses and of the salaries of some civil servants.
107	Embassy from a Japanese principality.
120	An embassy from the Shan Kingdom in Burma offers the Loyang court dancers and tumblers from the eastern part of the Roman empire.

A.D.	History	A.D.	Civilization
c.125	The power of the eunuchs begins to increase.	124	*Chang Heng's armillary sphere.
c.125–150	The Han re-establish their domination of central Asia.	127	Fan Ying, a specialist in esoteric sciences, is called to the court.
132	First mention of official relations between China and Java.	132	*Seismograph and armillary sphere worked by a daily rotary movement built by Chang Heng.
135	The eunuchs are authorized to adopt sons.	139	*Death of Chang Heng, astronomer, mathematician and poet.
140	Irrigation works in the region of Kuei-chi in Chekiang. The incursions of the Hsien-pei oblige the Han to hand over a large piece of territory to them.	142	The *Chou-i ts'an-t'ung chi*, an alchemical work.
		147	†Arrival in Loyang of the Parthian monk An Shih-kao, the first known translator of Indian Buddhist texts into Chinese.
		151	The *Cheng-lun, Political Discussions*, by Ts'ui Shih, a writer of Legalist tendencies.
157	Census: 56,486,856 individuals.	c.165	Death of Wang Fu, author of the *Ch'ien-fu-lun*, a work of social and political criticism.
161	Indian embassy arrives in China via South-East Asia.	166	†First mention of Buddhist ceremonies at the court of Loyang. Death of Ma Jung, the great commentator on the Classics.
166	Embassy of merchants from the eastern part of the Roman empire.		
169	Great victory over the Ch'iang.	c.170	Death of Ts'ui Shih, author of the *Cheng-lun*.
170	Start of agrarian agitation.		

A.D.	Civilization	A.D.	History
173	*Invention of aiming sight for the crossbow.	175	Enlargement of the powers of the eunuchs.
175	The text of the Classics is engraved in three kinds of writing by Ts'ai Yung in the capital.	178	Sale of offices.
182	Death of Ho Hsiu, the only representative in his time of the traditions in new characters, and the continuer of Tung Chung-shu.	184	Great rebellion of the YELLOW TURBANS, whose troops very soon number over 300,000.
		189	Massacre of the eunuchs. Sack of Loyang by the troops of Tung Cho.
190	The Han collections and archives disappear in the sack of Loyang by Tung Cho's armies. c.190, the *Shu-shu chi-i*, *Mathematical Traditions*, attributed to Hsü Yüeh.	190	Beginning of the power of Ts'ao Ts'ao. c.190, the members of the Taoist sect of the Five Bushels of Rice create an independent state in Szechwan and southern Shensi. From 190 onwards communications with central Asia are cut.
192	Death of Ts'ai Yung, author of the *Tu-tuan*, on Han institutions. Death of Lu Chih, author of a treatise on the customs of the area of present-day Peking and of a commentary on the *Li-chi*.		
193	†Buddhist temple at P'en-ch'eng, in northern Kiangsu.	194	Famine in Ch'ang-an.
		195	Sun Ts'e occupies the lower Yangtze.
200	Death of Cheng Hsüan, the great commentator on the Classics.	200	Death of Sun Ts'e, who is succeeded by his brother, San Ch'üan.
		201	Ts'ao Ts'ao is practically master of all north China.
		208	Alliance between Liu Pei and Sun Ch'üan against Ts'ao Ts'ao. Famous defeat of Ts'ao Ts'ao's troops on the Yangtze (battle of the Red Cliff).

A.D.	History
211	Liu Pei establishes himself in Szechwan.
212	Sun Ch'üan establishes himself in Nanking, which he fortifies and christens Chien-k'ang.
220	Death of Ts'ao Ts'ao. His son, Ts'ao P'ei, assumes the title of emperor of WEI. End of the Han dynasty.
221	Liu Pei founds the empire of the SHU-HAN in Szechwan and makes Ch'eng-tu his capital.
222	Sun Ch'üan proclaims himself emperor of WU. Beginning of the period known as the THREE KINGDOMS.
230	Maritime expeditions of Wu.
234	Death of Chu Ko-liang, adviser of the Shu-Han.
243	Embassy from Fu-nan (Cambodia) in Nanking.
249	In Wei, *coup d'état* of General Ssu-ma I.

A.D.	Civilization
220	Death of the poet and general Ts'ao Ts'ao.
220–225	†Chih Ch'ien, a monk from an Indo-Scythian family of Loyang, translates in Nanking the *sutra of Amitabha* and the *Vimalakirti*, texts of the Greater Vehicle.
226	Death of the poet Ts'ao P'ei, son of Ts'ao Ts'ao and first emperor of the Ts'ao-Wei.
c.229	Treatise by ambassador Chu Ying of Wu on Cambodia, the *Fu-nan i-wu chih*.
232	Death of the poet Ts'ao Chih, son of Ts'ao Ts'ao. *c.232, a tradition ascribing to Chu Ko-liang the invention of the 'wooden ox', the wheelbarrow.
c.240–248	Engravure on stele of the text of the three Classics (*Shu-ching, Ch'un-ch'iu* and *Tso-shih-chuan*) in Loyang.
247	†Arrival in Nanking of the scholarly monk K'ang Seng-hui, member of a Sogdian family settled in Vietnam.
249	Death of the philosophers Ho Yen and Wang Pi, of the School of Mysteries (*hsüan-hsüeh*).
c.255	Death of the monk Chih Ch'ien, translator of Buddhist texts.
256	Death of Wang Su, legalist commentator on the Classics.
259	†Departure of the first known Chinese pilgrim for central Asia.

A.D.	History
263	End of the Shu-Han empire, annexed by Wei.
265	Ssu-ma Yen founds the dynasty of the *Chin* at Loyang.
268	Code of the T'ai-shih era (2926 articles) in the Chin empire.
280	Capture of Nanking and annexation of the Wu empire by Chin.

A.D.	Civilization
262	Death of the Taoist poet and musician Hsi K'ang.
263	Death of the poet Juan Chi.
265	*Death of the famous doctor Hua T'o, supposed to have been the founder of medical gymnastics, massage, and physiotherapy.
271	*Death of P'ei Hsiu, the first cartographer to use a north-south and east-west square pattern.
279	Discovery in a tomb in Honan of manuscripts on bamboo dating from the age of the Warring States and containing the *Annals of Wei* and the *Mu-t'ien-tzu chuan*.
282	*Death of Huang Mi-fu, author of the *Chen-chiu chia-i ching*, a treatise on acupuncture and moxibustion.
284	*Death of Tu Yu, jurist and commentator on the *Tso-chuan*, engineer and inventor of machines.
c.285	The *San-kuo-chih*, History of the Three Kingdoms (220–280).
286	†First translation of the *Lotus of the Good Law* at Ch'ang-an by Dharmaraksha.
300	Death of P'ei Wei and of Hsiang Hsiu, commentator on the *Chuang-tzu*, philosophers of the School of Mysteries.
c.300	The *Mai-ching, Treatise on the Pulse*, attributed to Wang Shu-ho.

A.D.	History	A.D.	Civilization
304	Li Hsiung proclaims himself King of Ch'eng-tu; Szechwan and part of Yunnan form an independent kingdom. Liu Yüan, a sinicized chieftain of Hsiung-nu tribes, founds the independent kingdom of Han in Shansi.		
310	Massive exodus of the Chinese upper classes towards the south.	310	†Arrival in Ch'ang-an of the Buddhist monk and thaumaturge Fo-t'u-teng. First map of the heavens by Ch'en Cho.
311	Loyang is sacked by Hsiung-nu mercenaries.	312	Death of Kuo Hsiang, commentator on the *Chuang-tzu* and philosopher of the School of Mysteries.
313	End of the commanderie of Lelang in Korea.		
316	Siege and capture of Ch'ang-an by the Hsiung-nu of Liu Yao. The Western Chin succumb to anarchy and the insurrections of sinicized Barbarians.	c.317	*The *Pao-p'u-tzu*, a work on Taoist techniques by the master Ko Hung.
317	Ssu-ma Jui proclaims himself emperor in Nanking: beginning of the dynasty of the EASTERN CHIN.	c.320	*Discovery of the precession of the equinoxes, known in Greece by 134 B.C.
319	Shih Le proclaims himself king of Chao in Hopei.	324	Death in the Eastern Chin kingdom of Kuo P'u, specialist in divination and commentator on the *Mu-t'ien-tzu* and the *Shan-hai-ching*.
347	The Chin advance to Ch'eng-tu and annex the territory of the Ch'eng-Han.	349	Kuan Sui observes that in the latitude of Nha-trang (Vietnam) the shadow on a sundial falls towards the south.
351	Foundation of the Kingdom of Ch'in in Ch'ang-an.		

A.D.	History	A.D.	Civilization
354	Foundation of the Earlier Liang in Kansu.		
357	Accession of Fu Chien, third sovereign of the Earlier Ch'in.		
364	Creation of the 'Yellow Registers' in the Chin Kingdom to take a census of immigrants from the north.		
		365	†The great Buddhist monk Hui-yüan, disciple of Tao-an, leaves Hsiang-yang for Chiang-ling. c.365, death of the calligrapher Wang Hsi-chih.
373	Fu Chien occupies Szechwan, Yunnan, and part of Kweichow.		
		374	†Bibliographical catalogue of Buddhist translations into Chinese by Tao-an (about 600 titles).
376	Fu Chien annexes the Kingdom of Liang in Kansu and extends his control to central Asia. All North China is united.		
		c.380	†The great Buddhist master Hui-yüan settles in Lu-shan (region of Chiu-chiang in Kiangsu).
		c.384	†Foundation of the great monastery of Ton-lin-ssu in Lu-shan.
385	Death of Fu Chien and decline of his empire.		
386	Foundation of the empire of the Toba-Wei or NORTHERN WEI.	c.386	†First suicide by fire of a Buddhist monk.
389	Foundation of the Later Liang.		
398	The Wei seize Yeh, capital of the Later Yen. Transfer to Ta-t'ung, the Wei capital, of inhabitants of Shantung and the north-east.		
		399	†The monk Fa-hsien leaves for India via central Asia.

A.D.	History
400–402	Rebellion of Sun En in Chekiang and southern Kiangsu.
402	Huan Hsüan, master of the central provinces of the Chin empire, rebels and marches on Nanking.
404	Fall of the dictator Huan Hsüan and restoration of the Eastern Chin in Nanking.
406	First measures of administrative centralization in the Northern Wei empire.
417	The Chin enter Ch'ang-an and put an end to the Later Ch'in.
420	Usurpation of Liu Yü, who founds the Sung dynasty in Nanking.
422	Northern Wei attacks on the Sung empire.
423	The Northern Wei occupy Loyang in Honan and build a wall over 1000 km long against the incursions of the Jou-jan.

A.D.	Civilization
c.401–404	†The monk Chih-yen's stay in Kashmir.
402	†Arrival in Ch'ang-an of the great Kuchean translator Kumarajiva.
404	†Chih-meng sets out with fifteen other monks for central Asia and India. Treaty of Hui-yüan affirming monks' independence of the secular authority.
411	Death of Ku K'ai-chih, first famous painter in Chinese history.
412	†Fa-hsien, back from India, Ceylon and Sumatra, lands on the coast of Shantung.
414	The *Fo-kuo-chi* (or *Fa-hsien-chuan*), *Treatise on Buddhist Kingdoms*, by Fa-hsien.
420	†Death of Kan Pao, author of the *Sou-shen-chi*, Taoist religious folklore. Fa-yung sets out for India with 25 other Buddhist monks.
427	Death of the famous Taoist poet T'ao Ch'ien (T'ao Yüan-ming).
c.430	The *Hou-han-shu*, *History of the Later Han*.
433	Death of the great poet Hsieh Ling-yün, who was influenced by Buddhism.

A.D.	History	A.D.	Civilization
439	Beginning of the period of the SOUTHERN AND NORTHERN DYNASTIES (NAN-PEI-CH'AO) (440–589).		
		444	†Under the influence of Kou Ch'ien-chih, Taoism is made the official religion of the Northern Wei empire.
450	Death of the famous minister Ts'ui Hao, principal architect of the reforms in the Northern Wei empire (Chinese administrative measures and Chinese penal law).		
		456	Death of the famous poet Yen Yen-chih in the Sung empire.
		460	†The monk T'an-yao is appointed director-general of the Buddhist clergy in the Northern Wei empire.
		477	†First description in a Chinese text of the stirrup.
478	Veto on marriages between aristocrats and commoners in the Wei empire.		
479	Hsiao Tao-ch'eng proclaims himself emperor and founds the Ch'i dynasty at Nanking.		
485	Implementation in the Wei state of a system of distribution of land (distinction between main-crop lands and mulberry orchards).		
		488	The *Sung-shih, History of the Sung* of Nanking (420–479).
		489	†Work starts on the Buddhist caves of Yün-kang, near Ta-t'ung.
493	The Wei move their capital to Loyang.		
		495	†Work starts on the Buddhist caves of Lung-men, near Loyang, new capital of the Northern Wei.

A.D.	History
502	Hsiao Yen proclaims himself emperor at Nanking and founds the Liang dynasty.
518	Sung Yün is sent on a mission to India by Empress Wu of the Wei.
525–527	Insurrections of soldiers and erstwhile nomads on the northern frontier of the Wei empire.

A.D.	Civilization
496	†Foundation of the Shao-lin-ssu, famous Buddhist monastery of the Sung-shan in Honan, which under the T'ang was to become one of the great centres of the Chinese *ch'an* sect.
c.500	The *Wen-hsin tiao-lung*, a famous work of literary criticism. The *Ku-hua p'in-lu*, the most ancient work of pictorial criticism. The *Ch'ien-tzu-wen*, a manual of elementary instruction.
502–509	†The Bodhisattva emperor Wu of the Liang, a fervent Buddhist.
508–525	†Period of great activity at the Buddhist caves of Lung-men, in the Northern Wei kingdom.
c.510	The *Shui-ching-chu, Commentary on the Classic of the Waters* (geography and folklore).
513	Death of the phonetician Shen Yüeh, adviser to Emperor Wu of the Liang.
c.515–518	†The *Hung-ming-chi*, a collection of apologias for Buddhism.
515	†The *Ch'u-san-tsang chi-chi*, a catalogue of Buddhist translations into Chinese by Seng-yu.
c.530	The *Wen-hsüan*, a celebrated anthology of literary texts from the Han to the Liang. †The *Kao-seng-chuan, Biographies of Eminent Monks*, by Hui-chiao of the Liang.

A.D.	History	A.D.	Civilization
534	Kao Huan moves the capital to Yeh (foundation of the Eastern Wei empire).		
535	Beginning of the Western Wei at Ch'ang-an.	536	†Death of the Taoist master T'ao Hung-ching in the Liang kingdom.
		c.540	The *Ch'i-min yao-shu*, a famous work on agricultural techniques (North China).
543	Construction by the Eastern Wei of defence walls against the Turks.		
544	Proclamation in Vietnam of the kingdom of Viet.	547	The *Lo-yang Ch'ieh-lan chi*, a description of Loyang and its monasteries.
548	Siege of Nanking by Hou Ching.		
550	Kao Yang seizes power at Yeh and founds the dynasty of the Northern Ch'i.		
552	The Turks create, between 552 and 555, a new empire of the steppes.	554	The *Wei-shu, History of the Wei*, by Wei Shou, who lived in the Northern Ch'i kingdom.
553	The Western Wei occupy Szechwan.		
555–556	Conscription of 1,800,000 men to build 1500 km of Great Walls in the north of the Northern Ch'i empire.		
557	Yü-wan Chiao founds the Northern Chou empire at Ch'ang-an. Ch'en Pa-hsien founds the Ch'en empire at Nanking.		
564	Code of law of the Northern Ch'i, ancestor of the Sui and T'ang codes.	574	†The Northern Chou take measures against the Buddhist clergy.

A.D.	History	A.D.	Civilization
577	The Chou annex the territory of the Ch'i. All North China is unified.		
581	General Yang Chien founds the SUI dynasty at Ch'ang-an.		
583	Sui victories over the Turks and the T'u-yü-hun.		
585–587	Construction of Great Walls in the north and of a canal in the Yang-chow region.		
589	The Sui armies enter Nanking. End of the Ch'en empire.		
		594	†The *Chung-ching mu-lu* by Fa-ching, a catalogue of Buddhist works translated into Chinese.
		597	†Death of Chih-i, founder of the Buddhist T'ien-t'ai sect.
		c.600	*First bridges suspended on iron chains.
604	Accession of Emperor Yang of the Sui.		
605	Completion of the system of big canals. Construction of Loyang.		
606	Construction of the big grain storehouses in Loyang.		
614	Emperor Yang's third expedition to Korea.		
617	Li Yüan, governor of T'ai-yüan in Shansi, makes an alliance with the Turks and marches on Ch'ang-an.		
618	Assassination of the Sui emperor Yang at Yang-chow. Li Yüan founds the T'ANG dynasty in Ch'ang-an.		
619	The T'ang institute the system of the three taxes: taxes in grain, compulsory labour and deliveries of cloth.		
		620	Oldest Chinese coins found on the east coast of Africa date from this time.

A.D.	History	Civilization
624	Promulgation of the agrarian laws (system of distributing main-crop land on a life tenure).	
629		†The monk Hsüan-tsang sets out from Ch'ang-an for India via central Asia.
630	Decisive T'ang victory over the eastern Turks. First Japanese embassy at the T'ang court.	
630–645	The T'ang advance into central Asia and control the lines of communication.	
631		†The Gospel is brought to Ch'ang-an by Nestorians from Iran.
638	Embassy from Sassanid Persia in Ch'ang-an.	
643	Embassy from Byzantium in Ch'ang-an.	
644	T'ang offensive by land and sea against Koguryo in Korea.	
645		†The *Hsü kao-seng chuan*, biographies of eminent monks of the VI and VII centuries. Return from India to Ch'ang-an of the monk Hsüan-tsang. The *Ta-t'ang hsi-yü chi*, *Treatise on the Western Regions in the Time of the T'ang*.
c.652		*The Indian Chia-she Hsiao-wei is employed in the astronomical office.
655	Expedition to Korea to help Silla, attacked by Koguryo and Paekche.	
656		*History of the Sui* (*Sui-shu*). *The *Suan-ching shih-shu*, *Ten Treatises on Mathematics*.
657	The T'ang and the Uighurs inflict a serious defeat on the Western Turks.	
659		*History of the Southern Dynasties* (*Nan-shih*). *The *Hsin-hsiu pen-ts'ao*, official pharmacopoeia.

A.D.	History	A.D.	Civilization
661	Chinese administration in Kashmir, in the valley of the Amu-Darya, in Bokhara and on the borders of eastern Iran.		
663	Chinese armies defeat the Japanese troops who had come to the help of Paekche.		
		664	†Death of the great Buddhist master Hsüan-tsang. The *Kuang hung-ming-chi*, a collection of apologias for Buddhism.
665	The T'ang possess 700,000 horses on the state stud farms.		
666–668	End of the kingdoms of Kogaryo and Paekche. Manchuria and Korea under Chinese control. Unification of southern Korea by the kingdom of Silla, an ally of the T'ang.	667	†Death of the monk Tao-hsüan, a specialist in the monachal discipline (Vinaya) and in the history of Chinese Buddhism.
		668	†The *Fa-yüan chu-lin*, a Buddhist encyclopaedia.
		670	*The *Shih-liao pen ts'ao*, a treatise on dietetics. *Death of the astronomer Li Ch'un-feng.
		671	The monk I-ching leaves China via Canton for SouthEast Asia and India.
		672	*Map of the heavens.
		673	Death of the great painter Yen Li-pen, the continuer of medieval traditions.
680	Tibetan incursions into north-west China and central Asia grow more frequent.	681	†Death of Shan-tao, first patriarch of the Buddhist Pure Land sect.
684	The empress Wu usurps power.		

A.D.	Civilization
c.690	†The *Ta-t'ang hsi-yü-ch'iu-fa kao-seng chuan*, an account by I-ching of the pilgrims who went to India in the T'ang age.
692	†The *Nan-hai chi-kui nei-fa chuan* by I-ching, an account of the state of Buddhism in India and South-East Asia.
694	†The Manichean religion authorized by the empress Tse-t'ien.
710	The *Shih-t'ung, Generalities on History*, by Liu Chih-chi.
713	†Death of the Cantonese monk Hui-neng, founder of the *ch'an* sect.
718–729	*The *K'ai-yüan chan-ching*, an Indian collection of astronomical texts in which the symbol for zero figures.
721–725	*Scientific expeditions by the monk I-hsing to measure the shadow of the solstices from the 40th to the 17th degree of latitude.
c.725	*I-hsing's astronomical water-driven clock with escapement.

A.D.	History
690	Empress Wu founds the new dynasty of the Chou (690–705).
691	Transfer of several hundred thousand families from the valley of the Wei to the area of Loyang.
692	Development of the recruitment of civil servants by examination. Re-establishment of the government-general of central Asia at Kucha.
694	Victory over the Tibetans and Turks.
705	Restoration of the T'ang dynasty.
710	Start of the system of appointing imperial commissioners to command military regions (*chieh-tu-shih*).
712	Accession of the emperor Hsüan-tsung.
725	The re-establishment since 705 of the state stud-farms puts 420,000 horses at the government's disposal.
733	The number of imperial civil servants rises to 17,680 and that of locally recruited staff to 57,416.
734	Reform of the system of canal transport by P'ei Yao-ch'ing.

A.D.	History	A.D.	Civilization
742	The defence of the frontiers is entrusted to ten imperial commissioners. An Lu-shan controls the armies of Hopei, Shansi, Shantung, and southern Manchuria.		
745–751	Chinese counter-offensive against the Arabs in Transoxiania and the regions to the south of Lake Balkhash.		
751	Chinese armies commanded by the Korean general Kao Hsien-chih are defeated by the Arabs near Alma Ata, on the River Talas.		
755–763	Rebellion of An Lu-shan.		
756	An Lu-shan proclaims himself emperor. Flight of the emperor Hsüan-tsung to Szechwan.		
757	Death of An Lu-shan. Shih Ssu-ming succeeds him as leader of the rebellion.		
758	Institution of the salt monopoly.		
		761	Death of Wang Wei, painter and poet.
762	The Uighurs sack Ch'ang-an and massacre the inhabitants.	762	Death of the poet Li Pai.
763	End of the rebellion of An Lu-shan. Emperor Su-tsung enters Ch'ang-an.		
After 768	The military governments of the Chieh-tu-shih act in an increasingly arbitrary fashion.		
		770	Death of the great poet Tu Fu.
778	The receipts from the salt monopoly form more than half the total revenues of the T'ang.		
780	Fundamental reform of taxation by Yang Yen: substitution of taxes on harvests for taxes on families.		

A.D.	History	A.D.	Civilization
		781	†Nestorian stele in Chinese and Syriac set up in Ch'ang-an.
787	Treaty of peace between the T'ang and the Tibetans. Alliance of the T'ang with the Uighurs and Nan-chao against the Tibetans.		
790	The T'ang have lost control of all the territories to the west of Yü-men-kuan (western Kansu).	797	†Controversy at Lhasa between Chinese and Indian monks.
		c.800	The *T'ung-tien* by Tu Yu, a history of institutions from antiquity to about 800.
		805	Death of the famous geographer Chia Tan.
806–820	Eunuchs control the government.	806–820	First bankers' bills ('flying money', *fei-ch'ien*).
		819	†Han Yü's denunciation of Buddhism. Death of Liu Tsung-yüan, first defender, with Han Yü, of the 'ancient style' (*ku-wen*).
821	Sino-Tibetan treaty concluded at Ch'ang-an and ratified at Lhasa the following year recognizing the independence of Tibet and the occupation of Kansu by the Tibetans.		
826	A clan of eunuchs puts the emperor Wen-tsung in power.		
840	Dispersal and division of the Uighur tribes.	c.841	The *T'ang-ch'ao ming-hua lu*, a work of pictorial criticism by Chu Ching-yüan.
		842–845	†Proscription of foreign religions and of Buddhism.
		c.844	Death of Li Ao, precursor of the 'neo-Confucian' philosophers of the XI century.

A.D.	History	A.D.	Civilization
845	Following the great proscription of Buddhism, recovery of copper, land, and serfs from the Church.	846	Death of the poet Pai Chü-i.
		847	*Notes on the Famous Painters of the Past, Li-tai ming-hua chi*, by Chang Yen-yüan.
		858	Death of the poet Li Shang-yin.
		c.860	The *Man-shu*, a monograph on Yunnan, (history, ethnography, botany, etc.).
863	Capture of Hanoi by the troops of Nan-chao.		
866	Nan-chao evacuates the north of Vietnam in face of Chinese attacks.	868	*First known book printed by the wood-block process. (Buddhist sutra found at Tun-huang.)
874–884	Itinerant rebellion of Huang Chao and Wang Hsien-chih.		
879	Sack of Canton by Huang Chao's troops.		
880	Huang Chao's troops march back to Honan. Loyang put to the sword and burnt.		
884	End of Huang Chao's rebellion.		
893	The Yellow River bursts its dykes and changes course.		
894	Nineteenth and last Japanese embassy to the T'ang court.		
895	Anarchy in Ch'ang-an.		
902–909	The empire split up into several independent kingdoms.		
907	Chu Ch'üan-chung founds the Liang dynasty in K'ai-feng. Beginning of the FIVE DYNASTIES.		

A.D.	History	A.D.	Civilization
916	Foundation of the Turco-Mongol kingdom of the Khitan in eastern Mongolia and Manchuria.	c.920	The Khitan adopt a script based on the Chinese one for their own language.
923	Foundation of the Later T'ang dynasty.	932-952	Wood-block edition of the Nine Classics produced at K'ai-feng.
936	Foundation of the Later Chin dynasty at K'ai-feng.		
939	Vietnam becomes independent.	c.940	First allusion in a Chinese text to the rudder.
947	Great invasion of the Khitan. Capture of K'ai-feng and fall of the Chin. The Khitan adopt the dynastic name of LIAO. Foundation of the Later Han dynasty at K'ai-feng.		
951	Foundation of the Later Chou at K'ai-feng.	955	†The Northern Chou take measures against the Buddhist clergy.
960	Foundation of the SUNG DYNASTY by Chao K'uang-yin at K'ai-feng.	966-976	†Last big pilgrimage of Chinese monks to central Asia and India.
		967	The *Chiu wu-tai shih, History of the Five Dynasties* (907-960). Death of the painter Li Ch'eng, an innovator in the technique of painting.
969	Progressive substitution of civil personnel for military personnel in the provinces.	(by) 970	*Conversion of rotary movement into alternating movement—and *vice versa*—by means of eccentric, crank-shaft and piston rod (c.1450 in Europe).

A.D.	History	A.D.	Civilization
971	The Sung armies enter Canton. End of the Southern Han Kingdom.	971–983	†The Buddhist canon printed in Ch'eng-tu.
973	First recruitment competitions under the Sung.		
975	The Sung enter Nanking. End of the Kingdom of Chiang-nan (Southern T'ang).		
978	The Sung annex the kingdom of Wu-Yüeh.	978	*Probable first use of the endless chain for the transmission of energy (XIXc. in Europe).
979	All the Chinese lands unified by the Sung.	981	First printing of the *T'ai-p'ing kuang-chi*, huge collection of stories from the Han to the Sung.
		983	The *T'ai-p'ing yü-lan* encyclopaedia.
983	Creation of the three departments of the economy (*San-ssu*): state monopolies, agrarian taxes and budget.	984	*First canal lock.
		986	The *Wen-yüan ying-hua*, a literary anthology of the VI–X centuries.
986	Victory of the Khitan over the Sung and expansion of the Khitan in the north-east (Manchuria).	987	†The *Sung kao-seng chuan*, biographies of eminent monks of the VII–X centuries.
		c.990	*Mention of the compass in a work of geomancy.
993	Creation of salt and tea commissariats in the main regions of the Sung empire.	1004	†The *Ching-te ch'uan-teng lu*, biographies of monks of the *ch'an* sect.
1004	Peace of Shan-yüan between the Sung and the Khitan. It obliges the Sung to pay a heavy annual tribute in silk and silver.	1010	The *Chu-tao t'u-ching*, an illustrated geography of the Sung empire in 1566 chapters.
1012	First large-scale imports of species of early-ripening rice from Champa into the Sung empire.		

A.D.	Civilization
1013	The *Ts'e-fu yüan-kui*, a collection of political texts and essays.
c.1022	†The *Yün-chi ch'i-ch'ien*, a big Taoist compilation.
1024	The first promissory notes, issued in Szechwan.
1027	*Construction of a vehicle to measure distances along roads.
1034– 1036	Catalogue of the imperial library made by Fan Chung-yen and Ou-yang Hsiu.
1040	*The *Wu-ching tsung-yao*, a big treatise on the art of war (describes magnetism through retentivity).
1041– 1048	First attempts at printing with movable type.
1053	Death of the reformer Fan Chung-yen.
1054	*Observation of a supernova.
1061	The *Hsin-t'ang-shu*, *New History of the T'ang* (618–907), by Ou-yang Hsiu.
1063	The *Chi-ku-lu* by Ou-yang Hsiu, a work on ancient epigraphy.
c.1070	The *Hsin wu-tai shih*, *New History of the Five Dynasties*, by Ou-yang Hsiu.

A.D.	History
1038	The Tangut found the empire of the HSIA or Hsi-hsia (Western Hsia).
1044	Treaty of peace between the Sung and the Hsia; it obliges the Sung to pay a heavy annual tribute in silks, silver, and tea.
1068	Application of the new fiscal, administrative and military laws (*hsin-fa*) of Wang An-shih.

A.D.	History	A.D.	Civilization
1073	Six thousand million copper coins cast during the single year 1073.	1073	*Death of the philosopher Chou Tun-yi.
1077	The Yellow River breaks its dykes downstream from K'ai-feng.	1077	*Death of the mathematician and naturalist Shao K'ang-chieh (Shao Yung). Death of the philosopher Chang Tsai.
		1080	*The *Meng-ch'i pi-t'an*, a collection of various notes; one of the main sources for the history of the sciences in China.
		1084	Ssu-ma Kuang's *Tzu-chih t'ung-chien*, a famous general history of China from 403 B.C. to A.D. 959. Printing of the *Suan-ching shih-shu*, a collection of mathematical works.
1085	The conservative Ssu-ma Kuang is called upon to govern. Abolition of the New Laws of Wang An-shih.	1085	Death of the philosopher Ch'eng Hao.
1086	Death of Wang An-shih and Ssu-ma Kuang.	1086	*Su Sung's map of the heavens.
1087	Creation of a merchant shipping office at Ch'üan-chou.	1088	*Su Sung's astronomical clock actuated by an escapement system and worked by water.
		1090	First attested use of the compass in Chinese ships.
1094	Wang An-shih's New Laws are gradually re-introduced and the reformers are recalled from exile.	1101	Death of the famous poet Su Shih (Su Tung-p'o).
		1103	*The *Ying-tsao fa-shih*, a big treatise on architecture.
		1105	Death of the famous poet Huang T'ing-chien.
		1107	Death of Mi Fu, painter and aesthete, author of a history of painting, the *Hua-shih*.
		1108	Death of the philosopher Ch'eng I.

History

A.D.	
1115	The Jürchen found the CHIN (Kin) empire in Manchuria.
1122	The Chin and the Sung hold the Liao empire in a pincer grip. Capture of Peking by the Chin.
1125	End of the Khitan empire of the LIAO. Big Chin invasion of North China.
1127	In face of the Chin attacks the Sung take refuge south of the Yangtze. Beginning of the SOUTHERN SUNG.
1132	Emperor Kao-tsung of the SOUTHERN SUNG takes up residence in Hangchow.
1138	Treaty of peace between the Sung and the Chin.
1148	The Yellow River changes course.
1151	The Chin transfer their main capital to Peking (Yenching).
1154	First issue of paper money in the Chin empire.
1162	Famous battle of Ts'ai-shi in Anhwei, in which the Sung defeat the Chin armies.

Civilization

A.D.	
1123	The *Hsüan-ho shu-hua p'u*, a catalogue of the paintings and pieces of calligraphy in the imperial collection.
1124	†The *Pi-yen-lu*, a collection of *kung-an* (themes for meditation) of the *ch'an* school.
1125	End of the reign of the emperor Hui-tsung, painter, aesthete and collector.
1141(?)	Death of the poetess Li Ch'ing-chao.
1147	Preface of the *Tung-ching meng-hua lu*, a description of K'ai-feng at the beginning of the twelfth century.
1162	Death of Cheng Ch'iao, author of the *T'ung-chih*, a historical encyclopaedia of a new kind.
1163	†Synagogue in K'ai-feng.

A.D.	Civilization	A.D.	History
1178	The *Ling-wai tai-ta* by Chou Ch'ü-fei, on the countries of South-East Asia and the Indian Ocean.	1194	The Yellow River moves from the north of the Shantung peninsula to the south of it.
1192	Death of the 'intuitionist' philosopher Lu Chiu-yüan.		
1193	*Celestial planisphere of Soochow (polar projection).		
1196	Chu Hsi's interpretations of the Classics are declared heterodox by the Sung court.	1206	Genghis Khan comes into power in Mongolia.
1200	Death of Chu Hsi.	1214	The Chin, under pressure from the Mongols, move their capital to K'ai-feng.
1209	Death of the famous poet Lu Yu.		
1225	The *Chu-fan-chih* by Chao Ju-kua, about the lands of South-East Asia and the Indian Ocean.	1227	End of the empire of the Western Hsia. Death of Genghis Khan.
1227	†Death of the Taoist master Ch'ang-ch'un, religious adviser to Ghenghis Khan.	1229	Yeh-lü Ch'u-ts'ai becomes administrator-general of north China for the Mongols.
		1233	The Mongols seize K'ai-feng.
		1234	End of the Chin, through the combined action of the Mongols and the Sung.
1235	In the Sung empire, death of Yen Yü, author of *Ts'ang-lang shih-shua*, a famous treatise on the art of poetry.		
		1236	First issue of paper money in the Mongol realm.

A.D.	Civilization
1242	The Mongols favour the Buddhist *ch'an* sect. *The *Hsi-yüan-lu*, the first treatise in forensic medicine, produced in the Southern Sung empire.
1247	*The *Shu-shu chiu-chang*, a treatise on mathematics by the Sung writer Ch'in Chiu-shao.
1260	†The Tibetan monk 'Phags-pa is entrusted with the direction of the religious communities of north China.
1261	†All the favours of the Mongol court are given to Tibetan lamaism.
1262	*Death of the Sung mathematician Ch'in Chiu-shao, the first to use the symbol nought.
1269	Adoption of the script invented by the Tibetan lama 'Phags-pa to transcribe Mongol.

A.D.	History
1239	The Mongols entrust the collection of taxes in north China to Moslems from central Asia.
1251	Beginning of Liu Ping-Chung's reforms in the Mongol empire.
1253	The Mongol armies reach Szechwan and Yunnan.
1257	Mongol incursions into Vietnam.
1260	Accession of Kublai Khan. The Mongols enforce the use of promissory notes to the exclusion of any other kind of money.
1264	Peking becomes the Mongol capital.
1267	Start of the construction of the ramparts of Mongol Peking (Khanbalik).
1271	The engineer and mathematician Kuo Shou-ching is entrusted by the Mongols with all problems of river regulation and irrigation. The Mongols take the dynastic title of YÜAN.

A.D.	History
1274	First attempt by the Mongols to invade Japan.
1276	The Mongol armies enter Hangchow.
1279	Suicide of the last Southern Sung emperor. All China occupied by the Mongols.
1279–1294	Construction of the northern section of the Grand Canal.
1281	Second attempt by the Mongols to invade Japan. The 'wind of the gods' (kamikaze) destroys the Sino-Korean fleet commanded by the Mongols.
1285	Champa and Cambodia recognize Mongol suzerainty.
1287	Fresh expedition to Vietnam.
1288	Vietnam recognizes Mongol suzerainty.
1289	The Yellow River changes course.
1292–1293	Mongol expedition to Java.
1294	Death of Kublai Khan.

A.D.	Civilization
1274	Preface of the *Meng-lian-lu*, a long description of Hangchow, the Southern Sung capital.
1275	†Nestorian archbishop of Peking. *Works of the Southern Sung mathematician Yang Hui.
1275–1291	Marco Polo in the service of Kublai Khan.
1277	†A Tibetan lama is appointed administrator-general of the religious communities in South China.
1279	*Kuo Shou-ching constructs astronomical instruments in Peking. *Death of the Sung mathematician Li Yeh (or Li Chih).
1289	*Foundation of the Islamic academy of Peking at the suggestion of the minister Moiz-al-Din.
1296	Death of Wang Ying-lin, author of the big encyclopaedia *Yü-hai*.

A.D.	Civilization
c.1300	Death of the Peking dramatist Wang Shih-fu, author of the *Hsi-hsiang-chi*. *Death of Jamal-al-Din, astronomer and geographer to the Mongol court.
1303	*The *Ssu-yüan yü-chien*, an important treatise on algebra by Chu Shih-chieh. The Yüan declare the 'neo-Confucian' doctrine and interpretation of the Classics official.
1307	*Giovanni di Monte Corvino appointed Archbishop of Khanbalik (Yüan Peking).
1313	*The *Nung-shu*, a treatise on agriculture by Wang Chen.
1317	The *Wen-hsien t'ung-K'ao*, a history of institutions from antiquity to the Sung age.
1320	The big atlas, *Yü-ti-t'u*.
1337	Death of the geographer Chu Ssu-pen.
1344–1345	Official histories of the Sung (*Sung-shih*), of the Liao (*Liao-shih*), and of the Chin (*Chin-shih*).

A.D.	History
1315	First recruitment competition under the Mongol regime.
1324	The Yellow River changes course.
1336	The Yellow River returns to its old course.
1346	Peasant revolts in the provinces affected by famine.
1351	Anti-Mongol insurrections spread. First mention of the Red Turbans (*Hung-chin*).
1355	Han Lin-erh, a rebel leader, proclaims himself emperor of the Sung. From this time onwards a considerable part of the empire is free from Mongol control.
1364	Chu Yüan-chang proclaims himself King of Wu.

A.D.	History
1368	Proclamation of the MING dynasty by Chu Yüan-chang. Peking liberated.
1369	The Mongol armies encircled in eastern Mongolia.
1380	Big political purges. Trial of Hu Wei-yung, old companion-in-arms of the founder of the Ming dynasty.
1387	All China liberated. General land register of the empire.
1398	Death of Chu Yüan-chang, founder of the Ming dynasty (end of the Hung-wu era).
1402	Chu Ti, prince of Yen, takes Nanking and proclaims himself emperor. Beginning of the Yung-le era: 1403–1424.
1403–1435	Construction of Great Walls in North China.
1405–1433	Big maritime expeditions of the Ming to South-East Asia, the Indian Ocean, the Persian Gulf, the Red Sea and the east coast of Africa.
1406	Occupation of Vietnam by the Ming armies.

A.D.	Civilization
1365	Preface of the *T'u-hui pao-chien*, a treatise on painting with biographies of 1500 painters from the III to the XIV century.
1366	The *Ch'o-keng-lu, The Interrupted Ploughing*, notes on the social history of China in the Mongol period.
1368	*Creation of a Moslem astronomical office in Nanking, the Ming capital.
1370	The *Yüan-shih*, an official history of the Mongol period.
1374	Death of the classical painter Ni Tsan.
c.1378	Publication of the *Chien-teng hsin-hua*, a collection of stories.
1387	Start of the compositions in eight parts (*pa-ku*) in the official competitions.

A.D.	History
1411–1415	Repairs to the Grand Canal of the Mongol period.
1421	Decision to move the capital from Nanking to Peking.
1426	The Secret Council of the Nei-ke becomes preponderant; reinforcement of absolutism.
1427	Vietnam becomes independent again.
1433	Return of Cheng Ho's last maritime expedition to the Indian Ocean and the Red Sea.
1440–1441	Construction of the Peking palaces.
1449	Serious Chinese defeat at T'u-mu in Shansi. The emperor taken prisoner by the Mongols.
1470–1480	Construction of Great Walls in North China.
1505	The eunuch Liu Chin becomes all-powerful in the government.
1511	Albuquerque arrives in Malacca.
1514	Opening of silver mines in western Yunnan.
1528	Repairs to the Grand Canal.
1530–1581	Extension of monetary taxation based on silver ingots.

A.D.	Civilization
1407	The *Yung-le ta-tien*, a huge collection of texts.
1415	The *Hsing-li ta-ch'üan*, the *Wu-ching ta-ch'üan*, and the *Ssu-shu ta-ch'üan*, manuals on the 'neo-Confucian' philosophy, the Classics and the Four Books.
1500	Death of the Cantonese philosopher Ch'en Hsien-chang.
1518	First edition of the philosophical conversations of Wang Shou-jen (Wang Yang-ming).
1520	*First use of cannon bought by the Ming from the Portuguese.
1528	Death of Wang Yang-ming.
c.1530–1540	First allusions to the ground-nut.

A.D.	History	A.D.	Civilization
1540 (from)	Renewal of Japanese piracy on the coast.	1541	Death of Wang Ken, a philosopher of the school of Wang Yang-ming.
		1543	Mei Cho denounces the apocryphal nature of certain parts of the *Shang-shu* in ancient characters, one of the Classics.
1550	Peking is besieged for a week by the Mongols.	1550	The *Nan-chao yeh-shih*, a history of the Yunnanese kingdoms of Nan-chao and Ta-li (649–1253).
1555	The Japanese pirates attack Hangchow and threaten Nanking. Earthquake in the north-west: 830,000 victims.		
c.1570	First imports of silver from America.	c.1570	The *Journey to the West, Hsi-yu-chi*, a famous novel recounting the adventures of the monk Hsüan-tsang and the monkey Sun Wu-K'ung. *Variolation in everyday use.
1570–1580	Generalization of monetary taxation based on silver ingots.	1573–	First mention of the cultivation of maize.
		1619	(The Wan-li era.) Zenith of Chinese printing.
		1574	*Edition in movable type of the big collection of tales, *T'ai-p'ing kuang-chi*.
		1578	*The *Pen-ts'ao kang-mu*, the famous big treatise on the pharmacopoeia by Li Shih-chen, is completed.
		1583	The Jesuit missionaries Ricci and Ruggieri settle in Kwangtung. The *Shu-yü chou-tzu lu*, on the countries of east and central Asia.
1584–1590	Construction of the tomb of Emperor Wan-li.	1584	*The prince imperial Chu Tsai-yü defines the tempered scale. †The *T'ien-chu shih-lu*, the first catechism in Chinese.

A.D.	History	A.D.	Civilization
1590–1605	'Mining fever'.		
1592	The Japanese land in Korea under the command of Hideyoshi. Chinese defeat at Pyongyang.		
1593	Chinese victory over the Japanese in Korea.		
1596	Second Japanese invasion of Korea. From 1596 onwards, riots by workmen and traders in the towns multiply.		
1598	Withdrawal of the Japanese from Korea.	1598	†Death of the Fukienese Lin Chao-en, founder of the syncretist San-i-chiao sect.
		1601	†Matteo Ricci settles in Peking.
		1602	†Atlas of the world in Chinese by M. Ricci. Death of Li Chih, the nonconformist philosopher.
		1604	Restoration of the private Tung-lin academy founded in the Sung age.
		1606	*The *Chi-bo yüan-pen*, a translation of the first six books of Clavius' *Elements of Euclid*.
		1607	†Printed edition of the Taoist canon.
		1609	The *San-ts'ai t'u-bui*, an illustrated encyclopaedia.
		1615	Death of the scholarly monk Chu-hung.
1615–1627	Conflict between the eunuch party and the Tung-lin party.		
		c.1619	The *Chin-p'ing-mei*, a famous novel of manners.
1621	The Jürchen take Shen-yang (Mukden) and Liao-yang.	1621	*The *Wu-pei-chib*, a big treatise on the military art.
		1623	*The *Chib-fang wai-chi*, Father Aleni's universal geography.

A.D.	Civilization
1623–1632	Publication of the *San-yen* and the *Erh-p'ai*, big collections of tales.
1635	*The *Ch'ung-chen li-shu*, a collection of scientific works written in collaboration by Jesuit missionaries and Chinese literati.
1636	Death of the painter Tung Ch'i-ch'ang.
1637	*The *T'ien-kung k'ai-wu*, a big treatise on technology.
1639	*Publication of the *Nung-cheng ch'üan-shu*, a treatise on agriculture by Hsü Kuang-ch'i.
1640	*Death of the famous geographer Hsü Hung-tsu (Hsü Hsia-k'o).

A.D.	History
1624	The Dutch establish posts on the coast of Taiwan.
1624–1627	Dictatorship of the eunuch Wei Chung-hsian.
1625	Terrible persecution of the members of the Tung-lin.
1626	Death of Nurhaci, founder of the Jürchen-Manchu power.
1627	Start of the big military and peasant revolts of the end of the Ming period.
1635	The Jürchen start to call themselves Manchus.
1644	Li Tzu-ch'eng enters Peking, where the Ming emperor commits suicide. He is driven out of the city by the Manchus. Beginning of the CH'ING dynasty. Chang Hsien-chung invades Szechwan.
1645	The Manchus make the Chinese wear the pigtail and Manchu clothes, and create enclaves in North China.
1646	The Manchus occupy Chekiang, Fukien, and Szechwan.
1647	Canton is taken by the Manchus.

A.D.	History	A.D.	Civilization
1649–1662	Piratical activities of Cheng Ch'eng-kung (Coxinga) on the coast of Fukien and in Taiwan.	1650	†First Catholic church in Peking, the Nan-t'ang. *After 1650, the *Wu-li hsiao-chih*, Fang I-chih's work on natural philosophy.
1657	Reopening of the official competitions.	1656	The *Huang-shu* by Wang Fu-chih, on political philosophy and the theory of Chinese nationalism.
1661	Accession of Emperor K'ang-hsi. Coxinga lands in Taiwan and drives the Dutch out. End of resistance by the Southern Ming.	1659	†*The Intolerable*, an anti-Christian pamphlet by Yang Kuang-hsien.
1662	The Ch'ing order the evacuation of all the coastal regions.	1663	The *Ming-i tai-fang lu* by Huang Tsung-hsi, a critique of absolutist institutions.
1668	Manchuria is closed to Chinese.	1664	†The Jesuit missionaries in difficulties.
1673	Wu San Kuei's rebellion against the Ch'ing and secession of the southern provinces.	1670	The *Sixteen Moral Maxims* (*Holy Instructions*) of K'ang-hsi.
1677	The Ch'ing reconquer Fukien and the north-western provinces.	1676	Ku Yan-wu's *Jih-chih-lu*, a collection of historical notes. Huang Tsung-hsi's *Ming-ju hsueh-an*, an intellectual history of the Ming age.

A.D.	History	A.D.	Civilization
		1679	Selection of compilers for the *History of the Ming*.
1680	The Ch'ing reoccupy Szechwan.		
1681	The Ch'ing reconquer Kweichow.		
1683	Final occupation of Taiwan by the Ch'ing.		
1685	Any fresh confiscation of land for the Banners is forbidden.		
1689	Treaty of Nerchinsk between the Ch'ing and the Russians.	1692	Death of the philosopher Wang Fu-chih.
1697	The Ch'ing armies occupy Outer Mongolia.	c.1700	The *Liao-chai chih-i* by P'u Sung-ling, a collection of tales in classical Chinese.
		1703	The *Ch'üan-t'ang-shih*, a complete collection of poets of the T'ang age.
		1704	Death of the philosopher Yen Yüan.
		1707	†Mgr. de Tournon anathematizes in Nanking the practices and customs of the Chinese.
		1710	*Fathers de Mailla and Regis are entrusted by K'ang-hsi with the task of drawing up a general map of the empire.
		1714	Death of the philosopher Hu Wei.
		1716	The *P'ei-wen yün-fu*, a big dictionary of rhymes, and the *Kang-hsi tzu-tien*, a dictionary of characters.
1723	Accession of the emperor Yung-cheng.		
1727	Treaty of Kiakhta between China and Russia.		

A.D.	Civilization
1729	Printed edition in movable type of the encyclopaedia *T'u-shu chi-ch'eng*, comprising 10,000 chapters. The *Ta-i chüeh-mi lu*, a work by the emperor Yung-cheng defending the legitimacy of the Manchu dynasty.
1735	The *History of the Ming (Ming-shih)* is completed.
c.1745–1749	The *Forest of Literati, Ju-lin wai-shih*, a big novel of social criticism.
1747	The *Yüan-ming-yüan*, the emperor Ch'ien-lung's summer palace, is rebuilt in Western style.
1758	Death of Hui Tung, a specialist in the Han commentators.
1763	Ts'ao Hsüeh-ch'in leaves unfinished at his death his great romantic, psychological novel of manners, the *Dream of the Red Chamber (Hung-lou-meng* or *Shih-t'ou-chi).*
1769	*The *Atlas of Ch'ien-lung*, a combined work by Jesuit missionaries and Chinese geographers.
1774–1789	The great 'literary inquisition' of the Ch'ien-lung era.

A.D.	History
1729	Creation of the Chün-chi-ch'u, the supreme organ of government (progress of centralization).
1735	Accession of the emperor Ch'ien-lung.
1746–	Revolts by the peoples of Chin-ch'uan in north-western Szechwan.
1751	The Ch'ing finally occupy Tibet.
1756–1757	Extermination of the Dzungars by the Ch'ing armies. Conquest of the Ili valley.
1758–1759	Conquest of the Tarim basin by the Ch'ing.
1762	200 million inhabitants recorded by census.
1766	Renewal of agitation in the Chin-ch'uan.
1767–1771	Sino-Burmese war.
1775	Ho-shen, a young general of the Banners, becomes the favourite of the emperor Ch'ien-lung. Advance of corruption. 264 million inhabitants recorded in census.

A.D.	Civilization
1777	Death of Tai Chen, mathematician, philologist and philosopher, the most eminent representative of the school of critical studies (*k'ao-cheng-hsüeh*).
1782	Conclusion of the *Ssu-k'u ch'üan-shu*, a complete collection of works in Chinese, and of the notes to it.
1799	*The *Ch'ou-jen-chuan* by Juan Yüan, notes on the history of mathematics and astronomy in China.
1801	Death of the historian and philosopher Chang Hsüeh-ch'eng.
1804	Death of Ch'ien Ta-hsin, author of works on mathematics, geography, history, epigraphy, and other subjects.

A.D.	History
1776	End of the Chin-ch'uan rebellions.
1781–1784	Revolts by Moslems in Kansu, following the creation of a new sect by Ma Ming-hsin.
1782	More than 10,000 Chinese colonists slaughtered by Vietnamese.
1787–1788	Bloody suppression of revolt in Taiwan.
1788–1789	Ch'ing expeditions to Vietnam.
1791–1792	Expedition by the Manchu armies to Nepal against the Gurkhas.
1795–1803	White Lotus rebellions in North China.
1796	Ch'ien-lung abdicates in favour of Chia-ch'ing, but in fact continues to reign.
1799	Death of the emperor Ch'ien-lung and of his favourite Ho-shen.
1811–1814	Rising of the Celestial Order sect (*T'ien-li-chiao*) in Shantung and Hopei.
1812	Census: 361 million inhabitants.

A.D.	Civilization
1814	The *Ch'üan-t'ang-wen*, a collection of all the prose works of the T'ang age (1000 chapters).
1825	The *Ching-hua-yüan*, a feminist novel by the linguist Li Ju-chen (printed in 1828).
1825–1829	The *Huang-ch'ing ching-chieh*, a big critical work by Juan Yüan on the commentaries on the Classics.
1829	Death of Liu Feng-lu, the founder of the great reformist school of the Classics in new characters (school of Kung-yang).
1841	Death of Kung Tzu-chen, disciple and continuer of Liu Feng-lu (school of Kung-yang).
1844	The *Hai-kuo t'u-chih* by Wei Yüan.

A.D.	History
1816	The East India Company decides to develop imports of opium into China.
1820–1825	The opium imports cause the Chinese balance of trade to fall into deficit.
1830	Census: 394,780,000 inhabitants. From 1830 onwards, very rapid growth in clandestine imports of opium.
1839	Lin Tse-hsü, appointed governor of the two Kwangs, takes radical measures against the imports of opium in Canton. These measures provoke acts of piracy on the part of the British.
1842	Treaty of Nanking (Hong Kong ceded to Great Britain; Canton, Shanghai, Amoy, Foochow, and Ningpo opened to imports of opium).
1843	First extra-territorial rights for foreigners. Hung Hsiu-ch'üan founds the Society of the Worshippers of God (*Pai-shang-ti-hui*).
1846	Census: 421,340,000 inhabitants.

A.D.	History	A.D.	Civilization
1850	Start of the T'ai P'ing rebellion in eastern Kwangsi.		
1851	Census: 432 million inhabitants. Hung Hsiu-ch'üan proclaims himself King of the Kingdom of Heaven.		
1853	Nanking, occupied by the T'ai P'ing, becomes the 'celestial capital' (T'ien-ching). Big revolts of the Nien in North China.		
1854	The T'ai P'ing threaten Peking. Tseng Kuo-fen organizes the army of the Hsiang in Hunan.		
1855	The Yellow River moves from the north to the south of the Shantung peninsula. Revolt of the Moslems of Yunnan.		
1858	Li Hung-chang organizes the army of the Huai. Treaty of Tientsin. Treaty of Aigun, which gives Russia the territories east of the Ussuri.	1859	Translation of Western works on algebra, analytical geometry and botany.
1860	Sack of Peking by the French and British.		
1861	Rising of the Moslems of Shensi and Kansu. Creation of the *Tsung-li ya-men* to deal with relations with foreigners.		
1862	The Moslem territories of Sinkiang secede. Extension of the *li-chin*, a tax on goods in transit, to all provinces.	1862	Creation of the Peking *T'ung-wen-kuan*, a school of Western languages and sciences.
1864	Tso Tsung-t'ang recaptures Hangchow. Siege and fall of Nanking. Suicide of Hung Hsiu-ch'üan and the principal leaders of the T'ai P'ing.		
1866	Arsenal at Ma-wei, near Foochow.		
1867	The Nien threaten Peking, but Li Hung-chang defeats them. Fukien naval academy.		

A.D.	History	A.D.	Civilization
1868	Tso Tsung-t'ang is given the task of suppressing the Moslem revolt in the north-east.		
1870	The Tientsin incidents. The Chiang-nan arsenal in Shanghai is one of the biggest in the world about 1870.		
1873	Record amount of opium imported into China. The rebellion of the Moslems of Yunnan is suppressed after massacres and widespread destruction. The whole of Sinkiang in revolt.		
		1874	Death of the reformist Feng Kuei-fen.
1875	The empress Tz'u-hsi governs on her own.		
1876	Convention of Chih-fu.		
1878	All Sinkiang pacified.		
1880	Start of the construction of a new battle fleet under the direction of Li Hung-cheng.		
1883–1885	Conflict between China and France.		
1890	Han-yang foundries.		
		1891	The *Hsin-hsüeh wei-ching k'ao* by K'ang Yu-wei.
		1893	Chang Chih-tung founds in Wu-han a modern school with four departments: foreign languages, mathematics, natural sciences and commerce.
1894	The T'ung-hak Rebellion in Korea unleashes the Sino-Japanese War. Tientsin-Shanghai railway.		
1895	Treaty of Shimonoseki: Taiwan and the P'eng-hu Islands (Pescadores) are ceded to Japan; war damages of 200 million *liang*. K'ang Yu-wei's reformist manifesto.	1895	K'ang Yu-wei founds the *Ch'iang-hsüeh-hui* (Association for the Study of Reinforcement) in Shanghai.

A.D.	History	A.D.	Civilization
1897	Germany annexes the Ch'ing-tao area in Shantung.	1897	The *K'ung-tzu kai-chih kao* by K'ang Yu-wei.
1898	The British annex the Wei-hai region in Shantung, and the Russians those of Ta-lien and Lü-shun in Liao-tung. The Hundred Days of reform end in failure. Execution of the reformer T'an Ssu-t'ung.		
1899	The French annex the Chan-chiang region (Kwang-chou-wan) in western Kwangtung.	1899	Discovery of the inscriptions of the end of the second millennium B.C.
1900	The Boxers occupy Peking and besiege the embassies. International expedition to Peking and declaration of war on China.	1900	Translation of Adam Smith's *Wealth of Nations* by Yen Fu. Discovery of the paper manuscripts of Tun-huang (V-Xc.).
1901	The Boxer indemnity: 450 million silver dollars. Death of Li Hung-chang.		
1903	Publication of the *Ko-ming-chün, The Army of the Revolution*, by Tsou Jung.		
1904–1905	The Russo-Japanese War ends in a dazzling victory for Japan.		
1905	Sun Wen (Sun Yat-sen) founds the 'United League' (*T'ang-meng-hui*) in Tokyo.		
1910	Division of north-eastern China into Russian and Japanese spheres of influence.	c.1906	About 1300 Chinese students in Japan.
1911	10 October: republican insurrection of Wu-ch'ang. Outer Mongolia passes under Russian control.	1908	Death of the philologist Sun I-jang.
1912	1 January: Sun Yat-sen inaugurates the Chinese REPUBLIC in Nanking. He soon yields power to Yüan Shih-k'ai, who transfers the republican government to Peking.	1912	General reform of the educational system. Foundation of Peking University.

A.D.	Civilization
1915	Foundation of the review *Hsin ch'ing-nien* in Shanghai.
1919	Movement of 4 May.
1924	Death of Lin Shu, translator and adaptor of Western literary works.
1927	Suicide of the philologian and historian Wang Kuo-wei.
1927–1937	Scientific excavations on the site of the last Shang capital near An-yang (XIV–XIc. B.C.).
1928	New system of national education. Creation of Academia Sinica.

A.D.	History
1914	Yüan Shih-k'ai dissolves the parliament. The Japanese occupy the German possessions in Shantung.
1915	Japan's 'Twenty-one demands'.
1916	Death of Yüan Shih-k'ai and beginning of the 'war-lord' period.
1919	The Paris Peace Conference gives Japan the former German possessions in China.
1921	Foundation in Shanghai by a number of intellectuals of the Chinese Communist party. Formation in Canton of a nationalist government led by Sun Yat-sen.
1923	The Soviet Union supports the Nationalist government.
1925	12 March: death in Peking of Sun Yat-sen, who had come for talks with the generals.
1926	July: departure of the expedition to the north (*pei-fu*).
1927	Chiang Chieh-shi (Chiang Kai-shek) crushes the revolution in Shanghai and sets up his own government in Nanking.
1928	Chiang Kai-shek organizes the second expedition to the north.
1929	Soviet republic of Southern Kiangsi.
1930–1934	Campaigns to encircle the soviet zone of Kiangsi.
1931	The Japanese invade Manchuria.

A.D.	History	A.D.	Civilization
1932	Japanese attack on Shanghai. Creation by the Japanese of the state of Manshukoku (Manchukuo).		
1933–1935	The Japanese advance in northern China.		
1934	Start of the 'Long March' (*ch'ang-cheng*). Chiang Kai-shek launches the 'New Life Movement'.		
1935	Conference of Tsun-i (northern Kweichow) which re-establishes Mao Tse-tung as leader of the Communist party.		
1936	6 December: Chiang Kai-shek taken prisoner at Sian and forced to direct his efforts against the Japanese.	1936	Death of the great novelist Lu Hsün (Chou Shu-jen) and of the re lutionary scholar Chang Ping-lin. Death of the geologist Ting Wen-chiang.
1937	Soviet government in Yenan. The Japanese launch a general offensive in North China and capture all the big cities.		
1938	The Nationalist government withdraws to Chungking.		
1940	Wang Ching-wei sets up a government in the pay of the Japanese in Nanking.	1940	Death of the philologist Lo Chen-yü and of Ts'ai Yüan-p'ei. The *Ts'ung-shu chi-ch'eng*, a big collection of texts.
1942–1943	Famine in Honan; estimated deaths—two million.	1942	In Yenan Mao Tse-tung lays down the official line on literature and art.
1945	14 August: capitulation of Japan.		
1947	Military successes of the Nationalists, who take Yenan and Nanking. The Communists make progress in Manchuria.	1946	The poet Wen I-to murdered by the Kuo-min-tang.
1948	Formation of a people's government in North China. The Yellow River goes back to its 1855 course and moves from the south to the north of Shantung.		

A.D.	History	A.D.	Civilization
1949	The Communists occupy the whole of northern China. The people's army crosses the Yangtze and occupies Shanghai and Nanking. PEOPLE'S REPUBLIC proclaimed in Peking on 1 October. The Nationalist government takes refuge in Taiwan.		
1950	Treaty between the Soviet Union and the People's Republic of China. Beginning of the Korean War and of Chinese intervention in Korea.		
1951	Campaign to suppress counter-revolutionaries.	1951–1955	Campaign against 'deviationist' intellectuals, at its height in 1955.
1953	First Five Year Plan. End of the Korean war. Census: 601 million inhabitants.		
1954	Defence pact between the United States and the Nationalist government of Taiwan.		
1955	Bandung Conference.		
		1956–1957	The 'Hundred Flowers' campaign.
1957	Influx of country people into the towns.	1957	Death of the painter Ch'i Pai-shih.
1958	Start of the 'Great Leap Forward' (*ta yüeb-chin*). Establishment of people's communes. Suppression of all private life and personal property.	1958–1961	Difficult period for all intellectuals during the 'Great Leap Forward'.
1959	Revolt in Tibet. At the Lu-shan conference Mao Tse-tung fends off his opponents.		
1960	August: the Soviet Union withdraws all its technicians from China and halts its development aid. 1960 and 1961 are years of terrible famine. At least 13 million die. Mao Tse-tung falls from power.		
1961	Priority again given to agriculture.		
1962	War between India and China over the Himalayan frontier.	1962	Death of Hu Shih.

A.D.	History	A.D.	Civilization
1963	People start to be forced back from the towns to the countryside.		
1964	October: first Chinese nuclear test. Beginning of the cult of Mao Tse-tung.		
1965	Lin Piao removes his opponents from the army.		
1966	Start of the 'Great proletarian cultural revolution'.	1966–1969	The Cultural Revolution is a cruel tragedy for intellectuals, the aged, and the former middle-class, and is manifested everywhere by the destruction of treasures from the past. The novelist Lao She is driven to suicide by the Red Guards. Reform of the theatre by Chiang Ch'ing.
1967	Anarchy and civil war. Dramatic decline in production.		
1969	Repression of the Red Guards. Twenty million youths sent to the countryside. End of the Cultural Revolution. Reconstitution of the Communist Party, with important contributions from the army. Sino-Soviet incidents at the Ussuri River.	1969	Death of the philologist Ch'en Yin-k'o, a victim of the Cultural Revolution.
1970	Beginning of birth control.	1974	Manifesto for democracy by the students of Canton.
1971	Death of Lin Piao.	1978	Democracy movement called 'Peking Spring' suppressed in 1979.
1972	Nixon in Peking.	1981	Death of novelist Mao-tun.
1973	Leaders removed by the Cultural Revolution return to power.	1986	Student movement for political reform.
1976–1978	Neo-Maoist interlude under the direction of Hua Kuo-feng.	1987	Astrophysicist Fang Li-chih expelled from the Communist Party.
1976	Death of Chou En-lai and of Mao Tse-tung.	1989 (April–May)	Peking students demonstrate against corruption and for democracy.

1978	The reformers return to power under Tseng Hsiao-p'ing. Beginning of de-Maoization.
1979	Opening of China to foreign enterprises. Resumption of dialogue with the United States. Fruitless and costly Chinese intervention in Vietnam.
1980	Trial of the 'Gang of Four'.
1981	Restraints on investment.
1982	Suppression of social categorization inherited from the Maoist period.
1983	Maoist-style campaign against 'spiritual pollution'.
1984	Large-scale return of economic reforms. Resumption of relations with the Soviet Union. Joint Sino-British declaration on Hong Kong.
1985	China returns to a moderate international policy. Reduction of effective military forces and renovation of the army.
1987 (January)	Liberal leader Hu Yao-pang removed from power. Beginning in 1987, resumption of *de facto* relations between Taiwan and the Chinese continent.
1989 (4 June)	Massacre at T'ien-an men Square. Return of the conservatives to power.
1990–1991	Pursuit of repression and return to practices and concepts of the Stalinist period.
1992	Teng Hsiao-p'ing travels to the South, where he launches the economic reforms once again.
1993	Economy overheats.

Bibliography

Since this book is addressed in principle to general readers rather than to specialists, all the publications in Chinese and Japanese which form the main bulk of the literature on China and her neighbours have been excluded from this bibliography. It concentrates on books written in English, although selected important works of French and German sinology have also been included. The suggestions made here being necessarily very incomplete, readers are referred to the following more detailed bibliographies: Tsuen-hsuin Tsien, *China: An Annotated Bibliography of Bibliographies* (Boston: G. K. Hall, 1978). For Western writings on China from earliest times through the 1950s, see Henri Cordier, *Bibliotheca Sinica*, 4 vols. (Paris: Guilmoto, 1904–1908; rpt. New York: B. Franklin, 1968); T'ung-li Yüan, *China in Western Literature: A Continuation of Cordier's Bibliotheca Sinica* (New Haven: Yale University Press, 1958); John Lust, *Index Sinicus: A Catalogue of Articles Relating to China in Periodicals and Other Collective Publications, 1920–1955* (Cambridge: Heffer, 1964). For subsequent literature, see the annual bibliography of the Association for Asian Studies, the *Bibliography of Asian Studies*, as well as the *Revue bibliographique de sinologie* (Paris and the Hague: Mouton, 1955–   ). The *Annual Bibliography of Oriental Studies* (*Tôyôgaku bunken ruimoku*), although mainly devoted to publications in Japanese and Chinese, contains a section on Western-language publications. A useful, annotated survey of major English publications on China may be found in the American Historical Association's *Guide to Historical Literature* (New York: Oxford University Press, 1995). Other bibliographies include Charles O. Hucker, *China: A Critical Bibliography* (Tucson: University of Arizona Press, 1962); Endymion Wilkinson, *The History of Imperial China: A Research Guide* (Cambridge, Mass.: Harvard University Press, 1973); G. William Skinner, *Modern Chinese Society: An Analytical Bibliography* (Stanford, Calif.: Stanford University Press, 1973); Ernst Wolff, *Chinese Studies: A Bibliographic Manual* (San Francisco: Chinese Materials Center, 1981); and Leonard H. D. Gordon and Frank J. Shulman, *Doctoral Dissertations on China: A Bibliography of Studies in Western Languages, 1945–1970* (Seattle: University of Washington Press, 1972). Frank J. Shulman, *Doctoral Dissertations on China, 1971–1975* (Seattle: University of Washington Press, 1978), continues this work. Subsequent volumes in the same series have been published by the Association for Asian Studies.

General works

Geography of East Asia and China: Pierre Pfeffer, *Asia: A Natural History* (New York: Doubleday, 1968); George B. Cressey, *Asia's Lands and Peoples: A Geography of One-Third of the Earth and Two-Thirds of Its People* (New York: McGraw-Hill, 1963); Christopher J. Smith, *China: People and Places in the Land of One Billion* (Boulder: Westview Press, 1991); Leo J. Moser, *The Chinese Mosaic: The Peoples and Provinces of China* (Boulder: Westview Press, 1985); Caroline Blunden and Mark Elvin, *Cultural Atlas of China* (New York: Facts on File, Inc., 1983); P. J. M. Geelan and Denis Twitchett, eds., *The Times Atlas of China* (London: Times Books, 1974); A. Hermann, *Historical and Commercial Atlas of China* (rpt. Chicago: Aldine Publishing Co., 1966); and S. Robert Ramsey, *The Languages of China* (Princeton: Princeton University Press, 1987).

General histories of China: Denis Twitchett and John K. Fairbank, general editors, *The Cambridge History of China* (Cambridge University Press), which began publication in 1978, is the most comprehensive history of China in English. To date (1995), ten of a projected total of fifteen volumes have been published. These are vol. 1, 'The Ch'in and Han empires, 221 B.C.–A.D.220'; vol. 3, 'Sui and T'ang China, 589–906, Part 1'; vol. 6, 'Alien regimes and border states, 907–1368'; vol. 7, 'The Ming dynasty, 1368–1644, Part 1'; vol. 10, 'Late Ch'ing, 1800–1911, Part 1'; vol. 11, 'Nationalist China during the Sino-Japanese War, 1937–1945, Part 2'; vol. 12, 'The Chinese Communist movement during the Sino-Japanese War, 1937–1945, Part 1'; vol. 13, 'Republican China 1912–1942, Part 2'; vol. 14, 'The People's Republic, Part 1: The emergence of Revolutionary China, 1949–1965'; and vol. 15, 'The People's Republic, Part 2.' One will note that the first volume begins with the consolidation of the Ch'in empire in 221 B.C., the editors having decided that, given the rapid pace of archaeological discoveries in China, it would not be possible to write a definitive history of earlier periods at this time. At the other end of the scale is Charles O. Hucker, *China to 1850: A Short History* (Stanford, Calif.: Stanford University Press, 1978, a compressed survey). A standard text is John K. Fairbank and Edwin O. Reischauer, *East Asia: Tradition and Transformation* (Boston: Houghton Mifflin, 1989).

Individual periods of Chinese history: Jacques Gernet, *Ancient China from the Beginnings to the Empire* (Berkeley: University of California Press, 1968); Joseph R. Levenson and Franz Schurmann, *China: An Interpretive History: From the Beginnings to the Fall of the Han* (Berkeley: University of California Press, 1969). Wolfram Eberhard, *History of China*, 4th ed. (London: Routledge & Kegan Paul, 1977), is particularly strong on the period of the Northern and Southern Dynasties (317–589). For more recent times, see Jack Gray, *Rebellions and Revolutions: China from the 1800s to the 1980s* (New York: Oxford University Press, 1990), and John K. Fairbank, *The Great Chinese Revolution, 1800–1985* (New York: Harper & Row, 1986). Major biographical dictionaries by period are Herbert Franke, ed., *Sung Biographies* (Wiesbaden: Franz Steiner, 1976); Igor de Rachewiltz, ed., *In the Service of the Khan: Eminent Personalities of the Early Mongol-Yuan Period, 1200–1300* (Wiesbaden: Harrassowitz, 1993); L. Carrington Goodrich and Fang Chaoying, eds. *Dictionary of Ming Biography* (New York: Columbia University Press, 1976); Arthur W. Hummel, *Eminent Chinese of the Ch'ing Period* (Washington, D.C.: United States Government Printing Office,

1943–4); Howard L. Boorman, ed., *Biographical Dictionary of Republican China* (New York: Columbia University Press, 1967–79); Donald W. Klein, *Biographic Dictionary of Chinese Communism,* 1921–1965 (Cambridge, Mass.: Harvard University Press, 1971); and Wolfgang Bartke, *Who's Who in the People's Republic of China* (Munich: K. G. Saur, 1987).

General surveys of history and civilization: See Etienne Balazs, *Chinese Civilization and Bureaucracy* (New Haven: Yale University Press, 1964); John K. Fairbank, *Chinese Thought and Institutions* (Chicago: University of Chicago Press, 1957). Michael Loewe, *The Pride That was China* (New York: St. Martin's Press, 1990, draws extensively on archaeological evidence. Patricia B. Ebrey, ed., *Chinese Civilization and Society: A Sourcebook,* 2nd ed. (New York: Free Press, 1993), presents a wide range of original documents arranged chronologically with the editor's commentary. Also see Paul S. Ropp, ed., *Heritage of China: Contemporary Perspectives on Chinese Civilization* (Berkeley: University of California Press, 1990). On law, see T'ung-tsu Ch'ü, *Law and Society in Traditional China* (Paris: Mouton, 1961), and K. C. Chang, ed., *Food in Chinese Culture: Anthropological and Historical Perspectives* (New Haven: Yale University Press, 1977).

Economy and demography: Ho P'ing-ti, *Studies on the Population of China, 1368–1953* (Cambridge, Mass.: Harvard University Press, 1959); Hans Bielenstein, 'Chinese Historical Demography, A.D. 2–1982,' *Bulletin of the Museum of Far Eastern Antiquities* 59 (1987), 1–288; Chi Ch'ao-ting, *Key Economic Areas in Chinese History* (rpt. New York: Paragon Books, 1963); Yang Lien-sheng, *Money and Credit in China: A Short History* (Cambridge, Mass.: Harvard University Press, 1952); Mark Elvin, *The Pattern of the Chinese Past* (Stanford, Calif.: Stanford University Press, 1973); Chao Kang, *Man and Land in Chinese History; an Economic Analysis* (Stanford, Calif.: Stanford University Press, 1986).

History of science and technology: Joseph Needham's multi-volume and wide-ranging *Science and Civilization in China* (Cambridge University Press, 1954–) is the standard reference. Also by the same author are *Clerks and Craftsmen in China and the West* (Cambridge University Press, 1970) and *The Development of Iron and Steel Technology in China* (London: Newcomen Society, 1958). See also Nathan Sivin, 'Science and Medicine in Imperial China – The State of the Field,' *Journal of Asian Studies* 47.1 (1988), 41–90; E-tun Sun and Shiou-chuan Sun, trans., *T'ien-kung k'ai-wu: Chinese Technology in the Seventeenth Century* (University Park: Pennsylvania State University Press, 1966); Edward H. Schafer, *Pacing the Void: T'ang Approaches to the Stars* (Berkeley: University of California Press, 1977); Paul U. Unschuld, *Medicine in China: A History of Ideas* (Berkeley: University of California Press, 1985); Manfred Porkert, *The Theoretical Foundations of Chinese Medicine: Systems of Correspondence* (Cambridge, Mass.: The MIT Press, 1974); and Derke Bodde, *Chinese Thought, Society, and Science: The Intellectual and Social Background of Science and Technology in Pre-Modern China* (Honolulu: University of Hawaii Press, 1991).

History of Chinese philosophy: See Feng Yu-lan (trans. Derke Bodde), *A History of Chinese Philosophy* (Princeton: Princeton University Press, 1983); and Kung-chuan Hsiao (trans. F. W. Mote), *A History of Chinese Political Thought* (Princeton: Princeton University Press, 1979). Major collections of primary texts are Wm. Theodore de Bary, ed., *Sources of Chinese Tradition* (New York: Columbia University Press, rev. ed., 1995), and Wing-tsit Chan, ed., *A Source Book in Chinese Philosophy* (Princeton: Princeton University Press, 1969). A useful, succinct survey is Frederick W. Mote, *Intellectual Foundations of China* (New York: Knopf, 1971). See also François Jullien (trans. Janet Lloyd), *The Propensity of Things: Toward a History of Efficacy in China* (New York: Zone Books, 1995), and John B. Henderson, *The Development and Decline of Chinese Cosmology* (New York: Columbia University Press, 1984). For the Confucian tradition, see David S. Nivison and Arthur F. Wright, eds. *Confucianism in Action* (Stanford, Calif.: Stanford University Press, 1959); Arthur F. Wright, ed., *The Confucian Persuasion* (Stanford, Calif.: Stanford University Press, 1960); and Arthur F. Wright and Denis Twitchett, eds. *Confucian Personalities* (Stanford, Calif.: Stanford University Press, 1962). See also Thomas A. Metzger, *Escape from Predicament: Neo-Confucianism and China's Evolving Political Culture* (New York: Columbia University Press, 1977).

History of Chinese religions: See first the bibliographies of Laurence G. Thompson, *Chinese Religion in Western Languages: A Comprehensive and Classified Bibliography of Publications in English, French, and German through 1980* (Tucson: University of Arizona Press, 1985) and *Chinese Religion: Publications in Western Languages, 1981 through 1990* (Ann Arbor, Mich.: Association for Asian Studies, 1993). An important general work is Marcel Granet, *The Religion of the Chinese People* (Oxford: Blackwell, 1975), with an introductory essay and bibliography of Granet's works by Maurice Freedman. Two important collections of primary data gathered in the field are J. J. M. de Groot, *The Religious System of China* (Leiden: Brill, 1892–1910); and Henri Doré, *Recherches sur les superstitions en Chine*, 15 vols. (Shanghai, 1914–29). Fundamental is Rolf A. Stein (trans. Phyllis Brooks), *The World in Miniature: Container Gardens and Dwellings in Far Eastern Religious Thought* (Stanford, Calif.: Stanford University Press, 1990). On Taoism, see the detailed, annotated bibliography by Anna Seidel, 'Chronicle of Taoist Studies in the West, 1950–1990,' *Cahiers d'Extrême-Asie* 5 (1989–1990), 223–347. Henri Maspero (trans. Frank A. Kierman, Jr.), *Taoism and Chinese Religion* (Amherst: University of Massachusetts Press, 1981), translates the most important of Maspero's studies on Taoism and contains a good introduction to the field by Timothy H. Barrett. See also Max Kaltenmark, *Lao Tzu and Taoism* (Stanford, Calif.: Stanford University Press, 1969); Holmes Welch and Anna Seidel, *Facets of Taoism: Essays in Chinese Religion* (New Haven: Yale University Press, 1979); Kristofer Schipper (trans. Karen C. Duval), *The Taoist Body* (Berkeley: University of California Press, 1993); Isabelle Robinet (trans. Julian F. Pas and Norman J. Girardot), *Taoist Meditation: The Mao-shan Tradition of Great Purity* (Albany: State University of New York Press, 1993); John Lagerwey, *Taoist Ritual in Chinese Society and History* (New York: Macmillan, 1987); and Judith M. Boltz, *A Survey of Taoist Literature: Tenth to Seventeenth Centuries* (Berkeley: Center for Chinese Studies, 1987). For Buddhism, see Kenneth S. Ch'en, *Buddhism in China: A Historical Survey* (Princeton: Princeton University Press, 1964), and the same author's *The Chinese Transformation of Buddhism* (Princeton: Princeton University Press, 1973). A survey is Arthur F. Wright, *Buddhism in Chinese History* (Stanford, Calif.: Stanford University Press, 1959). Fundamental for the earlier period is Erik Zürcher, *The Buddhist Conquest of China: The Spread and Adaptation of Buddhism in Early*

Medieval China (Leiden: Brill, 1959). For the history of Christianity in China, see A. C. Moule, *Christians in China before the Year 1550* (London: Society for Promoting Christian Knowledge, 1930); Jacques Gernet, *China and the Christian Impact: A Conflict of Cultures* (Cambridge University Press, 1985); and Kenneth S. Latourette, *A History of Christian Missions in China* (New York: Macmillan, 1929).

History of art: See Laurence Sickman and Alexander Soper, *The Art and Architecture of China* (Harmondsworth: Penguin, 1978); Michael Sullivan, *An Introduction to Chinese Art* (Berkeley: University of California Press, 1961); and William Willets, *Chinese Art* (London: Penguin, 1958). A basic textbook is James Cahill, *Chinese Painting* (New York: Skira/Rizzoli, 1985). For recent bibliography, see Jerome Silbergeld, 'Chinese Painting Studies in the West: A State-of-the-Field Article,' *Journal of Asian Studies* 46.4 (1987), 849–97. See also Osvald Sirén, *Chinese Painting: Leading Masters and Principles*, 7 vols. (New York: Ronand Press, 1956–8); James Cahill, *An Index of Early Chinese Painters and Paintings: T'ang, Sung, and Yüan* (Berkeley: University of California Press, 1980); Jerome Silbergeld, *Chinese Painting Style: Media, Methods, and Principles of Form* (Seattle: University of Washington Press, 1982); and R. H. van Gulik, *Chinese Pictorial Art as Viewed by the Connoisseur* (Rome: Is.M.E.O., 1958). A basic reference work is Suzuki Kei, *Comprehensive Illustrated Catalog of Chinese Paintings*, 5 vols. (Tokyo: University of Tokyo Press, 1982–3). For translations of textual sources, see Susan Bush, *The Chinese Literati on Painting: Su Shih (1037–1101) to Tung Ch'i-ch'ang (1555–1636)* (Cambridge, Mass.: Harvard University Press, 1971), and Susan Bush and Hsio-yen Shih, *Early Chinese Texts on Painting* (Cambridge, Mass.: Harvard University Press, 1985). A good introductory work on the Tun-huang caves is Anil de Silva, *Chinese Landscape Painting in the Caves of Tun-huang* (London: Methuen, 1964). On gardens, see Osvald Sirén, *Gardens of China* (New York: Ronald Press, 1949), and Maggie Keswick, *The Chinese Garden: History, Art, and Architecture* (New York: Rizzoli, 1978); on calligraphy, see Chiang Yee, *Chinese Calligraphy* (rpt. London: Methuen, 1961), and Tseng Yuho, *A History of Chinese Calligraphy* (Hong Kong: The Chinese University Press, 1993).

History of literature: A fundamental reference is William H. Nienhauser, Jr., ed., *The Indiana Companion to Traditional Chinese Literature* (Bloomington: Indiana University Press, 1986). This work contains ten introductory essays on Buddhist literature, drama, fiction, literary criticism, poetry, popular literature, prose, rhetoric, Taoist literature, and women's literature. These are followed by over 500 entries on individual authors, works, schools, and terms, each with bibliographical references to editions, studies, and translations. The most comprehensive one-volume anthology in translation is Victor Mair, ed., *The Columbia Anthology of Traditional Chinese Literature* (New York: Columbia University Press, 1994). Still useful are Richard John Lynn, *Chinese Literature: A Draft Bibliography in Western European Languages* (Canberra: Australian National University Press, 1979); Liu Wu-chi, *An Introduction to Chinese Literature* (Bloomington: Indiana University Press, 1966); Ch'en Shou-yi, *Chinese Literature: An Historical Introduction* (New York: Ronald Press, 1961); and James R. Hightower, *Topics in Chinese Literature* (Cambridge, Mass.: Harvard University Press, 1953). For the modern period, see C. T. Hsia, *A History of Modern Chinese*

Fiction (New Haven: Yale University Press, 1961); Michele Yeh, *Modern Chinese Poetry: Theory and Practice since 1917* (New Haven: Yale University Press, 1991); and Michele Yeh, *Anthology of Modern Chinese Poetry* (New Haven: Yale University Press, 1993).

Bibliographies by periods

Antiquity to the fifth century B.C.

Andersson, J. G., *Children of the Yellow Earth*. Cambridge, Mass.: MIT Press, 1973.

Allan, Sarah, *The Heir and the Sage: Myth, Art, Dynastic Legend in Early China*. San Francisco: Chinese Materials Center, 1981.

Allan, Sarah, *The Shape of the Turtle: Myth, Art, and Cosmos in Early China*. Albany: State University of New York Press, 1991.

Bagley, Robert W., *Shang Ritual Bronzes in the Arthur M. Sackler Collections*. Washington, D.C., and Cambridge, Mass.: Arthur M. Sackler Foundation and Arthur M. Sackler Museum, 1987.

Chang Kwang-chih, *The Archaeology of Ancient China*. 4th. ed., New Haven: Yale University Press, 1986.

Chang Kwang-chih, *Art, Myth, and Ritual: The Path to Political Authority in Ancient China*. Cambridge, Mass.: Harvard University Press, 1983.

Chang Kwang-chih, *Early Chinese Civilization: Anthropological Perspectives*. Cambridge Mass.: Harvard University Press, 1976.

Chang Kwang-chih, *Shang Civilization*. New Haven: Yale University Press, 1980.

Cheng Te-k'un, *Archaeology in China*, 3 vols. Cambridge: Heffer, 1959–63.

Creel, Herrlee G., *The Origins of Statecraft in China*. Chicago: University of Chicago Press, 1970.

Fong Wen, ed., *The Great Bronze Age of China*. New York: Metropolitan Museum of Art, 1980.

Granet, Marcel, *Chinese Civilization*. New York: Knopf, 1930.

Granet, Marcel, *Danses et légendes de la Chine ancienne*. Paris: Alcan, 1926.

Granet, Marcel, *Festivals and Songs of Ancient China*. London: Routledge, 1932.

Ho Ping-ti, *The Cradle of the East*. Chicago: University of Chicago Press, 1975.

Hsü Cho-yun, *Ancient China in Transition*. Stanford, Calif.: Stanford University Press, 1965.

Hsü Cho-yun and Katheryn M. Linduff, *Western Chou Civilization*. New Haven: Yale University Press, 1988.

Keightley, David N., 'Early Civilization in China: Reflections on How It Became Chinese,' in Paul S. Ropp, ed., *Heritage of China*. Berkeley: University of California Press, 1990, pp. 15–54.

Keightley, David N., *The Origins of Chinese Civilization*. Berkeley: University of California Press, 1983.

Keightley, David N., *Sources of Shang History: The Oracle-bone Inscriptions of Bronze Age China*. Berkeley: University of California Press, 1978.

Li Chi, *The Beginnings of Chinese Civilization*. Seattle: University of Washington Press, 1957.

Lynn, Richard John, *The Classic of Changes: As interpreted by Wang Bi* (trans.). New York: Columbia University Press, 1994.

Maspero, Henri (trans. Frank Kierman, Jr.), *China in Antiquity.* Amherst: University of Massachusetts Press, 1978.
Rawson, Jessica, *Ancient China: Art and Archaeology.* London: British Museum, 1980.
Shaughnessy, Edward L., *Sources of Western Zhou History: Inscribed Bronze Vessels.* Berkeley: University of California Press, 1991.
Walker, Richard L., *The Multi-State System of Ancient China.* Hamden, Conn.: Shoe String Press, 1953.
Watson, William, *Early Civilization in China.* London: Thames & Hudson, 1966.
Wilhelm, Helmut, *Change: Eight Lectures on the I Ching.* New York: Harper & Row, 1964.
Wilhelm, Richard, and Cary F. Baynes (trans.), *The I-ching or Book of Changes.* Princeton: Princeton University Press, 1967.

Warring states

Crump, James I., trans., *Chan-kuo ts'e.* London: Clarendon Press, 1970.
Crump, James I., *Intrigues: Studies of the* Chan-kuo ts'e. Ann Arbor: University of Michigan Press, 1964.
Duyvendak, J. J. L., trans., *The Book of Lord Shang: A Classic of the Chinese School of Law.* London: Probsthain, 1928.
N. Girardot, *Myth and Meaning in Early Taoism: The Theme of Chaos.* Berkeley: University of California Press, 1983.
Graham, A. C., trans., *The Book of Lieh-tzu.* London: John Murray, 1960.
Graham, A. C., trans., *Chuang Tzu: The Seven Inner Chapters and Other Writings from the Book* Chuang-tzu. London: Allen & Unwin, 1981.
Graham, A. C., *Studies in Chinese Philosophy and Philosophical Literature.* Albany: State University of New York Press, 1990.
Granet, Marcel, *La pensée chinoise.* 1934; rpt. Paris: Albin Michel, 1968.
Griffith, S. B., *Sun tzu: The Art of War.* Oxford: Clarendon Press, 1963.
Hawkes, David, trans., *Ch'u-tz'u: The Songs of the South.* London: Oxford University Press, 1959.
Knoblock, John, trans., *Xunzi: A Translation and Study of the Complete Works,* 3 vols. Stanford, Calif.: Stanford University Press, 1988–94.
Lau, D. C., trans., *The Analects.* Baltimore: Penguin, 1979.
Lau, D. C., trans., *Mencius.* Baltimore: Penguin, 1970.
Lau, D. C., trans., *Tao Te Ching: Chinese Classics.* Hong Kong: Chinese University of Hong Kong Press, 1982.
Legge, James, trans., *The Chinese Classics.* Rpt. 5 vols., Hong Kong: Hong Kong University Press, 1960.
Legge, James, trans., *Li chi, Book of Rites.* New Hyde Park, N.Y.: University Books, 1967.
Liao, W. K., trans., *The Complete Works of Han Fei Tzu.* London: Probsthain, 1939–59.
Li Xueqin, *Eastern Zhou and Qin Civilization.* New Haven: Yale University Press, 1985.
Loewe, Michael, ed., *Early Chinese Texts: A Bibliographical Guide.* Berkeley: Society for the Study of Early China and Institute for East Asian Studies, University of California, 1993.

Mei, Y. P., trans., *The Ethical and Political Works of Motse*. London: Probsthain, 1929.

Rickett, W. Allyn, trans., *Kuan-tzu: A Repository of Early Chinese Thought*. Hong Kong: Hong Kong University Press, 1965.

Rickett, W. Allyn, trans., *Guanzi: Political, Economic, and Philosophic Essays from Early China*. Princeton: Princeton University Press, 1985.

Schneider, Laurence A., *A Madman of Ch'u: The Chinese Myth of Loyalty and Dissent*. Berkeley: University of California Press, 1980.

Schwartz, Benjamin I., *The World of Thought in Ancient China*. Cambridge, Mass.: Harvard University Press, 1985.

Tokei, F., *Naissance de l'élégie chinoise: K'iu Yuan et son époque*. Paris: Gallimard, 1967.

Vandermeersch, Léon, *La formation du légisme*. Paris: Ecole française d'Extrême-Orient, 1965.

Waley, Arthur, trans., *The Analects of Confucius*. London: Allen & Unwin, 1938.

Waley, Arthur, trans., *The Book of Songs*. London: Allen & Unwin, 1954.

Waley, Arthur, *Three Ways of Thought in Ancient China*. New York: Macmillan, 1939.

Waley, Arthur, *The Way and Its Power: A Study of the Tao te ching and Its Place in Chinese Thought*. London: Allen & Unwin, 1934.

Waley, Arthur, *The Nine Songs: A Study of Shamanism in Ancient China*. London: Allen & Unwin, 1955.

Watson, Burton, trans., *Basic Writings of Mo tzu, Hsün tzu and Han Fei tzu*. New York: Columbia University Press, 1967.

Watson, Burton, trans., *The Complete Works of Chuang Tzu*. New York: Columbia University Press, 1968.

Watson, Burton, *Early Chinese Literature*. New York: Columbia University Press, 1962.

Watson, Burton, trans., *The Tso Chuan: Selections from China's Oldest Narrative History*. New York: Columbia University Press, 1989.

Watters, Geoffrey R., *Three Elegies of Ch'u: An Introduction to the Traditional Interpretation of the* Ch'u Tz'u. Madison: University of Wisconsin Press, 1985.

Wilhelm, Richard, trans., *Frühling und Herbst des Lü Bu We*. Jena, Germ.: Diederichs, 1928.

Empires of the Ch'in and the Han

Balazs, Étienne, 'Political Philosophy and Social Crisis at the End of the Han Dynasty,' in his *Chinese Civilization and Bureaucracy*. New Haven: Yale University Press, 1964, pp. 187–225.

Bielenstein, Hans, *The Bureaucracy of Han Times*. Cambridge University Press, 1980.

Bielenstein, Hans, 'Lo-yang in Later Han Times'. *Bulletin of the Museum of Far Eastern Antiquities* 48 (1976), 1–142.

Bielenstein, Hans, 'The Restoration of the Han Dynasty'. *Bulletin of the Museum of Far Eastern Antiquities* 26 (1954), 1–209; 31 (1959), 1–287; 39 (1967), 1–198; 51 (1979), 1–300.

Birrell, Anne, *Popular Songs and Ballads of Han China*. London: Unwin Hyman, 1988.

Bodde, Derk, *Festivals in Classical China: New Year and Other Annual Observances During the Han Dynasty*. Princeton: Princeton University Press, 1975.

Chavannes, Édouard, trans., *Les mémoires historiques de Se-ma Ts'ien*. Paris, 1895–1905; rpt. 5 vols., Paris: Adrien Maissonneuve, 1967.

Ch'ü T'ung-tsu and Jack Dull, eds. *Han Social Structure*. Seattle: University of Washington Press, 1972.

de Crespigny, Rafe, trans., *The Last of the Han: Being the Chronicle of the Years 181–220 A.D. As Recorded in Chapters 58–68 of the* Tzu-chih t'ung-chien *of Ssu-ma Kuang*. Canberra: Centre of Oriental Studies, Australian National University, 1969.

Diény, Jean-Pierre, *Aux origines de la poésie classique en Chine*. Leiden: Brill, 1968.

Diény, Jean-Pierre, *Les dix-neuf poémes anciens*. Paris: Presses Universitaires de France, 1963.

DeWoskin, Kenneth J., trans., *Doctors, Diviners, and Magicians of Ancient China: Biographies of Fang-shih*. New York: Columbia University Press, 1983.

Dubs, Homer H., trans., *The History of the Former Han Dynasty*, 3 vols. Baltimore: Waverly Press, 1938–55.

Dunn, Hugh, *Cao Zhi: The Life of a Princely Chinese Poet*. Beijing: New World Press, 1983.

Forke, Alfred, trans., *Lun-heng: Philosophical Essays of Wang Ch'ung*. 1907–11; rpt. New York: Paragon Books, 1962.

Gale, Esson M., trans., *Discourse on Salt and Iron: A Debate on State Control of Commerce and Industry in Ancient China*. Leiden: Brill, 1931.

Hervouet, Yves, *Un poète de cour sour les Han: Sseu-ma Siang-jou*. Paris: Institut des Hautes Études Chinoises, 1964.

Hsü Cho-yun, *Han Agriculture: The Formation of Early Chinese Agrarian Economy*. Seattle: University of Washington Press, 1980.

Hulsewé, A. F. P., *Remnants of Ch'in Law: An Annotated Translation of the Ch'in Legal and Administrative Rules of the 3rd Century B.C. Discovered in Yün-meng Prefecture, Hu-pei Province, in 1975*. Leiden: Brill, 1985.

Hulsewé, A. F. P., *Remnants of Han Law*. Leiden: Brill, 1955.

Kaltenmark, Max, trans., *Le Lie-sien tchouan*. Peking: Centre d'Études Sinologiques, 1953.

Knechtges, David R., *The Han Rhapsody: A Study of the Fu of Yang Hsiung (53 B.C.–A.D.18)*. Cambridge University Press, 1976.

Kramers, R. P., trans., *K'ung-tzu chia-yü: The School Sayings of Confucius*. Leiden: Brill, 1949.

Loewe, Michael, *Chinese Ideas of Life and Death: Faith, Myth and Reason in the Han Period*. London: Allen & Unwin, 1982.

Loewe, Michael, *Crisis and Conflict in Han China*. London: Allen & Unwin, 1974.

Loewe, Michael, *Everyday Life in Early Imperial China During the Han Period*. London: Carousel Books, 1973.

Loewe, Michael, *Records of Han Administration*. Cambridge University Press, 1967.

Morgan, Even, trans., *Tao: The Great Luminant. Essays from the Huai nan tzu*. London: Kegan Paul, 1935.

Miao, Ronald, *Early Medieval Chinese Poetry: The Life and Verse of Wang Ts'an (A.D. 177–217)*. Wiesbaden: Steiner, 1982.

Nienhauser, William H. Jr., et al., trans., *The Grand Scribe's Records: Volume 1, The Basic Annals of Pre-Han China.* Bloomington: Indiana University Press, 1994. *Volume VII, The Memoirs of Pre-Han China.* Bloomington: Indiana University Press, 1994.

Peerenboom, R. P., *Law and Morality in Ancient China: The Silk Manuscripts of Huang-Lao.* Albany: State University of New York Press, 1993.

Pirazzoli-t'Serstevens, Michele, *The Han Dynasty.* New York: Rizzoli, 1982.

Powers, Martin J., *Art and Political Expression in Early China.* New Haven: Yale University Press, 1991.

Roth, Harold D., *The Textual History of the Huai-nan tzu.* Ann Arbor, Mich.: Association for Asian Studies, 1992.

Sage, Steven F., *Ancient Sichuan and the Unification of China.* Albany: State University of New York Press, 1992.

Schipper, Kristofer, *L'Empereur Wou des Han dans la légende taoïste.* Paris: École Française d'Extrême-Orient, 1963.

Seidel, Anna, *La divinisation de Lao-tseu dans le taoïsme.* Paris: École Française d'Extrême-Orient, 1969.

Swann, Nancy L., *Pan Chao: Foremost Woman Scholar of China.* New York: Century, 1932.

Swann, Nancy L., *Food and Money in Ancient China.* Princeton: Princeton University Press, 1950.

Tjan Tjoe Som, trans., *Po hu t'ung: The Comprehensive Discussions in the White Tiger Hall.* Leiden: Brill, 1948–52.

Vervoorn, Aat., *Men of the Cliffs and Caves: The Development of the Chinese Eremitic Tradition to the End of the Han Dynasty.* Hong Kong: Chinese University of Hong Kong, 1990.

Wang Zhongshu, *Han Civilization.* New Haven: Yale University Press, 1982.

Watson, Burton, trans., *Chinese Rhyme-Prose: Poems in the Fu Form from the Han and Six Dynasties Periods.* New York: Columbia University Press, 1971.

Watson, Burton, trans., *Courtier and Commoner in Ancient China: Selections from the* History of the Former Han *by Pan Ku.* New York: Columbia University Press, 1974.

Watson, Burton, trans., *Records of the Grand Historian of China.* New York: Columbia University Press, 1961.

Watson, Burton, *Ssu-ma Ch'ien: Grand Historian of China.* New York: Columbia University Press, 1958.

Wilber, Clarence Martin, *Slavery in China during the Former Han Dynasty.* Chicago: Field Museum of Natural History, 1943.

Wu Hung, *The Wu Liang Shrine: The Ideology of Early Chinese Pictorial Art.* Stanford, Calif.: Stanford University Press, 1989.

Yü Ying-shih, *Trade and Expansion in Han China: A Study in the Structure of Sino-Barbarian Economic Relations.* Berkeley: University of California Press, 1967.

Medieval period (from the end of Han to the Sui)

Balazs, Étienne, 'Le traité économique du Souei chou,' *T'oung-pao* 42 (1953), 113–329.

Balazs, Etienne, *Le traité juridique du Souei chou.* Leiden: Brill, 1954.

Chen Shih-hsiang, trans., *Biography of Ku K'ai-chih*. Berkeley: University of California Press, 1953.

Dien, Albert E., ed., *State and Society in Early Medieval China*. Stanford, Calif.: Stanford University Press, 1990.

Eberhard, Wolfram, *Conquerors and Rulers: Social Forces in Medieval China*. 2nd ed., Leiden: Brill, 1965.

Eberhard, Wolfram, *Das Toba-Reich Nordchinas: eine soziologische Untersuchung*. Leiden: Brill, 1949.

Ebrey, Patricia Buckley, *The Aristocratic Families of Early Imperial China: A Case Study of the Po-ling Ts'ui Family*. Cambridge University Press, 1978.

Fang, Achilles, trans., *The Chronicle of the Three Kingdoms (220–265)*. Cambridge, Mass.: Harvard University Press, 1965.

Frodsham, John D., and Ch'eng Hsi (trans.), *An Anthology of Chinese Verse: Han, Wei, Chin, and the Northern and Southern Dynasties*. Oxford: Oxford University Press, 1967.

Frodsham, John D., *The Murmuring Stream: The Life and Works of the Chinese Poet Hsieh Ling-yün (355–433), Duke of K'ang-lo*. Kuala Lumpur: University of Malaya Press, 1967.

Gulik, R. H. van, *Siddham: An Essay on Sanskrit Studies in China and Japan*. Nagpur: Sarasvati–Vihara Series 36, 1956.

Hightower, James R., *The Poetry of T'ao Ch'ien*. Oxford: Clarendon Press, 1970.

J. Holmgren, *Annals of Tai: Early T'o-pa History According to the First Chapter of the* Wei-shu. Canberra: Australian National University Press, 1982.

Holzman, Donald, *Poetry and Politics: The Life and Works of Juan Chi*. Cambridge University Press, 1976.

Jenner, W. J. F., trans., *Memories of Loyang: Yang Hsüan-chih and the Lost Capital (493–534)*. Oxford: Oxford University Press, 1981.

Johnson, David, *The Medieval Chinese Oligarchy*. Boulder: Westview Press, 1977.

Juliano, Annette L., *Art of the Six Dynasties: Centuries of Change and Innovation*. New York: China Institute in America, 1975.

Kao, Karl S. Y., *Classical Chinese Tales of the Supernatural and the Fantastic*. Bloomington: Indiana University Press, 1985.

Knechtges, David R., trans., *Wen xuan, or Selections of Refined Literature* [by Hsiao T'ung (501–31)]. Princeton: Princeton University Press, 1982 (vol. 1), 1987 (vol. 2).

Kohn, Livia, trans., *Laughing at the Tao: Debates among Buddhists and Taoists in Medieval China*. Princeton: Princeton University Press, 1995. [Chen Luan's *Hsiao-lun tao* of 570].

Legge, James, trans., *A Record of the Buddhistic Kingdoms, Being an Account by the Chinese Monk Fa-Hsien of His Travels in India and Ceylon*. Oxford, 1886; rpt. New York: Paragon Books, 1966.

Mather, Richard B., *The Poet Shen Yüeh (441–513): The Reticent Marquis*. Princeton: Princeton University Press, 1988.

Mather, Richard B., trans., *Shih-shuo hsin-yü: A New Account of Tales of the World*. Minneapolis: University of Minnesota Press, 1976.

Mizuno, S., and T. Nagashiro, *Yün-kang, the Buddhist Cave-Temples of the Vth Century in North China*. 16 vols., Kyoto, 1951–6.

Rogers, Michael C., *The Chronicle of Fu Chien*. Berkeley: University of California Press, 1968.

Shih, Robert, trans., *Biographies des moines éminents (Kao seng tchouan) de Houei-kiao*. Louvain: Institut Orientaliste, 1969.

Shih, Vincent Yu-chung, trans., *The Literary Mind and the Carving of Dragons by Liu Hsieh*. New York: Columbia University Press, 1959.

Teng Ssu-yü, trans., *Family Instructions for the Yen Clan*: Yen-shih chia-hsün [by Yen Chih-t'ui]. Leiden: Brill, 1968.

Zürcher, Erik, *The Buddhist Conquest of China: The Spread and Adaptation of Buddhism in Early Medieval China*, 2 vols. Leiden: Brill, 1959.

Sui, T'ang, and the Five Dynasties

Acker, W. R. B., trans., *Some T'ang and Pre-T'ang Texts on Chinese Painting*. Leiden: Brill, 1954.

Backus, Charles, *The Nan-chao Kingdom and T'ang China's Southwestern Frontier*. Cambridge University Press, 1981.

Barrett, T. H., *Li Ao: Buddhist, Taoist, or Neo-Confucian?* Oxford: Oxford University Press, 1991.

Beckwith, Christopher I., *The Tibetan Empire of Central Asia: A History of the Struggle for Great Power among Tibetans, Turks, Arabs, and Chinese during the Early Middle Ages*. Princeton: Princeton University Press, 1987.

Bingham, Woodbridge. *The Founding of the T'ang Dynasty: The Fall of Sui and Rise of T'ang, a Preliminary Survey*. 1941; rpt. New York: Octagon Books, 1975.

Cahill, Suzanne E., *Transcendence and Divine Passion: The Queen Mother of the West in Medieval China*. Stanford, Calif.: Stanford University Press, 1993.

Chavannes, E., *Documents sur les Tou-k'iue occidentaux*. 1903; rpt. Paris: A. Maisonneuve, 1942.

Demiéville, Paul, *Le concile de Lhasa, une controverse sur le quiétisme entre bouddhistes de l'Inde et de la Chine au VIIIe siècle de notre l'ère chrétienne*. Paris: Presses Universitaires de France, 1952.

Demiéville, Paul, trans., *Entretiens de Lin-tsi*. Paris: Fayard, 1972.

Ebrey, Patricia Buck, and Peter Gregory, eds., *Religion and Society in Tang and Sung China*. Honolulu: University of Hawaii Press, 1993.

Edwards, E. D., *Chinese Prose Literature of the T'ang Period*. London: Probsthain, 1937–8.

Fitzgerald, C. P., *Son of Heaven, a Biography of Li Shih-min*. Cambridge University Press, 1933.

Gernet, Jacques (trans. Franciscus Verellen), *Buddhism in Chinese Society: An Economic History from the Fifth to the Tenth Centuries*. New York: Columbia University Press, 1995.

Gray, Basil, *Buddhist Cave Paintings at Tunhuang*. Chicago: University of Chicago Press, 1959.

Gregory, Peter, *Tsung-mi and the Sinification of Buddhism*. Princeton: Princeton University Press, 1991.

Grousset, René, *In the Footsteps of the Buddha*. London: G. Routledge, 1932.

Guisso, R. W. L., *Wu Tse-t'ien and the Politics of Legitimation in T'ang China*. Bellingham: Western Washington University, 1978.

Hartman, Charles, *Han Yü and the T'ang Search for Unity*. Princeton: Princeton University Press, 1986.

Hayashi, Ryoichi, *The Silk Road and the Shoso-in*. New York: Weatherhill/ Heibonsha, 1975.

Henricks, Robert, trans., *The Poetry of Han-shan: A Complete, Annotated Translation of Cold Mountain*. Albany: State University of New York Press, 1990.

Herbert, P. A., *Examine the Honest, Appraise the Able: Contemporary Assessments of Civil Service Selection in Early T'ang China*. Canberra: Australian National University, 1988.

Hung, William, *Tu Fu: China's Greatest Poet*. Cambridge, Mass.: Harvard University Press, 1952.

Johnson, Wallace, trans., *The T'ang Code: Volume One: General Principles*. Princeton: Princeton University Press, 1979.

Levy, Howard S., trans., *Biography of An Lu-shan*. Berkeley: University of California Press, 1961.

Levy, Howard S., trans., *Biography of Huang Ch'ao*. Berkeley: University of California Press, 1955.

Mackerras, Colin, *The Uighur Empire (744–840)*. Canberra: Australian National University, 1968.

Mair, Victor, *T'ang Transformation Texts: A Study of the Buddhist Contribution to the Rise of Vernacular Fiction and Drama in China*. Cambridge, Mass.: Harvard University Press, 1989.

Mair, Victor, *Tun-huang Popular Narratives*. Cambridge University Press, 1983.

McRae, John, *The Northern School and the Formation of Early Ch'an Buddhism*. Honolulu: University of Hawaii, 1986.

Nielson, Thomas P., *The T'ang Poet-Monk Chiao-jan*. Tempe: Arizona State University, 1972.

Nienhauser, William H., Jr., *Bibliography of Selected Western Works on T'ang Dynasty Literature*. Taipei: Center for Chinese Studies, 1988.

Nienhauser, William H., Jr. et al., *Liu Tsung-yüan*. New York: Twayne Publishers, 1973.

Nienhauser, William H., Jr., *P'i Jih-hsiu*. Boston: Twayne Publishers, 1979.

Owen, Stephen, *The Great Age of Chinese Poetry: The High T'ang*. New Haven: Yale University Press, 1981.

Pelliot, Paul, *Histoire ancienne du Tibet*, Paris: A. Maisonneuve, 1961.

Perry, John Curtus, and Bardwell L. Smith, eds., *Essays on T'ang Society: The Interplay of Social, Political and Economic Forces*. Leiden: Brill, 1976.

Pulleyblank, Edwin G., *The Background of the Rebellion of An Lu-shan*. London: Oxford University Press, 1955.

Reischauer, Edwin O., trans., *Ennin's Diary, the Record of a Pilgrimage in China in Search of the Law*. New York: Ronald Press, 1955.

Reischauer, Edwin O., *Ennin's Travels in T'ang China*. New York: Ronald Press, 1955.

Rotours, Robert des, *Traité des examens*. Paris: E. Leroux, 1932.

Rotours, Robert des, *Traité des fonctionnaires et traité de l'armée*. Leiden: Brill, 1947–8.

Rotours, Robert des, *Histoire de Ngan Lou-chan*. Paris: Presses Universitaires de France, 1962.

Saeki, Y., *The Nestorian Documents and Relics in China*. Rpt. Tokyo: Maruzen, 1951, 1955.

Schafer, Edward H., *The Divine Woman: Dragon Ladies and Rain Maidens in T'ang Literature*. Berkeley: University of California Press, 1973.

Schafer, Edward H., *The Golden Peaches of Samarkand: A Study of T'ang Exotics*. Berkeley: University of California Press, 1963.

Schafer, Edward H., *The Vermilion Bird: T'ang Images of the South*. Berkeley: University of California Press, 1967.

Solomon, Bernard S., trans., *The Veritable Record of the T'ang Emperor Shun-tsung*. Cambridge, Mass.: Harvard University Press, 1955.

Teiser, Stephen F., *The Ghost Festival in Medieval China*. Princeton: Princeton University Press, 1988.

Twitchett, Denis, *Financial Administration under the T'ang Dynasty*. Cambridge University Press, 1963, 2nd ed., 1970.

Twitchett, Denis, *Printing and Publishing in Medieval China*. London: Wynkyn de Worde Society, 1983.

Twitchett, Denis, and Arthur F. Wright, eds., *Perspectives on the T'ang*. New Haven: Yale University Press, 1973.

Verellen, Franciscus, *Du Guangting (850–933): Taoïste de cour à la fin de la Chine médiévale*. Paris: Institut des Hautes Études Chinoises, 1989.

Waley, Arthur, *The Life and Times of Po Chü-i*. London: Allen & Unwin, 1949.

Waley, Arthur, *The Poetry and Career of Li Po*. London: Allen & Unwin, 1950.

Waley, Arthur, *The Real Tripitaka, and Other Pieces*. London: Allen & Unwin, 1952.

Wagner, Marsha L., *Wang Wei*. Boston: Twayne Publishers, 1981.

Wang Gung-wu, *The Structure of Power in North China during the Five Dynasties*. 1963; rpt. Stanford, Calif.: Stanford University Press, 1967.

Watters, Thomas, trans., *On Yuan Chwang's Travels in India. 629–645 A.D.*, 2 vols. Rpt. New York: AMS Press, 1971.

Wechsler, Howard, *Mirror to the Son of Heaven: Wei Cheng at the Court of T'ang T'ai-tsung*. New Haven: Yale University Press, 1974.

Wechsler, Howard, *Offerings of Jade and Silk: Ritual and Symbol in the Legitimation of the T'ang Dynasty*. New Haven: Yale University Press, 1985.

Weinstein, Stanley, *Buddhism under the T'ang*. Cambridge University Press, 1987.

Whitfield, Roderick, and Anne Farrer, *Cave of the Thousand Buddhas: Chinese Art from the Silk Route*. New York: George Braziller, Inc., 1990.

Wright, Arthur F., *The Sui Dynasty*. New York: Knopf, 1978.

Yampolsky, Philip B., trans., *The Platform Sutra of the Sixth Patriarch: The Text of the Tun-huang Manuscript with Translation*. New York: Columbia University Press, 1967.

The Sung dynasty

Balazs, Étienne, and Yves Hervouet, eds., *A Sung Bibliography*. Hong Kong: The Chinese University Press, 1978.

Bol, Peter K., *'This Culture of Ours': Intellectual Transitions in T'ang and Sung China*. Stanford, Calif.: Stanford University Press, 1992.

Birdwhistell, Anne D., *Transition to Neo-Confucianism: Shao Yung on Knowledge and Symbols of Reality*. Stanford, Calif.: Stanford University Press, 1989.

Carter, Thomas F., *The Invention of Printing in China and Its Spread Westward*, revised edition by L. C. Goodrich. New York: Ronald Press, 1955.

Chaffee, John William, *The Thorny Gates of Learning in Sung China: A Social History of Examinations*. Cambridge University Press, 1985.

Chan, Wing-tsit, trans., Chin-ssu lu. *Reflections on Things at Hand: The Neo-Confucian Anthology* [by Chu Hsi and Lü Tsu-ch'ien]. New York: Columbia University Press, 1967.

Chan, Wing-tsit, *Chu Hsi and Neo-Confucianism.* Honolulu: University of Hawaii Press, 1986.

Chan, Wing-tsit, *Chu Hsi: New Studies.* Honolulu: University of Hawaii Press, 1989.

Chaves, Jonathan, *Mei Yao-ch'en and the Development of Early Sung Poetry.* New York: Columbia University Press, 1976.

Chung, Priscilla Ching, *Palace Women in the Northern Sung.* Leiden: Brill, 1981.

Cleary, Thomas, and J. C. Cleary, trans., *The Blue Cliff Record.* Boulder: Shambhala, 1977.

Davis, Richard L., *Court and Family in Sung China, 960–1279: Bureaucratic Success and Kinship Fortunes for the Shih of Ming-chou.* Durham, N.C.: Duke University Press, 1986.

de Bary, Wm. Theodore, and John Chaffee, eds., *Neo-Confucian Education: The Formative Stage.* Berkeley: University of California Press, 1989.

Djang, Chu, and Jane C. Djang, trans., *A Compilation of Anecdotes of Sung Personalities.* New York: St. John's University Press, 1989.

Ebrey, Patricia Buck, trans., *Ch'u Hsi's Family Rituals: A Twelfth-century Chinese Manual for the Performance of Cappings, Weddings, Funerals, and Ancestral Rites.* Princeton: Princeton University Press, 1991.

Ebrey, Patricia Buck, trans., *Family and Property in Sung China: Yüan Ts'ai's Precepts for Social Life.* Princeton: Princeton University Press, 1984.

Ebrey, Patricia Buck, *The Inner Quarters: Marriage and the Lives of Chinese Women in the Sung Period.* Berkeley: University of California, 1993.

Egan, Ronald C., *The Literary Works of Ou-yang Hsiu (1007–72).* Cambridge University Press, 1984.

Egan, Ronald C., *Word, Image, and Deed in the Life of Su Shi.* Cambridge, Mass.: Harvard University Press, 1994.

Fong, Grace S., *Wu Wenying and the Art of Southern Ci Poetry.* Princeton: Princeton University Press, 1987.

Franke, Herbert, *Studien und Texte zur Kriegsgeschichte der Südlichen Sungzeit.* Wiesbaden: Harrassowitz, 1987.

Franke, Herbert, ed., *Sung Biographies,* 4 vols. Wiesbaden: Steiner, 1976.

Gardner, Daniel K., trans., *Learning to Be a Sage: Selections from the Conversations of Master Chu, Arranged Topically* [Chu Hsu, *Chu-tzu yü lei*]. Berkeley: University of California Press, 1990.

Gernet, Jacques, *Daily Life in China on the Eve of the Mongol Invasion.* New York: Macmillan, 1967.

Glahn, Richard von, *The Country of Streams and Grottoes: Expansion, Settlement, and the Civilizing of the Sichuan Frontier in Song Times.* Cambridge, Mass.: Harvard University Press, 1987.

Graham, A. C., *Two Chinese Philosophers: Ch'eng Ming-tao and Ch'eng Yi-ch'uan.* London: Lund Humphries, 1958.

Gulik, R. H. van, trans., *T'ang Yin Pi Shih: Parallel Cases from under the Peartree.* Leiden: Brill, 1956.

Gundert, Wilhelm, trans., *Bi-yän-lu: Niederschrift von der Smaragdenen Felswand,* 3 vols. Munich: Carl Hanser, 1960–73.

Haeger, John W., ed., *Crisis and Prosperity in Sung China*. Tucson: University of Arizona Press, 1975.

Hansen, Valerie, *Changing Gods in Medieval China, 1127–1276*. Princeton: Princeton University Press, 1990.

Hargett, James M., *On the Road in Twelfth-Century China: The Travel Diaries of Fan Chengda (1126–1193)*. Wiesbaden: Steiner, 1989.

Hirth, Frederick, and W. W. Rockhill, trans., *Chau Ju-kua: His Work on the Chinese and Arab Trade in the Twelfth and Thirteenth Centuries, Entitled Chu-fan-chi*. 1911; rpt. Taipei: Ch'eng-wen, 1970.

Hymes, Robert P., *Statesmen and Gentlemen: The Elite of Fu-chou, Chiang-hsi, in Northern and Southern Sung*. Cambridge University Press, 1986.

Jay, Jennifer W., *A Change in Dynasties: Loyalism in Thirteenth Century China*. Bellingham: Center for Asian Studies, Western Washington University, 1991.

Kasoff, Ira E., *The Thought of Chang Tsai (1020–1077)*. Cambridge University Press, 1984.

Kato, S., 'On the Hang or the Association of Merchants in China,' In *Memoires of the Research Department of the Tôyô Bunko*. Tokyo, 1936.

Kinugawa, Tsuyoshi, ed., *Collected Studies on Sung History Dedicated to Professor James T. C. Liu in Celebration of His Seventieth Birthday*. Kyoto: Dohosha, 1989.

Kleeman, Terry F., trans., *A God's Own Tale: The Book of Transformations of Wenchang*. Albany: State University of New York Press, 1994. [*Wen-ch'ang hua shu*, a Southern Sung Taoist text].

Kracke, Edward A., *Civil Service in Sung China: 960–1067*. Cambridge, Mass.: Harvard University Press, 1953.

Lachman, Charles, trans., *Evaluations of Sung Dynasty Painters of Renown: Liu Tao-ch'un's* 'Sung-ch'ao ming-hua p'ing'. Leiden: Brill, 1989.

Ledderose, Lothar, *Mi Fu and the Classical Tradition of Chinese Calligraphy*. Princeton: Princeton University Press, 1979.

Lee, Thomas H. C., *Government Education and Examinations in Sung China*. Hong Kong: Chinese University of Hong Kong, 1985.

Lin, Yutang, *The Gay Genius: The Life and Times of Su Tungpo*. New York: John Day, 1947.

Liu, James T. C., *China Turning Inward: Intellectual — Political Changes in Early Twelfth Century*. Cambridge, Mass.: Harvard University Press, 1988.

Liu, James T. C., 'An Early Sung Reformer, Fan Chung-yen,' in John K. Fairbank, ed., *Chinese Thought and Institutions*. Chicago: University of Chicago Press, 1957, pp. 105–31.

Liu, James T. C., *Ou-yang Hsiu: An Eleventh-Century Neo-Confucianist*. Stanford, Calif.: Stanford University Press, 1967.

Liu, James T. C., *Reform in Sung China: Wang An-shih and His New Policies*. Cambridge, Mass.: Harvard University Press, 1959.

Lin Shuen-fu, *The Transformation of the Chinese Lyrical Tradition: Chiang K'uei and Southern Sung tz'u Poetry*. Princeton: Princeton University Press, 1978.

Lo Jung-pang, 'The Emergence of China as a Sea-Power during the Late Sung and Early Yüan Periods,' *Far Eastern Quarterly* 14.4 (1955), 489–503.

Lo, Winston W., *An Introduction to the Civil Service of Sung China, with an Emphasis on its Personnel Administration*. Honolulu: University of Hawaii Press, 1987.

Ma, Lawrence J. C., *Commercial Development and Urban Change in Sung China*. Ann Arbor: Department of Geography, University of Michigan, 1971.

McKnight, Brian E., *Law and Order in Sung China*. Cambridge University Press, 1992.

McKnight, Brian E., *The Quality of Mercy*. Honolulu: University of Hawaii Press, 1981.

McKnight, Brian E., trans., *The Washing Away of Wrongs: Forensic Medicine in Thirteenth-century China*. Ann Arbor: Center for Chinese Studies, University of Michigan, 1981.

McKnight, Brian E., *Village and Bureaucracy in Southern Sung China*. Chicago: University of Chicago Press, 1971.

Meskill, John, ed., *Wang An-shih: Practical Reformer?* Boston: Heath, 1963.

Munro, Donald J., *Images of Human Nature: A Sung Portrait*. Princeton: Princeton University Press, 1988.

Murray, Julia K., *Ma Hezhi and the Illustration of the Book of Odes*. Cambridge University Press, 1993.

Palumbo-Liu, David, *The Poetics of Appropriation: The Literary Theory and Practice of Huang Tingjian*. Stanford, Calif.: Stanford University Press, 1993.

Pelliot, Paul, *Les débuts de l'imprimerie en China*. Paris: A. Maisonneuve, 1953.

Sargent, Eugene Galen, *Tchou Hi contre le bouddhisme*. Paris: Presses Universitaires de France, 1955.

Schirokauer, Conrad, and Robert B. Hymes, eds., *Ordering the World: Approaches to State and Society in Sung Dynasty China*. Berkeley: University of California Press, 1993.

Shiba, Yoshinobu, *Commerce and Society in Sung China*. Ann Arbor: Center for Chinese Studies, University of Michigan, 1970.

Smith, Paul, *Taxing Heaven's Storehouse: Bureaucratic Entrepreneurship and the Sichuan Tea and Horse Trade, 1074–1224*. Cambridge, Mass.: Harvard University Press, 1991.

Tillman, Hoyt C., *Confucian Discourse and Chu Hsi's Ascendancy*. Honolulu: University of Hawaii Press, 1992.

Tillman, Hoyt C., *Utilitarian Confucianism: Ch'en Liang's Challenge to Chu Hsi*. Cambridge, Mass.: Harvard University Press, 1982.

Trauzettel, Rolf, *Ts'ai Ching (1046–1126) als Typus des illegitimen Ministers*. Berlin: K. Urlaub, 1964.

Williamson, Henry Raymond, *Wang An-shih: A Chinese Statesman and Educationalist of the Sung Dynasty*, 2 vols. London: Probsthain, 1935.

Winkelman, John H., *The Imperial Library in Southern Sung China, 1127–1279: A Study of the Organization and Operation of the Scholarly Agencies of the Central Government*. Philadelphia: American Philosophical Society, 1974.

Yoshikawa, Kojiro, *An Introduction to Sung Poetry*. Cambridge, Mass.: Harvard University Press, 1967.

Liao, Chin, Hsia, and Mongol empires

Allsen, Thomas T., *Mongol Imperialism: The Policies of the Grand Qan Möngke in China, Russia, and the Islamic Lands*. Berkeley: University of California Press, 1987.

Budge, E. A. Wallis, trans., *The Monks of Kublai Khan, Emperor of China; or, The History of the Life and Travels of Rabban Sauma, Envoy and Plenipotentiary of the Mongol Khans to the Kings of Europe, and Markos Who as Mar Yahbh-Allaha III Became Patriarch of the Nestorian Church in Asia.* London: Religious Tract Society, 1928.

Cahill, James, *Hills Beyond a River: Chinese Painting of the Yüan Dynasty.* New York: Weatherhill, 1976.

Chan Hok-lam, *The Historiography of the Chin Dynasty: Three Studies.* Wiesbaden: Steiner, 1970.

Chan Hok-lam, *Legitimation in Imperial China: Discussion under the Jurchen-Chin Dynasty (1115–1234).* Seattle: University of Washington Press, 1984.

Chan Hok-lam and Wm. Theodore de Bary, eds., *Yüan Thought: Chinese Thought and Religion under the Mongols.* New York: Columbia University Press, 1982.

Ch'en, Paul Heng-chao, *Chinese Legal Tradition under the Mongols: The Code of 1291 as Reconstructed.* Princeton: Princeton University Press, 1979.

Ch'en Yüan, *Western and Central Asians in China under the Mongols.* Berkeley: University of California Press, 1966.

Cleaves, Francis Woodman, trans., *The Secret History of the Mongols.* Cambridge, Mass.: Harvard University Press, 1982.

Crump, James I., *Chinese Theater in the Days of Kublai Khan.* Ann Arbor: Center for Chinese Studies, University of Michigan, 1990.

Dardess, John W., *Conquerors and Confucians: Aspects of Political Change in Late Yüan China.* New York: Columbia University Press, 1973.

Dunnell, Ruth *Buddhism and the State in Eleventh Century Xia: Studies on the Sources of Early Tangut History.* Honolulu: University of Hawaii Press, 1995.

Endicott-West, Elizabeth, *Mongolian Rule in China: Local Administration in the Yüan Dynasty.* Cambridge, Mass.: Harvard University Press, 1989.

Farquhar, David, *Chinese Government under Mongolian Rule: A Research Guide.* Wiesbaden: Steiner, 1990.

Franke, Herbert, *China under Mongol Rule.* Aldershot, Variorum, 1994.

Franke, Herbert, *From Tribal Chieftain to Universal God: The Legitimation of the Yüan Dynasty.* Munich: Bayeriche Akademie der Wissenschaften, 1978.

Gridley, Marilyn, *Chinese Buddhist Sculpture under the Liao.* New Delhi, Aditya Prakashan, 1993.

Hsiao Ch'i-ch'ing, *The Military Establishment of the Yüan Dynasty.* Cambridge, Mass.: Harvard University Press, 1978.

Idema, Wilt, and Stephen H. West, *Chinese Theater, 1100–1450: A Source Book.* Wiesbaden: Steiner, 1982.

Kessler, Adam T., *Empires Beyond the Great Wall: The Heritage of Genghis Khan.* Los Angeles, Natural History Museum of Los Angeles County, 1993.

Komroff, M., *Contemporaries of Marco Polo.* New York: Boni & Liveright, 1928.

Kychanov, E. I., and Herbert Franke, *Tangutische und chinesische Quellen zur Militärgesetzgebung des 11–13 Jahrhunderts.* Munich: Bayeriche Akademie der Wissenschaften, 1990.

Langois, John D., ed., *China under Mongol Rule.* Princeton: Princeton University Press, 1981.

Lee, Sherman, and Wai-kam Ho, *Chinese Art under the Mongols: The Yüan Dynasty (1279–1368).* Cleveland, Cleveland Museum of Art, 1968.

Li, Chu-tsing, *The Autumn Colors on the Ch'iao and Hua Mountains: A Landscape by Chao Meng-fu*. Ascona, Artibus Asiae, 1965.

Lynn, Richard John, *Kuan Yün-shih*. Boston: Twayne Publishers, 1980.

Mote, Frederick W., *The Poet Kao Ch'i, 1336–1374*. Princeton: Princeton University Press, 1962.

Moule, A. C., and Paul Pelliot, trans., *Marco Polo: The Description of the World*, 2 vols. London: Routledge, 1938.

Moule, A. C., *Quinsai, with other Notes on Marco Polo*. Cambridge University Press, 1957.

Olbricht, Peter, *Das Postwesen in China under der Mongolenherrschaft im 13. und 14. Jahrhundert*. Wiesbaden: Harrassowitz, 1954.

Olschki, Leonardo, *Marco Polo's Precursors*. Baltimore: Johns Hopkins Press, 1943.

Olschki, Leonardo, *Guillaume Boucher: A French Artist at the Court of the Khans*. Baltimore: Johns Hopkins Press, 1946.

Pelliot, Paul, *Notes on Marco Polo*, 3 vols. Paris: Imprimerie nationale, 1959–73.

Ratchnevsky, Paul, *Un code des Yuan*. Paris: E. Leroux, 1937.

Rossabi, Morris, *China among Equals: The Middle Kingdom and Its Neighbors, 10th–14th Centuries*. Berkeley: University of California Press, 1983.

Rossabi, Morris, *Khubilai Khan: His Life and Times*. Berkeley: University of California Press, 1988.

Schurmann, Herbert Franz, *Economic Structure of the Yüan Dynasty*. Cambridge, Mass.: Harvard University Press, 1956.

Shimada, Masao, 'The Characteristics of Northern Region Liao Bureaucracy and the Significance of the Hereditary Official System,' *Memoirs of the Research Department of the Tôyô Bunko*, 1983.

Tao Jing-shen, *The Jurchen in Twelfth-Century China: A Study of Sinicization*. Seattle: University of Washington Press, 1976.

Tao Jing-shen, *Two Sons of Heaven: Studies in Sung-Liao Relations*. Tucson: University of Arizona Press, 1988.

Tillman, Hoyt Cleveland, and Stephen W. West, eds., *China under Jurchen Rule*. Albany: State University of New York Press, 1995.

Waley, Arthur, *The Travels of an Alchemist*. London: Routledge & Kegan Paul, 1931.

West, Stephen W., *Vaudeville and Narrative: Aspects of Chin Theater*. Wiesbaden: Steiner, 1977.

Wittfogel, Karl A., and Feng Chia-sheng, *History of Chinese Society: Liao (907–1125)*. Philadelphia: American Philosophical Society, 1949.

Wixted, John Timothy, *Poems on Poetry: Literary Criticism by Yuan Hao-wen (1190–1257)*. Wiesbaden: Steiner, 1982.

Yoshikawa, Kojiro (trans. John Timothy Wixted), *Five Hundred Years of Chinese Poetry, 1150–1650: The Chin, Yuan, and Ming Dynasties*. Princeton: Princeton University Press, 1989.

Yule, Henry, trans., *The Book of Ser Marco Polo*. 3rd ed. revised by Henri Cordier, 2 vols. London: Routledge, 1938.

The Ming dynasty

Barnhart, Richard M., *Painters of the Great Ming: The Imperial Court and the Zhe School*. Dallas: Dallas Museum of Art, 1993.

Beattie, Hilary J., *Land and Lineage in China: A Study of T'ung-ch'eng County, Anhwei, in the Ming and Ch'ing Dynasties*. Cambridge University Press, 1979.

Berling, Judith, *The Syncretic Religion of Lin Chao-en*. New York: Columbia University Press, 1980.

Billeter, Jean François, *Li Zhi, philosope maudit (1527–1602): Contribution à une sociologie du mandarinat chinois de la fin des Ming*. Geneva — Paris: Librairie Droz, 1979.

Black, Alison Harley, *Man and Nature in the Philosophical Thought of Wang Fu-chih*. Seattle: University of Washington Press, 1989.

Boxer, Charles R., *Hidalgos in the Far East, 1550–1610*. The Hague: Nijhoff, 1948.

Boxer, Charles R., ed., *South China in the Sixteenth Century, Being the Narratives of Galeote Pereira, Fr. Gaspar da Cruz, O.P., Fr. Martin de Rada, O.E.S.A*. London: The Hakluyt Society, 1953.

Cahill, James, *The Distant Mountains: Chinese Painting of the Late Ming Dynasty, 1570–1644*. New York: Weatherhill, 1982.

Cahill, James, *Parting at the Shore: Chinese Painting of the Early and Middle Ming Dynasties, 1368–1580*. New York: Weatherhill, 1978.

Chan, Albert, *The Glory and Fall of the Ming Dynasty*. Norman: University of Oklahoma Press, 1982.

Chang Chun-shu, *Crisis and Transformation in Seventeenth-Century China: Society, Culture, and Modernity in Li Yu's World*. Ann Arbor: University of Michigan Press, 1992.

Chang, K'ang-i Sun, *The Late-Ming Poet Ch'en Tzu-lung*. New Haven: Yale University Press, 1991.

Chang T'ien-tse, *Sino-Portuguese Trade from 1514–1644*. Leiden: Brill, 1934.

Chaves, Jonathan, *Singing of the Source: Nature and God in the Poetry of the Chinese Painter Wu Li*. Honolulu: University of Hawaii Press, 1993.

Ching, Julia, and Willard G. Oxtoby, ed., *Discovering China: European Interpretations in the Enlightenment*. Rochester, N.Y.: University of Rochester Press, 1992.

Ching, Julia, trans., *The Records of Ming Scholars*. Honolulu: University of Hawaii Press, 1987. [Huang Tsung-hsi's *Ming-ju hsüeh-an*].

Ching, Julia, *To Acquire Wisdom: The Way of Wang Yang-ming*. New York: Columbia University Press, 1976.

Clapp, Anne, *Wen Cheng-ming: The Ming Artist and Antiquity*. Ascona, Switz.: Artibus Asiae, 1975.

Dardess, John W., *Confucianism and Autocracy: Professional Elites in the Founding of the Ming Dynasty*. Berkeley: University of California Press, 1983.

de Bary, Wm. Theodore, *Neo-Confucian Orthodoxy and the Learning of the Mind-and-Heart*. New York: Columbia University Press, 1981.

de Bary, Wm. Theodore, *The Liberal Tradition in China*. New York: Columbia University Press, 1983.

de Bary, Wm. Theodore, *Self and Society in Ming Thought*. New York: Columbia University Press, 1970.

de Bary, Wm. Theodore, *The Unfolding of Neo-Confucianism*. New York: Columbia University Press, 1975.

de Heer, Philip, *The Caretaker Emperor: Aspects of the Imperial Institution in Fifteenth-Century China as Reflected in the Political History of the Reign of Chu Ch'i-yü*. Leiden: Brill, 1985.

Dennerline, Jerry, *The Chia-ting Loyalists: Confucian Leadership and Social Change in Seventeenth-Century China.* New Haven: Yale University Press, 1981.

Dreyer, Edward L., *Early Ming China: A Political History, 1355–1435.* Stanford, Calif.: Stanford University Press, 1982.

Dunne, George H., S. J., *Generation of Giants: The Story of the Jesuits in China in the Last Decades of the Ming.* Notre Dame, Ind.: University of Notre Dame Press, 1962.

Duyvendak, J. J. L., *China's Discovery of Africa.* London: Probsthain, 1949.

Egerton, Clement, trans., *The Golden Lotus: A Translation from the Chinese Original of the Novel*, Chin P'ing Mei, 4 vols. London: Routledge & Kegal Paul, 1939.

Farmer, Edward L., *Early Ming Government: The Evolution of Dual Capitals.* Cambridge, Mass.: Harvard University Press, 1976.

Fisher, Carney T., *The Chosen One: Succession and Adoption in the Court of Ming Shizong.* Sydney: Allen & Unwin, 1990.

Franke, Wolfgang, *An Introduction to the Sources of Ming History.* New York: Oxford University Press, 1969.

Goodrich, L. Carrington, and Fang Chaoying, eds., *Dictionary of Ming Biography, 1368–1644*, 2 vols. New York: Columbia University Press, 1976.

Gulik, R. H. van, trans., *Dee Gong An: Three Murder Cases Solved by Judge Dee.* Tokyo: Toppan Printing Co., 1949.

Hanan, Patrick D., trans., *The Carnal Prayer-Mat.* New York: Ballantine, 1990. [trans. of novel *Jou p'u tuan*].

Hanan, Patrick D., *The Invention of Li Yü.* Cambridge, Mass.: Harvard University Press, 1988.

Handlin-Smith, Joanna, *Action in Late Ming Thought: The Reorientation of Lü K'un and Other Scholar-Officials.* Berkeley: University of California Press, 1983.

Henke, Frederick Cooper, trans., *The Philosophy of Wang Yang-ming.* 1916; rpt. New York: Paragon Books, 1964.

Ho Ping-ti, *The Ladder of Success in Imperial China.* New York: Columbia University Press, 1962.

Huang, Ray, *1587, a Year of No Significance: The Ming Dynasty in Decline.* New Haven: Yale University Press, 1981.

Huang, Ray, *Taxation and Governmental Finance in Sixteenth-Century Ming China.* Cambridge University Press, 1974.

Hucker, Charles O., *The Censorial System of Ming China.* Stanford, Calif.: Stanford University Press, 1966.

Hucker, Charles O., ed., *Chinese Government in Ming Times: Seven Studies.* New York: Columbia University Press, 1969.

Hucker, Charles O., *The Ming Dynasty: Its Origins and Evolving Institutions.* Ann Arbor: University of Michigan, 1978.

Hucker, Charles O., *The Traditional Chinese State in Ming Times (1368–1644).* Tucson: University of Arizona Press, 1961.

Ko, Dorothy, *Teachers of the Inner Chambers: Women and Culture in Seventeenth-Century China.* Stanford, Calif.: Stanford University Press, 1994.

Lach, Donald, *Asia in the Making of Europe.* Chicago: University of Chicago Press, 1965–

Levathes, Louise, *When China Ruled the Seas: The Treasure Fleet of the Dragon Throne, 1405–1433*. New York: Simon & Schuster, 1994.

Li Chi, trans., *The Travel Diaries of Hsü Hsia-k'o*. Hong Kong: Chinese University of Hong Kong, 1974.

Liang Fang-chung, *The Single-Whip Method of Taxation in China*. Cambridge, Mass.: Harvard University Press, 1956.

Meskill, John, *Academies in Ming China: A Historical Essay*. Tucson: University of Arizona Press, 1982.

Mills, J. V. G., trans., *Ma Huan, Ying-yai sheng-lan: The Overall Survey of the Ocean's Shores*. Cambridge University Press, 1970.

Paluden, Ann, *The Imperial Ming Tombs*. New Haven: Yale University Press, 1981.

Parsons, James B., *The Peasant Rebellions of the Late Ming Dynasty*. Tucson: University of Arizona Press, 1970.

Peterson, Willard J., *Bitter Gourd: Fang I-chih and the Impetus for Intellectual Change*. New Haven: Yale University Press.

Plaks, Andrew H., *The Four Masterworks of the Ming Novel*. Princeton: Princeton University Press, 1987.

Ricci, Mateo, 1522–1610 (trans. Louis J. Gallagher, S. J.), *China in the Sixteenth Century: The Journals of Matthew Ricci, 1583–1610*. New York: Random House, 1953.

Rossabi, Morris, *The Jurchens in the Yüan and Ming*. Ithaca: Cornell University, 1982.

Roy, David, trans., *The Plum in the Golden Vase or, Chin P'ing Mei. Volume One: The Gathering*. Princeton: Princeton University Press, 1993.

Serruys, Henri, *Sino-Jürced Relations during the Yung-lo Period, 1403–1424*. Wiesbaden: Harrassowitz, 1955.

Shi Nai'an and Luo Guanzhong (trans. Sidney Shapiro), *Outlaws of the Marsh*, 2 vols. Bloomington: Indiana University Press, 1981. [The novel *Shui-hu chuan*].

Spence, Jonathan D., and John E. Wills, Jr., eds., *From Ming to Ch'ing: Conquest, Region, and Continuity in Seventeenth-Century China*. New Haven: Yale University Press, 1979.

Spence, Jonathan D., *The Memory Palace of Matteo Ricci*. Harmondsworth: Penguin, 1985.

Struve, Lynn A., *Voices from the Ming-Qing Cataclysm: China in Tigers' Jaws*. New Haven: Yale University Press, 1993.

Taylor, Romeyn, trans., *The Basic Annals of Ming T'ai-tsu*. San Francisco: Chinese Materials Center, 1975.

Trigault, Nicholas, 1577–1628 (trans. Louis J. Gallagher, S. J.), *The China That Was: China as Discovered by the Jesuits at the Close of the Sixteenth Century*. Milwaukee, Bruce, 1942.

Waldron, Arthur, *The Great Wall: From History to Myth*. Cambridge University Press, 1990.

Wang I-t'ung, *Official Relations Between China and Japan, 1368–1549*. Cambridge, Mass.: Harvard University Press, 1953.

Yu, Anthony C., trans., *The Journey to the West*, 4 vols. Chicago: University of Chicago Press, 1977–83.

Yü Chün-fang, *The Renewal of Buddhism in China: Chu-hung and the Late Ming Synthesis*. New York: Columbia University Press, 1981.

From 1644 to 1798

Bartlett, Beatrice S., *Monarchs and Ministers: The Grand Council in Mid-Ch'ing China, 1723–1820*. Berkeley: University of California Press, 1991.

Beurdeley, Cécile and Michel, *Giuseppe Castiglione: A Jesuit Painter at the Court of the Chinese Emperors*. Rutland, Vt.: Charles Tuttle Co., 1971.

Cahill, James, *The Compelling Image: Nature and Style in Seventeenth-Century Chinese Painting*. Cambridge, Mass.: Harvard University Press, 1982.

Chang Chun-shu, *The Making of China: Main Themes in Pre-Modern Chinese History*. Englewood Cliffs, N.J.: Prentice Hall, 1975.

Chou Ju-hsi et al., *The Elegant Brush: Chinese Painting under the Qianlong Emperor, 1735–1795*. Phoenix: Phoenix Art Museum, 1985.

Elman, Benjamin A., *From Philosophy to Philology: Intellectual and Social Aspects of Change in Late Imperial China*. Cambridge, Mass.: Harvard University Press, 1984.

Feuerwerker, Albert, *State and Society in Eighteenth Century China: The Ch'ing Empire in Its Glory*. Ann Arbor: Center for Chinese Studies, University of Michigan, 1976.

Fu Lo-shu, ed., *A Documentary Chronicle of Sino — Western Relations, 1644–1820*. Tucson: University of Arizona Press, 1966.

Giles, Herbert A., trans., *Strange Stories from a Chinese Studio*. 1880; rpt. New York: Boni & Liveright, 1925. [*Liao-chai chih-i* of P'u Sung-ling].

Gimm, Martin, *Kaiser Qianlong (1711–1799) als Poet: Anmerkungen zu seinem schriftstellerischen Werk*. Stuttgart, Steiner, 1993.

Goodrich, L. Carrington, *The Literary Inquisition of Ch'ien-lung*. Baltimore: Waverly Press, 1935.

Hawkes, David, trans., *The Story of the Stone*, 5 vols. Harmondsworth: Penguin, 1973–1982. [*Hung-lou meng* by Ts'ao Hsüeh-ch'in].

Hegel, Robert E., *The Novel in Seventeenth Century China*. New York: Columbia University Press, 1981.

Huang Pei, *Autocracy at Work: A Study of the Yung-cheng Period, 1723–1735*. Bloomington: Indiana University Press, 1974.

Jami, Catherine, and Hubert Delahaye, eds., *L'Europe en Chine: Interactions scientifiques, religieuses et culturelles aux XVIIe et XVIIIe siècles*. Paris: Institut des Hautes Études Chinoises, 1993.

Johnson, David, Andrew Nathan, and Evelyn S. Rawski, eds., *Popular Culture in Late Imperial China*. Berkeley: University of California Press, 1985.

Johnson, Linda Cooke, ed., *Cities of Jiangnan in Late Imperial China*. Albany: State University of New York Press, 1993.

Kahn, Harold L., *Monarchy in the Emperor's Eyes: Image and Reality in the Ch'ien Lung Reign*. Cambridge, Mass.: Harvard University Press, 1971.

Kessler, Lawrence D., *Kang-hsi and the Consolidation of Ch'ing Rule, 1661–1684*. Chicago: University of Chicago Press, 1976.

Keene, Donald, *The Battles of Coxinga*. London: Taylors Foreign Press, 1951.

Kuhn, Philip A., *Soulstealers: The Chinese Sorcery Scare of 1768*. Cambridge, Mass.: Harvard University Press, 1990.

Lessing, Ferdinand D., *Yung Ho Kung: An Iconography of the Lamaist Cathedral in Peking*. Göteborg, Elanders, 1942.

Liu, Adam Yuen-chung, *The Hanlin Academy: Training Ground for the Ambitious, 1644–1850*. Hamden, Conn.: Archon Books, 1981.

Liu, Adam Yuen-chung, *Two Rulers in One Reign: Dorgon and Shun-chih, 1644–1660.* Canberra: Australian National University, 1989.

Michael, Franz, *The Origin of Manchu Rule in China.* Baltimore: Johns Hopkins, 1942.

Naquin, Susan, and Evelyn S. Rawski, *Chinese Society in the Eighteenth Century.* New Haven: Yale University Press, 1987.

Nivison, David S., *The Life and Thought of Chang Hsüeh-ch'eng (1738–1801).* Stanford, Calif.: Stanford University Press, 1966.

Oxnam, Robert B., *Ruling from Horseback: Manchu Politics in the Oboi Regency, 1661–1669.* Chicago: University of Chicago Press, 1974.

Plaks, Andrew H., *Archetype and Allegory in the* Dream of the Red Chamber. Princeton: Princeton University Press, 1976.

Pratt, Leonard, and Chiang Su-hui, trans., *Shen Fu: Six Records of a Floating Life.* Harmondsworth: Penguin, 1983.

Rawski, Evelyn S., *Education and Popular Literacy in Ch'ing China.* Ann Arbor: University of Michigan, 1979.

Ropp, Paul, *Dissent in Early Modern China: Ju-lin wai-shih and Ch'ing Social Criticism.* Ann Arbor: University of Michigan Press, 1981.

Spence, Jonathan D., *The Death of Woman Wang.* New York: Viking Press, 1978.

Spence, Jonathan D., *Emperor of China: Self-Portrait of K'ang Hsi.* New York: Knopf, 1974.

Spence, Jonathan D., *The Search for Modern China.* New York: W. W. Norton, 1990.

Spence, Jonathan D., *Ts'ao Yin and the K'ang-hsi Emperor: Bondservant and Master.* New Haven: Yale University Press, 1966.

Strassberg, Richard, *The World of K'ung Shang-jen: A Man of Letters in Early Ch'ing China.* New York: Columbia University Press, 1983.

Struve, Lynn A., *The Southern Ming, 1644–1662.* New Haven: Yale University Press, 1984.

Sze Mai-mai, trans., *The Mustard Seed Garden Manual of Painting.* New York: Bollingen Foundation, 1956.

Wakeman, Frederic, Jr., *The Great Enterprise: The Manchu Reconstruction of Imperial Order in Seventeenth-Century China,* 2 vols. Berkeley: University of California Press, 1985.

Waley, Arthur, *Yuan Mei, Eighteenth-Century Chinese Poet.* New York: Allen & Unwin, 1956.

Wang, John, ed., *Chinese Literary Criticism of the Ch'ing Period (1644–1911).* Hong Kong: Hong Kong University Press, 1993.

Will, Pierre-Etienne, *Bureaucracy and Famine in Eighteenth-Century China.* Stanford, Calif.: Stanford University Press, 1990.

Wills, John E., *Embassies and Illusions: Dutch and Portuguese Envoys to K'ang-hsi, 1666–1687.* Cambridge, Mass.: Harvard University Press, 1984.

Wills, John E., *Pepper, Guns, and Parleys: The Dutch East India Company and China, 1662–1681.* Cambridge, Mass.: Harvard University Press, 1974.

Wu Ching-tzu (trans. Yang Hsien-yi and Gladys Yang), *The Scholars.* Peking: Foreign Language Press, 1957. [The novel *Ju-lin wai-shih*].

Wu, Silas H. L., *Communication and Imperial Control in China: Evolution of the Palace Memorial System, 1693–1735.* Cambridge, Mass.: Harvard University Press, 1970.

Wu, Silas H. L., *Passage to Power: K'ang-hsi and His Heir Apparent, 1661–1722*. Cambridge, Mass.: Harvard University Press, 1979.

Zeitlin, Judith T., *Historian of the Strange: Pu Songling and the Classical Tale*. Stanford, Calif.: Stanford University Press, 1993.

Nineteenth century

Beeching, Jack, *The Chinese Opium Wars*. London: Hutchinson, 1975.

Biggerstaff, Knight, *The Earliest Modern Government Schools in China*. Ithaca: Cornell University Press, 1961.

Bland, J. O. P., and Edmund Backhouse, *China under the Empress Dowager, Being the History of the Life and Times of Tz'u hsi*. Peking: Vetch, 1939.

Cameron, Nigel, *The Face of China as Seen by Photographers and Travelers, 1860–1912*. Millerton, N.Y.: Aperture, 1978.

Chan Win-wai, *Buddhism in Late Ch'ing Political Thought*. Hong Kong: Chinese University Press, 1985.

Chang Chung-li, *The Chinese Gentry: Studies on their Role in Nineteenth-Century China*. Seattle: University of Washington Press, 1955.

Chang Hao, *Chinese Intellectuals in Crisis: A Search for Order and Meaning (1890–1911)*. Berkeley: University of California Press, 1987.

Chang Hao, *Liang Ch'i-chao and Intellectual Transition in China, 1980–1907*. Cambridge, Mass.: Harvard University Press, 1971.

Chang Hsin-pao, *Commissioner Lin and the Opium War*. Cambridge, Mass.: Harvard University Press, 1964.

Ch'en Ch'i-t'ien, *Tso Tsung T'ang: Pioneer Promoter of the Modern Dockyard and the Woolen Mill in China*. 1938; rpt. New York: Paragon Books, 1961.

Chiang Siang-tseh, *The Nien Rebellion*. Seattle: University of Washington Press, 1954.

Chu, Samuel C., *Reformer in Modern China: Chang Chien (1853–1926)*. New York: Columbia University Press, 1965.

Chu Wen-chang, *The Moslem Rebellion in North-West China, 1861–1878*. The Hague: Mouton, 1966.

Ch'ü T'ung-tsu, *Local Government in China under the Ch'ing*. Cambridge, Mass.: Harvard University Press, 1962.

Cohen, Paul A., *Between Tradition and Modernity: Wang T'ao and Reform in Late Ch'ing China*. Cambridge, Mass.: Harvard University Press, 1974.

Cohen, Paul A., *The Missionary Movement and the Growth of Chinese Anti-Foreignism, 1960–1870*. Cambridge, Mass.: Harvard University Press, 1963.

Crossley, Pamela Kyle, *Orphan Warriors: Three Manchu Generations and the End of the Qing World*. Princeton: Princeton University Press, 1990.

Esherick, Joseph, *The Origins of the Boxer Uprising*. Berkeley: University of California Press, 1987.

Fairbank, John K., *Trade and Diplomacy on the China Coast: The Opening of the Treaty Ports, 1842–1854*. Cambridge, Mass.: Harvard University Press, 1964.

Fay, Peter Ward, *The Opium War, 1840–1842*. Chapel Hill: University of North Carolina Press, 1975.

Feuerwerker, Albert, *China's Early Industrialisation: Sheng Hsüan-huai (1844–1916) and Mandarin Enterprise*. Cambridge, Mass.: Harvard University Press, 1958.

Feuerwerker, Albert, *Rebellion in Nineteenth-Century China*. Ann Arbor: University of Michigan, 1975.

Fields, Lanny B., *Tso Tsung-t'ang and the Muslims: Statecraft in Northwest China, 1869–1880*. Kingston, Ont.: Limestone Press, 1978.

Graham, Gerald Sandford, *The China Station: War and Diplomacy 1830–1860*. New York: Oxford University Press, 1978.

Hail, William James, *Tseng Kuo-fan and the Taiping Rebellion*. New Haven: Yale University Press, 1927; rpt. New York: Paragon Books, 1964.

Hao Yen-p'ing, *The Comprador in Nineteenth Century China*. Cambridge, Mass.: Harvard University Press, 1970.

Hart, Robert, Sir, 1835–1911, *The I.G. in Peking: Letters of Robert Hart, Chinese Maritime Customs, 1868–1907*. Cambridge, Mass.: Harvard University Press, 1975.

Hart, Robert, *Entering China's Service: Robert Hart's Journals, 1854–1863*. Cambridge, Mass.: Harvard University Press, 1986.

Hart, Robert, *Robert Hart and China's Early Modernization: His Journals, 1863–1866*. Cambridge, Mass.: Harvard University Press, 1991.

Hibbert, Christopher, *The Dragon Wakes: China and the West, 1793–1911*. London: Longman, 1970.

Hsiao Kung-ch'üan, *Rural China: Imperial Control in the Nineteenth Century*. Seattle: University of Washington Press, 1960.

Hsü, Immanuel C. Y., *China's Entrance into the Family of Nations: The Diplomatic Phase, 1858–1880*. Cambridge, Mass.: Harvard University Press, 1960.

Hsü, Immanuel C. Y., *The Ili Crisis: A Study of Sino-Russian Diplomacy, 1871–1881*. Oxford: Clarendon Press, 1965.

Joseph, Philip, *Foreign Diplomacy in China, 1894–1900*. 1928; rpt. New York: Octagon Books, 1971.

Kiernan, Victor Gordon, *British Diplomacy in China, 1880–1885*. 1939; rpt. New York: Octagon Books, 1970.

King, Frank H. H., *Money and Monetary Policy in China, 1845–1895*. Cambridge, Mass.: Harvard University Press, 1965.

Kuhn, Philip A., *Rebellion and Its Enemies in Late Imperial China: Militarization and Social Structure, 1796–1864*. Cambridge, Mass.: Harvard University Press, 1970.

Laitinen, Kauko, *Chinese Nationalism in the Late Qing Dynasty: Zhang Binglin as an Anti-Manchu Propagandist*. London: Curzon Press, 1990.

Latourette, Kenneth S., *A History of Christian Missions in China*. 1929; rpt. New York: Russel & Russel, 1967.

Li Chien-nung (trans. Ssu-yu Teng and Jeremy Ingalls), *The Political History of China, 1840–1928*. Princeton: Van Nostrand Co., 1956.

Li Ju-chen (1763–1830), *Flowers in the Mirror*. Berkeley: Owen, 1965. [Abridged translation by Lin Tai-yi of *Ching-hua yüan*].

Liang Ch'i-ch'ao, *Intellectual Trends in the Ch'ing Period*. Cambridge, Mass.: Harvard University Press, 1959.

Liu Kwang-ching, *Anglo-American Steamship Rivalry in China, 1862–1874*. Cambridge, Mass.: Harvard University Press, 1962.

Mackerras, Colin, *Modern China: A Chronology from 1842 to the Present*. New York: W. H. Freeman & Co., 1982.

Mannix, William Francis, *Memoirs of Li Hung-chang*. Boston: Houghton Mifflin, 1913.

Marsh, Robert Mortimer, *The Mandarins: The Circulation of Elites in China, 1600–1900*. Glencoe, Ill.: Free Press, 1961.

Meng, S. M., *The Tsungli yamen: Its Organization and Functions*. Cambridge, Mass.: Harvard University Press, 1962.

Meskill, Johanna Menzel, *A Chinese Pioneer Family: The Lins of Wu-feng, Taiwan, 1729–1895*. Princeton: Princeton University Press, 1979.

Michael, Franz, *The Taiping Rebellion*. Seattle: University of Washington Press, 1966.

Ono, Kazuko, *Chinese Women in a Century of Revolution, 1850–1950*. Stanford, Calif.: Stanford University Press, 1989.

Perry, Elizabeth J., *Rebels and Revolutionaries in North China, 1845–1945*. Stanford, Calif.: Stanford University Press, 1980.

Polachek, James M., *The Inner Opium War*. Cambridge, Mass.: Harvard University Press, 1992.

Porter, Jonathan, *Tseng Kuo-fan's Private Bureaucracy*. Berkeley: Center for Chinese Studies, 1972.

Rankin, Mary Backus, *Elite Activism and Political Transformation in China: Zhejiang Province, 1865–1911*. Stanford, Calif.: Stanford University Press, 1986.

Rawlinson, John L., *China's Struggle for Naval Development, 1839–1895*. Cambridge, Mass.: Harvard University Press, 1967.

Scalapino, Robert A., *Modern China and its Revolutionary Process: Recurrent Challenges to the Traditional Order, 1850–1920*. Berkeley: University of California Press, 1985.

Schrecker, John E., *The Chinese Revolution in Historical Perspective*. New York: Greenwood Press, 1991.

Shih, Vincent Y. C., *The Taiping Ideology: Its Sources, Interpretations and Influences*. Seattle: University of Washington Press, 1967.

Shimada, Kenji, *Pioneer of the Chinese Revolution: Zhang Binglin and Confucianism*. Stanford, Calif.: Stanford University Press, 1990.

Spector, Stanley, *Li Hung-chang and the Huai Army, a Study in Nineteenth-Century Chinese Regionalism*. Seattle: University of Washington Press, 1964.

Spence, Jonathan D., *To Change China: Western Advisors in China, 1620–1960*. 1969; rpt. Harmondsworth: Penguin, 1980.

Stuart, John Leighton, *Fifty Years in China: The Memoirs of John Leighton Stuart.* New York: Random House, 1954.

Teng Ssu-yü, *Chang Hsi and the Treaty of Nanking, 1842*. Chicago: University of Chicago Press, 1944.

Teng Ssu-yü, *China's Response to the West: A Documentary Survey, 1939–1923*. Cambridge, Mass.: Harvard University Press, 1954.

Teng Ssu-yü, *Historiography of the Taiping Rebellion*. Cambridge, Mass.: Harvard University Press, 1962.

Teng Ssu-yü, *New Light on the History of the T'ai-p'ing Rebellion*. Cambridge, Mass.: Harvard University Press, 1950; rpt. New York: Russell & Russell, 1966.

Teng Ssu-yü, *The Nien Army and Their Guerrilla Warfare*. Paris: Mouton, 1961.

Teng Ssu-yü, *The Taiping Rebellion and the Western Powers: A Comprehensive Survey*. Oxford: Clarendon Press, 1971.

Wakeman, Frederic, *Strangers at the Gate: Social Disorder in South China, 1839–1861*. Berkeley: University of California Press, 1966.

Waley, Arthur, *The Opium War Through Chinese Eyes*. London: Allen & Unwin, 1958.
Wagner, Rudolf G., *Reenacting the Heavenly Vision: The Role of Religion in the Taiping Rebellion*. Berkeley: University of California, 1982.
Worswick, Clark, and Jonathan Spence, *Imperial China: Photographs, 1850–1912*. New York: Crown Publishers, 1978.
Wright, Mary C., *The Last Stand of Chinese Conservatism: The T'ung-chih Restoration, 1862–1874*. Stanford, Calif.: Stanford University Press, 1957.

First half of the twentieth century

Akimova, Vera Vladimirovna, *Two Years in Revolutionary China, 1925–1927*. Cambridge, Mass.: Harvard University Press, 1971.
Bailey, Paul, *China in the Twentieth Century*. Oxford: Blackwell, 1988.
Barber, Noel, *The Fall of Shanghai*. New York: Coward, McCann & Geoghegon, 1979.
Bedeski, Robert E., *State-Building in Modern China: The Kuomintang in the Prewar Period*. Berkeley: Center for Chinese Studies, 1981.
Benson, Linda, *The Ili Rebellion: The Moslem Challenge to Chinese Authority in Xinjiang, 1944–1949*. Armonk, N.Y.: M.E. Sharpe, 1990.
Bergere, Marie-Claire, *The Golden Age of the Chinese Bourgeoisie, 1911–1937*. Cambridge University Press, 1989.
Bianco, Lucien, *Origins of the Chinese Revolution, 1915–1949*. Stanford, Calif.: Stanford University Press, 1971.
Boorman, Howard L., ed., *Biographical Dictionary of Republican China*. New York: Columbia University Press, 1967.
Braun, Otto, *A Comintern Agent in China, 1932–1939*. Stanford, Calif.: Stanford University Press, 1982.
Chan, Wing-tsit, *Religious Trends in Modern China*. New York: Columbia University Press, 1953.
Chang, John K., *Industrial Development in Pre-Communist China*. Chicago: Aldine, 1969.
Chen, Jerome, *Mao and the Chinese Revolution*. New York: Oxford University Press, 1967.
Chen, Joseph, *The May Fourth Movement in Shanghai*. Leiden: Brill, 1971.
Ch'en Yung-fa, *Making Revolution: The Communist Movement in Eastern and Central China, 1937–1945*. Berkeley: University of California Press, 1986.
Cheng, Ronald Ye-lin, *The First Revolution in China: A Theory*. New York: Octagon Books, 1970.
Chow Tse-tsung, *The May Fourth Movement, Intellectual Revolution in Modern China*. Stanford, Calif.: Stanford University Press, 1960; rpt. 1967.
Clifford, Nicholas Rowland, *Spoilt Children of Empire: Westerners in Shanghai and the Chinese Revolution of the 1920s*. Hanover, N.H.: University Press of New England, 1991.
Clubb, O. Edmund, *Twentieth Century China*. New York: Columbia University Press, 1978.
Coble, Parks M., *The Shanghai Capitalists and the Nationalist Government, 1927–1937*. Cambridge, Mass.: Harvard University Press, 1980.
Cohen, Paul A., *Discovering History in China: American Historical Writing on the Recent Chinese Past*. New York: Columbia University Press, 1984.

de Crespigny, Rafe, *China This Century*. New York: Oxford University Press, 1992.

Dennerline, Jerry, *Qian Mu and the World of Seven Mansions*. New Haven: Yale University Press, 1988.

Eastman, Lloyd E., *Seeds of Destruction: Nationalist China in War and Revolution, 1937–1949*. Stanford, Calif.: Stanford University Press, 1984.

Esherick, Joseph, *Reform and Revolution in China: The 1911 Revolution in Hunan and Hubei*. Berkeley: University of California Press, 1976.

Fei Hsiao-tung, *From the Soil: The Foundations of Chinese Society*. Berkeley: University of California Press, 1992.

Fei Hsiao-tung, *Peasant Life in China, a Field Study of Country Life in the Yangtze Valley*. London: Kegan Paul, 1939.

Feuerwerker, Albert, *The Chinese Economy, 1912–1949*. Ann Arbor: University of Michigan, 1968.

Feuerwerker, Albert, *Economic Trends in the Republic of China, 1912–1949*. Ann Arbor: University of Michigan, 1977.

Franke, Wolfgang, *A Century of Chinese Revolution, 1851–1949*. Columbia: University of South Carolina Press, 1970.

Galik, Marian, *The Genesis of Modern Chinese Literary Criticism (1917–1930)*. London: Curzon Press, 1980.

Gillin, Donald G., *Warlord: Yen Hsi-shan in Shanhsi Province, 1911–1949*. Princeton: Princeton University Press, 1967.

Goldman, Merle, ed., *Modern Chinese Literature in the May Fourth Era*. Cambridge, Mass.: Harvard University Press, 1977.

Grieder, Jerome B., *Hu Shih and the Chinese Renaissance: Liberalism in the Chinese Revolution*. Cambridge, Mass.: Harvard University Press, 1970.

Grieder, Jerome B., *Intellectuals and the State in Modern China: A Narrative History*. New York: Free Press, 1981.

Guillermaz, Jacques, *History of the Chinese Communist Party*. New York: Random House, 1972.

Hamilton, John Maxwell, *Edgar Snow: A Biography*. Bloomington: Indiana University Press, 1988.

Harrison, James P., *The Long March to Power: A History of the Chinese Communist Party, 1921–1972*. New York: Praeger, 1972.

Honig, Emily, *Sisters and Strangers: Women in the Shanghai Cotton Mills, 1919–1949*. Stanford, Calif.: Stanford University Press, 1986.

Hoyt, Edwin Palmer, *The Rise of the Chinese Republic: From the Last Emperor to Deng Xiaoping*. New York: McGraw-Hill, 1989.

Hung Chang-tai, *Going to the People: Chinese Intellectuals and Folk Literature, 1918–1937*. Cambridge, Mass.: Harvard University Press, 1985.

Hsia, C. T., *A History of Modern Chinese Fiction, 1917–1957*. New Haven: Yale University Press, 1961.

Hsü, Immanuel C. Y., *Readings in Modern Chinese History*. New York: Oxford University Press, 1971.

Hsü, Immanuel C. Y., *The Rise of Modern China*. 4th ed., New York: Oxford University Press, 1990.

Hummel, Arthur, trans., *The Autobiography of a Chinese Historian (Ku Chieh-kang)*. Leiden: Brill, 1931.

Isaacs, Harold, *The Tragedy of the Chinese Revolution: China's National Revolution of 1926–1928*. London, 1958.

Jeans, Roger B., *Roads Not Taken: The Struggle of Opposition Parties in Twentieth-Century China.* Boulder: Westview Press, 1992.

Johnston, Reginald Fleming, *Twilight in the Forbidden City.* New York: Appleton-Century, 1934.

Jordan, Donald A., *The Northern Expedition: China's National Revolution of 1926–1928.* Honolulu: University of Hawaii Press, 1976.

Lang, Olga, *Pa Chin and His Writings.* Cambridge, Mass.: Harvard University Press, 1967.

Lary, Diana, *Warlord Soldiers: Chinese Common Soldiers, 1911–1937.* Cambridge University Press, 1985.

Lattimore, Owen, *China Memoirs: Chiang Kai-shek and the War against Japan.* Tokyo: University of Tokyo Press, 1990.

Lee, Leo Ou-fan, ed., *Lu Xun and His Legacy.* Berkeley: University of California Press, 1985.

Lee, Leo Ou-fan, *The Romantic Generation of Modern Chinese Writers.* Cambridge, Mass.: Harvard University Press, 1973.

Lee, Leo Ou-fan, *Voices from the Iron House: A Study of Lu Xun.* Bloomington: Indiana University Press, 1987.

Lee, Ta-ling, *Foundations of the Chinese Revolution, 1905–1912.* New York: St. John's University Press, 1970.

Levenson, Joseph R., *Liang Ch'i-ch'ao and the Mind of Modern China.* 1953; rpt. Berkeley: University of California Press, 1967.

Levenson, Joseph R., *Confucian China and Its Modern Fate.* Berkeley: University of California Press, 1958.

Li, Lincoln, *Student Nationalism in China, 1924–1949.* Albany: State University of New York Press, 1994.

Lin Yu-sheng, *The Crisis of Chinese Consciousness: Radical Antitraditionalism in the May Fourth Era.* Madison: University of Wisconsin Press, 1979.

Lin Yu-t'ang, *A History of the Press and Public Opinion in China.* Chicago: University of Chicago Press, 1936.

Link, Perry E., *Mandarin Ducks and Butterflies: Popular Fiction in Early Twentieth-Century Chinese Cities.* Berkeley: University of California Press, 1981.

Lu, Hsun, *The Complete Stories of Lu Xun.* Bloomington: Indiana University Press, 1981.

Lyell, William A., *Lu Hsun's Vision of Reality.* Berkeley: University of California Press, 1976.

Ma, L. Eve Armentrout, *Revolutionaries, Monarchists, and Chinatowns: Chinese Politics in the Americas and the 1911 Revolution.* Honolulu: University of Hawaii Press, 1990.

Malraux, Andre, *Man's Fate.* New York: The Modern Library, 1934.

Martin, Bernard, *Strange Vigor: A Biography of Sun Yat-sen.* Port Washington, N.Y.: Kennikat Press, 1970.

Meisner, Maurice J., *Li Ta-chao and the Origins of Chinese Marxism.* Cambridge, Mass.: Harvard University Press, 1967.

May, Gary, *China Scapegoat: The Diplomatic Order of John Carter Vincent.* Washington, D.C.: New Republic Books, 1979.

Pa Chin, *Family.* Garden City, N.Y.: Anchor Books, 1972.

Pepper, Suzanne, *Civil War in China: The Political Struggle, 1945–49.* Berkeley: University of California Press, 1978.

Powell, Ralph L., *The Rise of Chinese Military Power, 1895–1912.* Princeton: Princeton University Press, 1955.

Pu Yi, Aisin-Gioro (trans. W. J. F. Jenner), *From Emperor to Citizen: Autobiography of Aisin-Gioro Pu Yi.* Peking: Foreign Languages Press, 1964. [Autobiography of 'The Last Emperor'].

Purcell, Victor, *The Boxer Uprising: A Background Study.* Cambridge University Press, 1963.

Purcell, Victor, *The Chinese in South-East Asia.* London: Oxford University Press, 1965.

Rankin, Mary, *Early Chinese Revolutionaries.* Cambridge, Mass.: Harvard University Press, 1971.

Rawski, Thomas, *Economic Growth in Pre-War China.* Berkeley: University of California Press, 1989.

Reardon-Anderson, James, *Yenan and the Great Powers: The Origins of Chinese Communist Foreign Policy, 1944–1946.* New York: Columbia University Press, 1980.

Roberts, J. A. G., ed., *China Through Western Eyes. The Twentieth Century: A Reader in History.* Stroud, Eng.: A. Sutton, 1992.

Rummel, Rudolph J., *China's Bloody Century: Genocide and Mass Murder Since 1900.* New Brunswick, N.J.: Transaction Publishers, 1991.

Salisbury, Harrison Evans, *The Long March: The Untold Story.* New York: Harper & Row, 1985.

Schneider, Laurence A., *Ku Chieh-kang and China's New History: Nationalism and the Quest for Alternative Traditions.* Berkeley: University of California Press, 1971.

Schwarcz, Vera, *The Chinese Enlightenment: Intellectuals and the Legacy of the May Fourth Movement of 1919.* Berkeley: University of California Press, 1986.

Schwartz, Benjamin I., *In Search of Wealth and Power: Yen Fu and the West.* Cambridge, Mass.: Harvard University Press, 1964.

Schyns, Joseph et al., *1500 Modern Chinese Novels and Plays.* Peking: Catholic University Press, 1948; rpt. Ridgewood, N.J.: Gregg Press, 1965.

Seagrave, Sterling, *The Soong Dynasty.* New York: Harper & Row, 1985.

Sheridan, James E., *China in Disintegration: The Republican Era in Chinese History, 1919–1949.* New York: Free Press, 1975.

Sheridan, James E., *Chinese Warlord: The Career of Feng Yü-hsiang.* Stanford, Calif.: Stanford University Press, 1966.

Snow, Edgar, *Edgar Snow's China: A Personal Account of the Chinese Revolution.* New York: Random House, 1981.

Snow, Edgar, *Red Star Over China.* 1938; rpt. New York: Grove Press, 1993.

Spence, Jonathan D., *The Gate of Heavenly Peace: The Chinese and Their Revolution, 1985–1990.* New York: Viking Press, 1981.

Stuart, John Leighton, *The Forgotten Ambassador: The Reports of John Leighton Stuart, 1946–1949.* Boulder: Westview, 1981.

Stueck, William Whitney, *The Wedemeyer Mission: American Politics and Foreign Policy during the Cold War.* Athens: University of Georgia Press, 1984.

Sun Yat-sen, *Memoirs of a Chinese Revolutionary: A Programme of National Reconstruction for China.* London: Hutchinson, 1927.

Sun Yat-sen, *Prescription for Saving China: Selected Writings of Sun Yat-sen.* Stanford, Calif.: Hoover Institution Press, 1994.

Tan, Chester C., *The Boxer Catastrophe*. New York: Columbia University Press, 1955.

Thompson, Laurence G., *Ta t'ung shu: The One-World Philosophy of K'ang Yu-wei*. London: Allen & Unwin, 1958.

Thornton, Richard C., *China: A Political History, 1917–1980*. Boulder: Westview Press, 1982.

Wang, C. C., *Chinese Intellectuals and the West*. Chapel Hill: University of North Carolina Press, 1966.

Welch, Holms, *The Practice of Chinese Buddhism, 1900–1950*. Cambridge, Mass.: Harvard University Press, 1967.

White, Theodore Harold, *Thunder Out of China*. Rpt. New York: William Sloane Associates, 1961.

Wilbur, C. Martin, *Documents on Communism, Nationalism, and Soviet Advisors in China, 1918–1927: Papers Seized in the 1927 Peking Raid*. New York: Columbia University Press, 1956.

Wilbur, C. Martin, *Missionaries of Revolution: Soviet Advisers and Nationalist China, 1920–1927*. Cambridge, Mass.: Harvard University Press, 1989.

Yang, Benjamin, *From Revolution to Politics: Chinese Communists on the Long March*. Boulder: Westview, 1990.

Yeh, Michele, *Anthology of Modern Chinese Poetry*. New Haven: Yale University Press, 1993.

Yeh, Michele, *Modern Chinese Poetry: Theory and Practice since 1917*. New Haven: Yale University Press, 1991.

Yeh Wen-hsin, *The Alienated Academy: Culture and Politics in Republican China, 1919–1937*. Cambridge, Mass.: Harvard University Press, 1990.

Zarrow, Peter Gue, *Anarchism and Chinese Political Culture*. New York: Columbia University Press, 1990.

Since 1949

Altschiller, Donald, ed., *China at the Crossroads*. New York: H. W. Wilson Co., 1994.

Barnett, A. Doak, *China's Economy in Global Perspective*. Washington, D.C.: Brookings Institution, 1981.

Barnett, A. Doak, *China's Far West: Four Decades of Change*. Boulder: Westview Press, 1993.

Barnett, A. Doak, *Communist China: The Early Years, 1845–1955*. New York: Praeger, 1964.

Barnouin, Barbara, *Ten Years of Turbulence: The Chinese Cultural Revolution*. London: Kegan Paul, 1993.

Bartke, Wolfgang, *Biographical Dictionary and Analysis of China's Party Leadership, 1922–1988*. Munich: K. G. Saur, 1990.

Baun, Richard, *Burying Mao: Chinese Politics in the Age of Deng Xiaoping*. Princeton: Princeton University Press, 1994.

Brook, Timothy, *Quelling the People: The Military Suppression of the Beijing Democracy Movement*. New York: Oxford University Press, 1992.

Butterfield, Fox, *China: Alive in the Bitter Sea*. New York: Times Books, 1982.

Chi Wen-shun, *Ideological Conflicts in Modern China: Democracy and Authoritarianism*. New Brunswick, N.J.: Transaction Books, 1986.

Copper, John Franklin, *China Diplomacy: The Washington–Taipei–Beijing Triangle*. Boulder: Westview Press, 1992.
Daubier, Jean, *A History of the Chinese Cultural Revolution*. New York: Vintage Books, 1974.
Dietrich, Craig. *People's China: A Brief History*. New York: Oxford University Press, 1994.
Dittmer, Lowell, *China's Continuous Revolution: The Post-Liberation Epoch., 1949–1981*. Berkeley: University of California Press, 1987.
Domes, Jurgen et al., *After Tiananmen Square: Challenges for the Chinese–American Relationship*. Washington, D.C.: Brassey's, 1990.
Domes, Jurgen, *China after the Cultural Revolution: Politics between Two Party Congresses*. Berkeley: University of California Press, 1977.
Domes, Jurgen, *The Government and Politics of the PRC: A Time of Transition*. Boulder: Westview Press, 1985.
Duke, Michael S., *Blooming and Contending: Chinese Literature in the Post-Mao Era*. Bloomington: Indiana University Press, 1985.
Duke, Michael S., ed., *Modern Chinese Women Writers: Critical Appraisals*. Armonk, N.Y.: M. E. Sharpe, 1989.
Dwyer, Denis, ed., *China: The Next Decades*. Harlow, Eng.: Longman Scientific, 1994.
Etheridge, James M., *China's Unfinished Revolution: Problems and Prospects since Mao*. San Francisco: China Books and Periodicals, 1990.
Fang Li-chih, *Bringing Down the Great Wall: Writings on Science, Culture, and Democracy in China*. New York: Knopf, 1991.
Feuchwang, Stephan, ed., *Transforming China's Economy in the Eighties*. Boulder: Westview Press, 1988.
Feuerwerker, Albert, ed., *History in Communist China*. Cambridge, Mass.: Harvard University Press, 1968.
Gittings, James, *China Changes Face: The Road to Revolution, 1949–1989*. New York: Oxford University Press, 1989.
Gittings, James, *The Role of the Chinese Army*. New York: Oxford University Press, 1967.
Goldblatt, Howard, ed., *Worlds Apart: Recent Chinese Writing and Its Audiences*. Armonk, N.Y.: M. E. Sharpe, 1990.
Goldman, Merle, *China's Intellectuals: Advise and Dissent*. Cambridge, Mass.: Harvard University Press, 1981.
Goldman, Merle, ed., *China's Intellectuals and the State: In Search of a New Relationship*. Cambridge, Mass.: Harvard University Press, 1987.
Goldman, Merle, *Literary Dissent in Communist China*. Cambridge, Mass.: Harvard University Press, 1967.
Goldman, Merle, *Sowing the Seeds of Democracy in China: Political Reform in the Deng Xiaoping Era*. Cambridge, Mass.: Harvard University Press, 1994.
Gong, Ting, *The Politics of Corruption in Contemporary China: An Analysis of Policy Outcomes*. Westport, Conn.: Praeger, 1994.
Guillermaz, Jacques, *The Chinese Communist Party in Power, 1949–1974*. Boulder: Westview Press, 1976.
Guillermaz, Jacques, *A History of the Chinese Communist Party*. New York: Random House, 1972.
Harding, Harry, *China's Second Revolution: Reform after Mao*. Washington, D.C.: Brookings Institution, 1987.

Hicks, George, ed., *The Broken Mirror: China after Tiananmen*. Chicago: St. James Press, 1990.
Hinton, Harold C., ed., *The People's Republic of China, 1949–1979: A Documentary Survey*, 5 vols. Wilmington, Del.: Scholarly Resources, 1980.
Hsü, Immanuel C. Y., *China Without Mao: The Search for a New Order*. New York: Oxford University Press, 1990.
Hsueh Chun-tu, ed., *China's Foreign Relations: New Perspectives*. New York: Praeger, 1982.
Joseph, William A. et al., eds., *New Perspectives on the Cultural Revolution*. Cambridge, Mass.: Harvard University Press, 1991.
Leung, Beatrice, *Sino–Vatican Relations: Problems in Conflicting Authority, 1976–1986*. Cambridge University Press, 1992.
Leys, Simon, *The Chairman's New Clothes: Mao and the Cultural Revolution*. New York: St. Martin's Press, 1977.
Leys, Simon, *Chinese Shadows*. New York: Viking, 1977.
Li Lu, *Moving the Mountain: My Life in China from the Cultural Revolution to Tiananmen Square*. London: Macmillan, 1990.
Li Wei, *The Chinese Staff Control System: A Mechanism for Bureaucratic Control and Integration*. Berkeley: University of California, 1994.
Liang Heng, *Son of the Revolution*. New York: Knopf, 1983.
Liebenthal, Kenneth, *Policy Making in China: Leaders, Structures, and Processes*. Princeton: Princeton University Press, 1988.
Lin, Bij-jaw, ed., *The Aftermath of the 1989 Tiananmen Crisis in Mainland China*. Boulder: Westview Press, 1992.
Lin Jing, *Education in Post-Mao China*. Westport, Conn.: Praeger, 1993.
Link, Perry E., *Evening Chats in Beijing: Probing China's Predicament*. New York: Norton, 1992.
Link, Perry E., ed., *Rose and Thorns: The Second Blooming of the Hundred Flowers in Chinese Fiction, 1979–80*. Berkeley: University of California Press, 1984.
Link, Perry E., ed., *Stubborn Weeds: Popular and Controversial Chinese Literature after the Cultural Revolution*. Bloomington: Indiana University Press, 1983.
Link, Perry E. et al., eds., *Unofficial China: Popular Culture and Thought in the People's Republic*. Boulder: Westview Press, 1989.
Liu Pin-yen, *China's Crisis: China's Hope*. Cambridge, Mass.: Harvard University Press, 1990.
Liu Pin-yen, *A Higher Kind of Loyalty: A Memoir by China's Foremost Journalist*. New York: Pantheon Books, 1990.
MacFarquhar, Roderick, *The Hundred Flowers Campaign and the Chinese Intellectuals*. New York: Praeger, 1960.
MacFarquhar, Roderick, *The Origins of the Cultural Revolution*, 2 vols. New York: Columbia University Press, 1974.
Mao Tse-tung, *The Secret Speeches of Chairman Mao: From the Hundred Flowers to the Great Leap Forward*. Cambridge, Mass.: Harvard University Press.
Mao Tse-tung, *Selected Works*. Peking: Foreign Languages Press, 1965.
Meisner, Maurice, *Mao's China: A History of the People's Republic*. New York: Free Press, 1977.
Michael, Franz et al., *China and the Crisis of Marxism–Leninism*. Boulder: Westview Press, 1990.

Mosher, Steven W., *China Misperceived: American Illusions and Chinese Reality*. New York: Basic Books, 1990.

Munro, Donald J., *The Concept of Man in Contemporary China*. Ann Arbor: University of Michigan Press, 1977.

Myrdal, Jan, *Reports from a Chinese Village*. New York: Pantheon, 1965.

Nathan, Andrew J., *China's Crisis: Dilemmas of Reform and Prospects for Democracy*. New York: Columbia University Press, 1990.

Nolan, Peter, and Dong Fureng, eds., *The Chinese Economy and Its Future: Achievements and Problems of Post-Mao Reform*. Cambridge: Blackwell, 1990.

Ogden, Suzanne, *China's Unresolved Issues: Politics, Development, Culture*. 2nd ed., Englewood Cliffs, N.J.: Prentice Hall, 1992.

Onate, Andres D., *Chairman Mao and the Communist Party*. Chicago: Nelson-Hall, 1979.

Pusey, James R., *China and Charles Darwin*. Cambridge, Mass.: Harvard University Press, 1983.

Pusey, James R., *Wu Han: Attacking the Present through the Past*. Cambridge, Mass.: Harvard University Press, 1969.

Prybyla, Jan S., *The Chinese Economy: Problems and Policies*. Columbia: University of South Carolina Press, 1981.

Rai Shirin, *Resistance and Reaction: University Politics in Post-Mao China*. New York: St. Martin's Press, 1991.

Rittenberg, Sidney, *The Man Who Stayed Behind*. New York: Simon & Schuster, 1993.

Salisbury, Harrison Evans, *The New Emperors: China in the Era of Mao and Deng*. Boston: Little, Brown, 1992.

Schram, Stuart R., *Mao Tse-tung*. New York: Simon & Schuster, 1966.

Schram, Stuart R., ed., *The Scope of State Power in China*. New York: St. Martin's Press, 1985.

Schram, Stuart R., *The Thought of Mao Tse-tung*. Cambridge University Press, 1988.

Schran, Peter, *The Development of Chinese Agriculture, 1950–1959*. Urbana: University of Illinois Press, 1969.

Schurmann, Franz, *Ideology and Organization in Communist China*. Berkeley: University of California Press, 1966, 1968.

Scott, A. C., *Literature and the Arts in Twentieth Century China*. Gloucester, Mass.: Peter Smith, 1968.

Segal, Gerald, ed., *Chinese Politics and Foreign Policy Reform*. London: K. Paul International, 1990.

Shapiro, Judith, *Cold Winds, Warm Winds: Intellectual Life in China Today*. Middletown, Conn.: Wesleyan University Press, 1986.

Silbergeld, Jerome, *Contradictions: Artistic Life, the Socialist State, and the Chinese Painter Li Huasheng*. Seattle: University of Washington Press, 1993.

Terrill, Ross, *China in our Time: The Epic Saga of the People's Republic from the Communist Victory to Tiananmen Square and Beyond*. New York: Simon & Schuster, 1992.

Thomas, Hugh, ed., *Comrade Editor: Letters to the People's Daily*. Hong Kong: Joint Publishing Co., 1980.

Thurston, Anne F., *Enemies of the People*. New York: Knopf, 1987.

Wang Hui, *The Gradual Revolution: China's Economic Reform Movement*. New Brunswick, N.J.: Transaction, 1994.

Wasserstrom, Jeffrey N., and Elizabeth J. Perry, eds., *Popular Protest and Political Culture in Modern China: Learning from 1989.* Boulder: Westview Press, 1992.

Witke, Roxane, *Comrade Chiang Ching.* Boston: Little, Brown, 1977.

Wu Tien-wei, *Lin Biao and the Gang of Four: Contra-Confucianism in Historical and Intellectual Perspective.* Carbondale: Southern Illinois University Press, 1983.

Yang Chiang, *Six Chapters of Life in a Cadre School.* Boulder: Westview Press, 1986.

Yeung Yue-man and Hu Xu-wei, eds., *China's Coastal Cities: Catalysts for Modernization.* Honolulu: University of Hawaii Press, 1992.

Index

NOTE: word by word alphabetization is followed: thus Chen-la precedes Cheng Ch'iao ch precedes ch'; u precedes ü: thus chung, ch'ung, chu, ch'u, chü, ch'ü Provinces are spelt as one word (Honan, Yunnan); names of cities are usually hyphenated (Yang-chou) although occasional vestiges of the old Postal System remain (Foochow)